T0319756

CREDIT, *Fashion*, SEX

ECONOMIES OF REGARD

IN OLD REGIME FRANCE

CLARE HARU CROWSTON

DUKE UNIVERSITY PRESS

Durham and London

2013

Designed by Amy Ruth Buchanan
Typeset in Minion Pro by Tseng
Information Systems, Inc.

Library of Congress Cataloging-
in-Publication Data
Crowston, Clare Haru.
Credit, fashion, sex : economies of regard in
Old Regime France / Clare Haru Crowston.
pages cm
Includes bibliographical references and index.
ISBN 978-0-8223-5513-7 (cloth : alk. paper)
ISBN 978-0-8223-5528-1 (pbk. : alk. paper)
1. Credit—France—History—17th century.
2. Credit—France—History—18th century.
3. Fashion—France—History—17th century.
4. Fashion—France—History—18th century.
5. Sex—Economic aspects—France—History—
17th century. 6. Sex—Economic aspects—
France—History—18th century. I. Title.
HG3729.F82C76 2013
330.944′03—dc23
2013013824

DUKE UNIVERSITY PRESS GRATEFULLY
ACKNOWLEDGES THE FLORENCE GOULD FOUNDATION,
WHICH PROVIDED FUNDS TOWARD THE
PUBLICATION OF THIS BOOK

DUKE UNIVERSITY PRESS GRATEFULLY
ACKNOWLEDGES THE CAMPUS RESEARCH BOARD
AT THE UNIVERSITY OF ILLINOIS AT URBANA-
CHAMPAIGN, WHICH PROVIDED FUNDS TOWARD
THE PUBLICATION OF THIS BOOK.

TO ALI, LILI, REZA, AND KIAN BANIHASHEM

Who make the world turn

CONTENTS

ILLUSTRATIONS & TABLES

Illustrations

Tables

MONEY & MEASUREMENTS

1 livre	=	20 sous
1 sol	=	12 deniers
1 écu	=	3 livres
1 pistole	=	10 livres
1 louis d'or	=	24 livres
1 aune	=	1.18 meters or 46.5 inches

ACKNOWLEDGMENTS

It has been impossible to think and write about credit for more than a decade without incurring material and moral debts to an ever-wider circle of institutions and individuals. I am delighted to thank them here publicly, although I can never hope to repay their generosity in full. This project received funding from the National Endowment for the Humanities and the Mellon Foundation as well as from the University of Illinois at Urbana-Champaign's (UIUC) Academy for Entrepreneurial Leadership, Center for Advanced Study, and Conrad Humanities Scholar program. A subvention from the UIUC Research Board provided crucial assistance for the book's publication. I am extremely grateful for the financial support of all of these institutions, without which this book would never have reached readers. I also warmly thank the staffs of the Archives nationales, the Bibliothèque nationale, the Archives de Paris, the Institut national d'histoire de l'art, and the History and Philosophy Library at UIUC, until recently led by Mary Stuart, for their expert assistance over the years. I take full responsibility, of course, for any errors in the content of my work.

My greatest debt, as always, is to Steven Laurence Kaplan, my intellectual mentor since the first days of graduate school and now cherished friend. Rare is the adviser who lavishes close attention on every word his student writes, rarer still is the one who reads and rereads the manuscript of her second book, providing probing, detailed, and insightful commentary on almost every page. I am deeply indebted to Steve for his years of unconditional support and encouragement and to his wife Marie-Christine for her hospitality on numerous occasions. I am also very grateful to Lynn Hunt for her time and attention over the years and for her wise and generous reading of the manuscript, which came at an extremely important moment.

I have been fortunate over the years to present my work in multiple environments and to receive comments and criticism from brilliant colleagues in a range of fields and disciplines. I delivered portions of the manuscript to meetings of the Society for French Historical Studies, the Western Society for French History, and the Society for Eighteenth-Century Studies. For their work organizing sessions, delivering papers, and providing critical comments, I am grateful to Judith Bennett, Julie Hardwick, Michael Kwass, Janine Lanza, Tim LeGoff, Thomas Luckett, Jacob Melish, Kristin Neuschel, Oded Rabinovitch, Judith Sirkus, Dan Smail, Rebecca Spang, Carol Symes, and Chuck Walton. I am indebted to Claire LeMercier and Claire Zalc for inviting me to address their seminar at the Ecole normale supérieure and would like to recognize Natacha Coquery, Dominique Margairaz, and Alessandro Stanziani for their very helpful responses to my work. I also welcomed the opportunity to present to the Eighteenth-Century Studies Group at the University of Michigan and the Modern France Workshop at the University of Chicago. My thanks to Dena Goodman and Ruth McAdams and to Paul Cheney and Eleanor Rivera, respectively. I was honored to deliver the Annual Burkhardt Lecture at Ball State University and to address the Missouri Valley History Conference at the beginning of this project, and I thank Merry Wiesner-Hanks for inviting me to speak at the Attending to Early Modern Women Conference in its late stages.

At the University of Illinois, I am deeply obliged to the History Workshop and the Pre-Modern World Reading Group, which together read and responded to virtually every portion of this book over the last several years. Members of these groups include a long list of colleagues who never cease to amaze me with their generosity of time and spirit: James Barrett, Terri Barnes, Antoinette Burton, Jim Brennan, Tamara Chaplin, Ken Cuno, Dianne Harris, Caroline Hibbard, Kristin Hoganson, Fred Hoxie, Nils Jacobsen, Diane Koenker, Craig Koslofsky, Mark Leff, John Lynn, Bob Morrissey, Kathryn Oberdeck, Dana Rabin, Leslie Reagan, John Randolph, Mark Steinberg, Carol Symes, and Maria Todorova. I enjoyed and greatly benefited from discussions with Harry Liebersohn about the gift, with John McKay about economic history, with Susan Curtis and Huseyin Leblebici of our College of Business about historical entrepreneurship and accounting, and with Doug Kibbee, the late Larry Scher, and Marcus Keller about French literature (and I thank Marcus particularly for his help translating the book's epigraph). Interacting with graduate students is one of the best aspects of our work, and I have leaned heavily on insights gained from students at workshops and seminars. My sincere thanks to Ersin Akinci, Jacob Baum, Ryan Bean, Michelle Beer, Amanda Eisemann, Tara Fallon, Katie Godwin, and Lance Lubelski for all they have shared with me. I am particularly grateful to Tom Bedwell, Janet Abrahamson and the additional staff of the History Department for everything they do above and beyond the call of duty, to Adam Martinsek and the staff of the Illinois Statistics Office for their work on the project, and to Tara Fallon, Stefania Costache, and Alena Lapatniova for their work as research assistants and help with the tedious chore of creating databases. This long list of colleagues whose input was indispensable in bringing this manuscript to fruition is testimony to the intellectual hothouse that is UIUC and its History Department in particular. I could not imagine a more congenial home for my teaching and scholarship. For making it all possible in very challenging times, I thank Ruth Watkins, dean of the College of LAS at UIUC, for her unstinting support for me, our department, and the humanities at Illinois.

Over the years, I have tremendously enjoyed and benefited from informal discussions and exchanges with colleagues in North America and France. I have cherished time with and lessons learned from Roger Chartier and Gilles Postel-Vinay, both valued mentors of many years. The honorary fellow Cornellian Philippe Minard provided crucial input in the early stages of conducting my research. Natacha Coquery has proven an exceptionally generous interlocutor, most recently providing me access to her outstanding manuscript on Parisian retail trades before publication. Over the years, I have very much appreciated ongoing conversations with David A. Bell, Gayle Brunelle, Sara Chapman Williams, James Collins, Jonathan Dewald, Daryl Hafter, Julie Hardwick, Thomas Kaiser, David K. Smith, Jay Smith, and Allan Tulchin. I am grateful to all of them for their expert feedback on the project over the many phases of its development. I must also thank Avner Offer for graciously according me his blessing to use his "economy of regard" in the book's title.

My editor at Duke University Press, Valerie Millholland, has my wholehearted thanks for taking on the book and for all that she has done to shepherd it toward production. I am also grateful to Miriam Angress for her many patient efforts on my behalf, to project editor Susan Albury, copyeditor Alex Wolfe, book designer Amy Ruth Buchanan, and the numerous other individuals at Duke who have played a role in its publication. The two anonymous readers provided by Duke gave me extraordinarily useful readings of the manuscript, and I thank them for their time and attention. I benefited enormously from the help of John Reisbord, who not only found ways to trim the manuscript considerably (yes, there was an even longer version) but also provided extremely insightful and helpful comments and suggestions on its contents. I am grateful to the staffs at Art Resource, the Boston Museum of Fine Arts, Waddesdon Manor, and the Reproduction Service at the Bibliothèque nationale de France for their assistance in obtaining images and reproduction rights for the book.

Portions of chapters 5 and 6 appeared as "The Queen and her 'Minister of Fashion': Gender, Credit and Politics in Pre-Revolutionary France," in *Gender and History* 14, no. 1 (April 2002): 92–116. I am grateful to then editor Kathleen Canning and the article's anonymous readers for their feedback. An early rendition of chapter 7 appeared as "Family Affairs: Wives, Credit, Consumption and the Law in Old Regime France," in *Family, Gender, and Law in Early Modern France* (Pennsylvania State University Press, 2009). I thank the book's editors, Suzanne Desan and Jeffrey Merrick, and the anonymous reviewers for their close reading of the article and the press for authorization to reprint portions of that text. Portions of the book's conclusion appeared in "Credit and the Metanarrative of Modernity," *French Historical Studies* 34, no. 1 (winter 2011): 7–19. I thank Dan Smail for organizing the forum in which the article appeared and the anonymous reader of the article for his or her insightful comments.

This book emphasizes the crossover of the social and the economic, the private and the personal, and there could be no better proof for this argument than the process of its writing. Colleagues recognized above for their intellectual input must reappear to be thanked sincerely for their enduring friendship over the years. I am especially grateful to Antoinette Burton, Kathy Oberdeck, and Dana Rabin for the innumerable ways they have supported me as I struggled to bring this project to a close. Antoinette, an inimitable model of professionalism, productivity, and solidarity, may have been the only individual capable of convincing me to just send the damn thing in already. Kathy and William Munro and their children Fiona and Cara have provided a beloved second family to the Banihashem-Crowstons, and Dana Rabin has been there from the first day in the NICU through many birthdays and other ups and downs. I am also thankful to Masumi Iriye, David O'Brien, Dianne Harris, Larry Hamlin, Jim and Jenny Barrett, Don and Lorraine Crummey, Kristin Bouton, and Jacobo Rodriguez for both listening to me drone on about my work and providing marvelous distractions from the grindstone. My dear friends Sara Beam, Martin Bruegel, Cynthia Koepp, Mary Gayne, Janine Lanza, Emmanuelle Sruh, Sydney Watts, and Michael Wilson have shared the long path toward this book, and I thank them for decades of friendship.

The warmest thanks must go to members of my family, who have shared the burden of this book with me for so long. My parents, Taka and Wallace Crowston, my sister Catherine and her daughter Hana, my brother Kevin, my sister-in-law Marie, and Steven Nixon provided constant encouragement and support in the form of regular family vacations, phone calls, emails, and Skype. My in-laws Azar and Mohsen Banihashem and Rolf and Maryam Sachs and their children Phillip, Frederik, and Roya are the most fabulous and supportive relations anyone could desire. Spending time with them has added immensely to the pleasures of all visits across the Atlantic for me and my family. To my husband Ali, my children Lili, Reza, and Kian, my step-son Amir and his wife Monet, words cannot express how grateful I am for their patience and forbearance, their joyous and unconditional love. This project was conceived before my children, and there has never been a moment in their lives when I was not pledging to spend more time with them after "the book" was done. I have been more shameful in drawing out my credit than any Old Regime aristocrat, but now that the promised moment has finally arrived, I look forward with delight to returning the time they have so generously extended to me. No other payback could be so sweet.

Note on translations: Unless otherwise indicated, quotations from French language sources have been translated by the author.

(OPPOSITE)
François Métra, et al., *Correspondance secrète, politique et littéraire
ou mémoires pour servir à l'histoire des cours, des sociétés et de la
littérature en France* vol. 17 (London: John Adamson, 1789), 264–65.
Sources identify the target of the
song as Louis Le Tellier, Marquis de
Louvois and attribute authorship to
Louis René Quentin de Richebourg,
marquis de Champcenetz. See Fars
Fasselandry, Paysac, vicomtesse de,
*Mémoires de Madame la vicomesse de
Fars Fausselandry* (Paris: Ledoyen,
1830), 233–35.

Following the lessons of ******   [De L****** suivant les leçons,
I make songs and debts.   Je fais des chansons et des dettes;
The former are artless,   Les premières sont sans façons,
But the latter are well done.   Mais les secondes sont bien faites.
It's to escape boredom   C'est pour échapper à l'ennui
That a prudent man looses his way: Qu'un homme prudent se dérange:
What wealth is solid today?   Quel bien est solide aujourd'hui?
The surest is the one you eat.   Le plus sûr est celui qu'on mange.

Ah, who is not in debt today?   Eh, qui ne doit pas maintenant?
It's the most constant fashion,   C'est la mode la plus constante,
And the smallest little schemer   Et le plus petit intriguant
Boasts a thousand creditors.   De mille créanciers se vante.
In vain those Messieurs protest.   En vain ces Messieurs sont mutins;
Their number never frightens me   Jamais leur nombre ne m'effraie;
They resemble our whores: Ils ressemblent à nos catins:
The more we have, the less we pay.   Plus on en a, moins on les paie.

The courtier owes his favor   Le courtisan doit sa faveur
To some secret machinations: A quelque machine secrète:
The coquette owes her youthful air   La coquette doit sa fraîcheur
To a few hours of make-up: A quelques heures de toilette:
Everything's on loan, even wit   Tout s'emprunte jusqu'à l'esprit,
And in these fickle times   Et c'est dans ce siècle volage
What we have on the greatest credit   Ce qu'on a le plus à crédit,
Is what we use up the most.   Est ce qui s'use davantage.

But with a little gaiety   Mais avec un peu de gaîté,
Anything goes in France;   Tout s'excuse, tout passe en France;
In the arms of voluptuous pleasure   Dans les bras de la volupté,
How can we think of expense?   Comment songer à la dépense?
Old parents, in vain you preach: Vieux parens, en vain vous prêchez:
You are annoying missionaries;   Vous êtes d'ennuyeux apôtres;
You made us pay for your sins   Vous nous fîtes pour vos pêchés
And you live too long for our own.   Et vous vivez trop pour les nôtres.]

INTRODUCTION

W̶riting in 1783, Louis-Sébastien Mercier complained that the nation "ascribes no sense to the words *credit, circulation*."[1] Decrying their hostility toward the Caisse d'escompte (a government-backed proto-bank), he accused the French people of failing to understand the role of collective belief in economics as well as in politics. As he put it: "Tell this people that wealth should reside rather in the minds of citizens than in their coffers, and likewise that power has effect only because each individual mind believes it to be real, they will be unable to hear you."[2] This book is devoted to proving how poorly Mercier understood the French people, in this instance at least, and how badly he and writers of his ilk misjudged contemporary conceptions and practices of credit. As this book will argue, the French attached not one but multiple closely interrelated senses to the word *credit* (or *crédit*). They used it to describe the informal workings of influence and reputation in politics, social life, religious faith, and cultural production. They were also quite familiar with practices of economic credit, having conducted much of their daily business on credit—as producers and consumers—for centuries. Indeed, this book's two central arguments are that credit was one of the most important concepts people had in Old Regime France to comprehend the dynamics of their lives and that by following them as they discussed, dealt in, and debated credit, we can achieve a much better understanding of their world.

Thus, the French people, at precisely the moment Mercier was writing, actually had a rich and deep, fine-grained, expansive, and nuanced answer to the question of "what is credit and how does it operate," one that they had used for centuries at the time he was writing. It was not the people who could not hear Mercier, but Mercier who, in this case, could not or chose not to hear the people. His declaration is all the more surprising because the many volumes of *Le Tableau de Paris* are replete with precisely the usages of credit described above.[3] Perhaps what the French resisted hearing was not the word *credit* but the creation of a centralized institution run by powerful elites in which decisions about value were no longer local and subject to their own processes of assessment. One might argue, indeed, that it was because they were such experts at credit themselves—and so familiar with the volatility of its value, the potential gap between appearances and reality, and the constant conversion of one kind of credit into another (be it political, social, or cultural)—that they were wary of government-backed efforts to intervene in credit markets and issue paper notes stamped with a fixed value. And as it turned out, they were perfectly right to be wary.[4]

This book began as an attempt to write about the second word Mercier evokes, *circulation*. My initial plan was to examine three Old Regime systems of circulation: the credit economy, the fashion economy, and the libidinal economy. I hypothesized that these economies might be analyzed as conceptual homologies that were also deeply intertwined in practice. That book may still be awaiting its author, but what I discovered along the way led me in a new direction. Using the array of online databases now available to researchers, I discovered that when early modern French people invoked the term *crédit*, they more often meant an informal sort of influence and power than access to financial resources.

This is therefore not a book about financiers or discount markets. It is also not a book about the discipline of political economy that emerged over the course of the eighteenth century and has attracted a great deal of renewed attention from historians.[5] Instead, it is a book about what I call "expert practitioners" of credit, the legions of men and women who dealt in credit transactions, both in the politics of daily life and as buyers and sellers in retail commerce. Thus, I focus on how writers, courtiers, merchants, and other individuals understood and used credit before, during, and indeed for decades after political economy imposed an understanding of the economy as an empirically existing, discrete, and coherent system. In contrast to the claims of political economy, this book emphasizes the way many French men and women thought about and experienced the domains of economy, society, politics, and culture as overlapping and inseparable. Much of their concern in their daily lives was with gaining access to valuable resources; however, for them value was not reducible to money. Instead, they engaged in a constant effort of conversion among different currencies of value. As important as money could be goods as varied as obtaining an official post, forging friendship with a powerful man or woman, and securing a marriage partner, a wig, a lace kerchief, or an invitation to a dinner party.

Not only irreducible to money, such resources were also not for sale to all comers. Markets themselves were often restricted, excluding entry to those without certain types of trading privileges. Moreover, even those goods apparently governed by monetary value often turned out to be extremely difficult to assess definitively. Price itself was open to negotiation, sometimes even after the item had been produced, delivered, used, and discarded. Debts of money might be reimbursed late or only in part. Thus, even values that were numerical and expressed in monetary terms often required credit, in the form of influence and power, to be realized. This situation was, of course, encouraged by the fact that money itself was an unreliable entity. Coin was rare and awkward to transport; more importantly, its value in relation to the livre, the official unit of account, could be altered by government fiat.

These comments will not be terribly surprising to those familiar with early modern European society. What is new and important is to realize that French men and women themselves had a concept to describe the multidimensional world they inhabited. The word *credit*, as they used it, gives a name to everything historians already know about the operation of power in this period and shows, in addition, that contemporaries themselves were fully aware how influence and reputation shaped access to political, social, cultural, and economic resources and how similar dynamics affected and intimately connected all of these realms. Indeed, it suggests that our own perception of distinct realms of human existence is a historical construct born of the disavowal of the credit regime I have described and thus foreign to the early modern period.

Based on these observations, this book will analyze how contemporaries conceived and practiced credit across an array of activities, experiences, and representations. Harkening back to my original project, it will also argue that credit and the values it represented can profitably be examined in relation to two other systems of circulation: fashion (and fashionable clothing in particular) and the interrelated nexus of sex and gender. But first, to clarify what contemporaries meant by *credit*, it may be useful to pause briefly and examine Old Regime dictionary definitions of this intriguing term.

Defining Crédit in the Seventeenth Century

One of the first French dictionaries, Jean Nicot's *Thresor de la langue françoyse* (1606), provides a definition of credit in the form of thirty-five examples of contemporary usage. At the beginning of the seventeenth century, to judge from this dictionary, credit already held its current economic meaning, but as a minor usage of the term. Offering the Latin equivalent as "*fides*," the first example of usage associates credit with reputation: "The credit or belief and esteem that one has for another." The second example pairs credit with the positive results of a good reputation: "The credit and favor someone has." The remaining examples reveal that credit may be lost, that it is acquired through deeds, that you could be in credit or excluded from credit. They also demonstrate that individuals or groups could hold credit, that it could be large or small, and that one person could amass more than others. Credit needed to be maintained; others would try to diminish it; lost credit could possibly be regained. Financial aspects of credit explicitly enter the picture only in the two final examples, which are "a credit or a debt . . . that someone owes us" and "to take money on credit."[6]

Three dictionaries published in the last decades of the century provide a more balanced depiction of the economic and moral meanings of the term.[7] The first, Pierre Richelet's *Dictionnaire françois*, published in 1680, gives first place to credit's economic definition, "what one lends to another in the belief that he will repay it." He furnishes the following examples: "Have good credit with merchants. Give credit. Buy on credit, sell on credit. Who gives on credit loses his goods and his friend." Significantly, Richelet speaks not just of money lent but money lent based on the belief that one would be repaid. The second definition of the word echoes the social definition given by Nicot: "power, authority, reputation, favor."[8]

Antoine Furetière's *Dictionnaire universel*, published in 1690, which presented itself as a philosophical rather than etymological text, offers three definitions of credit. The first referred to reputation: "Belief, esteem that one acquires in public by one's virtue, probity, good faith, and merit. The Greeks put themselves in credit by their learning; the Romans by their valor; the Christians by the holiness of their doctrine and their morals." This definition emphasizes the perceived antiquity of credit as a form of reputation as well as its collective nature, going so far as to deem it a *public* phenomenon. Furetière's second definition of credit introduces the notion of power that may be obtained as a result of reputation: "Credit is also said of the power, the authority, the wealth that one acquires by means of that reputation one has acquired. This minister has acquired a great credit at court over the mind of the prince. This president [chief justice of a law court] has put himself in credit with his corps by his learning." These examples depict credit as a key instrument in public life whereby reputation confers wealth, power, and authority.[9]

The third definition notes, finally, that a credible reputation could also serve to gain access to loans of money or merchandise: "Credit is used more commonly in commerce for the mutual loan made of money and merchandise, based on a trader's reputation for probity and solvency." Furetière goes on to list some of the ways the word was used in commerce: "Merchants' books are numbered at the top of the page and distinguished by debit or credit. This banker has good credit in the marketplace, his bankruptcy has scarcely diminished his credit." Furetière also observes that the shop credit merchants accorded to great nobles (*grands seigneurs*) frequently ruined their businesses.

Furetière's list of colloquial usages of the term deepens the ambiguity introduced by his reference to bankruptcy. As he explains, to do something "*à crédit*" is to engage in a futile activity, one that is "without foundation" or for pleasure only. For example, one goes to great pains to do something "à crédit," meaning that no one appreciates the efforts. When a merchant says "that he will give credit from the hand to the purse," it means he will accept only cash. Introducing gender and sexuality to the term for the first time, Furetière repeats another sardonic proverb: one says "of a girl who is pregnant before marriage, that she has taken a loaf in the oven on credit."

Decades in the making, the first edition of the *Dictionnaire de l'Académie française* appeared in 1694. Unlike the two other dictionaries, it did not organize entries in alphabetical order but grouped them around common root words. The word *crédit* was situated within a group related to the word *croire*, underlining once again the root of the term in concepts of faith and belief. Like Richelet, the academy gave the economic sense of the word first, emphasizing the importance of reputation and belief for acquiring economic credit. The authors added the following examples of usage: "Good credit, great credit, he has credit, good credit with merchants in the marketplace. If he needed one hundred thousand écus, he would find them through his credit. He maintains his credit well, he preserves his credit well. That affair ruined his credit." In addition to these examples, the dictionary offers a straightforward commercial definition of "to extend credit": "To sell merchandise, foodstuffs, without demanding payment before a certain time."[10]

The nonmaterial definition of the term appears in the next entry, "à crédit." This entry begins in a negative vein, explaining, like Furetière, that "à crédit" could mean "in vain," "futilely," or "without proof or foundation." Following this explanation, the authors give the moral definition of the word:

Credit means, figuratively, reputation, good esteem that bestows belief and consideration on someone. He is in credit, in great credit. He has great credit, a great deal of credit in his corps, at court, among foreigners, in a given country. He put himself in credit by such a means. That put him in credit, acquired credit for him. His credit is capable of a great deal. He used all of his credit for it. He has all this through the credit of such a person. He has lost a great deal of his credit, all of his credit. He has forfeited much of his credit. His credit is greatly diminished. To use one's credit. To abuse one's credit.[11]

What may we conclude from these dictionaries? Together, they suggest that, throughout the seventeenth century, the economic and the moral senses of credit coexisted and were closely linked. From Nicot to the *Dictionnaire de l'Académie française*, a heightened attention to the economic usage emerged, and there is less inequality between the two senses of the word in the 1680s and 1690s than in 1606. Still, whatever precedence is given, the material and immaterial meanings of credit exist side by side, with a common reliance on the notions of belief and reputation as key to obtaining social, political, or financial credit. The two senses of the word are also linked by a shared concern with the difficulties of acquiring and maintaining credit and the potential for increasing or losing it. No matter what it consists of, credit is precarious and subject to the depredations of others. It is also amenable to quantitative analysis: whatever the type of credit, it can be assessed and expressed in terms of being greater or smaller.

To judge from the dictionaries, credit is not only fragile but also vulnerable to misuse and fraud. If belief is at the core of credit, there is always the possibility that confidence may be misplaced or illusory and that the power conferred by credit is unwarranted. Thus a bankrupt merchant's credit might flourish and a trusting girl might bear a child that no man would recognize. Further, although there are many similarities between financial and moral credit, the dictionaries suggest that different forms of reputation lay at the heart of social and financial credit. Whereas the former arose from general notions of esteem and trust, the latter derived specifically from a belief in the person's aptitude for reimbursing loans. The dictionaries mapped these two forms of confidence onto distinct social groups. In discussing the influence and power derived from social credit, they referred to courts, princes, royal ministers, corporate groups, and nations. Financial credit, by contrast, was the concern of merchants and their clients or moneylenders and those seeking to borrow money. Nonetheless, these groups overlapped and interacted; especially close relations tied the "grands seigneurs," as Furetière called them, whose lifestyles outweighed their incomes, to the merchants who furnished them.

Outside of dictionaries, the term credit often appears in texts of the seventeenth and eighteenth centuries as one half of a set of paired terms, illuminating the nexus of linked concepts to which it belonged. Among the most common pairs were: credit and reputation,[12] credit and merit,[13] credit and power (both *puissance* and *pouvoir*),[14] credit and authority,[15] credit and friendship,[16] credit and rank,[17] credit and renown, credit and glory,[18] credit and riches, honor and credit, place and credit, favor and credit,[19] credit and novelty, name and credit, credit and esteem,[20] and credit and consideration. One gender-specific pairing referred only to women: beauty and credit.[21] Together, these examples situate credit once more within a spectrum of ideas about power, rank, reputation, and influence; credit was associated with all of these words without being a direct synonym for any of them. These pairings also underline the ambivalent moral valence ascribed to credit. In many cases, the combination of the term with a positive value like honor or merit functioned in an ironic manner to expose the worldly considerations operating alongside ostensible virtues. Where merit and honor did not suffice, the interest of credit might successfully intervene.

In all of these representations of credit, it is worth noting, women are remarkable mostly for their absence. While there is no explicit statement that the term referred solely to masculine forms of reputation and behavior, the individuals described (merchants, princes, and presidents) were all male, with the exception of the unfortunate victim of seduction. We are left to infer that the audience that conveyed powerful reputation and the individuals who gathered its fruits were men.

This overview of definitions and usages of credit leads to the central questions animating this book: How were the different forms of credit evoked in these sources related to each other? To what extent did the existence of a single word imply similar concepts and practices across different domains of life? How did credit relate to other contemporary concepts and practices of power, influence, and evaluation? How much credence should we accord to the mapping of different forms of credit onto hierarchies of social status, such as the opposition between the moral credit of grands seigneurs and the financial credit of merchants posited by Furetière? Or might we more constructively turn this question around and ask instead how struggles over credit contributed to the construction and reconstruction of social groups and identities? Did women have so little role to play in credit exchange, either in its economic or figurative sense?

The issues raised by the dictionaries thus help to crystallize the research agenda for the chapters that follow. The book examines multiple genres of contemporary writing in order to tease out concepts and uses of credit across a wide spectrum of life, including the royal court, marriage, religion, cultural production, sexual relations, and monetary debt. Noting the potential for abuse and ill-founded confidence raised by the dictionary definitions, I question the ethical connotations of credit and examine the development from the late seventeenth-century onward of a critique of credit as a capricious and arbitrary form of dominion, particularly in its close ties to the exercise of power by the royal government. The book responds to the silence in the dictionary definitions by paying particularly close attention to women's capacity to acquire credit, investigating the impact of gender on the circulation of credit in its multiple forms and women's alleged use of sexual desire and seduction both as a generator of credit in and of itself and as a lever through which it could be converted into political power.

Responding to Furetière's emphasis on the "public" nature of credit, the book inquires into the role of audiences in judging and assessing credit. I emphasize the embodied nature of credibility and the importance of performance and appearances as means of displaying and acquiring it. This leads me back to the notion of fashion and its affinities with credit; in my reading, they constitute two, often overlapping systems for assessing and assigning value based on access to asymmetrical flows of information. The book also investigates the particular ways that both credit and fashion put into question the relationship between the individual and the social group. Elite women's consumption of clothing on credit is one telling example of the opportunities it provided for individuals to defy the normative strictures of their social role. Finally, and perhaps most importantly, the book confronts depictions of credit wielded by aristocrats, magistrates, and wealthy merchants—such as those presented in the dictionaries—with the work of Parisian fashion merchants and their management of reputation and the risky opportunities of credit. At the heart of the book is a study of the daily labor of men and women making credit in one of the foremost trades of the eighteenth-century consumer revolution.

The book thus responds to a claim recently made by William Sewell that "the current separation of economic history from cultural and political history is positively harmful to both." He suggests both that the "dynamics of capitalism in this era are incomprehensible if divorced from the dynamics of fashion" and that the "history of fashion cannot be a purely cultural history."[22] By restoring credit to the multiple economic, cultural, and political dimensions it occupied in the eighteenth century, this book echoes and takes up Sewell's challenge; as I hope to show, the dynamics of credit were at the heart of Old Regime life, and they are inseparable both from fashion and from economic development. Indeed, it is credit that provides a crucial bridge linking them together.

Fashion and Les Marchandes à la Mode

To tie the knot between credit as a form of power and influence, on the one hand, and economic credit, on the other, this book focuses on a trade that seems to encapsulate their relationship in the most striking manner possible. Fashion merchants existed as early as the seventeenth century and came into prominence in the second half of the eighteenth century. Both male and female practitioners, they sold dress decorations and fashionable accessories, primarily items worn on women's head and shoulders, such as headdresses, bonnets, shawls, and capes. In 1776 the royal government recognized the trade's importance by granting it status as a guild in the aftermath of Controller General Turgot's failed attempt to abolish the guild system.

Fashion merchants were thus both beneficiaries and catalysts of the consumer revolution that historians have documented in the cities of northwestern Europe and British North America in the second half of the eighteenth century. Like other retail merchants, fashion merchants sold most of their wares on shop credit and were obliged, in turn, to purchase their own supplies on account. Fashion merchants reveal to us the common people (and women in particular) engaged in multiple credit circuits, just like the courtly elite. To run a successful business, they needed to extend and obtain credit, so they were constantly engaged in juggling incoming and outgoing accounts. Like other merchants, they relied on their reputation and their network of social relations to qualify as creditworthy. They therefore add important depth to our understanding of how *credibility* operated in the commercial world of the Old Regime. Moreover, since their livelihood depended on helping clients in the competitive arena of ostentatious consumption and appearances, they were drawn into the elite world of political and social credit. Without an understanding of the dynamics of worldly display, they could not survive in business.

Alongside political credit at court and economic credit in commerce, fashion merchants thus provide a third perspective: the key role of cultural credit in what I have called, following Avner Offer, Old Regime "economies of regard."[23] This was possible because of the distinct status of fashion in eighteenth-century Paris. As the city gained in importance relative to the court and the composition of *le monde* broadened to include nonnoble men of letters, professionals, and *rentiers*, the king and his court could no longer command fashion. However, the latest fashions were not simply available on demand to those with enough money to pay for them. Instead, fashion innovation took the form of individual, custom-made pieces for particular clients who designed them in collaboration with the most sought-after merchants. An individual noblewoman or wealthy commoner could accrue expert knowledge about fashion through her social activities. Acquiring the actual items of fashion, however, required access to creative talent and skill, as well as specialized materials and techniques that only fashion professionals could provide. Increasingly the most successful *marchandes de modes* acquired cultural credit of their own through their capacity to create items acknowledged as the latest style. As a result, it became necessary to purchase one's dresses and accessories from the most acclaimed merchants if one wished to have the newest and most prestigious fashions. This unequal reciprocity opened new possibilities for those at the pinnacle of their profession to develop a form of celebrity within le monde of Paris and the court. Rose Bertin, a central figure in this book, was the brightest star in the firmament alongside many lesser suns.

Articulations of Credit

A key aim of this book is to demonstrate the articulation of the sociopolitical credit of le monde with the merchants' economic world of credit. In some ways the retail merchant occupied an entirely different world than the aristocrat. His or her "credit" relied not on winning the favor of a king's mistress or placing the perfect bon mot into salon conversation. Instead, merchants—as described in contemporary manuals and dictionaries of commerce—needed to establish a reputation for probity, sobriety, and industriousness, for keeping orderly books, selling high quality goods, and, perhaps most importantly, for paying accounts on time and in full. Apart from the difference in cultural values, the difference in the scale of money involved is astounding. Spectacular successes aside, many merchants and almost all artisans operated modest businesses, dutifully keeping track of every sol and denier. By contrast, their clients operated in a world of ostentatious luxury consumption involving lavish expenditure secured through credit guaranteed by landed estates, annuities, royal pensions, and offices.

This enormous discrepancy in the scale of credit transactions was one indicator of the extreme inequality between merchant and client; it was both by-product and bulwark of the corresponding gulf in social status between the two parties. The inequality between them was perhaps best expressed in the aristocratic tenet that a gambling debt was a debt of honor (that is, between equals), while a debt to a tradesman was a mere inconvenience. An irate tradesman could be the cause of humor, embarrassment, or even legal calamity but never a source of dishonor. We will see that this inequality manifested itself in extreme delays and nonpayment of accounts.

And yet, for all these discrepancies, the dynamics of credit drew these two worlds together in complex and enduring ways. First, it was arguably credit, in its multiple forms, that provided the most regular and reciprocal interaction between them. Nobles' quest for credit among their peers drove them to seek the goods and services of merchants and artisans. As they did so, they entered credit relations that could span decades. These relations opened the possibility of some form of recognition and mutual obligation between social unequals, as nobles and wealthy commoners came to depend on the talents, skills, and innovation of the most successful merchants. Merchants' success depended directly on their capacity to understand the relationship between fashion and social power, and they had every interest in demonstrating their capacity to provide clients with a competitive edge. The fact that both client and merchant found it completely normal that a household whose wealth could be calculated in the millions would wait one year to satisfy a bill of one hundred livres signals a shared occupancy of a world that emphasized relationships and processes over discrete transactions.

A second factor drawing client and merchant together was that, whatever the difference in social scale, both had to manage multiple credit relations. They faced the same exigencies in calculating who owed what and when, how much had to be satisfied at once or could be put off, how likely someone was to demand payment or to satisfy it, whether to grant a debtor's request for extending terms or whether one's request to a creditor would be granted. Their business officers, servants, and social prestige cushioned noble families from pressure to a certain extent, but the stakes of debt for them were as high as for a humble tradesman or woman.

The twin expansion of fashion and trade credit in the second half of the eighteenth century thus forged new relations between elite consumer and plebeian purveyor; it also helped to blur traditional social boundaries by undercutting the display of distinction. Increased consumption of goods was made possible by credit and, when purchasing on credit, Parisians sought items of fashion, like clothing, bonnets, parasols, writing desks, and other goods. The availability of fashion to new sectors of the populace helped disseminate an aristocratic practice of self-fashioning and competitive display through wider social groups. They adopted fashion not to emulate the nobility (except for the highest reaches of bourgeois society) but to help in their own strategies for obtaining credit in all its senses among their own peers. As commentary from bemused observers attested, the marchandes de modes led the way in donning new fashions that helped break down the traditional visual cultures of social taxonomy.

Any historian familiar with the world of work would be unsurprised to learn that, just like nobles, merchants and artisans had to engage in the politics of personal power in a society still dominated by patronage relations. Whether at a court or in a guild, in a workshop or a salon, who you knew, the strength of your personal connections, the debts and favors you could call in, and your individual skill at mastering the dynamics of reputation and influence were all key to the outcome of events. As it created vertical ties between social groups, credit created networks and factions within them, fostering cooperation and solidarity as well as competition.

Information Economies

In seeking to uncover links between economics and other realms, this book draws on work in literary history and the history of the book as well as the new field of information history that has emerged from it.[24] I have benefited from scholarship on the literary world of the seventeenth and eighteenth centuries, which has emphasized the multiple forms that "publication" could take. In addition to printed documents circulated through commercial markets, these included letters and manuscript texts as well as gossip, conversation, songs, oral verse, jokes, and other forms of verbal communication. This broad view of publication, and the importance of the oral context, especially in dense urban environments, help us understand the circulation of anecdotes and stories about changing styles of dress and leading fashion merchants.[25]

Another important field of literary history has focused on the impact of the expansion of the credit economy on signifying systems, particularly on the formation of new genres like the novel. Mary Poovey has intriguingly described money itself as a genre and analyzed its simultaneous emergence with the new genres of the novel and political economy. For Poovey, all three were important means of mediating value in the wake of the late seventeenth-century English Financial Revolution. She further argues that the genres of the novel and political economy served to naturalize and legitimate money by securely bifurcating signification into "fact" and "fiction," thereby enabling the "truth claim" of currency to be more easily accepted. Ian Baucom argues in a similar spirit that the transformation of human bodies into abstract commodities in the transatlantic slave trade may be seen as the epitome of the abstraction of value operated by modern capitalism. Like these scholars, I am fascinated by the problem of value in the seventeenth and eighteenth centuries and the way that calculations of value spanned fields now considered distinct.[26] I depart from these literary historians, however, in considering eighteenth-century actors not as novices needing to learn about credit from novels and other literary genres but as experts long familiar with the wheeling and dealing of credit.

Considering the early modern world in terms of information systems provides another way of overcoming boundaries that exist between "mainstream" history and economic history, which tend, as William Sewell noted above, to be written in isolation from each other. According to Jean-Yves Grenier, information possessed a particular value in the Old Regime economy, which was transitioning from a premarket to an industrial society. As he put it:

> In this type of economy, information is rare, poorly distributed, often secret and even more highly valued because it is the source of important profits. This characteristic is more easily perceived by its difference from societies without markets, where it [information] is at once more ritualized and less necessary because the goods exchanged vary little and are well-codified, and from industrial economies where techniques of production and of information transfer occupy a central place. The growing diversity of merchandise produced and exchanged across more and more vast spaces means that knowledge of products, of the state of the market and the evolution of consumption is a prerequisite to master transactions and reduce uncertainty. And such information can only be acquired through practice.[27]

Grenier provides crucial insight in this passage into the tensions between the privileged and uneven access to information, on the one hand, and the demand for information driven by the ever-increasing quantity and types of goods in circulation, on the other. This insight can be applied broadly to many types of information. Studies on early modern information systems, a field that has emerged in the last decade, emphasize the thirst for news and its circulation in multiple forms. From newspapers to posted advertisements and official proclamations, prints, hand-written newssheets, songs, and gossip, news circulated through eighteenth-century Paris with surprising rapidity through a complex range of media, as Robert Darnton has shown.[28]

News spread quickly, but it also—as Grenier emphasizes—spread unevenly. Drawing on these insights, this book conceives of both credit (in its material and immaterial forms) and fashion as systems of information exchange in which crucial advantages accrued to those who possessed the latest and most up-to-date information. Moreover, since both systems relied on collective and informal judgments of value, the ability to display one's access to information was itself a tool of distinction. Bluffing and posing were as important tactics as securing reliable information and choosing when and with whom to share it.

Bourdieu: Capital or Credit?

Much of what I have argued so far will seem familiar to readers of Pierre Bourdieu and in particular those acquainted with his writings on forms of capital. I am indeed indebted to Bourdieu, whose tripartite formulation of economic, social, and cultural or symbolic capital offers a set of extremely useful heuristic categories as well as an important reminder that, even while emphasizing linkages and relations, analytical distinctions must be made among different types of capital. As he explained, "capital can present itself in three fundamental guises: as *economic capital*, which is immediately and directly convertible into money and may be institutionalized in the form of property rights; as *cultural capital*, which is convertible, on certain conditions, into economic capital and may be institutionalized in the forms of educational qualifications; and as *social capital*, made up of social obligations ('connections'), which is convertible, in certain conditions, into economic capital and may be institutionalized in the forms of a title of nobility."[29] Bourdieu's definition of social capital as consisting of one's network of social connections and his emphasis on the importance of cultural knowledge and habits as a form of capital are both extremely important to this book. In drawing on Bourdieu's categories of capital, I add fashion as a form of cultural capital and political capital in the form of relationships with holders of office that allow influence over decision making.

However, I maintain distance from Bourdieu's analysis in one crucial aspect and that is his insistence that the other forms of capital are derivative of the economic. As he stated in this text: "it has to be posited simultaneously that economic capital is at the root of all the other types of capital and that these transformed, disguised forms of economic capital, never entirely reducible to that definition, produce their most specific effects only to the extent that they conceal (not least from their possessors) the fact that economic capital is at their root, in other words—but only in the last analysis—at the root of their effects." In making this claim, Bourdieu declared a desire to avoid the two extremes of "economism," that is, imagining that because they were reducible to economics one could ignore the specific efficacy of cultural and social capital, on the one hand, and, on the other hand, indulging in a facile "semilogism" that "reduces social exchanges to phenomena of communication and ignores the brutal fact of universal reducibility to economics."[30]

This formulation, in my view, does not avoid the problem of "economism" but merely raises new questions about the meaning and status of "economics" itself. Bourdieu argues against a notion of economics strictly reduced to money and profit, arguing instead for a "general science of the economy of practices, which would treat mercantile exchange as a particular case of exchange in all its forms."[31] However, by insisting on "economic capital" as the disguised root of the other forms of capital, he privileges ontologically economic capital and undermines the ways in which social and cultural capital act as generators of value. This is particularly problematic for the early modern period, when so many precious goods were not for sale on open markets. Moreover, the function of credit in Old Regime economic exchange brought it closer to the dynamics of symbolic and cultural capital as described by Bourdieu, in that the lapse of time involved in economic exchange was closer to the deferred rhythms he describes for cultural capital than to the staccato rhythms of monetary exchange. Since most economic exchange occurred through some form of credit, the saliency of the monetary transaction itself as a model for social relations is questionable for this period.

One of the main points of this book therefore is that economic capital in terms of money, wealth, and property was one crucial way of assessing value, but it was not primordial. At stake in exchanges of credit and attempts to raise one's own and lower that of others was not merely the acquisition of economic capital but gaining advantage in the struggle over access to limited resources. Here, I mean resources writ large: status, reputation, honor, power, as well as wealth. It is vital to recall that the time period covered by this book was precisely the moment when the meaning and contents of the category "economic" itself were being deliberated. If we mean by "economic" strategic thinking and behavior aimed at increasing possession of scarce resources, then certainly all the forms of credit I describe were "economic." This would mean, in turn, in Bourdieuian terms that we should speak of economies of capital acquisition rather than ceding hegemony to economic capital.

By using the word *credit* across political, social, cultural, and economic fields, early modern actors demonstrated centuries before Bourdieu that they understood the essential commensurability of values generated in those fields. Thus, I prefer to retain their formulation and refer to different forms of "credit" rather than "capital," with its assumption that at the bottom of exchange lay the bedrock reality of economic capital and a social system based on economic class.

The Political Economy of Credit vs. Credit as Practice

Another area where this book draws heavily on Pierre Bourdieu, as well as on Michel de Certeau, is in its emphasis on understanding credit in terms of practice rather than theory.[32] My initial goal of writing a book that would examine "homologies" of credit, fashion, and the libidinal economy arose from my assumption, born perhaps of the on-going ideological sway of political economy, that each constituted a discrete and autonomous circuit that could be compared with the others. Instead, I would now emphasize the constructed nature of the eighteenth-century "discovery" of the economy as an enclosed, controlled, and rational circuit. This discovery drew on the prestige of scientific models of the macrocosm of the universe and the microcosm of the human body, including Harvey's discovery of the circulation of blood in 1628. As Todd Lowry has noted, in this conception of the economy, "individual transactions became more than a series of random events and instead took their place as a part of a circular flow of exchange."[33] Following earlier theorists like Richard Cantillon and François Quesnay, Adam Smith identified money as the "great wheel of circulation," "by means of which every individual in the society has his subsistence, convenience, and amusements regularly distributed to him in their proper proportions."[34] This enabled new experts like Smith to "discover" objective characteristics of the economy and the laws governing its function, just as experts did for the physical universe or the body.[35]

This conception of the economy represented a rationalization and reification of a system experienced in practice as considerably less coherent or predictable. Eighteenth-century actors' experience of economic life bore more resemblance to the humoral system described by Barbara Duden than to the circulation of the blood discovered by Harvey. According to Duden, eighteenth-century German women's perception of their body was of a multitude of vital fluids moving within it.[36] These fluids were prone to blockages, to leaking from the wrong orifices, and to transforming from one type of fluid into another and then back again. Even the sexed division of the body was not inviolate, as men were known to lactate and menstruate. There are, of course, limits to what this analogy will bear, and I am not suggesting the humoral theory as a model for understanding the eighteenth-century economy; however, it is a helpful contrast to the closed, rational, and systematic circulatory model used by Smith and other pioneers of political economy.

Therefore, more important for this study than eighteenth-century theories of the economy are its practices of credit. Although much of this book focuses on published writings produced by elites, I am for the most part not concerned with formal conceptualizations of economy among elite intellectuals. In this way, the book differs from the important work of scholars such as Jean-Claude Perrot, John Shovlin, Michael Sonenscher, and Paul Cheney, who focus largely on political economy as formally delineated by theorists. In discussing credit, this book emphasizes that references to credit as a form of power are ubiquitous in published and unpublished sources from the Old Regime that address multiple domains of life. Explicit theories of this conception of credit, however, are almost nowhere to be found. Credit constituted the common sense of the Old Regime; to borrow a Bourdieuian term, it was part of the habitus that directed and guided practice without requiring explicit theorization.[37] This is why, I believe, it did not produce much in the way of overt theorization (with the fascinating exception of one chapter in Charles Pinot Duclos's *Considéra-tions sur les moeurs de ce siècle*) and perhaps why its multiple dimensions have not often been studied together. Once one begins to look for credit, however, it quickly becomes apparent how frequently it was used as a shorthand to explain how power was acquired and exercised.

These commitments raise a significant methodological problem. How is it possible to reconstruct underlying concepts that are not theorized and the practices they produce? I have adopted two different methodological approaches to this problem. The first was to make use of databases of published sources available online, specifically *Eighteenth-Century Collections Online* and *The Making of the Modern World* (both available through subscription from Gale-Cengage), the Project for American and French Research on the Treasury of the French Language (ARTFL; another subscription-based database produced through the University of Chicago), Gallica (a free access site with online versions of a selection of the holdings of the Bibliothèque nationale de France), the HathiTrust Digital Library, Google Books, and others. It was typing the word *crédit* into these databases that produced the insight that credit signified much more than a form of economic capital. I used a variety of text searches of materials in these databases to achieve broad, rather than in-depth, coverage of sources from the seventeenth and eighteenth centuries.

This method clearly poses a number of problems. First, my source base does not constitute a discrete corpus, defined either by contemporaries or by me. The databases arguably open the field so wide and so capriciously as to render any analysis incoherent and scattershot. Moreover, given the number and range of sources consulted, I cannot claim the level of critical reading of complex texts that has been the norm for cultural and intellectual history. My decision to sacrifice canonical coherence and close reading was taken self-consciously and with a painful awareness of what I was losing, not only with regard to my analysis of the primary sources themselves but also of the voluminous second-ary literature devoted to each of the texts in question. I decided, nonetheless, to risk a strategy of wide reading over multiple fields and genres in order to cover as much material as possible in a reasonable period of time and therefore gain as wide as possible an apercu on the usage of the term *crédit*.

My second methodological approach also involved digital history, but in a wholly different register. I procured (through my own labor and that of hired graduate assistants) digital photographs of fashion merchants' account books and bankruptcy statements, which I then (again using my own and graduate student labor) entered into computerized databases. Graduate students and faculty working at the University of Illinois Statistics Office performed statistical analysis of the account books.

The ultimate goal of this project is to read these sources, and the interpretations they enable, with and against each other. I thus seek to combine readings of literary and narrative sources with an empirical analysis of the activities of male and female merchants and artisans and their clients. To give a specific example, I read the "meaning" of credit for the fashion merchant Rose Bertin in chapters 5 and 6 in part through a close (often quantitative) study of her economic activities.[38] Rather than seeking to recuperate Bertin's "authentic" voice from published accounts of her words, I examine the tension between her manipulation of words, as reflected in reports from the Parisian rumor mill, and her concrete management of commercial affairs, as revealed by surviving archival records. Indeed, it is at this intersection between Bertin's elusive and echoing voice and the traces of her professional practice that I wish to situate this study.[39] Ultimately, this methodological approach — and the convergence between economic and cultural history that it reveals — undermines perceived gaps between different fields of history and hopefully challenges the rather sterile territorialism that continues to divide the historical profession.

The Chronology of Credit

One of the most vexing questions in writing this book has been the question of change over time. In an important article arguing for the dual moral and financial meanings of credit as a window into noble relations, Jay Smith posits a fundamental shift over time from the moral to the financial senses of credit. He finds that, whereas late seventeenth-century dictionaries gave priority to the "personal" and "subjective" sense of credit over its material connotations, during the eighteenth century successive dictionaries downgraded the status of nonmaterial credit and added a range of new commercial usages of credit. By 1771, Smith points out, Trévoux's dictionary relegated credit in its nonmaterial sense to a "metaphorical" usage.

Smith interprets this semantic shift as evidence of a profound cultural and social transition from a set of values that emphasized personal connections and commitments to ones based on abstract systems. As he states, "relationships that had been transitory and negotiable were to be regarded as abstract and permanent, with the monarchy serving as a fixed point at the center of the political matrix. The exchange of goods and services that underlay and signified political obligation would be routinized and rendered predictable. The value of the assets exchanged in political life would be determined less by the status and character of the person who bore them and more by the ease with which they could be transferred and exchanged for other useful assets."[40] Thus, from adeptly symbolizing the personal bonds at the heart of elite culture, credit equally adeptly signified the impersonal and quantifiable power relations created over the eighteenth century.

Smith's narrative ends "several years before the French Revolution" with a courtier's remark that no one said "I serve the king" anymore except the *grands valets* at Versailles; instead they proclaimed, "I serve the state."[41] With the tumbrils of the French Revolution wheeling onstage, we look back through the lens of credit to see that the decline of collective, personal values in favor of abstract power relations went hand in glove with the desacralization of the monarchy, the rejection of noble values, and the monetization of human relations.

While there is much to appreciate in this analysis of shifting attitudes toward credit, I nonetheless find myself resisting this teleology. First, it is clear from a quick look even at early twentieth-century dictionaries that the nonmaterial sense of credit survived for at least two centuries beyond the revolution. As the conclusion will discuss, credit remained a viable analytical category for explaining the currents of influence running through political institutions such as the National Assembly during the French Revolution and the royal court of the Restoration. Further research would undoubtedly reveal similar usage of the term further into the nineteenth century. Second, I remain unconvinced that the changes described by Smith can be ascribed to the society and culture as a whole. In reading written descriptions of credit from the mid-seventeenth century through the end of the eighteenth century, what struck me most was how little they changed over time. It was clear that I could write the same story with virtually the same quotations from the first half of the seventeenth century to the end of the eighteenth century at least. As a lived element of habitus, credit resisted sudden change. Third, if nonmaterial credit has a longue durée, its origins also stretch far earlier than the court of Louis XIV. In his study of thirteenth-century Marseilles, Dan Smail discusses the important economic role of credit and the fact that it was embedded in social and cultural relations, concluding that "credit, in short, is power."[42] Closer to my period, the writings of François Rabelais, to give just one example, contain references to "credit" in both financial and nonmaterial senses.

Having insisted on the limits of a linear trajectory from Louis XIV to the revolution, I do, of course, acknowledge Smith's point that—without eclipsing older notions—new conceptions of credit emerged in the mid-eighteenth century, bound up with both the emergent discipline of political economy, on the one hand, and efforts to rethink monarchical power and aristocratic culture, on the other. Credit is indeed a useful way to rethink political change over the eighteenth century, because it suggests that one of the most important issues at stake was the proper relationship between credit as informal power and influence and credit as economic capital, particularly in the form of public credit. Chapter 2 engages these chronological developments, examining criticisms of political credit as a capricious form of power and reading efforts at radical reform of public credit as, at least in part, a response to this critique. Similarly, I reread attacks on women's role in the "public sphere" of Old Regime France, described by Joan Landes and others, as another response to perceptions of the potentially despotic and corrupt use of political credit. Chapter 6 thus examines the relationship between Marie-Antoinette and her fashion merchant Rose Bertin as a moment when the political credit of the monarchy, the cultural credit of fashion, and the fiscal problems of the crown collided in spectacular fashion. In the midst of all of these crises, however, it is important to remember that commonplace discussions of political, social, and cultural credit continued, often among the same theorists who fulminated against capricious forms of power. As we see in the discussions of Charles Duclos in chapters 2 and 3, to take an ideological position against abusive influence or unmerited power was one matter; it by no means required one to forgo in correspondence or light-hearted writings a commonplace and widely recognized category of human interaction.

The following chapters introduce several sets of matched pairs: the feuding cousins Bussy-Rabutin and Madame de Sévigné (Chapter 1); the real-life and imaginary fashion consumers, Angélique the notary's wife and Marie-Angélique Françoise de Bercy, robe noble (Chapter 4); and the queen Marie Antoinette and her fashion merchant Marie-Jeanne, better known to history as Mademoiselle Bertin (Chapter 6). These pairs illustrate the unlikely couplings produced by the bonds of credit as well as the social inequalities they engendered and the conflicts they produced within families and other collective groups. Credit wove Old Regime French society together and cast it asunder; in addition to being an epochal world-historical event, the French Revolution may have been yet another crisis in the credit cycles of the nation.

CHAPTER 1

CREDIT AND OLD REGIME ECONOMIES OF REGARD

> Women in the capital enjoy not only the greatest possible free-
> dom, but also the most incredible credit. By secret and specific
> manoeuvers, they are the invisible spirit of all affairs, they suc-
> ceed almost without leaving home; they determine the pub-
> lic voice in circumstances when it seemed initially undecided.
> —Louis-Sébastien Mercier, *Le Tableau de Paris*

*I*n the playwright Marivaux's *La Double inconstance* (1724), Arlequin boasts: "I am in credit, for people do what I want" ("Je suis en cré-dit, car on fait ce que je veux").[1] This bold claim nicely summarizes the nonmaterial sense of the term *credit* that is the focus of this chapter. In Old Regime France fictional characters and real people frequently employed the word *credit* to signify a crucial form of nonmaterial capital that could take on political, social, and cultural guises. As we will see, texts of this period portray credit as an intangible, often hidden, and yet highly efficacious form of power that operated within and across numerous registers of life: from patronage networks at court and elsewhere to courtship and marriage transactions, intellectual life, missionary work, and trade and economic activity.

To date, historians' attention to nonmaterial usages of the term have focused on patronage politics at the royal court and in particular at Louis XIV's Versailles. This sense of credit referred to the influence and power a courtier accrued from his or her social and political connections as well as from a range of assets like birth, fortune, and individual charisma. While the court was certainly a central forum for the exchange of credit in its political and social manifestations—and thus constitutes a starting point for the chapter—the focus on courtly credit has obscured the importance of the concept as a key explanatory mechanism for the operation of power throughout Old Regime society and culture. As this chapter will show, belief in credit as a hidden but omnipresent lever of power shaped the perceptions of men and women throughout French society, whether at court, in salons, workshops, abbeys and churches, the tavern, the street, or the boudoir.

Scholars have hitherto neglected this central "category of analysis" of Old Regime France in part because there is so little formal writing on nonmaterial forms of credit. This was not because credit was unimportant. Rather, credit was the common sense and realpolitik of the era, the open secret of the operation of power, and the constant low-level current thrumming through their lives. It did not call for philosophical speculation or explanation because "everyone knew" that flows of credit directed events. French writers referred to it constantly but in shorthand and throwaway phrases, precisely because its dynamic was so familiar and so universally accepted and understood. This shorthand — ubiquitous once the eye becomes attuned to it — has also escaped notice because of the distance between the Old Regime understanding of credit and our own. We have (for the most part) lost the notion that credit can be used to procure anything but commodities in the market; they believed it was a much more pervasive force, one that was at work in all aspects of their lives.

Credit could not only be found in many different realms of life, it also provided a common currency for transferring capital from one domain to another. As we will see, credit had putative equivalencies in favor, money, personal connections, and intellectual influence. The exchange rates of this credit system were constantly subject to negotiation that could be friendly or fiercely competitive. A focus on credit thus highlights the inextricability of the economic from the social, cultural, or political in this period. For the writers I analyze below, these domains constantly overlapped and individual and collective strategies for advancement necessarily operated simultaneously across registers. They found credit so useful and pervasive as a form of currency precisely because they could make use of it in so many different transactions.

This chapter guides the reader through distinct milieus in which contemporary sources — ranging from memoirs to letters, plays, sermons, almanacs, and novels — showcase the use of credit as a form of influence and power. Through a series of case studies — of the royal court, of law courts, of the intellectual world, of missionary work, and of marriage and courtship — we examine how contemporaries understood credit in its nonmaterial guises, how they described themselves and others making use of it, and how they imagined credit across political, social, and economic life. To add more concrete depth to this broad overview, we turn to a focus on the multiple and overlapping meanings of credit in the writings of two well-known late seventeenth-century writers, Bussy-Rabutin and Madame de Sévigné. This affords a closer understanding of the way two individuals — elite and educated — experienced interwoven strands of credit running through their own lives. They also underline a central theme of this chapter: women's capacity to wield credit in its multiple forms. Finally, we turn our attention from the elites to the common people. While credit might appear to be the monopoly of the well connected and wealthy, a number of sources suggest that similar dynamics were at work among commoners and that ordinary people were equally familiar with the nonmaterial meanings of credit.

It should be noted at the outset that my analysis does not consider any of the documents it addresses, even those purporting to be true reports of daily events (such as letters or memoirs), as transparent depictions of an empirically existing entity called "credit." Instead, I am interested in how contemporaries conceived of a range of forms of influence and power they subsumed under the category of "credit" and their descriptions of behaviors and attitudes they explained as being motivated by struggles to obtain and manage it. I am also not able, in covering such a broad terrain, to accord full attention to the complexity of each text or its place in the author's overall oeuvre or the genre and period to which it belongs. It is thus not the empirical truth of credit that I seek to reconstruct, or its contextualization within a close reading of a text or set of texts, but the beliefs and behaviors that the authors, mostly elite, of these texts found to be credibly associated with this concept, whether in texts written in the guise of factual accounts, those openly declaring themselves as fictions, or those (perhaps the most common category) that straddled the line between what we now recognize as fiction and nonfiction.[2]

Credit and Court Patronage

The secondary literature on noneconomic forms of credit focuses primarily on the court and noble patronage.[3] Scholars such as Arlette Jouanna, Sharon Kettering, Jay Smith, and Jonathan Dewald have all noted aristocrats' use of the term "credit" to describe the exchange of influence and power within the patronage system. These historians tend to agree that the reign of Louis XIV marked a turning point within this system. Arlette Jouanna, for example, argues that as Louis XIV claimed ever-greater control of the distribution of resources he also seized the reins of social credit, displacing the local connections that had formed the basis of noble credibility. For their part, Jonathan Dewald and Jay Smith emphasize the growing monetization of French society from Louis XIV onward. Jonathan Dewald claims that Louis's intensified fiscality—the engine of both state making and dynastic war—contributed significantly to the rise of a money economy and a concomitant expansion of economic credit. These changes did not, however, lead to a sharp break with traditional values. Instead, the monarchy harnessed money as another tool of control: "Money was as likely to be an element of political power and social deference as of economic exchange. . . . It functioned less as a challenge to established patterns of power and subordination than as a newly effective implement for their exercise."[4] It is these circumstances, Dewald suggests, that made credit "a central metaphor of seventeenth-century public life."[5]

Smith makes a similar case, arguing that the term *credit* usefully highlights the intertwining of "interest" and "values" in seventeenth-century noble worldviews and thus provides a solution for historiographical debates on the sincerity of the flowery language of patronage.[6] For Smith, nobles' frequent use of the word underlines the mixture of economic and moral calculation in their everyday lives: "*Debts* were moral as much as they were monetary; *obligations* found expression through proofs of selflessness; *rewards* took the form of coin but also of honors, status, and other markers of respect; *credit* stood for all of the moral and financial resources one's reputation could command."[7] Based on changing dictionary definitions of the word, Smith argues that over the course of the eighteenth century the financial sense of the term "credit" gradually eclipsed its nonmaterial ones, serving as testimony—he argues—of the growing autonomy of the economic sphere.[8]

A numerical count of the frequency of the word *crédit* (per ten thousand words of text) by fifty-year periods on the database of the Project for American and French Research on the Treasury of the French Language (ARTFL) confirms these historians' sense that the importance of credit as a conceptual category peaked in the Old Regime. The top five chronological periods for usage in order were: 1700–1749 (0.81), 1550–1599 (0.75) (mostly in the works of Montaigne and Jean Bodin), 1600–1649 (0.56), 1750–1799 (0.56), and 1650–1699 (0.44).[9] The top ten users of the word (per ten thousand words of text), two of whom were women, were also situated in the Old Regime. They were, in order: Jean-Claude Fernier, Pierre Berthelot (d. 1615), Jean Rotrou (1609–1650), Marie de Gournay (1565–1645), René-Louis de Voyer de Paulmy, the marquis d'Argenson (1694–1757), the Abbé de Vertot (1655–1735), Madame de Villedieu (d. 1683), Guy Patin (1601–1672), and Gabriel Naudé (1600–1653).[10] The contexts in which these and other authors used the word *crédit* varied a great deal, as we see below, but references to the financial sense of the term constituted a minority of cases.

These results (which draw on a sample of about three thousand canonical French publications) suggest that the period from 1550 to 1800 represented a high point in the cultural saliency of credit, particularly with regard to nonmaterial uses of the word.[11] It was thus not the reign of Louis XIV itself that gave rise to the category of credit as a form of power and influence. This periodization suggests instead that the political instability of the Wars of Religion, followed by the slow rise in royal power (with the significant, disruptive interlude of the Fronde), raised new questions about how authority was generated and power was exercised, while at the same time the expansion of financial credit in public and private life provided new ways of framing and expressing bonds of obligation and reciprocity. It would not do, however, to place too much emphasis on the chronological origins of the nonmaterial usage of the term as the relatively few sources in the ARTFL database prior to 1600 exclude the possibility of definite conclusions about origins. The fact that the single thirteenth-century source in the database, by the trouvère Rutebeuf, contains ten references to credit in its nonmaterial form suggests that this was a trope of long-standing in French culture. This chapter accordingly focuses on a synchronic, rather than a diachronic, reading of credit, leaving chapter 2 to address the issue of change from the seventeenth through the eighteenth centuries.

The subjects treated by the top ten authors reveal that the court was but one arena for the exchange of credit. The court of Louis XIV at Versailles nonetheless provides an apt starting place for this chapter not only because of the existing historiography on courtly credit but also because the author in the ARTFL database who used the word the most was Louis de Rouvroy, duc de Saint-Simon.[12] Saint-Simon and other commentators on court culture provide a number of insights into how observers and participants understood the circulation of credit. In their writings the court is a forum for ostentatious, competitive display, a small and centralized milieu in which displaying and witnessing functioned as modes for assessing value and transmitting judgments. The sources also show that individuals at court—including women—lavishly praised their superiors' credit and candidly discussed their own and others' credit standing. Credit may have been informal, but it was not illicit or secret. The myriad forms of royal payout described by Dewald generated tremendous financial credit; they also fostered the accumulation of cultural credit (in the form of a lavish lifestyle, fashionable clothing, courtly poise, and so on) and social credit (in the form of dowries for good marriages, hosting important personages, and so forth) that could be transformed, through careful maneuvering, into political credit. Because credit traversed these domains, a very broad—if highly unequal—array of materials was available to individuals, families, and coteries seeking to increase their credit. These consisted of, most importantly, social rank, offices, kin networks, social connections, property, and wealth in addition to honorary positions, individual talent, experience and skill, ostentatious consumption, and possession of valued information. Some of these possessions could be transmitted over generations, but many were contingent on external circumstances and individual aptitudes.

A young courtier would have found an invaluable, if embittered, guide in the duc de Saint-Simon. His aristocratic pride and his opposition to Louis's political innovations led him to keep close track of the fluctuations in the privilege and power of others, and his cynicism attributed many types of exchange to trafficking in credit. For example, he explained that the Secretary of State for War François-Michel Le Tellier's advocacy of the Dutch War in 1673 was an attempt to undo Jean-Baptiste Colbert's influence by a decisive victory over Protestants inside and outside of France. As he states, "Le Tellier and his son Louvois, who had the Department of War, trembled at the success and credit of Colbert and had no difficulty putting a new war into the king's head."[13] According to Saint-Simon, the ministers and their entourages explicitly used the word credit to describe their power. He recounts, for example, that an intimate friend once asked Le Tellier to solicit a favor from the king on a matter that would be decided in his private meetings with the monarch. In response, Le Tellier told him simply that he would try his best. The friend took offense at this modest reply and told him "frankly that, with the place and credit [Le Tellier] had," he expected more from him.[14]

For Saint-Simon, the only rival to the ministers' credit was Françoise d'Aubigné, marquise de Maintenon, Louis xiv's mistress and, from 1683, secret wife. According to Saint-Simon, "for three quarters of the favors and the choices, and a further three quarters of the fourth quarter of what passed through the ministers' work in her quarters, it was she who disposed of them.... It was almost the same for accentuating or diminishing offences, making good on letters and services, or letting them go, and thus preparing a fall or a fortune."[15] Both mistress and ministers owed their influence to their personal ties to the king; their common interest in controlling Louis led them, according to the duke, to form a secret conspiracy to direct his decisions. Before their working meetings with the king, he tells us, Madame de Maintenon would summon ministers to a private meeting in which she indicated her choices for the benefices to be discussed with Louis. They would then enact an elaborate charade to maintain the illusion that the king was making his own choices. Saint-Simon resentfully concluded that "among them [was] a circle of reciprocal needs and services, which the king never suspected at all."[16]

Failure to please the royal consort, Saint-Simon claimed, could result in disaster, even for the highly placed. Her power over the lives of more humble individuals was even greater: "If the ministers, and the most accredited, were in this situation with Madame de Maintenon, one can judge what she was capable of with regard to all other sorts of people who were much less able to defend themselves. Many people thus had their necks broken without being able to imagine the cause and gave themselves a great deal of trouble to discover and remedy it, and without effect."[17] Thus, even while participating in mutually beneficial exchanges of credit with favored ministers, she also used her superior credit to crush those beneath her. The only branch of government that escaped her control, according to Saint-Simon, was foreign affairs, which were discussed in Council of State meetings that she did not attend.

Madame de Maintenon's own writings demonstrate that her credit was not a fiction invented by the vindictive Saint-Simon but something she consciously cultivated and deployed. In a long letter to her brother on February 28, 1678, scolding him on his extravagant lifestyle and recommending close supervision of his wife, she also promised her aid: "Please tell Monsieur Viette to let me know the state of Monsieur Truc's affair, because if my credit does not suffice, I will pluck longer strings."[18] These efforts apparently had limited success, for she lamented to a third party in a letter of December 1682: "You have too great a conception of favor in general and mine in particular. . . . All my credit and all my efforts have made of my brother [merely] a bourgeois de Paris."[19] On other occasions she acknowledged the rivalry between herself and the king's ministers, the theme so frequently sounded by Saint-Simon. For example, she wrote to the Comtesse de Saint Germain on March 13, 1688: "Monsieur de Louvois seems despondent that his credit has begun to fall: he envies me my favor; he attributes the king's disgust to me; he wants to make himself necessary by some new war."[20] These letters show Madame de Maintenon's lucid sense of the efficacy of her informal power and of its occasional limitations. She also knew, like Louvois, how to denigrate her credit as a tactical maneuver, emphasizing her limited powers to placate a supplicant while preserving her capital for more important affairs.

Madame de Maintenon and those around her viewed credit as a crucial element of court women's assets. Her letters include advice, exhortations, and commendations to her circle of friends and relatives—many of them women—regarding their use of credit. Madame de Maintenon herself received counsel about the appropriate exercise of her credit from priests and spiritual directors, demonstrating that, if her relationship with the king outraged Saint-Simon, the power she derived from it did not appear covert or scandalous to men of the church. Père Bourdaloue, one of the candidates she considered for a new spiritual director in the late 1680s, for example, wrote exhorting her to do good works with discernment, "that is to say that you do not consume the talents, mind, credit that God has given you to do good works of little consequence, whilst you could be doing much more important ones that you perhaps do not do."[21] The bishop of Chartres, Paul Godet des Marais, ultimately became her spiritual director. In one of numerous letters of instruction he wrote for his pious charge, the bishop told her: "Do not exhaust your credit on the affairs of private individuals: save yourself for the general affairs of the church, for the good of the state and that of the king." In another letter, he wrote: "it is for the great interests of the church and the state, when you clearly see the good, that you must use your credit, and even exhaust it in the service of God, if necessity demands it."[22] A subsequent letter returned to this theme: "You must make good use [*faire valoir* or, literally, make value] of your place, your credit, your talents, the gifts God has given you: you must not make usury of them. Withdrawing through fear, falling into the fault of the lazy servant who feared losing his goods, and buried them, is to expose yourself to the same punishment and you know that it was terrible."[23] The bishop acknowledged the force of credit and its potential for beneficial application. However, given its worldly nature, he believed the higher spiritual path was to redirect profits gained through credit toward pious ends. The link is explicit here between financial and political credit, both of which must be given up as gratuitous gifts to God.

Madame de Maintenon was not the only female courtier whose credit attracted attention from Saint-Simon and other observers. As studies of female patronage would lead us to expect, beyond mistresses and queens, noble women wielding credit appear in innumerable sources from the seventeenth and eighteenth centuries.[24] For example, the bishop of Chartres's fellow bishops similarly highlighted the credit possessed by powerful court women and commended them for using it for spiritual rather than worldly ends. In his funeral oration of 1669 for Henrietta-Maria, queen of England, Bishop Jacques-Bénigne Bossuet made three references to the queen's credit, which, he states, she used to lessen the plight of Catholics in England. In his funeral oration of 1670 for the duchesse d'Orléans, Bossuet praised the duchess for using her powerful credit not to oppress but to help others.[25] In his funeral oration of 1683 for Maria-Theresa, wife of Louis XIV, Bishop Esprit Fléchier stressed, again, the theme of using credit to support religion: "Thus nothing touched her as deeply as the interests of her religion. What mission has there been that she has not either assisted with her credit or supported with her beneficence?"[26] He also praised the queen for according credit to virtue instead of wealth: "To be called to her side, it was not enough to follow her, it was also necessary to imitate her in her pious practices. Wisdom and order reigned everywhere:

modesty was more esteemed than beauty and virtue found more credit than fortune."[27] These eulogies raise the possibility of an abusive use of credit by powerful women, but the theme was not particularly gendered. For example, Saint-Simon declared approvingly of Alexandre Bontemps, the first valet of the king's chamber, that "he never did harm to anyone and always used his credit to oblige others."[28] So accepted was courtly women's credit that the 1721 edition of Furetière's dictionary cited Fléchier's eulogy of Maria-Theresa to illustrate the following definition of crédit: "belief, esteem that one acquires in public by one's virtue, probity, good faith and merit."[29]

Spokesmen for the church thus acknowledged the powerful credit possessed by court ladies; for them, credit was a potentially praiseworthy element of court life, but one vulnerable to misuse and corruption. They painted an idealized portrait of the great lady, who devoted her credit to the defense of religion and the support of virtue. For these moralists, the logic of credit opposed the logic of economics; instead of seeking a return on their credit, they should spend it freely in the service of God and the state. The public good must triumph over any private or self-interested benefits. As we will see in the next chapter, this ironic and idealistic strain in conceptualizing credit was appropriated by a new generation of eighteenth-century secular moralizers. As the financial functions of credit attracted ever more attention, some commentators strove to purify credit by returning it to its putative origins in the gift economy and thus projected onto the past a notion of credit based solely on esteem, virtue, and reputation.

It is worth underlining the matter-of-factness with which contemporaries acknowledged women's possession of credit. This is particularly striking, given the fact that dictionary definitions of the term make almost no reference to women. Because it was informal and tied not only to birth and title but also to intangible factors like personal charm, charisma, friendships, and other loyalties, both men and women were able to acquire and deploy credit. To place this discussion within the existing historiography on women and power in the Old Regime, *credit* is the word some eighteenth-century critics used to sum up the informal power exercised by women in monarchical society, the power that was viewed as symbolic of the regime's corruption by late eighteenth-century writers like Rousseau and the Baron d'Holbach.[30]

In addition to describing the machinations of men and women possessed of credit, Saint-Simon's memoirs also reveal individuals with a surprising lack of credit, despite their close ties to the royal family. For example, he describes Madame de Maintenon's trying relationship with her outspoken brother and unfashionable sister-in-law: "Her brother, as long as he lived, grieved her; he came to her at all hours, spoke of nonsense, and often made sorties. Of credit with her, not the least in the world. Her sister-in-law never appeared at court, nor in society [*le monde*]. Madame de Maintenon treated her well through pity, without it ever carrying through to the smallest credit."[31] (In return, Madame de Maintenon herself lamented in December 1701 in a letter to her friend, the Cardinal de Noailles: "I have no credit over my brother's mind.")[32]

Even more surprisingly, Saint-Simon reveals the total lack of credit held by the heir to the throne, Monseigneur, the king's son. Although his proximity to power might lead one to expect him to hold credit second only to the king, the opposite was true. As Saint-Simon explained: "He did not have a shadow of credit with his father; it sufficed even that his taste was noted in favor of someone for that someone to perceive harmful repercussions; and the king was so jealous to show that he [Monseigneur] could do nothing that he [the king] did nothing for any of those who sought to pay court to him not even for any of his *menins*, albeit chosen and named by the king, who would have found it very bad that they did not serve Monseigneur with great assiduity."[33] Louis's success in imposing his will thus manifested itself here in the denial of his credit to the dauphin, who lacked the personal skills and will to defy his father. Much to Saint-Simon's chagrin, the circuits of courtly credit thus ran directly counter to official hierarchies of rank: while the first in line to the throne had no influence, a female mistress held tremendous power. It was not credit itself that shocked the duke but the king's perversion of the channels through which it should flow.

Moreover, not all royal mistresses or queens sought the credit their position might have provided. In a biography of Princess Henrietta (the first wife of the duc d'Orléans), Madame de Lafayette contrasts the official rank of Louis XIV's mother with her disinterest in the credit that might have accompanied it: "the Queen Mother held by rank the first place in the royal family and, according to appearances, should have held it by her credit, but the same disposition that made authority a heavy burden while it was entirely in her hands prevented her from thinking of recovering part of it when she no longer held it."[34] Of Louise de La Vallière, attendant to Henrietta and early mistress of the Sun King, Lafayette remarked: "it is also true that the lack of wit of La Vallière meant that she did not pursue the advantages and the credit that such a great passion could have led another to take: she only thought of being loved by the king and loving him."[35]

A final—and crucial—point to note regarding the politics of credit at court is the constant and complex interplay between financial and political credit. Extended and repeated credit from a host of merchants and financiers was indispensable for obtaining political and social credit (merchants to supply the lavish food, drink, furnishings, coaches, and clothing for display of rank and financiers for the loans needed to purchase royal offices and titles). Unfortunately for the merchants, the ever-rising cost of increasing their credit led noble clients to neglect paying their debts. In the hierarchy of credit, the final conversion—from trade credit to cash—was the rarest and most difficult.

While merchants struggled to obtain payment, powerful individuals constantly sought to convert their influence into hard cash. Saint-Simon reveals, for example, that Marie Anne de La Trémoille, princesse des Ursins, derived substantial financial benefits from her position at the Spanish court, where she served as chief of household to the teenaged queen of Spain, a position arranged by Madame de Maintenon: "The King of Spain [grandson of Louis XIV and former duc d'Anjou] sent her fifteen hundred pistoles, even though he surely needed money more than she; . . . without the credit of the Abbé d'Estrées, who found one hundred thousand écus, he would not have been able to leave Madrid."[36] The princess thus took advantage of her political credit to obtain money that the king of Spain could only acquire through the mediating financial credit of the French ambassador. In addition to revealing the constant two-way conversion between economic and social credit, contemporary documents also underline the distinction between mere wealth and credit. The doctor Guy Patin wrote, in one example, that "Monsieur Vautier [the physician of Cardinal Mazarin] is very rich, he has a good abbey, much hard cash, but little credit."[37] Patin's letter reveals that not everything was available for purchase and not all wealthy individuals possessed the influence or connections necessary for efficacious actions.[38] This anecdote reminds us that credit was not reducible to money, and money alone was no guarantee of the influence or power inherent in credit. Indeed, credit was such a useful category because it encompassed not only the relatively small array of goods available on the open market but also all of the material and immaterial resources to which access was difficult and uncertain.

The warrior and member of the French Academy, Roger de Bussy, comte de Rabutin (known as Bussy-Rabutin), offers a striking example of the complex intertwining of political and economic credit in an extended anecdote in his memoirs:

> When I bought the charge of maître de camp général of the cavalry, M. Fouquet took a promise of twenty thousand livres that I had from the prince de Condé, and the old ordinances of my appointment as royal lieutenant that amounted to ten thousand francs, and sent me ten thousand écus. For the

pleasure that he did me and the marks of his friendship that he made me hope for, he demanded from me a promise written and signed in my hand, to sell him my charge in three years at the king's pleasure, for the ninety thousand écus that it cost me, and he promised me in return by the same bill to help me with his credit and his money to enter into an important position in the king's household or provincial government, when I gave up the charge of maître de camp général. His plan was to have this charge fall into the hands of whoever married his daughter. Following this promise, he made me a thousand assurances of friendship; and he not only assured me that he would make sure my stipend was paid; but that I would further receive from him all the favors that one could expect from a *surintendant* [a high royal financial officer] with whom one is friends.[39]

In this incident, Fouquet, the powerful superintendent of finances (later imprisoned for alleged financial corruption), imposed a series of transactions on Bussy-Rabutin. First, he exchanged Rabutin's credit money (a promissory note of twenty thousand livres and the ten-thousand-livre value of his lieutenant's post) for thirty thousand livres in cash, a sum Rabutin would never have realized from the papers he held. In exchange, the superintendent asked Rabutin to sign a note promising to sell Fouquet his new position of maître de camp in the cavalry for its cash price. Fouquet sweetened the deal with promises to assist Rabutin with "his credit and his money" to obtain an important political post and to ensure full payment of his military stipend, which was normally paid in fractional installments, if at all. The point of these exchanges was to obtain the cavalry post for Fouquet's future son-in-law. Fouquet wielded his credit here not just as a promise to aid Bussy subsequently but to force him to consent to the exchange in the first place.

This complex transaction, or set of transactions, collapsed, however, when Fouquet suspected Bussy-Rabutin of having formed a liaison with a young woman who had refused his own advances. Although Fouquet later acknowledged his error in doubting the woman's virtue, he never forgave Bussy-Rabutin the imagined slight and "when she spoke to him sometimes of [his] interests, he responded that one did not receive [him]." Having acquired her own credit with the superintendent, the young woman was unable to extend it to the unfortunate Bussy-Rabutin. This situation had financial as well as political repercussions for Bussy-Rabutin, who ultimately received less than a quarter of his military stipend.[40] Although Bussy-Rabutin is too discreet (in this instance) to mention her name, the woman in question has been identified as his cousin, Madame de Sévigné, who was much pursued after being widowed in 1651 at the age of twenty-five and was also a close friend and correspondent of Madame de Lafayette.[41] Madame de Sévigné's famous correspondence, as we will see below, offers its own rich insights into the multiplicity of credit.

This anecdote reveals the range of values that contemporaries calculated, exchanged, and converted: financial credit, cash, military posts, royal offices, stipends, friendship, influence, and marriage, among others. Cash, financial papers (like promissory notes), and official salaries were sufficiently discrete as to form three distinct currencies. The canniest seventeenth-century men and women were able to come up with the most advantageous formulation of these forms of capital. The worth of each currency was derived not from its abstract or formally assigned value but from a complex and collective process of assessment that was inseparable from wider social relations, cultural norms, and political processes. The slippery relationship between the nominal value of money and its real value in exchange was encouraged and underlined by the fact that the French livre itself was a unit of account, not a coin, which the royal government repeatedly devalued in relationship to silver and gold between 1690 and 1725.[42]

From Royal Courts to Courts of Law

The royal court was a key arena of credit relations, but contemporaries also believed credit was the decisive form of power in quite another court system: the Parlements and other courts of law. Guy Patin (1601–1672), a doctor who became dean of the medical school at the University of Paris, was a keen participant in and observer of this phenomenon. Patin wrote many letters during the Fronde that highlight the intervention of credit in the judicial process in those fractious years as a means of forging alliances and breaking rivals. As one letter explained of the growing power of Cardinal Mazarin: "Cardinal Mazarin had the bishop of Beauvais driven from the council of the queen and from Paris and had him sent back to his diocese, eight days after having had the credit to have the duc de Beaufort, second son of Monsieur de Vendôme, arrested and sent as a prisoner to the bois de Vincennes."[43] Whatever his formal authority, Patin suggests, Mazarin could not have detained such a powerful figure if he did not possess substantial informal power and influence as well. Patin also frankly discussed his capacity to use his own credit to bend the course of the law. As he wrote to Monsieur Belin, a fellow doctor in Troyes, Champagne, "It seems to me that the *chambre des enquestes* where I have the most credit is the second one; if your trial goes elsewhere, we will follow it."[44]

As at the court of Versailles, the allocation of credit did not always follow official hierarchies. For example, the Jansenist Robert Arnauld d'Andilly wrote of efforts by the central government to have the Parlement of Toulouse register a peace treaty after the successful siege of Montpellier in 1622. Arnauld described the request he received to seek the assistance in this effort of his friend, Monsieur de Bertier de Montrave, who "even though he was only the second president, had much more credit than anyone else in his company."[45] Judicial titles, like other forms of office, were up for sale but, again, money alone did not suffice to purchase them. Madame de Sévigné described a meeting with the twenty-seven-year-old chief justice of the *chambre de comptes* of Nantes, remarking that she had met the young man many times without ever imagining he could become a magistrate. She continued: "However he has become one by his credit, and for forty thousand francs, he has purchased all the experience necessary to be at the head of a sovereign court."[46] In all probability even the young man's cash was just another form of credit, raised in the forms of loans by the young man's family; for almost no family, however wealthy, would have had forty thousand livres in cash at hand.

Another parallel with the royal court was women's capacity to draw on their credit to manipulate decision-making. In a letter to the president of the Parlement of Paris (the most important of the nation's sovereign law courts), the poet Vincent Voiture referred to an appeal on his credit by a woman anxious for a beneficial outcome to a lawsuit: "Madame de Marsilly imagined that I had some credit with you, and I, who am vain, did not want to tell her the contrary. She is a person who is beloved and esteemed by the whole court and who disposes of the whole parlement. If she has good success in an affair in which she has chosen you for judge, and she thinks that I have contributed something, you would not believe the honor that that would do me in society [le monde] and how much more agreeable I would be to all honorable people."[47] By invoking his credit with one interlocutor, he hoped to acquire it with another, who herself was a powerful credit broker at court and in Parlement. The currency of credit could thus be transferred from one institution and one set of relations to another.

Credit in Intellectual Life

The courts of the king and of his royal magistrates operated in tandem, with crisscrossing circuits of credit flowing both through sanctioned hierarchies and against them. Another field in which contemporaries used credit to explain the workings of power was that of intellectual life and publishing. *La*

Bibliothèque françoise by Charles Sorel—himself the beneficiary of a pension from Fouquet—furnishes multiple examples of credit as a form of credence and influence acquired by authors, ideas, and even intellectual styles. With reference to Michel de Montaigne, for example, Sorel noted critics' complaint that "he makes masculine or feminine several nouns against custom and against nature." Sorel defended Montaigne by claiming that "this reproach is not worth great consideration, and indeed one should note that several of the words have since passed into common use, which occurred perhaps by the credit he gave them, being a privilege of great authors, to make words."[48] This passage provides a striking parallel to Montesquieu's later comments on banks and value: "In states that conduct economic trade, they have fortunately established banks that, by their credit, have formed new signs of value."[49] Institutions or individuals possessed of sufficient credit gained the capacity to issue new forms of value, whether in financial or cultural terms.

Over time styles of writing themselves fell into and out of credit: "Perhaps one esteemed some clarity of style, and some facility of expression that was in credit, and of which we have lost knowledge and practice; so many there were that imagined that that was a model to write letters well, as each thing has its season."[50] On another occasion Sorel referred to the "great credit" acquired by the published letters of Jean-Louis Guez de Balzac and the resulting cascade of publications emulating his style.[51] Remarking on the credit acquired by the published letters of poet Vincent Voiture, he added that "this agreeable and informal style is now in credit for amusing oneself among friends, and one must give glory to M. de Voiture for having invented it."[52] More concretely, books could also bring credit to their owners, according to Gabriel Naudé in his *Advis Pour Dresser une Bibliothèque* (*Advice on Establishing a Library*): "if the libraries that one purchases are good and noteworthy, they serve to augment the credit and reputation of those who are enriched by them."[53]

Even a celebrated author such as Jean-Louis Guez de Balzac (whose literary and personal reputation Sorel staunchly defended against critics) worried about his credit standing; he declared of his opponents: "nothing has been forgotten to give credit to my enemy and to make me lose my reputation."[54] Defiantly, Guez de Balzac dismissed his opponents' talents: "the audacity with which they say that they know gives them more reputation and more credit than their science."[55] Read on their own, these comments might seem like isolated and banal references to intellectual credibility. Viewed within the broader commentary on credit, they show us an intellectual milieu in which personalized and collective mechanisms of reputation and influence were of paramount importance. Like the court, the intellectual world was a relatively closed and highly hierarchical community, whose denizens struggled for the reputation that led to material and immaterial rewards and within which assessments of value shifted according to shared perceptions of credibility and merit. The key role of royal and noble patronage in legitimating and supporting literature in this period also meant that the flows of courtly credit discussed above encompassed the literary arena.[56]

In the early decades of the seventeenth century the letters of Nicolas Peiresc (1580–1637) reveal the importance of credit relations for scholars wishing to gain access to research materials. He wrote one colleague to "beg you to favor with your assistance the said Sieur Du Chesne so that he can see and can freely extract what will be necessary for him in your abbey and elsewhere where you have credit. He is a person of great erudition and whose virtue and merits are in very great esteem among all men of letters."[57] On another occasion he wrote: "You have made me aware of a life of Constantine in Greek. Let me know, I beg you what it is and if it is within your reach and if you would be willing to communicate where it is; is it possible that we will have enough credit to obtain it, either on loan or in property and in that case we will put it in your own hands first so that you can work on it if you are so inclined."[58] Given the limited size and material constraints of the intellectual world, the credit of a good scholarly reputation was not merely self-gratifying but an indispensable form of introduction. Books acquired and conferred credit, and it required credit to gain access to rare and precious works.

Even within this masculine intellectual world, women could wield influence. In a letter to Mademoiselle Paulet, a prominent seventeenth-century salonnière, Vincent Voiture wrote: "I beg you very humbly, Mademoiselle, you who procure me all sorts of goods, to employ all the credit you have with him, to have him do me the honor of remembering me; and if you can make him love me, I will give you six months respite for what you owe me."[59] This example highlights the crossing over between moral and financial credit in the intellectual world, just as at court. In exchange for using her credit to acquire a new source of patronage, Voiture promised an extension of Paulet's loan. His comments emphasize the ongoing nature of their exchange and the broad content of the "all sorts of goods" they exchanged. The same tactics and strategies—with a similar outcome—attended struggles for power and influence in the intellectual world as in the worlds of politics and law. Money was one goal, but credibility and efficacy were the common currency in all of these endeavors: at court, in the law, or in the world of ideas. They also served as crucial weapons in confrontations between rivals, be they individuals, families, or factions. Since writers and publishers were predominantly nonnoble in origins, they also demonstrate the crossover of aristocratic notions of credit and patronage into the mental world of the middle classes.

Credo: Credit and Religious Belief

The word *credit* derives from the Latin *credo* or belief; drawing on these origins, credit was also an important theme in discussions of religious faith and the reputation of religious institutions. Guy Patin fulminated against the hysteria aroused by the supposed demonic possessions at Louviers in 1642: "One didn't speak in earlier times of this devilry; it was the monks who put it in credit over the last hundred years or so, in order to gain value for their holy water."[60] *Tartuffe*, Molière's satire of religious hypocrisy, decries those who use false devotion to win credit, proclaiming: "these utter charlatans, these hired zealots, whose sacrilege and false grimaces abuse with impunity and play at will with that which mortals have of the most saintly and sacred, these men who, with a soul enslaved to interest, make of devotion a trade and merchandise, and wish to buy credit and dignities at the price of false winks of the eye and affected transports."[61] While bishops presented an idealized form of credit purged of economic calculation, Molière, in the same years, used the economic sense of credit to disparage false religion, which disguised venal self-interest under an illusion of piety.

One writer used the term to describe the spiritual authority generated by pious missionaries and as a category to analyze the workings of power in foreign states. In 1685 Louis XIV sent a group of five Jesuit monks, including Père Louis Le Comte (1655–1728), on a mission to China. The monks assumed the task of charting Chinese geography and assisting the efforts of Christian missionaries already active in Asia. In 1696 Le Comte published *New Memoirs on the State of China* based on his experience. For Le Comte, both the politics of the Chinese state and the activities of Western missionaries were best described in terms of strategies for acquiring and deploying credit. Deploring the death of Père Verbiest, a Flemish Jesuit who had preceded them in China, Le Comte noted that "he conserved the fervor of the existing faithful and he sustained the weakness of the new by the interest that he took in all of their affairs; he gave credit to missionaries in the provinces by his letters of recommendation; he saved Macao, which had become suspicious to the Tartars; the state itself, which he had served on several important occasions, was in no small way indebted to him; so that the Europeans, the Chinese, and the emperor viewed him almost equally as their father."[62] In such difficult circumstances, credit won could be easily exhausted: "They were on the brink of ruining Macao, and the order had already been given to expel all the Portuguese, when father Adam made a last effort to save them. It was there that all his credit ended that he had employed so usefully for the good of religion. Because a short time later he was himself the object of the bloodiest persecution that the church has suffered."[63]

According to Le Comte, Christian missionaries were obliged to adopt local elite practices in order to acquire the credit necessary to pursue their mission: "they adopt silk garments, according to local custom, when they visit people of quality; they sometimes even have themselves carried in chairs, or else they go on horseback followed by some valets. All of this is absolutely necessary to preserve their credit and the protection of the mandarins, without whom the Christians would be frequently oppressed; but this itself makes the life of the missionary very harsh: because since this expense takes almost all of his revenue or his pensions, which never approaches one hundred écus, the little that remains to him scarcely suffices to live on."[64] The Chinese elite thus held a series of expectations about the behaviors and appearance of a credible interlocutor, to which European visitors must conform. At least in Le Comte's mind, appearances were as important in this foreign court as they were at Versailles.

To succeed in their scientific and religious projects, French monks were required not only to emulate Chinese customs but also to attain a nuanced understanding of Chinese politics. Credit was a category through which Le Comte did so, noting that "Prince Sosan is so respected throughout the empire, either for the honor he bears of being a close relative of the emperor, for his title of grand master of the palace, or for his credit and skill."[65] In addition to lines of parentage and official titles, awareness of credit standings and individual dexterity in manipulating them were key to understanding the lines of power. As with Louvois and Colbert, the credit of one royal servant hemmed in that of another: "While all these things were taking place in Peking, the viceroy of Ham-Chéou, who had had the time to reflect on his conduct, was not tranquil in his province. The credit of prince Sosan troubled him, and he feared above all his just anger."[66] As the next section elucidates, the Chinese were not the only "others" subject to this scrutiny, for credit as a category of analysis ran through French historical and proto-ethnographic writing of the period.

Credit and Cultural Translation

As in the case of China, studies of past or distant societies relied on credit as a way to render the foreign familiar. The Swiss naturalist Charles Bonnet wrote in *La Palingénésie Philosophique* that "ostracism was a ten-year exile introduced by the Athenians against citizens whose wealth or whose credit rendered them suspect."[67] Roman society was an obvious candidate for such analysis, given the importance of the patron-client relation to Roman society. On Rome, the Abbé Mably wrote in *Parallel between Romans and Frenchmen* (1740) that "the office of censor above all and the religious offices that at first conveyed so much credit in the Republic and which were reserved to the patricians alone successfully outweighed the authority of the tribunes."[68] According to Mably, it was Julius Caesar's acquisition of credit that threatened his adversaries; he thus wrote of "Caesar whose burgeoning credit threatened Pompey with a dangerous rival." The Abbé Raynal noted in his *Philosophical and Political History of the Settlements and Trade of the Europeans in the East and West Indies* (1770) that Pompey possessed formidable credit in his own right, attributing Caesar's recall to Rome to "the credit of Pompey."

Moving forward in time, in his account of the Frankish invasion of Gaul (which he portrayed as a friendly overture in response to a Gaulish invitation), the Abbé Dubos discussed the credit of Gaulish queens with their kings in much the same way contemporaries evoked the credit of their queens: "Everyone has heard of the credit that Tanaquil had over the mind of her husband Lucumon, known so well in Roman history under the name of old Tarquin, and of the confidence that Germanicus had in his wife Agrippine."[69] Fast-forwarding several centuries, Jeanne Chapelain's *La Pucelle* attributed Jeanne d'Arc's trial and execution to resentment of the credit she had acquired.

As these scattered examples suggest, credit was an important category of analysis for Old Regime historians, playwrights, translators, and other writers. They used credit to explain foreign or historic societies in a way that was immediately comprehensible to readers familiar with the *commerce du monde* of Old Regime France. In their view the goals of credit wielding were the same, as were the dynamics of power and the relations that traversed the public-private divide. Whether in a republic, an empire, or a "despotic" Eastern monarchy, undercurrents of power flowed through personal ties of affection, obligation, and reciprocity, and they were all cast against a collective scrutiny that assessed fluctuating levels of reputation, influence, and power. Regardless of the accuracy of their analysis, these sources reveal their authors' perception that credit was a universal and ubiquitous mechanism of political power.

One means to gauge the importance of credit as a category to familiarize foreign and historical others is to compare early modern French translations of Roman authors with the Latin originals. This comparison is all the more instructive in that the "translations" of the period were rarely literal and almost always infused with contemporary concerns. To take one example, the early modern period witnessed a rediscovery of Tacitus (A.D. 56–117), whose frank accounts of the machinations at the imperial court resonated deeply with courtiers across Europe. The so-called Tacitist movement in European political theory began in the late sixteenth century and lasted until the French Revolution, producing multiple translations of his work. These translations served as a guide to kings and courtiers alike who read him as an advocate of realpolitik.[70] In the mid-seventeenth century Perrot d'Ablancourt was one of the first and most important French translators of Tacitus. To read d'Ablancourt's translation of Tacitus's *Annals* is to find the Roman historian using the term *credit* to signify political power and influence in a number of passages. The original Latin, however, uses many different words to convey these ideas, including *ambitu*, *gratia*, and *arts*, all of which he translated as "crédit." D'Ablancourt even inserted the word into sentences lacking any clear equivalent for the term.[71] Thus, it was in the loose protocols of seventeenth-century translation that Rome became an empire run by credit. Tacitus himself did not use a singular concept to refer to power and influence, but his mid-seventeenth-century French readers could learn from him the lesson that power flowed in the Roman Empire through the same circuits as in the French monarchical regime.

Examination of English publications translated into French shows similar dynamics at work. In Samuel Richardson's *Pamela*, published in 1740, the title character declares the following: "My poor parents are so low in the world, they can do nothing but break their hearts for me."[72] The contemporary French translation, by the Abbé Prévost, renders her despair as: "Mes parens sont si pauvres, et ont si peu de crédit dans le monde que tout ce qu'ils peuvent faire pour moi c'est de mourir de chagrin." Whereas the Abbé Prévost imposed the notion of credit on Richardson's hierarchical depiction of society, other translators substituted the term for particular English words, such as *authority* or *force*. For example, in a passage from Henry Fielding's *Amelia* of 1751, one character declared, "you know the great authority which that worthy man had over the whole town."[73] In P. F. de Puisieux's French translation this statement became: "vous n'ignorez pas le crédit que ce digne homme s'est acquis dans toute la ville."[74]

Particularly intriguing is the occasional use of "crédit" as a replacement for the English word *interest*. For example, Richardson's Pamela is held against her will at the behest of her lustful master, lamenting: "And I have not interest to save myself!"[75] What more natural term to employ for this notion than that of *crédit*, which is the choice Prévost made. When a character in Fielding's *Amelia* relates the promises of aid he has received from a noble lord, his interlocutor responds joyfully: "I do assure you, if you have his interest, you will need no other." Puisieux's French version reads: "Je vous assure que si vous êtes aidé de son crédit, il ne vous en faut pas d'autre."[76] Thus, in eighteenth-century usage, the English word *interest* could fill some of the same functions as *crédit* in France.[77]

Domestic Credit

Much closer to home, credit also explained the motivations and the machinations at work within French families and, in particular, between spouses. In practical terms marriage was, of course, a prime opportunity to obtain new sources of credit, be they financial, social, or political. As a character in Molière's comédie-héroique *Dom Garcie de Navarre* (first produced in 1661) declared of a projected marriage: "he seeks in the hymen of this illustrious girl the support of the great credit in which her family finds itself."[78] Madame de Lafayette wrote of the dauphine in *La Princesse de Clèves*, "Messieurs de Guise, whose niece she was, had greatly increased their credit and their respect by her marriage."[79] In Pierre Corneille's *Le Menteur*, Dorante asks for Clarice's hand in marriage, declaring: "you are going to put me in such credit in the city, but such a great credit that I fear jealous people."[80]

Marriage was an important means to obtain credit, but it was also necessary to deploy credit to forge alliances. In *Mémoires sur les Grands jours tenus à Clermont en 1665–66* Esprit Fléchier recounted the story of a provincial intendant begged by a friend to use his credit to win a beloved's hand: "While the intendant entertained himself, Fayet, who was among his closest friends, spoke to him confidentially one day of his affairs and begged him to use his credit with the girl's parents to have them finally consent to his request and, if he dared to say, to the inclinations of their daughter, and he instructed him in different specificities to be able to negotiate more successfully." Things did not work out as planned, however, when the intendant substituted his own suit for that of the friend and married the girl himself.[81]

The role of credit in marriage was due, in part, to the dynastic and material interests at stake in the forging of alliances. There was also a sense, however, in which credit derived from the deepest feelings and emotions. Contemporaries frequently referred to the heart or the soul as the seat of credit. Writing of Jeanne d'Arc in *La Pucelle*, Jean Chapelain wrote: "the girl doubles her credit in all hearts."[82] Of the one character (Elmire) to whom Molière's Tartuffe was emotionally susceptible, the plain-spoken maidservant noted: "she has some credit over Tartuffe's mind; he goes along with whatever she says and could well have a soft heart for her."[83] In Molière's *Le Dépit amoureux*, Ascagne uses the tie of credit to persuade his sister to change her course of action: "My sister, if over you I might have credit, if you are susceptible to the pleas of a brother, abandon such a plan and do not take Valère away from a young thing whose interests are dear to me and who, by my word, has the right to move you."[84] In the sense used by these authors, credit did not mean merely merit-worthy reputation, as we continue to use the word today, but the stock of influence one individual held over others, akin to the dynamics we have seen at court and elsewhere.

Despite his apparent cynicism about the role of credit in the courts, the doctor Guy Patin attributed his father's credit in the city of Paris to the man's honor and the love of his friends: "my father was called François Patin, a good man if there ever was one. If everyone resembled him, we would have no need of notaries. He came to Paris every year for the affairs of his master, where he had all the credit imaginable, and I have found there a quantity of friends that I did not know at all, who embraced me a thousand times because of him."[85] Patin measured his father's credit not in the financial support available to him but in the friendship and affection offered by virtual strangers. The relationship between credit and emotion was one element of women's ability to acquire credit in the form of influence over powerful men. This positive attribute, however, had its negative aspect, as the role of sexuality and seduction threatened to debase the pure virtue supposedly at the heart of the credit relation.

As elsewhere, the dual nature of credit was a useful way to reflect on the tensions between individual interest and sincere esteem. The role of credit in relations of love was thus not always perceived in a beneficent light, and the contamination of love by interest and calculation could be powerfully conveyed by the metaphor of credit. In Molière's *Le Misanthrope* the vain and calculating Marquis Acaste says to his friend Clitandre: "I have neither the figure nor the disposition to erase a beauty's coldness. It is for poorly formed people, those of common merit, to burn constantly for harsh beauties, to languish at their feet and suffer their severity, to seek the aid of sighs and tears, and to attempt by a very long courtship to obtain what is denied their small merit. But men of my stamp, marquis, are not made to love on credit, and pay all the expenses. However rare is the merit of beauties, I think, thank God! That we are worth our price like them, and that to have the honor of a heart like mine, there is no reason that it cost them nothing, and that, at least, to weigh everything on a just scale, the advances must be made at shared expense."[86] Acaste's miscalculation—the object of his affections remains indifferent to him—reveals his foolish and base character, making him a just object of the misanthrope's scorn.[87]

Varieties of Credit in Daily Life

We have seen examples of the multiple uses of "credit" in its social or political form in a wide variety of texts. Two cousins, both remarkable letter writers, permit a closer reading of how individual men and women thought about credit, how their conception of it was inflected by gender, and how they conceived of the multiple forms of credit operating within their daily lives. Bussy-Rabutin was a military man, a member of the French academy, and an author of a scurrilous account of court life that led to imprisonment in the Bastille in 1660 and a seventeen-year exile at his estates in Burgundy. Most celebrated for her correspondence with her daughter, Marie de Rabutin-Chantal, marquise de Sévigné, known as Madame de Sévigné, exchanged many letters with her cousin.[88] Both cousins' letters contain numerous reflections on credit in its multiple dimensions.

Bussy-Rabutin relied heavily on credit relations in his bids to return from exile and regain his place at court. In a letter of 1671 to his friend and fellow writer Mademoiselle de Scudéry, he commented on how courtiers often failed to use their credit to help their friends: "When courtiers forget their absent and unfortunate friends, it is not that their hearts sleep as you say, they are only too awake; but it is that they attend to their own interests; and there are few who have enough credit for their own affairs and those of others."[89] In a subsequent letter to Scudéry, he discussed the negative effects of the lack of confidence that the Duc de Saint-Aignan displayed in his friends.[90] He continued: "If he does not acquire me any good graces from Monsieur Colbert, I will have to believe that he is a feeble friend, or that he has no credit with him. If I had not had great proofs of his friendship, I would believe rather the former than the latter, because by all appearances he must be on very good terms with Monsieur Colbert." In a subsequent letter, where he deplored the false friendships one found at court, he told her: "As for you, madame, if you had as much credit as I am assured that you have good wishes for me, I would have no reason to complain of my fortune."[91] For Bussy-Rabutin, as for his contemporaries, one mark of true friendship was a willingness to proffer credit to those in need; false friends placed self-interest above the heart and reserved their credit for their own affairs. His remarks also highlight the uncertainties surrounding credit. Lacking a formal scale of measurement, there was always room for doubt about how much individuals possessed and with whom they enjoyed it.

Bussy-Rabutin interpreted his fall, and his potential for returning to grace, through the dynamics of credit. In May 1674 he wrote to the premier président of the Parlement at Dijon: "I believe that my more or less prompt return depends a fair amount on circumstances, and the credit and ardor of those who will serve me."[92] In a letter to the Bishop of Verdun, he stated: "As for my disgrace, it is one of those injustices of fortune that one sees sometimes at court. Trifles with enemies in credit are much more harmful than crimes without enemies."[93] A year later, he was not confident of the powers of credit to help him: "However, I work so as to have nothing to reproach myself with and I await from time and circumstance the aid that I do not foresee should arrive by my efforts or by the credit of those who love me."[94] In 1677, writing to the wife of a parlementary president (la Présidente d'O), he audaciously declared: "I say nothing to you of the trial I have in your chamber [that is, her husband's chamber]; because my cause is too worthy to employ so great a credit as your own; I save you for doubtful affairs. It's true that since you do not count the favors you do for your friends, and that this one will not prevent me from receiving others from you, I permit you to win this trial for me."[95] This quotation speaks not only to the famous Bussy-Rabutin wit but also to the assumption that a head magistrate's wife was easily capable of decisive intervention in the course of justice. In Bussy-Rabutin's flattering formulation, unlike economic credit, credit extended to friends was not susceptible to base calculation.

In the end Bussy-Rabutin's fears of the inefficacy of his friends' credit were justified. He would have to wait until 1682 to be allowed to return to court. He returned shortly thereafter to his estates in Burgundy, where he died in 1693. Despite his political disgrace, Bussy-Rabutin's literary renown endured. Richelet's dictionary definition of credit cited an excerpt from one of his poems to illustrate the influence a lover acquires over the beloved: "When on a young heart a lover that one esteems / Has acquired some credit, / One begins to doubt that love is a crime / As great as one says" ("Quand sur un jeune coeur un amant qu'on estime / A pris quelque crédit, / On commence à douter si l'amour est un crime / Aussi grand qu'on le dit").[96] For Bussy-Rabutin, credit was at the center of court intrigue but also the heart of real friendship and part of the bonds of love. I maintained the awkward *on* ("one") construction to emphasize the collective nature of the judgments formed. The lover is esteemed by an anonymous but informed public, whose convictions on the dangers of romantic love are challenged by the lover's positive influence.

The link between credit and love also reappeared repeatedly in the celebrated correspondence of Bussy-Rabutin's cousin, Madame de Sévigné. The famous correspondent used the term *credit* in at least five distinct, although interrelated, ways. First, she spoke of credit when referring to the maneuvers of power among the elite to which she belonged. She was an enthusiastic observer of the power relations at court, discounting, for example, rumors that

Madame de Nevers had replaced the king's mistress: "The credit of Madame de Fontanges is brilliant and solid."[97] In a letter to her daughter she gleefully noted the decline of public credit in England: "The affairs of England are going well; the credit of the prince of Orange gets smaller every day. A practical joker put on the door of Whitehall: house for rent on Saint-Jean day."[98]

Closer to home, Madame de Sévigné was keenly involved in various "affairs" related to her friends and family, and her letters vividly analyze the operation of credit in local power struggles. For example, in a letter to the Comte de Guitaut (dated November 23, 1673), she describes a campaign in which she was involved to obtain a post in the Marseilles city government for the Marquis de Duous, cousin of her son-in-law the Marquis de Grignan. This campaign ran counter to the desires of the bishop of Marseilles, who was offended that "we dare put his credit to the test." Madame de Sévigné commented that if the campaign were successful the bishop would oppose everything relating to the Marquis de Grignan—who was lieutenant general of Provence—in the provincial assembly.[99] In another letter Madame de Sévigné rejoiced to her daughter on victory in "*nos affaires de Provence*," declaring "here is the credit of the cabal vanquished, here is insolence brought down." But she also cautioned prudence: "But, in the name of God, be modest in your victory."[100] A week later, in reference to the same affair she told her daughter: "I have hoped for a long time that you would put to work the credit of your high-ranking friends."[101]

If she used *credit* as a term to analyze other people and their interactions, Madame de Sévigné, like Madame de Maintenon, was also a prudent judge of the limitations of her own credit. In a letter to her daughter, Madame de Sévigné agreed to support a request from her daughter to assist the Marquis de Roquesante, a member of the Parlement d'Aix, who had been exiled to Quimper by the king after he voted against the death sentence for Fouquet.[102] She was not optimistic, however, about her ability to influence his fate: "You know, my daughter, what the name de Roquesante is to me and what veneration I have for his virtue. You may believe that his recommendation and your own are very considerable for me; but my credit does not meet my good intentions. You have told me so much good of the president [of the Parlement] of whom it is no question that one would be honored to serve him, if one had some influence in the chamber. I will speak out on the off chance, but in reality everything is so hidden at Versailles that we must await in peace the oracles that emanate from it."[103]

Politics was merely one arena, however, in which Madame de Sévigné identified the operation of credit. Family life was another. Famous for her passionate love of her daughter, Madame de Sévigné sometimes expressed this love in the language of credit. In one letter, Madame de Sévigné told her daughter that they must accept their love for each other on credit: "My dear child, you say that your friendship is not very visible in certain areas. Mine is not either; we must give credit to each other. I see your friendship very well and I am happy with it; be the same for me." Mutual esteem, founded on confidence and trust, was essential in families as well as in patronage.[104] She could be sterner, for example, warning her daughter "you lose all credit by the force of things you say to confound others."[105] In her worries over her daughter's health, she also appealed to the credit that others held with her: "Is it possible that you wish to give me this bitter and constant pain? Are you afraid of getting well? Monsieur de la Rouvière, Monsieur De Grignan, do all of them have no credit with you?"[106]

The echo here of more worldly usages of the term reveals the role of influence, patronage, and deference as models of family relationships. By the same token, such private usages of the term *credit* reflected and reinforced contemporaries' expectations that courtiers display regard for virtue and practice "real" friendship, not just power politics. There was no clear dividing line between public and private relationships and the behavior that accompanied them. Love should guide relations at court and family members should honor the obligations that they owed people whom they esteemed and respected.

Like her cousin Bussy-Rabutin, Madame de Sévigné was also cited as an authority on credit. Féraud's dictionary chose a mocking reference to credit in Madame de Sévigné's correspondence as an illustration of a figurative and familiar sense of the word: "*Give credit* to someone for something; to exempt him from it" ("*Faire crédit* à quelqu'un de quelque chose, l'en dispenser"). Referring to a pathway she had constructed in her garden, Madame de Sévigné stated: "It is so beautiful, so well planted that my son should kiss the steps I take there every day, but since it contains twelve hundred steps, and that would be a rather violent exercise with a blood as heated as his, I give him credit for this gratitude."[107]

Beyond politics and family affection, Madame de Sévigné also used credit to refer to the good reputation people acquired by noteworthy deeds. Indeed, the reputation could be more important than the deed, as she noted in the aftermath of the battle of Maestricht in 1676: "Monsieur De Schomberg is heaped with praise and he is given credit for a victory in the event that he did fight, and it has the same effect. The good opinion one has of him is founded on so many battles won that one can very easily believe that he has won this one as well."[108] Referring to her friend and relative, the Cardinal de Retz, she wrote to the Comte de Guitaut: "I give him credit for his conduct." This is not a purely emotional gesture, as she reveals in the sentence that immediately follows: "All his friends have found themselves so well off for having trusted in him that I wish to trust him again; he can cover the stakes because of the regularity of his life."[109] The cardinal's "friends" had accrued substantial benefits from their friendship, leading Madame de Sévigné to calculate that her continued faith in him was merited. This letter is also revealing in outlining Madame de Sévigné's criteria for according her credit: "You will not see him running from gathering to gathering holding conversations and judging beautiful works; he will retire at an early hour, make and receive few visits, see only his friends and people who suit him, and no one who would be contraband to the regularity of his life." The cardinal's exemplary conduct consisted of limiting his own circulation (retiring early, limiting his visits) and the circuits of friendship in which he participated. Like a good merchant, his intake and output were carefully regulated and controlled; his friends could thus be sure that his "friendship" and the resources he brought to it were not exhausted by excessive expenditure.

The events of the cardinal's life and her own reporting of them reinforce this reading of a type of economic calculation behind Madame de Sévigné's admiration. After being imprisoned for his involvement in the Fronde, the cardinal found his way back to Louis XIV's favor and served the king as a diplomat. He had huge debts and in 1675 publicly resolved to abandon his remaining income to creditors. Madame de Sévigné referred to this decision in a preceding passage of the letter that refers to the cardinal's departure for Saint-Germain, where "he has a trial to have judged, which will finish paying his debts; that is well worth the trouble of soliciting it himself."

Finally, Madame de Sévigné also used the word *credit* in a purely financial sense. Finances—in the form of expenses, investments, debts, military pensions, and others—were constant themes of the correspondence, and much of it took the form of credit rather than hard cash. In her flood of maternal advice, Madame de Sévigné included counsel on her daughter's financial credit relations: "My uncle the abbé saw this D'Harouys this morning. You may dispose of all of his worth, and it is for that reason that you did very well to respectably send his letter of credit back to him."[110] She sympathized with her daughter on the unsatisfactory sale of a military company (formed for the latter's son): "You are very unfortunate not to have been able to sell your company for ten thousand francs. What a misunderstanding! Everything works to do you harm. You will lose one thousand francs by this, and cash money, because your nine thousand francs will be paid on credit, and with poor grace."[111]

Madame de Sévigné's correspondence reveals the lack of liquidity that made credit so important for everyone from nobles to shop workers; this was a constant challenge in an economy in which borrowing and lending were constant features of life. She wrote a letter to Bussy-Rabutin deploring her economic situation: "Do you know that I received only yesterday your letter from March 19th from that respectable merchant who gives credit and does not press too much? Please God that there will soon be others as accommodating! They have been miserable lately. Everyone knows I'm telling the truth. We are in despair. We don't have a sou left, we find nothing to borrow, the financiers won't pay, we don't dare make counterfeit money, we don't wish to throw all to the wind and yet everyone goes to the war with an entourage." As this letter reveals, even wealthy nobles such as Madame de Sévigné relied on credit relations with merchants. She knew how to esteem a "respectable" merchant who was willing to be patient in credit relations. Her correspondence also reveals the bonds that could develop between such a merchant and his or her loyal clients. This merchant, who was acting as courier between the cousins, could expect future assistance from his elite patrons. She continued: "But getting back to our merchant . . . I assure you that I'll do him all the favors I can."[112] Financial and moral credit owed to the merchant formed two interwoven strands in the tangled skein of credit relations that Madame de Sévigné maintained.

At times the two overlapped in ways that are difficult to disentangle. Discussing a visit to Nantes, where she succeeded in selling some land for two thousand écus in cash and three or four thousand livres in promissory notes, she told her daughter: "You will ask me if no one could handle this affair for me; I will tell you no. It needed my presence and the credit of my friends."[113] It is unclear from the context whether she referred to material or social credit. In another example, she wrote to her daughter, "Le *bien bon* [Madame de Sévigné's maternal uncle, the Abbé Christophe de Coulanges] loves you and begs you to be always clever, cash-paying [*comptant*], calculating, and reckoning, because that is everything; and what does it matter to have money as long as one knows how much is due? Your landholders do their duty much better than ours. You pay your arrears better than any person at court; that is what does you a great honor and a great credit." Paying one's debts was apparently so rare at court that doing so brought great honor and credit. Again, Madame de Sévigné seems to be referring to moral credit; however, we cannot avoid the implication that this moral credit will be an effective means of obtaining fresh economic credit. Moreover, the practices of counting and calculating surely traversed from the purely monetary domain to the management of political and social affairs.[114]

The credit that was such an important catalyst to the correspondence between Madame de Sévigné and her cousin also led to the breakdown of their affection. In 1658, with the Spanish attacking Dunkerque, Marshall Turenne called the French troops into action. Desperate to gather his regiment to join the battle, the cash-strapped Bussy-Rabutin turned to his wealthy cousin with a request for a loan. Each cousin, upon his or her marriage, had received a promise of thirty thousand livres in the estate of their common uncle, the bishop of Chalon. Since the bishop was expected to die soon, Bussy-Rabutin proposed that Madame de Sévigné advance him ten thousand livres on his expectation. After she refused to accord this request, he offered to give her as security for the loan the "*ordonnances de ses appointements*" and to make her his chief heir if he died in battle.[115] Madame de Sévigné again refused to help. She later defended herself by claiming not to have had the money he requested, although at the moment of her refusal she had recently received more than twenty thousand livres in cash as reimbursement of a loan to a bourgeois of Paris. Her refusal led to a break between the cousins and to Bussy-Rabutin's caustic portrait of her that was published (without his consent) in *L'Histoire amoureuse des Gaules*, which states: "Madame de Sévigné's friendship has other limits: this beauty is only friends as far as her purse."[116]

In this comment, Bussy-Rabutin deplored his cousin's failure to forward him financial credit; a few years later he would be deploring his friends' failure to forward their credit at court. The issues were fundamentally the same, however. Leading troops in battle was the raison d'être of the sword nobility. Failure to do so on Bussy-Rabutin's part could only lead to a disastrous collapse of his credit at court.

It is noteworthy in the context of this chapter that the Marquise's letters did not arise from a purely private exchange between mother and daughter. Madame de Sévigné's letters frequently include comments in the hand of other family members and friends present at the time of writing; she herself included messages intended for members of her daughter's entourage as well as enclosing separate letters for them. The act of writing and reading letters was part of a shared aristocratic sociability. Moreover, the letters themselves had already begun to be copied and circulated in manuscript form during her lifetime, and she thus wrote in the expectation of a much wider readership. Like the credit circuits Madame de Sévigné describes, her letters straddle the public-private divide. Like credit, they were validated by the collective gaze of a circle of friends, allies, and family members, who shared in their production and reproduction. As Michele Longino Farrell comments, "Friends function in Sévigné's letters as witnesses, participants, critics, judges, and fans and play an essential role in enabling, regulating, censoring, and ensuring the playing out of the mother-daughter relationship."[117] One could say the same of the role of friends in the exchange of credit. The letters not only describe credit, they also helped to produce forms of social credibility for Madame de Sévigné, her daughter, and their circle.

"Mais allons aux morts sans crédit": The Credit of Ordinary People[118]

The examples above delineate multiple forms of credit at the heart of court patronage, cultural production, household negotiations, and many other facets of life. So far, however, they beg a crucial question: Was this immaterial notion of credit limited to the world of court aristocrats, men of letters, office holders, and other cultural and social elites? According to one member of that elite, it was. Critical of what he perceived as the despotic powers of the royal government, the Abbé Malby nonetheless retained a dim view of the capacities of the common people: "The third estate is nothing in France, because no one wishes to belong to it. . . . The common people (*le peuple*) is merely that part of the population without credit, respect, fortune, that can do nothing for itself."[119] Thus, to belong to the Third Estate—especially that large portion of the order that lacked corporate affiliations—meant by definition that one was dispossessed of credit.

This view was widely shared but by no means unanimous. This final section of the chapter turns our attention away from credit exchanges among elite actors to inquire into the movement of credit among the common people. Sources drawn from both popular and elite writers suggest multiple dynamics of credit pulsing through the lives of working men and women. First, in instances of resistance or rebellion, individuals of high social standing drew on their credit with the crowd as a source of support and legitimation. Credit operated in this way as a type of protopublic opinion. Second, we also find that the inverse was true: the poor and powerless frequently made claims on the credit of higher-status patrons. These claims suggest that the common people were aware of the "credit" their superiors possessed and attempted to leverage it for their own needs and interests. Moreover, in a third set of cases, educated authors voiced their conviction that individuals among the people could exercise credit within their own circles and even over their social superiors. Finally, the *Bibliothèque bleue*, a series of cheap published books aimed at the rural and urban working population, confirms that the language of credit circulated in texts available to nonelites.

The memoirs of Jean-François Paul de Gondi, Cardinal de Retz, provide one illuminating window into the dynamics of credit in relations between working people and the elite and among the lower orders themselves. In 1643 Anne of

Austria named him archbishop of Paris, and by the time of the outbreak of the Fronde in 1648, he had succeeded in his efforts to win popularity and influence with the city's inhabitants. The cardinal's memoirs, drafted in the 1660s, are addressed to an unknown woman, whom many believe to have been Madame de Sévigné, a distant relative and frequent correspondent. In his detailed account of the events of the Fronde, Retz repeatedly turned to the language of credit to explain the dynamics of the uprising and his own active participation as both sympathizer with the rebels and representative of the forces of order. Retz refers on several occasions to his credit among the people and the appeals he received from the crown to employ his credit to calm sedition.

Retz emphasizes the risks involved in calling in that credit, due to the suspicions of the common people. At times, the archbishop sought support for his maneuvering from other members of the ruling classes, such as "Miron, maître des comptes, colonel of the quarter of Saint-Germain De L'Auxerrois, man of worth and of heart and who had a great deal of credit among the people."[120] Retz also, however, referred to leaders among the working people who exercised power in their own right within their communities. On one occasion, for example, he sought information from "Le Houx, butcher, but a man of credit among the people and of good sense," who told Retz that his fellow butchers at the Place aux Veaux were preparing to take up arms.[121] Retz formed alliances with leaders of the people, but he was also vulnerable to their disaffection. As he described one perilous encounter: "by a singular misfortune, I found, at the end of rue Neuve-Notre-Dame, du Buisson, a wood merchant who had a great deal of credit in the ports. He was absolutely with me; but that day he was in a bad mood. He beat my postilion; he threatened my coachman. The populace, who ran over in a crowd, turned over my carriage."[122] Only the intervention of the market women of the Marché-Neuf saved Retz.

Servants were an obvious category of working people who accrued credit over others, including their own masters and mistresses. Saint-Simon ascribed enormous credit to the king's valets, high-ranking men but vastly inferior to the royal family they served. Authors recognized credit among ordinary servants as well. For example, in Marivaux's *Les Fausses Confidences*, Dorante is afraid to speak up against a false tale spread by a chambermaid: "because I would have turned against me that girl, who has credit with her mistress."[123] In return workers in search of jobs were also depicted as relying on the credit of their friends and patrons. In Restif de la Brétonne's *Histoire de Sara* the title character urges the narrator to help her find employment: "In the afternoon, Sara pressed me to use my credit and my friends to get her some work. 'I wish to work,' she told me; 'I will live contentedly in the midst of mediocrity; even of misery; find me work.'"[124] Just as at court one used credit to obtain an office or a pension, in the working world women pleaded for and used credit to obtain jobs and clients. Credit was thus a vector by which power and its privileges trickled down from elite to ordinary people.

Like Retz, other writers ascribed the possession of credit to working people in their own neighborhoods and trade corps. In a passage of his popular philosophical dialogues *Les entretiens d'Ariste et d'Eugène*, the Jesuit priest Dominique Bouhours expounded on the vital role of secrecy in political and military affairs. To illustrate the point, the character Ariste described the plotting of the Duc de Bragance to free Portugal from Spanish rule. In addition to secret meetings with the nobility, the duke and his comrades "opened themselves up to a few artisans who had the most credit among the people," whom they provided with arms.[125] By the late eighteenth century, it was even possible to conceive of the dynamics of credit encompassing communities of enslaved people. In his well-known account of life in the French Caribbean colonies, Louis-Élie Moreau de Saint-Méry ascribed credit to both male and female slaves. In an anecdote intended to demonstrate the rote nature of women's manifestations of mourning at slave funerals, Saint-Méry described the intervention of "a negresse who had great credit over the others" who told the other women "*pencore crié, mon va ba zot' la voi*," which Saint-Méry translated as "Do not shout yet, I will give you the signal."[126] In criticizing the lack of order in Le Cap, the capital of the colony, he remarked: "As for the slaves, it seems that the police have no duties that concern them." Saint-Méry complained that slaves armed themselves with heavy sticks, rented rooms, gambled, and gathered in large groups, all direct violations of the law. The only individuals subject to arrest were "those who do not have the right of impunity through the credit of their masters." More fortunate slaves not only enjoyed police protection, he continued, but had their own "creatures."[127] In this anecdote the dynamics of protection and influence straddled the boundaries between freedom and slavery. Credit, derived in part from their close ties to powerful masters, allowed them to defy openly the basic laws of slavery.

While these examples suggest that educated writers believed that the common people possessed credit, one might object that their texts offer no indication that the concept of credit was familiar to working people themselves. If we turn to texts that circulated among popular audiences, however, it becomes apparent that writers addressing plebeians assumed that their audience was familiar with both material and nonmaterial usages of the term. For example, numerous references to credit exist in the *Bibliothèque bleue*, the series of inexpensive books distributed by peddlers to peasants and urban artisans from the seventeenth to the mid-nineteenth century.[128] Just as the texts in the *Biblio-thèque bleue* ranged from prayer books and hagiographies to almanacs, song-books, and novels, references to credit include the religious, the comical, and the practical.

For example, an unhappily married woman might take interest in the play *The Wife Unhappy with Her Husband*, published in 1738, in which the title char-acter seeks help from a friend whom she believes has "so much credit" with her bad-tempered and violent husband.[129] If the couple reconciled and the woman found herself pregnant, she could consult *Le miroir d'astrologie naturelle* of 1745, which would inform her that if she gave birth to a daughter in late July, the girl would be subject to childhood diseases, well-loved for her kindness, and very fond of travel. Indeed, the handbook forecast that her daughter would leave home for a foreign country, where "she will have a lot of credit" as a re-sult of her prudence and discretion and go on to marry well, acquire powerful friends, and recover from a spell of dementia to end her days peacefully with her family.[130] A son born in May would share a future of travel and social as-cension: "he will be a lover of science and will make his mark with people of the highest quality; he will know how to maintain his post with honor; he will be inclined to travel to faraway countries where he will be very well received; he will meet with good credit and benevolence from great lords."[131]

Texts in the *Bibliothèque bleue* also reflected experiences in the world of work. For all the commentary on their credit with their masters, servants en-dured humiliation, hard work, and poverty. They could find echoes of their frustrations and resentments in the verses of *L'état de servitude ou la misère des domestiques*. In this poem of 1738, a lackey deplores the misfortunes that led to his life of service, declaring: "I am a great rascal to have become a Lackey / When Heaven, justly angry with me / Has left me without wealth, without credit, without employment / Must it in a wrathful spirit / Entangle me in the chains of such harsh slavery?"[132] From the servant's perspective enunciated here, lack of credit led to a life comparable to bondage, rather than endowing him with the credit of his masters. More cynical readers might take pleasure in the *Fameuse harangue . . . de messeigneurs les savetiers*, which includes an aspi-rant to mastership who uses his "credit, favor, and money" to evade the require-ment of a masterpiece. The text comments satirically that "one should have regard for some people that one does not have for others when they are protec-tors and conservers of the state."[133] Saint-Simon himself could not have sum-marized more clearly the powers endowed by influence and social connections.

Many readers turned to publications in the *Bibliothèque bleue* for religious instruction and consolation. They would find a number of texts that explained the workings of God through the metaphor of credit. For example, *La grande Bible des noëls tans vieux que nouveaux* of 1772 taught them that the angel Gabriel chided Joseph for accusing Mary of infidelity, telling him "you are in credit," because his wife Mary was pregnant with the child of God in fulfillment of divine prophecy.[134] A passage in the *Life of St. Patroclus* called on the grace and intervention of the divine savior "by the merits and the powerful credit of that illustrious Martyr."[135] As this passage suggests, the very definition of a saint might be that of an individual who possessed credit with God and used it to intervene with heaven on behalf of mortals. More prosaically, readers of the *Prophéties perpétuelles*—which claimed both divine and astrological guidance—would find among its predictions the news that financial paper had been and would be "in credit" every twenty-eight years beginning in 1583 and continuing to 2058, but "in great discredit" at the same rhythm from 1563 to 2055.[136]

This chapter has made four main arguments. To the extent that historians have examined nonmaterial forms of credit in early modern France, they have focused on the court and noble patronage. While the court was a key site for wielding credit and perhaps rightfully dominates the historiography, contemporary sources use the term to describe the powers of reputation and influence in many other domains, including religion, intellectual life, courtship, and family relations. As they reveal, credit was the informal, often hidden, dynamic that explained why things happened the way they did in myriad arenas of life. The term was ubiquitous precisely because it was so useful and resonated so powerfully with the way they understood the operation of power. Second, women played a central and widely recognized role in nonmaterial forms of credit. Women modestly denied having credit or protested that their credit was much overestimated, but their capacity, as women, to possess and wield credit was never in doubt. The epigraph that opens the chapter aptly summarizes perceptions of women's credit as a form of power, demonstrating the persistence of such ideas through the 1780s. Third, a constant process of conversion and reconversion took place among different forms of credit and across the material and nonmaterial divide. Contemporaries were quite able to distinguish between financial tools of credit (bills of exchange, promissory notes, and so on) and nonmaterial forms (patronage ties, spiritual credence, fashionability, and so forth). Nonetheless, their interactions often involved the exchange of multiple forms of credit, and they were quite adept at calculating exchange values. Monetary value was but one among a series of other values, not the primary end of transactions or the "real" underlying value. Fourth, elite observers believed they discerned the dynamics of credit among the working people, and popular sources confirm that the term circulated in its nonmaterial sense through texts intended for common people.

Not only were contemporaries self-conscious about their use of nonmaterial forms of credit, many objected to what they saw as abuses of credit and the power it conveyed. Their critique highlights the perceived distance between the moral values upon which credit was ostensibly based and the self-interest that it appeared to serve. The next chapter takes up these points in greater detail, focusing on the late seventeenth to the mid-eighteenth century, a period characterized both by a rising critique of credit and by strong continuities in references to its nonmaterial forms.

CHAPTER 2

CRITIQUES AND CRISES OF THE CREDIT SYSTEM

Villain, he does not even have enough credit to be a dangerous villain.

— Jacques-Pierre Brissot de Warville, *Réplique à la première et dernière lettre de L.-M. Gouy, 10 février 1791*, on Louis-Marthe Jouy,
self-proclaimed "defender of the slave trade and slavery"

One ought normally to desire the death of the benefactor from
whom one is not yet discharged of obligation and I am never
surprised to hear of accounts being settled by a murder.

— Marquis de Sade, *Juliette*

*I*n the second volume of his *Système social* (1773), the Baron d'Holbach advocated an "ethocracy," a state founded on the basis of the
public good. For Holbach, the credit system described in chapter 1
constituted the antithesis of such a state. As he proclaimed: "To have great
credit is often to have the terrible right to be unjust, to violate the rules with
impunity, to be able to do wrong and insolently flaunt justice and law. A woman
in credit at court, having been asked to take interest in an affair that was shown
to be very just and very simple, responded proudly: 'I only involve myself in
affairs that are unjust and impossible.'"[1] Holbach's target in this passage, as
revealed in the accompanying footnote, was the Princesse des Ursins, whose
credit he would have seen denounced in the memoirs of Saint-Simon and in
the work of his friend Charles Pinot Duclos, whose unpublished *Secret Memoirs of the Reigns of Louis XIV and Louis XV* drew heavily on the duke.

Holbach's diatribe represents the culmination of a long stream of protest
against the unchecked and arbitrary power represented by credit, which developed alongside the commonsense understanding of credit as an efficacious
form of influence and reputation. Taking our cue from Holbach, this chapter
addresses a series of questions: Who opposed and criticized the credit system

and on what grounds? And how did such criticism relate to crucial political events and debates of the eighteenth century? I do not claim that the thread of critique traced in this chapter is the only possible chronology; indeed, I encourage scholars to trace their own timelines of the types of credit described in chapter 1. Nonetheless, the particular moments scrutinized in this chapter constitute a significant evolution over time in critical thinking about the abuses of credit and particularly about its covert impact on the exercise of royal power and governmental administration. Historicizing credit in this manner reveals the connections between discourses on credit and the existing literature on absolutism, female agency, and reform ideologies in France during this period.

The chapter proceeds through three chronologically organized phases of inquiry. The first examines criticism written under Louis xiv that targeted and castigated, rather than merely acknowledging, the gap between credit as belief and faith, on the one hand, and credit as self-interest and source of material profit, on the other hand. I focus on writings from satirists and critics of the court, such as Jean de La Bruyère, as well as members of the range of religious minorities—Protestants, Jansenists, and Quietists—persecuted under Louis xiv. Their commentary situates perceptions of credit within the tensions and factionalism of Louis xiv's court as well as with regard to intense late seventeenth-century concerns over the role of theatricality in social life and the ever-present conflict between artifice and reality.[2]

The second section of the chapter turns to the last years of the reign of Louis xiv and the regency that followed his death in 1715. The absence of a strong monarch and the struggle over the Duc d'Orléans's appointment as regent introduced a new political dimension to this moralizing critique. Writers questioned the role of credit in governing France and in particular the influence women exercised as credit brokers at court. The enormous expenses and debt generated by Louis xiv's foreign wars called forth urgent efforts to repair public credit, a project inescapably intertwined with the fate of political credit networks in the royal government. The collapse of royal credit led to the boldest experiment in public finance to that date, the John Law project, first considered in the last years of Louis xiv's reign and authorized by the regent shortly after he came to power. Although the topic of royal finance is too complex and vast to receive adequate attention here, this chapter posits the intertwined tangle of public credit—which forged symbiotic bonds among king, ministers, office holders, and private financiers—as yet another facet of the credit systems described in chapter 1. For most of Louis xiv's reign, France's credit lay in the hands of private financiers and venal office holders, whose collateral lay in their wealth, personal reputation, and their legal title over the collection of taxes and other forms of state revenue. Law's bank sought to replace the credit of such wealthy and powerful individuals with confidence generated by public opinion. The bank's spectacular failure meant that those systems and their beneficiaries remained in place to the end of the Old Regime.

The third and final movement in the chapter takes us to the reign of Louis xv. This period produced the only text of the eighteenth century to devote sustained, original attention to nonmaterial credit: Charles Duclos's *Considérations des moeurs de ce siècle*. Duclos's work deliberately evoked La Bruyère's *Caractères ou les moeurs de ce siècle*; however, instead of satirizing the court in the name of true aristocratic values, Duclos argued for an expansion of the values of honor and virtue to a new elite of men of letters, with the public good, rather than social stability, as the prized goal.

Despite his stance in favor of a new meritocratic elite, Duclos's text failed to acknowledge, let alone propose solutions for, the problems raised by an earlier generation. In light of the Law project, Duclos's work is noteworthy in its attempt to reimagine a credit system devoid not only of self-interest but of any reference to financial credit at all. Moreover, Duclos has nothing to say about women's role in the credit system, which is completely effaced in *Considérations*. These absences are all the more remarkable in that he was a familiar figure in salon society, a protégé of Madame de Pompadour, and his other writings demonstrate a frank intimacy with all the forms of credit described in chapter 1. Duclos thus epitomizes the position of the homme de lettres in the mid-eighteenth century, whose explicitly critical stance remained enmeshed in traditional forms of patronage and worldly sociability. To call for a new elite culture of merit and service did not necessitate coming to terms with the interweaving of financial and social credit nor with the role women should play in such a reformed elite. The absence of financial issues from this work may also signal an implicit acknowledgment that, by 1751, writers had established the "economy" as a discrete entity to be treated by experts in specialized texts.

To emphasize the complexity of processes of continuity and change, the chapter ends with a brief examination of Madame de Pompadour, mistress of Louis xv and mentor to Duclos. Pompadour's career reflects the restored power of private financiers—such as her family's protectors, the Pâris brothers— who had regained their role as brokers of the French national debt after Law's downfall. Pompadour's self-avowed capacity to wield credit echoes her earlier counterpart, Madame de Maintenon, and thus points to strong continuities in the power and patronage of royal favorites. However, decades of criticism of the abuses of power had left their mark. Contemporary sources in which the king's mistresses speak most candidly of their credit turn out to be forgeries.[3]

These falsified documents suggest a new awareness among mid-eighteenth-century writers of the potency of credit as a denunciatory metaphor, particularly when associated with women and the way they leveraged sex into power.

This chapter thus reveals the emergence from the late seventeenth to the mid-eighteenth century of a heightened perception of credit as exercising a pernicious impact, particularly on politics and government administration. Attempts to think through the implications of this perception produced a range of reactions, epitomized here by the radically different projects of John Law and Charles Duclos. For all their differences, the two men shared an impulse to remove credit from the shadowy amalgam of courtiers and private financiers and to redirect the dynamics of reputation, faith, and influence toward the service of the nation and public good. Both projects failed to bring about their vaulting ambitions, but the problems they evoked and the attention they drew to the role of political credit in national life provided an important foundation for the next generations.

Critique under Louis XIV: Credit as Hypocrisy, Venality, and Self-Interest

COURTLY DIS-CREDIT

One proof of the long history of credit as a form of political and social capital is the equally long tradition of criticizing and satirizing it. Like the many uses of credit described in chapter 1, denunciations spread across multiple domains. Thus, in his *Satires*, published in 1646, Jacques Du Lorens offered a cynical perspective on strategies for acquiring spiritual credit: "To put himself in credit everyone has his approach; the hypocrite attends more than one mass each day, to display his zeal and fervor in the faith to others more credulous than I; his words are sweet and if he never takes oaths, he yet makes no contract that does not smell of usury."[4] In a lighter moment Du Lorens also joked that it was the nobleman's distribution of free food that conveyed credit, rather than his birth: "Do not think that it is your merit or virtue they are seeking, they are rushing to your stew; it gives you more reputation, credit, and friends than your extraction, your civility and your humble sword."[5] Du Lorens sardonically contrasts the "true" values of nobility—birth, gentility, military valor—that were ostensibly at the heart of credit with mere gluttony. And, if Du Lorens's analysis was correct, then anyone, regardless of their background, could gain credit if they satisfied the appetites of those around them.

In his *Aristippe ou de la Cour*, published in 1654, Jean-Louis Guez de Balzac elaborated on the theme of courtiers who acquired influence at court without the advantages of high birth: "Such people usually introduce themselves at court through means that are lowly and at times scarcely respectable; they sometimes owe the beginning of their fortune to a well-danced sarabande, to the agility of their body and to the beauty of their face; they make themselves valued by shameful services, whose payment cannot be requested in public: they put themselves in credit by the sole recommendation of vice."[6] This satire constituted a reversal of texts such as Nicolas Faret's famous treatise on court life, which instructed ambitious individuals how to advance at court. The courtier's attributes that Faret urges his readers to acquire—skill in dancing, bodily elegance, and beauty—are here rejected as deceitful appearances.[7] Guez de Balzac relates such skills directly to sexual favors—*shameful services*—that must be kept secret. The public power of credit, he suggested, was acquired through the private practice of vice.

Once the court settled with the king at Versailles in 1682, the stakes of credit, and the opportunity for critique, heightened. One of the most important moralists of the late seventeenth century was Jean de La Bruyère (1645–1696), whose *Les Caractères ou les moeurs de ce siècle* appeared in eight editions during his lifetime. Tutor to the Duc de Bourbon and member of the Académie française, La Bruyère criticized contemporary society from an insider's perspective. His writings satirized what he characterized as the hypocrisy of court society, the arrogance and excessive self-interest of courtiers, the lack of true friendship at court, and the valorization of money, pomp, and fashionable appearances over merit and virtue.[8]

In one example of his attack on the self-interest of courtiers, he wrote: "They go to bed at court and get up on interest, it is what they digest morning and evening, daytime and night; it is what makes them think, speak, be quiet, be active; it is in this spirit that they approach some people and neglect others, that they rise and fall; it is by this rule that they measure care, kindness, esteem, indifference, and contempt."[9] La Bruyère compared life at court to a game of chess, with its carefully calculated risks and strategies: "Life at court is a serious and melancholy game that requires application: one must arrange one's pieces and batteries, devise a plan, follow it, fend off those of one's adversary, take risks sometimes, and follow whims; and after all of these reveries and measures, one is put into check, sometimes checkmate; frequently, with well-managed pawns one can promote a queen and win the game: the most skillful wins or the luckiest."[10] Luck and skill existed in an arbitrary relationship to each other; there was no clear path leading from talent and hard work to success.

Echoing the complaints of Bussy-Rabutin, La Bruyère remarked on the false promises made at court and the reality that courtiers were usually unwilling to use their credit on behalf of ostensible friends. Instead of using their talents to advance their friends' interests, they used them to find pretexts to refuse: "Courtiers do not employ what they possess of wit, skill, and finesse to find ways to oblige friends who implore their help, but only to devise plausible reasons, specious pretexts or what they call the impossibility of being able to do it; and they persuade themselves that they have thereby satisfied in their regard all the duties of friendship or gratitude."[11]

In addition to disparaging those who did not help their friends, he also expressed disgust at the obsequiousness shown to power: "From the same depths of arrogance from which one proudly elevates oneself above inferiors, one basely crawls before those above oneself. It is the peculiarity of vice, which is founded neither on personal merit nor on virtue but on riches, offices, credit, and vain science, to lead us equally to despise those who have less than we do of these types of goods and to esteem too highly those who have a greater amount than ourselves."[12] This exposure of the lack of true value of the powerful accompanied an assault on money and self-interest: "There are dirty souls, covered with mud and filth, besotted with gain and interest; capable of a sole delight, which is that of acquiring or of not losing; inquisitive and eager about their 10 percent interest; solely occupied by their debtors; always concerned about the discount or discredit of coinage; plunged and seemingly engulfed by contracts, title deeds, and mortgages. Such individuals are neither relatives, friends, citizens, Christians, nor even men: they have money."[13]

Money, in this passage, is a contaminating and corrosive filth that begrimes avaricious courtiers. Positive human relations—with family, friends, and God—give way to an abyss of financial calculations. For La Bruyère, the negative quality of money and paper credit was linked to their volatility. Such men were always worrying about acquiring or losing money and about the gain or loss in value of their holdings. Because of the shifting nature of the money to which they were so attached, their own identity was equally uncertain and transient. Recalling that the years of La Bruyère's writing corresponded to a series of government devaluations of the value of the livre, the French unit of account, one might be tempted to be more sympathetic to the targets of his attack.

What renders La Bruyère's critique all the more fascinating and complex is that he was not objecting to materialism or the stain of money from the perspective of traditional aristocratic values or Christian ethics. La Bruyère in fact had roots in the sphere of government finance; his father had been a municipal finance officer and he himself purchased the office of treasurer of finance of the city of Caen in 1673, although he continued to live in Paris and does not seem to have played an active role in the city's governance. Nevertheless, he did demonstrate strong interest in commercial matters, and as one recent scholar has noted, his moral writings abounded with economic terms—"*monnaie, achat, coûte, epargne, marchander, prix, argent* and *commerce*"—which he used both metaphorically and literally to convey a notion of human interaction as a form of reciprocal exchange in which interest was a constant motivating factor.[14] It was the excess of self-interest, rather than the mere fact of it, that aroused his ire. La Bruyère thus attacked attachment to money from the perspective of one familiar with the risks of financial investment and fluctuating value. This experience appears to have made him highly sensitive to the overlaps between economies of power and money and the interplay of interests of all kinds in reciprocal exchange. His reaction to such risks was to advocate stability, in terms of both social identity and fortune.[15]

As La Bruyère's critique suggests, affiliation between the gift economy and credit was a crucial element of the moralizing critique. Studies of early modern Europe and patronage relations have emphasized the partial survival of a gift economy into the early modern period.[16] The language of the gift was common within patron-client relations at court and between provincial elites and their followers. The exchange of presents, favors, hospitality, and other forms of reciprocity structured vertical and hierarchical relations within the nobility and between nobles and their dependents. Following Marcel Mauss, historians have argued that what was presented as a disinterested exchange of gifts motivated by affection and esteem constituted in fact a logical, systematic exchange of mutual obligation over time intended to display status and to construct and maintain social relations.

How did this gift economy coexist with credit? Was credit the "reality" underneath the self-professed gift? Did credit, as discussed in chapter 1, represent a devolution or corruption of an ostensible gift economy, thus engendering possible disappointment, bitterness, and cynicism when the gift was revealed to be a mere loan? When courtiers, writers, suitors, and other individuals wrote openly about their credit relations, it is clear that what they presented in some guises as a gift, they understood very well to be a form of credit. They were ethnographers as well as practitioners of their own social codes and very much aware of the spectrum of coercion and gratuitousness encompassed by reciprocity. The words *debt* and *obligation* occur as frequently as *gift* or *present* in noble correspondence and memoirs.[17] This is not to say that they did not also genuinely feel obliged by exchange or indignant when someone failed to reciprocate appropriately, but they also clearly understood the dynamics of reciprocal obligation, its unfolding over time, and its role in creating and sustaining unequal power relations. In that sense, credit and the gift were two ways of talking about, engaging with, and understanding reciprocal forms of exchange. The gift was not an originary form subsequently corrupted by credit and money, but the two were always co-present in each other, at least during the early modern period and probably within ancient societies as well. As Mauss wrote, "the gift necessarily entails the notion of credit."[18]

Credit's affinity with the gift encouraged people to assimilate such diverse things as favors, money, genres of writing, and material objects into forms of exchange. This affinity, however, was also what allowed critics to complain that others were not following the rules that called for performing favors as free gifts out of esteem and affection and the sincere desire to form social bonds. Of course, the very notion of a free gift in their diatribes was naive at best and disingenuous at worst, but it carried a potent ideological charge, particularly given the dual factors of noble values of generous and uncalculating giving and the Christian emphasis on the gratuitous gift of charity. This understanding of credit as occupying the same spectrum of exchange as the gift, or the same "economy of regard" to use Avner Offer's phrase, helps not only to understand the criticism of moralists like La Bruyère but also the normative ethics of Duclos, which I discuss below.[19]

If the gift stood at one end of the spectrum of exchange, outright monetary exchanges, such as gambling, occupied another end. Whereas credit relied on hierarchical distinctions, rooted as it was in personal yet unequal relations, gambling could be seen as the great leveler. In his writings on gambling La Bruyère expressed consternation at the mingling of individuals of vastly different social status at the gaming table: "One says of gambling that it equalizes conditions; but they are sometimes so bizarrely disproportionate and there is between one condition and another an abyss so immense and so profound, that one's eyes suffer to see such extremities approach each other: it is like off-key music; it is mismatched colors, like speech that swears and offends the ear, like those noises or sounds that make you shudder; it is in a word the reversal of all propriety."[20] For La Bruyère such a contradiction of the natural order of social relations evoked sensory and bodily distress.

La Bruyère's text suggests that credit functioned in many ways as the antithesis of gambling. It was about reciprocity based on personal relations established and maintained over time, while gambling—like any monetized transaction—could be anonymous and did not build lasting relations. Credit was based on minimizing risk by creating ties based on faith in another's probity; gambling was a celebration and courting of risk. Credit smiled on prudent caution, while gambling rewarded luck (although noble culture prized games of skill over games of chance) and refused to recognize social rank or ties. As he noted: "a sad severity reigns on their faces, implacable one for the other and irreconcilable enemies as long as the session lasts, they no longer recognize liaisons, alliance, birth, nor distinctions: chance alone, blind and fierce deity, presides over the group and rules sovereignly; they all honor it with a profound silence."[21] While La Bruyère deplored the abuse of credit and its descent from social relations into self-interest, he saw gambling as a complete negation of social mores. Credit used wrongly was vice parading as virtue; gambling was the abandonment of any pretense of virtue at all.[22]

THE RELIGIOUS CRITIQUE

Critics posited true noble values as one counterpart to the abuses of credit. Another, as Du Lorens has already suggested, was religion. Blaise Pascal, in *Les Provinciales* (1656–1657), defied the power of those with credit over him, contrasting the divine authority of God with the worldly power of credit: "I fear you neither for myself nor for any other, being attached neither to any community, nor to any individual at all. All the credit that you may have is useless in my regard. I hope for nothing in the world, I dread nothing, I want nothing; I need, by the grace of God, neither wealth nor the authority of anyone."[23] He also spoke bitterly of the credit of the Jesuits and the impunity they derived from it: "One should no longer be surprised to see the Jesuits as slanderers; they do it with a clear conscience and nothing can prevent them, because, due to the credit they have in society, they can slander without fearing the justice of men."[24] In his denunciation of credit we may paradoxically recognize Pascal's acknowledgment that it is credit that binds society and sanctions those who defy its conventions. Only by cutting himself from ties of community or patronage could he be free from the bondage of credit.

Marie Jeanne Guyon, the French Quietist mystic, also used the term to characterize the oppressive power of the clergy, who contested the validity of her spiritual visions: "Monsieur the Curé no longer wishing to confess me, there was no one else who wished to take care of me. And coming close to me he said quietly: 'They will ruin you.' I told him loudly: 'You have all the power, Monsieur, I am in your hands. You have all the credit; I only have my life left to lose.'"[25] Credit whispered its secrets of power, while genuine piety boldly declared truth. Voltaire himself, who viewed Quietism and Jansenism as forms of hysterical religious enthusiasm, cruelly concurred with Madame Guyon's self-assessment, describing her as a "woman without credit, without a real mind, and who had nothing but an overheated imagination."[26] His description of her beliefs nonetheless lends insight into Guyon's opposition to the worldly values of credit: "She preached total renouncement of the self, the silence of the soul, the destruction of all one's powers, the interior cult, pure and disinterested love that was neither debased by fear nor by the hope of reward."[27]

As these examples suggest, denunciation of the abusive use of credit was a theme of Jansenists and others in conflict with the Gallican church. The late seventeenth-century Jansenist Pierre Nicole complained that credit elevated ambitious people over their superiors: "It happens only too often that those who have the most credit take pleasure in bringing down those whom birth and merit should elevate above them. There is no doubt nothing harsher or more effectual than this treatment, nor anything that leads more to impatience and anger."[28] He also castigated those who performed favors only in exchange for credit: "Thus they perform a veritable traffic of their credit and their speech. And one can say, without slandering them, that they are but merchants of a higher condition."[29] Nicole does not claim that credit itself is essentially mercantile, an affair for base shopkeepers and traders. Instead, he calls for a disinterested credit of the heart or soul, a gift economy of credit free from self-interest. Rather than being a metaphor derived from economic credit, he viewed this form of credit as categorically different from and superior to commercial trafficking. He also lamented the silencing of those without credit: "if we feel that we do not have the credit or esteem necessary to make our warnings welcomed, we should usually accept that God excuses us from saying what we think."[30]

Other dissenting faiths held similar views. In 1684 the Protestant theologian and preacher Jacques Abbadie employed credit as a foil in his discussion of religion, contrasting the humility of Christ with the power of his opponents: "Jesus Christ had neither money to give, nor titles to promise; and skill, refinement, politics, wealth, and credit were entirely on the side of the scribes, the Pharisees, the doctors of law, his implacable enemies, who lost no opportunity to harm him and whose hypocrisy he loudly condemned in all their meetings."[31] Abbadie similarly emphasized the modest social position of the apostles: "We know that those who first preached the Gospel were not men of high standing or of great credit in the world."[32]

These sources unveil perceptions of the inherent violence of the existing credit system. Viewed from the religious margins, credit holders seemed to defy the constraints of law, social status, and Christian imperatives of mercy and compassion to wield a brutalizing power. It was thus the capricious and arbitrary nature of credit that its victims feared. Operating outside of formal laws and explicit norms, such informal authority afforded no legal or institutional means of recourse. By contrast, from within the dominant Gallican church, as we saw in chapter 1, the saints themselves could be conceived as those blessed with the credit of God.

Jansenist attacks on the credit of the Jesuits had a long posthumous influence. As the jurist Simon-Nicolas Henri Linguet wrote in the 1760s at the time of the Jesuits' banishment from France: "Those unhappy Jansenists were nothing but persecuted; they never had the consolation to be the persecutors. But they had good writers who covered their victorious adversaries in ridicule and ignominy. Blaise Pascal, Antoine Arnauld, Pierre Nicole, became famous at the expense of the Society [of Jesus]. Their many and purely written works inundated France. The credit of the Jesuits, which made them hated, also made people read with eagerness books where they were openly insulted."[33] Linguet further specified that women and the lower orders were particularly susceptible to Jesuitical error. With reference to the spiritual retreats held by Jesuit priests, he wrote: "That is not the spirit of religion; but in the end the common people and women had a taste for these practices because they were novel and the Jesuits authorized them because they gave them credit."[34] Rather than from true spiritual valor, the Jesuits derived their influence from the credulity and curiosity of the lower orders.

In suggesting that women were particularly susceptible to manipulation by the Jesuits, Linguet joined a line of earlier commentators with doubts about the legitimacy of women's connections to credit. Bishop Bossuet himself, who had recommended La Bruyère for his position with the Duc de Bourbon, indirectly raised this question in his eulogy of Henriette-Anne d'Angleterre, duchesse d'Orléans. In praising her use of credit, he stated: "always gentle, always peaceful as well as generous and benevolent, her credit would never be odious."[35] While bishops like Bossuet frankly acknowledged and praised court women's sway, they felt obliged to emphasize that their patronesses used it for good purposes rather than bad. The *Dictionnaire de l'Académie française* of 1694 defines "odious" as something that "incites aversion, hatred, indignation."[36] Bossuet's comments thus suggest that, when brandished by a woman who did not share the duchess's diplomatic approach, credit appeared to others as a blunt and brutal tool of power.

The Regency: The Discredit of Louis XIV and His Reign

Such concerns emerged much more openly after the death of Louis XIV in 1715. With the passing of the Sun King, his five-year-old great-grandson inherited power. Almost constant warfare during Louis XIV's reign had devastated the country's finances and the bitter winter of 1709–1710 produced famine and death. Adding to the instability was the fact that Louis XV was the sole heir of his predecessor, leaving Philip V of Spain as the next in line for the throne. Having just ended the long and grueling War of the Spanish Succession over the issue of Bourbon rule in Spain, the possibility of another dynastic war loomed over France.

Louis XIV's will named his nephew Philippe, duc d'Orléans, as regent; Philippe assumed this title, but only after a power struggle with the king's illegitimate son, the Duc de Maine. The weakened authority of the crown, combined with grave financial crisis, created a potent atmosphere for rethinking the bases of monarchical rule. The circumstances of the regency also had important ramifications for perceptions of credit, in both its financial and political forms. In this section we examine two forms taken by this reassessment: first, a critique of women's role in credit at court and, second, the spectacular episode of the John Law project. The two are linked in that the first was seen as emblematic of the problems of political credit in the absolutist regime and the second constituted an attempt to solve those problems by replacing a public credit system controlled by well-connected financiers with a national bank guaranteed by the collective confidence of the nation.

SEX AND THE POLITICS OF CREDIT

Doubt over the legitimacy of women's informal power was not new, but it reached a new level under the regency. Many observers had resented the influence of Madame de Maintenon and other court ladies, and the death of Louis XIV presented new possibilities for expressing opposition. One of the best-known texts of the period, Montesquieu's *Persian Letters*, contains many passages noting the prominent role of French women in court patronage, their outspokenness and vanity, and their excessive involvement in public affairs. Letter 107, one of the letters in which Montesquieu's own voice emerges most clearly in the text, provides an explicit commentary on these issues. As Rica writes:

> When I arrived in France, I found the late king absolutely governed by women. And yet, at his age, I believe there was no monarch on earth who needed them less. I heard a woman saying one day: "we must do something for that young colonel; his worth is well known to me; I will speak to the minister." Another said: "It is surprising that that young abbé has been forgotten; he must be made a bishop: he is a man of birth and I can speak for his morals." You must not, however, imagine that the speakers were favorites of the king; they had perhaps spoken with him twice in their

lives: something that is nonetheless quite easy to do with European princes. But, in fact, there is no one with a position at court, in Paris or the provinces, who does not have a woman through whose hands pass all the favors and sometimes all the injustices he can do. These women are all connected with each other and form a sort of republic whose always active members help and serve each other: it is like a new state within a state and a man at court, in Paris, in the provinces, who sees the actions of ministers, magistrates and prelates, if he does not know the women who govern them, is like a man who sees a machine at work but without knowing anything of the springs that drive it.[37]

Taken as a whole, Montesquieu's text presents a more nuanced analysis of women's role in public life than conveyed by this passage. The Persian harem clearly stood as a model of despotic government, and its bloody collapse at the end of the novel signaled the inherent instability of despotic rule. By making the female harem the epitome of despotism, Montesquieu implied that women's relative liberty was a crucial measure of the nature of a regime and that oppression of women in the household paralleled the tyrannical fiat of rulers. Without providing a clear alternative, the text suggests that some middle ground between the confinement and subjugation of women by despotism and the excessive involvement of women in French monarchical politics must be reached.[38]

At least one political commentator shared Montesquieu's concerns about female credit and went much further in proposing corrective action. In 1719 Abbé Charles-Irénée Castel de Saint-Pierre responded to the regency government of the Duc d'Orléans with a work titled *Discourse on Polysynody Wherein We Show that Polysynody, or the Plurality of Councils, Is the Most Advantageous Form of Ministry for a King and His Kingdom.* As the title suggests, the overall point of the work was to urge the adoption of a system of government based on multiple royal councils. The first part of the work was divided into twenty chapters, each of which argued for a particular benefit of the council system. The chapter titles included: "Individual Interest Will Less Often Be Opposed to the Public Interest"; "Kings Will Be Better Instructed of Their Affairs"; "Fewer Injustices and Humiliations on the Part of the Strongest," "More Men of Quality Will Apply Themselves, with More Success, to Governmental Affairs," and "More Love for the Fatherland." The second part of the book listed a series of potential objections to his plan and his response to each of them.

Chapter seventeen of part one was titled "The State Will Suffer Less from the Credit of Women." Here Saint-Pierre argued that one of the benefits of a council system would be to reduce the influence of women at court. It should be emphasized that he sought to reduce women's involvement in political affairs, not eliminate it. In his view the nature of human society itself made it impossible to prevent women from acquiring credit over men "to the extent that they please, that they take initiative, that they are led by ambitious people, and that they have cunning and skill to profit from favorable moments so as to succeed in their enterprises." Even more than ordinary men, kings were vulnerable to being governed by women, Saint-Pierre declared, because of the competition to please them and the reluctance of advisors to alert them to the wiles of adventuresses. The king's mistresses then chose ministers not according to their qualities but solely on the basis of "a perfect devotion to their ambition and their whim."[39]

Even if it were possible, Saint-Pierre thought it undesirable to eradicate women's credit over men. While he decried the excessive influence women acquired through their powers of sexual seduction, he did not advocate a separation of the sexes or a diminution of the social intercourse between them. In this reluctance he echoes passages in Montesquieu that viewed close relations between men and women as a positive characteristic of French social life.[40] For all its dangers, women's capacity to generate and sustain male sexual desire was too essential a foundation of procreation, family, and thus of the kingdom itself, to attempt to remove it altogether. Just as credit revealed problems in the intersection of gift and market economies, so did it highlight the necessary but threatening connections among household, libidinal, and political economies and the way such links enabled women to transfer credit from one economy to another.

Without undoing gendered social relations themselves, the best one could hope for was to diminish women's political influence and render it less dangerous to the state. Returning to his central theme, Saint-Pierre proposed that one of the best means to reduce women's credit in government was to adopt rule by council. First, because authority would be shared among many ministers, even the most beloved and powerful mistress's influence would be reduced to naming council members, who would possess much less power than ministers. Second, by giving each council the right to propose three individuals for a vacant place, women's potential harm would be limited to influencing the choice among the three, each of whom would have been vetted by the council. Third, should a chosen candidate prove "odious," it would be much easier to remove him. Fourth, even though each council member might be controlled by a woman, the very number of protectors would minimize the influence any one woman could exercise: "Thus the councilors pushed by different women, would be always opposed to each other, and the opposition of some would prevent the bad effects of the authority of others."[41] Rule by council was thus the opposite of the reign of a prime minister, who might be ruled by a single woman.

This was indeed outspoken criticism of women's harmful credit at court as well as explicit recognition that women's sexual relations with powerful men would inevitably endow them with political power. Saint-Pierre offers no examples or proof of this claim so it is difficult to gauge whether he intended his comments as empirical observation or rhetorical flourish. His text assumes, as did Montesquieu's, a readership that would simply accept as given his characterization of female power.

It is worth noting that Saint-Pierre acted on his own advice several years later as cofounder of the Club de l'Entresol. The club, which met from 1724 to 1731, was very much akin to a literary salon and boasted Montesquieu and the Marquis d'Argenson as members. Unlike the salons, however, the club was officially restricted to men. Redoubting the influence of women in the salons and perhaps desiring to show a positive example of a society free of their meddling, Saint-Pierre and his collaborators thus created a masculine space for serious discussion of public affairs. In private life he followed quite a different path, living out his own lessons on the inadvisability of restricting sexual relations among the sexes. He openly advocated the clergy's duty to marry and procreate and, according to Jean-Jacques Rousseau, he kept "a servant girl of an age to make [babies] and slept with her every Saturday."[42]

Saint-Pierre's book was highly radical for its time, earning him expulsion from the Académie française. His club was also closed after several years of existence at the behest of the royal government. Yet Saint-Pierre was not alone in his concerns about women's credit and the excessive influence they derived from it. In addition to Montesquieu's comments in *Persian Letters*, the Jansenist priest Jacques-Joseph Duguet made similar arguments in *Institutions d'un prince*, published posthumously in 1740.[43] Written to instruct the heir to the Duke of Savoy on the duties of a Christian prince, Duguet declares that the prince must not sell his credit or accede to individual solicitations. As part of these instructions, he counsels against giving any part of government to women and against corrupting luxury or gambling at court.

Together, these writers' complaints form an important backdrop to Rousseau's infamous denunciation of the role of women in French public life in *Letter to d'Alembert on the Theater*.[44] They show that within the long-term development of criticism of monarchical rule, women's role in court society was targeted as a crucial symptom of the failings of the regime. To appreciate the depth of frustration with the machinations of credit at court, and the tenacity of such networks, one must situate them alongside the dramatic effort to reform France's public credit system under John Law.

Saint-Pierre's controversial work appeared on the eve of one of the most important episodes of the regency and indeed of French public life in the eighteenth century. Louis XIV's wars, and the explosion in size of the French army they produced, placed unprecedented strains on French finances. The final conflict of Louis's reign, the War of the Spanish Succession (1701–1714), proved especially disastrous. Annual state expenditure rose from 175 million livres in 1702 to 264 million livres in 1711. In 1715, with the return of peace, state expenditure fell to 146 million livres annually but taxes only brought in 69 million livres.[45] By this point the elaborate system of public credit carefully crafted by Jean-Baptiste Colbert had all but collapsed.

Colbert's fiscal regime consisted of two major branches: the direct property tax, or *taille*, and indirect taxes accruing from the sales of goods, revenue from internal tariffs, and income from the king's domain. Colbert had joined indirect taxes on goods into a single unit, known as the general farm, and leased their collection to a consortium of private financiers. A group of venal office holders, known as the receivers general, collected the direct property tax, from which nobles, the clergy, major cities, and other privileged groups were exempt. The system operated not merely as a means to collect taxes but, even more importantly, as a source of collateral for its collectors. These wealthy and powerful men first contributed substantial sums as payment for their offices (in the case of the receivers general) or their leases (in the case of the general farmers). They also advanced money to the crown periodically by issuing promissory notes to royal creditors based on their expected fiscal revenue. On orders from Versailles, they also reimbursed individuals holding different forms of government debt with their own notes. The process through which such individuals obtained their government offices was one more of the hidden secrets of absolutist government, heavily based on the "credit," in all its senses, of the would-be official. The circulating reciprocal exchange of credit Saint-Simon portrayed between Madame de Maintenon and Louis's ministers provides an apt model for the system: men of high credit extended their own collateral to the crown and in return derived fresh credit with potential lenders, social relations, business or marriage partners, and other interested parties, which would in turn cycle back to benefit the state.

When times were good, financial paper produced by this system allowed the government to meet its debts without cumbersome specie payments and pro-

FIGURE 2.1 Nicolas Desmaretz, controller general of finance (1708–1715). *Source*: Bibliothèque nationale de France.

vided a stimulus for commercial exchange and artisanal production. Decades of war and stagnant trade from 1688 onward, however, meant that the revenues that served as collateral for all this paper shrank drastically, dealing a fatal blow to the credit of the crucial intermediary figures. Successive controllers general turned to a series of extraordinary measures, creating cascades of new venal offices, extorting loans from existing office holders, alienating the collection of different forms of revenue, offering exemptions from taxation for one-time payments, and devaluating the value of the livre with regard to silver and gold coins. Experiments with new forms of taxation led in 1695 to a temporary capitation tax that was based on social status rather than wealth and from which no social category was exempt. The government reimposed the tax in 1701 and raised it by 5 percent in 1705, extending this surcharge to all other sources of revenue, including the taille.

In 1710, at the height of the War of the Spanish Succession, Controller General Desmaretz (figure 2.1) struggled once more to breathe new life into the system. In addition to a host of additional "extraordinary" impositions, he convinced the king and his council to impose a new nation-wide income tax of 10 percent (the *dixième*). Apart from generating new revenue, Desmaretz sought to retire existing government paper by requiring that payments for a range of new offices, annuities, and other one-time impositions be made in a combination of coin and paper. Desmaretz's ambition was thus to restore the existing multitiered credit system, not to install a fundamentally different method of public finance.[46]

Despite his efforts and the confidence he initially enjoyed within commercial and banking circles, Desmaretz could not overcome the strains of decades of war. Moreover, his efforts to impose taxes on nobles through the capitation won him the enmity of those who would take power in the regency. Once Louis XIV died, the regency government quickly set out to recover control of Desmaretz's crucial set of responsibilities and the patronage positions he controlled.[47] He was dismissed from the government in spite of the looming financial crisis and his long experience and dedication in attempting to overcome it. As one tangent of the attack on Desmaretz, officials accused his son-in-law, Charles Henri Malon, seigneur de Bercy, of corruption in dealings with private financiers who loaned money to the crown. According to court memoirist Dangeau, rumors circulated of secret nighttime rendezvous with financiers to plot currency speculation based on their insider knowledge.[48] These rumors open a window into the use of gossip and scandal as a means of discrediting opponents in the royal government and its financial system. Despite efforts by partisans at court to return him to power, de Bercy's disgrace was permanent.

At the time of Desmaretz's departure, the country held over 2 billion livres in debt, owed annual interest payments of approximately 90 million livres, and possessed a weak and unreliable revenue stream with which to meet its obligations. Into this abyss stepped the Scottish economist (and gambler and speculator) John Law, who arrived in the kingdom in 1714 with a proposal for a radical transformation of French public finance. As early as 1705 Law had argued in favor of the establishment of a land bank in Scotland, claiming that increasing the supply of credit would allow his country to gain new prosperity and strength. Drawing an analogy with the circulation of blood in the human body, discovered by William Harvey in 1628, he claimed: "When blood does not circulate throughout the body, the body languishes; the same when money does not circulate."[49] By 1711 Law had abandoned the idea of a land bank and returned to an earlier conviction that credit could be based on a national bank and trading company.

From the beginning of financial crisis in the last decades of the seventeenth century through the death of Louis XIV, hundreds of reform-minded individuals—known as *donneurs d'avis*—submitted proposals to the government, ranging from broad-ranging projects for fiscal reform to suggestions for new sources of extraordinary revenue, to means of eliminating corruption in the allocation or collection of taxes. Writers now famous as precursors of economic theory, such as Vauban and Boisguilbert, wrote and circulated their treatises not in an ivory tower of abstract speculation but in this context of project jobbing to address the crisis in public finance.

Like many other ambitious men seeking to profit from crisis to gain an entrée to power, John Law submitted a memorandum to the royal government promising to restore and expand public credit through the creation of a national bank. Desmaretz's goal, since his appointment in 1708, was to rebuild Colbert's credit system; for Law, the only solution was to abandon all the old means of generating revenue. Instead, France would have a royal bank that would issue paper money in order to stimulate trade and commerce and, most importantly, pay off existing loans. In 1716 the Council of Finances authorized Law to establish a private Banque générale, which would accept and manage deposits and discount bills of exchange. The government also allowed the bank to issue a limited number of notes valued in écus that could be exchanged on demand for specie.

Based on its initial success in putting its notes into circulation, the bank received the title of Banque royale in 1718. The crown purchased the shares of existing shareholders and proclaimed that it would back the notes of the bank—and receive all profits—making it effectively an arm of government. To encourage the adoption of banknotes in favor of metal coins, the government ordered in December 1718 that buyers and sellers of transactions above six hundred livres must use either gold coins or bank notes but not the more common silver coins. In April 1719 it ruled that creditors could demand payment in bank notes in towns where the bank had established offices.

Law's plan to make the bank part of the royal government faced the major obstacle that investors had very little confidence in the crown's capacity to guarantee its paper, based on its dismal record over the previous decade. Inspired by the model of the joint operations of the Bank of England and the East India Company, Law's innovation was to use the profits from colonization and foreign trade to provide the bank's capital. He thus combined the bank's operations with those of the Compagnie de l'Occident, a royal trading company he created in 1717 with a monopoly over the vast region watered by the Mississippi River. From December 1718 to June 1719 the company greatly expanded its geographical range by taking over the struggling Compagnie des Indes Orientales and the Compagnie de la Chine as well as the Compagnie du Sénégal. This vast conglomerate, renamed the Compagnie des Indes, now claimed control over all French trade outside of Europe. In July 1719 the company expanded its reach even further by purchasing the right to mint coins and, in August, it purchased the general farm as well as the offices of those who collected direct taxes. The company had effectively put the crown's traditional credit brokers out of business.

Like Desmaretz, Law realized that existing debt had to be erased before new currency could circulate. To this end, the bank offered its shares in exchange for government annuities and other forms of public debt. Moreover, Law decreed that shares in the company could only be purchased with banknotes, thus encouraging investors to turn in their public annuities for bank paper. The bank's currency was also used to pay interest on government debt, thereby not only releasing the government from the expense of interest payments (they could just print more notes) but also encouraging the circulation of banknotes and the company shares they could be used to purchase.

If one benefit of the scheme would be to retire government debt at low cost, another would be to increase greatly the circulation of money. This would take the form of the paper generated by the bank as well as an increased amount of coinage in circulation, due to the government's decreased reliance on taxation. Dating back to his publication in 1705, Law was convinced that increasing the monetary supply was the key to encouraging commerce and trade and thus strengthening the state. The scheme had profound social and political, as well as financial, goals. Law argued that creating a French currency that was independent of international specie trading would allow the nation to be more self-sufficient and lessen the domestic effects of volatility in world currency markets. Law also believed that encouraging rentiers to return their funds to circulation in a public market would decrease social inequality in France by ending the privileged position that owners of government debt enjoyed.

Law's system represented a fundamental shift in techniques for generating confidence in public credit. Rather than relying on private financiers, whose self-interest might well conflict with collective needs, the state would derive its credit from public opinion, that is, from its subjects as a whole and their faith in the system. In a sense Law thus intended to replace the political credit system of the court and the royal government—and along with them the financiers who kept the royal government afloat—with a more transparent system of public credit. No more would patronage, hidden deals, and influence peddling allow individuals to usurp state finance; instead, the nation itself would control and benefit from the new system.[50]

Law's scheme captured the imagination of investors across Europe and, in a frenzy of speculation, the price of company shares skyrocketed from a real value of 150 livres in 1717 to 10,000 livres in December 1719. The apparent success of the system in triggering economic growth resulted in Law's appointment as controller general in January 1720 and the merger of the company and the bank in February of that year. The rise in value of bank notes was accompanied by more strenuous measures on the part of the government to replace metal coin with paper and to prevent a sudden run on the bank. A royal edict forbade the repayment of debts of more than 100 livres with coin, and by February 1720 another edict made it a crime to possess more than 500 livres in metal coin.

Law had reached the pinnacle of his power and influence, but his descent was to prove even faster than his rise. Fear began to spread about the astronomical rise in the value of company shares. As investors sought to transfer their funds back to more secure forms of property, such as land and metal coins, the values of the shares began to fall. To prevent a collapse in share prices, Law issued an edict in March 1721 fixing the company's share price at nine thousand livres and ordering the bank to trade them at that price. The result was a collapse in the real value of the bank notes. By May 1721 a new decree had to be issued cutting the value of both notes and shares in half. The speculative bubble quickly burst, leaving thousands of investors with worthless paper. Fearing for his safety, Law fled France in December 1721.

The John Law system was a formidable boon to debtors, including many peasants, who were able to repay their debts at a fraction of their nominative value. However, many were left penniless. A commission established to deal with the aftermath of the experiment reestablished the public debt at roughly the same level and the old system of tax farming, annuities, and private financiers returned. Debate continued over the validity of Law's ideas and the long-term impact of the project throughout the eighteenth century and continues among historians today.[51]

Michael Sonenscher's recent study of public credit argues that eighteenth-century commentators assessed Law's project more positively than historians have previously acknowledged. For example, he cites Voltaire's statement in 1738 that if Law had succeeded he would have rendered France the most powerful nation in the world and that the country had accrued many benefits even from his failure. The Marquis d'Argenson had an even more positive assessment: "Properly examined, public credit is not a debt. . . . It is, rather, the fabrication of a new kind of money. It is a form of value that is a companion to circulating coin and acts in the same way. It should be maintained, not extinguished. It is never a charge upon the king or the state but is infinitely useful to them both."[52] D'Argenson concluded that Law's system, overall, had prevented the looming collapse of credit and improved the French economy, despite the suffering of some individuals.

The larger point of Sonenscher's book, however, is not to identify such optimists but to emphasize the views of those who, like Montesquieu, believed that the growth of public credit threatened to lead France down the path toward despotism. Sonenscher argues that anxieties about the consequences of royal debt constituted a fundamental, and hitherto overlooked, element of eighteenth-century political debate. This was because of what he terms the "Janus-faced" nature of public credit: on the one hand, it could generate prosperity and stimulate the creation of constitutional structures to regulate it; on the other hand, government debt was "a product of war and continuous preparations for war."[53] Thus, the very mechanism that seemed to be premised on freedom and stability could also be co-opted by a violent revolutionary regime that appropriated public credit and private property for its own tyrannical purposes. Sonenscher proposes that this understanding of what a "revolution" would look like predated the events of 1789 and helped to shape their outcome.

In analyzing the violent capacities unleashed by reliance on public credit, Sonenscher might have noted that one element of state coercion at work in the Law experiment was the claim to monopolize overseas commerce, including the trade in enslaved Africans. In its 1717 charter, the Compagnie de l'Occident promised to bring 6,000 settlers and 3,000 slaves to the colony over the next twenty-five years. By acquiring the Compagnie du Sénégal, Law's trading conglomerate gained a monopoly over the slave trade with Senegal. In June 1719, two company ships brought the first enslaved Africans to Louisiana, with a combined cargo of 451 individuals. In September 1720, the company expanded these rights with a royal edict conveying monopolies over the slave trade with the Guinea coast and with the colony of Saint-Domingue as well as exemption from taxation and a cash bonus for each slave transported. In exchange for these privileges, the Compagnie des Indes promised to deliver three thousand enslaved people to French colonies each year. Law thus premised his new system of public credit directly on the expansion of slavery; violence and coercion, backed by state power, were to generate collective confidence in the value of the bank's notes. Although the company could never meet the slave quotas without help from private traders, the Compagnie des Indes was one of the few elements of Law's system to survive his downfall in 1721.[54]

In the context of this book, the period of John Law's financial innovations throws stark light on the manner by which debates about public credit inevitably led to questions about the circulation of political and social credit. Fear of the arbitrary and potentially despotic nature of government debt financing rested, implicitly or explicitly, at least in part on distrust of the political and social credit mechanisms governing access to and control over state finance. One of the aspirations of those calling for a new constitution, a central feature of the debates Sonenscher studies, was to impose regular and transparent conditions for access to power, including control of state finances, and thus to eliminate the capricious forms of credit maneuvering we have studied to this point.

The Pâris brothers and their protégé, Mademoiselle Poisson, later Madame de Pompadour, stood at the combined nexus of the politico-financial credit system that controlled the French state. Her ascension and hold on power signified to many the ongoing interconnections of politics with financial credit and the vital need to reform both arenas.

Louis XV: Continuity and Change

DUCLOS AND THE ETHICS OF CREDIT

The most explicit commentator on credit as a form of political capital in eighteenth-century France was Charles Pinot Duclos (1704–1772). Born in Brittany to a merchant family and educated in Paris, Duclos (figure 2.2) achieved an illustrious career at the center of French cultural life. He replaced Voltaire as *historiographe de France* when the philosophe left France for Prussia and was named to the Académie des inscriptions in 1739. Elected to the Académie française in 1747, he became permanent secretary of this august body in 1755. Duclos was an active member of salon society and enjoyed the protection of Madame de Pompadour.[55]

Duclos was a prolific author of works of history, novels, and other forms of literature, and he oversaw collaboration on the 1762 edition of the *Dictionnaire de l'Académie française*. His memoirs of the reigns of Louis XIV and XV, which draw very heavily on the work of Saint-Simon, were published posthumously after the French Revolution. Among his many publications, *Considérations sur les moeurs de ce siècle* (1751) had the greatest impact on contemporaries and appeared in eleven editions before his death in 1772. The book was written as a contribution to moral philosophy for readers who made up *le monde* of the Old Regime: courtiers, government administrators, successful men of letters, and salon participants. Duclos's goal was to reorient his readers toward the public good and away from self-interest or cliquish society life. Like La Bruyère's earlier work, whose title he self-consciously echoed, Duclos's text sought to unmask what he viewed as the hypocrisies and artifice of polite society and to explain the true principles and motivations behind people's behavior. In common with his predecessor, Duclos accepted that self-interest was an inevitable part of human motivation; it was, once more, the excess of self-regard that marred society. He argued that a new and enlarged elite—that would include both nobles and educated men of letters—should revive and reform traditional noble values, such as honor, virtue, and patriotism.[56]

One of the main claims of Duclos's book was that a significant shift had taken place in the operation of power in France. According to Duclos, the

FIGURE 2.2 Charles Pinot Duclos (1704–1772). *Source:* © Musée Antoine Lecuyer / RMN-Grand Palais / Art Resource, NY.

"great lords" who had once exercised power now retained only their magnificent titles. In their place, officers of the crown now held true power in the realm. Some nobles, he granted, did succeed in acquiring credit through service to the royal government; however, it was more common for courtiers to be in need of services than to be in a position to dispense them. As he stated:

> The former [*les grands*] are obliged to have recourse to men with positions, and often have more need of them than the common people, who, condemned to obscurity, have neither the opportunity nor the presumption to hope for anything. It is not that there are no lords with credit, but they owe it only to the consideration that they have made for themselves, to the services they have rendered, to the need the state still has for them. But the great who are only great, having neither power nor direct credit, seek to play a role by ploys, suppleness and intrigue, [that are] characteristics of weakness. Honorary titles, finally, command little but respect, positions alone give power.[57]

Duclos's chapter 6, titled "On Credit," focused on the power held by *gens en place*," that is, men who held formal appointments in the royal government. Because these men held true power, according to Duclos, they alone had the capacity to dispense credit. Duclos's account of the circulation of credit accordingly focused on the way crown officers—and most importantly royal ministers—dispensed favors and influence. His vision of credit thus represented a narrow slice of the broad notions of credit discussed in chapter 1. While

Furetière's dictionary definition began by identifying credit as a reputation for excellence and then discussed the influence one might derive from a good reputation, Duclos skipped over the issue of influence to focus on power. He opened the chapter with the blunt declaration that "credit is the use of the power of another." Duclos also highlighted the inequalities and subordination inherent in credit. The third sentence of the chapter stated that "credit indicates thus a sort of inferiority, at least relative to the power that one uses, whatever superiority one has in other respects."[58] However great his title, a noble who sought favors from a minister of lesser social status thereby acknowledged his true inferiority. For Duclos, credit revealed the real chain of being in the realm and exposed the lie of the official one: "speaking of credit, one vaunts that of a simple individual with a great lord, that of a lord with a minister and that of a minister with the king." As he summarized, "credit is thus the relation of need to power."[59]

Based on this relational theory of credit, Duclos outlined a complex network of individuals involved in its exchange. His definition implicated at least four people in each credit transaction: (1) the individual who requested a service, (2) the person he wished to benefit with the service, (3) the credit holder who used credit to obtain the service, and (4) the granter of credit who provided the service. This list provides further insight into the complex hierarchies and relations that structured the world to which Duclos belonged. As he stated, to use influence for a favor for oneself was simply to be a protégé of the individual who bestowed the grace; credit consisted in using that influence to obtain a benefit for someone else. His comments also reveal the ambiguities in this credit system, for each individual in the list could be said to possess credit. Individual 1 had to possess credit with individual 3 in order successfully to request the favor for individual 2, but it was 3's possession of credit with his superiors that allowed him to grant credit to 1. Moreover person 2 must have possessed some form of credit with person 1 to convince that individual to put in motion the credit of number 3. This model puts into play a cascade of hierarchical levels of credit, in which individuals take on multiple and interrelated roles.

Most significantly, Duclos suggested that these hierarchies did not correspond to, indeed they actively undermined, the official social taxonomy. Noble titles alone had little currency in the credit system. The royal government, however, did. Duclos thus attempted to ensure closure of the system at its summit by according total and sovereign power over the credit system to the king. He declared that "the idea we have of credit is so well-established that there is no one who would not find it ridiculous to hear of the credit of the king."[60] In this comment Duclos reiterated the dictionaries of the late seventeenth century, which had insisted that it was impossible to speak of the king's credit because no one occupied the position of superiority necessary to accord him credit.

Duclos, of course, was well aware that a rising tide of publications focused precisely on the king's financial credit. He had lived through the John Law experiment as an adolescent; his own family lost money from it and he explicitly denounced Law in his *Secret Memoirs of the Reign of Louis XIV, the Regency and the Reign of Louis XV*, commenting that never was a "despotism more frenetic."[61] He must have been well aware of the torrent of debate over the consequences of the system and of the renewed impact of military conflict on French finances during the War of the Austrian Succession (1740–1748). Although sharply critical of the nobility and cognizant of the challenges proffered to traditional social values by the expansion of royal power, Duclos was not prepared to question the monarchical regime. He therefore closed off the potentially radical implications of his analysis of credit by reaffirming the supremacy of the monarch.

For Duclos, the problem with the credit system was not that it undercut the status of the ancient nobility but that through it the nobility was tarnished by excess self-interest and venality. He explained that there were four means by which individuals acquired credit. The best was through esteem, which "could be seen as a form of justice rendered to merit."[62] Duclos did not define the word *merit* explicitly in this text, although it was one of the key values that he wished to inspire in society and a central term of his analysis. Indeed, much of the text functioned as a series of contrasts based on assessments of merit: between those with and without merit, between merit-worthy and shameful actions, between individuals who acquired favor without merit and those who possessed merit but no influence, and between wealth and merit.[63] The closest Duclos came to a definition in *Considérations* was in his explanation that the "man of merit" was one who "having all the qualities and advantages of his estate does not tarnish them in any way."[64] The *Dictionnaire de l'Académie française* of 1762, whose publication he oversaw, defined the word as "that which renders [someone or something] worthy of esteem," explaining that, "with regard to people, we mean excellent qualities, either of the mind or of the heart."[65]

The second means of acquiring credit, according to Duclos, was through "inclination," meaning personal affection and attachment. This was a less honorable method for acquiring credit but—given the realities of the human heart—was more reliable than the first. Both of these channels, however, were much less common than what he identified as the last two means: hope and fear. In turn, hope and fear, for Duclos, "were two effects of the same cause":

self-interest. People seldom wished to accord credit to those with merit, he declared, because it felt too much like performing a duty rather than granting a favor. Inclination based on friendship and merit usually lost out to the desire for more immediate and less honorable pleasures. Moreover, office holders had little use for friends, devoting themselves instead to personal ambition and political machinations. Their position gave them so many opportunities to see the crapulous aspects of human behavior that they were justified, he admitted, in discounting avowals of friendship.

"Friendship" (*amitié*) was another key term in Duclos's text and one that he similarly elucidated not through a single definition but through contrast with its absence or opposite and by its association with related, positive terms like "love," "merit," and "esteem." He stated, for example, that "ties of blood" did not determine friendship, and that one only enjoyed "friendship, esteem, respect, and consideration" from those whom one knew personally. The *Dictionnaire de l'Académie française* of 1762 defined "amitié" as "affection that one has for someone, which is ordinarily mutual."

Although he found them to have little influence on credit in practice, Duclos insisted that, without merit and friendship, "credit would be nothing more than a tribute paid to interest, a pure exchange, ruled by hope and fear."[66] When it came closest to its economic avatar, credit was at its most base and ignoble. What enabled credit to take on a positive moral effect was its mediation through positive values like virtue, esteem, and love. Without their purifying effects, credit sank into a mere exchange of interests, exposing the base self-regard of the individuals involved. Interest, Duclos elucidated, could take many forms. It could consist of enhanced reputation: "One does not refuse those whom one can oblige with glory and from whom glory is the interest one procures." Even more important was the hope for a return favor of some kind; as he stated, "this expectancy is a more perceptible interest for the majority of men." The most powerful form of interest, however, was not material reward but fear: "We grant almost everything to those whose resentment we fear." This fear was inspired particularly by individuals at court, "whose status we despise but whom domestic intimacy [that is, with the king] or circumstances may render dangerous."[67]

This statement complicates, in its own fashion, the revisionist social hierarchy posited by Duclos. Duclos's discussion to that point had focused on the motivations for a more powerful person to accord credit to an inferior (or how individual 1 set in motion the credit of individual 3), who was already in possession of credit. By giving fear such a prominent place among the motivations for granting favors, Duclos suggested that person 3 (the "gens en place") feared the power of others, such as the lowborn but well-connected people at court, to whom they felt they must accord credit, willingly or not. Thus, individual 1 who sought credit was already empowered by his possession of credit from an alternate (and equally powerful) source. The king may have stood alone at the summit of the credit system, but—according to Duclos—he sponsored discrete and competing credit networks. Personal access to the king and his family could generate credit superior to that of a crown minister. The result was a blurring of the lines of power: "So many circumstances compete and intersect sometimes in the smallest favors, that it would be difficult to say how and by whom they are granted."[68] Rather than reinforcing or even simply reversing the existing chain of being, credit—in its degraded form—created new, overlapping, excessive, and ultimately unintelligible circuits.

The best proof of these excesses was that the possession of credit itself had become, according to Duclos, a way to acquire more credit: "the sole reputation of having it is one of the surest ways to consolidate, extend, and even to obtain it."[69] There were many individuals, Duclos declared, who were so eager to appear in credit that they encouraged solicitations they could not fulfill. The danger of seeking the reputation of being *en crédit*—which Duclos derided as a "frivolous good"—is that there were always more favor seekers than even the most powerful credit could satisfy: "There is no credit that is not inferior to the reputation that it acquires."[70] Thus in seeking to build a reputation for possessing credit, one risked becoming known only for one's inability to meet requests. The ingratitude and self-righteousness of those who sought favors rendered these hazards all the greater.

Duclos ended the chapter by explaining that his desire was not to discourage those who wished to benefit others. On the contrary, he wished to encourage them to act on disinterested and noble sentiments, to perform services only through generosity and for the pleasure of helping others. His goal—here and throughout *Considérations*—was to reinsert the supposedly original principles of virtue and esteem back into what had become a system of self-interest and power politics, in other words to reform the nobility and also elaborate a new set of truly "noble" values accessible to plebeians as well as patricians. He did not explain, however, how disinterest and generosity could break the cycles of fear, greed, and selfishness he described or bring order to the tangled webs of credit. His only response to the permeation of noble life and monarchical rule by money was to ignore the existence of financial credit altogether.

In addition to providing the sole theoretical model of political and social credit in the literature, Duclos's book is valuable for the constellation of words that appear alongside credit and the relations he established among them. As with the terms "merit" and "friendship," Duclos's authorial strategy through-out the text was to elucidate the meaning of his key terms by associating sets of values together and contrasting them with their opposite. In addition to speci-fying that credit was "use of the power of another," Duclos thus defined a num-ber of terms he used in conjunction with credit. According to Duclos, probity was "the observation of the law," while virtue stemmed from an inner moral instinct that "insists that we do right and inspires the desire to do so." Honor was another value tightly linked with virtue: "Honor is the instinct for virtue and it imparts courage to it."

Apart from these high moral values, Duclos also discusses the role of "repu-tation" and "renown." Both, he tells us, were important wellsprings of society and originated with the same principle: "the desire to occupy a place in men's opinions." They differed only in that reputation had a more humble character. Any person could have a "respectable reputation" (*une réputation honnête*); "one obtains it by social virtues and the constant practice of one's duty."[71] Repu-tation, while not brilliant or widely recognized, had positive moral effects on society. Renown was the equivalent of fame. Princes received it as a birthright, while lesser beings might seek to acquire it. The desire for fame could have positive results for society, but, turned into a mania, the thirst for fame led to humiliating and hypocritical behavior. If interest was the Achilles heel of credit, pride was that of reputation.

The worst aspect of reputation, according to Duclos, was the speed and fre-quency with which reputations rose and fell, most often with little connection to the true merits of their subjects. Part of the fault lay with those who dis-sembled to maintain a false reputation. The largest share of blame, however, belonged to those who created the reputation, the "cabal" or the "public" that was often surprised at the reputation it had created and, finding no apparent justification, "only conceived greater admiration and respect for the phantom it created." Here, Duclos drew an explicit link not with moral but with financial credit: "These reputations resemble those fortunes that, without real capital, rely on credit and are only the more brilliant."[72] Duclos's only explicit refer-ence to financial credit in the book, this passing comment suggests his distrust of the phenomenon.

Contrasted to the artificial and illusory nature of reputation was "consider-ation," which Duclos defined as "a sentiment of esteem mixed with a sort of personal respect that a man inspires in his favor."[73] Rather than being based on the whims of the cabal, consideration arose from personal knowledge. It could be possessed by men of any estate and be accorded to an individual by his social superiors, equals, or inferiors. Consideration was obtained, he stated, "by the union of merit, decency, and self-respect."[74]

Even consideration, however, could be usurped. Behind many alleged men of merit, he commented, lay a surprising emptiness. The appearance of merit drew simply on "an air, a tone of importance and self-satisfaction; a hint of impertinence does not hurt." The opposite of the man of consideration, Duclos declared, was the "*espèce*." This neologism referred to a man who, "lacking the merit of his estate, participates in his own degradation."[75] He failed himself more than others. Duclos nonetheless concluded the chapter on a benign tone, noting that renown came with superior talent and great effort while reputation was less widespread, that false reputations were unreliable, that the most respectable (*honnête*) was the most useful, and that each individual should aspire to the consideration appropriate to his estate. He did not, however, offer answers for the multiple problems of hypocrisy and pride he discussed. Despite his upbeat conclusion, the victory of true virtue and merit seem as unreliable as false reputation. The only unfailing elements, it appears, were artifice and ambition, the gullibility of the public, and the recurrence of illusion.

We see throughout Duclos's analysis of the workings of credit and the dangers of false reputation the heavy imprint of his reading of Saint-Simon. Duclos's emphasis on the way ministers usurped credit from great nobles, his schematic flowchart for the exchange of credit, his cynicism about the selfish interests guiding courtiers, and his nostalgia for an imaginary world of lost values in which reputation was indelibly tied to merit—these all resonate strongly with Saint-Simon's depiction of credit at the court of Louis XIV. Like Saint-Simon decades before, he argued that there were, effectively, no more great lords; everyone who appeared at Versailles participated in the intrigues and power plays at court.

Although he relied on Saint-Simon for his analysis of power, Duclos broke with him in crucial ways. Whereas the duke reviled the loss of aristocratic influence, the parvenu Duclos made the case in favor of social ascension. He argued that at least two new social groups had infiltrated le monde: the rich (whom he divides among financiers and merchants) and men of letters, the group to which Duclos himself belonged and whose claims for inclusion he ardently defended. Duclos thus denied essential differences among the social classes who composed le monde. Except for the way they expressed themselves, he remarked, there was little difference between the courtier and the bourgeois. Those groups, bourgeois and noble, who composed le monde and created public opinion constituted his intended audience and the target of his moralizing.

Indeed, Duclos laid his best hopes for moral regeneration in the beneficial influence of men of letters, who demonstrated neither the arrogant futility of the nobility nor the self-interest and material concerns of the bourgeoisie. Their enlightened wisdom, he argued, could renew the moral character so lacking in a system that relied on birth or fortune. At the same time, Duclos explicitly excluded "*le bas peuple*" from his hopes for regeneration. While he deplored their poverty and lack of education, he simply discounted their capacity to rise above their pursuit of daily necessities. Duclos's vision was thus a typically "enlightened" mixture of the radical and conservative. He not only abandoned the poor to their fate, he also left unclear how to reconcile this progressive social vision of an expanded elite composed of exceptional commoners and nobles with the explicitly aristocratic origins of the values he espoused or with the injunction, cited above, that each individual should aspire for consideration appropriate to his estate. In his reformed society commoners would acquire credit through their merit and virtue, but it is unclear how far he intended this credit to carry them in social or political terms.

What is particularly fascinating, for our purposes, is Duclos's refusal to acknowledge the conversion among different types of credit that was a constant aspect of his society. Economic credit surfaced only once in the book, as an analogy for the artifice of false reputation. In his discussion of the differences between financiers and merchants—the former are merely channels for the circulation of money, while the latter are sources of abundance—he had nothing to say about the use of credit by either group. Most strikingly, economic credit, for Duclos, apparently bore no relation to the exchange of influence and favors discussed in his chapter on credit. Instead, the inclusion of interest tainted social credit with the stain of economic exchange. For him to rescue the moral value of credit relations, he had to banish any analogy with its economic counterpart. In other words, he had to recast credit as a pure gift system devoid of any materiality or self-interest. This move not only veiled the common origins of the two forms of credit in notions of belief and credibility—roots that were explicitly emphasized in the academy's dictionary written under his direction—but also obscured the extent to which economic credit continued to bathe in the same language of trust, confidence, reputation, and esteem. His position highlights the resistance men of letters such as Duclos may have had to discussing the obvious homologies among economic and moral credit in their projects for social reform, even as they enacted and discussed them in their letters.

In the aftermath of the Law system one influential commentator thus reacted to public credit by disowning it entirely and relegating it, implicitly, to a wholly discrete realm to be dealt with by its own commentators and experts. Instead of seeking to reform corrupt politics by wresting the king's credit from the hands of private financiers, as John Law struggled and failed to accomplish, Duclos sought instead a moral regeneration of the system of power through the rebirth of virtue and merit.

To judge from an even more influential and widely read text, the *Encyclopédie*, some readers echoed this division of credit into two distinct realms with no overt connections between them. His rivals in the *Encyclopédie* thus offered two successive entries on credit. The first was a lengthy discussion by the economic writer François Véron Duverger de Forbonnais, who cited Duclos briefly before moving on to discuss financial credit in informed and extended detail. The second was an entry on "moral credit" by Denis Diderot that drew very heavily on Duclos's text in chapter six of *Considérations*. In these influential texts of the mid-eighteenth century we see economic circulation severed from social relations and cultural values. This normative projection bore little resemblance to the ongoing amalgam of different forms of credit in the lives of many individuals, including the authors of the texts themselves.

The Marquise de Pompadour

In addition to its silence on financial matters, a second noteworthy feature of Duclos's lengthy treatment of credit is his utter silence on the issue of women's involvement in credit networks. His reading of Saint-Simon notwithstanding, the tacit assumption of the text is that the court and its politics constituted an exclusively masculine world. The ethical and moral issues he targeted involved sword noblemen, robe ministers, obsequious servants, intellectuals, and other male members of le monde. His work reads as though he had taken the complaints of Montesquieu, Saint-Pierre, and Duguet one step further by imagining a moral universe of power in which women had no part.

What is so striking about the absence of women in *Considérations sur les moeurs de ce siècle* is that Duclos's other publications indicated his full understanding of the role that women played in patronage. His *Secret Memoirs of the Reign of Louis XIV, the Regency and the Reign of Louis XV* virtually plagiarized Saint-Simon's memoirs of Versailles in its account of Louis XIV and the regency. Duclos echoed Saint-Simon, for example, in recounting the credit scheming of Madame de Maintenon and her credit exchanges with the Princesse des Ursins (a French courtier sent to Spain to attend the first Bourbon queen of Spain and act as secret agent for the French crown).[76] In later sections of the work he borrowed the metaphor of credit to describe the power

FIGURE 2.3 Jeanne Antoinette Poisson, Marquise de Pompadour (1721–1764). Painting by François Boucher. *Source*: © National Gallery of Scotland / The Art Archive at Art Resource, NY.

and influence of his own patron, the Marquise de Pompadour (figure 2.3), the longest-lasting and most important mistress of Louis XV. He characterized, for example, the efforts of the Austrian ambassador to France to further the cause of a new Franco-Austrian alliance in terms of credit: "He strove first of all to persuade the ministers, and above all Madame de Pompadour, whose credit seemed to him the most important to be dealt with."[77] He also described the effects of Pompadour's "powerful credit" on the fortunes of the Abbé de Bernis, whom she took under her protection.[78]

Certainly anyone familiar with Madame de Pompadour could not have been ignorant of the credit she wielded at court or the hostility her own connections with financiers inspired. Like Madame de Maintenon, the credit of Madame de Pompadour garnered constant scrutiny, in her case much more often critical than complimentary. Attacks on Pompadour's perceived influence over Louis XV and his government represented in some sense a culmination of the criticisms expressed under the regency by Montesquieu and Saint-Pierre.[79] Pompadour was born into a bourgeois family with close relations to the Pâris family of tax farmers and financiers; some speculated that her real father was Pâris de Marmontel, one of the Pâris brothers. Another man rumored to be her biological father, a farmer general named Le Normant de Tournehem, sponsored Pompadour's education and lessons in dance and music. Pompadour gained access to high society through her relations in the world of finance and the entree they provided to Parisian salons, where she attracted admiration for her beauty and artistic skills. Her relationship with Louis xv began in 1745, and she remained at court until her death in 1764, although sexual relations with the king ceased in 1750.

After a brief period of approbation, court and city opinion turned against Pompadour, aided by vituperative rumors, songs, and poems circulated by those loyal to the queen and the *dévot* party. Negative portrayals of Pompadour often focused on her lowly origins and links to state financiers. These links served to taint Pompadour with base self-interest and greed, charges heightened by knowledge of the sums she spent on artistic patronage and building projects. She was accused of inflicting ruinous debt on the crown, leading to new taxes, like the *vingtième*, a renewed version of Desmaretz's dixième tax imposed by Controller General Machault in 1749.[80] In the combined accusations that Pompadour was bleeding the state dry and that she was sapping the king's vitality through libidinous excess, we find a conception of overlapping circuits of libidinal and financial economy. One woman's insatiable appetites exhausted the vital forces of money and sexual vigor. As we will see, all of these accusations resurfaced with regard to Marie-Antoinette twenty-five years later.

One of the most important contemporary sources regarding perceptions of Pompadour are the journals of the Marquis d'Argenson. The marquis served as foreign minister from 1744 to 1747, when he lost his office to Pompadour's candidate, the Vicomte de Puisieulx. His younger brother, the Comte d'Argenson, was lieutenant general of Paris police in 1720 and secretary of state for war from 1743 to 1757. Both were interested readers, if not avowed supporters, of the Enlightenment texts of Voltaire and the *Encyclopédie*. Like the marquis, the Comte d'Argenson lost his position as minister as a result of Pompadour's interference. Despite significant differences and tensions between them, the d'Argenson brothers shared disdain for the undue power wielded by the royal favorite, a recurring theme in the marquis's journals.[81]

Through the late 1740s and early 1750s, the Marquis d'Argenson closely watched the rivalry between Madame de Pompadour and her cousin, the Comtesse d'Estrades, lady-in-waiting to Mesdames, the daughters of Louis xv. He jubilated in the apparent rise of d'Estrades's credit and what he hoped was the imminent disgrace of Pompadour. On September 20, 1752, he reported that "the Comtesse d'Estrades has more credit than ever. Madame de Pompadour sees that she will be lost through her. . . . My brother is her councilor and directs her. Thus here is a credit raised higher than it had been struck down. This credit is that of the royal family."[82] The Comte d'Argenson conspired with d'Estrades to have the latter's niece, the Comtesse de Choiseul, replace Pompadour in the king's affections. However, the disgrace of the Comtesse d'Estrades in August 1755, at the behest of Pompadour, marked the failure of this plot and the beginning of the count's downfall. To the disgust of the d'Argenson brothers and many others at court and throughout the country, Pompadour's power over the king continued into the 1750s despite the fact that her sexual relations with the king had ended several years earlier and he had taken new mistresses. Thus Pompadour not only successfully converted credit acquired through the libidinal economy into political credit, she was able to maintain capital in the political realm despite her withdrawal from circulation in the sexual one.

As d'Argenson wrote, "the party of the Marquise de Pompadour has more influence than ever over the government, and the king appears subject to this corps of favorites (male and female), the ministers are bewildered and have no more credit. My brother maintains himself as he can, still openly broken with the marquise."[83] A few days later he continued this train of thought: "the Marquise de Pompadour has remained powerful in credit even though she no longer fulfills the functions of a mistress, having become the center of royal solace for affairs. She acts as a control over the ministers, and above all against my brother."[84] On February 1, 1757, the king dismissed the Comte d'Argenson from his post, along with Machault, secretary of state for the navy.

The Marquis d'Argenson drew a direct comparison between the powers of Madame de Pompadour and those of Louis XIV's last mistress and secret wife. Having been named a lady-in-waiting to the queen in February 1756, to the consternation of the court, she would, he predicted, "become superintendent of the queen's household and will be a Madame de Maintenon, and the example of Louis XIV will be followed. She will procure many favors for the queen, and we will see that princess very powerful and in high credit. The favorite will influence the ministry even more."[85] Like Saint-Pierre and Montesquieu before him, d'Argenson found this state of affairs unnatural and dangerous. For an individual in private life to trust and confide in a mistress caused little scandal and could even encourage a beneficial gentility of conduct, the marquis conceded, but for the head of the kingdom such dependence was an outrage to duty, decency, and public dignity. He blamed the state's financial ruin on Pompadour's greed and the extravagant favors she proffered to win the affection of the royal family. He also attributed, in earlier letters, the diplomatic bungling that led to the disastrous Seven Years' War on her support for abandoning France's traditional ally, Prussia, in favor of an ill-conceived alliance with Austria.

Like other observers, d'Argenson believed that Pompadour's links to the world of financial credit explained much of her power, particularly in the years following the cessation of intimacy with the king. Thus, he claimed in his journal that her credit with the king stemmed not from sexual favors or affection but instead from her close relationship with the Pâris family of financiers. As he noted in December 1748, "the strength of the Pâris brothers comes mainly from their hold over the purse strings. The king fears them as a result. He has money, him and his kingdom, based on what he believes, based on what he sees, depending on whether he pleases those messieurs. They say that that is what keeps him in the chains of the mistress, of whom he's tired. Today all financial credit lies with the Pâris [brothers]; the king has great consideration for finance. Indeed what would become of the machinery of state without the illusory machinery of this credit as it is today." Contemplating a way to rid the court of Pompadour's influence, he reflected that "the great thing would be to present the king with financial projects that would let him do without the Pâris [brothers]."[86] Some thirty years after the failure of Law's system, critics of the public credit system still dreamed of ridding themselves of the influence of private financiers. This anecdote aptly draws together the strands we have traced from the time of the regency: credit machinations at court, women's leveraging of sex into power, and the subjugation of royal financial credit to political credit networks.

A noteworthy element of public reaction to Pompadour was that even falsified documents attributed to her characterize her power through the language of credit. The scant surviving correspondence of Pompadour contains few open references to the question of her influence and thus little use of the term *credit*.[87] However, the spurious letters attributed to her, published by François Barbé de Marbois in the early 1770s, abound with discussion of her credit, as part of the broad thematics of cynicism, abuse of power, and decadence evoked throughout the letters. The collection included, for example, a fake letter dated from August 1760 in which Pompadour reproached the Duc de Richelieu, declaring: "I have a little credit; I have always used it to serve those whom I believed distinguished by it. Often, I admit, I have had the misfortune to be mistaken, and I took ambitious little men for men of merit. You are not the only one of this number; but you are the only one to have been basely ungrateful, and to have attributed to your personal merit the favors you owed to the goodness and weakness of others."[88]

A spurious letter dated from 1762 depicted her writing in a happier tone to the Comtesse du Barail: "You may be assured that the young Marquis will not be forgotten, unless I lose all my credit: yet is it not my duty to recommend people of merit and those I esteem?"[89] Another letter dated from the same year showered the philosophe Voltaire with praise for his part in publicizing the Calas affair, in which a Protestant in Toulouse had been tortured and executed for killing his son, ostensibly to prevent the latter's conversion to Catholicism. The text of the letter has Pompadour pledging to throw all of her weight behind the cause of vindicating Calas: "I will boldly use all my credit to avenge the cause of justice and oppressed virtue."[90] Pompadour supposedly refused to play a similar role in defending the Jesuit order. A letter on the subject to the archbishop of Paris included the following postscript: "I have received this minute a large package of letters. They are bishops who beg me to employ my credit in favor of the Society."[91] This was an undertaking Pompadour had already vehemently rejected in the body of the letter. These fake letters, written and published in the 1770s, reveal that contemporaries expected the private correspondence of a royal mistress to include open references to her influence and her tactics for deploying it. Placing the language of credit into the mouth of the king's favorite constituted one strategy for achieving verisimilitude in libels of the court.

As the French state experienced fresh waves of financial calamity in the 1770s and 1780s and denunciation of the regime began to mount in genres ranging from pornography to fake correspondence and legal briefs, credit—and in particular female credit—increased in potency as a sign of the capriciousness and tyranny of absolutist rule. The Baron d'Holbach, cited at the opening of the chapter, provides one striking example of these concerns. A second may be found in one reader's reaction to another spurious published correspondence, that of the Comtesse du Barry, the mistress who followed Pompadour in the king's favor. In a review of *Lettres originales de Madame la comtesse du Barry* published in *Correspondance littéraire* in 1779, Jacques-Henri Meister acknowledged that the letters were fakes. Nonetheless, he insisted, they were "all the more true for having been invented." One of the elements that he claimed lent the letters the most authenticity was their depiction of du Barry's corrupt wielding of favor: "One sees the greatest dignitaries, the most powerful figures of the kingdom debase themselves at her feet, beg for her credit, exhibit incomparably more greed than she does."[92] It was thus, once more, the evocation of a royal mistress's credit that helped cast the letters as a convincing and politically useful text.[93]

As Old Regime political and fiscal structures grew increasingly unstable, credit relationships attracted increased scrutiny. Just as writers and administrators asked new questions about the foundations of government, state institutions, the relationship between church and state, and other fundamental issues, they also reexamined credit, the complex, invisible force that animated the machinery of society and government. And, as was the case in other areas of inquiry, intensified concern about credit relationships did not result in a clean break from the past or a clear, new consensus about the nature of credit. Instead, as eighteenth-century people struggled to understand and control their changing world, they mixed the familiar and the innovative; their responses to the challenges they perceived were shaped both by lofty ideals and the practical realities of their lives.

This chapter has traced several strands of criticism of credit from the late seventeenth through the mid-eighteenth century. We began with two broad categories of attack under Louis XIV: first, satires of the hypocrisy of court mores and, second, protests at the heavy-handed imposition of orthodox Catholicism by members of minority religious groups. Although these two perspectives were distinct (we should recall that La Bruyère published a polemic against the Quietists),[94] they shared a presumption that nonmaterial forms of credit were acceptable only when backed by virtue and righteousness and that self-interest and worldly concerns indelibly tainted the exchange of credit.

With the death of Louis XIV criticism of credit acquired new political implications, as those arguing for a reform of monarchical rule came to identify political credit as a particular problem in need of attention. John Law's project to transform public credit was predicated on his (ultimately unsuccessful) bid to replace the power and influence of private financiers with a national bank backed by the power of public confidence. Another motif through which critics began to attack the mechanisms of political credit was that of the excessive influence wielded by women on public affairs through their possession of credit acquired through sexual relations with powerful men.

In 1751 Charles Duclos's moral treatise *Considérations sur les moeurs de ce siècle* proposed a regeneration of French public life, to be led by a new elite that would overcome excessive self-interest and revive the values of honor, virtue, and merit. In his lengthy chapter "Sur le crédit" Duclos completely elided the complex challenges of public credit and the role of women's credit in political affairs, the two aspects of credit that attracted the most attention in the decades prior to its publication. Given his personal history and worldly engage-ments—indeed given the evidence of his own correspondence and other pub-lications—it is clear that Duclos was well aware of both themes. His silence on these matters was perhaps a strategy to avoid offending his patrons: even if he agreed on women's credit as a problem, why risk losing the support of Madame de Pompadour by dwelling on the question? Arguing for a merit-based credit system also allowed Duclos to claim the possibility for men of letters, such as himself, to participate in exchanges hitherto dominated either by men of high noble birth or royal office holders. More broadly, it is also possible to read these lacunae as evidence for the cultural and intellectual shift—identified by Michel Foucault in *The Order of Things*—that began to separate the entangled strands of political, social, cultural, and financial credit that were the focus of chapter 1. Nonmaterial exchange of credit should henceforth take place in a pure realm of merit and virtue, while financial credit would operate in a discrete field sub-ject to analysis only by experts.

This suggestion is supported by the choice of the editors of the *Encyclo-pédie*, who devoted two separate articles to credit, one on financial credit by the economist Forbonnais and another on "moral credit," heavily influenced by Duclos, and attributed to the philosopher Diderot. This division surely reflects the emergence of political economy, a discipline that reified economic mat-ters as a discrete and distinct phenomenon to be treated by specialists. It also points to the analytical limitations of men of letters like Diderot and Duclos, who were unable to come to terms with the fact that the entanglements wed-ding these realms together remained very real and problematic.

The chapter closed with the case of Madame de Pompadour, who high-lights the complexities of continuity and change over the period covered in this chapter. Pompadour reveals women's ongoing exercise of credit at court in a manner very similar to those of earlier royal mistresses. However, it is telling that contemporary documents in which royal mistresses boasted of their credit were forged; indeed, readers may have accepted them as real precisely because they depicted her shamelessly flaunting her credit. By the second half of the eighteenth century, therefore, the audience for literature attacking the regime found it convincing to read about the self-conscious and cynical manipulation of political credit by powerful women at court. The spotlight Saint-Pierre and others had cast on women's credit remained brightly illuminated through the middle of the century and beyond.

The legacy of the first decades of the eighteenth century was thus to high-light credit as a political problem, to render women's credit as a symbol of the capriciousness of the regime as a whole, and to discredit the coexistence and constant conversions between different forms of credit (especially between libidinal and political economies). The next chapter takes this investigation of notions of credit and credibility—and the fears over illusion and artifice—in a new direction by examining overlapping conceptions of fashion and credit from the late seventeenth through the mid-eighteenth century. Chapter 7 will continue the story of continuity and change with the career of Marie-Antoinette and her spectacular credit history.

CHAPTER 3

INCREDIBLE STYLE

INTERTWINED CIRCUITS OF CREDIT, FASHION, AND SEX

*I*n 1744, several years before publishing *Considérations sur les moeurs de ce siècle*, Charles Duclos offered a lighter version of credit in the fairy tale *Acajou et Zirphile*. Duclos wrote the piece as a bet, in which he wagered that he could compose a narrative based on ten existing engravings by the painter François Boucher. The resulting tale, a parody of the popular genre, tells the story of Prince Acajou and Princess Zirphile (figure 3.1), whose true love is thwarted by their evil guardians. Bewitched by magic grapes, Acajou abandons Zirphile and descends into libertinage. His success as a libertine provides a lesson in the perverse relationship between seduction and social reputation: "After having had enough celebrated women to put himself in credit, he resolved to seduce some solely to have them lose the reputation for virtue that they held. If he learned that there was a woman tenderly beloved by a dear husband, she immediately became the object of his attentions and such were the irregularities that inspire the title of *homme à la mode* that he succeeded by everything that should have made him fail."[1]

Acajou's career as a libertine underlines the affinities between the man of credit and the homme à la mode, suggesting that the dynamics of reputation and influence that gave power to the former were identical to the ones that brought acclaim and attention to the latter. In the competition for reputation, one man's gain was another man's loss, as Acajou acquired credit by cuckolding his lovers' husbands. Sex, not merit or virtue, lay at the heart of this version of credit, and it was perversely his reputation for seduction that made Acajou so attractive to otherwise chaste wives. This fairy tale adds a new perspective to the role of sex in credit systems; rather than revolving around women who leveraged power through male sexual desire, here it is men who gain credit by seducing women. Acajou's experience is all the more striking for the fact that women make no appearance at all in the chapter of *Considérations* that Duclos devotes to credit. For Duclos, women, sex, and fashion were hidden motors of

FIGURE 3.1 *Acajou et Zirphile*. Charles Pinot Duclos's fairy tale was inspired by a series of paintings by François Boucher. This one, from the engravings published with the tale, shows the title characters menaced by evil fairies. *Source*: Bibliothèque nationale de France.

the credit system, acknowledged in light-hearted social satires but banished from weightier works of moral commentary.

This chapter seeks to unravel the multiple strands tied up in the story of Acajou and Zirphile, and in particular the dynamics of fashion in Old Regime France as they interwove with the credit relations examined in the previous chapters. The sources analyzed here—court manuals, plays, moral treatises, dictionaries, and libertine novels—begin to link discourses on credit reviewed thus far to the material worlds in which they were embedded and embodied, a task that the remaining chapters of the book will complete. As we have seen, individuals' capacity to acquire and maintain credit in its many guises relied not merely on rank or fortune but also on performances of credibility carried out in view of an audience. The performative nature of credit meant that material objects—like clothing, carriages, and furniture—and embodied interaction with such objects were crucial elements of credit accumulation and exchange.

A great deal of scholarship has focused on dress and appearances in Old Regime France, much of it exploring the relationship between absolutism and representations of power and, as a corollary, the role of fashion and ostentatious consumption at the royal court. Historians and literary scholars have also examined the multiple discourses treating fashion, from theological treatises that thundered against its vanity and worldliness to satirical plays that mocked social parvenus' ridiculous attempts to follow elite fashion. This literature has emphasized the role of fashion as a visual manifestation of social taxonomy in the Old Regime, arguing that competitive struggles over differentiation and emulation served as a major catalyst for the movements of fashion. Scholars have also underlined contemporaries' perception of fashion as something essentially French, arguing both that the fashion industry constituted a central element of the French economy and that a love of fashion and a talent for style and innovation constituted crucial components of the emerging French national identity. Another key finding—although not without controversy—is that fashion shifted from being a relatively gender-neutral topic in the seventeenth century to being primarily, and negatively, associated with women by the end of the eighteenth.[2]

This chapter does not attempt to retread the details of the copious literature on fashion, but rather to situate its findings with regard to the analysis of credit traced in previous chapters. The first section of the chapter interrogates the role of clothing and appearances in strategies of worldly credibility and the complex interaction of king, court, city, and commerce in the late seventeenth-century "fashion system," a phrase I use to refer to the dynamic of change in fashions, their cultural and social significance, the industries that produced and disseminated fashionable goods, and the consumers who purchased and displayed them. The section begins by examining advice proffered by mid-seventeenth-century court manuals on the use of fashionable dress to succeed at court, then analyzes efforts by Louis XIV and his government to take control of the production of appearances, and, finally, offers a critical reading of accounts of fashion provided by a variety of contemporary observers. These sources present a complex and ambiguous account of the dynamic of fashion in the late seventeenth century and the mechanisms of credibility it engendered.

Fashion meant much more in this period, however, than bows and ruffles. The second section of the chapter moves on to consider fashion as an all-encompassing dynamic that seemed to contemporaries to touch ever-increasing aspects of their lives. Just as credit flows spanned multiple spheres of life, so the rhythms of fashion pulsed through everything from clothing to furnishings, from words to religious beliefs and even to individuals themselves. In this section we take a step back from the focus on attire to examine parallels and discontinuities between the systems of fashion and credit as depicted in texts in multiple genres. This section highlights the similarity of fashion and credit as information economies constitutive of—rather than merely reflective of—social hierarchies. The dynamics driving fashion and credit resembled each other in their relationship to time, their capacity to encompass multiple goods and forms of behavior, and their role in processes of commodification. As the story of Acajou illustrates, fashion and credit could be envisioned as homologous and intersecting circuits of influence and reputation.

Finally, in the third section of the chapter, we examine the ultimate extension of fashion, suggested by the Duclos tale, which saw human beings themselves turned into objects of fashion. The phrase *homme à la mode* appeared regularly in late seventeenth-century literature, most often in reference to a court favorite. In this guise the man of fashion could be akin to the trustworthy man of credit. However, by the first decades of the eighteenth century, as Duclos's tale suggests, references to the homme à la mode more often described him as a ladies' man, elevated to the rank of fashion by his sexual relations with women. Instead of profiting from male desire to leverage power for themselves, their female victims unwittingly bestowed power on their seducers. The woman of fashion appeared less frequently in the literature, but references to *femmes à la mode* through the first half of the nineteenth century demonstrate that Old Regime debates over women's access to the power and influence generated by worldly acclaim left a long legacy in French culture.

Court, City, and Commerce: The Transforming Fashion
System of the Late Seventeenth Century

Printed commentary on fashion, its role in princely courts, and on the blurred lines between appearance and artifice was long-standing by the time Louis XIV assumed personal rule in 1661. Fashion was a controversial subject in seventeenth-century France, as it has indeed been since its birth (or rebirth) in the High Middle Ages. Numerous contemporary critics lamented the vanity of fashion, its fickleness and ephemeral nature, its celebration of worldly rather than spiritual values, and its special temptation for what was largely accepted to be the weak moral character of women.[3]

For courtiers, however, there could be little question of the need for appropriate aristocratic display. Manuals written to guide newcomers provide one perspective on the role of appearances and bodily discipline in the struggle for credibility. Nicolas Faret's *The Art to Please at Court*, published in 1632, instructed readers to choose a faithful friend who could provide trustworthy information on the ins and outs of court life, including "the parties and cabals that are in credit."[4] One of the most vital pieces of information this friend could provide regarded appropriate attire. According to Faret, fine dress was potentially more important for success at court than birth or merit, opening "doors often closed to those of high status, and even more to virtue."

For Faret, dressing the part entailed not only knowledge of the basic wardrobe worn at each court but also of the reigning fashions of the day. It was crucial, however, not to confuse fashion with mere novelty. The point of fashion was not simply to attract attention but to gain the approving notice of those in credit. As he stated:

> In everything, one must be curious about fashion; I don't mean that of a few fools among the young people at court, who to stand out sometimes hide half of their figure in large boots, sometimes plunge themselves from their underarms to their heels in their breeches, and sometimes drown the entire outline of their face in the brims of hats as wide as the parasols of Italy. But I mean that fashion, which being authorized by the most approved among the great and the honorable people, serves as a law to all the rest.[5]

Faret thus distinguished between the extravagant and singular fashions invented by young court dandies and those "authorized" by its most "approved" members. Discovering and obeying the rules laid down by this elite was key to success at court and thus to winning the credit so necessary for success. Despite his insistence on adherence to "received usage," however, Faret did leave open a significant potential for individual prowess. The difference between a bizarre ensemble and a "new style" lay in the wearer's capacity to persuade others to adopt it. Failure to gain followers would expose an individual to humiliation and ridicule, while success offered enhanced prestige and reputation and, implicitly, an increase in one's own credit at court.

Faret's text also invokes a central tension between the appropriate authority of noble title and the possibility of social ascension. His acknowledgment that appearances were more important than the rank conferred by birth or by inner virtue resonates with the book's stated goal of inculcating outsiders, including wealthy commoners, with the tools needed for a successful career at court. And yet at other points in the text Faret explicitly insists on the innate superiority conveyed by noble blood, declaring that "we must admit that those who are of good background usually have good inclinations, that others have them only rarely. . . . Certain seeds of good and evil run in the blood, which sprout over time in our souls and give birth to our good and bad qualities."[6] Moreover, he also instructs the reader that, while the opinion of the court is crucial for one's reputation, "the solid foundation of this opinion is indeed virtue and merit."[7] Thus, his manual leaves unresolved a central tension between the value of inherent qualities—often associated with blood—and the possibility for those outside the traditional aristocracy to carry off a convincing performance of the role of courtier. Credit operated within this gap between strict rank and individual prowess at displays of credibility.

Antoine de Courtin's treatise on civility of 1671 made Faret's case for the need for appropriate dress even more strongly. According to Courtin, civility was merely "the modesty and respectability that everyone should maintain in their speech and actions."[8] His basic rules included covering one's private parts, performing activities related to our animal nature (eating, coughing, spitting, and so on) in the least bestial manner possible, obeying social conventions such as standing or being seated, and giving precedence to others.[9]

These rules underlined the role of embodied behavior in performing social taxonomies within the space of the court and worldly sociability. Just as civilized humans should distinguish themselves from animals, so should they occupy or give up symbolic forms of space (including the space of their own bodies) to mark social distinctions. Common social conventions included: "to uncover one's head to show respect, to give way at a doorway, the upper end of a room or table, the right-hand side or the upper end of the pavement in a street."[10] As his first example reveals, not the body alone but the interaction between clothing and the body was crucial to the performance of social deference. Men were to remove their hats in the company of superiors and doff them in response to such a salutation from a male of any social class. In superior company men should not fidget or play with their hat or gloves or the tassels on their sword hilts. For women, the mask, the veil, and the dress all served to signify deference. They must remove the mask and veil in addressing superiors, unless riding in an open coach, and should not hitch their dresses up at the sides.[11]

With regard to clothing, Courtin insisted above all on the need for dress suited to the individual characteristics of each person, believing that "propriety composes a large part of decorum and serves as much as any other thing to convey the virtue and character of a person: because it is impossible, that seeing someone in ridiculous clothing, that one does not immediately conceive that the person is ridiculous him- or herself."[12] As in all things, astute judgment of what was appropriate attire, with regard to age, social status, and body shape, was paramount. One might imagine that the rigidity of social codes upon which Courtin insisted would lead him to reject fashion but instead he declared: "the law that one must observe to be appropriately dressed, is fashion[;] it is beneath this absolute mistress that reason must bend, without reasoning further, if we do not wish to depart from civil life."[13] Conceived as the antithesis of reason, the law of fashion nonetheless constituted the dividing line between civility and its opposite. To reject fashion—depicted as an imperious female ruler—was to place oneself beyond the boundaries of polite society.

Courtin did not define his use of "reason" in this text but a diatribe against Dominique Bouhours's *Remarques nouvelles sur la langue françoise* published in 1677 provides insight into his conception of the term: "The authors of observations on language equivocate over what is to be understood by reason. It means in fact conformity with an established principle, and where no such principle has been established, it is pointless to speak of reason. Usage may simply not be in conformity with reason, and as for authority, it is often at variance with itself."[14] Thus, when Courtin contrasted reason with fashion, he did not refer to the universal rationality of eighteenth-century philosophes but to the difference between established codes of dress and new innovations. Indeed, he signified, constant changes of fashion—akin to "usage" in the passage above—made it impossible to cling to any one standard of attire. As in language, no single authority could pass judgment on the conflicts between reason and usage.

Like Faret, Courtin believed it was as ridiculous to reject fashion as it was to take it to extravagant extremes. The person who would ignore the reigning styles altogether invited public humiliation: "by appearing, for example, before the world with a pointed hat now that they are worn low in form, he would put himself at risk of being pursued and pointed out." There were also those who courted ridicule by going to the other extreme and wildly exaggerating existing fashions: "if pants are made wide at the bottom, they make them two aunes wide; if the bottom of the dress of a lady should trail by half an aune, they make it one-and-a-half."[15]

The way to avoid these two extremes was to rely on current usage at court for guidance. For Courtin, as for Faret several decades earlier, the social prestige of the most admired courtiers equated with the cultural capacity to set the fashion. Like Faret, Courtin advised his readers to seek out a special friend at court to serve as model and mentor:

> That is why those who do not go to court should find someone who has commerce there and make of that person a model, selecting him more or less from his own condition, his age, and his size, and not only must the one who will serve as guide be accustomed to the court, but also, to arrive at my principle, he must possess character and virtue: because those who have judgment and wisdom reduce as much as possible the luxury and frivolity of fashions, and reduce them to some utility, to some convenience, and above all to the modesty that should be the rule of all of the conduct of a Christian, as we have taken for the foundation of this treaty, and a type of paradox is then enacted, in that fashion, which is capricious, bizarre, and often scandalous, becomes reasonable and modest.[16]

Success and skill in manipulating fashion, for Courtin, lay in figuring out how to adapt reigning styles to one's age, circumstance, and body type. Those destined for the church should aim for modest versions of the current style; the elderly should also adopt reserved versions, and short people should wear reduced versions. The skilled practitioner of fashion thereby performed a miraculous sleight of hand, transforming caprice and scandal into reason and modesty.

Civility manuals thus underlined the strain between fashion as an established code and as a swift and capricious current, arguing for the need to hew to the former to avoid being swept away by the latter. They welcomed the possibility for outsiders to assimilate into court society but only at the price of accepting its existing social and cultural codes. Their texts thus simultaneously acknowledge the capacity of fashion to generate social credibility and contain its powers by insisting that authoritative fashion can only issue from those of high rank. This position proved influential, despite the persistence of religious and moralizing attacks on fashion. It was even prescribed in the new

Christian and universal version of civility promoted by Jean-Baptiste de la Salle at the beginning of the eighteenth century. De la Salle's *Rules for Christian Propriety and Civility*, written as a conduct manual in 1703 for poor children attending schools of the Christian Brothers, strongly echoed Faret's and Courtin's precepts regarding appropriate appearances. De la Salle thus decried excessive expense on clothing and advised students to reject "capricious and bizarre" fashions. Yet he also insisted that they respect existing conventions. Not only should students' dress be clean and modest, but it should also avoid "singularity" by following established fashion. Rather than exhibiting the folly of those who seek to invent fashions, the students should follow "reasonable" fashions, and he reassured them that such fashions did indeed exist.[17]

For de la Salle, the empire of fashion stretched from the king's court to poor children attending charity schools, as he transformed an aristocratic means of distinction into a universal Christian model of conduct. Based on its numerous editions and use as a pedagogical guide in schools across France, Roger Chartier has argued that "these rules were perhaps one of the most efficacious agents for the implantation of elite models of comportment among the lower echelons of society."[18] Thus, de la Salle created a crucial normative framework through which the notion of fashion was legitimized and disseminated, within "reasonable" limits, for a plebeian audience.

LOUIS XIV: KING OF FASHION OR MERCANTILIST ECONOMIST?

Already under Louis XIII, one commentator remarked that "the King makes fashion on each occasion that he deigns to,"[19] and at Versailles his successor, Louis XIV, set out to bring apparel within the rigid new etiquette system he imposed on his court. As de la Salle's text indicates, the notion of fashion far outstripped the king's court, and yet Louis XIV's emphasis on ostentatious appearances at court and, even more importantly, the economic policies adopted by his controller general, Jean-Baptiste Colbert, had profound effects on the evolution of fashion and its dissemination to wider segments of society.

Many scholars have commented on the central role that the king and queen's dressing and undressing ceremonies occupied in court etiquette as moments when the royal body was celebrated by courtiers and they could jockey for a few moments of intimate engagement with their sovereign.[20] In addition to orchestrating rituals of dress surrounding his own body, Louis personally enunciated and enforced a series of rules about the styles of male and female dress to be worn at his court. The king manipulated details within the required garments to confer additional elements of distinction. For example, he dictated that the lengths of women's trains be determined by rank of nobility. For men, he issued licenses to a small number of courtiers to wear a special jacket, the *juste-au-corps de brevet*, which was blue with red trim and golden embroidery. Louis kept careful watch over the appearance of those at court and he severely rebuked those who failed to observe his regulations.

In addition to mandating the form and details of garments to be worn at court, he imitated his predecessors by issuing acts of sumptuary legislation. An edict of November 1660, *Déclaration contre le luxe des habits, carrosses et ornemens*, reiterated a long series of earlier prohibitions against the use, by nobles and commoners alike, of gold or silver thread in cloth for clothing, home furnishings, and carriages.[21] The declaration further ordered nobles to dress their servants in woolen cloth rather than silk and forbade the use of imported lace. This order forms a striking juxtaposition not only with the rights of the patent holders for the juste-au-corps de brevet, but also with Louis's own dress on August 26, 1660, at his formal entry to Paris with his new queen, Maria-Theresa. According to one of his mother's ladies-in-waiting, "his coat was embroidered with gold and silver, as fine as it should be, given the dignity of the person wearing it."[22] For Louis, the splendor of gold and silver apparently befitted the French sovereign and his family, not all of his nobles or any of the lower social orders.

Rules establishing dress at court provided a focus of emulation to those outside the small circle of courtiers and therefore affected the many thousands employed in the luxury trades in Paris and elsewhere. The mercantilist policies of Jean-Baptiste Colbert had a more direct and even more widespread impact. To reduce foreign imports, Colbert strove to establish new manufactures for products hitherto not produced in France and to improve quality standards in existing industries. In addition to his well-known support of the Lyons silk manufacture, Colbert took personal action to establish a high quality lace trade in France, with the help of mistresses imported from Venice and the Netherlands.[23] In the 1670s he issued a series of royal edicts outlining detailed rules for the production of cloth, dying techniques, and other manufacturing processes. He also promulgated a new Code de commerce or Commercial Code to regulate trade and ordered all artisans to form guilds in cities and towns where guilds existed. A direct result of the last measure was the incorporation of all female seamstresses' guilds in Paris and Rouen in 1675, which served as finishing outlets for the increased volume of textiles produced.[24]

As Colbert's activities suggest, the royal government's attitude toward fashion was mixed. Policies to increase French production at the expense of foreign industries had the dual aim of stimulating exports to other countries and expanding domestic consumption. Increasing employment — in the garment industry and elsewhere — would facilitate these goals not only by adding to the number of hands to make goods but by providing wages for working people to purchase more products for themselves. Nonetheless, mercantilist administrators from Colbert downward believed that the state must play a central role in deciding which products should be manufactured and how they were produced and distributed. Fashion should flourish and descend the social scale but only under government control and regulation.

It proved, however, impossible to control a phenomenon defined by innovation, especially given the weak powers of the royal government to police and punish offenders. The government's most controversial ruling over fashion, which occurred after Colbert's death in 1683, aptly illustrates this point. Cotton calicoes imported from India and the Middle East (called *toiles peintes* or *indiennes*) captured a growing market in the second half of the seventeenth century to the detriment of French silk and woolen cloth producers. In October 1686 a decree of the royal council forbade both the import of these calicoes and the practice that had arisen of using wood block printing to produce calicoes with domestic linen, hemp cloth, or imported cottons. (Such industries had sprung up in southern France and Normandy in the 1660s).

Instead of suppressing the market for these goods, the edict only succeeded in creating a lively smuggling trade. In response the government reiterated the laws multiple times, increasing the fines on manufacturers and smugglers. It also extended the ban on printing cloth to silk and other fabrics with the justification that the low quality of printing techniques would harm the reputation of French textiles. These bans continued until 1759, inspiring impassioned debate on the effects of government economic regulations. Throughout the period of prohibition, many men and women at court and elsewhere openly defied the ban and escaped the prescribed penalties.[25]

The king and his government thus exercised tremendous symbolic and regulatory power over the fashion industries but within severe practical limits. Under Louis XIV, the king's dictates did a great deal to shape what the court and its emulators wore. The protectionist economic policies of Colbert and his successors increased the production of domestic luxury products along with the outlets to furnish clothing to wider markets, making fashion more accessible to his subjects. However, both the king's personal rulings and those of the government failed to eliminate demand for desired products, nor could the king monopolize the constant cycles of fashion.

Contemporaries were well aware of this state of affairs. In 1690 Antoine Furetière's dictionary revealed perceptions of the ambivalent state of authority in
French fashion. Furetière defined "*mode*" as "custom, manner of living, of
doing things; fashion is also used for everything that changes according to
time and place." He added that it "is said more particularly of styles of dressing
oneself following the received usage of the court. The French change fashions
everyday. Foreigners follow the fashions of the French, except for the Spanish,
who never change fashions. The most extravagant are those who invent fashions. Merchants profit from changes in fashion."[26] For Furetière, as for many
observers, fashion was quintessentially French and a source of national pride.
He was less clear, though, about the source of fashion. On the one hand, he
insisted that the court was the supreme arbiter of style; on the other hand, he
could not help but notice the rapidity with which fashions changed under the
influence of anonymous innovators at court and a burgeoning mercantile sector, both beyond the monarch's direct control.[27]

Two decades earlier Jean Donneau de Visé had expressed similar uncertainties. Donneau was an established writer and salon participant with connections
to the court nobility. In January 1672 he published the first edition of the new
journal *Le Mercure galant*, one of only three periodicals approved and funded
by the royal government, the others being the *Gazette royale*, which printed
diplomatic and political news, and the *Journal des savants*, dedicated to reports on scientific findings. Between 1672 and 1724, with a brief interruption
from 1674 to 1677, *Le Mercure galant* published literary reviews, poems, stories,
obituaries, marriage announcements, and news on military affairs, noteworthy
trials, and cultural happenings. It was also the first French journal to include
regular reports on men's and women's fashions. In January 1678 Donneau
began issuing a quarterly supplement titled *L'Extraordinaire du Mercure galant*
with even more attention to fashion accompanied by illustrations drawn by
Jean Bérain and engraved by Jean le Pautre (figure 3.2).[28]

Under Donneau's editorship, the journal encapsulated the intersection of
three distinct forces shaping fashion, royal policy, the prestige of the court,
and the vitality of commerce. Donneau and his collaborators—fellow writers
and well-connected *mondains* like Bernard Bovier de Fontenelle and Charles
Perrault—aimed to amuse male and female readers who shared their cultural
horizons, to reflect back to them both in genre and content the worldly sociability they shared, and to provide critical responses to the latest events. They

FIGURE 3.2 Detail from *Le Mercure galant*. This engraving from *Le Mercure galant* emphasizes the minute details of fashion described in the journal. *Source*: Bibliothèque nationale de France.

also attempted to provide those outside the capital with the vicarious pleasures of participating in *le monde*. These goals combined at all times with the necessity of maintaining approval from the king and his government.

With *Le Mercure galant*, information about fashion entered the domain of quasi-commercial dissemination. The journal took the form of a series of letters—supposedly written to a lady in the provinces avid for news of Paris and the court—dated on a weekly basis. In an early letter dated July 22–29, 1672, Donneau provided an extremely lengthy account of the latest styles as well as a series of reflections on the system of fashion itself. Because this extended discussion raises a series of key issues about the origins and transmission of fashion and its differentiation by social group, it is worth exploring in some detail. Donneau couched his reporting in this text not merely at one but at two removes, presenting it as a letter to his provincial correspondent recounting a long dialogue that had taken place between the narrator and two ladies. After informing his reader about the latest military news he had heard at a salon (*assemblée*), the narrator notes, "I was obliged to leave the assembly to go speak to two women of my acquaintance who were walking and gestured to me to approach them." This frame within a frame placed Donneau and his reporting within three major modes of worldly sociability: letter writing, leisurely strolls in public spaces, and the salon. It also established the witty and semi-satirical attitude toward fashion that he maintained throughout his editorship: "After having gossiped for a while and uttered some slander against everyone they knew who was strolling along, the conservation turned to fashion."[29]

The first comment the ladies make about fashion is to lament their uncertainty about what to wear given the rapid evolution of styles, which they attribute to the efforts of courtiers to distinguish themselves from those lower down the social scale: "one must admit, they said, that one hardly knows how to dress, fashions die before they are born and all people of quality have hardly begun to follow a fashion when the monkeys of the court make them abort, because the great lords leave [the fashions] as quickly to take new ones; and that is why the bourgeois who think they are in fashion never are."[30] This opening sally depicts fashion as the result of a swift and confusing exchange of information among at least three groups of people: the great lords and their imitators at court who determine fashion, the "people of quality" who observe and try to follow them, and the bourgeoisie whose access to information is slower and less reliable. This classification functions as much as a form of judgment and an effort to fix a normative taxonomy as it does as a form of social analysis: the ladies distance themselves equally from the "monkeys" at court and from the gauche social climbers of the bourgeoisie, situating themselves and the readers of the journal as the beleaguered gens de qualité.

The women's dialogue then turns to a particular garment, mantuas (*manteaux*), made from hand-painted or printed cloth. The mantua was a new dress style in the early 1670s, consisting of a loose kimono-shaped garment that tied at the waist. As *Le Mercure galant* tells us, even noblewomen adopted the mantua, wearing it instead of the official court dress, except for appearances at the royal court where Louis's dress code remained in force. The ladies remark on the profusion of mantuas in the streets of Paris made from fabric with Chinese patterns. The style was originally made with very expensive hand-painted imported fabrics, they explain, but the mantua had now become very widespread due to the availability of low-cost printed fabrics. The popularity of the dress style has inspired one of the ladies, Lucresse, to launch a similar innovation in home furnishings: "I have had some beautiful screens painted in the same style . . . and because I think that no one has had the same foresight, I hope to bring it into fashion." To this ambition, her friend Clarice responds dismissively: "Your screens are but a trifle. . . . I was yesterday at the home of one of my friends who has had an alcove tapestry painted with figures of my height. There is nothing more beautiful." Undaunted, Lucresse retorts in turn: "I saw something [even] more curious and more original," silk stockings imported from China painted with decorative figures.[31]

Having reclaimed the competitive advantage, Lucresse goes on to inform her two listeners of the latest styles in jewelry and mantuas and then assures them that she has noticed many other new fashions and that "if you wish to give me an audience, I will speak to you of more than fifty, without mentioning those we have already discussed." With her friends' assent, Lucresse launches into a highly detailed catalog of fashions for a cornucopia of distinct articles. Returning to the subject of the mantua dress, Lucresse also provides her listeners with further insight into their diffusion across social hierarchies. As she says, "one hardly sees a person of high rank who does not have one of these kinds of mantua or a mantua from China that is painted and not printed. Still, they have recently started printing ones that are almost as beautiful as the painted ones; but the first ones they printed were only for grisettes [poor working women, originally so-called for the low quality gray cloth they wore] and on taffetas, while now there are satin ones that are so beautiful, it is hard to tell if they are printed or painted."[32]

Lucresse pauses in her catalog to declare: "I would never finish, if I wished to speak to you of a million fashions involving only trifles, and to speak to you of many others that die almost as they are born."[33] She picks up her thread again to describe, over five pages of text, the latest styles in furniture. When she finally stops to take a breath, her friend Clarice interrupts to point out all that was missing from the list and in turn contributes her own detailed account of new styles omitted by her friend. The two women finally turn to the narrator to ask him to fill them in on the latest in men's fashions. His response indicates that it is not only women's fashions that he regards with a satirical eye. He tells his listeners that "men acknowledge fashion's empire even more than the most inconstant and ridiculous flirts of Paris."[34] To prove his point, he regales them with the minutiae of styles in men's jacket sleeves and the four distinct forms they have taken over the past year alone. These changes, he emphasizes, actually detracted from the intrinsic beauty and quality of the materials used, but they were imposed by what he describes as an innate French impulse to change fashions.

This prolonged discussion of fashion ends with Lucresse and Clarice agreeing on an explicitly "trickle-down" model of fashion, in which new styles passed from the pinnacle of the court to a series of social groups in a downward cycle of emulation and adaptation. The commentary issues as a collective consensus from these well-informed observers:

> And it was then said that fashions pass from the court to the ladies of the city, from ladies of the city to rich bourgeois women, from rich bourgeois women to grisettes, who imitated them with lesser cloth and that where ladies of the court and the city put precious stones, the bourgeois women put rhinestones and the grisettes put gold-plated buttons, and that when the grisettes could not wear fine ones they used fake ones in the same places. It was added that fashions passed from these grisettes to ladies of the provinces, from ladies of the provinces to bourgeois women of the same places; and that from there they passed to foreign countries; in such a way that when they started their runs there, those which had been invented at court in the meantime had already begun to grow old.[35]

Having summarized the overall dynamics of fashion, the conversation ends and the narrator leaves the women. He chastises himself momentarily for the frivolity of the conversation, but admits "my shame soon ceased, when I had told myself that most people of high rank [gens de qualité] and even those who had demonstrated qualities of mind, often discussed new fashions and that this subject entered as naturally into conversation as cold and heat, rain and good weather."[36]

I have cited this discussion of fashion—which covers more than thirty pages of the journal—at length as much for what it reveals about modes of discussing and transmitting information about fashion as for what we may glean about contemporary fashions themselves. The first point to make regards the journal's publication date, 1673. The fact that the volume was not published for at least six months after the ostensible date of the letter clearly indicates that "news" of the latest fashions delivered in the letter was not Donneau's priority. Instead, as his witty and ironic conversational style suggests, Donneau intended his reporting to amuse as much as to instruct. Remarking that gens de qualité discuss fashion as frequently as the weather, Donneau insists that fashion was a constant subject of conversation in le monde and that oral exchanges such as the one involving the narrator, Clarice, and Lucresse served as a key means by which information about fashion circulated. Such conversations— alongside visual observations in the salons, pleasure gardens, boutiques, and other urban sites that appear frequently in the journal—were so important for the exchange of information that the journal itself presented its news through the mise-en-scène of worldly encounters.

Even as satire, the long lists of fashions in this volume and elsewhere reveal much about worldly struggles for distinction. In addition to major changes in the types of garments worn and their cut, Donneau noted hundreds of micro-details in materials, trimmings, and accessories: the shape and material of buttons, the color and placement of ribbons, styles of lace, the number of frills on a cuff, the color and fabric of a garment's interior lining. The sheer number of details that were intelligible and coherent to observers underlines the challenges confronting those who wished to remain in fashion and the extremely close scrutiny given to appearances in the struggle for distinction. According to Donneau's narrative, ladies strolling through the streets of Paris strove to discern the quality and cost of the materials worn by the individuals they encountered in order to match garment to social rank. In the example of the printed mantuas the combination of an expensive cloth, satin, with a relatively inexpensive technique, printing, testifies to the subtle gradations of products sold by innovative manufacturers and the challenges facing those who wished to fix rank onto specific garments.

Moreover, both men and women shouldered this burden. The plethora of information on male fashion, as well as the narrator's semi-ironic but extremely well informed role in the conversation with Lucresse and Clarisse, suggest that both men and women in le monde followed fashion as a matter of course. It was as much a part of worldly sociability for men to appear in stylish attire and to keep track of passing fads in buttons and ribbons as it was to attend the latest play or spout witty verse at an elegant dinner. As Donneau remarked in a later volume of the journal: "one must be in fashion unless one wants to pass either for ridiculous or stingy."[37] This was as true for the man of letters aspiring to worldly acceptance as for the courtier at Versailles.

Still, despite displaying his own knowledge and interest, the narrator presents fashion as a particularly female zone of competition. Men needed to know enough to make a decent showing, while women struggled to outmaneuver each other in both knowledge and innovation. He presumably intended readers—including the journal's large female readership—to be both amused by Lucresse and Clarice's competition over their encyclopedic mastery of the latest styles and the creation of new ones and to find such competition plausible. Donneau clearly believed that readers, whom his text situates as "ladies of the city" and their mixed-sex equivalent the gens de qualité, would not only be eager to read so many details of fashion but would recognize satirical versions of themselves in the talkative, self-promoting, and back-biting ladies who exchanged expressions of gallantry with the opposite sex.

This extended report on fashion is particularly fascinating in the story it tells about the way fashion both united and divided socioeconomic groups. While Lucresse and Clarisse agree that styles come from the court and that the motor of fashion lay in the highest nobles' determination to distinguish themselves from the lower born, their account also emphasizes the role of commerce in facilitating this cycle; it is cloth manufacturers, artisans, and shopkeepers who provide cheaper counterparts to noble styles at a level affordable to each niche in society. The text also reveals, moreover, Donneau's perception that fashion could work against the grain of social hierarchy. As Lucresse explains, the use of printed fabrics for skirts originated as a populuxe version of hand-painted cloth for working women (grisettes), which proved so comfortable and affordable it spread through the capital.[38] Indeed, given the role of eyewitnessing in transmitting information about fashion, Lucresse and Clarice ranked Parisian grisettes higher in their taxonomy of style than wealthier women outside the city. Fashion was an urban, particularly Parisian, form of cultural credit in which the grisette could be "richer" than a provincial noblewoman (see figure 3.3).

If we turn to subsequent issues of *Le Mercure galant*, we find a similarly rich mix of authority and ambiguity. Donneau's reporting often reinforced the court-centered vision of fashion provided by Lucresse and Clarice. He frequently informed readers of the garments and accessories worn by the royal family in order to enthrall them with evocations of princely luxury and to allow them to emulate the items they could afford to purchase for themselves. For example, the journal publicized minute details of a fur muff presented to the dauphine, the king's hunting boots, his dislike of shoulder tassels, and his decision to wear ribbons in order to encourage their consumption and provide much-needed employment for poor ribbon makers.[39] Donneau also reminded readers about the relationship between fashion and royal authority. He referred on several occasions to the prohibition on gold and silver cloth, lauding the just severity of Nicolas de la Reynie, the new *lieutenant de police*, while also noting the fashionable rage for such items among individuals who continued to flout the ban in places where they did not risk official notice.[40]

However much authority he accorded to the royal family in setting fashion, Donneau just as emphatically underlined the reciprocal relationship between the court and the capital. For those seeking to emulate courtly styles, he provided the names and addresses of Parisian artisans who furnished the royal family and could provide reliable versions of court styles. At times, Donneau explicitly credited such individuals with the creation of new styles.

Despite his deference to the court and its purveyors, his presentation of fashion was also strikingly open to individual needs and preferences. He de-

FIGURE 3.3 Elegant ladies' promenade. Two ladies, akin to Lucresse and Clarisse, stroll in the Tuileries Gardens in this late seventeenth-century engraving. *Source*: Bibliothèque nationale de France.

limited specific fashions according to the social status, wealth, age, spatial location, and body type of its wearers. For example, he explained that ribbons were always in vogue among the young "because they adorn at little cost."[41] The length of the male suit jacket was shorter at court than in the city of Paris.[42] In some cases he ascribed differences in fashions simply to individual "fantasy," an apparently socially neutral form of taste. Indeed, according to Donneau's fictional interlocutors, French fashion of the last quarter of the seventeenth century saw a growing acceptance of such personal choice: "We have never seen in France what we see today; there are no more general fashions, because there are too many particular ones; one hardly sees two people clothed in the same manner; everyone dresses according to his [or her] fantasy, and one no longer appears extravagant, as in the past, when one is not turned out like the others."[43] For Donneau, therefore, usage increasingly trumped authority.

A final element to explore in Le Mercure galant's reporting is the sense it conveys of the rhythm of the fashion year. Donneau's decision to issue quarterly supplements in 1678 reflected the importance of seasonal changes in attire. This cycle was determined not only by the weather but also by the movements of the royal court and the sales schedule of the merchants who served it. The royal court sojourned at Fontainebleau from September to November each year for the hunting season. Many courtiers therefore placed orders for warmer winter clothes upon their return after the feast day of Saint-Martin (celebrated on the second Sunday in November). Merchant manufacturers timed the release of new fabrics accordingly. One of the most frequently mentioned merchants in Le Mercure galant, for example, is Monsieur Gaultier.[44] In October 1678 Donneau announced that Monsieur Gaultier was promising a brand-new color that would be among the "fleet of very rich cloth" he was expecting to receive on Saint-Martin's feast day. The other great moment of seasonal transition was in springtime, with many new orders clustering around the Easter holiday.

Despite the best laid plans of court and city, Donneau's observations quickly taught him that the months of the calendar were an unreliable guide to what people actually wore. One problem stemmed from the capriciousness of the weather. As he complained in the Extraordinaire du mercure quartier de janvier 1678, "I return to fashion, not yet those of the present season, but to winter outfits, which the rigors of the weather have caused many women to retain until now."[45] Unexpected events could also affect the fashion cycle. The most important human factor was mourning for members of royal and princely families at home or abroad, which could enforce black attire on the court and prominent commoners for months at a time. In April 1672 Donneau complained that mourning wear, in honor of the Duchesse d'Orleans who died in March of that year, had "suffocated" many fashions that "never saw the light of day and most remained in the imagination of those who invented them."[46] War apparently wreaked less havoc on consuming patterns among the elite: Donneau mentioned the effects of Louis's foreign wars on new styles only once, with regard to the declaration of war against England in 1689.

Donneau's efforts to impose regular periods on his fashion reporting also suffered from the rapid pace of renewal. His reporting revealed that while some fashions lasted for several seasons, others changed within a single season. With reference to an engraving of the woman's grand habit, he urged readers to note the sleeves, which are the first that "have appeared in the manner in which you see them." While the image accurately conveyed the novelty of the form, he explained, the decorations were wrong: "Do not be surprised to see a row of ribbons on them. They were still worn that way at the beginning of the current season. That fashion did not continue, and few people wear them presently."[47] In October 1682 Donneau commented that in the time it took to have an outfit made in imitation of another one, it was uncertain that the style would remain in vogue.[48] Given this unpredictability, his role was as much to reassure readers that a length of skirt or a type of cloth was still in style as to introduce the newest modes.

Reading Donneau alongside Faret and Courtin, it is clear that all three perceived the origins of fashion as multiple and ambiguous. One source of authority was the monarch, who personally set down rules of dress, issued patents for waistcoats, and dictated the length of the dresses of court ladies who appeared before him. Another set of guidelines consisted of the commonly accepted rules of etiquette and cultural notions of appropriateness, what Courtin might have called "reason": the old should be more circumspect, the young could indulge in greater experimentation, and so forth. Within these rules and expectations, however, there was room for "usage," that is, innovation and self-expression. The most important source of innovation was individuals who sought to draw attention to themselves, with the risks of humiliation commensurate with the potential gains in prestige. As Donneau's journal suggests, these three dynamics of fashion were increasingly bound up with the merchants, manufacturers, and artisans that supplied the court and the city and who were a crucial source of innovation in their own right. Another source of innovation came from grisettes and other members of the Parisian populace, whose styles might work their way up the social ladder. While the official version of court society posited credit as a direct outcome of social rank, the sources of fashion underline multiple possibilities for demonstrating credibility, and thus capturing unwarranted prestige, through individual prowess and innovation.

THE CREDIBILITY OF FASHION

Not everyone approved of the social openings created by fashion; indeed, it posed a series of ethical dilemmas much commented on by seventeenth-century theologians and moralists, especially those critical of the court and its mores. As with credit, one strain of criticism was religious, although in the case of fashion it was not only the marginalized but also the mainstream of the Gallican church that condemned fashion as sinful vanity and pride.[49] Echoing the assault on artifice and hypocrisy discussed in the previous chapter, secular critics also disparaged the ways in which fashion could be used to masquerade a social position and honor that one did not actually possess. Fashion was, as writers on fashion commonly acknowledged, flighty, whimsical, capricious, and ephemeral. To make things worse, everyone knew that fashionable clothing was most often purchased on shop credit, which often turned out to have no solid substance behind it at all.[50]

As we might expect from his attitude toward credit, Jean de La Bruyère saw fashion as a force that corroded virtue. While sensible people acknowledged the superficiality of worldly display, they too often gave in to its demands. "One says 'one must have modest clothes.' People of merit desire nothing further, but le monde wants finery[;] one provides it; it is avid for superfluity; one displays it. Some only esteem others for beautiful linen or a rich cloth; one does not always refuse to be esteemed at this price. There are places where one must make one's value felt: a wider or narrower gold braid allows you entrance or refuses you."[51] Whereas Faret and Courtin matter-of-factly acknowledged the role of appearances in forging credibility, La Bruyère denounced them as fraud.

In his chapter on "Judgments" in *Les caractères ou les mœurs de ce siècle*, La Bruyère attempted to neutralize the destabilizing effects of fashion by denying its very efficacy. He argued that a woman was more beautiful, and more dangerously appealing, without the embellishments of fashionable clothing. For men, the concern was not aesthetics or sexual seduction but probity and merit. La Bruyère argued that fashionable clothing added nothing to a real man of worth (*homme de bien*): "Similarly, a man of worth is respectable in himself, and independently of all the externals which he would use to render his personage more grave and his virtue more specious: a pious air, an excessive modesty, singularity in dress, a large hat adds nothing to probity, reveals no merit, they paint it in make-up, and perhaps render it less pure and less ingenuous."[52] As we saw in chapter 2, La Bruyère perceived a deepening rift in French elite society between inner merit and outward display; outside appearances and be-havior should have no bearing on inner worth and served only to sully it. The double meaning of "*bien*," connoting both moral and financial worth, recalls the similar duality contained in his use of the word *credit*.

Although the text was not published until 1747, one of the harshest criti-cisms of women's role at court under Louis xiv occurred in François de Sali-gnac de la Mothe-Fénélon's *Examen de conscience sur les devoirs de la royauté*, ostensibly written for the edification of the Duc de Bourgogne, to whom he was tutor. He wrote the text in 1687, before the turn to Quietism that lead to his exile from court. Couched as a series of directions for the examination of a prince before confession, it contained stinging criticism of moral standards at court. Direction xi began with the following question: "Have you not authorized an immodest liberty among women?"[53] Fénélon asserted that the only appropriate role for women at court was to serve the queen and royal princesses. The prince should ban other women from court life and choose ladies-in-waiting for their morality and decent conduct. He should exclude the young and beautiful from service to reduce temptation for himself and his male courtiers.

Direction xii reinforced this point by requiring the sovereign to "punish luxury and halt the ruinous inconstancy of fashions."[54] According to Fénélon it was love of fashion and luxury that corrupted court women and led them to ruinous expenses. This resulted not only in private vice but danger for the nation, for the natural goal of their unbridled avarice and passion was to please the king and attract his attention. In turn Louis's own taste for magnificence, Fénélon charged, had encouraged the parade of new fashions and ostentatious expenditure. In a dizzying cycle of emulation, great nobles imitated the royal family, were in turn imitated by lesser nobles, then by financiers, and finally by the bourgeoisie, who "wish to walk in the footsteps of the financiers, whom they have seen emerge from the mud."[55] Thus the taste for luxury passed from the court to the people. Where de la Salle saw the civilizing process at work and Donneau remarked on a natural cycle of emulative flight and chase, Fénélon perceived only infectious corruption and decadence. Perched at the summit of this great chain of consumption, the king was the source of the cascade of luxury coursing through his kingdom, and only he could put an end to it. This tract was republished in 1747 and again in several editions through the second half of the eighteenth century, exposing generations of readers to its attack on women's power and influence at court and the corrupting role of fashion in French society.

The gap between appearances and substance and the use of the former to ape the latter could be a source of humor as well as indignation. Molière's *Le*

Bourgeois gentilhomme, published in 1670, satirically explored the dilemmas of social forgery, fashionable appearances, and hollow credit. Commissioned by Louis XIV, the play was originally performed at the royal theaters of Chambord and Saint-Germain and then in Paris at the Palais-Royal, where it met with great success. Monsieur Jourdain, the social-climbing bourgeois merchant of the title, takes Faret's lessons to heart, recognizing fashion as one of the essential accouterments of an aspiring noble. His money cannot, Louis XIV would have been reassured to see, buy Jourdain the grace that he seeks, and his extravagantly fashionable clothing merely exposes him to ridicule. By contrast, his noble "friend" Dorante trades his social credit (access to the king, friendship with a marquise) for the hard cash necessary to pay his debts and maintain noble appearances. These include—according to the precise memorandum kept by Jourdain, successful merchant that he is, despite himself—1,832 livres to Dorante's feather merchant, 2,780 livres to his tailor, and 4,379 livres, 12 sous, and 8 deniers to a merchant.[56] For Molière, the nobleman is born and bred for fashion, but his extravagant lifestyle leaves him without the means to pay for it. The commoner longs for the cultural credit that fashion would bring him but lacks the necessary training and innate grace to pull it off. He also longs for the sexual favors of the marquise, highlighting once more the role of sexual desire in setting dynamics of credit and fashion into motion.

The exchange of social for financial credit forges relations of false and hypocritical friendship between aristocrat and bourgeois. Molière heightens the dramatic tension by tantalizing the audience with the possibility of reciprocity across social divides, but then he reveals that the exchange must fail. In this satiric yet ultimately conservative vision of society, harmony reigns when each man returns to his place. Cléonte, the young suitor of Jourdain's daughter, is a scion of the *noblesse de robe*; his honesty and hard work represent a reproach both to Dorante's arrogant privilege and Jourdain's misguided social pretensions, just as Madame Jourdain's commonsense dignity offers a defense of appropriate bourgeois values.[57]

Set against Donneau de Visé's nuanced presentation of the relationship between court and city, the tendentiousness of Molière's account takes on bold relief. Given the capacities for innovation and strategic marketing that *Le Mercure galant* ascribed to merchants serving the court, it is of course highly implausible that a successful merchant such as Jourdain could remain so ignorant of the reigning usage of fashion and be so easily gulled by his tailor. Indeed, one might argue that it was precisely because the gap between the appearance and behaviors of successful commoners and court nobles was shrinking that Molière's comedy played well for a royal audience.

Florent Carton Dancourt issued a fascinating response to *Le Bourgeois gentilhomme* in his *La Femme d'intrigues*, published in 1692, which recounts the scheming of Madame Thibaut and her suitor Cléante (an ironic echo of Molière's Cléonte), a man she believes to be a noble army officer.[58] Madame Thibaut, the title character of the play, is a cunning woman with multiple schemes in motion. She has established a brisk trade in secondhand sales of luxurious clothing, jewelry, and furniture entrusted to her by aristocrats in need of hard cash (the play was also known under the title of *La Revendeuse à la toilette*). She succeeds not only in reaping high profits from this trade but has also established herself as a patronage broker (*faiseuse d'affaires*), conniving to suborn the distribution of official posts and to find wealthy spouses for her greedy clients. The opening of the play finds Madame Thibaut having used the pawned goods in her possession to pass herself off as a "widow of quality" to win her own promise of marriage from the noble officer Cléante.[59]

The opposite of the naive and bumbling Monsieur Jourdain, Madame Thibaut has no interest in gaining access to court; she brusquely informs a client: "At court! No, I hardly go to that country."[60] Social climbing holds little attraction for her, perhaps because her business dealings have rendered her all too familiar with the venality, loose morals, and false appearances of the court aristocracy. The only values she clings to are money and material advancement. Unbeknownst to Thibaut, she has met her match in Laramée, a sergeant in Cléante's unit who has used money advanced by his superior officer to perform his own masquerade. Laramée has received considerable sums of money from Cléante to perform errands on his behalf in Paris: to recruit new troops for the regiment, settle accounts with the officer's wool merchant, and place an order for two new suits. As Laramée boasts to an acquaintance: "I have received orders to have two suits made for him by his tailor [and] to pay cash for them; I am taking them on credit and serving myself." The absent Cléante is the most honorable character in the play, the rare aristocrat who pays his bills in cash. Laramée has used the purloined funds to pass himself off as his superior officer and proved capable of fooling even the jaded Madame Thibaut.

Credit enters the play once more with the character of Le Marquis, who visits Madame Thibaut to request her assistance in finding a wealthy widow to marry. In response to her inquiries into the state of his own fortune, he responds: "First of all, there is no year, however bad it is, that I don't get seven or eight hundred pistoles from the hands of Gaultier [the real-life silk merchant publicized in *Le Mercure galant*], that's in cloth: but what difference does it make? Doesn't one have to be dressed?" He adds to that figure approximately six or seven thousand livres worth of lace and linen he obtains annually from merchants in Picardy, as well as what he receives in saddles and carriages each year from two well-known saddlers. Thibaut interrupts him to clarify: "That is to say, Monsieur le Marquis, that all of your revenue is in the capital of credit [*fonds de crédit*]." He responds airily, "Capital in land or capital in credit, what difference does it make? Do I not receive that much each year?" Despite this nonchalant tone, the marquis is self-interested enough to point out that since he has "great funds in credit . . . , to diversify things the lady must have great funds in land." He quickly accepts Madame Thibaut's offer of the hand of the sixty-year-old widow of a wealthy fish merchant, but the match falls through when the widow discovers his list of debts.[61]

Both Thibaut and Laramée are exposed in the end, she by a police commissaire to whom a fraudulent sale has been denounced and he by the impending arrival of the real Cléante. This convenient ending offers no hope, however, that any of the remaining twenty-six schemers and sharp dealers who have appeared during the play's five acts will reform their ways. Perhaps too outspoken and sweeping in its denunciation of the machinations of the aristocracy and Parisian bourgeoisie, the play did not do well in the theater and continued for only twenty-three performances.[62]

Despite its lack of popular success, the play provides an important counterpart to *Le Bourgeois gentilhomme*, reminding us, as it must have reminded Parisian audiences, that merchants were not mere dupes of a society dominated by aristocratic values, but were shrewd and profit-seeking collaborators who were indispensable in creating noble appearances. In the figure of Thibaut the playwright provides another model of the woman of credit: not a sexualized courtier converting libidinal capital into political influence but an asexual, calculating merchant who takes advantage of worldly economies of regard to fill her purse. The play also emphasizes the crucial role of mercantile credit—and of merchants of cloth and clothing and other items associated with luxurious appearances in particular—in keeping aristocratic lifestyles afloat, so much so that the marquis calculated his entire income in terms of the goods he received each year on credit. The assumption behind his calculation is that he will not reimburse the merchants and, paradoxically, that his credit will never expire. By naming real merchants, Dancourt signaled his desire to impose some level of verisimilitude on the play; although the marquis is a caricature, his actions do not take place in the realm of pure farce. Such frank depictions of debt and greed within high society apparently did not seem very funny to the audiences of the Comédie française, who greeted the play with lukewarm acclaim. They certainly found echoes, however, in the account books of Parisian merchants studied in chapters 4 and 5.

Fashion and Credit: Intertwined Circuits of Authority and Influence

To this point, we have focused on fashion primarily as it affected clothing and we have begun to examine the connections between fashionable dress and social credibility. Yet fashion's empire reached far beyond clothing to encompass not only other forms of consumption but also other commodities, diverse forms of cultural production, and even modes of comportment. In these cases contemporaries often explicitly linked the status of being in fashion with that of possessing credit. For writers of the time, the authority and influence that fashion conferred on an object, style, behavior, or person was akin to the authority and influence conveyed by credit.

Returning to Furetière's dictionary of 1690, we note that he begins the definition of "fashion" (*la mode*) with: "custom, manner of living, of doing things; fashion is used also for all that which changes according to time and space." Reaching back to 1642, François de Grenaille's *La Mode* was subtitled "or the Character of Religion, Life, Conversation, Solitude, Compliments, Clothing, and the Style of the Times." Within its covers, Grenaille listed a plethora of aspects of life susceptible to fashion. He tells us of "the fashionable life, fashionable compliments, fashionable conversations, fashionable weapons, [and] fashionable homes and clothing."[63] According to Grenaille, even fields of learning and literature such as theology, philosophy, jurisprudence, eloquence, and poetry were all driven by fashion. By the late seventeenth century playwrights had turned this observation into its own type of fashion. In addition to the Dancourt titles discussed above, other plays from the late seventeenth century include *Paris ou la Mentor à la mode*, *Les maris à la mode*, *Le Courtisan à la mode*, *Les Panaches ou les coiffures à la mode*, and *Le marquis à la mode*.

Indeed, Jean de La Bruyère's dislike of fashion stemmed in large part from the expansion of its domain to so many facets of life. In his chapter titled "On Fashion" he lamented that "a foolish thing that reveals our pettiness, is the subjection to fashion when it extends to that which concerns taste, food, health, and conscience. Wild game meat is out of fashion and for this reason insipid; it would be a sin against fashion to cure a fever with bleeding." For the moralist, a sign of fashion's unbridled sway was its intrusion even into questions of life and death: "The duel is the triumph of fashion and the place where it exercises its tyranny most spectacularly; this usage has not allowed the coward freedom to live; it has led him to be killed by someone more brave and confused him with a man of heart."[64] La Bruyère was complaining of a dynamic of fashion, of a thirst for novelty, of according authority to novelty for its own sake, that he felt was widespread among his elite readers.

Saint-Simon, the court memoirist, clearly perceived affinities between fashionability and credit and we find in his memoirs several instances where the two forces meet or overlap. In one example Saint-Simon depicts the setting in motion of fashion by Madame de Maintenon as a counter to the effects of credit: "She showed the king pressing letters from Messieurs Thiberge and Brisacier, superiors of the Foreign Missions, whom, to counter the Jesuits whose credit hindered her, she had put into fashion with the king."[65] In another example, speaking of the salonnière Ninon de l'Enclos, he notes that due to the respectability and decency of her gatherings, she had "for friends those who were among the most select and elevated at court, so much that it became the fashion to be received by her." He goes on to praise the tone, liveliness, and ambience of her gatherings, her knowledge of the court, and her conversation, which he described as charming, disinterested, loyal, and trustworthy. Unsurprisingly, this woman of the moment also possessed credit, which she used to reward her friends: "She often helped her friends with money and credit, entered for them into important undertakings, [and] kept very faithfully the considerable deposits of money and secrets that were confided to her."[66]

Saint-Simon thus depicts money, secrets, and credit as precious items in circulation at court, all of which were accumulated by the woman who commanded fashion. This statement recalls the Quietist depiction of authority whispering its power in the previous chapter. The circulation of credit and fashion operated not only by disseminating information but by concealing, misrepresenting, and whispering it. In part it was the capacity of these goods to propagate untruth that worried contemporaries. Speaking of negative gossip spread by the Duke and Duchess of Orleans, Saint-Simon spoke of the "execrable accusations so much in fashion due to the credit and currency that Madame de Maintenon and Monsieur du Maine endlessly strove to give them."[67]

In some instances credit and fashion intersected in more tangible ways. As Saint-Simon recounted: "This Madame de Puysieux had great credit with the queen mother, and in society a singular consideration. She married her son to the sister of the Duc de La Rochefoucauld, favorite of Louis XIV, and ruined him with extravagant expenses, among others to consume one hundred thousand écus in collars of Genovese lace, which were very much in fashion at the time."[68] Social credit with the queen mother thus enabled an ambitious woman to marry her son to a family in royal favor and in turn to exploit his financial credit to procure the cultural credit of fashionable clothing. Fashion and credit were not identical forces, but they traversed the same circuits and their dynamics could conjoin or oppose each other.

To return to the dictionary as an instructive source on usage, Abel Boyer published the first edition of his English-French dictionary in 1702, after which it reappeared in multiple editions throughout the eighteenth century. For the French word *vogue*, Boyer provided as synonyms "crédit, estime, reputation" (he translated it with the English word *vogue*).[69] Boyer thus indicated that the two words *credit* and *vogue* belonged to a constellation of terms signifying reputation and power. Under the heading of the English word *authority* (whose synonyms he gives as "power, credit"), he offered the following translation: "Authorité, Puissance, Pouvoir, Considération, Estime, Réputation, Vogue."

Other words in the dictionary bear out the strong relationship between credit and fashionability (or vogue), which frequently appear as synonyms. For example, as synonyms for the verb *fleurir* (to flower or flourish), he provided: "*être en credit, en honneur, en vogue.*" In the dictionary's edition of 1727, under the entry for "date," he translated the colloquial phrase *to grow out of date* as "*n'être plus en crédit, ou en Vogue, être hors de Saison.*"[70] He also rendered *to promote or prefer a book (or recommend it to the world)* as "*mettre un Livre en vogue, ou en crédit, le pousser dans le Monde.*" For the phrase *to reign* (to be in vogue), he suggests "*régner, être en crédit ou en vogue.*" In the same edition he translated the English word *vogue* for the first time, rendering it as "*vogue, estime, crédit, réputation.*" He appended examples of common usages of the word: "a thing in vogue (or in fashion), *une chose qui est en vogue, qui est à la mode, qui a grand cours.*" The two words also shared the same antonym. Thus, Jacques Savary des Bruslons's *Dictionnaire universel de commerce* defined the word *décrédité* as follows: "*which has no more credit.* That man is totally *discredited*, he could not find a sol to support his business. A *discredited* shop is a shop where one sees no more customers. A *discredited* cloth is one that is no longer in fashion."[71]

These examples suggest crucial similarities—as well as important differences—between fashion and credit systems. Fashion and credit (in its dual sense of material and immaterial credit) were informal systems for assessing and according value, whose function lay primarily in the access they allowed to other valued goods, tangible and intangible. It was thus not the possession of fashionable items in and for themselves that mattered. Instead, it was the status of being someone who was à la mode—someone who had the inside information and the financial means to achieve that status—that produced cultural capital, which could in turn be converted to its social and political equivalents.[72] Similarly, in the case of credit, it was not the possession of credit itself that mattered but the commodities and money (in the case of financial credit) or the influence and power (in the case of social credit) it enabled as well as the further access to goods, relations, and influence.

To take the comparison further, both fashion and credit were constituted in large part by informal, anonymous, and collective, yet seemingly efficient, systems for disseminating and evaluating information. Who bore the authority to declare an item of clothing, a genre of literature, or a word to be of the latest fashion? Who decided how much debt an individual was capable of sustaining and reimbursing or who—at the court of Louis XIV or other social milieus—dictated the effective power and prestige of an individual? In all cases collective social judgments emerged based on information that circulated through asymmetric, hierarchical, and semipublic networks. Although informal, these networks were highly effective. For financial credit, Philip Hoffman, Jean-Laurent Rosenthal, and Gilles Postel-Vinay have shown the efficacy of informal networks run by notaries in generating credit in the financial sector.[73] In the case of fashion the efficiency of the system is suggested by the January 1678 edition of the quarterly supplement *L'Extraordinaire du Mercure galant*, which listed for its readers' edification at least fourteen new fabrics that had been introduced solely for the current season. Seasonal change was already well established by the 1670s, with an impressive variety and number of commodities issued on a seasonal basis. The fact that France developed only one, short-lived journal solely devoted to fashion until the 1780s further suggests that informal visual and aural witnessing sufficed for many decades to transmit news about the constant flow of new fashions.

There were, of course, privileged informants in these systems. One was the Parisian merchant, whose expertise lay not only in making and selling fashionable goods but also in keeping track of changing fashions and launching new ones. One of Donneau's fictionalized protagonists declared that she had been out buying new skirts the previous day: "because of this I informed myself on those that are the most in fashion."[74] An exceptionally adept practitioner of the trade was fashion merchant Rose Bertin, discussed in chapters 5 and 6, who carried great authority in declaring new styles (such as the controversial *robe à la chemise* worn by Marie Antoinette in her portrait by Elisabeth-Louise Vigée-Lebrun). Another set of data specialists consisted of the local notaries who advised their clients about the solvency of potential debtors, as described by Hoffman and his coauthors.[75]

In neither case, however, could these powerful knowledge brokers control the status of the myriad objects and individuals at play in the system; nor did they possess complete information. Instead, limits on the circulation of information served as one means to construct social hierarchies and collective identities. Le monde was not a static social formation within which individuals competed for regard; rather, worldly individuals' practices of seeking out and displaying fashions, daring to launch new ones, and recognizing or dismissing other peoples' sallies, all served as processes through which le monde came into being, reproduced itself, and evolved. Finding out what styles, accessories, colors, and so on remained in fashion, which were about to fade, and what new ones were coming into being required significant investments of time, money, and social capital, as the breathless conversations in *Le Mercure galant* testified. Success or failure had real consequences in terms of prestige, which translated into influence and connections and the rewards they proffered. To reconstitute the inclusions and exclusions constituted by these information systems, historians might pay closer attention to strategies for obtaining, circulating, and also hiding or distorting such information.[76]

Another common feature of fashion and credit was that they both hinged essentially on time. Fashion's very basis was its ephemeral nature. A turn of speech or a color could only be considered fashionable to the extent that it had emerged from obscurity to occupy center stage but would soon fade in favor of the next comer. The short-lived nature of fashion drove elite consumption, leading figures like Dorante back to his tailor (and back into debt) despite the fact that his existing clothes were not threadbare or irreparably soiled. One historian's study of fashion in the reign of Louis XIII accordingly remarked on the frequent use of the metaphor of running to describe fashion. Contemporaries often referred to "*la mode qui court*" and "*la mode qui trotte*" (literally the "fashion that runs" and the "fashion that trots").[77]

Credit was also fundamentally concerned with time. To speak only of trade credit, it involved obtaining goods and services at the present moment with the promise of payment in the future, guaranteed in part by a record of satisfactory borrowing and reimbursement in the past.[78] Credit involved projecting past behavior and current value into the future. One might object that here is a primary difference between fashion and credit, for surely the point of trade credit was that one must be able to rely on some permanence between today's reputation and tomorrow's repayment and on an essential identity between the commodity purchased today and the value of the money received in the future. However, even in this case it was clear to observers that credit was never fixed; it ebbed and flowed constantly. Agile merchants ensured this was the case by multiplying the number of their suppliers, and thus their sources of credit, all the while reassuring each of their fidelity. The trick, for merchants as well as power brokers at court and elsewhere, was to track these shifting tides as closely as possible so as to form the most reliable predictions of future value.[79]

Given its constantly evolving nature, organic metaphors proliferated for credit just as for fashion. *Le Mercure galant* used the metaphors of birth and death, referring in some cases to the "abortion" of fashions before they could be born. In the Boyer example above he speaks of the flowering of credit and the potential for credit, as for fashion, to be "out of season"; many other contemporary sources refer to the growing and shrinking of credit and also accorded autonomous agency to credit itself (that is, *son crédit peut beaucoup* or "his credit is capable of a great deal"). The most striking organic metaphor, *le crédit est mort* ("credit is dead"), referred to a systemic withdrawal of credit and was the object of numerous images in the eighteenth and nineteenth centuries. Fashion ran, credit grew and shrank, and, in extreme cases, they withered and died.[80]

One window into the affinities between credit and fashion in terms of time is provided by the definition of the term *cours* (a word translated today in English as course, currency, or price). According to the *Encyclopédie*, this was a "term much used in *commerce*, where it has diverse meanings." It could denote long trade expeditions by sea, such as voyages to the Indies; it could also be used to indicate the length of a piece of cloth." More to our point, "cours, signifies also the *credit* or *discredit* that the letters of a merchant, trader or banker have in commerce. They have currency [*cours*] when they are found to be good, and one wishes to accept them: when they are found to be bad, and no one wants to accept them, they no longer have currency." The same meaning applied to more public forms of financial credit: "Cours is taken in the same sense, for the favor that letters introduced into commerce acquire or lose in public." Finally, it was a term applied to the effects of fashion as well: "Cours is said also among merchants for the good or bad sale of cloth, foodstuffs. It is fashion that give currency to new fabrics; those in out-dated styles have no more currency."[81]

The common thread here is the notion of an uninterrupted current or track, along which confidence and belief set both credit and fashion running on their course. When this faith dissolved, the circuit ground to a halt. The endless acts of deferral involved in setting prices, which run along the tracks inscribed by fashion and credit, evoke the process of deferral inherent in the production of meaning and the concept of the "trace" described by Derrida and other poststructuralist theorists.[82] Like the "meaning" produced by language, the "value" produced by both fashion and credit relied on reference to prior and subsequent signs (words, objects, money, favors) rather than any fixed or stable foundations.

A final similarity to underline is the role of the individual in both credit and fashion systems. As Georg Simmel insisted, dress furnishes a meeting point between the collective and the individual, a place where social structures and hierarchies intersect with personal choices and tastes.[83] The same could be said of credit. In a society still explicitly grounded in corporate social relations, both credit and fashion were essentially held and deployed by individuals. One cannot, of course, deny the role of collective affiliations in generating the capacity to acquire credit and to be fashionable. To that extent, both credit and fashion served the function of upholding existing social structures and hierarchies. Both systems, however, also offered considerable opportunities for individual skill and competence. Indeed, they depended on individual trajectories of success or failure, for if either were entirely predictable, there would be no dynamic to drive the system. Social status and wealth could not guarantee an individual's capacity to display mastery of fashionable dress, speech, and gesture or of the social maneuvering required to amass social credit. A son could rely to a certain extent on the informal bonds of social credit accrued by his father—or his reputation for honest and fair trading—but he could just as easily fail to maintain that capital through his own ineptitude.[84] Once again, attention to these value systems, which cut across social hierarchies and even the intimacy of families and couples, suggests an alternate way of understanding the complexities of social life. Moreover, the opportunity for strategic maneuvering reveals that individuals were not merely subjects of these signifying systems but were capable of thoughtful and decisive action in manipulating them or of idiosyncratic incompetence and failure.

L'homme à la mode: Libidinal Economies of Credit and Fashion

THE MAN OF FASHION IN THE LATE SEVENTEENTH CENTURY

Contemporary sources remarked on the extension of fashion to touch many aspects of life; they also marveled at the way individuals themselves became objects of fashion. As with other cultural phenomena, they held differing opinions about the character type they identified as the homme à la mode. Saint-Simon used the expression on several occasions in his memoirs, offering insight into contemporary usage of the term. Of the Baron de Breteuil, Saint-Simon stated: "He was a man who did not lack wit but who had a rage for the court, for ministers, for men with official posts or in fashion, and above all for earning money by promising his protection."[85] In speaking of a high-born officer of the royal family, he commented that the man was "very much in fashion in le monde, and with very little wit, a very gallant man and well-received everywhere." Another royal servant, the king's valet, acquired his status of homme à la mode through his service to the king's sexual pleasures: "Lavienne, bathkeeper in Paris very much in fashion, became [the king's bath-keeper] during the time of [the king's] love affairs. He pleased him with drugs that rendered him more than once capable of giving more satisfaction, and this path led him to become one of the four first valets de chambre."[86]

What qualities allowed a man to become an homme à la mode under Louis XIV? In the case of Lavienne it was his capacity to guarantee the king's virility. In the case of the Maréchal de Clérembault, "very much in fashion" according to Saint-Simon, he tells us that: "He was a man of great spirit, decorated, agreeable, pleasant, ingratiating and agile, with a great deal of finesse, always in good standing with ministers, much to the liking of Cardinal Mazarin and also much to the liking of high society and always among the best [people]."[87] The patronage of the powerful—the king, a minister, a mistress in favor—certainly helped, but the personal charms of being pleasing and enjoyable company were also necessary to elevate an individual to the collective acclaim of fashion. In contemporary sources an homme à la mode was a personage with polished manners, wit, and elegance in dress. Regardless of his inherent merit or virtue, this was someone whom everyone wanted to know and have at their dinners and other social gatherings.[88] Skill at conversation was of paramount importance, for "the *bon mot* makes the man of fashion."[89]

A similar depiction of the homme à la mode comes from the pen of another royal valet. Reputed to be an illegitimate grandson of Henri IV, Charles Du Fresny, sieur de la Rivière, was named valet de chambre to Louis XIV. He later served as designer of the royal gardens and became a playwright and editor of *Le Mercure galant* at the death of Donneau de Visé in 1710. Du Fresny's credit problems were well known at court. His extravagant spending gave rise to gossip that he had been obliged to marry his laundress because he was too poor to pay her bill.[90] In honor of his royal blood the regent tried to rescue him after Louis XIV's death with a gift of two hundred thousand livres, which Du Fresny supposedly lost in financial speculation during the John Law period.

Du Fresny's major literary work was *Amusemens sérieux et comiques* (1699), a series of anecdotes about Parisian life that inspired Montesquieu's *Persian Letters* (the narrator of du Fresny's text is accompanied by a visitor from Siam to whom he explains Parisian customs). One chapter of *Amusemens* begins with a satirical description of a meeting resembling a Parisian salon: "These assemblies are a type of bourgeois society that are formed in imitation of court society." The description continues:

> The bourgeois circle is an informal gathering, a free council, where the affairs of others are judged sovereignly without hearing the parties involved. These courts hear both sublime and plebeian affairs, everything is within

their jurisdiction; there, caprice presides, and it is there in fact that one finds as many different opinions as there are faces: the same judge is at times severe and at times indulgent, sometimes grave, sometimes light-hearted; and they act there as I have done in my *Amusements*; they pass in an instant from the serious to the comic, from the great to the petty; and sometimes a sudden comment on the hairstyle of a woman impedes a decision on a moral issue that was on the floor. They pronounce twenty decrees at once; the men voice their opinions when they can; and the woman as much as they wish; they accord each woman two votes.[91]

This account satirizes the worldly gatherings evoked by Donneau, where talk of the weather easily turns to gossip or the latest fashions. Du Fresny explicitly contrasts the "bourgeois" Parisian gathering with "court circles," but his acknowledgment of complicity in the rhetorical style of the urban gathering suggests complicity with this milieu rather than outright rejection of it. Du Fresny's description of the gathering focuses in particular on the overlap of fashionable clothing with the phenomenon of being an item of fashion oneself. As the narrator explains to his Siamese companion:

It is not love, for example, but pure curiosity, that causes the eagerness for the cavalier who just came in; first of all, curiosity to see his outfit close-up; it is a suit of his own invention, covered in imaginative embroidery, and thoroughly planned out; the design pleases them, it is bizarre, extravagant and well-reasoned: to study its effect, the cavalier shut himself up for five or six mornings with his embroiderer; this brilliant masterpiece deserves all of the ladies' attention. Another reason for their curiosity: this handsome man has recently come into vogue; he is the latest fashion, and only provincial women are allowed not to know him.[92]

The studied and fashionable clothing worn by the cavalier is thus matched by the man's own reputation of being himself the latest fashion. The wised-up Siamese responds with a commentary on the ephemerality of the phenomenon of being in fashion: "'Very well,' the Siamese told me, 'I've already been taught to what extent Parisian ladies are scrupulous about fashion; they would be ashamed to wear an outfit from the previous year; according to the rule of fashion, this handsome man will seem very ugly to them in the coming year.'"[93] As in La Bruyère, outward appearances contrast negatively with inner merit. It turns out that the "*joli homme*" has no wit or intellect. His only way of addressing women is with his looks, and they soon pass on to a more entertaining character.

Not surprisingly the elevation of men and women themselves to be items of fashion attracted disapprobation from moralists like La Bruyère: "Someone was in fashion, either for commanding armies and negotiations, or for eloquence at the pulpit, or for verses, who no longer is. Are there men who degenerate from what they once were? Is it their merit that is spent or the taste one had for them?" Like other kinds of fashion, the vogue for individual men was ephemeral. The man of fashion, by definition, could not endure: "A man of fashion lasts little, because fashions pass; if by chance he is a man of merit, he is not destroyed, and he remains somewhere; equally estimable, he is only less esteemed."[94] In his chapter titled "The Great" La Bruyère sketches the character of an ambitious and false courtier whom he calls Pamphile. He comments on men of this nature: "They do not accept maxims, principles even less: they live by adventure, pushed and pulled by the wind of favor and the attraction of riches. They have no opinion that is their own, that belongs to them; they borrow as much as they need: and the one to whom they have recourse is hardly a man of wisdom, ability or virtue: he is an homme à la mode."[95] Those attracted to the man of fashion treat opinions like debts, borrowing easily without thought for repayment. Without fixed principles, they are directed by fashion and self-interest. The polished manners and pleasant conversation of the homme à la mode for La Bruyère disguise the inner vacuity of his ilk.

Fénélon was another who complained about the power conveyed on fashionable men. His vision of the homme à la mode, like that of Saint-Simon, is of the *homme en place* (someone occupying official posts in government):

Have you not heaped too many posts on the head of one man, either to satisfy his ambition or to spare yourself the trouble of having many people with whom you must speak? As soon as a man is an homme à la mode, he is given everything; one would like him alone to do everything. It is not that one loves him, for one loves nothing; it is not because one finds him perfect, because one is delighted to criticize him frequently; but because one is lazy and unsociable. One does not wish to have to reckon with so many people.[96]

The state inevitably suffers from the incapacity of one man to face so many responsibilities, and the fashionable man himself is overwhelmed and exhausted. Taken as a fact of life by worldly writers, the homme à la mode embodied for moralists the failings of high society. Pleasing rather than merit-worthy, the homme à la mode was destined to shine brightly and then fade quickly, leaving a vacuum of leadership and honor behind him.

In condemning the man of fashion, commentators like La Bruyère and Fénélon attacked the falsity of court society and the bestowal of fame and power on a man elevated by capricious adulation. After the beginning of the eighteenth century the tenor of the discussion began to shift as the definition of the homme à la mode came to center on his sexual liaisons with women. The judgment elevating him to "fashion" was no longer le monde but specifically the women who belonged to it. As one text summed up this new perspective in 1740: "Nothing puts a man more in fashion than to be recommended by women of a certain rank."[97] The ephemeral reputation of the homme à la mode thus resulted, to a certain extent, from the fact that it was the taste of women that won him the title.[98]

One of the best places to view such questions at work is the libertine novel, which emerged in the same decades that the Abbé de Saint-Pierre and Montesquieu criticized powerful women's credit. Charles Duclos himself wrote highly successful libertine fiction including *The Story of Madame de Luz* and *The Confessions of the Comte de ****, which appeared in eight editions in its first year and was translated into English and German.[99] While such novels did not provide realistic depictions of behaviors and practices, they served as important cultural sites of thinking about struggles over forms of social representation and the links among sex, fashion, reputation, and power.[100] They thus provide their own response to the question of women's sexuality and its links to reputation and influence that animated political critics like Montesquieu and the Abbé Saint-Pierre in the same years.

One of the most popular libertine novels was *Les égarements du cœur et de l'esprit* (1736–1738) by Claude Prosper Jolyot de Crébillon. It takes the form of a memoir by an aristocrat named Meilcour, who recounts his entry to high society at the age of seventeen. He falls under the tutelage of the libertine rake Versac, who has gained the title of homme à la mode by countless seductions. In outlining a libertine manifesto to Meilcour, Versac voices the strategies of the eighteenth-century homme à la mode for manipulating fashion and credit to attain celebrity, with its corollaries of influence and fortune. Like Faret and Courtin a century earlier, if in a far more cynical register, Versac advises Meilcour to study the usages of le monde and to adopt those most appropriate to his station. He frankly admits that the reigning fashions of dress and behavior are ridiculous, but argues that they are necessary to survival and success in the milieu. Thus, in addition to the study of women, he tells Meilcour:

> It is a mistake to believe that one can maintain in society that moral innocence that one commonly has when one enters it, and that one can always

be virtuous and natural there, without risking one's reputation or one's fortune. The heart and the mind must be spoiled, [for] everything there is fashion and affectation. Virtues, charms, and talents are purely arbitrary, and one can only succeed there by constantly disfiguring oneself. These are the principles that you must never lose from view: but it is not enough to know that, to succeed, you must be ridiculous. You must study with care the tenor of society in which our rank has placed us, the follies [*ridicules*] most appropriate to our estate, those, in a word, that are in credit, and this study requires more finesse and attention than you can imagine.[101]

In response to Meilcour's perplexed question, what do you mean by "*ridicules en crédit*," the author provides the following riposte: "'I mean,' he responded, 'those that, depending on caprice, are subject to vary [and] have, like all fashions, but a certain time to please and that while they reign outshine all others. It is in the time of their vogue that you must seize them; it would be as fruitless to accept them when the world is beginning to tire of them, as it would be risky to hold on to them, when they are utterly banished.'"[102] For Versac, as for earlier commentators, the dynamics of fashion and credit are closely related. He asks Meilcour, in turn, whether he could possibly believe that Versac, who promotes or at least perfects most of the successful oddities of fashion, launches them by sheer caprice without being guided by his knowledge of the world. He assures his young pupil that his own success is proof of the worth of his strategy. Asked on what basis one can ascertain when a fashion is about to fall, Versac responds: from the "low esteem in which it is held by women."

Twenty years later a libertine in another text by Crébillon offered a similar perspective on his success: "It was at first in spite of myself through the whim of a few women who then set the fashion that I became fashionable. The reputation created by my first affairs inevitably attracted others to me, and without having conceived the project of having all women, soon there were none in Paris . . . who did not believe themselves obliged to have me, and whom in turn I did not feel obliged to take."[103] In the voice of the libertine, what late seventeenth-century moralists condemned was now boldly celebrated as the path to success for the canny careerist. Versac frankly agrees with the charge of hypocrisy leveled by the moralists, declaring: "as long as a folly pleases, it is grace, adornment, wit; and it only receives the name it deserves when one has worn it out and grown tired of it." Far from lamenting this state of affairs, he advises the naive Meilcour to seize the reins of fashion and win the race for success. He also confirms, without regret, the role of women's capricious taste in launching and maintaining fashions.[104]

Versac's advice found an echo in other libertine coming-of-age novels. The narrator of one text describes his first undertaking upon entering le monde to have been to start "by scrupulously informing myself of the folly in fashion, or rather the reigning tone."[105] Another young narrator describes his tutelage in the hands of an "homme à la mode, a famous man, a hero, a buffoon in a word. That man spoke to me only of subjugated women, of the superior talent to maintain simultaneously dozens of intrigues, of the profound knowledge of the heart of women, of the art of governing them."[106] Le chevalier d'Arcq's libertine novel *Le roman du jour, pour servir à l'histoire du siècle*, published in 1754, features another libertine character who offers advice remarkably similar to that of Versac. In response to the young narrator Mircourt's protestation that modesty must be the most appropriate attitude for his age, he responds: "But yes! Monsieur . . . what you're saying there is the height of absurdity. That is what dreary parents preach all day long. Their heads full of the prejudices of the old court, they prefer to censure fashionable adornments rather than submit to them, and regard with chagrin in their successors the advantages which they can no longer enjoy." Instead of following useless adages, he counsels, one must learn to please women.[107]

Although characters like Versac celebrate their freedom from conventional morality, the ultimate lesson of such tales usually defers to social mores and censorship by emphasizing the doomed nature of their rebellion. In some sense they therefore offered but a new twist on the moralizing literature of the seventeenth century. They also comforted the passionate denunciations of the homme à la mode expressed by some female authors who identified dangers for women posed by this version of the man of fashion, who manipulates, dominates, and ultimately betrays his mistresses. In her *Réflexions nouvelles sur les femmes*, published in 1727, the salonnière and writer Madame de Lambert declared: "Sincerity, good faith, the purity of feeling, all these things are regarded by young people as ancient virtues, enemies of pleasure and good company. A man, to be in fashion, must cheat, deceive, malign, and slander all women; he must seduce well-behaved ones, abandon them without remorse, and publicize afterward their favors."[108] Another proto-feminist author, Madame de Puisieux, concurred that the homme à la mode presented a dangerous moral void: "What would become of a young homme à la mode beside a respectable woman, who made him feel the horror of his disorder? In truth, it is impracticable, society would destroy itself; no more house parties, no more society dinners: one would hide oneself from gallant commerce as from a crime; the passions would become reasonable, decent, and steady."[109]

To return to the central themes of this book, how did the man of fashion relate to the man of credit? It is clear that the informal, socially adjudicated authority and power enjoyed by the man of fashion was akin to that enjoyed by men in credit. *Les Dehors Trompeurs ou l'homme du jour* (The false appearances or the man of the moment), a play published in 1740 by Louis de Boissy, the comic poet, playwright, and editor of the *Gazette de France* and *Le Mercure de France*, was the most popular play of the season and remained in production to the time of the revolution. The play drew an explicit link between becoming an homme à la mode through seduction and acquiring credit. The character of the marquis declares that "society is surprising in its bizarre nature. The gambler who swindles is covered in infamy, and the treacherous lover who cheats and betrays becomes homme à la mode and puts himself in credit."[110] Boissy is struck here by the incongruity in the treatment of two similar forms of cheating—at gambling and in love.

An anonymous poem of 1767, "Läis et Phriné," drew the same connection between the credit a man acquired by seduction and his elevation to fashion: "Lindor made a thousand conquests / And saw his credit crest. / Among all types, the name suffices / L'homme à la mode is an idol / Placed in favor by some fool[ish woman] / Raised by nothing, destroyed by nothing / And for nothing makes our ears ring."[111] A play in 1764 ascribed the creation of credit to luck and the favor of "*gens à la mode*" and predicted that such credit would be as ephemeral as fashion itself: "If I know Madame Arminte, the marquis, from one day to another, may displease her, inconsistency and flightiness are the distinctive character of fashionable people, and my lucky rival could in an instant lose all the credit that I know not what good fortune has given him so quickly."[112]

The gendering of the relationship between becoming a man of fashion and acquiring credit thus evolved considerably over time. In the late seventeenth century a man of fashion acquired his title through the mixed-sex audience of le monde; by the mid-eighteenth century it was mostly women who conveyed the title, and the dynamic behind the exchange was one of sexual seduction. To the extent that the libertine's conquests were motivated by vanity and desire for reputation rather than sexual desire itself, we may argue that currents of sexual desire were harnessed to the same dynamics of social authority and power that drove credit and fashion.

Women themselves were depicted as *femme à la mode* during the eighteenth century but less frequently than men.[113] Like homme à la mode, the term was used to describe a woman who had acquired a sparkling reputation in fashionable society. According to a character in *Les Petits émigrés*, by the Comtesse de Genlis, the femme à la mode must fulfill several criteria. She must have two or three "intimate friends" to demonstrate her sensibility and another dozen "intimate liaisons" with whom to exchange visits and endless notes and letters. Finally, it was vital that "she show herself publicly each day in two or three different places; that she be found at all the dinners with some splendor, at all the brilliant balls and parties; that she make great expense in jewels and clothing; that she take all necessary precautions to be promptly informed of all the latest fashions; and that, to sustain her reputation, she invent some herself or at least that she exaggerate the extravagance of all the received ones."[114] As de Genlis's satirical depiction reveals, following and displaying fashions in clothing was inseparably associated with becoming a lady of fashion.

References to femme à la mode multiplied in the nineteenth century.[115] The novelist Honoré de Balzac used the term much like his eighteenth-century predecessors. In his *L'interdiction*, published in 1836, a precursor to *The Human Comedy*, he paints the picture of the femme à la mode in the personage of the Marquise d'Espard, who attempts to win legal and economic autonomy by having her husband declared legally insane. The doctor Bianchon professes his "horror" at the coldness and self-interest of the fashionable woman, declaring that "a woman of fashion and a man in power are two analogues: but with this precise difference, that the qualities through which a man elevates himself above others heighten him and render his glory, while the qualities through which a woman arrives at her empire of a day are appalling vices." For Balzac, the fashionable woman was thus another face of the despised woman in credit who used her influence—most often acquired through sexual seduction—to pervert the course of justice. However, the novelist did not allow the doctor's lambast to pass unanswered. The ambitious young Rastignac protests to Bianchon that a man such as himself must always prefer the femme à la mode to her most chaste and modest counterpart. She is the "diamond with which a man cuts all glass," possessed of the crucial qualities of "fortune, power, splendor, and a certain contempt for all that is beneath them."

The novella's ambiguous ending—which leaves unclear whether the marquise wins her lawsuit and whether Rastignac succeeds in seducing her—suggests no easy resolution to this dispute. Balzac thus points toward a dual inheritance from the Old Regime in the form of worldly strategies of wielding reputation and influence as well as ambivalence about women's part in such affairs.[116]

Fashion and credit constituted overlapping Old Regime economies of regard in which reputation, influence, and authority were constantly shifting values.

Individuals pursued fashion and credit not merely for material gains but to establish and maintain their own currency within these economies. The rewards they hoped to acquire consisted of tangible prizes (like royal pensions and gifts, salaries from official posts, access to financial credit, sex) as well as intangible ones (such as honor, advantageous marriages, invitations to exclusive social gatherings, membership in honorary orders, and friendships with influential people).

Credit and fashion functioned as information systems based on rapidly evolving and unequally accessible forms of knowledge. Because of the uneven distribution of knowledge about what was currently in fashion, those with access to the latest styles not only benefited from the prestige of displaying them in public but also from heralding their status as privileged holders of important information. Establishing one's status as a significant node of information served to attract new informants—eager to exchange the latest news—and also conveyed the capacity to "create" news, that is, the authority to decide what information was reliable and worth sharing instead of being dismissed and discarded. In the case of fashion the most successful participants in the system were able to impose styles of dress and many other items as *the* latest fashion. The system also created privileged informants in the form of professional experts who derived authority from their role as nodes in the system. Similar dynamics functioned with regard to credit, considered in its social, political, or cultural guises. However, the very closeness of the relationship between fashion and credit was what troubled some observers and served to undermine the credibility of both systems.

Economies of regard produced forms of social inequality that drew on but also cut across the traditional rankings of society as well as collective units like the family. Unlike the normative taxonomy of official estates and corporate orders, this system allowed for, even relied on, individual virtuosity and ineptitude. The social boundaries of fashion and credit discussed above were clearly limited to a small elite, yet such processes also subsumed the everyday lives and experiences of ordinary people. They did so both in terms of the ideological impact of these codes of conduct (and the emulation they inspired) and, more practically, by constant demands for the renewal of goods and services and the difficulties purveyors of these goods and services encountered in transforming credit into cash. Restricted access to fashion, like access to credit, was an important way of reinforcing social, cultural, and economic inequality. Like power, powerlessness took on multiple forms. Chapters 5 and 6 will be devoted to examining the culture and practice of credit among female fashion merchants.

The status of gender within these systems was complex and ambivalent. Women participated actively in systems of social and political credit, serving as credit brokers as well as users and bestowers of credit who explicitly discussed their credit standing with others. In late seventeenth-century representations of fashion, similarly, both men and women strove to acquire fashionable clothing and behaviors and to improve their standing by displaying an insider's knowledge of fashion. From court etiquette manuals to the first fashion journal and contemporary dictionaries, both men and women faced the necessity of active participation in fashionable display. Indeed, it was men who rose most frequently to the status of items of fashion in and of themselves. By the early eighteenth century both credit and fashion began to take on new valences as critics of informal, highly unequal, and arbitrary systems of power began to focus on the role of women in shaping their dynamics. The delegitimation of these forms of power and the spotlight on women's authority within them were intertwined processes.

However, this shift was neither total nor inevitable. Men did not stop participating in fashion, nor was women's informal power ever wholly denounced or eradicated. The next chapter discusses the evolution of the production and distribution of fashion during the eighteenth century and, in particular, the role of fashion merchants and credit within these developments. As we will see, the growth of the fashion industry in the second half of the eighteenth century provided women with a range of new opportunities to produce and consume clothing and fashionable accessories. In turn these developments gave women new possibilities for exercising power and influence: celebrity stylists wielded unprecedented cultural authority, and women enthusiastically entered credit networks both as buyers and sellers.

CHAPTER 4

CREDIT IN THE FEMALE
FASHION TRADES OF
EIGHTEENTH-CENTURY PARIS

*I*n the same year he introduced Parisian audiences to Madame Thibaut, the scheming *revendeuse à la toilette*, Dancourt produced another, more successful, play spotlighting a working woman. His *Les Bourgeoises à la mode* of 1692 placed a *marchande de modes* on stage for the first time in French history. Like Molière's *Le Bourgeois gentilhomme*, the play depicts the laughable aspirations of the social-climbing bourgeoisie, in this case represented by Angélique, the young wife of a notary who squanders her husband's money by emulating a noble lifestyle. Scene 6 of act 1 opens as the lackey announces a new arrival: "Madame Amelin, your fashion merchant." This announcement prompts the chambermaid, Lisette, to warn her mistress: "It's money that she wants from you." Angélique's frank retort is clearly a laugh line: "I don't have any to give her." Instead of finding a means to repay her credit, Angélique sets in motion an outrageous scheme to obtain a large sum in cash from the merchant.[1]

This chapter focuses on the marchandes de modes, a privileged group of information brokers in Old Regime economies of regard. Although the origins of their trade are unknown, they seem to have emerged from the shadows of the mercers' guild in the last decades of the seventeenth century and grown increasingly numerous and commercially important in the eighteenth century. In 1776 they acquired an independent guild in Paris and Rouen after Controller General Turgot's failed abolition of the guild system. Both men and women practiced the trade, but it was the many women among them, and their predominantly female clientele, that caught the attention of contemporary commentators.

Their wares enabled worldly clients to vie for the prestigious reputation associated with displaying fashionable appearances. The most successful fashion merchants not only reproduced existing fashions but also possessed the imagination, skill, and authority necessary to invent new ones. Virtuoso fashion merchants thus became indispensable collaborators in elite appearances, challenging traditional hierarchies between aristocratic client and modest purveyor and between manual labor and artistic creation.

If fashion merchants played a crucial role in providing access to the cultural credit of style, the trade itself was driven by the exigencies of financial credit. The spendthrift aristocrats of Molière and Dancourt, who owed immense sums to the merchants who provided their fine clothing, spoofed the well-known consuming habits of the day. Like other merchants — wholesale or retail — fashion merchants sold the majority of their wares on extended credit accounts, not cash. The fact that they sold extensively on credit meant, in turn, that they had to purchase their supplies on account. The marchande de modes was both creditor to her wealthy clients and debtor to wholesale suppliers. Their profession thus imposed concerns with reputation and self-presentation that, while not identical to those of their clients, followed similar dynamics. A key difference was that fashion merchants possessed none of the inherent resources of the elite in title, real property, or investments and thus faced greater constraints in reassuring creditors. On the financial front they had to convey the appearance of conducting solvent businesses that could repay debt. In their social behavior, they had to appear honest and hardworking and deploy social connections and individual skills to forge lasting relationships with suppliers and clients. In cultural terms, marchandes de modes had to master swiftly changing fashions and convince others to recognize the styles they created as new contributions to la mode.

While economic historians have focused primarily on public finance and formal instruments of exchange, our focus here is the relatively understudied realm of shop or trade credit. Shop credit was highly informal, often oral in nature, and always less regulated and supervised than loan contracts, letters of exchange, government annuities, and other financial paper, but it was no less crucial to the economy. This study draws on, and seeks to contribute to, a growing literature emphasizing the ubiquity of shop credit among artisans and merchants in the towns and cities of preindustrial Europe. It also challenges previous historians' emphasis on merchants' reputation as being above all a question of honesty and integrity. The dynamics of fashion placed distinctive challenges on female merchants to integrate style, flair, and individual creativity into the traditional model of the upstanding merchant. With these additional demands came the possibility of bypassing the taint of manual labor and claiming a new persona as creative genius and talented artist.[2]

This chapter opens by tracing the origins and growth of the trade within the context of the overall evolution of the Parisian textile and garment industries. Although traces of the fashion merchants as a distinct occupational group date from the late seventeenth century, it was from the 1760s onward that they received increasing notice. Commentators—in genres ranging from encyclopedias to newspapers, plays, and philosophical treatises—emphasized fashion merchants' contribution to multiple forms of production. They noted the surplus value marchandes de modes endowed on the materials they used, which allegedly sold for many times more than the price of their constituent elements. They also remarked upon the cultural knowledge produced by fashion merchants and other luxury purveyors through the fanciful names they bestowed on their wares. Commentators within and outside France viewed their wares as contributing to an essentially French culture of style and ostentatious display, which reaped substantial profits to the nation.

To probe further the intertwined credit of appearances and accounting, the second section of the chapter scrutinizes the relations between elite client and fashion merchant through two case studies, the fictional one of Dancourt's Madame Amelin and the real-life consuming career of a prominent member of the Parisian robe nobility, Madame de Bercy, wife of the president of the Grand Conseil. These examples illustrate the shared risks assumed by patron and purveyor. Each time a client donned a new outfit, he or she put his or her own credit on the line, since wearing an item that looked ridiculous instead of the latest mode constituted a significant failure of credibility. In turn, fashion merchants took risks of their own, selling their wares of extremely limited shelf life on very generous terms of credit, which customers fulfilled late, in part, or not at all. The burden of shared risks heightened the mutual—if unequal— dependency between merchant and client. The marchandes de modes had little choice but to acquiesce to such terms, because their own credibility as fashion creators rested on their ability to acquire high-status patrons who would serve as walking advertisements for their talents. At the same time, their clients relied on trusted purveyors to guide them through a maze of fashion whose borders constantly shifted.

These findings are explored in greater detail in chapter 5. For the moment, we pause to inquire, in the third section of the chapter, into the legal and practical codes governing the use of shop credit and what skills and types of knowledge fashion merchants needed to manage financial relations with suppliers and clients. The chapter ends by returning to the question of cultural credit and the potential for successful fashion merchants to acquire a form of celebrity within *le monde* of Parisian high society. Rose Bertin, the brightest star in the fashion merchant firmament, will receive due attention in chapters 5 and 6;

here we focus on an early precursor, Mademoiselle DuChapt, who captured the attention of the philosophes but has largely slipped from historical memory.

Fashion Merchants and the Eighteenth-Century Fashion System

GROWTH AND EVOLUTION OF THE PARISIAN GARMENT TRADES, 1675–1789

The depiction of Madame Amelin in *Les Bourgeoises à la mode* prefigured many late eighteenth-century stereotypes about her trade. These attributes included her creative talents, her professional autonomy, and, above all, her frustrated attempts to obtain payment on her credit accounts from wealthy female clients. What is noteworthy is that her character strode on stage at least half a century before contemporaries began discussing fashion merchants in an outburst of fictional and nonfictional commentary, culminating in the many exuberant passages that Louis-Sébastien Mercier and Nicolas Restif de la Brétonne devoted to the marchandes de modes. The play thus challenges both contemporary and historiographical convention, identifying the trade as a well-known element of Parisian life by the 1690s, at least. As background for our examination of fashion merchants' relationship to credit systems, we begin by tracing the origins of the trade and its place within the broader context of the Parisian garment industry and French commerce in the late seventeenth and eighteenth centuries.[3]

As in other economic sectors, the guild system established legal parameters for the activities of merchants and artisans who made and sold fashionable clothing and accessories. Members of the wealthy and diverse merchant mercers' guild, one of the elite Six Corps that topped the Parisian guild hierarchy, were famously "makers of nothing, sellers of everything." The trade encompassed twenty-one different forms of specialization, including merchants of cloth for men's and women's clothing and purveyors of fashionable accessories and the decorative items used to embellish women's dresses. The guild numbered approximately two thousand members in the mid-eighteenth century, rising to perhaps three thousand on the eve of the guilds' temporary abolition in 1776.[4] While cloth, ribbons, and other materials for making clothing came from mercers, for much of the seventeenth century the tailors' guild—around two thousand strong—held the unique privilege to make custom-made articles of clothing for men, women, and children. Used clothing was sold by the fripiers' guild as well as by unlicensed ambulatory merchants. An exception in the predominantly male guild world, the all-female linen drapers' corporation handled the sale of linen cloth and linen household goods.[5] By the mid-1600s female seamstresses constituted another important niche in the garment trades, making women's and children's clothing in defiance of the tailors' statutes. They acquired an autonomous, all-female guild in 1675 in Paris and Rouen, as the royal government sought to profit from guild fees to help defray expenses of the Dutch Wars. Many provincial tailors' guilds accorded some form of work license to seamstresses in the succeeding decades.[6]

Women in guilds possessed the same business prerogatives as male masters, including the right to accord credit to customers and to receive it from suppliers. Female entrepreneurs also benefited from a distinct legal status, that of "public merchant" (*marchande publique*), which had existed in French law since the Middle Ages. This status allowed married women financial autonomy for all business-related affairs, overriding the legal coverture ordinarily exercised by husbands over their wives.[7] The law required no formal approval for a woman to operate as a "public merchant"; indeed, this category implicitly applied to any woman legitimately exercising an independent trade, whether or not she belonged to a guild.

The medieval origins of this legal category testify to the long-standing importance of female entrepreneurs in France; nonetheless, strong evidence exists that women and girls began to enter the skilled labor market in larger numbers in the second half of the seventeenth century. For northwestern Europe as a whole, the historian Jan de Vries has argued for an "industrious revolution" in this period during which families reoriented both production and consumption away from self-sufficiency and toward the market, using wages from paid work to purchase consumer goods. In France the evolution of women's work in the garment trades provides considerable support for this thesis. After its creation in 1675, the seamstresses' guild quickly became one of the largest in Paris. Its membership of approximately three thousand mistresses accepted over four hundred new apprentices each year on average and employed perhaps ten thousand workers. In the same period Controller General Colbert spearheaded an initiative to create high-quality lace manufactures staffed by women and girls in a number of provincial cities. Associations of lay sisters similarly established schools in cities and towns in the late seventeenth and early eighteenth centuries to teach poor girls sewing, embroidery, tapestry making, and other employable skills.[8]

The industrious revolution of these female garment workers helped propel what historians have referred to as a mid-eighteenth century "consumer revolution," in which clothing was one of the most important sectors of expansion.[9] By comparing the contents of a large sample of probate inventories from 1700 with another sample from 1789, Daniel Roche's *The Culture of Clothing* documented a remarkable growth in the size and value of Parisian wardrobes over the eighteenth century. Women led the way in the growth of consumption across all classes, with the exception of the nobility where ostentatious display remained the norm for both sexes. Consumption not only increased, it altered dramatically. Roche found that by 1789 female wage earners, domestic servants, and the wives of artisans and shopkeepers had replaced their brown and grey wool skirts of 1700 with dresses of more comfortable cotton and linen cloth, dyed in bright colors with stripes, polka dots, and other patterns. Moreover, Cissie Fairchilds has found that by 1789 men and women of modest means accessorized their outfits with a range of "populuxe" goods, cheap reproductions of luxury items such as watches, fans, parasols, and snuffboxes.[10] Fashion itself had thus reached into the ranks of wage earners, domestic servants, and artisanal families. While the harsh contrasts of poverty and wealth did not recede from Parisian streets, the findings of Roche and others emphasize the significant growth of fashionable consumption between these extremes.

A number of different factors enabled this revolution in consumption. Seamstresses and other garment workers played a crucial dual role, providing cheap hands to sew new clothes and using their wages to buy less expensive versions of their clients' orders. Lower-cost fabrics played a significant part as well.[11] In the 1770s newly stylish and much less expensive cotton and linen cloth replaced silk for everyday wear. Silk cloth itself, which remained de rigueur for formal attire, became less expensive as manufacturers in Lyons responded to the swifter pace of fashion with thinner, less durable fabric that could be replaced more frequently.[12] Part of the drop in prices also came from the unpaid toil of enslaved people on colonial plantations, who produced cottons and most of the indigo dye (the only natural colorfast blue dye) imported from European colonies in the New World.[13] The result of these changes was the limited democratization of fashion uncovered by historians. Much of the trickle-down of fashion occurred through the secondhand trade: cheap labor and lower-cost fabrics allowed affluent consumers to renew their wardrobes more quickly, which in turn led to a more rapid dissemination of their castoff garments through the bustling, multitiered secondhand market.

THE BIRTH OF THE FASHION MERCHANT

Daniel Roche bracketed his study by the dates 1700 and 1789, leaving many unanswered questions about the origins of the consumer revolution and its pace over the eighteenth century. Research conducted since the publication of *The Culture of Clothing* suggests that fundamental changes in production and consumption had already emerged in the second half of the seventeenth century. This was the era of de Vries's industrious revolution and, in France, the energetic tenure of Controller General Colbert, which inaugurated the seamstresses' guild as one of its many interventions in economic life. *Le Mercure galant*'s reporting, discussed in chapter 3, confirms that many elements of the eighteenth-century "fashion system" were firmly in place by the 1670s. In its pages the narrator depicted fashionable appearances as being derived from an impressive profusion of garments, accessories, and materials sold by specialized merchants on a seasonal basis. Already in the 1670s, to judge by *Le Mercure galant*, shopping in the boutiques of Paris was an important leisure pastime of the elite, serving both as a means to gather information about the latest styles and to display one's mastery of them. Dancourt's Madame Amelin suggests, moreover, that fashion merchants played their own role in the early years of the industrious and consumer revolutions. From the 1690s at least, they constituted a recognizable trade group selling the accessories and finery needed to render garments into the reigning styles of the day.

Direct evidence is scanty, but scattered references to the *marchandes de modes* confirm that they occupied a recognized place in Parisian commercial culture in the first half of the eighteenth century. It was in this period that Mademoiselle Duchapt, or la Duchapt as she came to be known, acquired notice among worldly writers for her work as a fashion merchant for Parisian and court ladies.[14] In the Comte de Caylus's *Histoire de Guillaume Cocher*, published in 1737, Madame Minutin's life story represents a type the author presumed was well-known to his readers, the poor shopgirl with only her looks to recommend her. As she states, "before my marriage, I was but a simple grisette, shopgirl for a fashion merchant of the rue Saint-Honoré."[15] The mid-century commercial press also testifies to the trade's entrenchment within the city's urban culture. An advertisement in the *Annonces, affiches et avis divers* of 1755 heralded the availability of a ground floor boutique on the rue Croix des Petits Champs. According to the advertiser, its high quality, up-to-date furnishings rendered the shop space "appropriate for a drinks seller [*limonadier*], an apothecary, a fashion merchant, and so forth."[16] Another advertisement from the same year announced the sale of two counters, a glass panel, and an eighty-drawer cabinet suitable for "a tassel merchant, a merchant mercer, a fashion merchant, and so on."[17]

With publication of the *Encyclopédie* and other dictionaries in the 1760s, the fashion merchant's trade attracted sustained attention from the new self-appointed experts on commerce and industry (figure 4.1). Their writings emphasized the ties linking fashion merchants to the mercers' guild. The *Encyclopédie* article "*Mode, marchands & marchandes de*" explained that "marchandes

FIGURE 4.1 Fashion merchant's shop from the *Encyclopédie* (1777). The *Encyclopédie* illustration of the fashion merchant's shop emphasized the femininity of the space of the shop and the elegance of both clientele and employees. *Source*: University of Central England Digital Services. © The National Trust, Waddesdon Manor.

de modes belong to the corps of mercers, who can do the same commerce as them; but since it is very extensive, the fashion merchants have resolved to sell only that which involves the attire and clothing of men and women, and what is called ornaments and decorations. Often it is they who attach them to garments, and invent ways of attaching them. They also make headdresses and construct them like female hairdressers." The author added that "it has been a very short time that these merchants have been established and bear this name; it is only since they have completely abandoned the mercers' trade to take up the fashion trade."[18] Similar depictions of fashion merchants as a recent entry to the trade corps, with close institutional and familial ties to merchant mercers appear in François-Alexandre Garsault's *L'Art du tailleur*, published in 1769, and Abbé Pierre Jaubert's *Dictionnaire raisonné universel des arts et métiers*, published in 1773.[19]

Judging from these texts, fashion merchants' situation in the 1760s was akin to that of seamstresses a little over a century earlier. Just as seamstresses had done to tailors, marchandes de modes profited from the inability of their corporate rivals to meet rising demand from female consumers. The Parisian mercers seem to have responded by trying to bring as many of the women into the guild as possible, either by renting them privileges outright or allowing masters' female relatives to work as fashion merchants. This is similar to the solution devised by master tailors in a number of provincial cities, who allowed women to become adjunct members of their corporation—with no administrative role—after acknowledging that their efforts to discourage the seamstresses' illegal labor had failed utterly.[20]

Archival documents affirm the existence of close ties between fashion merchants and mercers. The marchande de modes Marie Anne Philidor, who accepted an apprentice by notarial contract in April 1761, was married to a merchant mercer.[21] Three additional training contracts, also from 1761, all involved the same fashion merchant, Louise Marguerite Haillot, who was similarly married to a merchant mercer. On February 5, 1762, yet another mercer, Jean Baptiste Dominique Vietty, appeared before the king's procurator at the Châtelet of Paris with his wife Marie De Larue to demand that an absconded apprentice return to complete her apprenticeship in "the commerce of fashion." His wife had accepted the girl as her own apprentice, at a fee of three hundred livres.[22] On April 25, 1762, Etienette Charles, widow of a merchant butcher in Dijon, appeared at the notary's office to sign the marriage contract of her daughter, Bonnard Sage, a fashion merchant, to Nicolas Fagard, a clock maker of the rue de Condé in Paris. The bride's witness in the contract was her sister's husband, Jean Dufey, a merchant mercer.[23]

Archival sources also document licensing agreements between fashion merchants and the mercers' guild. The financial statement of a fashion merchant drawn up during bankruptcy proceedings noted that she had paid 375 livres at midcentury to rent a privilege from the guild, much less than the 1,600 livres a man would have paid to become a master mercer.[24] Other individuals bypassed the corporation and came to private, technically illegal, agreements with master mercers. In her 1777 bankruptcy statement Marie Anne Defrenay listed three female merchants who worked respectively under the names of a merchant mercer, a merchant of gauze fabric, and a trader.[25]

To combat illegal workers, the mercers combined integrationist efforts with heavy-handed repression. In July 1758, to give one example, the officers of the guild, accompanied by a police commissaire, conducted raids on men and women who violated its corporate monopolies. Given the multiple forms of commerce their privileges encompassed, they caught up many different types of vendors in their net, including one woman "who peddled and exhibited for public sale different merchandise of flowers and fashions" and another "who peddled for sale in different homes diverse merchandise of fashions and gauze."[26] On July 3, 1758, the mercers' officers caught "a female individual who exhibited for public sale two new linen shirts, seven pairs of pockets, two pairs of embroidered cuffs, two pieces of batiste cloth, three pairs of cotton stockings, [and] six pairs of gloves and mittens" as well as strikingly bold women "who exhibited for public sale diverse goods of the mercers' trade and fashions displayed on a table standing on the street beside the door of the Châtelet prison."[27]

Ultimately, like the seamstresses a century earlier, fashion merchants succeeded in carving out a commercial niche substantial enough to win a guild of their own. After the brief abolition of the guilds in 1776, the royal edict that recreated the corporate system established a new fashion merchants' guild that was independent of the mercers. It was called the Community of Makers and Merchants of Fashions-Featherworkers-Flowermakers, indicating that it had subsumed the small guild of featherworkers that had existed prior to 1776.[28] The fashion merchants' statutes presumed their clients to be predominantly women, for whom they could make and sell items for the head and shoulders (figure 4.2), including hats (figure 4.3), headdresses, shawls, and capes. They also held the right to make and sell the decorations—made from ribbons, rhinestones, lace, and other fine materials—to garnish their clients' dresses. Like all other post-1776 guilds, it was officially open to both men and women.[29] Fashion merchants in the city of Rouen received an independent guild in the same period.

Lacking quantitative documentation on the trade, it is difficult to give precise figures for its size. Records from a royal commission that audited guild finances show that 452 individuals joined the new fashion merchants' corporation in its first six years.[30] The price for entry was three hundred livres, comparable to what they had paid to rent privileges from the mercers' guild. These prices were significantly lower than the one-thousand-livre price of membership in the post-1776 mercer-drapers' guild, but they were considerably higher than the hundred-livre fee charged by the seamstresses. To the several hundred mistresses of the guild must be added thousands more dependent workers. Rose Bertin was said to employ twenty to thirty workers in her shop, but the average for less illustrious members of the profession seems closer to one to three employees. If we put the average at two, that would give approximately one thousand workers for the 450 guild mistresses, to whom we could add approximately four hundred apprentices. These are likely minimal figures, given that not all merchants would have joined the new corporation, particularly if they had preexisting ties to merchant mercers and their guild. It is also impor-

FIGURE 4.2 *La Marchande de modes* (1746). This painting, by François Boucher, depicts a well-dressed fashion merchant displaying trimmings during her client's morning toilette. The merchant's position on the floor underscores the deference she proffers to her client, whose wealth is evident in the luxurious interior. The date of the painting suggests the marchande de modes was a well-known Parisian figure by the mid-eighteenth century. *Source*: © National Museum Sweden / Scala / White Images / Art Resource, NY.

FIGURE 4.3 Fashionable hats. This engraving from the *Magasin des modes nouvelles, françaises et anglaises* depicts fashionable hats of 1787. Hats were one of the most common items sold by fashion merchants. *Source*: Bibliothèque nationale de France.

tant to note that fashion merchants subcontracted a great deal of work to other artisans—such as seamstresses, tailors, launderers, artificial flower makers and embroiderers—and thus put to work a much larger number of men and women in a variety of different trades.

Parisian commercial almanacs name only a small elite of the profession. Of 337 mercers listed in Rose de Chantoiseau's Parisian trade almanac of 1769 and its supplement, 22 described themselves as fashion merchants or keepers of a "fashion shop"; 9 were women.[31] In year V of the French Revolution (1798–99), the *Almanach du commerce et de toutes les adresses de la ville de Paris* divided fashion merchants by sex, listing 24 women and 32 men.[32] An almanac of 1809 noted 115 fashion merchants in Paris, 56 men and 59 women. This group included 12 single women, 43 wives (including two partnerships of married women), and 2 widows.[33] Whatever the perception of the feminized nature of this trade, therefore, its elite seemingly contained as many men as women.

These almanacs unfortunately do not encompass the 1770s and 1780s when the Old Regime trade was at its height. It is likely that fashion merchants increased substantially in number from 1769 to 1789 and that the figures from year V of the revolution represent a significant decline, due to noble emigration and the economic collapse caused by war. In addition to the loss of clientele, traders had to contend with a wave of secondhand luxury goods castoff by nobles trying to raise cash for emigration or auctioned by authorities from their seized estates. The figures of 1809 show a recovery but one that was presumably not complete until economic growth returned to France around 1820.[34]

As we have seen, complaints about the swift pace of fashion, its extension to a dizzying array of items and ever more branches of life, were nothing new to France in the 1760s and 1770s. This was standard fare in *Le Mercure galant* and other printed sources a century earlier. The new periodical press of the second half of the eighteenth century suggests, nonetheless, that important changes had occurred, primarily in commentators' explanation of the origins of fashion, its speed, and the dynamics of its circulation. Late seventeenth-century writings on fashion acknowledged the influence of Parisian merchants in generating new fashions, yet they agreed on the paramount role of court aristocrats, who adopted new styles as a tool of distinction to escape the predatory emulation of the socially ambitious bourgeoisie. By the mid-eighteenth century the complicated amalgam of king, court, and city documented in those sources had shifted decisively toward the third element of the triad. References to the dress of the royal family and the court at Versailles were rare in the press, as individual innovations and rivalries among worldly women drew even closer attention.[35] Men's fashions in clothing and accessories continued to garner substantial coverage in the periodical press but more often ceded center stage to women.

Perhaps the most dramatic shift from the late seventeenth to the eighteenth century was the appearance of the marchande de modes, often credited as the creative genius and chief instigator behind the ever-quickening renewal of fashion. In *Le Tableau de Paris*, for example, the social commentator Louis-Sébastien Mercier credited fashion merchants with the central role in inventing and commercializing new styles. As he stated: "Nothing equals the gravity of a fashion merchant combining *poufs* and giving a hundred-fold value to gauze and flowers. Every week you see the birth of a new form in the construction of bonnets. Invention in this area makes a celebrated name for its author. Women have a profound and heartfelt respect for the happy geniuses who vary the advantages of their beauty and their face."[36] Like Mercier, observers were struck not just by the imaginative creativity of fashion merchants but also by the economic value they created by combining cloth, ribbons, and other trimmings into new and sought-after combinations. The October 1761 issue of the

Brussels-based *Journal de commerce et d'agriculture* contained lengthy commentary on the trade. The journal's editor was Jacques Accarias de Sérionne, a Frenchman who served as a minor royal administrator before being forced to relocate to Brussels due to losses in colonial trade. Accarias de Sérionne began the article by noting that "the whole art of the worker, known as the *fashion maker* [*faiseuse de modes*], consists of giving to different goods, which are gathered from diverse manufactures and used to make a single one, a new value that is found much more in its taste, its outward impression, in its novelty or caprice, than in its real utility."[37] He provided a long list of items designated by the term *modes*: "under the name of *fashion* in general is included mantles, fichus, palatines, etc., infinite forms of bonnets and head-pieces, necklaces, sleeve cuffs, bodice fronts, bracelets, dress decorations, those for skirts, tassels, bows, silk, gold and silver garlands, all colors of silk bonnet ties, lace, even garters, sword tassels, epaulettes, men's jacket decorations, etc." The production of this variety of items drew on an even more bewildering array of raw and finished materials: "To make all of these pieces of finery and ornaments, whose form and figure vary constantly under new names, they use solid and flowered gauze; *marlis*, [which is] another type of gauze; *milleret* [a fine-ribbed cloth used to trim dress decorations]; chenille; silk lace in black, white and other colors; jet; garnets; fake pearls; light silk fabrics; ribbons in all colors; cloth with figures woven of gold, silver, and silk, [and that are] solid, striped, flowered, à la crème, in heavy grain, in fine grain, or napped, etc.; [and] *comète* ribbons [which are a] thin, very narrow ribbon that is worked into garlands to make flowers."[38]

These passages echo the late seventeenth-century *Le Mercure galant* in their emphasis on the profusion of stylish items and the different materials from which they were made; what is new is the focus on the labor force that produced and sold the goods that constituted fashions, rather than the worldly ladies who consumed them. As the journal commented, "manufacturers, artists, are almost all masters of varying fashion from time to time." Accarias de Sérionne attempted to put a precise number on the value added created by fashion merchants in Brussels, commenting: "If one adds to the value that art has already given to the gold, silver and silk, that which is added to it by the hands of the faiseuses de modes, one finds here that the value that the handiwork adds to the raw materials, to bring them into the form that makes them *fashions*, is more than 500 percent."[39] Mercier, in a throwaway line quoted above, placed the figure for Paris for the work of the marchandes de modes at a "one-hundred fold" increase in value.

The result was a tremendous profit, especially for Paris, whose reign as the capital of the European fashion industry endured to the end of the eighteenth century and beyond. As Accarias de Sérionne noted, "the manufactures that furnish all of these raw materials of *fashion* are spread throughout Paris, its surroundings, and in some French provinces. But Paris seems to appropriate for itself the exclusive right to make use of them and to produce *fashions* not only for all the cities of France but in all those of Europe where women pride themselves on being adorned and well-dressed. Because one only seeks in this sort of merchandise that which is new, of the latest taste and the latest fashion; and it is Paris who decides: it is Paris that is in this domain the legislator of fashion and taste."[40] This domination constituted a major success for French industry and a very sizable source of revenue, which Accarias de Sérionne estimated at several million livres annually. French success was only limited by the commercial timidity of its traders, who had thus far failed to emulate the English model of establishing branch offices in other countries to facilitate exports.[41] He urged modistes in other European cities, especially Brussels, to seize the opportunity to undercut high French labor prices with manufactures of their own.

Such potential gains, however, brought with them heightened risks. Accarias de Sérionne acknowledged that the value conveyed by fashion merchants' exquisite taste "lasts only as long as the reign of the fashion that produces it."[42] If a product failed to sell while it was in fashion, merchants would be left with items in stock that were worth even less than the expensive materials from which they had been fabricated. This was a classic concern about industries that relied on fashion raised by Jacques Savary in the 1670s in *Le Parfait négociant*. Based on his own experience as a merchant mercer, Savary advised that if a piece of merchandise could be worn only during the winter months and a client wished to purchase it at the end of the season, "one must sell it cheaper than at the beginning, so that it does not remain for the following winter, because it will perhaps no longer be fashionable, and one risks losing from the purchase [of raw materials] to the sale."[43] The *Journal de commerce et d'agriculture* echoed these comments a century later stating that "without the aid of fashion, the most expensive and original items fall into disgrace and lose almost all of their value." At that point the taste and expertise of the fashion merchant alone could renew the value of the item: "The recourse of the worker then consists of taking them apart so as to use the raw materials in items made in a new taste or a new fashion."[44]

These comments on the centrality of marchandes de modes in the process of innovation found echoes in the renewed coverage of fashion in the periodical press that arose in the 1760s. Following Donneau de Visé's death in

1710, *Le Mercure galant* paid only sporadic attention to fashion and after 1731 ceased reporting on it altogether.[45] After two decades of relative silence, a new weekly periodical emerged in 1759, *La Feuille nécessaire*, which gave regular reports on the latest styles of garments and accessories. Its successor *L'Avant-courreur* (1760–1773) continued this practice, albeit sporadically. The *Journal des dames*, a journal targeted specifically at women and also founded in 1759, supplemented its high-minded focus on literature with occasional reports on fashion. By 1761 its distribution reached thirty-nine French and forty-one foreign cities.[46] A decade later, the *Journal de Paris* (1777–1840), the first daily newspaper in France, provided regular reports on fashionable clothing and accessories for men and women. Its reports were reproduced throughout France and neighboring countries in such titles as *L'Esprit des journaux*, the *Journal étranger de littérature, des spectacles et de politique* (published in London on a bimonthly basis in 1777), and the Liège-based *Feuille sans titre* and its successor *L'Indicateur*, which appeared from 1777 through 1779.

While these journals included fashion as a minor concern alongside other news, in April 1768 the *Correspondance littéraire* announced the appearance of a monthly periodical, *Le Journal du Goût ou le Courrier de la mode* that would be exclusively devoted to "everything new related to dress and decoration."[47] Like most contemporary periodicals, the journal was ephemeral and ceased publication in 1770, having suffered, perhaps, from the constraints on fashion imposed by the extended period of mourning dress following the queen's death in late June 1768. The first long-lasting journal solely dedicated to fashion was the *Cabinet des modes* of 1785, which endured under different names and editors to the Terror of 1793.[48]

Newspapers were not the only print media concerned with fashion. Marchandes de modes, like other retailers, ordered elaborate engraved trade cards (figures 4.4 and 4.5)—if possible featuring the arms of royal or princely patrons—to distribute to current and potential clients. In 1778 the first of what would total over four hundred engravings appeared under the title of *Galérie des modes*. These images of the latest styles in clothing and accessories, often created by well-known artists, were published over the next decade under this name.[49] Considerable overlap occurred among different genres of publication. In addition to its fashion reporting, the *Journal de Paris* publicized and reviewed fashion prints, philosophical and historical studies of fashion, and theatrical performances such as the pantomimes "The Used Clothes Seller-Fashion Merchant" and "The Awakening of the Fashion Merchants," produced at the Ambigu comique in 1782 and 1785, respectively. The journal also published satirical letters to the editor, ostensibly from elegant ladies, recounting

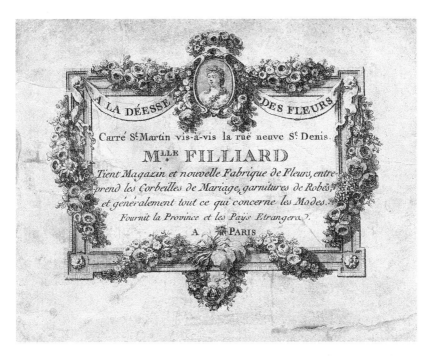

FIGURE 4.4 Trade card of Mademoiselle Filliard (ca. 1770–1790). According to her card, Madame Filliard manufactured and sold silk flowers, dress trimmings, and "generally everything to do with fashion." She assured customers that from her shop, "the Goddess of Flowers," she could transmit orders to the provinces and abroad. *Source*: University of Central England Digital Services. © The National Trust, Waddesdon Manor.

their viciously competitive struggles to acquire news of the latest fashions and the goods themselves. *La Feuille sans titre* not only reproduced fashion reporting from the *Journal de Paris* but also reprinted engravings from the *Manuel des toilettes*, a periodical that published engravings of hairstyles with detailed accompanying text explaining how to re-create each style.

The commercial press coexisted with older means of distributing information about fashion, in particular the fashion dolls that had long been sent across Europe and to the colonies dressed in miniature versions of the latest styles. Such dolls had travelled between royal courts since the fourteenth century at least and became more prominent in the eighteenth century as a means to disseminate the latest Parisian fashions. The January 17, 1711 issue of the London *Spectator* noted the following: "I presume I need not inform the polite part of my readers, that before our correspondence with *France* was unhappily interrupted by the war, our ladies had all their fashions from thence; which the milliners took care to furnish them with by means of a jointed baby, that came

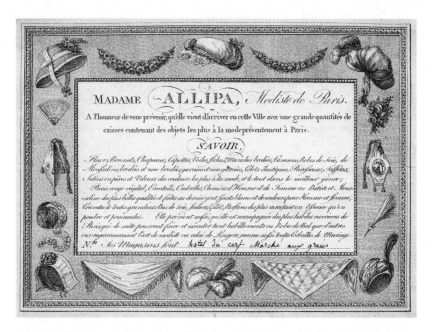

FIGURE 4.5 Trade card of Madame Allipa (ca. 1800). This card for a travelling sales-woman announced that "Madame Allipa, Parisian modiste, has the honor of informing you that she is recently arrived in this city with a great quantity of trunks containing the latest in Parisian fashions." The card listed the amazing profusion of articles she carried, some of which were illustrated on its borders. They included bonnets, hats, hoods, veils, fans, umbrellas, men and women's shirts, stockings, perfume, rouge, and dresses in many fabrics and styles. Madame Allipa also claimed to be "accompanied by the most skillful workers of Paris," who could execute all custom orders. *Source*: University of Central England Digital Services. © The National Trust, Waddesdon Manor.

regularly over, once a month, habited after the manner of the most eminent toasts in Paris."[50] According to the *Correspondance littéraire*, a collection of thirty such dolls, coiffed by the hairdresser LeGros, was displayed at the fair of Saint Ovide in Paris in 1763.[51]

Well-known fashion merchants continued to clothe fashion dolls throughout the eighteenth century as a form of advertising and as special commissions for clients. As Louis-Sébastien Mercier commented, "the famous doll, the precious mannequin, courteous [wearer] of the newest fashions, the *inspirational* prototype travels from Paris to London each month, and goes from there to spread its grace throughout Europe. It goes from north to south: it reaches Constantinople and Petersburg, and the fold made by a French hand is repeated in all nations, humble observers of the taste of the rue Saint-Honoré."[52]

At Marie Antoinette's request, Rose Bertin sent fashion dolls every month to the queen's sisters and mother to keep them up to date on the latest fashions. Bertin also created a life-sized mannequin in the queen's likeness that was sent to London and other foreign courts, just as a previous fashion merchant had devised a life-sized doll of Madame de Pompadour.[53]

The coexistence of dolls and journals through the second half of the eighteenth century suggests the importance of multiple vectors for the circulation of fashion information through the eighteenth century. Firsthand knowledge of fashion, either by voyaging to Paris oneself or by touching and seeing a fashion doll, only slowly gave way to the role of printed text and image. This was presumably why Paris was slow, compared to England, to publish fashion journals. Not only was the periodical press less lively in the French capital but Parisian men and women could obtain much more accurate and timely information by promenading through the city, paying social calls, and visiting the boutiques of fashion merchants and other provisioners.

Fashion in the Periodical Press

The burgeoning periodical press manifested diverse attitudes toward fashion, ranging from the satirical to the laudatory, philosophical, historical, and straightforward explanations of the styles of the day. It was not uncommon to find this range represented within the pages of a single issue. Despite all this diversity, the periodical press agreed, as early as the late 1750s, that the fashion merchant was the central figure within the commerce of style. *La Feuille nécessaire* thus lamented on March 12, 1759 that, despite its editors' best efforts, they had not been able to discover any new fashions worth reporting. "The most highly credited [female] merchants," they noted, "say sadly that our ladies are still hairstyled and dressed as they were a month ago."[54] This was but a temporary setback. Six months later, in September 1759, the editors could once more celebrate the "inventive genius of our artists of fashion who offer ladies every day new resources to lend value to their charms." The editors singled out Madame Daniel, marchande de modes of the rue Saint-Honoré, whose new bonnets were "perfectly good" and "very elegant in form."[55] Advertisements for Madame Daniel's work reappeared in the pages of *La Feuille nécessaire*'s successor, *L'Avant-coureur*, through 1761. From October to December 1761 the foreword of each monthly issue of the *Journal des dames* requested that fashion merchants inform the editors of their new creations, proclaiming that "they should occupy a place in the *Journal des dames*."[56] Dominated by praise of the work of female artists, writers, and scholars, these issues also publicized the work of male and female artisans and merchants, including Madame Buffaut, a fashion merchant of the rue Saint-Honoré.[57]

The actual fashions described by the periodical press help explain why fashion merchants succeeded in occupying such a central role in Parisian commerce. As the journals continually emphasized, the most significant elements of fashionable dress in this period were women's headware and the decorations of their dresses, precisely the items of dress that belonged to the fashion merchants' domain. It was not until the 1780s that women's fashion began to include regular innovations in types of dresses and new garments, such as the caraco, a short, fitted jacket formerly confined to working women that became the most popular informal style among women of all classes in Paris. Until that time the novelty of women's dresses resided mostly in the color and design of the fabric and the materials, colors, and design of the trimmings on the dress.

The same was true of women's headware. In most cases the new styles that fashion merchants introduced did not consist of wholly new forms of hats or bonnets but rather of new ways of combining and arranging materials and the innovative addition of flowers, feathers, and facsimiles of real-life objects. In January 1778, for example, the *Journal de Paris* reported on Mademoiselle Saint-Quentin's new *bonnet à la vendangeuse* (grape-picker's bonnet) topped with a life-like sprig of artificial grapes, noting that "variety in fashion consists less, as we know, in the form of garments than in the trimmings and garnishes that accompany them."[58] The December 11, 1788 edition of the *Cabinet des modes* echoed this sentiment, explaining that the reason it devoted so much attention to women's bonnets and hats was that "everyone knows that our ladies' inventiveness for bonnets and hats never runs dry, and that it is this aspect of their dress that they diversify the most." Acknowledging that women rarely created entirely new styles, they insisted that, "by their variation, they lend an air of novelty to the preexisting [styles] they reproduce."[59]

As with fashion merchant Mademoiselle Saint-Quentin's bonnet, the press frequently gave credit to merchants and artisans, and especially to fashion merchants, for inventing the new styles it reported. This credit consisted of general odes to the creativity of Parisian entrepreneurs, such as the *Feuille sans titre*'s prediction in June 1776 that "*nos modistes*" would soon come up with new creations to tempt elegant consumers away from the simple "hedgehog" hairstyle that required only a comb and a few ribbons and was thus ruining their business.[60] Journal editors, however, also developed privileged relationships with particular merchants, exchanging laudatory coverage for up-to-date and detailed information on their latest creations. Just as *La Feuille nécessaire* had its favorite in Madame Daniel, so the *Journal de Paris* championed Mademoiselle Saint-Quentin. Mademoiselle Saint-Quentin was mentioned at least seven times in its pages for creations as diverse as a life-sized doll outfitted in authentic Spanish dress, a hat that doubled as a folding hood, hats with artificial feathers, readymade dress decorations, a new type of mantle, a novel style of hat, a formal mourning bonnet, and a hat suitable for horseback riding.

The journal continued to advertise her wares regularly and almost exclusively for the next few years, noting the relocation of her boutique from the rue Saint-Honoré to the rue de Cléry in May 1779, still under the sign "au Magnifique" (figure 4.6).[61] A final notice appeared in the edition of July 4, 1780 in the voice of Saint-Quentin herself, stating that she was leaving Paris for the provinces and wished to thank the editors of the journal for "the goodness you have shown me and the faithfulness with which you have always lent yourself to all that could be useful to me by announcing to your subscribers the novelties that could also flatter them." She also expressed the hope that a public explanation of her departure would forestall the jealous and ill-spirited gossip it might arouse.[62] The journal editors apparently did not obtain a new informant, for no other merchant appeared regularly in its pages until 1790, when it began publishing a lengthy annual advertisement for a Dame Teillard, who maintained a shop in the galleries of the Palais Royal with a large stock of ready-to-wear dresses and other garments sold at fixed prices.[63]

In the 1780s the *Cabinet des modes* similarly favored only a few select individuals, including the fashion merchant Mademoiselle Rousseau and a mistress seamstress Demoiselle Tournon, to whose shop on the rue Salle-au-Comte it repeatedly directed readers interested in acquiring the latest styles of dresses and caracoes discussed in the journal. It is worth noting that, despite the lavish praise heaped on them, these figures were not the most celebrated members of their field. Rose Bertin, fashion merchant to Queen Marie Antoinette, featured heavily in the manuscript gossip sheets circulating in Paris, but she was scarcely mentioned in the fashion press. Her greatest rival, Jean-Joseph Beaulard, was the subject of a satiric ode published in *La Feuille sans titre* in March 1777, but he did not advertise any of his own creations in the journal.[64] Recourse to the commercial press was a novel strategy that must have seemed unnecessary and undignified in the eyes of a Bertin or Beaulard, who insisted on the exclusivity of their clientele and their preoccupation with orders from the court.

In addition to crediting marchandes de modes with creating fashion, contemporary periodical literature also claimed that they dictated its increasingly swift pace. Donneau de Visé's fashion reporting in *Le Mercure galant* was largely framed by the seasons, with occasional acknowledgment of changes in

FIGURE 4.6 The boutique of Mademoiselle Saint-Quentin (1777). This sketch by Gabriel Jacques de Saint-Aubin illustrates the shop of the fashion merchant frequently featured in the *Journal de Paris*. As the caption indicates, the shop was located on the rue Saint-Honoré under the sign "au Magnifique." The shop was dominated by a statue of Minerva, shown in the background. *Source*: © Louvre/RMN-grand Palais/Art Resource, NY.

the details of sleeves or color combinations within seasons. Fashion reporting in the second half of the eighteenth century continued to note the seasonal punctuation of male and female attire; for example, the *Magasin des modes nouvelles françaises et anglaises* (the new title of *Cabinet des modes* from December 1786) reported on the adoption of taffetas in early June and the turn to autumnal wear in early September.[65] However, the press also suggested a much more rapid cycle of innovation. Instead of issuing seasonal reports, the *Courrier de la Modes* of 1768 published on a monthly basis; by 1785 the *Cabinet des modes* appeared on a bimonthly basis, accelerating to once every ten days from November 1786.

Satirical literature insisted on an even faster pace of renewal. A facetious proposal for an "Academy of Fashion," published in *La Feuille sans titre* in February 1777, called for the academicians' daily rulings on new styles to be published in a thrice weekly "gazette."[66] A fictitious letter to the editor in October of that year explained that the 9,877 privileged hairstylists of Paris appointed deputies among their ranks on a rotating basis to scour the "boulevards, public walkways, dance halls, and spectacles" of Paris looking for innovative styles. A sketch artist accompanied each deputy to capture the new looks, which were shared at a nightly meeting in the cellar of a wine merchant. The next morning stylists offered their customers the results of the night's findings, paying a fee of two sous for every use of the new look within six days of its sighting, one sol during the following six days, and nothing thereafter, "the hairstyle being considered outdated after twelve days."[67] The postscript to the letter noted the fervor that attended the next issue of the *Manuel des toilettes*, revealing the piece to be a humorous advertisement for the journal.

We may trace representations of the chronological frame of fashion's diffusion through one striking example. On July 17, 1788, two ambassadors of the South Asian ruler Tippoo-Saïb arrived in Paris with their retinue after a journey from the Mediterranean port of Toulon. They began to appear in public near the end of the month and were formally received by Louis XVI at Versailles on August 10. The August 20 issue of *Magasin des modes nouvelles* declared an incipient vogue in Indian styles to be inevitable, a prediction it triumphantly announced as fulfilled on August 30 with engravings of the *robe à la Tippo-Saïb* and the *redingote à l'indienne*. By September 10, the London newspapers were reporting the *robe à la Tippo-Saïb* as the latest Paris vogue.[68] The ambassadors' visit continued to affect fashion, according to the *Magasin des modes nouvelles*, through September 20, when the journal printed an engraving of a woman dressed in a "harem robe" ("*négligé du serrail*").[69] By September 30, however, South Asian credit had apparently dissipated, for the issue of *Magasin des modes nouvelles* for that day refers to the latest "Chinese turban bonnet" and makes no mention of the Indians. In early November, the editors acknowledged: "it is no longer the Indians who give rise to fashions. Since they have left Paris, fashions only owe their name and their form to the taste and imagination of [female] Merchants, or sometimes to the taste and imagination of sectaries or benevolent authors of fashion."[70] Six weeks had passed between the ambassadors' arrival in Paris and the appearance in print of a woman dressed in the garments they inspired; in total, Tippoo-Saïb's reign of fashion apparently lasted only one month.

As the *robe à la Tippo-Saïb* reveals, fashion commented on the news and in turn it was news; a symbiotic relationship existed between the "novelty" of current events and styles in apparel. The swift work of fashion merchants allowed worldly women to comment in a highly visible manner on the events that caught public attention. Their choice of which events to recognize in hats and dresses in turn helped determine journalists' reporting on the news. A successful naval engagement, inoculation, the success of a new play, an exotic addition to the royal zoo, visits from foreign dignitaries, all were events memorialized by a brief fashion in hats and bonnets. Highly ephemeral, these fashions could shape public perceptions of current affairs and convey success or failure—in commercial, political, or social terms—on the individuals involved in them.

In most cases, it was the name attached to the fashion—rather than any particular content of its shape or materials—that mattered. Emphasis in the Tippoo-Saïb episode on the terminology of fashion was reflected in many contemporary sources suggesting that contemporaries cared as much about knowing and possessing the names of new items as wearing the garments themselves. Several articles in Denis Diderot's *Encyclopédie* thus commented on the constant neologisms inspired by fashion merchants, casting them as producers of cultural knowledge not just commodities. To maintain a reputation within worldly society, men and women needed to demonstrate their recognition of the current styles worn by peers; they also required this knowledge to interact confidently with prominent fashion merchants and seamstresses and obtain the items they desired. Indeed, names were so important that, as the editors occasionally acknowledged, the "newness" of a style often lay as much in its appellation as in its appearance.

The profusion and perceived extravagance of these titles provoked comparisons to the endless taxonomies of natural history. Jacques Savary des Bruslons's *Dictionnaire universel de commerce* of 1759 remarked on the abundance of items produced and sold by fashion merchants. In defining the word *coëffe* (or headdress), it stated that these items had an "infinite number" of names (figure

4.7). The author continued: "There is nothing that resembles so much the abuse of nomenclature in natural history, as that of the fashion merchants; the least little differences in the form of an individual makes naturalists imagine a new name or a new phrase; the least little difference in an outfit, alters or changes, for fashion merchants, the denomination of an outfit." Thus, he explained, they referred to different forms of headdresses, depending on minute variations in their style (which the dictionary described in some detail) as *coëffe à la bonne femme*, *coëffe à la duchesse*, *coëffe à la miramione*, and *coëffe au rhinoceros*.[71]

Marchandes de modes' role in French production in the second half of the eighteenth century was thus regarded as both extremely important and hilariously silly. Economists acknowledged their capacity to multiply the value of their materials many times over merely by arranging them in novel combinations; they were aware of how important the textile industry was to the French economy and by extension the finishing sector occupied by fashion merchants. However, they warned that any industry based on the perceived value of fashion was subject to high risks and bankruptcy. Satirists and dictionary editors alike echoed these warnings in their assessment of the cultural production of fashion merchants. They were struck by the cultural credit of fashion merchants who could dictate a constantly changing lexicon that came to constitute a new arena of competition among the worldly. The self-appointed duty of the fashion journals was thus to instruct consumers in the relationship between each new signifier and the minutiae of the signified (in new ways of knotting ribbons, contrasting the color of the lining with the fabric of a dress, on which side of the hat the flower was placed, and other details). Fashion merchants attracted attention in part because their trade resonated so strongly with contemporary debates over the source of value and questions about the illusory ties between what was argued to be "real" value and untrustworthy signifiers of value (like paper money, credit, flowery language, and fashion).[72] It was clear that France exceeded all other nations in generating wealth through luxury production, but the brisk winds of fashion threatened to topple this unstable edifice, bringing penury to thousands of workers and bankruptcy to the French economy.

SEX AND THE SHOP

A second form of danger associated with the trade resulted from another type of circulation: the alleged sexual promiscuity of its labor force. Long-standing stereotypes associated all female tradeswomen, such as milkmaids, fishwives, linen drapers, and flower sellers, with loose morals. Any woman engaged in public commerce was vulnerable to accusations of commerce of a more sor-

FIGURE 4.7 New headdresses and their names (1778). This engraving from the *Gallerie des modes et costumes français* illustrates the new headdresses of 1778, including the "Cradle of Love Hat" on the upper left, the "Hedgehog Coiffure" on the upper right, and the "Asian Pouf" on the lower right. *Source*: The Elizabeth Day McCormick Collection, photograph copyright 2013. © Museum of Fine Arts, Boston.

did nature. The luxury boutique of the fashion merchant attracted particular attention, for it brought women of the working classes into contact with elite customers. Since both men and women patronized fashion merchants' boutiques, the shop enabled and encouraged encounters between wealthy men and poor women. Commentators like Mercier and Restif de la Brétonne depict bustling boutiques whose windows served as much to display the coquettish young women working within as the wares on the shelves. They characterized female fashion workers not as innocent victims of sexual predators but ambitious schemers, eager to attract wealthy lovers. The satirical project for an "Academy of Fashion," discussed above, specified that the boutique run by the academy should have large plate-glass windows so the workers could be easily seen from the street.[73]

The archetype of this sly shopgirl was Madame du Barry, the royal mistress whose lowly origins shocked public opinion and did much to discredit Louis XV. In his scandal-mongering *Anecdotes sur Madame la Comtesse Du Barri*, Pidansat de Mairobert recounted the rise of Madame du Barry from subservient worker to royal courtesan via the fashion merchant's boutique. Mairobert explained that her mother was a cook who scraped together enough money to place her beautiful daughter in apprenticeship with a fashion merchant, Sieur Labille. According to Mairobert, it was known to all Parisians—including the girl's mother—that such a position was tantamount to prostitution: "This trade, very respectable in and of itself, has become so decried that a wise and prudent mother avoids giving it to a young and pretty girl. To introduce her to such a place is to expose her a great deal; properly speaking it is, as they say, to put her on the sidewalk."[74]

The extent of unemployment and poverty among female workers meant that such accusations were often based on fact. The reports of Parisian police inspectors who oversaw prostitution in the capital from the late 1740s onward contain the life stories of many young women kept as courtesans by wealthy men. The temptation to accept an offer of sexual patronage was great; a young woman could hope for a furnished apartment with servants and an allowance for fashionable clothing, fine food, and other luxury goods. Relations with male patrons were highly unequal, yet they contained some degree of reciprocity. Just as the young women relied on the carte blanche of their clients to acquire the accouterments of a comfortable lifestyle, so their patrons flaunted their attractive courtesans to enhance their own worldly prestige and reputation. At its heart the relationship thus represented an exchange of the credit of wealth and social status for the credit of ostentatious display (of youth, beauty, and sexual attractiveness), each side leveraging their own capital to tap into that of the other.

In some cases the benefits provided to the women also included a path back into legitimate commerce. According to a report by the police inspector Marais, a young woman named Madeleine Queru required her wealthy lover to rent her a license from the mercers' guild to practice the fashion merchant's trade and to supply two thousand livres worth of merchandise. With this assistance, she opened a boutique on the rue Royale. Another young woman abandoned life as a courtesan to become a shopgirl in a boutique on the rue Montmartre, telling her disappointed patron, according to Marais, that "all of her views turned toward a more solid establishment."[75]

The trade's reputation for fostering sexual license posed challenges to the credibility of its practitioners. No respectable merchant could afford to have her shop perceived as a den of promiscuity rather than an honorable place of business. Even if their worldly clients took an indulgent view of libertinage, their wholesale suppliers of silk cloth, lace, ribbons, and other goods were prominent businessmen who were deeply concerned with their own reputation. As Mairobert's comments suggest, the owners of the boutiques themselves seem on the whole to have successfully avoided the moral taint attached to their shopgirls. The fashion merchant as entrepreneur was often portrayed as the intentional or unwitting midwife to her shopgirls' seductive wiles (figure 4.8). What concerned the proprietor of the business was not her sexual relations with clients but the constant difficulty of managing credit relations, both with recalcitrant customers and demanding suppliers.

The Credit of Fashion

Fashion merchants were not alone in struggling to balance the assets with the debits in their credit accounts. Both contemporary commentators and modern historians confirm that day-to-day commerce in seventeenth- and eighteenth-century Europe depended utterly on credit in its wide variety of forms. In his merchant guidebook *Le parfait négociant*, Jacques Savary insisted that before opening shop a merchant must make himself known to clients and suppliers through his work as an assistant. Without prior reputation, a merchant could not acquire credit, and without credit, Savary intoned, "it is impossible that a merchant can subsist; because to say that one would conduct commerce from one's own capital, without borrowing from anyone, that cannot be conceived; there is no trader, however rich he might be, who does not owe and to whom nothing is owed."[76] Savary was well positioned to make this assertion, having

FIGURE 4.8 *The Fashion Merchant's Visit.* This painting by Philibert Debucourt depicts a wealthy client profiting from the distraction created by a fashion merchant to slip a letter to a female admirer. The merchant herself is innocent of seduction, but her presence enables the scene. *Source*: © Musee Cognacq-Jay / RMN-Grand Palais / Art Resource, NY.

conducted a highly successful career as a merchant mercer and served as principal author of the Commercial Code of 1673 promulgated under Controller General Colbert.

Historians have confirmed Savary's observation. As Craig Muldrew wrote in a study of credit in early modern England: "Almost all buying and selling involved credit of one form or another, . . . and it was credit, above all, which dominated the way in which the market was structured and interpreted."[77] In a study of commercial credit in France, Thomas Luckett similarly concluded that by the eighteenth century "credit had replaced money as the principal medium of exchange." Reliance on credit, according to Luckett, fundamentally shaped commercial culture and was the primary source of conflict within it. As he concluded, "For anyone who owned a business, credit was a daily preoccupation, an endless labyrinth, a constant headache."[78]

Studies of craftsmen and merchants in specific trades further demonstrate the heavy weight of credit in retail commerce.[79] Steven Kaplan has described the "great chain of credit" that ran through provisioning trades and "enveloped virtually everyone, at one time or another, from the producers to the myriad intermediaries and then to the bakers and to all manner of consumers."[80] Kaplan used the term *pratik* to describe the tie that bound individual sellers and buyers in a "most-favored client connection." The relation had advantages for both sides, for it "lowered the costs of search in the trading arena, attenuated the imperfections of the information system, increased the security of transactions, . . . and generally helped bring order to the market."[81] Similar dynamics operated in the luxury trades. Natacha Coquery describes the "war of attrition" that existed between aristocratic clients and their merchants, finding that a ten-year wait for payment was not uncommon.[82]

What was true from the retailers' perspective was equally true from the point-of-view of the working family. As Julie Hardwick writes, "borrowing was a critical element in making a living, whether to fund commerce, or to make up the difference between what their households needed to live and what they earned by borrowing. . . . The management of complex and fragile networks of debt and credit was a crucial element in early modern households, and their experiences, repeated hundreds of thousands of times, were central to the macro- as well as micro-economy."[83] Thus, from production to consumption, from the elite luxury trades to provisioning the basics of life, credit was the ubiquitous thread running through French economic life.

This reliance on credit, in turn, rendered reputation a crucial concern for all individuals and households; credit, as Craig Muldrew tells us, "referred to the amount of trust in society, and as such consisted of a system of judgments about trustworthiness."[84] Often seen by modern economists as evidence of market inefficiencies, relying on reputation was in fact not a backward or uneconomic practice, according to Phillip Hoffman. Instead, it was a workable "solution to the problem of trust—or in the jargon of economics, moral hazard—inherent in extending credit."[85] Moreover, in his study of rural land markets, Hoffman found that reputation constrained the powerful landlord renting his land as much as it did the lowly tenant farmer seeking to rent it. It created bonds of obligations that impinged as much on social superiors as inferiors. The economic importance of credit, and the primary role of reputation in obtaining it, in turn, gave a particular cast to conceptions of wealth. A man's or woman's fortune could be assessed as much in their credit standing within their communities as in the amount of specie in their coffers.[86] Given the endemic economic insecurity of the period—due to frequent wars, recurrent crop disasters producing volatile prices, government-imposed fluctuations in the value of coin, and other forms of default—it made sound strategic sense to seek wealth in the form of credit, a good reputation, and the resources they leveraged.[87]

Fashion merchants both confirm the literature on credit and provide new perspectives on it. The shared risks of fashion bound merchants to their clients in a manner that unsettled established hierarchies between trade and gentry. However, credit also set them at odds with their patrons, as the quickening rhythms of style clashed with the much slower pace of credit payment. The emergence of a new type of entrepreneur—both creative genius and artisanal worker—set into motion novel forms of reputation far removed from the sober, upright tradesman of the commercial dictionaries. The feminization of the trade—in its practitioners, clients, and the cultural associations of their productions—also imposed particular legal and cultural constraints on the exchange of credit.

TWO PERSPECTIVES ON THE POWER RELATIONS OF CREDIT

We may enter the credit world of fashion merchants by juxtaposing two sets of relations between client and merchant, the first between the fictional Madame Amelin and Angélique, the flighty notary's wife, and the second between the real-life Marie-Angélique-Françoise Taschereau de Baudry, later Madame de Bercy, and her purveyors. Dancourt wrote his play at the same moment that Molière produced *Le Bourgeois gentilhomme*, two works that juxtapose the social ambitions of the well-to-do bourgeoisie with the debts of the elegant aristocracy. *Le Bourgeois gentilhomme* told the story of a merchant striving to pass as noble, extending credit to an indebted aristocrat whose connections could open doors at court. *Les Bourgeoises à la mode* added a new twist to that plot with the introduction of women as agents, both of social masquerade and of commercial success. The play depicts an upstart bourgeois woman, the wife of a notary, who draws on the talents and credit of a successful female merchant to emulate the noble lifestyle; a side plot involves Madame Amelin's son, who uses his mother's money to pass himself off as a noble chevalier.

A member of the robe nobility, Marie-Angélique was socially far superior to the fictional Angélique. She was the daughter of an *intendant de finances*, one of only three occupants of this extremely expensive and important royal office, each of whom was responsible for one region of the country and reported directly to the controller general. And yet, while she occupied a much higher milieu of society and was far richer than Angélique, Marie-Angélique was no more reliable in paying her bills than her fictional counterpart. Moreover, her life was marred by financial scandals of the sort that court nobles found typical of the taint of the bourgeoisie, similar to those that sullied the reputation of her contemporary, Madame de Pompadour. We learn from juxtaposing the two Angéliques that over a period of almost one hundred years ambitious Parisian women drew on credit with their fashion merchants to craft the appearances necessary to maintain and improve their social position.

Act 1, scene 7, of *Les Bourgeoises à la mode* introduces Madame Amelin on a visit to her client. She denies having come to collect money but nonetheless produces a lengthy bill in response to Angélique's blunt question: "How much do I owe you, Madame Amelin?" (Angélique addresses her servants by their first names and with the familiar "*tu*," but she dignifies her fashion merchant with the title of Madame and the formal "*vous*.") The first item on the merchant's bill is "for the idea of an extraordinary headdress," an article that suggests both Madame Amelin's role in the creative process and the possibility that some padding has gone into the preparation of the memorandum. Angélique protests that the bill is "furiously long" and declares that she is too lazy to read the whole thing. Madame Amelin directs her to the bottom of the bill where the total of 310 livres is noted. Angélique instructs her chambermaid to go ask her secretary for the sum in coin, ending scene 7.[88]

In scene 8 Angélique puts her scheme in motion, beginning by commiserating with Amelin about the difficulties of her trade. Madame Amelin tells her: "I am owed more than ten thousand livres, of which I will never see ten pistoles [a hundred livres]." Amelin is also distressed about her son's fall into luxurious ways: he is spending time with beautiful ladies and gambling with noblemen, passing Amelin off as his old wet-nurse rather than his mother. The audience soon learns that he is also masquerading as a noble chevalier to court Angélique's daughter. Madame Amelin delivers the moral of the play, declaring to her client: "Alas! Madame, it's the way everyone is today. One wishes to appear what one is not and that is what leads many young people to ruin."[89]

After Angélique leaves the room, the maid Lisette returns to tell Madame Amelin that they do not have 310 livres worth of cash to pay her. She further informs the fashion merchant that even when Angélique wins at gambling she does not pay her bills: "Oh if she won a thousand pistoles, she would rather die than settle the least debt; money from gambling is a sacred thing, dash it, those are funds for pleasure that you never touch for necessities." As instructed by her mistress, Lisette puts forth a convoluted proposal in which Angélique will satisfy Amelin's bill not by paying her but by borrowing 600 écus from her (equivalent to 1,800 livres). The fashion merchant will deduct 310 livres from the borrowed sum for her bill, and Angélique will refund the whole at a later date. As collateral, Lisette proposes a diamond worth 3,000 livres. Madame Amelin agrees to this scheme and rushes out to fetch the coins. Left alone Lisette reflects sadly on "the character" of her mistress, "who dreams only of ruining her husband; she buys expensive, sells cheap, [and] pawns everything."[90]

Chapter 7 will return to the subject of consuming women and their alleged credit failures. Here let us focus on the character of the fashion merchant, who dispenses credit to her flighty clients to encourage their orders but suffers greatly in her attempts to collect it. The play suggests a well-developed social image of the trade, known to Parisians as early as the last decade of the seventeenth century. The wealthy bourgeois and noble audiences viewing its productions, along with the humbler men in the parterre, saw on stage an independent female merchant, with more cash than her clients and a son who aspired to enter the world of his mother's clientele. Madame Amelin is shown as an honest and upright if somewhat grasping woman, mortified by her son's shame at his proper social place. Nothing in the play suggests that the audience would be surprised by or unfamiliar with her character; instead she seems to represent a well-known type.

In turn, Madame Amelin may serve as a telling foil for the real-life merchants and artisans who supplied one equally real Parisian noblewoman. The circuits of fashion, financial credit, and credit as a form of influence and power intersected spectacularly in the person of Marie-Angélique-Françoise Taschereau de Baudry. Marie-Angélique was the daughter of an intendant of finances, described in contemporary sources as a man of "scandalous wealth" who reportedly left five hundred thousand écus (three million livres) hidden in his home when he died.[91] In 1734 she brought a dowry of four hundred thousand livres to her marriage to Nicholas de Bercy, grandson of Controller General Desmaretz and rising scion of the robe nobility. With a spectacular location overlooking the Seine river, the Château de Bercy (figure 4.9) became an important site of Parisian elite sociability during the mid-eighteenth century.

A wealthy and prominent member of the Parisian robe, the Marquise de Bercy spent a lifetime procuring expensive dresses and accessories to display her status. Her payments to fashion merchants and seamstresses are recorded in an impressive collection of purveyors' receipts, spanning more than four decades of her long life, held at the Musée Galliera in Paris. They begin with a bill submitted to then Mademoiselle Baudry at the time of her wedding in 1734 and end in the early 1770s. The dated invoices each include a total of the amount owed along with a list of individual orders by date with the price and details of the items and services provided. The records include bills from eighteen different purveyors, including four seamstresses, thirteen fashion merchants, and a corset maker. From February 7, 1734 to May 29, 1772, they total 10,350 livres

FIGURE 4.9 The Château de Bercy. Visitors came to stroll through the gardens of the château, designed by Le Nôtre, to admire its famous wood paneling and to attend the many balls, dinner parties, and theatrical performances hosted by the well-connected Nicholas and Angélique de Bercy. *Source*: Bibliothèque nationale de France.

for goods and services for her wardrobe (as well as some of her daughter's). De Bercy's seamstresses charged fees for making and altering her garments and for some of the raw materials used, while fashion merchants supplied cloth, ribbons, lace, and other goods used to decorate her dresses and for mantles, hats, bonnets, headdresses, and other fashionable accessories.

The bills do not include large-scale purchases of cloth used to make her dresses, the price of which would have far exceeded the sums noted here. They do, however, document the payments she made to have new dresses made and decorated and for accessories to garnish them, orders that she placed at an impressive pace as befitted the wife of a prominent royal officer. From 1735 to 1769, de Bercy paid her seamstress for making an average of eight new dresses each year. After 1769, aged approximately sixty years old, her purchases slowed down considerably, with only two or three new dresses recorded per year from 1770 to 1773, when the record ends.

De Bercy's bills attest both to her loyalty to favored artisans and her adherence to Parisian fashion. Her seamstress, Mademoiselle Gaillard, a mistress of the guild, served de Bercy for over thirty years. Gaillard's successor, mistress Saulmont, worked for her for more than fifteen years. Prominent among the thirteen fashion merchants she patronized was Marie Madeleine Duchapt, one of the most celebrated fashion merchants of the mid-eighteenth century, whom she patronized for eight years. While sustained over a number of years, de Bercy's loyalty to fashion merchants was much less long-lived than to seamstresses, suggesting that the dynamics of fashion influenced the choice of marchandes de modes themselves and not just their wares. The risks of the trade may have also rendered fashion merchants' careers more volatile and short-lived than that of seamstresses, who did not purchase supplies and thus faced fewer risks of bankruptcy.

The bills submitted by seamstresses and fashion merchants largely corresponded to the normative specializations of their trades. The fashion merchants submitted bills for mantles, scarfs, and other accessories and for the materials and labor involved in making the trimmings for dresses and skirts. One common charge is for a "*bavaroise*," a ruffle made with a thin, ruched length of fabric attached to the front of the dress from the collar to the waist.[92] Although the dates on bills for dresses and dress decorations do not correspond completely, there are occasional, suggestive overlaps. For example, on September 13, 1735, seamstresses Gaillard noted a charge of 6 livres and 5 sous for sewing a dress of white flowered cloth. On September 9 of the same year, fashion merchant Duchapt charged de Bercy 113 livres and 6 sous for a bavaroise decoration, three neck scarves, twenty-two aunes of ribbon, and several other head coverings. On April 14, 1736, Gaillard charged 6 livres for sewing a white silk dress, and on the same day a fashion merchant charged 3 livres for "the making of a facing," perhaps for the same dress. Four days later, on April 18, Gaillard charged 6 livres for remaking a dress, which would have involved removing the seams, recutting the fabric, and sewing it into a more fashionable style. On the same day fashion merchant Duchapt noted a charge of 11 livres for decorating a robe with a bavaroise and 2 livres for "regarnishing" an article; these may well have been coordinated efforts to refurbish a dress containing valuable quantities of silk cloth.[93]

To judge from these invoices, fashion merchants and seamstresses provided complementary rather than competitive services to their client. The bills provide no evidence, however, on how they coordinated their labor and who supervised the process. This is a key question, for it would have been extremely important to match colors, textures, and styles of decorations to the fabric and cut of the dress itself. Neither seamstress nor fashion merchant charged for the material of the dress itself, so a third key figure, the cloth merchant, is also missing from the records. At roughly five or six livres per aune for at least ten aunes required for a dress (and much more if worn over voluminous hoop skirts), the cost of silk would have been fifty livres at a minimum.[94] De Bercy's seamstresses almost always billed only for the labor involved in cutting and sewing garments, with occasional small amounts for cloth or other supplies. De Bercy's fashion merchants charged for the raw materials for decorations and accessories, as well as labor, justifying their much higher bills.

It seems likely that a new dress began with a visit to the cloth and/or the fashion merchant (or a request for samples by mail or messenger) and was then followed by a series of consultations among the three parties, with the seamstress perhaps called in for her opinion on new styles or ones that were hard to fit correctly. The frequent occasions upon which de Bercy purchased accessories along with dress decorations from her fashion merchants suggest that it fell to the latter to guide her through the creation of a complete outfit, from headpiece to gloves, jewelry, and neckerchiefs, all made or chosen to match her dress and its embellishments. Because only her business offered such full services, the fashion merchant took responsibility for the final look, leaving even the wealthy and powerful merchants of silk, lace, and other fabrics as secondary players in the creation of fashion. Given the stakes at risk for their reputation and their own expertise in current styles, the clients themselves would have played a central role in decision making.[95]

Extending from the year of her wedding to her old age, de Bercy's receipts reveal her continual reliance on credit from her purveyors and the power dynamics at work within credit relations. By modern standards the payment terms of her credit with merchants were extremely generous. Most purveyors presented her with an annual bill, meaning that they had to wait up to a year to be paid for some orders; in some cases the period was even longer.[96] For 551 orders charged to her account, the average number of days between the date the charge was noted and the date of payment was 605 days. Although the bills do not specify, it seems safe to assume that the date the charge was noted was the date of delivery, not the date the order was placed, which means that the delay between the time the merchant would have needed to purchase raw materials and employ laborers to begin making the item and the date of payment was even longer. Moreover, the records do not state if de Bercy paid in coin or with promissory notes. If she chose the latter, her purveyors would encounter the additional uncertainties and delays required to negotiate financial paper as well as any discounts incurred in the exchange.

There were variations in de Bercy's deferrals in paying specific purveyors, with a tendency toward longer periods of credit as she aged. From 1734 to 1742, de Bercy placed orders with the marchande de modes Duchapt on thirty-seven occasions. The average interval for payment of an order was 196 days or a little over six months. From 1735 to 1757 she placed a total of 166 orders with her seamstress Mademoiselle Gaillard (with orders referring once more to days on which she placed an order, rather than the actual total of items ordered). Gaillard waited on average 257 days, or more than eight months, to be paid. A fashion merchant named Mademoiselle Patte, who supplied de Bercy from September 1736 until September 1749, waited an average of 1,315 days or more than three and a half years. And for Saulmont, the mistress seamstress who took over from Gaillard in 1757 and continued working for de Bercy until May 1772, the period was 1,143 days on average or a little over three years.

One explanation for the increased delays is the expense of providing for a family. As Madame de Bercy had more bills to cover, including those of her grown children, it took longer to satisfy the accounts. Supporting this interpretation is the fact that many of the bills were for items for her daughter, who married in 1762. The family also faced the expenses of her husband's advancement in royal service. Interest payments on loans taken to purchase his offices would have constituted a heavy drain on family finances. Nonetheless, the deferments were hardly due to penury. Mademoiselle de Baudry's dowry reportedly totaled 400,000 livres but it took her 308 days to pay the 369 livres and 4 sous charged by Mademoiselle Duchapt for items in her trousseau. Fifteen years later d'Argenson claimed that her husband offered a 300,000-livre bribe in November 1749. Contrast this largesse with the 96 livres his wife paid seamstress Gaillard on December 18, 1749 to pay for orders delivered three to eight months earlier. Moreover, an order she received of 1.5 aunes of laces worth 6 livres and 15 sous from Mademoiselle Patte on September 18, 1749 was not paid until December 1, 1751, more than two years later.

The juxtaposition of the family's reportedly fabulous wealth with one, two, or three years delay in paying relatively paltry sums is startling to the modern reader. One reality their credit arrangements reflect is the paucity of specie within the early modern economy. For all their riches on paper, the family probably did not have large sums in coin readily at hand to pay the many furnishers who supplied them (Duchapt was only one among dozens).[97] De Bercy's dowry would have been composed of multiple elements (including annuities, clothing, jewelry, linen, and possibly real estate and expectations on family inheritance), with specie making up a minor portion if any. Similarly, although d'Argenson referred to the bribe allegedly proffered by her husband in écus (a silver coin), it is difficult to believe that he proposed to hand over such an enormous quantity of specie.

If it were simply a question of a shortage of coin, however, de Bercy might have settled her accounts promptly with a letter of credit. Instead, her lengthy delays speak to a culture in which commercial exchange was not a singular transaction but a process extending over time. The moment of settling accounts punctuated a long-term exchange between client and artisan, and de Bercy's accounts testify to the durable relations thereby produced. Another partial explanation for her reluctance to pay may lie in the dynamic of shared risk that bound patrons and purveyors together. The higher the client's account, the more the merchant's own survival depended on eventual repayment of the debt. Delayed payments on the client's part may thus have represented one means of eliciting loyal and engaged service from those who served her, effectively binding the merchant to the client's cause and increasing his or her stake in the expansion of the client's social credit. Thus, the very existence of credit could be used as a lever to obtain more.

Bound together they may have been, equal partners in risk they were not. De Bercy's tardy payments signal the deference she commanded from her socially inferior purveyors; another indicator of inequality was the heavy pressure she maintained on wages over time. In 1735 Gaillard charged de Bercy six livres for making a dress and between one and a half and three livres for making a skirt. Thirty years later Gaillard continued to receive the same rates. When de Bercy switched to a new seamstress in 1757, mistress Saulmont merited only six livres for making a dress and skirt ensemble. While prices for food and rent skyrocketed in Paris over the eighteenth century, the labor of a seamstress earned no more than it had thirty years earlier. This wage stagnation was even less favorable to the artisan than the findings of the economic historian Ernest Labrousse, who posited at least nominal wage increases in this period (against a 25 percent loss in real terms).[98]

What of the prices charged by her fashion merchants for the dress decorations and accessories they furnished? As a general rule of eighteenth-century commerce, merchants did not set fixed or published prices for their wares. Both merchant manuals and literary sources commonly claimed that prices for goods on credit were higher than on cash because they carried implicit interest charges. In this example, on the contrary, the prices were lowered after the moment of sale, and the merchant never received the amount she charged. Out of a total of 10,305 livres billed, reductions on specific items in the bills totaled 421 livres or 4 percent.

De Bercy's household imposed such reductions unevenly, with the seamstress Gaillard suffering the most. A summary drawn up by de Bercy (probably at the end of August 1745) clearly shows the pattern of forcing reductions as a regular part of business. In this document, which summed up her account with Gaillard for the years 1743 to 1745, de Bercy noted that for 1745 she owed 117 livres and 8 sols and had "removed" 12 livres and 10 sous; for 1744 she owed 104 livres, 13 sous, and 6 deniers and had refused 8 livres and 10 sous, and for 1745 she had deducted 12 livres from the 57 livres due. These reductions amounted to a 12 percent reduction in the bill. She had made two partial payments on the account, the first of 72 livres on January 17, 1745 and the second on August 27, 1745 of 150 livres; she paid the remainder on December 7, 1746. Gaillard thus not only had to suffer a significant reduction in her bill, she had to wait almost two years to receive payment on the orders she delivered in early 1743.[99] Since Gaillard was a seamstress and did not supply raw materials to de Bercy, the deductions solely targeted the cost of her labor in making garments for her client. At least one of the noblewoman's provisioners attempted to forestall such reductions in advance. Mademoiselle LeBlond wrote on the bottom of the bill she submitted for a mourning dress: "I hope that Madame will please remember that *étamine* [a light woolen fabric] is at 5 livres and 10 sous [per aune] and the rest at an overly modest price." Despite this plea, de Bercy's household refused 4 livres of the bill of 22 livres and 15 sous.[100]

De Bercy's provisioners might have been sheltered from the effects of these long terms of credit if there had been a routine moment when accounts were paid. An annual settlement day would have at least provided some reliability to the income they could expect to receive and a basis for negotiating with their own creditors. It would appear, however, that no regular schedule of payments existed. Over the consuming career documented by these bills, de Bercy's disbursements stretch over the twelve months of the calendar (figure 4.10). There were, nonetheless, privileged seasons, if not distinct days or even months, for settling accounts. If we combine January and December, they account for twenty-seven out of ninety-four payments or 28 percent. April through July together accounted for another forty-seven payments or 50 percent. If we take just one example, that of Mademoiselle Gaillard, we see the pattern confirmed: December and January account for 40 percent of her payments and April through July another 50 percent (figure 4.11).

De Bercy's settling of accounts thus corresponds, roughly, to her pattern of orders, which peaked in the spring months of April, May, and June, with a smaller spike in December and January. This pattern reflects the impact of the two most important Catholic festivals, Easter and Christmas. The summer months, when many nobles retreated to their provincial estates, represented a lull in both orders and payments (figure 4.12).[101] For de Bercy, it appears that neither her social calendar nor the weather imposed a substantial renewal of consumption until December.

Madame de Bercy was but one individual among the many thousands who patronized fashion merchants over the eighteenth century, and her case is placed in a wider context in the following chapter. What the two Angéliques

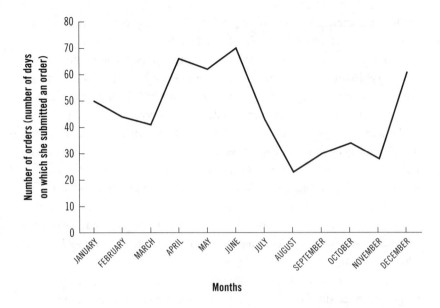

FIGURE 4.10 Madame de Bercy's orders by month (1732–1772). *Source*: Musée Galliera, Paris, France. Drawn for this book by Bill Nelson.

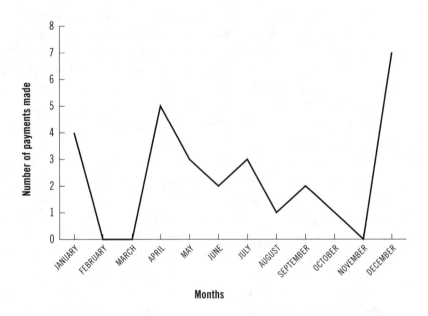

FIGURE 4.11 Madame de Bercy's payments to Mademoiselle Gaillard. *Source*: Musée Galliera, Paris, France. Drawn for this book by Bill Nelson.

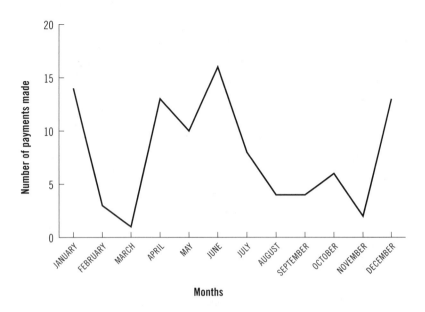

FIGURE 4.12 Madame de Bercy's payments by month. *Source*: Musée Galliera, Paris, France. Drawn for this book by Bill Nelson.

allow us to conclude provisionally, nonetheless, is that even in the most seemingly routine commercial transactions, money did not change hands in a straightforward manner. The price charged by a merchant was subject to negotiation and remained conditional even after the item was delivered. Customers did not pay any price, moreover, for months or sometimes several years after receiving the goods. The transaction, in many cases, lasted longer than the item in question, whose fashionability had expired long before cash changed hands. Finally, credit agreements apparently did not entail any regular payment schedule. Madame de Bercy's merchants seem to have had little means of predicting when and how much they might be paid. Thus, the tyranny of credit and its use by the high and mighty to exercise power over the weak did not just exist as a trope in the mind of Quietist mystics; it was the practice of everyday commerce in the luxury trades.

What merchants received in exchange for their submission was a long-term relationship with their client and the implicit collateral of their custom. It was presumably no accident that the individual who suffered the greatest reductions in her bills was also the one who served Madame de Bercy the longest. In a time of chronic un- and underemployment, such loyalty was a precious asset and a crucial source of reassurance to suppliers.

This daily cascade of borrowing and lending was shaped by laws and commercial customs, which contained general provisions governing borrowing and lending among merchants and specific rules on women's capacity to conduct credit relations. King Charles IX of France first established a specialized court in 1563 to hear conflicts involving merchants that largely arose from disputes over unpaid debts. In 1673 Colbert promulgated the Code de commerce, or Commercial Code, as part of a larger series of laws governing economic production and exchange. The law remained in force until the Napoleonic Code of 1804, which reiterated many of its provisions.

The code of 1673 clearly assumed the centrality of credit in commerce and many of its stipulations concerned buying and selling on account. Article 7 of title 1 of the code required all merchants, wholesale or retail, to demand payment within a year of delivering goods. Article 8 specified that artisans who sold on credit—such as "bakers, pastry makers, butchers, roast meat sellers, cooks, seamstresses, trimmings makers, saddlemakers, harness makers, and other similar trades"—had to demand payment within six months.[102] Whereas previous royal regulations counted the six- or twelve-month limit from the day of delivery of the last item in a client's account, the code of 1673 stipulated that the deadline began as soon as the first article was delivered. These provisions sought to limit the difficulties purveyors encountered in receiving satisfaction of their accounts, placing the onus on them to seek payment within a reasonable time frame. The code acknowledged that artisans as well as merchants sold on credit, but it assumed they had a more limited capacity for managing risk.

While accounts based solely on oral agreements needed to be settled swiftly, the code stipulated that any written acknowledgement of the debt on the client's part would retain legal status for thirty years, the standard term of validity for debt in the Old Regime. In consequence one commentator on the edict urged that "it is something that a retail merchant should carefully observe, to draw up and deliver his accounts, or to obtain from his debtors promises or obligations, if he cannot be paid for them in the time allowed by the ordinance."[103]

In order to secure the validity of their accounts, merchants had to have accurate information about what was owed to them. Title 3 of the code set out ten articles governing commercial accounting, focusing primarily on the manner in which merchants should maintain their account books. The first article required merchants and traders, both wholesale and retail, to keep a journal, recording all the details of their commerce.[104] This was called the *grand journal*, known in English as a ledger; merchants generally maintained this journal in alphabetical order according to the client or supplier's last name. Later commentators noted that in addition to the ledger, it was customary for merchants to maintain a *livre journal* or *brouillard* in which they recorded daily transactions as they occurred. The term *brouillard* (literally "fog") conveyed the unvetted nature of the book, subject to imprecisions corrected subsequently in the ledger. A third common type of journal was the *livre de caisse*, which recorded actual sums of money received and paid (as opposed to orders placed on credit).

The reward for those who followed the procedures outlined in the code was that they could use their books as evidence in the merchant court. This was an important provision since in practice merchants habitually did not require written acknowledgement of orders supplied on credit and often lacked explicit proof of their accounts. In light of the evidentiary weight accorded to account books, the code established a series of safeguards against fraud. Article 3 of title 3 required that the first and last page of merchants' account books be signed and numbered by the clerk of the merchant court. With regard to the daily journal, the law enjoined merchants to number each page and use them in strict chronological order, while forbidding them to leave pages blank or to write in the margins (all provisions frequently violated, as chapter 5 will show, by practicing merchants). A later commentator on the code, Philippe Bornier, also emphasized that the merchant's reputation within the community and the apparent reliability of his bookkeeping practices should impact the court's willingness to place faith in his books:

> Although private writings do not command belief if they are not countersigned, it is nonetheless true that the account book of a merchant constitutes proof against him, and that against debtors an oath can be demanded to supplement the proof of the book, provided that it be accompanied by the following criteria: that the merchant have the reputation of being a man of integrity and fidelity; that he writes his journal himself; that he has the reputation of writing nothing but what he is legitimately owed; that he mentions the cause for which he is owed; that he writes what he owes to others, as well as what is due to him; and finally that it may be judged by other circumstances whether he is a respectable man [*homme de bien*] and of good renown.[105]

According to Bornier, one measure of the merchant's scrupulousness was whether all entries in the ledger could be found in the daily journal and vice versa. Together, these comments emphasize the crucial role of reputation and collective judgment for according credit and the arbitration of disputes regarding it. The double meaning of homme de bien, which connoted both a respectable man and a man of assets, reflects the intertwining of personal reputation and economic fortune within credit.[106] The role of collective judgment was so important in commerce that it could replace the usual emphasis on written documentation in the courts. In commercial law a man's word, and the worth accorded to it by those who dealt with him, could rival the preference established since the sixteenth century for written proof.

These stipulations also emphasize the interweaving of public and private in the merchants' conduct. On the one hand, credit was vital to the public interest. The Commercial Code deemed account books to be "public" documents, and Jacques Savary insisted that "it is important for public interest that traders have books."[107] On the other hand, the law acknowledged a merchant's private interests and need for commercial secrecy. Article 9 of title 3 thus stipulated that merchants could only be forced to present their journals in court for cases involving inheritance, marital property, and bankruptcy. In case of a dispute between two merchants, if one party wished to use his books to prove a debt, the court could order their production. According to Bornier, such viewings took place in the privacy of the merchant's home, where the judges themselves would gather to view them.[108] Like the credit of aristocrats at court, a merchant's reputation represented the meeting point of public and private: the site where his private activities were recognized and judged by a broader collective.

Just as the private activities of a merchant had a crucial impact on the public good, so should public concerns inflect his private conduct. Savary argued that it was for the merchant's own good that he be obliged to maintain proper account books. As he put it: "if they have books that contain all of their affairs, they will have a greater knowledge of them and in consequence will trade more prudently in buying and selling their merchandise."[109] He conceded that there would always be those who "wish to live in disorder" and who would refuse to keep track of their expenses, especially "useless and superfluous" ones such as gambling, women, and wine. This refusal, he claimed, stemmed from fear that if they went bankrupt, their creditors would discover their incontinent ways and force a more responsible lifestyle upon them.[110]

Recognizing the primordial importance of early education to instill proper conduct, the first articles of the code of 1673 addressed the issue of apprenticeship. They began by situating apprenticeship within the framework of the corporate system, requiring merchant apprentices to complete the time of training required by their guilds. The code also recognized family as an acceptable alternative to guild surveillance, stipulating that sons of merchants who lived at home to the end of their seventeenth year should be considered to have completed their training. The code provides a rare glimpse into the knowledge and skills a finished apprentice was expected to attain, explaining that "those who aspire to mastership will be interrogated on their books and registers by double and single entry, on letters and bills of exchange, on the rules of arithmetic, on the aune, on the pound and *poids de marc*, on measures and qualities of merchandise, as much as is appropriate for the trade he intends to conduct."[111]

Women and Credit

The Commercial Code implicitly presumed the merchants involved in credit transactions to be men, and my use of the masculine pronoun to this point has mirrored the assumptions written into the code. It nonetheless referred on numerous occasions to women, implicitly acknowledging their significant participation in commerce both as household members and independent entrepreneurs. Before examining these references more closely, it is worthwhile recalling the legal status of women in Old Regime France, for these parameters framed the stipulations of the 1673 code. Although law regimes varied considerably across France, a common feature of women's legal status was the incapacity of married women. Wives generally retained ownership of the dowry they brought to marriage and of wealth earned or inherited thereafter, but their husbands held sole authority to manage those resources. Married women could not sign contracts without written consent of their husbands and thus could not engage debt on their own authority. Widows and single women over the age of majority (usually set at twenty-five years) enjoyed legal and financial autonomy in most, but not all, areas of France. Major exceptions to the rules governing married women existed for "public merchants," who held legal capacity for their commercial dealings, and for women who obtained a "separation of goods," a legal status conveying limited financial autonomy.[112]

Within these broad parameters, what rules and expectations applied to women in commerce? Commentators clearly expected that managing credit would be a vital aspect of a female merchant's business, just as for her male counterparts. In clarifying the legal capacity of the *marchande publique* in the expanded 1715 edition of *Le Parfait négociant*, Savary explained that a husband's creditors were not legally entitled to seize his wife's merchandise or the money owed to her by clients. This was because those assets were a "public pledge" that had served as collateral for the creditors who "have lent and everyday lend their merchandise, their money, and other things belonging to the trade that she conducts." He went on to insist that the wife's freedom from potential interference by her husband was essential to fostering the trust necessary for her to obtain credit for her business: "otherwise there would be no security in trading and exchanging with the woman [who is a] public merchant."[113] In Savary's view, therefore, it was the needs of credit that justified the status of marchande publique itself.

Indeed, not only did the law prohibit her husband from interfering with her commerce, Savary elaborated, the wife must not allow him to become involved even if she had no personal objection to his participation. This was necessary because the basic guarantee that a merchant's assets matched his or her liabilities could only be safeguarded if the reins of commerce resided in a single hand. Were the interests of the couple to be conjoined, wives might be tempted to assume commercial debt to obtain capital or merchandise for their husbands.[114] In driving home this point, Savary went so far as to contend that the credit the wife received was based on belief that she would "make use of them as a good father of a family." Just as the stability of the family derived from maintaining authority in the hands of one person (the father or his substitute), so the stability of commerce relied on the sovereign authority of the merchant. When she assumed authority over a business, the female merchant acted like a patriarchal father, much the way widows assumed paternal authority over their families. And yet, Savary was careful to point out, marchandes publiques remained under the legal control of their husbands for everything unrelated to their businesses. To protect wives from the possibility of coercion from their husbands (who might be tempted to seize their wives' merchandise or dowry to satisfy their own creditors), the law rendered husbands responsible for their wives' commercial as well as personal debts. Thus, the husband bore legal responsibility for his wife's liabilities but could take no active role in running her business or to prevent her from forming debt.

ESTABLISHING CREDIBILITY: SKILLS, EXPERIENCE, AND TALENT

If commentators agreed that female merchants required credit, what paths to obtaining it existed for *marchandes* and what obstacles did they have to overcome to obtain it? Family and social connections provided one crucial opening for women seeking financial backing for their businesses. As we saw above, many fashion merchants enjoyed ties to merchant mercers, either through kinship relations, by renting privileges from the guild, or through informal patronage. The prestigious mercers' guild would have served as a substantial source of collateral to potential creditors through its own institutional heft and the collective credit standing of its members. After 1776 marchandes de modes had their own corporation to fulfill this role.

To capitalize on family and institutional connections, however, fashion merchants had to establish personal credibility. Just like courtiers at Versailles, official titles, social connections, and wealth were important factors but insufficient for an individual to capitalize on his or her potential for credit. Studies of the rise of the English novel have argued that a principal function of the new realist fiction of the eighteenth century was to teach readers how to assess moral character, a crucial skill in what these scholars describe as an emerging credit economy, which required a new set of competencies in assessing the trustworthiness of others.[115] These claims miss the point established so well by Craig Muldrew and others that such readers would have been long accustomed to dealing in credit as buyers and sellers in a commercial culture that had functioned on credit for centuries. It is probably more accurate to argue that realist novels reflect lessons long learned rather than instructing callow and inexperienced readers. These studies are nonetheless useful in emphasizing the close scrutiny that men and women maintained over those to whom they extended credit and the watchful eye kept on minutiae of facial expressions, tone of voice, and body language. As they point out, the criteria for fostering confidence included demonstrated traits of self-discipline, honesty, integrity, skill, intelligence, sobriety, and a strong work ethic. Attempting to meet all these criteria was challenging enough, but the additional requirements for innovation and creative flair posed additional obstacles for aspiring marchandes de modes.

François Garsault's description is a useful reminder of the multifaceted nature of the trade: "They themselves call what they do a talent, and this talent consists primarily of constructing and garnishing headdresses, dresses, skirts, etc. That is to say to sew and arrange, following the fashion of the day, the decorations that ladies and themselves are perpetually imagining, which mostly consist of gauze, ribbons, netting, pinked cloth, fur, etc. But they also construct actual garments, like short capes, fur-lined capes, and court mantillas."[116] As this description emphasizes, fashion merchants needed intimate knowledge of the substance and price of materials produced in multiple locations by many different manufacturers. They also required practical skills in sewing and "arranging" decorations made from a wide variety of materials as well as cutting and sewing outerwear. Since they mostly sold loose-fitting garments, like capes and shawls, fashion merchants might not have had to learn complex fitting and cutting techniques employed by seamstresses, but they would need to be able to sew such garments together and also to stitch the yards of ribbon, lace, and other decorations to the dresses they embellished. Moreover, fashion merchants had to learn to manipulate the many different materials used to construct headdresses.

In addition to these skills, practitioners of the trade needed creativity and imagination sufficient to justify the designation of their trade as a *talent*, a term connoting artistic ability rather than mere craft skill. A successful fashion merchant was familiar with the latest styles and able to customize them for each client's needs and desires. To achieve acclaim, she also needed to create new styles and successfully impose them as the latest fashion. Succeeding in this endeavor required innate talent as well as access to specialized and up-to-date information: what was appropriate attire for which social events and which social groups; who was wearing what for which occasions. This must have been the most challenging requirement for fashion merchants and the most difficult for mistresses to teach. The *Cabinet des modes*, which began publication in 1785, claimed to include fashion professionals in its target audience. Until that point—and beyond it, for those unable to afford the substantial subscription price—this information was acquired through personal observation and experience.

We know little about how fashion merchants and their shopgirls acquired these skills and forms of knowledge. Prior to 1776 there was no fashion merchants' guild to oversee or impose apprenticeship, and there is no indication that mercers required formal training from those requesting to rent privileges. Notarized contracts confirm that some young women—or their parents—sought a degree of formal training in the trade, but they are extremely taciturn about the precise set of skills apprentices would be taught. Given the mixed nature of the trade—involving both producing items and conducting a commerce in them—it is unclear if apprentices were trained as artisans to make fashionable items or as merchants to trade in cloth, ribbons, and other items. In a small-scale business we must assume that the fashion merchant would do both. High-level merchants subcontracted a great deal of their labor, but even Rose Bertin kept a staff of up to thirty workers. A majority of her workforce must have engaged in productive labor, while the privileged senior employees greeted and assisted clients in the shop.

The pathway to expertise would have begun with apprentices helping to sort and store materials, cleaning the shop, accompanying their elders to deliver orders or obtain supplies, and also preparing food, carrying messages, and running errands. As she accomplished these menial tasks, she would gradually become familiar with the raw materials, finished products, and the culture of commerce in the trade. If the mistress fulfilled her end of the deal, she would gradually introduce the apprentice to more complex skills of making or selling fashions or more likely have her employees do so. An ambitious young girl with aspirations to open her own boutique one day would also need basic skills in reading, writing, and arithmetic. Because of the importance of keeping credit accounts, such skills were indispensable for establishing an independent business.

Historian Martine Sonnet has documented the growth of female education in eighteenth-century Paris, concluding that between 1760 and 1789 one
place in school was available for every three or four girls between the ages of
seven and fourteen.[117] It seems safe to assume that many prospective fashion
merchants acquired rudimentary literacy at school and that they constituted
an elite among the Parisian populace. Numeracy is a more perplexing question, since the curriculum of girls' schools notably lacked attention to arithmetic. Parish and charity schools for boys routinely included some arithmetic,
a field of study usually replaced in the girls' schools by needlework.[118] Fashion
merchant account books, discussed in the next chapter, testify to a limited but
shared set of mathematical skills, mostly consisting of addition and subtraction. They must have been able to do rudimentary multiplication and division
as well, for example, in order to calculate the amount of cloth they would need
for a client's order and to handle the complexities of French currency. It is unclear where and how they learned to calculate. Girls' schools may have done a
better job than advertised of providing mathematical skills or girls may have
learned from their mothers, who usually kept the books for the small family
businesses that formed the backbone of the Parisian economy.[119]

While some schooling was extremely helpful to would-be fashion merchants, they also needed forms of knowledge that could only be acquired on
the job. They needed to be intimately familiar with a wide array of products of
different quality, origin, and price, including an ever-changing variety of fabrics, ribbons, thread, rhinestones, feathers, fake flowers, and lace. This knowledge was complicated by the fact that each region of France used its own system of weights and measures. A good fashion merchant had to recognize the
quality and the defects of the merchandise she ordered, be able to communicate effectively with wholesale merchants, and calculate the costs of tolls and
transportation. To set up her own shop, several years of experience as a trusted
worker alongside her mistress was a crucial prerequisite, as Savary stressed repeatedly. No amount of savings or family capital could substitute for experience and the personal contacts with clients and potential suppliers.

Once a fashion merchant was ready to set up her own shop, she faced a new
set of constraints. The expansion of shopping in fashionable boutiques as an
elite pastime raised the bar for merchants in the luxury trades. They had to acquire shops in prime commercial neighborhoods (and sometimes move locations to accommodate changing tastes), decorate them attractively, and create
a favorable ambiance for elite leisure. Savary's *Le parfait négociant* provides
insight into the considerations that entered into the display of goods. One important question, Savary noted, was the physical orientation of the boutique. In

a northern city in an era with limited artificial light, sunlight entered the shop from different directions at different times of the day and year. Varying light conditions showed cloth to advantage or disadvantage, based on the color, the type and technique of dye, the weave of the cloth, and other factors. Choosing where and how to install shelves and which items to put on which shelf was therefore a tricky business. If it was impossible to rent a shop with a favorable orientation, Savary instructed, the merchant should construct wooden shutters to shield the interior from direct sunlight.[120] As a prospective supplier entered a fashion merchant's shop, he or she would be assessing the capital invested in furnishings and stock as well as the expertise demonstrated in how it was displayed. Clients would be passing similar judgments on the level of luxuriousness and comfort of the shop, the quality of the merchandise, and the social status of its clientele.

The shop was not merely a place to display merchandise and sell to customers. It was also a central site for information sharing of various kinds. During the day the merchant's shop was an ideal site for mistress and workers to observe and listen to clients of superior social and economic status. Such encounters not only provided news about the latest fashions but also about the social and financial vicissitudes of their worldly customers. After the shop closed it became a center of commercial gossip, providing a semipublic stock-taking of the state of the trade and individual credit ratings. Jacques Savary urged journeymen for wholesale merchants to conduct frequent visits to the shops of retailers who purchased from their masters:

> It is [how] one learns everything that is going on in trade; since it is in the evenings that the wholesale merchants go to collect and settle accounts with the retail merchants, one finds several of them together, and they never fail to speak of the things that are going on in commerce. One will say that business failures have occurred in a given city; the other will say that a merchant had obtained letters of respite or protection against his creditors; someone else, that some traders have received letters of protest for the payment of which they have been summoned by the consuls [of the commercial court]; that some ship has sunk in which this person or that was interested. Another will say that people are having trouble obtaining payment from these or those retail merchants; in sum, everything that is going on in commerce.[121]

The shop was thus a multifaceted hub of the information systems that drove both fashion and credit. To maintain credit from suppliers, merchants had to be available in their boutiques during and after the hours of business and make regular rounds of other retail and wholesale shops. The multiple roles of the boutique in the transmission of information highlight the different roles played by fashion merchants themselves and the need for merchants to adopt distinct behaviors and patterns of speech depending on their audience. Savary noted that wholesale merchants had to speak differently than retail merchants. The flowery language a retail merchant used to convince worldly clients would, he remarked, ill suit a wholesale merchant whose peers expected to hear a straightforward expression of the quality and price of his goods.[122] The situation was even more complex for fashion merchants, who had to learn to speak in several registers, one way with suppliers and colleagues, another with shopgirls and apprentices, and in an entirely different manner with duchesses and marquises. Achieving just the right combination of deference and confidence to speak to a noble client, or a prosperous wholesale silk merchant, demanded social acumen and experience. As we will see in chapter 6, Rose Bertin's acclaim resulted in no small measure from her audacious speech, which shocked and impressed audiences in her shop and at court. In addition to being able to cross class boundaries, fashion merchants had to traverse gender divides, appealing to a predominantly female clientele but purchasing supplies mostly from male merchants of silk, lace, and other goods.[123]

Skillful use of the body and attire were also crucial in this trade. In order to attract and maintain elite clients marchandes de modes had to fashion their appearances to inspire confidence in their honest and upstanding character as businesswomen and in their style and taste as designers. In a letter of 1776 the wife of the British ambassador to France, Lady Stormont, provides one glimpse of a fashionable merchant: "I sent this morning for Madame Montclair, a milliner. . . . She arrived poudree and frisee like the best drest lady in London."[124] An engraving from the *Galérie des modes* depicts an elegant marchande de modes delivering her wares (figure 4.13). Transforming their own appearance from common worker into stylish lady, fashion merchants served as living reminders of fashion's capacity to foster social ascension.

These points suggest the distinctiveness of this profession, at least with regard to the normative image of mercantile reputation as outlined by commentators like Jacques Savary and Philippe Bornier. Merchant manuals emphasized the paramount importance of maintaining a reputation for integrity and industry. To successfully project such an image required exercising strict control over one's personal life: making the right choice of a spouse, engaging in appropriate leisure activities, and carefully regulating consumption of alcohol and food. In the case of fashion merchants, respectability and probity were certainly expected by elite clients, but it was only one aspect of their professional

FIGURE 4.13 Elegant *marchande de modes* delivering her wares. The caption of this image from the *Galerie des modes* emphasizes the fashion merchant's elegant dress and skill in creating a seductive appearance: "A large hood of black taffetas with the brim turned back, trimmed with gauze, covers her head and hides a part of her charms from the greedy eyes of passersby; but her cloak is arranged to show her figure to the best advantage. She is clad in a simple dress trimmed with the same material, of which the flounce is also made, and lifted up behind in the shape of a polonaise. Openwork silk mittens, showing the bracelet: green paper fan . . . the little goose wants nothing." *Source*: The Elizabeth Day McCormick Collection, photograph © 2013 Museum of Fine Arts, Boston.

persona. Clients sought the gifted and innovative creator who could give them an edge in the ostentatious display that constituted one important arena of elite competition.

Celebrity

At the peak of the profession, the balance between old-fashioned mercantile integrity and the "art" and "talent" of the creator tilted decisively toward the latter. What was new about fashion merchants in the first decades of the eighteenth century was their ability to impose themselves not merely as a recognizable social type but as individual celebrities, recognized and discussed in the manuscript and print literature of le monde. In this period the first celebrated individual fashion merchants emerged who could acquire not just a reputation for honesty but something like the "*renommée*" discussed by Duclos in *Considérations sur les moeurs de ce siècle*.[125]

Perhaps the first of these fashion celebrities was Marie Madeleine Duchapt. Little is known about her today, but fragments in archival and literary sources suggest that she was an important precursor to Rose Bertin's stardom in her field. One source of information on Duchapt is the bills she submitted to Madame de Bercy. On October 25, 1734 Mademoiselle Duchapt, as she signed herself, furnished 369 livres worth of apparel to Marie-Angélique de Baudry on the eve of the latter's wedding. From December 1734 to April 1739, the fashion merchant signed bills to the new Madame de Bercy as "Loisant," signifying that her own marriage, to Martin Arnaud Loisant, a merchant and bourgeois of Paris, must have followed within weeks of her client's nuptials.[126] Unlike de Bercy, Duchapt did not enjoy a lengthy married life, for we find bills from her signed as widow Loisant starting in August 1739. From 1744 onward, Duchapt appeared with a new partner, Madame Boutray. By December 1747 Madame Boutray had apparently branched out on her own, submitting two bills to de Bercy from her boutique, A la renommée des dames de France. It was located at the epicenter of the Parisian fashion trade on rue Saint-Honoré at the corner of the rue des Bourdonnais.

In addition to de Bercy, Mademoiselle Duchapt acquired clients in the highest circles, including a mistress of Louis xv, Madame de Mailly. According to the memoirs of the Duc de Luynes, Duchapt travelled with Madame de Mailly to Spain to clothe the royal favorite for a Bourbon marriage in 1739. Luynes recounts that the king himself joined Mailly in good-heartedly teasing the fashion merchant and her assistants.[127] As with Bertin in the latter decades of the century, stories about Duchapt circulated in published literature and manuscript letters and resurfaced in memoirists' accounts in later years. Duchapt's celebrity in the 1740s and 1750s drew the attention of the philosophes who pointed to her acclaim as living proof of the frivolity of the day. In *Bagatelles morales*, for example, the Abbé Coyer offered a facetious set of instructions for an English lady, ostensibly intended to help her become a *petite-maîtresse* (an equivalent of the *femme à la mode*). Coyer wrote: "The graces nature has granted you, Madame, do not equal those of art. There are graces in dressing. Your dresses are in good taste, but they are not from Duchapt."

As Coyer suggests, Mademoiselle Duchapt's renown was so great that she was often referred to simply as "la Duchapt"; she seems to have been the first female merchant to achieve this distinction. In a letter of September 1752 to the salonnière Madame du Deffand, Voltaire used Duchapt to contrast the greatness of Louis XIV's era with the banality of his own age, declaring: "He was, with his defects, a great king, and his century was a very great century. What do we have today but la Duchapt?"[128] While the intimate pairing of Rose Bertin and Marie Antoinette caused controversy and scandal some thirty years later, for Voltaire it was the disparity of naming the fashion merchant alongside the Sun King that epitomized the decline of the nation: the peerless grandeur of royalty versus ephemeral fashion, a sacred male sovereign versus a common female merchant.

Twenty years later Voltaire remembered Duchapt more fondly, suggesting that his earlier reference was more satirical than damning. In a letter to the Comtesse de Saint-Jullien in 1772, he asked his correspondent to recommend the lace produced in Ferney to "the [female] merchant who alone upholds the honor of France, having succeeded Madame Duchapt." Voltaire assured the countess that the artisan who had previously produced the lace for Duchapt was eager to do the same for her successor and to bring twelve workers along with her to France to serve her. He clearly presumed that Duchapt was either retired or dead at that date but did not seem to know who had taken over her place at the summit of the trade.[129]

Jean-Jacques Rousseau was, predictably, less forgiving of the influence of fashion merchants like Duchapt. In *Emile* he argued for a natural and simple appearance as the most flattering and appropriate to a young woman. Duchapt, once more, served as the personification of frivolous fashion. As he proclaimed: "If a young girl has good taste and a contempt for fashion, give her a few yards of ribbon, muslin, and gauze, and a handful of flowers, without any diamonds, fringe, or lace, and she will make herself a dress a hundredfold more becoming than all the smart clothes of la Duchapt."[130] Rousseau here makes explicit what Coyer had satirically implied: that natural beauty should outshine the artifice of mercenary merchants. He also, disingenuously, uses the reference to a celebrated merchant to demonstrate his own engagement with the mores of his time and repudiate critics who mocked him as unworldly and gauche.

Duchapt's establishment did not escape the insinuations of precarious sexual morality associated with the fashion merchant's boutique. In book 7 of *The Confessions* Rousseau discusses the libertine dinner parties he used to attend at the home of a tailor's wife, Madame La Selle, in front of the cul-de-sac de l'Opéra. According to Rousseau, military officers as well as financiers and merchants attended the dinners. He further noted that "the passage leading to Madame La Selle's house also led to the shop of Madame Duchapt, a celebrated fashion merchant, who at the time employed some very pretty girls, with whom our gentlemen used to go and chat before or after dinner."[131] While this hint of libertinism was directed at her employees rather than Duchapt, the fashion merchant herself was the subject of a pornographic work, entitled "Sainte Nitouche: Ou histoire galante de la Tourière des Carmelites suivie de l'histoire de la Duchapt, célèbre marchande de modes." The text told a predictable tale of Duchapt's impoverished yet virtuous youth, her placement in apprenticeship with a debauched fashion merchant by an imprudent aunt, her first liaison with a lascivious nobleman in exchange for one hundred louis d'or, followed by an energetic career as a courtesan and libertine, and eventual penitent retreat to a Carmelite convent.[132] The story reveals, of course, nothing about her real life or actual sexual relations, but it does suggest that celebrity could be a double-edged sword.

Duchapt has survived in the works of philosophes, at least one libel, and in scant archival traces. She is an important reminder that the intensity of Rose Bertin's starlight has cast a shadow on other renowned practitioners of her trade. Bertin was a virtuoso in a field that provided unprecedented possibilities for men and women to acquire a new type of celebrity as artists and creators, whose talents led to influence and recognition well beyond that of a simple merchant or artisan. Bertin achieved a new level of celebrity by manipulating consciously the way her words and gestures were reported. With Duchapt we see an earlier phase, where an individual virtuoso merchant commanded the attention of the cultural elite who used her as the epitome of her generation but whose own words escape the historical record.

Fashion merchants emerged onto the Parisian scene in the late seventeenth century and rose to prominence over the succeeding decades. They benefited from the rising consumption of clothing and accessories made possible by the so-called industrious revolution; in turn they contributed to the increased pace of fashion and its extension to the middling and working classes. Emerging from the corporate umbrella of the mercers' guild, they occupied a position superior to humble seamstresses, who earned wages for sewing but were not considered "artists" and "creators" like the marchandes de modes.

Fashion merchants were privileged nodes in the information system of fashion in Paris and other cities. They derived new forms of cultural prominence in the mixed media that satisfied the thirst of le monde for news, gossip, and entertainment. Their expert knowledge of fashion, and access to materials and skilled workers, allowed them to endow goods with a distinctive cultural capital. They thus became indispensable collaborators to elite women who sought their help in competitive struggles over ostentatious display. The most successful fashion merchants could achieve a new form of celebrity with their work, a potential most dramatically epitomized by Rose Bertin, who will be discussed in the following two chapters.

Nevertheless, fashion merchants occupied a strikingly inferior position in credit dealings with their clients. Even the celebrated Duchapt had to wait for many months to have her bills paid. These delays, and the reductions in price and the irregularity of payments, all speak to a commercial culture in which elite clients took for granted the deference of the artisans and merchants who supplied them. From the very nature of their trade, fashion merchants were visible reminders of the fragile link between fashionable appearances and credit. With their skills they were capable of transforming any woman into the height of fashion. The wares that they carried through the streets of Paris could be intended for a duchess or an opera dancer, and the women who benefited from their services might be difficult to distinguish from each other, despite the close scrutiny of a Lucresse or Clarice. The best proof of the social magic they performed was their own transformation—before the eyes of bemused Parisian observers—from humble workingwomen into the semblance of fashionable and elegant ladies. They thus seemed to critics of the second half of the eighteenth century, like Louis-Sébastien Mercier, to epitomize the social blurring enabled by fashion and the frivolity of an age that judged by appearances alone. The fact that everyone knew their goods were sold on credit only heightened the sense of instability and illusion created by fashionable appearances. Another type of knowledge—that some of the courtesans they dressed had originally worked as shopgirls in fashion merchants' boutiques, including Madame du Barry, despised mistress of Louis XV—suggested that more than clothing could be purchased from the marchandes de modes.[133]

CHAPTER 5

FASHION MERCHANTS

MANAGING CREDIT, NARRATING COLLAPSE

On Saturday, May 5, 1781, the *Journal de Paris* announced that, by order of the criminal lieutenant of the Châtelet of Paris, police officials had applied wax seals to the doors, bureaus, and cabinets in the apartment of Marie-Jeanne-Victoire Moreau, fashion merchant of the rue de la Monnaie. In eighteenth-century Paris it was common practice to summon officials to secure the home and property of a deceased individual in order to protect the integrity of the estate for heirs and potential creditors. The *Journal de Paris* regularly published announcements of such sequestrations. Moreau stood out from the thirteen other individuals it listed that day, however, in that she was still alive. The lieutenant's ruling, the journal specified, had followed upon the woman's "absence and business failure."[1] Rather than being requested by grieving kin, the police action resulted from legal demands filed by creditors.

The brief entry in the *Journal de Paris* stands in sharp contrast to the prolix statements rendered by bankrupt merchants themselves, in which they recounted the anxiety, humiliation, and harassment that accompanied business failure. Indeed, Moreau's absence probably resulted from fears that creditors were pursuing her incarceration for debt. In August of that year she reappeared to convene an assembly of her thirteen creditors, hoping to negotiate a settlement that would satisfy their demands and allow her to maintain her business. At the outset of the meeting Moreau laid bare her dire financial straits. With over 71,000 livres in liabilities, she possessed only 43,000 livres in assets. To make matters worse, a full 35,000 livres of those assets consisted of accounts unpaid by clients, almost half of which she held no hope of recovering. She begged her creditors to forgo the interest and legal fees she owed them, along with one half of the principal, and to accord her four years to pay the remaining principal. Conceding that recovering half of their debt was better than nothing at all, the assembled group accepted these terms, promising to rescind the order they had obtained for seizure of her goods and promising not to request her incarceration. Despite these assurances, one or more of her creditors continued to take legal measures against Moreau, leading her to file a renewed statement of accounts six months later.[2]

This chapter focuses on fashion merchants' strategies and practices for managing the credit they accorded to clients and that they received in turn from suppliers. It opens by investigating bookkeeping habits among fashion merchants, including the unfortunate demoiselle Moreau, as revealed in account books deposited during bankruptcy proceedings at the Juridiction consulaire, the merchant court that heard cases of commercial litigation. We then examine the summit of the trade through a study of the credit relations of Rose Bertin, fashion merchant to Marie Antoinette. Although Bertin's account books have disappeared, information about her business affairs survives in statements she deposited with revolutionary authorities and in the client accounts retained by her heirs as part of their efforts to realize their inheritance.[3]

Bertin was a virtuoso who occupied the apex of her trade. The third section of the chapter places her activities in a broader context through a study of a larger group of merchants based on account books and financial statements deposited with the Juridiction consulaire at the moment of bankruptcy. Although by their nature the documents are biased toward failure, they also include prominent members of the trade whose businesses flourished before encountering difficulty from external circumstances. Many of them continued working in the trade after filing bankruptcy papers, an outcome the process itself served to foster.

Analysis of merchants' account books allows for close study of how they allocated credit to clients and how that credit was reimbursed, while their declarations of liabilities permit investigation of the credit they received from wholesale suppliers. Together, these sources reveal the gulf of inequality separating fashion merchant from client. Like Marie-Angélique-Françoise Taschereau de Bercy, clients routinely forced their fashion merchants to wait one, two, or more years to settle their accounts. When they did submit payment, they often failed to pay the full amount they owed. The merchants in our sample commonly had half or more of their orders unpaid at the time they went bankrupt. They might have survived these losses if they had charged a hefty surcharge on the materials they sold to their clients, as the contemporary literature accused them of doing. The best proof that they did not do so was that they often owed to their collective group of suppliers as much or more than the bills they submitted to their clients. This divergence attests to the weakness of their position between wholesale supplier and wealthy client.

Credit had multiple conversions in eighteenth-century France, from patronage relations at court to the influence of credit-worthy literary genres, a wife's credit over her husband's heart, and the ability to purchase clothing on account. The hardest domino to topple, it would seem, was the final one: the conversion of all these forms of credit into money placed in the hands of working people.

Keeping Track of Credit

FASHION MERCHANTS AS ACCOUNTANTS

Eighteenth-century commercial law recognized two forms of business failure. The first, *faillite*, concerned failure caused by external circumstances or misjudgment in which the entrepreneur had behaved in good faith. This was the term the *Journal de Paris* used for Marie-Jeanne-Victoire Moreau in tacit acceptance of her claims to be an honest victim of misfortune. The second, *banqueroute*, referred to a fraudulent act in which a merchant or artisan declared insolvency in order to mask assets from creditors. Faillite is closest to the English usage of "bankruptcy," and for simplicity's sake I will use the terms interchangeably in this chapter. None of the cases I studied involved charges of *banqueroute*.

The account books studied here entered the archival record solely because the entrepreneurs involved could no longer pay their debts and were forced to file for faillite in the hopes of obtaining a settlement with their creditors. The sources are thus biased toward failure and do not allow investigation of the many businesses that successfully navigated credit relations. Despite these limitations, these account books are precious sources, given the lack of alternative documentation for the small businesses that formed the core of the Parisian economy. It is also important to underscore how prevalent faillite was among retailers in this period, even among the most prominent firms. The frequency of bankruptcy and the fact that many entrepreneurs continued their businesses in the wake of faillite helps counter at least some of the bias of the sources. Even Rose Bertin was the subject of rumors of bankruptcy in 1787, which contemporaries found entirely plausible, given the frequency of insolvency among high-level enterprises.[4]

Based on the surviving documents, it is clear that fashion merchants maintained at least three types of journals. In their daily journal (*livre journal* or *brouillard*) they recorded in chronological order all of the orders they received and, in most cases, cash payments that represented full or partial payment of their accounts. Some fashion merchants recorded cash sales along with credit accounts in their daily journals, while others devoted a separate section or a separate journal to cash sales.[5] When they received payments, merchants usually recorded the date, the client's name, and whether the sum satisfied the account in full or in part.

With credit sales the merchants were generally quite specific not only about the client who placed the order but also about the details of the item sold. They noted the type of object as well its color, the materials from which it was made, and sometimes even its quality ("beautiful," "splendid," "fine," "inferior"). Cash sales most often did not include such details but recorded merely the date, the item sold, and the price. Because each cash sale constituted a discrete transaction, there was little need to recall particular information about the item sold. With credit, by contrast, it was important to retain enough detail to remind clients about the specificities of the goods they ordered when seeking repayment one or more years subsequent to the sale.

Merchants drew on information recorded in the daily log to create a master journal or ledger called the *grand journal*. The ledger was organized by client based on the date he or she first appeared in the shop. One double-sided page of the ledger was devoted to each client's account, with the orders written in chronological order on the left page and payments received listed on the right. Despite the dual entries, this was a form of single-entry bookkeeping, as were all the fashion merchant account books examined in the Juridiction consulaire archives. The merchants kept track of the price of outgoing orders and of incoming payments, but they did not systematically tally them against each other. Merchants with a large client base often created an alphabetical index to the grand journal, so they could easily locate each client's page or pages. (For clients with many orders, a second page would be commenced, but because the clients were organized by the date of their first order, the second page could occur much later in the journal).

Maintaining a legible and correct daily journal must have been a laborious daily chore; recopying entries from the daily journal to the ledger would have taken even more time, perhaps relegated to a weekly or monthly chore. To make recopying the information easier, merchants generally did not include any details of the orders in the ledger, noting merely the price and date. The Code de commerce called on merchants to keep their own books, but delegating the task to a clerk was common for firms of any size. Rose Bertin entrusted the task to her own nephews, while others hired professional bookkeepers.

Surviving account books suggest that fashion merchants had no conception of what accountants today refer to as "cost accounting." Cost accounting is a type of internally directed analysis (as opposed to financial accounting, which is used to convey information to other firms or the public) by which modern firms study the cost of producing items, including direct costs of labor, raw materials, and indirect costs such as overhead, debt financing, rent, maintenance, taxes, and the salary of the proprietor. Modern managers compare costs with prices to assess profitability and make decisions about what products to produce, how to make and market them, and what price to charge. They also compare the projected cost of making an item with the actual cost in order to determine the efficiency of production processes. Because it serves as a basis for future planning, cost accounting involves not just current or historic prices but estimating future prices. In modern firms such analysis takes place at regular monthly or quarterly intervals, and the system itself is frequently evaluated and adapted.

There is no evidence that fashion merchants engaged in any such analysis, nor should this be surprising, for cost accounting was rare in Europe until the second half of the nineteenth century.[6] Bookkeeping manuals from the seventeenth and eighteenth centuries were written by and for merchants, who traded in raw materials or finished goods, rather than for manufacturers. As a result, their concern with accounting focused on transactions that took place on the market, that is, between a supplier and a merchant or a merchant and a customer, not within the production process itself.

As we have seen, fashion merchants differed from the mercantile model in that they both produced and sold goods. Thus, they made complex choices about the different materials they used to fabricate headdresses, hats, and other items and then about how to sell them. Was it better to use this type of ribbon or another? Was it worth the risk to buy a popular style of silk gauze or feathers in bulk at a discount rate? To what extent could one trade quality for price when procuring lace or artificial flowers for a client's order? How did seasonal patterns of demand affect what sold best to which clients? If one launched a new style involving a larger quantity or higher quality of materials, would it be possible to charge enough to cover the expense? Or would it be worthwhile to accept a lower profit margin in return for higher sales of a successful new "fashion"?

The account books do not reveal any systematic analysis of such questions. Instead, they are almost transparent to the market in that when the merchant fulfilled custom orders she usually charged the client separately for each length of cloth, ribbon, or lace that she used and then added a surcharge for labor. This was the case for merchants from the most humble to the most illustrious, including Rose Bertin. This pattern of billing meant that it was difficult for fashion merchants to charge a very high markup because their clients could assess the individual cost of all the materials and of labor and then presumably compare the cost of ribbons, cloth, and other goods with what they paid to other suppliers. As merchant manufacturers, they might have profitably revised traditional mercantile methods of maintaining and, more importantly, presenting accounts. They did not.

This situation seems to contradict an argument sometimes offered for the lack of attention to cost accounting among eighteenth-century merchants: that it was unnecessary because their margin of profit was so substantial. As we will see below, the bankruptcy cases suggest, on the contrary, that fashion merchants often failed precisely because of insufficient profit margins.[7] What is so interesting about their accounting techniques is that there is no evidence of any attempt to master the flow of information about sales, credit accounts, or purchasing in order to improve the profitability of the business. They did not conceive of numeric information about income and expenditure in strategic terms, although they surely had a sophisticated tactical understanding of the need to acquire and manipulate information about fashions, raw materials, and credit ratings.

One explanation for these blinders may be that the purpose of their business was not monetary profit alone or above all else. Given the extreme delays in obtaining cash payment typical of this economy, they may have measured success in terms of maintaining their credit standing with suppliers of professional and household goods and managing the gap between outgoing and incoming credit so as to maintain a business, rather than in terms of revenue strictly speaking. In a premodern economy as described by Craig Muldrew and others, in which credit standing equaled wealth and reputation was paramount, it is plausible that these women wanted to be independent and respected merchants as much as they wanted to be rich merchants. They wished to maintain their credit so as to conduct an honorable and independent trade, support themselves and their families, and win public confidence and respect. As Jacques Savary explained, a good merchant, who united the qualities of experience, prudence, courage, and integrity, "will always maintain himself with honor in commerce and will acquire great reputation, which will be more advantageous for his children than if he left them with great riches."[8] Credit—in all its senses—could be more important than profit as conceived by modern accounting methods.

To attain this goal, the prestige accrued by creating a fashionable new hat may have seemed as desirable as revenue the hat would generate several months or years later. It was this cultural credit that kept the orders coming and convinced suppliers to continue to furnish raw materials on account. In this sense marchandes de modes resembled the courtiers of chapter 1, who calculated value in multiple currencies. Fashion merchants of course hoped for wealth and prosperity and needed to reimburse their creditors, but their economic and cultural context showed them certain strategies for achieving these goals while masking others.

Failing sophisticated cost accounting techniques, the Commercial Code of 1673 tried to impose at least some awareness of their financial situation on merchants by requiring them to conduct an inventory of all property, paper assets, and debts immediately following publication of the code and again every two years. It is clear that this requirement was followed only by the most successful and best regulated enterprises; I found no evidence of regular inventories among fashion merchants. For many of them the first systematic assessment of their assets and liabilities occurred only at the moment of failure.

For all the crucial business information included in the daily journal and the ledger, they failed to record much of the day-to-day life of the merchants' commerce. Only one fashion merchant in our sample followed the requirement of the ordinance of 1673 to record all supplies purchased on credit or cash in the daily journal. The others presumably maintained separate journals for such purchases, but these do not appear in large numbers in the archives. (It is possible that if they accepted their creditors' claims, they were relieved of the obligation of submitting those books.) Another type of account book recommended by Savary but largely missing from the sources is a journal to record letters of exchange and other financial paper accepted or issued and the dates when they would come due. I also found no examples of notebooks used to record payments to workers, either shopgirls or craftswomen. Most businesses employed a small labor force of one to three shopgirls, presumably too few to require a separate accounting mechanism.

There were also many elements of the business and its credit transactions that could not be recorded in any account book. For example, account books do not document the original contact between client and merchant. How was the issue of credit broached and by which party? Was there a discussion about how much credit the merchant would extend or when it would be collected? Did the merchant ask for any proof of solvency or base her judgment simply on the appearance or address of the client? What types of information regarding the credibility of potential clients circulated and by what means? In some instances merchants recorded information about a new client that helps us understand what they felt they needed to know, such as the name of the contact that had led the individual to their door, perhaps a sister or a neighbor. They also noted the street where the client lived or the landlord of the building. Sometimes the woman's occupation seemed to suffice with no surname or contact information.

Some notations are surprisingly terse. On April 21, 1787, fashion merchant Marie-Thérèse Gicquel noted fulfilling an order on credit worth fifteen livres from "a lady that I do not know." On April 17, 1788, she extended credit to a woman described only as "Madame who has a two-year-old child." We do not know if either client ever repaid the trusting merchant. In her bankruptcy statement Marie Denise Prévost included as part of her assets a number of accounts outstanding belonging to clients whose names she did not know.[9] Such statements, which are not uncommon in retailers' account books, suggest a commercial world in which identity could be established through personal recognition and social relations rather than formal criteria, such as full names or addresses. Personal contacts weighed heavily on economic exchange, and the demands of reputation within the neighborhood acted as a substantial lever for good faith.

Another element missing from the record is the placing of the order itself and any preliminary negotiations regarding it. The account books note the date an item was delivered, either on credit or for cash, but some orders must have taken weeks or even months to fulfill. How did the merchant remember the details of what had been agreed with her client? She must have taken notes as a reminder of what was going to be made. Did she fix a price in advance or was it negotiated upon delivery, based on the actual labor and material costs involved? These details are nowhere to be found in the account books. Also absent are references to any intermediate steps between the placing of an order and its final delivery: fittings, alterations, and substitutions.

It was this long and intimate process of agreeing upon the style and materials for a new headdress and then adjusting the results that Rose Bertin referred to as her "work" with Queen Marie Antoinette. As Bertin's insistence on the term conveys, the creation of new styles was "work," and it involved time, effort, and imagination from the merchant and, in many cases, from the client herself. While servants conducted many commercial transactions on behalf of elite women, the subtleties of fashion—and in the 1770s and 1780s the popularity of elaborate headdresses that represented the latest public events—often meant the client herself would have to be involved to obtain the best results. A lady's maid needed to know about the current fashions and styles and be able to dress her mistress's hair and care for her clothing, but only the lady herself could judge if a particular hat achieved the intended effect on her head.

One key element of these interactions upon which the account books shed little light was their physical location. Rose Bertin reportedly outraged public opinion when she declared that she would travel to Versailles for the queen but that all other clients would find her in her shop. Literary and visual evidence suggests that it was indeed common for fashion merchants to visit elite clients in their homes, a scene vividly captured in Boucher's *La Marchande de modes* (figure 4.2). And yet this was also the period when shopping became an important elite leisure practice. In all likelihood fashion merchants made strategic choices, as did Rose Bertin, visiting the homes of prestigious clients but allowing others to visit the shop. A fashion merchant's success could be gauged by the extent to which her boutique became an accepted site of elite sociability and a hub of the Parisian (and thus European) fashion information system.

Finally, although we may calculate in the account books the extent of unpaid accounts at any given time, the books themselves do not note such calculations. Moreover they do not show us the interaction between merchant and client over time, as the latter failed to pay the account and as the former either furnished new orders despite such lapses or refused to do so. It is clear from the outrage generated by Rose Bertin that clients were accustomed to deference from their purveyors. This expectation is palpable in a letter written by the seamstress Gaillard to Madame de Bercy in 1749: "The need in which I find myself for money has made me take the liberty of asking you for a 120-livre down payment. I count on your goodness and that you will not find it wrong [of me]." Gaillard was fortunate to receive a favorable and relatively rapid response from her client. It is striking that the seamstress feared that asking for a partial payment before the account was due would be perceived as unacceptable presumption, even though she had served this client for over fifteen years at the time she wrote the letter.[10]

ACCOUNT BOOKS AND THE PRIVATE-PUBLIC DIVIDE

If many aspects of the transactions between merchant and client are missing from the account books, they nevertheless unveil crucial elements of fashion merchants' commercial practices. One conclusion they permit regards the limited, yet sufficient, education the merchants had received. Assuming most kept their books themselves, the penmanship of fashion merchants ranged from excellent to very poor. They often spelled phonetically and used multiple spellings for the same client's names. They sometimes forgot or made mistakes about the titles of noble clients. They could add and subtract, but mistakes of addition and subtraction of relatively simple sums were not uncommon. Fashion merchants also varied a great deal in the regularity of their bookkeeping, sometimes neglecting to keep the daily journal for days or weeks at a time.

It must be acknowledged that the irregularity and errors of the fashion merchants' spelling are not unusual for the period. Men of the working classes continued to rely on phonetic spelling throughout the eighteenth century, a characteristic they shared with women across the social spectrum. According to Marie-Claire Grassi's study of eleven hundred manuscript letters written by noblewomen and men between 1700 and 1860, gender was a key factor in determining orthography. From 1700 to 1770 more than 90 percent of male letter writers used standard spelling compared to only 25 percent of women.[11] Dena Goodman interprets this study not as evidence of women's "backwardness" but as a result of gendered differences in education.

Another revelation of the account books is the merchants' high level of professionalization. Although their spelling was irregular, they kept regular and fairly precise records of their business. They also followed standardized accounting practices used by retail merchants in other trades.[12] When required to present their accounts to the Juridiction consulaire, they duly presented sets of books for scrutiny. Most had the discipline necessary to keep at least two sets of books and to transpose information from one book to another in a regular fashion. An instructive parallel is the journal of the New England midwife Martha Ballard, covering the years 1785–1812, analyzed by Laurel Thatcher Ulrich. Ostensibly maintained as a record of the babies she delivered and the payments she received, the journal contains a wealth of information regarding Ballard's family and social networks, her health, and religious attitudes. Ulrich concluded that Ballard's work identity and practice were deeply embedded within a rich family, community, and spiritual life.[13] In contrast, fashion merchant account books offer no indication of when the proprietor or her family members were ill, when workers quit suddenly, or when she was a victim of theft or malicious gossip. We know from the statements they presented at the moment of bankruptcy that such calamities regularly occurred, but they left no trace in the account books.

The professional lives of fashion merchants thus did not overlap with their personal lives to the extent of a rural midwife. It was presumably their professional demeanor and standards that allowed fashion merchants to obtain credit from merchants and attract the patronage of wealthy clients. However, one must not exaggerate the separation between the personal and the professional. Their firms were family businesses. In the statements they deposited with the court—if not in their daily account books—they detailed the expenses of illness, of maintaining the family home, and of caring for their children. This was a common strategy for all merchants, male and female, which served both to legitimate the consumption of assets and to project an image of the merchant as a good family provider, worthy of past credit and future accommodation.[14] But these details were only publicized due to the coercion of bankruptcy proceedings, when the merchant had already faced the humiliation of being forced to give up her account books. Intended for a limited public consumption—by clients, workers, and suppliers—the books were a key element of the merchant's presentation of a creditworthy façade.

Accounting for Rose Bertin

CLIENTS AND CREDIT AT THE PINNACLE OF THE TRADE

Like most merchants in eighteenth-century France, Rose Bertin ran her business on credit. Her wealthy clients rarely paid upfront for the goods and services she supplied, preferring to maintain an account that they paid in installments. In return Bertin herself relied on credit to purchase raw materials and services from a host of artisans and merchants. Despite her celebrated reputation, she was thus caught, as so many of her colleagues were, between the tardiness of her prestigious clientele and the demands of her suppliers. After her death her heirs boasted that because of her comfortable situation Bertin had never pressed her clients for payment or even demanded formal acknowledgments of their debts. Despite these proud claims, financial stability, for Bertin and other merchants, was a precarious attainment at best. She survived, despite rumors of bankruptcy in 1787, because the queen acted as a tacit guarantor of her liabilities. As this chapter attests, many of Bertin's colleagues were not so fortunate.[15]

At her death in 1813, the probate inventory conducted on Bertin's estate testified to the precise and exhaustive bookkeeping her business had entailed. The notary listed forty-eight daily journals or "brouillards," which dated from June 24, 1777 to September 13, 1793 and covered 9,420 pages. The inventory listed two additional sets of journals, comprising the grand livre, which had been drawn from the brouillards. A separate register contained an alphabetical index of the grand livre. A final journal noted in the inventory was a book listing her own credit accounts with provisioners.[16]

These account books have long disappeared, but a limited number of records regarding her business remain. Several years after her death Bertin's heirs hired lawyers to recoup more than 400,000 livres in unpaid accounts from one hundred and eighty-three clients, an effort that ultimately generated some seven thousand pages of documentation. These records consist of detailed copies of Bertin's accounts for each client as well as correspondence between the clients (or their descendants) and the Bertin family lawyers and internal memoranda. Together, these documents offer a crucial source of information about the fashion merchant's business, including the names of clients, the types of goods and services furnished, prices, and the extent of unpaid accounts. However, these

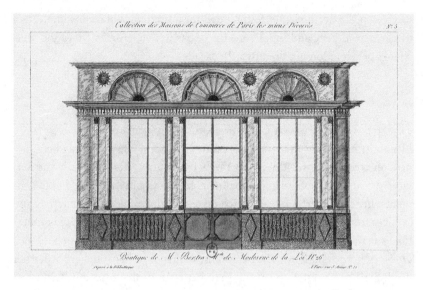

Boutique de M. Bertin M.lle de Modes rue de la Loi N.º 26

FIGURE 5.1 Boutique of Rose Bertin. This engraving shows the Bertin boutique as it appeared in the early nineteenth century, after her move from the rue Saint-Honoré to Number 26, rue de la Loi (now rue de Richelieu). *Source*: Bibliothèque nationale de France.

records only include clients whose accounts remained in arrears in 1813 and are not a reliable index of Bertin's overall clientele. The surviving memoranda also offer little insight into the rhythm of payments over time, and it is not clear if the documents contain each individual's entire set of orders or merely those that remained unpaid at her death.[17]

Despite these drawbacks, the surviving records testify to the wide geographic reach and high social status of Bertin's clientele, characteristics amply echoed in contemporary memoirs and journals. Bertin not only served the French queen and court noblewomen but also the royal families of Russia, Sweden, Spain, and Portugal and nobles in many European countries as well as wealthy Americans. Bertin's clientele was also impressively large in size. Her unpaid accounts alone included almost two hundred individuals, much less than the over one thousand clients she herself claimed to serve. A letter from 1785 written by John Adam's daughter about a visit to Bertin's Parisian boutique (figure 5.1) while traveling in France underlines these points. As she wrote: "We went to see Mademoiselle Bertang, who is milliner to the Queen of France and to all Europe. She is now employed in making clothes for l'infante d'Espagne, and the Princess of Portugal. . . . She is the first milliner in Europe; every year she sends the fashions to all parts of the world. We went to a large room, where there were twenty girls at work; the hotel seemed to be large and full."[18] At its height in the 1780s, Bertin's commerce must have been among the most important retail operations in France.[19]

To these distinguished clients Bertin furnished a highly diverse array of goods and services. According to surviving records, she billed her clients for at least 210 different items, including both finished goods and the many different types of textiles, ribbons, feathers, and other materials she used to make custom orders. Judging from her accounts, Bertin did not routinely supply her clients with new dresses, but she did make an exception for the lavish dresses worn for a client's first presentation at court. For the most part, she concentrated on the much more lucrative task of furnishing headwear—consisting of custom-made hats, poufs, and bonnets, among other items—and decorating dresses with elaborate ruffles, swags, and trimmings in ribbon, lace, rhinestones, and gold or silver cloth. A third element of her commerce was the sale of outerwear, such as finished shawls, neckerchiefs, and mantles. To complete the ensembles she devised for clients, Bertin supplied jewelry and many different kinds of accessories.

In addition to goods, Bertin charged clients for a number of services, including labor costs for making dress decorations and headwear as well as for mending, altering, and cleaning their goods. She also passed on charges from a number of different artisans, including seamstresses to whom she occasionally subcontracted the work of dressmaking. She does not mention other artisans in her bills for making headwear or dress decorations, suggesting that her own employees performed this labor. For her many non-Parisian clients, Bertin took charge of sending finished orders to other cities and countries.

Although she focused on items of the female wardrobe, not all of her clients were women. Men patronized Bertin for handkerchiefs, lace cuffs, and sword hilt tassels for themselves and stylish hats and shawls for their wives, daughters, or mistresses. They also appear in the records as male servants of royal and noble households tending to their mistresses' orders.[20] What commentators like Louis-Sébastien Mercier presented as an all-female world thus included men as consumers, payers, and intermediaries.

Judging from these accounts, the pace of orders varied a great deal over time. Some clients placed only one or two orders with Bertin, while others made orders several times a year over many years. The Baron Duplouy was a regular customer whose account extended from December 24, 1778 to May 30, 1791. During these thirteen years, Bertin listed orders on nineteen separate dates. Altogether, she charged the baron for a total of ninety-five separate items or services, covering at least twenty-five different types of objects. All of his orders were for the female wardrobe, three specifically for a female child. There is no indication of the woman or women for whom the garments and accessories were intended, although many were custom-made. By May 1791 the baron's bill amounted to 3,699 livres and 13 sols. Bertin recorded just one payment toward the bill in thirteen years, a sum of 12 livres on December 19, 1780. The remaining 3,687 livres remained unpaid. Friendly relations between the two apparently continued, to judge by an 1808 letter in which the baron informed Bertin that he had sent a barrel of sassafras tea to her country estate, having heard from her companion that she was partial to the beverage.[21]

Bertin's most important customer both in terms of prestige and the number and price of orders was Queen Marie Antoinette. Records from the royal household reveal that the queen ordered 87,597 livres worth of goods and services from Bertin in the year 1785 alone. This figure declined to 60,225 livres in 1787 and 61,992 in 1788, as the queen's household retrenched in response to financial crisis. The queen's expenditure on clothing shrank even further during the French Revolution, as her account in Bertin's collection reveals. Beginning in January 1791 and ending in August 1792, the queen's account for this twenty-month period equaled only 53,035 livres (a still sizeable sum considering the queen's virtual imprisonment from June 1791 onward).

Bertin's records also reveal that the queen was no more reliable than any other aristocratic lady in paying her bills. In the quarter of October 1791 Bertin included 3,390 livres for three years of interest at 5 percent on 22,600 livres due from the year 1788. She also charged 4,600 livres interest on more than 46,000 livres due from 1789. A note at the bottom of the page indicated that the queen's household had agreed to pay only 4,000 livres in interest. Bertin's ability to impose interest payments is rare among the fashion merchants in the sample, who routinely suffered reductions of their bills but did not charge upfront interest fees. Bertin also levied interest on other princely clients. For example, on April 26, 1777, the Russian Princesse de Baratinsky signed a statement of account acknowledging a substantial debt to Bertin: "I recognize owing to Mademoiselle Bertin the sum of 14,174 livres that I promise to pay to her order on May 1, 1777 without interest; in case I do not reimburse my letter on the due date, interest will commence from that day at 6 percent."[22] Based on surviving records, Bertin received neither the interest nor the remaining principal.

Despite her tardiness, the queen's household was not entirely negligent. Since the total charge for 1788 was 61,992 livres, we may conclude that her household had in fact paid 39,392 livres or 63 percent of her bill. Bertin thus received a significant proportion of her bill, enough to meet pressing expenses and reassure her creditors. Moreover, if she had added a surcharge to her fees in anticipation of such partial payments, her losses may have been considerably less.

Records from the royal household also confirm anecdotal reports that Bertin was the most important of all the artisans and merchants who furnished the queen. In 1785 Marie Antoinette ran up expenses of 258,002 livres for her wardrobe. She owed this money to fifty-nine individuals or groups who furnished raw materials, clothing, and accessories or who repaired and maintained her clothing. Bertin's share alone represented fully one-third of the total expenditure. In 1787 the total was 217,188 livres for sixty-one individuals, giving Bertin 28 percent; in 1788 the total was 190,721 livres for fifty-four individuals, giving Bertin 32 percent. Those who viewed Bertin as the chief culprit in encouraging the queen's lavish tastes were thus quite right in their understanding of the fashion merchant's preeminent role in furnishing the queen. They were also correct in suspecting that the queen's expenses far outstripped her income. As the queen's annual budget for her wardrobe was 120,000 livres, her spending on clothing and accessories represented a large excess expenditure each year.[23]

These figures may be compared to those of Mademoiselle Eloffe, another court fashion merchant. According to registers published in the late nineteenth century by the Comte de Reiset, Eloffe worked for 262 clients between 1787 and 1793. Her first and third most important customers were two daughters of Louis XV, Princesses Adelaïde and Victoire, whom she billed 76,427 livres and 57,700 respectively over this period. The queen occupied second place at 72,547 livres, enough to incur the jealousy of Bertin but not to rival her standing as the most important royal fashion merchant. Fourth place belonged to the Comtesse d'Artois, the wife of Louis XVI's younger brother, the future king Charles X, whom Eloffe billed for a total of 43,284 livres of goods and services. Below this level the charges dropped off sharply. The next highest spenders—the Comtesses de Luxembourg and Chatellux and the Marquise de Donnissan—had bills ranging from 8,000 to 9,000 livres each. Altogether, women identified by Reiset as belonging to the royal court numbered 145 clients versus an additional 117 noble and nonnoble women outside the court. Even among the former, their orders did not approach those of the royal family; almost a third (55) purchased less than 100 livres worth of goods. Her bills submitted to the royal family and the court totaled 364,623 livres, two-thirds of which belonged to the top four clients. These figures do not mean, however, that court ladies did not spend a great deal on fashions; Eloffe must have been extremely busy working for her main clients, forcing court noblewomen to turn to marchandes who had more time to satisfy their needs.[24]

Eloffe's published journal, unfortunately, does not provide any information on payment of her accounts. It does confirm, however, the vast range of materials sold by fashion merchants, the subject of awe and derision among observers. In his list of terms named in the journal, Reiset includes 189 different types of finished goods or materials, including four types of bonnets and seven sorts of neckerchiefs (fichus).[25]

SUPPLYING MADEMOISELLE BERTIN

Given the tardy payment of her accounts, Bertin in turn relied heavily on credit from her own workers, subcontracted artisans, and suppliers. She emphasized this dependence in a petition addressed to revolutionary officials justifying her departure from France as necessary to raise money to meet her debts. In a document written at the end of 1793, Bertin claimed to have paid more than 450,000 livres to creditors since her departure in July 1792. Included in this sum were almost 300,000 livres to satisfy promissory notes, 66,625 livres to a single lace merchant, and another 73,504 livres paid to "different workers."[26]

The detailed table Bertin provided outlining these payments imparts further detail about her credit relations. We may divide her creditors into three types: those who furnished their labor for products she sold to clients, those who supplied raw materials, and those who provided ancillary services. Bertin's table included forty individuals in the first category. They included three of her own workers and thirty-seven other artisans divided into seventeen trades, such as seamstresses, tailors, linen workers, and embroiderers. In the second category we find thirty-nine merchants or merchant manufacturers specified as belonging to eleven different branches of commerce (ribbons, lace, cloth, feathers, and so on). The third category comprised twenty-seven individuals in seventeen different occupations, including a notary and artisans who worked in the construction, furnishing, and equine trades. The amounts she owed varied a great deal. She listed some 20,070 livres paid to workers and artisans in the garment trades, more than 41,221 to merchants, and almost 10,000 livres to ancillary artisans and professionals.[27]

As these figures reveal, Bertin's business was the center of a complex web of artisans, merchants, and service providers, all of whom accorded her credit for their goods and services. Her role thus extended far beyond that of fashion visionary; she acted as an organizer and intermediary, bringing together raw materials and specialized artisans to furnish a large array of luxury goods, often geared specifically to individual clients' orders. She also regularly sent goods abroad and engaged factors in several European cities. The table further suggests that, while labor costs generated significant credit problems, it was the expense of raw materials that weighed most heavily on Bertin's finances.

If we examine the sexual division of her creditors, we find that women were prominent among artisans of the first category, where they numbered seventeen versus sixteen men (and seven whose sex was not given). Among merchants we find twenty-four men and only twelve women (with three whose sex was unclear). Among ancillary trades we find twenty-seven men and no women. As this division reveals, both men and women performed labor on credit for Bertin; however, women only did so in the garment trades, while men performed an array of skills from needlework to construction and carpentry. Women were less numerous among merchants, who needed sufficient capital to invest in expensive textiles and survive lengthy delays in payment of their substantial accounts. Given this gender discrepancy, it is not surprising that Bertin owed more money to men than women. According to this document, she paid 21,822 livres to women and 37,758 to men (another 7,449 went to people of unknown sex). If we add the 66,625 livres Bertin paid to the male lace merchant, the gender discrepancy is even greater. Notorious for her relations with the queen and other noblewomen, Bertin's business in fact brought her into transactions with male clients, as well as with many male merchants and artisans on whom she depended for credit.

Rose Bertin provides an outstanding example of a woman capable of borrowing and lending substantial sums of money. Her own credit patterns suggest that it was much more common for women to work as modest artisans rather than as merchants. Still, Rose Bertin was hardly unique. Her most important client, Marie Antoinette, relied on a handful of female purveyors. In 1785 the queen's wardrobe accounts included charges from twenty-one women and twenty-eight men. Among the women, we find four fashion merchants and five merchants of cloth, lace, or ribbons. A similar situation existed in 1787 and 1788, when she employed three female fashion merchants and four female cloth merchants.[28] On a much smaller scale, this pattern of employing female purveyors recurred among the court aristocracy and the wealthy inhabitants of Paris.

Managing Credit, Narrating Crisis

FASHION MERCHANTS AS ACCOUNTANTS

Bertin managed to stave off bankruptcy, but many of her counterparts in the trade were not so fortunate. Commercial law required merchants entering bankruptcy proceedings to provide financial statements detailing assets and liabilities and to surrender their account books as proof for the claims made in the statements. Merchants could also list, albeit for informational purposes only, any losses incurred during the course of business, such as the theft or destruction of merchandise, the expense of moving shop, and income forfeited during illness or absence. Many merchants also included an estimate of the cost of keeping house for themselves and their families. Financial statements thus straddled merchants' personal and professional lives, underlining the porous nature of such boundaries in their own experience and their conception of profit and loss as taking on fluid yet interrelated forms. Although not all of the statements provide such information, where they do we find valuable insight into the merchants' understanding of the causes of their failure and their strategies for justifying default.

Of course, information provided in the bankruptcy documents is not only biased toward failure but also contains both intentional and inadvertent mistakes and omissions. In the analysis below I attempt to control for errors by comparing information in the account books with the financial statements; however, given the uncertainties, the figures should be read as providing an overall impression of debts and credits rather than as precisely accurate information. Indeed, since so many of the resources involved were on paper rather than real and were subject to negotiation between parties, any attempt to fix precise sums is not merely hopeless; it would misrepresent the very nature of the exchanges under consideration.

Apart from the documents submitted by merchants, the court produced its own records of its proceedings. Typically, the magistrates—who were themselves successful businessmen rather than legal professionals—established a panel of merchant experts to oversee negotiations between debtors and creditors. A bailiff informed creditors of the filing and invited them to present proof of their claims to the court. A court clerk kept records of their appearances. Based on the statements they filed and the information provided by the financial statement and account books, the panel encouraged creditors to achieve a settlement with the defaulting individuals, which generally took the form of new delays for meeting the debts and possibly a reduction in the amount owed. The court took note of any agreement reached, sometimes in a formal notarized statement. Some, but not all, of these documents survive in the case files studied here.

Table 5.1 shows the chronology of all cases of faillite among fashion merchants available in the archives of the Juridiction consulaire. It shows a sharp increase in the number of cases from the 1770s onward, which reflects both the rise in number of fashion merchants in this period and the financial crisis of those years. Drawn from these archives, my sample consists of thirty-nine financial statements deposited with the Juridiction consulaire from 1758 to 1791

TABLE 5.1 Chronology of cases of fashion merchant bankruptcy in the archives of the Juridiction consulaire

DECADE	NUMBER OF CASES	DECADE	NUMBER OF CASES
1720s	1	1770s	34
1740s	1	1780s	46
1750s	4	1790–1792	10
1760s	7	Total	100

(see the archival sources consulted in the bibliography under Archives de Paris, D4B6, for a full list of these dossiers). My chosen case studies mirror the larger set in being biased toward the 1770s and 1780s; I also sought to reflect the gendered composition of the profession by balancing female entrepreneurs with a small number of male ones.

Pinpointing the "owner" of the business, and by extension his or her gender, was often difficult, given the family economy of the retail world. The thirty-nine cases studied include five cases of an apparent partnership between husband and wife. Other partnerships included two pairs of sisters and one association between two apparently unrelated women. Eleven unmarried women declared themselves to be the heads of their own businesses, as did eleven wives and three widows. Among the eleven wives, four obtained a financial separation from their husbands at some point during their career. The cases also include six married male fashion merchants, whose records did not mention their wives' activities.

Additional examples of family-run businesses probably lurked beneath the independent ownership declared by both male and female merchants. Five of the married women's husbands were *bourgeois de Paris*, a vague title that left open the possibility that they took a behind-the-scenes role in their wives' activities, despite the injunctions of the Code de commerce. Moreover, it seems safe to assume that wives of male fashion merchants participated in their husbands' businesses. In the case of the most famous among them, Jean-Joseph Beaulard, at least one contemporary account refers to madame, rather monsieur. In December of 1781 the Chevalier de l'Isle wrote to his cousin, the Comtesse de Riocor, to laud Rose Bertin and urge his cousin to adopt her services. As he wrote, "listen, my good cousin, if your favor for Mademoiselle Adelaïde or Madame Beaulard is based on the certainty of finding with them outfits in the best taste and lower prices than anywhere else and you have no other reason for your preference, I ask you to consider my intimate friend Mademoiselle Bertin."[29] In the case of Leveque and Boullenois the financial statement submitted at the moment of bankruptcy referred to the "creditors of messieurs Leveque et Boullenois marchands de modes" but subsequently to the "receivables owed to sieurs et dames Leveque et Boullenois." Moreover, at least one of their account books referred to the proprietors as Leveque and Madame Boullenois. Family participation in the enterprise and the identity of its main proprietor could be blurry, especially in the day-to-day operation of business.

Apart from married couples, other family ties were clearly important. The two Alleaume sisters who operated a joint business may well have been the sisters of another Alleaume, a marchande de modes, who kept a separate shop with her husband who was also listed as a fashion merchant. Jean-Joseph Beaulard was himself the son of a well-known fashion merchant; his younger brother operated a Moscow branch on his behalf, while two additional brothers based in Paris worked as a merchant mercer and a master perfume maker.[30] Another woman in our sample, Marie-Thérèse Gicquel, may have been related to Louis Gicquel, a merchant mercer and one of the most important suppliers of silk cloth to the individuals in our sample.

As the Beaulard family suggests, at their highest levels the Parisian fashion trades were highly cosmopolitan, with branches and agents throughout France, Europe, and its overseas colonies. Rose Bertin's shop, Le Grand mogol, was a magnet for wealthy foreign visitors in Paris, and Bertin had extensive networks for distributing her products abroad. She herself travelled extensively in Europe prior to and during the revolution and sent employees in her place on occasion. She also worked with agents in the provinces and in foreign countries. These agents sometimes purchased goods outright for resale and sometimes, as in the case of her factor Monsieur Bernard in Madrid, sold them on her behalf. On November 26, 1802, Bernard announced that he had sold a white dress and a black shawl he had received from her: "which funds I pass to you by the attached letter of exchange, which is to say the dress 1,110 livres and the shawl 400 livres."[31] Such agents also served as brokers to help Bertin recover assets. A wool merchant in the city of Orléans, who acted as Bertin's commissioner for Spanish deliveries, purchased fine wool from a Spanish marquis on Bertin's behalf and settled that bill against the running account the wife of the marquis held with Bertin.[32] Her activities represented the peak of geographic expansion, but even Elizabeth Tatry, a mid-level merchant in our sample, left Paris to open a shop in Saint-Domingue.

Marchandes de modes also reached beyond Paris for their supplies, purchasing cloth, lace, and other goods from provincial merchants. The province of Normandy was an especially important source of lace and linen cloth. Given the role of Paris as the hub of European fashion, demand from its fashion merchants could have a significant impact on local economies far from the capital. The Marquis de Bombelles credited Rose Bertin with causing an explosive boom in the production of linen and gauze in Paisley, Scotland—and a corresponding depression in the Lyons silk industry—by her favor for the Scottish textiles, which "she has put into fashion from Paris to [Saint] Petersburg and from Moscow to the ends of the West Indies."[33]

Although the fashion industry distributed its products over a wide geographic territory and acquired materials from across France and foreign countries, it remained in many ways a nucleus of families and associates tightly concentrated in a single area. In the 1770s and 1780s the heart of the trade was the western half of the Right Bank, in the streets around the Palais-Royal, the rue de Richelieu, and the rue Saint-Honoré. Personal acquaintance and reputation remained essential for acquiring credit, even for merchants with national and international networks of sales and supplies.

THE CASE STUDIES: BANKRUPTCY UP CLOSE

From the thirty-nine dossiers of bankruptcy statements studied, I selected eight cases for more detailed investigation, transcribing the contents of their account books into a database (see the archival sources consulted in the bibliography under Archives de Paris, D5B6, for a list of these merchants).[34] In six cases a single individual was named as the owner of the business and the other two were partnerships. The first, in chronological order, was Barbe Catherine Cabaille, married to Jean Paul Châtillon, a bourgeois de Paris. The records of her business cover the years 1753 to 1760. The second was an anonymous "modiste," whose business records extend from 1762 to 1767. Unfortunately, we do not know where in Paris she conducted business or when she filed faillite; however, her case provides one relatively early case study, an important corrective to the predominance of later examples. Our third case study is Jean Baptiste Francois Bermont, whose surviving accounts cover the years 1772 to 1773. Bermont's business was located initially on the rue Tiquetonne, but he had moved to the rue Neuve St. Denis by the time he declared faillite in 1777.

The fourth business, the longest-lasting and most successful among the eight cases, was the partnership between the married couples Leveque and Boullenois. Their surviving account books span from 1774 to 1791. Their boutique was at number 89, rue Mazarine, one of the few Left Bank businesses in the sample, and their many clients included court nobles such as the Comtesse de Polignac, the Duchesse de Luynes, and the Princesses de Chimay, de Robecque, and de la Rochefoucault. I examined their ledger covering the period January 2, 1778 to July 20, 1791. During this period they billed the substantial sum of 310,377 livres or on average over 22,000 livres a year. To give two extremes of comparison, a purse maker studied by Thomas Luckett grossed 5,000 livres per year during the 1750s, while the prominent mercer Lazare Duvaux had almost 140,000 livres in sales in the year 1750 alone.[35]

Our fifth case study is Adélaïde Bernard, who lived with her husband on the rue Croix des Petits Champs. Her business records cover the years 1778 to 1781; she filed for bankruptcy in May 1781 and again in December 1782. Like several of the other married women in the larger sample, her economic difficulties prompted her to protect her assets by acquiring a legal "separation of goods" from her husband from the civil lieutenant of the Châtelet of Paris. Such a decree, which required witness testimony of the husband's gross financial mismanagement, obliged the husband to restore his wife's dowry and the portion of her fortune that did not enter the marital community at the time of marriage. This responsibility preceded all other financial obligations on the husband's part, rendering his wife the first creditor of the estate. This legal process served to protect the fortune women brought to marriage, which in French law remained the property of the woman and her own family. The sixth example was Marie-Jeanne-Victoire Moreau, whom we encountered above, an unmarried woman whose business records span from 1778 to 1784. Of her two surviving daily journals, I studied one that extended from 1778 to 1781.

The seventh case study consisted of a business run initially by two sisters, Scolastique La Croix and Josephine Catherine La Croix, wife of Claude Louis Joseph Bouly. By the time of the bankruptcy filing Scolastique had disappeared from the record. Josephine Catherine and her husband lived on the rue de Grammont. The account book covers 1783 to 1784, and the couple registered their failure on September 6, 1784. The eighth and final case involves Marie-Thérèse Gicquel, married to François Louis Julien, a master mason and contractor. Her business appears to have suffered considerable disjuncture. One account book covers part of 1783 and then jumps to 1787 and 1788. During the latter years her business was located on the rue Croix des Petits Champs, but she had moved to the rue de Gretry by the time of her bankruptcy in 1790.

These merchants varied considerably in terms of the length of time they operated their businesses and their volume of sales. Table 5.2 provides an overview of their enterprises based on sales recorded in their account books. The average sales per year shown on the far right is slightly misleading, given that sales varied significantly from year to year. Nevertheless, it shows an extremely

TABLE 5.2 Overview of merchants in sample of account books
(Archives de la Seine, D5B6)

MERCHANT'S NAME	SEX	DATES OF ACTIVITY	DURATION OF BUSINESS	VOLUME OF SALES RECORDED IN LIVRES (CASH AND CREDIT)	AVERAGE SALES PER YEAR IN LIVRES
Cabaille	Female	1753–1760	8 years	16,627	2,078
Anonymous	N/A	1762–1767	6 years	10,751	1,791
Bermont	Male	1772–1773	2 years	3,025	1,512
Leveque and Boullenois	Male/ Female	1774–1791	18 years	310,377 (from 1778 to 1791)	22,170
Gicquel	Female	1784, 1787–1788	3 years (noncontinuous)	27,892	9,297
Bernard	Female	1778–1782	5 years	51,921	10,384
Moreau	Female	1778–1784	7 years	104,615 (from 1778 to 1781)	26,154
Lacroix	Female	1783–1784	2 years	38,224	19,112

wide gap between the average annual sales of the least and the most successful merchants. At two thousand livres or less in annual sales, it is hard to see how the three merchants at the bottom of the pool could have covered the expenses of materials, overhead, and labor, let alone paid their own cost of living and that of any family members. Enterprises with twenty thousand livres in sales, by contrast, represented substantial small businesses.[36]

The merchants also varied significantly in the social makeup of their clientele. Just as some had higher sales and lasted longer in business (the two were not necessarily linked), some had far more socially distinguished clients than others. As a rough index of these disparities, table 5.3 shows the number of noble clients listed in each of the journals. I have divided "noble" clients between those who appear with the simple "de" indicating nobility and those bearing specific titles. We should note that the journal notations are not wholly reliable indicators of noble rank (some are referred to with "de" even though they held titles, while the account keepers sometimes wrongly ascribed different titles to the same individual). It should also be noted that nobility was no guarantee of wealth and that some commoners achieved both fortune and

TABLE 5.3 Percentage of nobles among fashion merchants' clients

MERCHANT'S NAME	NUMBER OF CLIENTS	NUMBER OF "DE"	NUMBER OF TITLES	TOTAL NUMBER OF NOBLES	PERCENTAGE OF NOBLE CLIENTS
Cabaille	122	12	11	23	19
Anonymous	175	23	5	28	7
Bermont	94	4	3	7	7
Leveque and Boullenois	261	120	16	136	52
Gicquel	542	38	16	54	10
Bernard	141	30	14	44	31
Moreau	237	47	49	96	41
Lacroix	95	24	37	61	64

social prestige. In the absence of other information on the clients I provide this table as one way of approaching the question of the social makeup of clientele and, in turn, one form of distinction within the trade.

The data reveal no clear relationship between the size of the clientele and the prestige of its members: Bermont had a small clientele with relatively few nobles, while Lacroix's equally small client base contained a majority of them. However, they do suggest a significant relationship between the status of a merchant's customers and his or her volume of sales: the merchants with the lowest annual sales figures (Cabaille, Anonymous, and Bermont) were also those with a relatively low number of noble patrons, and the highest earners all designated at least 40 percent of their clients to be nobles. In the second half of the eighteenth century noble status still conveyed significant advantages to retailers in Parisian luxury trades.

To gain further insight into the composition of the clientele of fashion merchants, I compared client lists drawn from the records of five merchants operating within the same chronological period, including two royal purveyors (Rose Bertin and Mademoiselle Eloffe) and four businesses from the bankruptcy cases, those of Bernard, Gicquel, LaCroix, and Leveque and Boullenois. This comparison yielded a total of 1,448 individual clients, with at least forty-eight of the clients patronizing two of the merchants and a handful patronizing three of them. (These are minimum figures because they do not include cases where it was impossible to identify the client precisely and also because we do not possess Bertin's full client list.) These figures suggest that, while some very wealthy women sought out multiple purveyors of fashions to whom they provided a crucial source of income, the trade was by no means monopolized by a small cluster of court ladies.

MANAGING CREDIT

Given the commercial culture of the day, fashion merchants had little choice but to sell on credit if they wished to attract clients. The risks involved must have seemed an unavoidable element of running almost any commercial enterprise, and they were, or so the merchants must have hoped, counterbalanced by the credit provided by wholesale suppliers. As expected, the account books confirm the weight of credit within the fashion industry. Of eight cases, only five businesses recorded cash sales (although it should be noted that two of the three without cash sales involved merchants who only left behind the ledger, which recorded only credit accounts). Of the remaining five cases, for which we do have records of sales on cash, only one merchant, Adélaïde Bernard, sold as much on cash as she did on credit. The remaining four merchants ranged from a low of 1.5 percent cash sales to a high of 30 percent. The example of Bernard aside, it appears that cash sales accounted for a minority of transactions in the trade.

Among the eight case studies, the number of clients varied considerably from a low of approximately 90 for Bermont to a high of over 600 for Gicquel. The average among the eight merchants was 261 clients. In addition to purchasing supplies, making or supervising the making of client orders, and subcontracting labor, fashion merchants therefore had to keep track of orders and payments for up to several hundred clients, as well as writing letters and making personal visits to request satisfaction of their accounts. It is perhaps not surprising that so many of their clients succeeded in eluding payment.

Another revelation of the account books is the length of time it took for clients to satisfy accounts and the high percentage of defaulted accounts. The highest billing merchants were also the most successful in obtaining payment. From January 2, 1778 to July 20, 1791, Leveque and Boullenois charged clients for 310,377 livres in orders and were paid 276,249 livres or 89 percent of what they were owed. Another merchant with a relatively high record of reimbursement was Marie-Thérèse Gicquel. From January 12, 1787, to May 16, 1788, she billed a total of 17,771 livres and was paid 13,267 (including one returned garment worth 6 livres) or 75 percent of the total.[37]

Others appear to have received a smaller proportion of what was due. The lowest was an anonymous merchant whose books cover the period November 13, 1762 to July 20, 1765. If we include orders explicitly noted "paid" as well as those simply crossed out, a mark customarily used to denote payment, the percentage of paid orders amounted to only 31 percent (unfortunately, her file does not include an accompanying financial statement that would help to confirm this figure). Barbe Cabaille, the earliest merchant in our sample, recorded a total of 16,627 livres in orders but only payments of 9,541 livres or 57 percent of her accounts.[38]

Marie-Jeanne-Victoire Moreau's ratio of accounts outstanding to payment was even lower, based on one of her account books, which extended from October 5, 1778 to April 30, 1781. During this period, she billed 103,057 livres in credit sales and received 52,727 livres in payment (including 608 livres in returned goods) or 51 percent of the total. She recorded giving reductions of 25 livres to four clients, hardly enough to explain the discrepancy. These figures meant that over a three-year period only half of Moreau's clients paid in full.

Jean Baptiste François Bermont, who described himself in court documents as a "former fashion merchant," had a similarly frustrating experience. In his surviving account book he billed clients from October 26, 1772 to April 24, 1773, for 2,748 livres in credit sales and received 1,144 livres (including one return). Only 41 percent of his bills were satisfied, leaving 1,604 livres unpaid. This figure is largely corroborated by Bermont's bankruptcy statement of June 1777, in which he declared 1,661 livres in unpaid accounts.

Our final case is harder to decipher. Two successive daily account books of Adélaïde Bernard document orders worth 26,488 livres from January 19, 1778, to July 4, 1782. She recorded payments of only 10,810 livres (including 48 livres for a returned hat), or 20 percent, with 15,678 livres left unpaid. However, in her bankruptcy declaration from December 1782 she claimed 23,480 livres in outstanding accounts from her "old account books" and an additional 1,352 livres that she billed subsequent to financial separation from her husband. These were the only journals she deposited with the court, so it would appear the two existing registers covered her entire period of business. It is unclear whether she was deliberately inflating her accounts payable to appear more creditworthy or if she simply failed to record all the orders she received in her daily journal. It is possible that both alternatives were true.

These journals reveal the challenges fashion merchants experienced in managing sales on credit. Like Madame de Bercy, clients routinely waited two or even three years before paying their accounts. These delays created serious problems of liquidity for fashion merchants. Given their relatively low social status, they had little leverage to exert on clients and they were accordingly vulnerable to suspicion from suppliers. They might therefore be forced into bankruptcy before they could obtain payment to pass along the credit chain. While their statements to the court make it clear that the defaulting merchants expected many of their clients to pay in the end, a number of clients did default entirely. Entrepreneurs often registered their awareness of these risks in their financial statements by dividing accounts outstanding into the categories of "good," "doubtful," and "bad" or "lost." For bad debts, they sometimes justified this assessment by noting the length of time the debts had gone unpaid or the bankrupt state of the client herself. Based on these examples, it appears that merchants retained hope for up to eight or nine years before placing the account in the "bad" column.

Clients' ability to pay their bills—and suppliers' willingness to wait for satisfaction of their own accounts—was determined not just by individual circumstances, but also by the broader economic conjuncture. Then, as now, wholesale and retail merchants expanded their provision of credit when economic growth fueled consumer demand and retrenched as recession lowered it. The periodic credit crises of eighteenth-century France tended to occur at the peak of these boom periods, when a sudden panic hit and the collapse of confidence left many firms and individuals overextended. Panic could ensue from many factors, such as the bankruptcy of a prominent merchant (which had a ripple effect among his creditors), the loss of a military battle, or any other news that seemed bound to disrupt the movement of goods and their prices. Historians have counted at least twelve such collapses during the fifty years prior to the French Revolution, most of which lasted for several months but any of which could bring fashion merchants to ruin by rendering their suppliers more exigent at the precise moment when their clients could no longer pay.[39] Another set of circumstances that produced commercial crisis was harsh weather leading to crop failure, a subsequent rise in food prices, and economic stagnation. These conditions might not lead consumers—particularly those whose social situation dictated ostentatious consumption—to restrict their consumption, but it meant that they were less likely to pay for goods purchased on account. Fashion merchants might therefore survive a credit crisis only to fall victim to the delayed effects of the ensuing recession.[40]

The merchants' bankruptcy statements and account books confirm that high levels of unpaid accounts played a significant role in forcing them into bankruptcy. Two of the businesses studied here clearly entered bankruptcy from a lack of liquidity, not because the basic enterprise was unsound. According to her statement, Adélaïde Bernard's clients owed 29,270 livres, which would have been more than enough to cover her 21,653 in debts, without counting an additional 3,000 livres worth of merchandise in her shop. Leveque and Boullenois similarly owed 26,279 livres, much less than their 38,640 livres in accounts outstanding. In their case it is clear that the loss of trade caused by the financial disaster of the late 1780s and the early years of the revolution contributed to the demise of what had been a profitable and flourishing business.[41] Their businesses, with tight but adequate profit margins, are probably representative of the situation of those enterprises that stayed afloat.

What of the other merchants in our sample? In her bankruptcy statement of August 1781 Marie-Jeanne-Victoire Moreau provided important insight into the 51 percent of her accounts that remained unpaid. Like other merchants in the same predicament, Moreau divided her outstanding accounts, which she declared to total 35,044 livres, into three categories. She claimed 19,802 livres in "good debts" against fifty-one clients. Debts she considered to be "doubtful" constituted 14,994 livres for twenty clients, while she was willing to write off 248 livres of "bad" debts owed by five clients. Her debts thus consisted of a slender majority (56.5 percent) that she expected to be paid and a large minority (43.5 percent) that she believed would definitely or probably not be satisfied.[42] One woman, the Vicomtesse de Fandeau, was responsible for much of Moreau's bad credit. According to Moreau's account book, the vicomtesse ran up an account of 12,351 livres and paid only 960 livres, leaving 11,391 livres unpaid up to the end of the book in April 30, 1781.[43] She was also Moreau's most regular client, with 351 items charged to her. Her second-most frequent client was Madame de Frêne Lamoignon with 284 items, worth 6,294.3 livres, whom Moreau listed in the August 1781 statement as owing 4,710 livres.

By October 1782, a little over a year later, ongoing pressure from creditors forced her to submit a new statement to the court. This time she divided her accounts in a slightly different way, reflecting her efforts in the meantime to collect from clients. Her first category was "*memoires arrêtés*," meaning accounts that she had formally drawn up and issued to clients, which represented slightly more than 18,000 livres. This group included only three clients, Vicomtesse de Fandeau and another woman from the doubtful category of August 1781, from whom she had still received nothing, and one client from the "good" category who had paid her 700 livres out of a total of 5,857 livres past due. The second category was "old accounts that have not been closed" (*comptes anciens non arrêtés*). In this category twelve of the eighteen names were from the earlier statement. Only one of them had paid Moreau and that client had only paid 102 out of a total of 1,050 livres owed. A third category, "current accounts," represented new sales conducted since the time of the first statement. Eleven out of the eighteen individuals in this category were people who had owed her money in her deposition of 1781, but it is notable that they owed her much less than they had a year earlier. For example, Madame Souza had reduced her debt from 4,110 livres to 38, the Comtesse de Pralin from 1,254 livres to 16, Madame

TABLE 5.4 Declarations of value of accounts payable
by likelihood of repayment

PERCENTAGE OF TOTAL CREDIT OWED BY CLIENTS	GOOD	DOUBTFUL	BAD OR LOST
0	0	1	8
10–19	0	3	1
20–29	2	3	2
30–39	2	6	2
40–49	4	1	3
50–59	3	1	0
60–69	3	0	0
70–79	1	1	0
80–89	1	0	0

Note: The percentages were calculated from the total amount of money owed, not the number of clients who owed money, while the numbers in each column are the number of merchants in our case study who declared a percentage in each category. For example, eight merchants considered 0 percent of their accounts outstanding to be in the "bad" category, but three of them considered between 40–49 percent of the total amount of accounts payable to be in that category.

Camillac from 1,412 livres to 315, and Madame St. Chaman from 126 livres to 27. This improvement suggests that Moreau's desperate situation had met with some sympathy from her regular clients who had agreed to pay off almost all of their accounts. This time her unpaid accounts totaled only 21,688 livres, almost two-thirds of which came from the statement of 1781. In her case, therefore, it appears that she carried unrealizable credits of 20,000 livres; in other words, roughly one-fifth of her billing was never met.

Moreau was far from alone in judging that many of her clients would never meet their commitments. Table 5.4 provides a breakdown of the various categories of debt for the sixteen merchants who took the time to divide outstanding accounts in their financial statements into "good," "doubtful," and "bad" debts (some merely used two categories, "good" and "bad"). We find that the proportion of debt considered good ranged from roughly 20 percent to 90 percent, with the median around 50 percent. The proportion of debt considered "doubtful" was smaller in most cases but still with a median between 30 and 39 percent of the total credits outstanding. Bad debt took up an even smaller proportion of the total, and yet seven merchants declared between 20 and 50 percent of their remaining unpaid credits to be hopeless.

In the larger sample of thirty-nine financial statements, accounts unpaid by the merchants' clients ranged from 0 (three cases) to 585,573 livres. The highest figure belonged to Jean-Joseph Beaulard, with the second-ranked merchant claiming a little less than 114,000 livres. If we exclude the extremes at the high and low ends, the average for thirty-five cases was 20,331.5 livres, with a mean of 7,651 livres and a standard deviation of 27,295 livres.

One question the accounts do not answer clearly is whether the amounts actually paid by clients took the form of cash or financial paper. Only three of the account books studied mention the latter. The company of Leveque and Boullenois noted three occasions on which clients made payments in promissory notes, akin to an IOU, two of which involved the same client.[44] Marie-Jeanne Moreau noted on one occasion that a regular client, Madame Audbert, submitted a partial payment of her bill on July 31, 1781 in the form of a note that was "payable at the end of next April." Such notes in effect constituted additional extensions for the client to satisfy the account. Marie-Thérèse Gicquel noted on three occasions that she had received payment in the form of financial paper. In two of these instances a client gave Gicquel a promissory note; the third case involved a more complex instrument, a bill of exchange. Gicquel recorded on April 28, 1784 that she had received 866 livres from a regular client, Mademoiselle de Malblanc, in the form of a "billet from Monsieur Baury, endorsed by Monsieur Oudre, to be paid by Monsieur Dupon de la Halière on July 20 in the sum of 800 livres and in her note for 66 livres [payable] at the end of July."[45] In contrast to the promissory note, the bill of exchange involved in addition to the drawer and the taker of the letter a third-party drawee (often a debtor of the drawer) who agreed to furnish the sum of money at the stipulated date. It had the advantage that it could involve drawees in distant locales and thus provided a convenient exchange medium for long-distance trade. Within the confined arena of the Parisian luxury trades, promissory notes could play a similar role and be traded as a form of currency.[46]

It would be wrong to assume that the rare explicit references to financial paper in the account books meant that coin was the rule. In all likelihood many payments took the form of promissory notes or, less frequently, bills of exchange. Although it is tempting to view payment in financial paper as yet another extension of credit—and thus another failure on the part of the merchant to obtain satisfaction of her account—possession of a client's letter of credit could work in a merchant's favor. She could, as suggested above, submit it to a supplier as a form of payment. More cunningly, instead of negotiating it right away, a fashion merchant might show the letter of credit to multiple suppliers, thus reassuring them of her solvency and staving off their demands, if only momentarily; coin, by contrast, could only change hands once and did not have the same effectiveness as a form of collateral. Nonetheless, financial paper typically exchanged at a discounted rate, given the transaction costs of obtaining payment, so they might well represent another type of forced reduction in the payment of an account.

Bankruptcy documents reveal that fashion merchants themselves made copious and repeated use of billets to meet their own debts to suppliers. It is not uncommon to find creditors in faillite proceedings possessed of multiple postdated promissory notes from marchandes de modes, indicating that the merchants had attempted to stave off business failure by structuring an extended reimbursement schedule. It was their repeated failure to meet those commitments that led them to the merchant court.

THE PRICE OF CREDIT

Fashion merchants were not hurt merely by clients who failed to pay their accounts; they also suffered from clients who demanded reductions in the amount they owed. Such demands are counterintuitive: one would expect that consumers purchasing on credit of one to three years would incur significant interest charges. Despite the Catholic prohibition of usury, interest did exist in eighteenth-century France. For example, creditors who took legal action against their debtors were entitled to demand interest payments; this was the "interest" that demoiselle Moreau begged her creditors to forgive at the meeting of May 1781. Even without recourse to the courts, a celebrated fashion merchant like Rose Bertin could demand interest for overdue payments. It was also assumed in the contemporary literature—a claim that has been echoed by historians—that merchants routinely imposed disguised interest when they sold items on credit at higher prices than for cash.[47] In his *Traité du contrat de vente*, published in 1762, the jurist Pothier posed the rhetorical question, "Can one sell what one sells on credit higher than the just price?" He responded that since merchants were forced to purchase their supplies at higher prices on credit, due to the fact that their own clients rarely paid in cash, it was entirely reasonable for a merchant to pass along the higher prices he paid for supplies in the prices he charged his clients. As Pothier concluded, "the credit that he provides should not be harmful to him."[48]

Pothier further cautioned, however, that the merchant could not raise prices higher than the expenses he incurred in buying on credit. By restricting himself to a mere indemnity, the merchant could charge interest in good faith without defying Catholic doctrine. Customers who wished to avoid paying the higher prices could easily do so by purchasing with cash. In *Le Parfait négo-*

ciant Jacques Savary similarly assumed that goods sold on credit carried higher prices. In discussing the skills apprentices must acquire he commented that they should learn all about their master's merchandise, especially whether it was purchased for cash or credit. In the latter case they should learn the time accorded for payment and the price differential between cash and credit.[49] In a later passage he acknowledged that "it is true that the fortune of retail merchants is made neither as considerably nor as quickly in cash sales as credit, because those who buy with cash are more difficult for the choice and the price of goods than those who buy on credit." He nevertheless insisted that the difficulties of obtaining satisfaction of credit accounts should encourage retailers to overlook the apparent disadvantages of cash.[50] His comments suggest that a customer paying with cash was so rare and valuable that he or she could afford to be extremely picky about the quality and prices of the goods purchased. Merchants could run up impressive figures in their account books by selling on credit, but then paid a price in time and risk to collect their money.

Consumers disagreed about the justice of what they took to be a well-established practice of disguising interest in the price of credit sales. Readers of *Les visions de Dom Francisco de Quevedo Villegat*, published in the *Bibliothèque bleue* in 1711, could read what a demon had to say about clothing merchants sent to hell for such practices: "It is they who maintain and feed all your disorders and your foolish expenses, to which they lead and attract you, with a lover they call Credit, by means of which they ruin you imperceptibly, because they sell you things for more than half again what they are worth, and, the time of payment having arrived, they seize your property, imprison your persons, have decrees issued against your houses, and finally as they had previously furnished that with which to dress yourselves as princes, they now skin you alive and turn you into beggars."[51] One hundred years later, by contrast, Madame de Genlis faulted not the practice but the imprudent consumer: "A merchant who sells on credit reasonably charges higher prices, because he wants to recover the interest on the money withheld from him; a woman who buys in this manner has no right to bargain and frequently even takes the merchandise without informing herself of the price; which means that in a year or two, often with only six or seven thousand francs in allowance, she finds herself with fifteen or twenty [thousand] in bills [that,] . . . consequently, she cannot pay."[52]

The reality according to the account books strongly contests the assumptions of both consumers and commercial experts. Instead of dictating high prices on the wares they sold, fashion merchants suffered regular reductions imposed by their clients. Jean-Joseph Beaulard lost so much to reductions that he included them as a category in the list of business losses he itemized in his

TABLE 5.5 Clients noted as paid in full who paid less than the credit orders noted in the account books

MERCHANT'S NAME	NUMBER OF CLIENTS NOTED AS "SOLDÉ" (PAID IN FULL)	NUMBER OF SOLDÉS WHO PAID AS MUCH OR MORE THAN THEIR CREDIT ORDERS	NUMBER WHO PAID LESS	NUMBER WHO PAID LESS AS A PERCENTAGE OF THE TOTAL CLIENTELE
Leveque and Boullenois	208	105	103	50
Bermont	16	6	10	63
Lacroix	62	39	23	37
Bernard	30	16	14	47
Gicquel	91	58	33	36
Moreau	101	43	58	57

financial statement of 1789 under the heading, "Discounts that my debtors imposed on me and coerced gifts to servants to maintain the custom of their masters according to the detailed statement taken from the journals." He claimed to have lost 17,375 livres over the course of his thirteen-year career in reduced prices and "coerced gifts."[53]

Unfortunately Beaulard's journals do not survive to provide corroboration of his claim, but analysis of account books deposited by six of our merchants seems to confirm it.[54] For six merchants with books offering the necessary information, we compared the orders placed by the merchants' clients on credit with the sums paid by the clients. For entries marked "to satisfy the account in full," we calculated whether or not the amount paid corresponded with the total price of orders previously noted in the account book. The results, shown in table 5.5, suggest that it was quite common for merchants to excuse clients from making full payment on their accounts. Not all customers received this privilege, but many did. The percentage of individuals within a merchant's clientele marked as *soldé* who did not pay the full amount ranged from a low of 36 percent to a high of 62 percent, with a mean of 51 percent and a median of 48.5 percent.

In cases where reductions were granted, they were often substantial. For Moreau, the average reduction was 36 percent (median of 24 percent) of the amount owed; for Leveque, the average was 37 percent (median of 35 percent); for Bermont, the average was 39 percent (median of 33 percent); for Lacroix, the average was 28 percent (median of 22 percent); for Bernard, the average was 39 percent (median of 37 percent); for Gicquel, the average was 40 percent (median of 38 percent). Together, these figures show that many clients, in some cases the majority of clients, lopped off a hefty chunk of their bill. To further investigate the dynamics behind such reductions, we sought correlations between the fact of receiving a reduction and the factors of noble title, length of time the bill was unpaid, the amount owed, and the frequency of a client's orders. The only variable that showed up in every case as significant was the amount owed, suggesting that the more a client owed, the more likely he or she was to receive a reduction. Other factors (frequency of orders or length of time since the order was placed or degree of nobility) did not statistically impact the existence of reductions.[55]

It is not clear how representative these patterns were of Parisian retailers on the whole, given the small size of our sample. One fashion merchant claimed that the fact that her clients were mostly married women made it harder to collect her accounts. Louise de France, in a financial statement submitted on December 7, 1791, claimed she had lost thirty-five thousand livres over the course of her career due to "reductions on the merchandise she furnished to her clients, almost always being forced to make sacrifices. The women being under the authority of their husbands, she would have lost everything if she had been rigorous."[56] Unfortunately, her account book has not survived, and her claims cannot be verified against the evidence of her daily practices. Madame de Genlis echoed this statement in her pedagogical treatise *Adèle et Théodore*, discussed in detail in chapter 7. This section of the treatise recounted the story of an impoverished fashion merchant whose clients' husbands routinely drove down the value of accounts presented to their wives. Arguing against this interpretation, however, is the close study of Natacha Coquery, who finds very similar levels of unpaid credit for two male trades, jewelers and tapestry makers.[57]

As Coquery argues, retailers were constrained from pursuing legal charges against their recalcitrant clients for multiple reasons. First, justice was expensive and it was extremely slow moving. Confronted with a constant shortage of cash, many small-scale entrepreneurs must have judged that they could not afford to take recourse to the courts, whose judgments were uncertain and liable to take as long to arrive as the defaulting client's payment. Second, and more importantly, were the steep risks imposed by taking action. As we have seen, it was the clients with the largest credit accounts who exercised the most leverage over the fashion merchants, demanding reductions on a par with their investment. Pursuing legal action against such clients meant losing their future custom and potentially that of their friends and relatives. In businesses based so heavily on reputation, turning to the law not only risked alienating valuable customers, it could send signals of alarm to one's creditors. If we add to these dangers the social deference expected by wealthy customers, retailers' inaction appears as a rational reaction to their circumstances rather than mere passivity. In most cases it took mounting pressure from their own creditors to persuade retailers to move from informal letters and visits to the bailiffs and civil litigation.

Of course, if the prices fashion merchants charged were exorbitant in the first place—the complaint of many contemporary observers—defaults and reductions would have represented merely the cost of doing business. Once again, the account books deny such an optimistic scenario. To return to the example of Moreau, her failure did not result primarily from the default of the Vicomtesse de Fandeau. Instead, it was the underlying discrepancy between Moreau's income and her expenditure. According to her declaration of August 1781, Moreau was owed 35,044 livres by clients, but she herself owed 71,096 livres, mostly to wholesale suppliers. These figures suggest that Moreau was unable to charge prices high enough to cover the extremely high cost of the luxurious materials she purchased to make items for her clients. Had all of her clients paid their accounts quickly and in full, Moreau could have held off her creditors longer, but it appears that the fundamentals of the business were unsound. It is significant, given her apparent position of weakness, to note the gendered pattern of Moreau's credit relations. Seventy-six clients, all female, owed her money, but she owed money to twenty-three creditors, only one of whom was a woman.[58]

Although information on the nature of the liabilities was not always included in account books, it is clear that most were debts to suppliers of materials used in the fashion merchants' trade, such as lace, ribbons, silk, and artificial flowers. They also owed money to artisans who provided subcontracted labor in ancillary trades, to craftsmen who decorated and improved their shops, to employees, and to purveyors of goods and services for personal needs such as wine merchants, bakers, apothecaries, and landlords. Fashion merchants not only called upon a wide range of purveyors of materials, they also frequently used more than one supplier of the same type of material. Reaching out to a number of different merchants allowed them to locate specialized materials to fulfill client orders and to distribute their credit dependency. If each supplier owned only a fraction of her debt, the results of one creditor's sudden demand for payment would be less catastrophic for the business. They may have also chosen suppliers in response to clients' insistence on obtaining materials from well-known and trusted purveyors. Fashion merchants themselves almost never appear on each other's list of creditors. Their ties of credit linked them to many other trades but not to each other.

Comparing the debts fashion merchants claimed from their clients to the

TABLE 5.6 Credits owed by merchants' clients as a percentage of the merchants' debt

PERCENTAGE RANGE	NUMBER OF CASES	PERCENTAGE RANGE	NUMBER OF CASES
10–19	6	80–89	1
20–29	4	90–99	1
30–39	2	100–109	1
40–49	3	110–119	3
50–59	1	120–129	1
60–69	6	Above 130	2
70–79	2		

amount they owed their own purveyors reveals a stark pattern. For thirty-three cases where the information was available, only seven merchants were owed as much as they owed. Indeed, fifteen merchants were owed less than 50 percent of what they owed (see table 5.6). (These figures actually underestimate the discrepancy, for I included "bad" accounts in the assets, whereas most merchants would write them off as a loss.) This finding underlines the fragility of fashion merchants with regard to the wholesale merchants with whom they placed their orders. Contrary to the claims of Mercier and other contemporary writers, who insisted on the high value that fashion merchants imposed on the materials they used, these entrepreneurs were clearly unable to pass along a sufficient markup on the products they sold to cover the cost of their raw materials. The rapid pace of fashion worsened the situation by drastically reducing the value of their stock and enforcing steep discounts. Clients' delay in paying accounts thus constituted only one element of the fashion merchants' failures; equally important were the financial leverage wielded by wholesale merchants and the inherent risks of the fashion industry.

Of course, commercial debt was merely one element of their overall financial situation. In their statements the merchants included a wide range of assets and liabilities. Assets included the estimated current market value of merchandise held in stock and the furnishings of their shop and home, as well as annuities, inheritances, and (in a small number of cases) real estate or other forms of real property. On the debit side of the ledger, they included outstanding wages and rent, loans of money (which often took the form of annuities they had constituted for other people in exchange for a large cash payment), and, in one case, dowries owed to married children. If we compare total assets

TABLE 5.7 Total assets as a percentage of total liabilities

PERCENTAGE RANGE	NUMBER OF CASES	PERCENTAGE RANGE	NUMBER OF CASES
10–19	1	90–99	1
20–29	4	100–109	2
30–39	1	110–119	1
40–49	2	120–129	2
50–59	3	130–139	3
60–69	4	140–149	1
70–79	5	Above 150	3
80–89	4		

to total liabilities, the picture is less bleak, as shown in table 5.7. Only eight out of thirty-seven merchants held assets worth less than 50 percent of their debts, and twelve declared assets worth more than their liabilities (again, they would presumably contest this conclusion since I included book credit that they described as "bad" or "lost" in their assets).

These findings suggest that wholesalers who extended credit to fashion merchants were not so rash as to provide supplies far beyond the total assets of the merchants' holdings. Whatever their success in attracting paying customers, fashion merchants enjoyed resources in the merchandise and furniture in their shop, the leases they held on commercial property, almost all located in the thriving Right Bank fashion district, as well as the more intangible reputation and following they had established. The value of the business itself, called the *fonds de commerce*, was intangible and yet at times subject to explicit calculation and exchange. A number of merchants reported in their financial statements the sums they had paid for a predecessor's fonds de commerce. In her bankruptcy statement of 1790 Marie-Thérèse Gicquel claimed to have paid 5,000 livres for the fonds de commerce of a business situated on the highly desirable rue Croix des Petits Champs. The Alleaume sisters had not yet reimbursed the 4,445 livres they had paid for their business when they declared bankruptcy in 1785. Another merchant reported spending 800 livres to acquire the clientele of his predecessor on the rue de Bussy. As this example emphasizes, the core of a retail enterprise was its regular customers rather than its tools, stock, or location.[59]

We should also consider the ratio of liabilities to assets by looking at the number of clients who owed merchants money versus the number of suppliers

TABLE 5.8 Proportion of supplier-creditors to client-debtors

PERCENTAGE	NUMBER OF CASES	PERCENTAGE	NUMBER OF CASES
10–29	4	90–109	4
30–49	5	110–129	1
50–69	4	130–200	6
70–89	1	Over 200	4

to whom merchants were indebted. For this comparison, I used only those merchants who furnished information on both suppliers and clients in their financial statements. As table 5.8 shows, the majority of these merchants, eighteen out of twenty-nine, owed money to a number of suppliers that was equal to or lesser than the number of clients who owed them. Many fashion merchants' enterprises were characterized by a few large debts to a small number of suppliers and many smaller credits with a much larger group of clients. This situation intensified the pressure they felt from their relatively small number of significant creditor suppliers, while reducing the effectiveness of their pursuit of the many clients who owed them small sums of money.

One strategy fashion merchants could use to acquire leverage and to write off book debt was to provide their wares to suppliers. Adélaïde Bernard's journal noted purchases of cloth and other items from Messieurs Marcilly and Osmont but also listed Mesdames Marcilly and Osmont as clients with running accounts. Their custom did not save Bernard from financial troubles but may have helped delay the moment of reckoning and disposed her creditors in her favor. Bernard also traded assets with her *fille de boutique* Mademoiselle Frissard, noting the items purchased by Frissard on the credit side of her ledger and the forty-eight livres she had borrowed from her employee as a debit.[60] The practice of exchanging credit and periodically tallying where the parties stood must have been an important way for fashion merchants to survive the lengthy delays they incurred in collecting cash for their accounts. This was a common practice in the Parisian business world of the eighteenth century and could have allowed marchandes de modes to stave off the demands of female professionals and male landlords, wine merchants, doctors, and bakers, whose wives and daughters may well have been delighted with a fashionable new hat. Marie-Thérèse Gicquel recorded the professions of ten of her clients (a hairstylist, female tapestry maker, linen draper, laundress, female knife maker, bookseller, drinks seller, and two female paper merchants), suggesting the possibility of some kind of quid pro quo arrangement.

GENDER, CREDIT, AND MARITAL STATUS

To gain a better understanding of the impact of gender on fashion merchants' access to credit and the nature of the social relations forged by borrowing and lending, this section takes a closer look at their patterns of debt to suppliers.[61] Overall, the thirty-nine merchants in the sample had an average of thirty-two creditors, with a low of twelve and a high of eighty-three. An analysis of their debts suggests that the accessibility of credit to fashion merchants was not strongly determined by gender. One way to approach this issue would have been to calculate levels of debt based solely on the gender of the presumed chief operator of the business. I chose instead to use the dual criteria of the gender and the marital status of the chief operator. Since husbands were legally responsible for debts contracted by their wives—even when the latter were independent entrepreneurs—we may assume that prospective suppliers would have assessed the creditworthiness of married women quite differently than single women or widows. Broken down, therefore, into the categories of male business operators, married women or couples, and single women (comprised of widows, unmarried women, and legally separated women), the gender distinctions are surprisingly small. The seven men on average carried 43,811 livres of debt, the married couples jointly declared an average of 30,076 livres, and the single women 36,767 livres. If we figure it in percentages, the results are similar. Men composed 17.5 percent of the sample and held 21 percent of the debt, couples made up 30 percent of the sample and had 25 percent of the debt, and single women were 52.5 percent of the sample and held 57 percent of the debt.

Neither marital status nor gender thus seems to have determined fashion merchants' capacity to obtain supplies on credit. It is when we turn to the wholesale suppliers themselves that the impact of gender becomes much more apparent, as we saw with Rose Bertin. Among the suppliers, an overwhelming 722 out of 945 (89 percent) were male and only 90 (11 percent) were female. The gender of the remaining 133 is unknown, but it seems safe to assume that they were male given that women were unusual and as such were usually identified in the statements. Male creditors together owned 1,205,080 livres of the total debt (85.6 percent) among fashion merchants, while female creditors owned only 104,216 livres of the total debt (7.4 percent). If we assume that the vast majority of the 98,721 livres belonging to creditors of unknown gender (7 percent) were male-owned, the totals would be closer to 92 percent male-owned debt and 7 percent female-owned debt. Thus a retail trade composed in majority of women, with a substantial pool of unmarried women, was deeply in debt to male merchants and manufacturers.

To clarify the impact of gender on credit relations, I compared lists of creditors among the thirty-nine bankruptcy statements I sampled. If we grant a total of roughly 500 enterprises of varying size (based on the 450 individuals admitted to the guild after 1776), our sample constitutes a little under 10 percent of the total. This is obviously a limited number, but it is enough to suggest patterns of behavior, particularly if we remember that even highly successful merchants, like Jean-Joseph Beaulard, found themselves in bankruptcy proceedings. Out of a total of 945 creditors (composed of individuals or firms), only 44 (or 4.5 percent) had granted credit to more than one fashion merchant in the sample (this is a minimum figure because I disregarded repetition of extremely common names when additional information, such as first name, profession, or address, was not provided). For these "repeat" creditors, the average number to whom they had extended credit was 3 (with a median of 3 and a range from 2 to 7). These figures signify, in turn, that the vast majority of creditors (901, to be exact) appeared only once. The network constituted by credit relations between fashion merchants and their suppliers thus appears very diffuse.

Further examination of the creditors, however, complicates this initial impression. All but four of the fashion merchants in this sample were linked to colleagues by at least one supplier; many shared several. Indeed, suppliers holding credits with more than one marchande de modes held 334,055 livres or almost 25 percent of the total sums owed. The most important creditor was Louis Gicquel, a merchant mercer, who owned almost 100,000 livres of debt from seven fashion merchants. The statements do not list all of the "repeat" creditors' professions, but it is clear that almost all were commercial suppliers: they were merchants and merchant manufacturers of lace (nine cases), of gauze cloth (seven cases), of silk (three cases), and ribbons (six cases), merchants of feathers and artificial flowers (six cases), and merchant mercers (three cases). Brandishing a disproportionately large amount of credit, this small core of merchants must have wielded considerable power within the fashion trades. The nucleus of suppliers was also a highly gendered group. Only two women appear more than once on the list of creditors. They were Madame Dupuis, a linen draper, with three fashion merchant debtors, and Madame Noel, a lace merchant, with two.

Furthermore, a considerable gender discrepancy existed between marchandes de modes' suppliers and their clients. The percentage of women among creditors listed in these financial statements ranged from 0 to 58 percent, with a mean of 12 percent and a median of 8 percent. By contrast, among those who owed money to fashion merchants, the percentage of women ranged from 31 percent to 100 percent, with a mean of 71 percent and a median of 74 percent. Five of the fashion merchants in the sample were men and nineteen were women. Assuming these results were representative, we may conclude that fashion merchants were predominantly women who were owed money by women but who owed money to men. The fashion trades could thus be viewed as a hub for transferring resources from elite women to male merchants and manufacturers, with a crucial passage through the hands of female retailers and artisans. Links between elite female clients and male purveyors were intensified by the fact that many fashion merchants passed on their clients' letters of exchange or accounts receivable to their suppliers in an attempt to forestall aggressive collection efforts. Such transactions allowed the suppliers to take direct recourse against the female clients, thereby creating another layer in the network of credit relations. Indeed, many of the textile dealers would have held their own debts with the same clients.

CASH OR CREDIT?

Only three fashion merchants out of the eight surveyed had significant sales on cash, permitting a limited comparison of prices charged for cash and credit sales for the same items. To conduct the comparison, I selected six of the most commonly sold items—bonnets, hats, neckerchiefs (*fichus*), mantles, *baigneuses* (a pleated bonnet), and poufs—and calculated the average cash price as a percentage of the average credit price. A fichu was a large, lightweight, square kerchief that was folded into a triangle and wrapped around the neck to fill in the open neckline of a dress. A mantelet was a short cape. A *baigneuse* was a specific type of bonnet, which was large and loose with soft pleats. The pouf was a headpiece composed of a frame of wire, covered with horsehair, cloth, and fake hair, on top of which were arranged flowers, feathers, and other objects, often following a theme or reflecting an important current event.

Comparison among the three merchants in our sample reveals quite different patterns (see table 5.9). Marie-Thérèse Gicquel made 22 percent of the sales in her account book on cash versus 78 percent on credit. In her case credit and cash prices were not very far apart: the cash price ranged from a low of 87 percent of the credit price for a mantle to a high of 120 percent of the price of a neckerchief. Josephine Catherine La Croix had a similar division of her sales, with 30 percent delivered on cash and 70 percent on credit. La Croix, however, charged considerably less on average for items sold on cash. For example, the average proportion of cash to credit ranged from a low of 55 percent on average for mantles to 82 percent for baigneuses. The final case was Adélaïde Bernard, with the largest proportion of cash sales in the group at 49 percent. She also charged much less on average for items sold on cash. At the low end, the average cash price of fichus was only 21 percent of the credit price and at the high end poufs sold for 76 percent of their average price on credit.

Before we conclude that purchases on credit really were more expensive than those on cash, it is worth noting that the standard deviation from the mean for La Croix and Bernard was, in general, substantially higher for credit sales than cash sales. This was because the upper range of prices was, overall, much higher for sales on credit than cash. These figures suggest, therefore, that cash sales represented the lower end of their commerce and perhaps consisted of a larger proportion of readymade goods. Custom-made orders, incorporating expensive materials and demanding the most time, seem to have been sold predominantly on credit rather than cash. For Gicquel, who charged more or less the same for cash and credit sales, the standard deviation was the same for both types of sales.

Only one merchant in our sample, Adélaïde Bernard, recorded the purchases she made as well as the orders she fulfilled.[62] Her journals are a unique but rich source because she not only recorded supply purchases and sales but also distinguished in both cases between credit and cash transactions. Her two surviving account books reveal that in addition to raw materials, like cloth or ribbons, she also routinely purchased finished items. In order to probe the relationship between the prices she paid suppliers for goods she purchased and those she charged clients, I analyzed six items: baigneuses, bonnets, hats, fichus, mantles, and gauze, a sheer fabric made of cotton or silk. The first five items represented finished goods, presumably sold as is, whereas the last was a material she employed to fill custom orders. Bernard purchased and resold four of these items most frequently (bonnets, hats, neckerchiefs, and gauze). Many of her purchases of bonnets, neckerchiefs, and hats were made on cash, and she did not note in those cases the name of her suppliers. She more often purchased gauze cloth on credit, dividing her custom among at least ten provisioners of gauze, who also sold her other materials and supplies.

She sold all four of these items at significantly higher prices than she paid for them, buying bonnets for an average of 2.5 livres on cash and 1.75 livres on credit and selling them on average for 7.2 livres on cash and 11.4 livres on credit. The same pattern is evident with hats, neckerchiefs, and gauze. In her case her profit margin stemmed from her practice (discussed neither in the Pothier nor the Savary passages cited above) of purchasing in large lots at discount prices and reselling goods as individual items, or in much smaller lots,

TABLE 5.9 Cash as a percentage of credit sales for three merchants

ITEMS SOLD AND MODALITY OF SALE	GICQUEL	LA CROIX	BERNARD
Bonnet	100%	56%	63%
Mean price credit:	10.4 (std = 5.1)	12.2 (std = 6.60)	7.2 (std = 2.7)
Mean price cash:	10.2 (std = 7.1)	21.7 (std = 15.5)	11.4 (std = 10.6)
Chapeau	113%	86%	47%
Mean price credit:	16.8 (std = 8.6)	21.5 (std = 11.9)	14.7 (std = 8.9)
Mean price cash:	14.8 (std = 8.8)	25 (std = 14.3)	31.5 (std = 30.2)
Fichu	123%	60%	21%
Mean price credit:	7.4 (std = 5.1)	10.1 (std = 3.4)	3.4 (std = 2.6)
Mean price cash:	6 (std = 3.8)	16.7 (std = 15.3)	16.1 (std = 29)
Mantelet	87%	55%	61%
Mean price credit:	26.1 (std = 8.4)	24 (std = n/a)	34 (std = 39)
Mean price cash:	30 (std = 12.6)	43.3 (std = 27.1)	55.6 (std = 52.6)
Baigneuse	94%	82%	49%
Mean price credit:	7.1 (std = 2.6)	9.2 (std = 3.4)	5.8 (std = 1.7)
Mean price cash:	7.5 (std = 3.5)	11.2 (std = 7.4)	11.7 (std = 9.3)
Pouf	125%	90%	76%
Mean price credit:	21.6 (std = 7.8)	30.3 (std=15.1)	20.2 (std=29.4)
Mean price cash:	17.3 (std = 8.9)	33.8 (std = 19.5)	26.5 (std = 34)

at higher prices. It was thus the scale of her purchases rather than an implicit imposition of interest that generated a profit margin.

Despite this evidence of canny business strategy, Bernard did not escape the humiliation and fear of rigorous pursuit by her creditors. She first filed for faillite in May 1781. Her account book continued until July 4, 1782, but soon after that date she was incarcerated for debt in the Hôtel de la Force prison. On August 12 her former worker Demoiselle Goussot appeared before the judges of the Juridiction consulaire to complain about an unpaid letter of credit for 300 livres that she had accepted from Bernard. Goussot explained that the letter was intended to cover 250 livres in cash she had lent Bernard to "meet debts for supplies for her trade in fashions." The rest consisted of her unpaid wages, "having continued to serve the defendant and her husband until the time she was incarcerated for debts." Bernard acknowledged the liability, adding that she had employed Goussot as a shopgirl at a salary of 150 livres a year. She further declared that her husband (from whom she had obtained a financial separation) had taken flight and that she intended to satisfy her creditors "when she has money that for the moment she does not have." Evidently fearing Bernard would follow her husband's example, Goussot demanded that she be remanded until the debt was satisfied.[63] Bernard's second business failure, filed in December 16, 1782, continued to state her profession as marchande de modes but did not specify whether she remained in prison.

As *marchandes publiques*, fashion merchants did not receive the normal protection against incarceration for debt that women normally enjoyed, and Bernard was not alone in suffering this frightening ordeal. Another fashion merchant, Marie Anne Defrenay, submitted a plaintive note to the Juridiction consulaire from her cell in the Fort L'évêque debtors' prison: "I have nothing deeper at heart than to give my creditors all possible satisfaction and the means to allow them the possibility to recover what is due to them, as long as they relieve me from the captivity where I am, which will become more harmful than profitable to them."[64] These cases are all the more striking in that imprisonment for debt was relatively rare in France. It usually resulted from discord among creditors or a suspicion that the individual filing faillite was hiding assets and might learn to be more forthcoming from a spell in prison. The parties responsible for incarcerating a debtor were obliged to pay for his or her food, so it was a step taken with reluctance and usually for only a brief period.

BANKRUPTCY TALES: MAKING SENSE OF FAILURE

Like Bernard, fashion merchants faced many risks, some intrinsic to their trade and others circumstantial. Their bankruptcy papers strove to portray them as honest business operators with a good faith commitment to honoring the promises made to creditors. They often highlighted the calamities leading to bankruptcy as a means to justify the merchant's predicament and place him or her squarely in the category of innocent faillite rather than that of the criminal banqueroute. Their narrative strategies are particularly transparent when the catalog of losses arrived at a figure that virtually balanced the debit side of the ledger, suggesting that all would have been well without the unforeseeable stroke of misfortune. Of course, the documents exaggerated these accidents and the monetary losses they produced. And yet there is no reason to believe that calamity did not strike or that the cupidity of others did not bring hardworking men and women to ruin. Like Natalie Zemon Davis's pardon tales, their authors framed bankruptcy statements according to their conception of what would make sense and seem plausible, and thus they are woven from the fabric of their authors' lives, albeit in brighter and more vivid colors.[65]

One virtuoso of the bankruptcy narrative was Marie-Thérèse Gicquel. Gicquel and her husband endured an apparent deluge of misfortune in their careers as, respectively, a fashion merchant and a mason and contractor. Gicquel and her husband's explanation of business failure lay not in sizeable unpaid accounts but in a long list of unpredictable losses and expenses visited upon their personal and professional lives, events that remind us of the risks particular to the fashion industry. For example, Gicquel claimed to have incurred a loss of 3,000 livres on fashionable goods that she purchased to sell during the Longchamp horse races, an important social moment for the display of new styles. Faced with disappointing sales, she had been obliged to sell them at deep discount and to have them dismantled and remade, since they were "no longer in fashion." She declared another loss of 2,000 livres for clothing made on order for a client who was supposed to debut at the Comédie française theater but who had been rejected and subsequently refused to take the order. She also listed 2,400 livres in merchandise that had been lost, stolen, or ruined by the "lack of care of the shopgirls" especially during Gicquel's illnesses and absences. The heavy fees she paid to purchase a new business, after losing the lease on her first boutique, may also have resulted from the exigencies of the fashion trade, which was heavily concentrated in certain highly desirable, and thus expensive, neighborhoods. To these losses connected to the fashion business, Gicquel added the expenses of medical care, the cost of supporting Gicquel's mother (a burden that Gicquel's brother allegedly refused to share), losses incurred in her husband's construction business when tools and materials were destroyed during the storming of the Bastille, and finally, a number of significant legal expenditures and other debits incurred as relations between the couple and their creditors moved toward the breaking point.

The couple's total liabilities thus amounted to 45,800 livres, which nicely balanced the 45,329 livres they owed to their creditors. The balance this list created between loss and debt was intended quite explicitly to show the court that Gicquel's business might have survived if not for unavoidable circumstances in which they merely played the part of innocent victims. Although we may find the figures to balance too neatly for absolute credibility, Gicquel's statement nonetheless reveals the costs and risks of the multiple credit transactions this family undertook and the specific perils of opening shop as a marchande de modes.

At the end of their statement the couple summarized their situation by stating that "the profits that they made in their commerce and enterprise were very modest due to the little trade and business that they each did and that these profits were not sufficient to offset the expense of their household and upkeep that they do not note here; however without the losses detailed above, they would have had enough to pay what they owe." Whatever the accuracy of the losses Gicquel detailed, she was certainly correct that her income did not cover her expenditures. The total sales recorded in her journal from January 1, 1784 to May 23, 1784 and from January 12, 1787 to May 16, 1788 amounted to a total of 27,892 livres. This represented 17,437 livres less than the debts she acknowledged to her suppliers. Like Moreau, it appears that income from her trade never covered its expenses. Part of her problem was surely bad luck as she claimed, though it seems likely that Gicquel's margin of profit was always too slender to allow her business to thrive.

Other bankruptcy accounts tell of different aspirations and different setbacks. For example, two unmarried women, Madeleine Charlotte Girard and Elizabeth Tatry, were partners in a joint enterprise in the late 1770s. Their operations included sales to Parisian clients as well as an attempt to export goods to the West Indies. Dissatisfied with their local agent, Tatry traveled to Cap Français in April 1778 to oversee their affairs personally. Despite these adventuresome efforts, the partners were obliged to initiate bankruptcy proceedings in June 1778. Their declaration to the consular court indicated that they owed 36,673 livres to twenty-three individuals, including merchants of silk, lace, fur, gauze, perfume, and ribbons. They would have used these materials themselves, alongside a few employees, to make the fashionable goods in their shop. Their largest debt was of almost 18,000 livres to Louis Gicquel, a merchant mercer who held debt on many of the fashion merchants in this study; the smallest debt, 115 livres, was to a painter who had presumably worked on their boutique. These debts were matched by 8,500 livres in unpaid accounts from over thirty clients, along with 5,000 livres in stock, almost 700 livres in furnishings from their shop, and 1,000 livres in personal clothing and furniture. The two partners also claimed to own 22,000 livres in merchandise sent to the West Indies.

A year later, in July 1779, Tatry and Girard had reduced their overall liabilities by only twenty-five livres and most of their remaining obligations remained close to the figures from the declaration of June 1778. The detailed new accounts they rendered to the court in 1779, however, revealed some significant shifts in their debts. They had apparently paid off three of their creditors and added five additional ones. Moreover, some merchants, like Louis Gicquel, had furnished them additional credit. Even while undergoing bankruptcy proceedings, the partners had not only managed to forestall their creditors but even obtained new sources of credit in the hopes of reviving their business. Unfortunately, Tatry and Girard's undertakings in the West Indies were less successful. In July 1779 they declared losses of almost 20,000 livres related to their business at Cap Français, which included 3,800 spent for Tatry's voyages there and back, 6,000 livres for goods damaged during the voyage, 2,400 livres for her rented house there, and 1,000 livres for the "rent of a negress and her food." They calculated as losses another 14,000 livres spent on wages for shopgirls and servants in Paris as well as on personal expenses and lost merchandise.[66] The amalgam of workers' wages and personal expenses suggests the blurry lines dividing the women's personal and professional lives. Given the lack of subsequent documentation, it is unknown whether they were able to revive their business after July 1779.

Marie Denise Prévost operated a more modest endeavor still, which led her to deposit a failure dossier in 1758. Prévost's deposition declared arrears of 5,361 livres. Among twelve creditors, the most important were a ribbon maker and a cloth merchant, to whom she owed 3,000 and 1,000 livres respectively. She also claimed losses of 13,345 livres, including 2,500 livres for a fifteen-month illness, 1,500 in goods stolen from her shop, 2,500 on furnishing and decorations for the shop, 1,125 in rent, 375 for an operating license from the mercers' guild over a two-and-a-half year period, and the same amount in wages to two shopgirls. Prévost's clients owed her 4,365 livres, with an average of 86 livres each for thirty-three clients. She also estimated her stock to be worth 1,500 livres.[67]

Not all fashion merchants declared losses in their bankruptcy statements, but those who did largely echo the types of claims made by Gicquel, Tatry and Girard, and Prévost. The category of "losses" had no official bearing on the tallying of accounts, which focused solely on calculating assets against liabilities. Failing merchants nonetheless took advantage of the provision allowing them to include losses "for information only" to provide explanations about the unpredictable and onerous expenses they had faced. The range of items included in the loss category is capacious and often ill assorted, reflective of their authors' eagerness to put as many details of their plight into the record as possible. Eight of twenty-nine statements itemized expenses for illness, six noted legal and/or notarial expenses (usually associated with prosecution for unpaid debts), four lamented the cost of interest charges on their debts, and five mentioned the price of their guild membership. Expenses related to setting up shop, mentioned in eleven cases, ranged from 366 to 8,900 livres. The latter figure included 5,600 livres for bribes spent to obtain a prime location for the boutique, a common source of expense and anxiety in the documents.

The merchants' statements also emphasize heavy losses due to the theft of merchandise (four cases), the loss of their goods' value through changes in fashion or physical destruction (seven cases, including fire and a sea voyage), and the failure of agents to sell goods entrusted to them or reimburse their value (two cases). Altogether thirty-five separate types of loss were mentioned in the documents. Of course, none of these claims may be taken at face value, but they do indicate the range of justifications merchants employed to present themselves as honorable and industrious entrepreneurs: they paid guild fees; they suffered predations from greedy landlords and thieves; they invested heavily in their shops yet were victims of unavoidable misfortune. The very existence of the loss category suggests that their audience of creditors and adjudicators accepted the role of contingency and was willing to take into account the precise circumstances of each failure when deliberating on its outcome.

Information on the result of bankruptcy negotiations is unfortunately lacking from most of the dossiers held in the archives of the merchant court. Available evidence suggests that the terms of settlement fashion merchants obtained were often as generous as those they had extended to their own clients. As noted above, Marie-Jeanne-Victoire Moreau was able to cut her debt in half and eliminate all legal fees and interest. Another merchant, Marie Elisabeth Rondu, sought sympathy from her creditors by listing a long string of losses she had endured, which consisted primarily of being obliged to move shop on several occasions when new owners purchased the buildings in which she was located. Like Moreau, she requested a 50 percent reduction in the principal of her debts and the annulment of all interest and fees. In exchange she promised to pay the remaining portion in twelve equal payments every three months over a four-year period.[68] Marie Madeleine Fremont, widow Berthelot, came up with a different strategy. While also requesting the cancellation of interest and fees on the debt, she did not ask for a reduction of the principal. Instead, she instructed her representative to request a ten-year delay in its payment, promising to pay one-tenth each year and pledging all of her property, present and future, as security to back the deal.[69]

It is unknown whether Rondu and Fremont enjoyed the same success as Moreau in obtaining generous terms from creditors. Another colleague, Marie Rose Lacoste, secured a long delay in paying her debts but only at the cost of abandoning her business as well as all of her property to her creditors. On the basis of this agreement, they agreed to allow her eight years to pay her remaining debts, in which interest and fees from the legal procedures against her were included.[70] Her creditors' harsh treatment may have been influenced by Lacoste's admission that she had never kept an account book. Such negligent bookkeeping practices did not argue in favor of extending her additional credit and granting her a chance to renew the business. Lacoste's subsequent life history, however, testifies to the resilience of Parisian entrepreneurs. A single woman in her faillite of 1765, in 1774 she reappeared in the records as the widow of Sieur Petit, a bourgeois de Paris, with new bills from another independent commerce. Thus, marriage to a man of means seems to have provided a fresh start for Lacoste, whose prior failure did not render her ineligible for marriage.

Rose Bertin's success in the two decades before the French Revolution is striking testimony to the central role women had gained in the fashion and garment industries over the eighteenth century. Hers was an exceptional story of celebrity and royal patronage, but it emerged from a wider context in which women had become key figures in making and selling articles of female clothing and accessories to a substantially enlarged purchasing population. Like other retailers, fashion merchants functioned on credit: they sold their products to clients through delayed payment agreements and relied in turn on credit from workers and suppliers. Their credit relations involved them in extended transactions with both male and female merchants and artisans, although they owed more money to men and acquired a wider array of goods and services from men. The vast majority operated on a far smaller scale than Bertin, but they also sold and purchased goods on credit. In selling labor or goods and in buying food, clothing, or other items, either for personal or professional consumption, credit touched the lives of women from all social categories, including working women.

Given their imbrication in different types of credit networks, women's reputations must have drawn on local knowledge of their creditworthiness. Did the woman work hard? Did she have a reliable pool of paying customers for her wares? Did she squander money or save it for a rainy day? Could she be trusted to reimburse money loaned to her or not? Records from the merchant court furnish examples of female credit in crisis and failure, but even these examples show us women who had succeeded in obtaining substantial advances from wholesalers and who devised plausible explanations of their business failure. Like their male counterparts, they fell ill, they suffered theft, and their goods were damaged by unforeseen circumstances. Fashion, the source of their livelihood, could also turn against them and decimate the value of their stock. The very fact that their cases entered the historical record attests to their participation in official procedures for regulating the flow and disruption of credit transactions.

Women's involvement in trade credit was in many ways empowering in the eighteenth century. Married, single, and widowed women appear to have enjoyed relatively equal access with male merchants to the credit of wholesale suppliers. Credit thus allowed women to develop relations with other men and women based on professional interest rather than through exclusively familial or affective ties. The world of fashion, in particular, offered women autonomous careers and a space to imagine new kinds of social relations and self-presentation. We have seen how far it carried Rose Bertin from her humble origins in a provincial city. Credit also helped foster long-term attachments between elite clients and their socially inferior provisioners. As was the case with Rose Bertin and Marie Antoinette, discussed in the following chapter, these relations could be reciprocal and transcend the level of anonymous monetary transactions. There were also, however, negative aspects to women's credit relations. Like their male counterparts, female merchants struggled to survive as they awaited long-overdue payments from clients whose lavish lifestyles were brokered on credit.

The findings of this chapter thus pose two pressing questions: How did fashion merchants survive at all, given their clients' long delays and reductions in paying accounts? And why did some survive where others did not? Each question requires multiple answers. First, fashion merchants survived because many of them did not face the circumstances recorded in these chapters or at least not in such extreme form. We must remember the inherent bias of the sources, which record failures to pay much more emphatically than those who actually did pay.

And yet this can only be a partial response, for evidence of the frequency of lengthy delays and defaults abounds in our own sources and in the historiography. A second answer is that the "culture of credit," which was such a burden to failing fashion merchants, also worked to their advantage. Suppliers knew very well that fashion merchants faced lengthy delays in obtaining payment—they faced them too and often from the same clients—and they were prepared to be patient as long as their confidence in the retailers survived and their own circumstances permitted it. The accommodation demanded by defaulting marchandes de modes testifies to their belief that they merited terms at least as generous as the ones enjoyed by their clients. Thus, a second factor allowing fashion merchants to survive was the very culture of credit that placed them in jeopardy. Closely related was a third factor, the practice of balancing credits among merchants. Although the evidence is thin, it is plausible that fashion merchants met some of their debts in kind by furnishing fashionable goods to the men and women who provided raw materials as well as other necessities like food, wine, medical care, lodgings, and so on. This would allow them to cancel some of their debt, even if they did not obtain cash payments from clients.

A key conclusion here is that categories of "success" and "failure" were fuzzy and very fluid. A "successful" merchant was not one who had no debts and did not rely on credit, but one whose suppliers kept the lines of credit open. A "failed" merchant was not necessarily finished in the trade but possibly subject only to more stringent negotiations and supervision. Merchants might walk the path from success to failure multiple times and in both directions. These considerations do not explain why one marchande de modes survived while another did not. Bankruptcy narratives suggest that contingency—in the form of illness, ruthless landlords, thieving shopgirls, the whims of fashion, an important client's default, revolution, and other calamities—played a crucial role. While maintaining a critical perspective on the details recounted with such stirring emotion in these cases, we may accept that transaction costs were steep and sometimes insurmountable. We must not overlook, however, the role of factors such as individual talent and acumen, personal connections, charisma, and habits of hard work and industry. A merchant acknowledged as a creator of new styles, for example, would be much less vulnerable to losing valuable stock to the caprices of fashion. The family story behind each business must have also played a vital part in its outcome. Most concretely, this chapter suggests that the simple key to survival was being able to charge high enough prices to cover expenses and to extract sufficient payment from clients; fashion merchants' weakness on both these points suggests the fragility of their position between their large, socially superior female clientele and a smaller number of powerful male merchants and manufacturers.

CHAPTER 6

MADAME DÉFICIT AND HER
MINISTER OF FASHION

SELF-FASHIONING AND THE POLITICS OF CREDIT

*I*n January 1787 rumors spread through Paris that the celebrated fashion merchant Rose Bertin had filed for bankruptcy, with debts of two to three million livres. Unlike the police action against Marie-Jeanne-Victoire Moreau, the report was not limited to a brief statement in the back pages of a daily newspaper. Instead, gossip spread like wildfire through *le monde*. Despite her notoriously high prices and rich clients, the rumors did not shock Parisians, for aristocratic clients' were notorious for tardiness in paying their bills. High-ranking observers, who resented Bertin's arrogance and unprecedented access to the queen, greeted the news with spiteful acclaim. As the Baronne d'Oberkirch wrote: "The empire of fashion is experiencing a great cataclysm. Mademoiselle Bertin, so proud, so high, so insolent even, who *worked* with her majesty, Mademoiselle Bertin displaying on her bills in large letters: *Fashion merchant to the queen*; Mademoiselle Bertin has just gone bankrupt. It is true that her bankruptcy is not at all plebeian; it is the bankruptcy of a great lady, two million! . . . We are assured that Mademoiselle Bertin will cede to all the tears and continue her business."[1]

In another twist to the story rumormongers claimed that Bertin herself had invented the alleged bankruptcy in order to obtain payment of her long over-due account with Queen Marie Antoinette. According to the diary of book-seller Siméon-Prosper Hardy, Bertin habitually resorted to such tactics to wrest compensation from the crown, and on this occasion had immediately received a note for four hundred thousand livres.[2] In this episode rumors of the bank-ruptcy of the foremost fashion merchant in the realm echoed collective aware-ness of the potential bankruptcy of her most lucrative and controversial client. Royal finances were stretched by the War of the Austrian Succession (1740–1748), then leveled by the Seven Years' War (1756–1763), a disaster for French colonial holdings, and finally decimated by French support for the American

War of Independence (1776–1783). In 1786 Controller General Charles Alexandre de Calonne submitted a secret memorandum to the king warning of the state's impending financial collapse. As Hardy circulated reports about Bertin's affairs, the Assembly of Notables was preparing to meet to consider Louis xvi's request for new taxes to stave off his own credit disaster.

Marie Antoinette's spending on fashionable clothing formed a tiny portion of the colossal French debt. And yet critics argued, and many in the public believed, that she bore a non-negligible share of responsibility for the crisis. Hostile attention focused in particular on her long-term relationship with Rose Bertin and the alleged expenses of Bertin's creations for the queen. The coupling of Marie Antoinette and Rose Bertin (figures 6.1 and 6.2) represents the ultimate fusion of the multiple strands woven through this book: political and financial credit, fashion, sexuality, and female agency. Marie Antoinette and Marie-Jeanne (the merchant's legal name) could not have been further apart in social origins: a poor daughter of the provincial working classes and the daughter of the Austrian empress, consort to the king of the largest and most powerful state in western Europe. Their meetings were real, consisting of at least twice-weekly sessions in the privacy of the queen's chambers at Versailles from 1775 until the queen's imprisonment in 1792. They also took the form of reported exchanges between queen and commoner that circulated in the pages of contemporary periodical literature, letters, and journals and in the witty anecdotes that made the rounds of salons, public promenades, and court festivities.

What these stories expressed was a perceived collapse of traditional boundaries: between aristocratic circuits of political credit and mercantile channels of financial credit; between rank and tradition, on the one hand, and social mobility and publicity, on the other; and between court-sanctioned dress codes and ephemeral novelties. With no favorite to rival her, the queen enjoyed unprecedented influence over her husband. She wielded power in part through fashionable display, encouraging court ladies to emulate her consumption as a means to demonstrate allegiance to the crown. The queen's chief collaborator in this effort was Rose Bertin, who gained her own unprecedented intimacy with the queen through a virtuoso creative gift and keen understanding of how to use display and apparel as techniques of power. A (foreign) woman thus controlled circuits of credit at the French court but was herself dependent on a master wielder of the credibility of fashion. The two were bound by confused and confusing ties of mutual dependence.

What made all of this possible, one might argue, was the inadequacy of Louis xvi's sexuality to the demands of rule, including both the eight years of impotency following his marriage in 1770 and the sexual indifference that

FIGURE 6.1 Marie Antoinette, Queen of France. This portrait, by Elisabeth Vigée-LeBrun, depicts Marie Antoinette in 1778, three years after meeting Bertin and at the height of her interest in fashion. In all likelihood Bertin furnished the queen the hat and dress trimmings worn in the portrait. *Source*: © Schloss Ambras / Erich Lessing / Art Resource, NY.

FIGURE 6.2 Marie-Jeanne (Rose) Bertin, fashion merchant to the queen. A medallion portrait of the famous fashion merchant by Jean-François Janinet, date unknown. It is one of the few surviving images of Bertin. *Source*: Bibliothèque nationale de France.

led him to be the first French monarch on record with no favorite, male or female. With a physically and temperamentally weak king, the normal circuits of power were obstructed, creating both the possibility of alternate circuits for the queen's libidinal energies and the potential for her to channel all power to herself.

To untangle the overlapping strands binding together queen and fashion merchant, this chapter examines four elements of their credit relations. The first section investigates the role of political credit in Marie Antoinette's ascension from dauphine to monarch as discussed in correspondence between her mother and the male advisers who represented the empress at the French court. This correspondence reveals overt discussion of how a princess should manage her credit relations at court as well as constant attempts to apply these policies to particular events and circumstances. Marie Antoinette's youthful inattention only further convinced her mentors of the need for a systematic policy on the appropriate use of credit. While nodding good-naturedly at their lessons, Marie Antoinette devised one response on her own to the dilemmas of her position at court. This was to use the visibility and novelty of her apparel to attract notice and generate a new kind of courtly credibility. In doing so she both continued traditional feminine ways of exercising power and broke controversial boundaries.

The second section of the chapter focuses on the other side of the pair, tracking the rise of the fashion merchant who enabled Marie Antoinette's self-fashioning as a princess à la mode after their meeting in 1775. We explore the importance of reputation for Bertin's commercial credibility and, in particular, her use of the theater of her shop and her performance of gestures and words to generate fascination with herself and her products. Discussion then turns to the ways Bertin deployed her credit with the queen as collateral for other forms of credit that brought her the accoutrements of her clients' noble lifestyles. What is particularly captivating in Bertin's case is the overlap between her public activities as a merchant and stories about her in publications belonging to the literary and aristocratic milieus of *le monde*. Anecdotes about Bertin spread both by word of mouth and in the published and manuscript literature that reported on current events, literary publications, and cultural happenings. Duchapt may have inspired great interest on the part of philosophes in the 1740s, but Bertin appears to have consciously sought this publicity and to have manipulated to a large degree the nature of her celebrity.

The chapter ends with an examination of the politicization of the relationship between the two women in the last years of the Old Regime. The attack from critics of the monarchy posited a collapse of boundaries, cascading from the queen's apartments at Versailles to the fashion merchant's boutique in Paris and ultimately to the Bastille and the sharp blade of the guillotine. These denunciations were the legacy of the critique of women's access to credit that emerged under the regency, discussed in chapter 2, and the suspicion of the relationship between fashionable appearances and credit in all its guises, discussed in chapter 3. Marie Antoinette's relationship with Bertin caused scandal partly for its unprecedented intimacy but also because it presented the living embodiment of decades of frustration among opponents of the crown.

The Regime of Credit: Strategies for the Making of a Queen

Marie Antoinette arrived in France in May 1770 as a young girl of fourteen, married to the heir of the throne of France. It was, from the outset, a highly controversial union. Austria was the traditional enemy of France, reviled as the ambitious and threatening power on France's eastern borders. In 1756 the Treaty of Versailles—orchestrated by Madame de Pompadour and the foreign minister Choiseul—initiated a Diplomatic Revolution whereby France replaced Britain as Austria's privileged partner, just as Prussia turned from France to Britain. Negotiated for over four years, the marriage in 1770 between the children of Austria and France was intended to cement the new and tenuous bond between the two nations.

The stakes of this marriage were thus extremely high, as public opinion in France remained hostile to Austria and the anti-Pompadour *dévot* party at court urged reversal of the alliance. Until her death in 1780, Maria Theresa kept close tabs on her daughter through a continuous exchange of letters, containing as much imperious scolding as maternal affection, as well as through a secret correspondence she maintained with the Austrian ambassador at the French court the Comte de Mercy-Argenteau and the Abbé de Vermond, who had been sent to Vienna as a French tutor prior to the marriage and accompanied Marie Antoinette to France as her reader and secretary.[3] This voluminous correspondence emphasizes the centrality of credit as a category through which the empress and her informers understood Marie Antoinette's position at court and tried to manipulate the young bride's power and influence.

Like other eighteenth-century courtiers, by "credit" they meant the power and influence an individual possessed with others, which allowed the credit holder to obtain advantages and favors. At court the king held the greatest credit, as evidenced by the extreme concern in these letters with Louis XVI's sentiments and affections. And yet, despite Bourbon claims to absolutism, credit devolved from his power through the ranks at court, sometimes crossing over nominal rankings of hierarchy and title. The correspondents also used the word *credit* to describe the affective power individuals held over each other. In her eyes, for example, the letters Maria Theresa wrote to her daughter were one way to maintain her own credit over her daughter, despite the distance that separated them. As she remarked to Mercy-Argenteau in a letter of December 1, 1770: "I know my daughter well enough to be quite assured that she will succeed at everything she desires and that she will be very bold. It is why I always restrain her and use my credit with her sparingly, mixing much tenderness with my reproaches."[4]

Mercy-Argenteau and Vermond observed affairs at court closely and reported on them at length to Vienna. Guided by the empress, they dispensed endless advice to the dauphine on how to manage concrete situations and individuals and strove to inculcate general principles for managing and increasing the credit available to her as one of the chief ladies of the court. Their concern was heightened, and more so over time, by the fact that the marriage remained unconsummated and Louis appeared uninterested in or incapable of fulfilling his dynastic obligations. As dauphine, and later as queen, Marie Antoinette thus occupied a unique and paradoxical situation vis-à-vis her husband. As the only woman in his life, she was ideally situated to exercise unchecked power over him, but their lack of sexual relations invalidated the two means through which women normally secured their position: seduction or motherhood.

One of the most pressing issues, given Marie Antoinette's youth and vulnerability and the acknowledged weaknesses of her husband, was to prevent powerful individuals from exercising undue influence over her. A great source of concern (which would continue into the first years of Louis XVI's reign) was the influence of King Louis XV's four aunts, long-time habitués of court intrigue. The aunts latched on to this impressionable newcomer as a means to counter the power of the king's despised favorite, Madame du Barry, who had joined the court a year before Marie Antoinette's arrival. Mercy-Argenteau's careful assessment of the rise and fall of the influence of the aunts, referred to collectively as Mesdames, illuminates the almost daily accounting that observers conducted of the day-to-day fluctuations of credit at court. On May 15, 1772, he wrote to the empress of the improper hold Mesdames held over her daughter, confessing that they "still possess a more extensive credit then would be desirable." By September he noted with relief that "through the remarks of Madame the Archduchess [Marie Antoinette], I remarked a lessening of Mesdames' credit," although he acknowledged that the influence bred by strength of habit and fear had not disappeared entirely.[5] In November he continued in this reassuring vein: "I should observe here, once and for all, that the credit and the influence of Mesdames on Madame the Dauphine has continually declined." By July 1773 he was surprised that the minister of foreign affairs, the Duc d'Aiguillon, was so ill-informed of the politics of the royal family that he attempted to use one of the aunts, Madame Adélaïde, as a conduit to Marie Antoinette.[6]

Alongside his attempts to distance those seeking to control the dauphine, Mercy-Argenteau and his collaborator Vermond struggled to impart general principles of credit management to an impetuous and inattentive adolescent. The key issue was how to respond to courtiers' attempts to employ her credit to obtain favors and recommendations for themselves, their friends, and family members. Mercy-Argenteau was alarmed to note that, under the influence of Mesdames, Marie Antoinette had been weak enough to let them persuade her to solicit favors on their behalf. He was quick to react: "I made Madame the Archduchess see that all of this clearly led to the compromising of her credit, and even the justice which is in her nature." Although the ministers to whom she most frequently turned, the controller general and the war minister, had so far proved amenable to her requests, Mercy-Argenteau reminded her that she risked embarrassing them with demands of weak merit and thus losing their respect and support.[7]

The dauphine had shown a similar weakness with her first lady-in-waiting, Madame de Misry, a woman who, "without talent or wit, does not cease her fondness for intrigue, a great desire to flaunt credit and enough impudence to impose in this regard." Misry apparently convinced Marie Antoinette to allow her to hold "audiences for certain women who solicited favors" in which she promised to use her influence over the dauphine to grant their requests. Mercy-Argenteau decried the woman's audacity and recommended, without success, that she be disgraced for abusing her position.[8]

On another occasion the dauphine had fallen victim to the machinations of a group of court ladies who sought her favor to obtain the position of superintendent of the household and finances of the dauphine for a young royal officer, described by Mercy-Argenteau as a "a very slight personage." To elude potential interference, the women cornered the dauphine at the moment she was entering her husband's apartments and convinced her to present their suit in her own name. When the king's agreement became known, a "clamor" arose from those who knew themselves to be more highly ranked and better qualified for the post. Marie Antoinette prevailed only by directly confronting the minister who was refusing to issue letters of appointment, at some cost to her reputation.

Alarmed by these incidents, Mercy-Argenteau took advantage of private conversations to outline the principles by which Marie Antoinette must manage her credit: "I greatly insisted on the prudence that is necessary in the choice of those one wishes to protect or to attach to one's service, on the nature of requests that one proposes to make to the king or his ministers, on the distrust that one should have of requests from others and that almost always lead to injustices or the favoring of mediocre individuals. One error of this kind alone may suffice to destroy the most well-established credit."[9] In the same letter he remarked that the dauphine had all the personal faculties necessary to obtain great influence over the king, her husband's grandfather, but was too timid to exercise them: "I would answer with my life that if she could force herself to take advantage of her ascendancy over the king, there would be neither favorite nor minister who could resist the weight, the influence, and the credit that Madame la Dauphine would presently acquire." He noted that the dauphine good-naturedly listened to his pleadings and generally agreed with his reasoning but then failed to alter her conduct.

Once Marie Antoinette became queen, upon the death of Louis XV in May 1774, the stakes of her credit soared, even as the continuing lack of sexual relations with her husband heightened malicious gossip and endangered her legitimacy as royal consort. Mercy-Argenteau immediately counseled Marie Antoinette against a number of dangers. The first was that Mesdames or other court factions would attempt to exert influence over the new king's weak character. If public opinion perceived such domination, he warned, "the queen's credit would receive a mortal blow." He also cautioned Marie Antoinette to insist that no prime minister be named to assist the king, since "the craft of a prime minister in France has always been to intercept and destroy the credit of queens." A third principle was that the queen should force herself to tolerate and please her husband despite what he acknowledged were the monarch's coarse manners and lack of charm. By using caresses and indulgence, "she will acquire absolute power over the king; but she must govern him without appearing to wish to govern him." A final element in his plan was that the queen must ensure that she always shared the king's bed. If he did manage to achieve sexual satisfaction, this injunction suggested, it must be with the queen and no other woman.[10]

The Abbé de Vermond shared Mercy-Argenteau's concerns and cautions. On June 7, 1774, Mercy-Argenteau included a long quotation from Vermond in a letter to Maria Theresa in which the abbé expounded upon the central role of credit in French politics. According to Vermond, it was impossible to ban patronage and protection in France, despite frequent abuses:

> That is impossible in France, without recasting the constitution of the monarchy, perhaps even the national character. V. E. [Votre Excellence, that

is, Mercy-Argenteau] knows better than I that from immemorial custom three-quarters of positions, honors, pensions are accorded not to service but to favor and credit. This favor is supposedly motivated by birth, alliance, wealth; almost always it has no true foundation but protection and intrigue. This order is so well established that it is respected as a type of justice even by those who suffer from it the most. A good gentleman who can neither dazzle by alliances at court nor by a splendid expenditure would not dare to hope for a regiment, however long-standing and distinguished might be both his service and his origins.[11]

Not only regiments and officer posts, Vermond continued, but even military honors, including the supreme distinction of the Croix de Saint-Louis, were given "through credit and favor." Bishoprics and abbeys "are even more thoroughly under the regime of credit," as were financial offices, magistracies, and other high posts in the royal administration and judiciary.[12]

The fascination with credit evinced throughout Maria Theresa's correspondence with Versailles suggests that the "regime of credit" described by Vermond was a European-wide phenomenon intimately familiar to the Austrian empress and her Belgian-born ambassador. However, the abbé's comments in the passage above also suggest that contemporaries saw the court of France as particularly marked by the dark side of credit, by exchanges in which "no true foundation" justified the bestowal of credit. Vermond's words echo Charles Duclos's analysis of French credit as dominating the circuits linking the official authority of the royal ministers and the informal prestige, connections, and self-interest of the court nobility.

Given the opportunities and the risks of the credit regime, how should the new queen respond to requests for her favor? While he counseled Marie Antoinette to avoid unnecessary or excessive use of patronage, Vermond judged that it was the queen's duty to promote the interests of members of her own household, whose official stipends were insufficient for the expenses of their ostentatious role at court. Moreover, if the queen failed to play any part in the patronage system, disappointed courtiers would turn elsewhere and her credit would dissipate. She must engage the system in order to retain ascendancy over it. In discussing the pitfalls encircling her, the example of Louis xv's self-effacing and pious queen was presented to Marie Antoinette as the model to be avoided at all costs. It was advice such as this, one presumes, that led to Vermond's poor reputation as a schemer who encouraged the queen to meddle in affairs at court.

Within a few weeks Marie Antoinette had satisfied her counselors that she had won the new king's confidence, thus assuring her standing. As Mercy-Argenteau joyfully noted in a letter to the empress, "the queen advances with a steady step toward the greatest credit, and she will invoke it successfully each time and whenever she wishes to make use of it."[13] By July this initial impression was confirmed by her success in demanding the dismissal of the foreign minister d'Aiguillon, leading Mercy-Argenteau to comment that "there can be no doubt that the queen enjoys the most marked and decisive credit over the mind of the king her husband." However, a new source of concern had arisen along with the queen's credit standing. Credit she might have with the king, but, despite the repeated counsel of Mercy-Argenteau and Vermond, she was proving incapable of using it wisely: "Isolated objects, often useless, sometimes harmful, set her in action, she uses force for them, she makes use of her credit and she succeeds, whereas other more important and truly useful objects attract no attention from her whatsoever."[14]

Like any other type of capital, courtly credit needed to be wisely invested in affairs promising lasting gain. Mercy-Argenteau cautioned that "if, in the long term, the use of her credit only bears on momentary objects of fantasy, if, instead of making herself useful, even necessary to the king by giving him good advice and calming his doubts, the queen limits herself simply to demanding this or that," and if she allows herself to appear bored or disinterested when the king discussed affairs of state with her, then the weak-willed king would look elsewhere for guidance. As a result, "the credit of the queen would disappear, [and] other people would acquire it at her expense."[15] Maria Theresa was even less optimistic about her daughter's capacity to excel in statecraft: "I doubt whether she will ever have a great share in affairs; the political system of France aside, her lack of application will always create too great an obstacle. I thus believe that we may be content if she preserves enough credit to influence the choice of ministers and prevent royal princes and princesses from gaining ascendancy over the king."[16]

Maria Theresa was both right and wrong. Although the queen remained distracted by the pleasures of life at court and did not seek systematic input into national affairs, she was capable of rousing herself for causes in which she took special interest, usually involving the maintenance of the Franco-Austrian Alliance and any individuals she credited with having favored the alliance. Thus she acted in secret, and with unexpected success, to have Monsieur de Guines—a former French ambassador in London recalled for abusing his diplomatic privileges—elevated to the title of duke by the king in May 1776. According to the Comte de Creutz, ambassador for Swedish King Gustavus III, she did so to reward Guines for his loyalty to the party of the Duc de Choiseul, chief architect of the Diplomatic Revolution and of her own marriage. He noted that "we have just seen the most resounding effect of her credit; there is no more doubt of the power she has over the king."[17]

Marie Antoinette also played a role in the dismissal of Controller General Turgot and the resignation of Chancellor Malesherbes, both of whom she resented for their role in Guines's recall from London. Her advisors from the imperial court were helpless to prevent such personally motivated attacks, leaving Mercy-Argenteau to issue a visionary warning: "Such effects of her credit could one day bring her just reproach from her husband the king and even the entire nation."[18] Thus, whatever her motivations, observers believed she successfully deployed her credit to intervene in the highest posts of the royal government. One inadvertent result of her exclusion of Turgot was the reversal of his abolition of the guilds, which temporarily saved the seamstresses' guild from oblivion and allowed for the creation in 1776 of a new fashion merchants' guild whose first officer was no less than her own purveyor, Rose Bertin. One wonders if Bertin herself raised the issue of guild status for her trade in one of the sessions she spent with the queen each week.

More damning to Marie Antoinette's credit, in the eyes of the court and public opinion, was the coterie of friends that formed around her. One of the central figures was Madame de Lamballe, whom she appointed to the lucrative position of superintendent of the queen's household. She became even closer to the Comtesse Jules de Polignac. From their first meeting in 1775 at a court festival, through the birth of her first child in December 1778, the queen's affection for Polignac eclipsed all others. These friendships reveal the extent to which money and financial credit were intertwined with the exercise of political credit. Her new friends wished to be at the center of court society and desired posts and titles for themselves and their friends, but they also sought money to pay off their debts and fund their lavish courtly lifestyles. The Comtesse de Polignac reportedly succeeded in extracting enormous profits from the queen's favor, including four hundred thousand livres to pay her debts, eight hundred thousand livres for her daughter's dowry, and the promise of land with an annual income of thirty-five thousand livres.[19] This was, in some ways, business as usual. The king's favorites had obtained even larger sums of money both from those who sought their favors and in direct gifts from the king. What surprised and dismayed the court and public opinion was the new role of a queen dispensing money to favorites, especially in a situation where the queen herself was the only favorite of the king.

Over time it was not merely her friends' venality and extravagance that displeased public opinion but the appearance of such failings within the queen herself. Much of the criticism of her expenditures centered on her growing love of fashion, which bloomed after another friend, the Duchesse de Chartres, introduced the young queen to her fashion merchant Rose Bertin.

The Queen's Self-Fashioning

Commentators on Marie Antoinette have frequently observed her use of clothing and fashion as tools of power.[20] The queen herself acknowledged in correspondence that one of the ways she had endeavored to project the "appearance of [political] credit" was through her clothing.[21] She did not invent the usage of clothing and dress as a means of impressing others and winning prestige and influence, having discovered upon arrival at Versailles how deeply ingrained clothing and display—and the rituals of dressing and undressing—were in the French practice of power. The importance of constructing an appropriately French self-presentation was imposed on then Archduchess Maria Antonia even before her marriage took place. As part of the negotiations leading up to the marriage, Louis xv dispatched a portrait painter to the Austrian court, along with a renowned hairstylist, who together produced a portrait showing the new Marie Antoinette in French dress with an appropriately Gallic hairstyle. She also had French dancing masters to teach her proper comportment at court along with French language tutors and a painful operation on her teeth to render her smile worthy of the Bourbon dynasty.

Marie Antoinette thus drew on long-standing French traditions of representing power and authority with the body and its clothing. Where she departed radically from this tradition, however, was by becoming an active participant in the fashion system itself. Louis xiv had issued rules regarding appropriate attire at his court for the purposes of status distinction; he also favored manufacturers with his custom to stimulate French domestic production. He did not descend, however, to personal involvement in the everyday dynamics of fashion, either as a creator of new fashions in collaboration with merchants and artisans or as a follower of the general trends. The credit conveyed by his crown guaranteed a ripple effect from royal fashions, yet he himself and his family stood above the vagaries of *la mode*. Within a few years of her arrival, Marie Antoinette began to break down the boundaries between royal attire and Parisian fashion and to use fashionable display to forge a particular niche at court. As Caroline Weber has argued, "she identified fashion as a key weapon in her struggle for personal prestige, authority, and sometimes mere survival."[22] As she did so, the dauphine drew first on existing fashions;

as time went by she more ambitiously sought to control the reins of fashion herself and thus to demonstrate to the world her cultural and social authority.

One of the most important sites of this display was the queen's hair and headdresses. At the time the headdresses worn by elite women at court and in the city had already captured public attention. In the 1770s the *pouf* became popular, a style that would last through the revolution. It was a complex construction requiring hours of painstaking labor to construct. It consisted of a wire frame that was padded and covered with false hair and placed upon the wearer's head, after which the stylist would weave the wearer's own hair, along with additional artificial hair, into the frame. The hair was curled and arranged to complement the overall themes and style of the pouf and covered in white powder. On top of this base were attached lace, gauze, ribbons, real or artificial flowers, feathers, and sometimes miniature replicas of ships, castles, animals, and other objects. Poufs were remarkable not only in their enormous size—which grew to two or three feet in height—but in their thematic styles, which celebrated the latest public events (figure 6.3).

Fashion engravings and periodical literature of the 1770s and 1780s provide numerous examples of the quickly succeeding themes of poufs and some hints as to their origins. In the January 28, 1775 edition of the gossip sheet the *Correspondance secrète*, the author attributed the summit of creativity in this area to the famous Sieur Beaulard, Bertin's predecessor at the top of their profession: "The fertility of imagination and the taste of Sieur Beaulard, fashion merchant, surpassed everything we have seen in this genre."

In response to the request of an English admiral's widow for a bonnet reflecting her late husband's career, Beaulard reportedly arrived two days later with a pouf on which gauze puffs "perfectly represented a turbulent sea, a thousand different baubles imitated ships."[23] He supposedly invented bonnets "à la bonne Maman," with hidden springs that the wearer could use to lower the bonnet's height to a modest height for visiting conservative parents or raise it when away from familial scrutiny. He also presented an artificial rose to the new queen that imitated both the appearance and smell of a real flower and opened to reveal a miniature portrait of her.

These spectacular successes did not prevent Beaulard's filing for bankruptcy (*faillite*) in August 1789, but they do show how imbricated fashion had become with public affairs. Robert Darnton has described the overlapping media of the eighteenth-century Parisian information system that encompassed gossip, rumors, handwritten newssheets, and published journals.[24] To this mix, we should add advertising, commercial publications, and items of fashion them-

Cœffure
à l'Indépendance ou le
Triomphe de la liberté

FIGURE 6.3 *Coëffure à l'indépendance ou triomphe de la liberté.* This head-dress, also known as the *"coëffure à la Belle poule,"* celebrated the victory of the French frigate *Belle poule* against the English *Arethuse* in a naval battle of the American War of Independence in 1778. *Source:* © Snark/ Art Resource, NY.

selves. In this period fashionable goods both represented current events in material form and constituted "news" in their own right. In February 25, 1775, for example, the author of the *Correspondance secrète* reported the breaking news that "the hairstyles of our women become higher and higher, and at this moment, a hairstyle that would have been seen a few months ago as ridiculously high is already no longer sufferable except among the bourgeoisie." Forced by the logic of ostentatious consumption to keep raising the bar, noblewomen were now wearing hats of two or three feet in height (figure 6.4). The source of this competition, he informed readers, was Marie Antoinette herself: "it is the Queen who gives the example for it."[25]

Marie Antoinette was reportedly taking the lead in other forms of fashion as well. In November of that year the *Correspondance secrète* noted that the queen had ordered silks from Lyon manufacturers in the same color as her blonde hair. The new color immediately "eclipsed" the popularity of puce, the previous must-have color of that autumn: "everyone who *knows* how to dress wears *blonde*. They have *blonde* outfits made, *blonde* dresses; for a few years we have been using *blonde* harnesses, and I don't doubt that one of our elegant bishops will soon appear in a *blonde* carriage." As in this instance, fashion commented on the news and it was news, especially when worn by the recently crowned queen.[26]

According to the memoirs of Madame de Campan, the queen's lady-in-waiting, Marie Antoinette's introduction to Rose Bertin played a crucial role in stimulating her interest in fashion: "One might say that the admission of a fashion merchant to the queen was followed by unfortunate results for her majesty. The art of the merchant, received in the inner quarters, in spite of the tradition that distanced without exception all persons of her class, provided her with the means to have adopted, every day, some new fashion. The queen, until that moment, had developed only a very simple taste for grooming; she began to make it a principal occupation; all women naturally imitated her."[27] Rose Bertin offered the queen the possibility of setting new fashions at an unprecedentedly rapid rate. Bertin also provided an opportunity for the queen to escape from the constraints of court life into a more private realm of imagination and play, just as she did with intimate friends at Le Petit Trianon. Upon her arrival at the French court, and especially after her coronation, Marie Antoinette was subjected to long and formal ceremonies of dressing and undressing, a ritual performed and controlled by her ladies-in-waiting. Accustomed to the more informal style of the Austrian court, Marie Antoinette found the ceremonies insufferable. According to Campan, spurred by her discovery of Rose Bertin,

FIGURE 6.4 *A Hint to the Ladies to Take Care of Their Heads.* This British image satirizes the elevated headdresses popular in the 1770s. *Source:* © Museum of London/HIP/ Art Resource, NY.

Marie Antoinette began to abandon these long-standing traditions of royal etiquette: "The Queen abolished all this formality. When her head was dressed, she curtsied to all the ladies who were in her chamber, and, followed only by her own women, went into her closet, where Mademoiselle Bertin, who could not be admitted into the chamber, used to await her. It was in this inner closet that she produced her new and numerous dresses."[28]

By abandoning her ladies-in-waiting to retreat to a private room with Rose Bertin, Marie Antoinette confounded distinctions between the city and the court and between commerce and nobility. She transgressed similar boundaries in the case of her famous hairdresser Monsieur Léonard, who as holder of a royal patent was ordinarily forbidden from taking other clients, a rule Campan believed was intended to "cut off all communication between the privacy of princes and society at large; the latter being always extremely curious respecting the most trifling particulars relative to the private life of the former." Instead of fearing gossip, the queen was concerned that "the taste of the hairdresser would suffer if he should discontinue the general practice of his art," and thus she insisted that he continue to work for women at court and in the city of Paris. Campan believed this departure from custom led to the dissemination of rumors and gossip about the court.[29] Marie Antoinette took that risk because even as reigning queen she could not autonomously decree fashions. Instead, she felt obliged to reflect and comment on the "taste" of the city. She relied on her purveyors as privileged informants on the Parisian fashion system, and they needed to participate in both worlds to fulfill the role she desired.

Rumors of the queen's dissipated ways and increasingly bold display of fashion reached Vienna in the first months of 1775. Fearing that her daughter was indulging in an "extravagance of fashion," Maria Theresa asked Mercy-Argenteau in February to verify the truth of a report she had heard that the king had given his wife a pretty feather, stating that it would suit her much better than the fashionable feathered headdress she was wearing.[30] The empress interpreted this as a gentle rebuke from the sovereign. In March she returned to the question, writing Mercy-Argenteau: "I receive news from more than one channel of the overly extravagant manner in which my daughter dresses her hair."[31] The same day she wrote directly to her daughter stating: "I cannot refrain from mentioning to you something that many gazettes repeat to me too often: it is the finery that you display; they say from the roots of your hair [it rises] thirty-six inches high, and with so many feathers and ribbons that raise the whole thing even higher! You know that I have always been of the opinion to follow fashions moderately, but never to exaggerate them." The empress further reminded Marie Antoinette that her youth and beauty precluded the need for such "follies," and that the rank of a queen was better displayed with simple attire.[32]

In response to this reproach Marie Antoinette acknowledged that "it is true that I am a little concerned with my appearance." She nonetheless defended her feathers by claiming that "everyone is wearing them," that "it would seem extraordinary not to wear them," and that at any rate the height of headdresses had greatly decreased since the end of Carnival season.[33] Two years later, however, the queen's devotion to fashion continued. When her brother Joseph II visited in May 1777 he handled numerous important matters, including a frank talk with his brother-in-law (and possibly a medical procedure) that resulted in the long-awaited consummation of the royal marriage. He also warned his sister against the frivolity of her conduct. As the *Correspondance secrète* reported: "The Emperor was at his sister's toilette. She wore on her head a quantity of feathers and flowers, and asked her brother: 'Do you not find me ravishingly coiffed?' 'Yes.' 'But that *yes* is very curt; does my hairstyle not suit me well?' 'My word, if you want me to speak frankly, madame, I find it very flimsy to bear a crown.'"[34]

Complaints from her own family stemmed in part from growing public disapproval of the queen's lifestyle. In the 1780s as the French economy deteriorated, accusations of the queen's extravagance and frivolity mounted. Her credit with the French people sank in tandem with the king's public credit. Before examining the political uses to which her relationship with Rose Bertin was put, let us turn to the credit strategies that underlay Bertin's rise to prominence.

The Making of Rose Bertin: Credibility and Reputation in Commerce

Eight years older than Marie Antoinette, Marie-Jeanne Bertin was born in 1747. She grew up in Abbeville in Picardy in a poor family; her father worked as a low-ranking policeman. Around the same age at which Marie Antoinette married the French dauphin, Marie-Jeanne took up her own life's work as an apprentice in the shop of a local fashion merchant. Given her subsequent success, she must have been an assiduous and exceptionally gifted pupil. Around 1770 Bertin left the provinces for Paris, arriving in the French capital in the same year as the new dauphine. She brought with her the family nickname Rose, which she apparently found more appropriate to her calling, although in legal documents she continued to use her birth name.

It is not known exactly how Bertin began her career in Paris. Early twentieth-century biographies assert that she came to the capital with her mistress, who subsequently established herself as one of the best-known fashion merchants in Paris. On March 6, 1773, the Parisian police received a declaration of theft from "Marie-Jeanne Bertin, fashion merchant, living on the rue Saint Denis vis-à-vis les Innocents." Bertin told the officer that she been robbed of four thousand livres worth of lace and other fabric. The prime suspect was a former worker, named L'Evêque, wife of a domestic servant.[35] By October of that year Bertin had sufficiently recovered from the loss to open a boutique on the fashionable rue Saint-Honoré, under the sign of the Grand Mogol.

Two years later, at the age of twenty-eight, Rose Bertin scaled the summit of her profession with her new role as a purveyor to the queen, which occurred after the Duchesse de Chartres presented her to Marie Antoinette. Based on the queen's patronage, Bertin attracted an extremely large clientele of French and foreign royals and aristocrats. She continued to work for Marie Antoinette until 1792, even supplying dresses to the imprisoned queen after the failed flight to Varennes. With the justification that she needed to go abroad to sell her stock so as to repay debts to her "poor sans-culotte workers," Bertin obtained a passport from revolutionary authorities permitting her to leave France in 1792. She returned sporadically after the end of the Terror and is believed to have reestablished residency in France in 1800. She died on September 22, 1813 at the age of 66.

What accounts for Rose Bertin's meteoric rise from newly arrived, poor provincial shopgirl to owner of a fashionable boutique and purveyor to the royal families of Europe? A crucial factor, much commented upon in contemporary sources, was her extraordinary creativity and imagination, which had been honed by years of work, first in the provinces and then in the capital. It was this capacity for constant reinvention and renewal that made her appealing and indispensable to Marie Antoinette. She also must have been a highly charismatic and socially intuitive person, able to surmount her lack of pedigree and education with charm, wit, and a studied familiarity with noble manners and ways of life. Alongside these qualities, Bertin was an extremely astute businesswoman. She not only acquired elite clients across Europe willing to pay hundreds and thousands of livres for new fashions, but she successfully financed her business on multiple levels of credit. Her passport request in 1792 was accompanied by a declaration that she owed five hundred thousand livres to merchants who supplied her with precious silks, lace, gemstones, and other fine goods on credit.

Rose Bertin's career offers a key vantage point for examining the role of reputation in shaping female merchants' credit in both economic and nonmaterial terms. Indeed, her career exemplifies an extreme concern with professional reputation, although not always in ways predicted by economic or gender historians. To date, most studies of credit in the early modern economy have focused on male tradesmen and the importance of a reputation for integrity, hard work, and responsibility. With regard to women, historians have usually emphasized the overwhelming importance of sexual reputation and marital status for a woman's "credit" in her community. All women were highly vulnerable to accusations of sexual misconduct, which could destroy a woman's respectability. Married women gained some protection from their position as mistresses of a male-dominated household, while widows and single women, especially single mothers, had less economic or cultural capital to draw on in defending themselves.[36]

While Bertin left no memoirs or other documents expressing personal sentiments, her intense interest in reputation and something of her strategies toward fostering it may be gleaned from contemporary accounts. In fact it is striking to note the extent to which memoirists, journal writers, and social observers recorded Bertin's words. If fashion in general was news, Bertin's pronouncements made headlines. Contemporary sources repeated a series of anecdotes about her, often echoing the same phrases. She clearly chose her words with care, using the semipublic space of her shop as a forum to project and protect a certain reputation. Her outspokenness and the shock value of her audacious self-presentation helped her acquire the celebrity she used to advertise herself and her wares.[37]

Bertin's celebrity demonstrates the speed with which news circulated in multiple forms and the ongoing importance of oral culture within le monde, an element stressed by Antoine Lilti in his study of Parisian salons.[38] In the relatively restricted world of Parisian elite sociability, personal meetings, visual witnessing, and oral speech remained integral aspects of information exchange. Bertin's success also testifies to her understanding of le monde and its affinities with the emerging commercial sector and its modes of publicity. Just as the worlds of aristocratic leisure and that of men of letters and literary production intersected in the salons described by Lilti, so Bertin's career reveals a three-way meeting of the aristocratic world of luxury consumption and leisure, the politico-literary world of reporting on culture and current events, and the commercial world of merchants. These three worlds were brought together by their common interest in fashion and its capacity not only to signify social status but also to convey an individual's status as a privileged possessor of desirable information about what constituted the latest modes. A key site for this multilayered encounter was the luxury boutique, the theater where Bertin performed her celebrity and the mini-court from which she ruled her empire of fashion.

If we may find Bertin's words echoing through scandal sheets, worldly gossip, and memoirs, it is just as important, however, to note the media from which she was absent. The *Journal de Paris*, the *Feuille sans titre*, and other daily and weekly newspapers that regularly reported on fashion never referred to Bertin. Their relationships with a small number of professional informants on fashion may have precluded editors from publicizing the work of competitors. Their silence on Bertin also suggests that multiple audiences existed for fashion news in this period. The *Journal de Paris* and other published newspapers addressed a Parisian set of readers more interested in the styles worn in the boulevards and theaters of the capital and where to obtain them. The *Correspondance secrète* and its ilk spoke to a worldly and politically engaged audience familiar with the court and eager for scandalous tidbits about the doings of the royal family and courtiers.

Rose Bertin's performances in her shop were thus depicted as newsworthy events of le monde, just like the latest bon mot in a fashionable salon, the success of a new play, or the sinking of a battleship. Unsurprisingly, it was the way she spoke of her relationship to the queen that attracted the most attention. The Baronne d'Oberkirch, for example, offers one well-known account of Bertin flaunting her relationship with Marie Antoinette. In reference to Bertin—whom she called the "famous fashion merchant of the queen"—Oberkirch recalled: "They say that one day a lady from the provinces came to ask her for a headdress for her presentation [at court]; she wanted something new. The merchant sized her up from head to toe and, no doubt satisfied with this examination, she turned with a majestic air to one of her girls saying: 'Show madame the result of my latest work with her majesty.'"[39]

The *Correspondance secrète* recounted a very similar story of a woman seeking mourning garments after the death of Maria Theresa in 1780: "She was presented with several sorts that she rejected. Mademoiselle Bertin, impatient and seeing that she was dealing with a petite-maîtresse with very difficult taste, cried out in order to be done with it: 'Show madame samples of my latest work with her majesty.'"[40] The anecdote in turn made such an impression on Madame de Campan that she repeated it virtually word for word in her own memoirs. Both authors remarked on the "ridiculousness" of the word *work* to describe the relationship between the queen and her subject. (The telling of the story is so similar that one suspects Campan used the *Correspondance* as an aide-mémoire when writing her memoirs.) In 1785 Bertin's words made the rounds of Parisian wags again, with the *Correspondance secrète* noting her claim that "this outfit was decided during my latest work with the queen."

The repetition of these anecdotes suggests that contemporaries were flabbergasted by Bertin's claim to a shared "work" relationship with the queen; the very definition of a noble—let alone a queen consort—was that he or she did not work, and if they did pass some time in manual occupations (like brewing coffee or making clocks), it was certainly not in partnership with a common grisette. It seemed such a ridiculous and exaggerated claim that they did not know whether to pity or mock Bertin.

Despite this disapproval, it is clear that the hundreds of hours Bertin and Marie Antoinette spent together at Versailles represented an intensive shared endeavor, recognized by both women as a form of creative labor. Moreover, it seems apparent that the two women were bound by ties of mutual dependence, despite the social and political abyss between them. If Marie Antoinette had been less determined and successful in her efforts to drive fashion, Bertin's career could not have flourished as spectacularly. In turn, if Bertin had been less skillful in generating appealing new styles and less assiduous in garnering acclaim for her creations, Marie Antoinette could not have projected her image through fashion to the extent that she did. Through a mutual process of self-fashioning, two skillful women exercised dominance, each in her own sphere.

Apart from boasting of her relationship with the queen, another tactic Bertin adopted to foster her reputation was to play with the accelerated rhythms of fashion and her clients' desire to acquire new fashions as quickly as possible. By collaborating several times a week in person, the queen and her fashion merchant set an almost daily pace to fashion. Yet Bertin reportedly refused to display her new "work" for Marie Antoinette immediately, stating that she and the queen had agreed on a one-week delay before making the styles public.[41] She ordered her worker to show one client, described as a "woman of quality," only the "one-month old bonnets." According to the Baronne d'Oberkirch, Bertin obliged her customers by displaying the dresses ordered by the Comtesse du Nord, future tsarina of Russia, but refused to duplicate the models until the countess had worn them herself at court. Bertin thus played heavily on her role as a creator of new fashions for royal customers, controlling the timing of the dissemination of new fashions and manipulating the tension between publicity and secrecy involved in their invention. Many mercers and fashion merchants laid claim to possessing the latest styles; Bertin's superior power lay in her capacity to dictate new styles through her influence at court and her capacity to show or hide the new fashions from her elite clients. At once a victim of noble clients through her credit relations, Bertin also wielded considerable authority over them.[42]

Lady Frances Crewe's account of a visit to Bertin's shop in 1786 further illustrates the strategies of self-presentation Bertin employed within the space of her shop: "She sat upon a sort of throne, at least an elevated chair in the center of a room surrounded by persons of all ranks and denominations, who were listening to her dictates upon the important article of dress. She was herself decorated too in much more splendid manner than the rest, having her fingers covered with large valuable rings, such as are in great vogue at present, and having, in short, watch and chains and trinkets of infinite value spread all over her."[43] By the expense and fashionability of her dress, as well as her physical domination of the room, Bertin presented a simulacrum of the authority of her royal client, wielding her knowledge and embodiment of "fashion" (as dictated by herself and the queen) to fix the attention of her audience. The gathered women played simultaneous roles of clientele, audience, and subjects of the royal fashion merchant, who used her cultural authority to overcome—if only momentarily and in the space of her shop—her social inequality.

From the above account, it is clear that Bertin's reputation did not rely, as historians have suggested for early modern tradesmen in general, on confidence in her integrity, honesty, or moral probity. None of the anecdotes about her refer to her moral character or her skill in creating high-quality goods; instead, they focus on her close relationship with the queen, her gift for innovation and imagination, and the haughty and arrogant demeanor she adopted with all clients beneath the level of Marie Antoinette. With Bertin and her male and female colleagues who adopted similar strategies, we appear to leave the world of traditional economic relations for more modern notions of celebrity and publicity. The possibility for an individual to acquire personal renown based on the products they sold was new (not just as artists but as merchant artists), but it still depended on an Old Regime monde in which court and city were inseparably bound together.

An intriguing comparison with Rose Bertin is provided by Josiah Wedgwood, the English pottery manufacturer studied by Neil McKendrick, among others. Bertin and Wedgwood both rose from modest provincial origins to acquire international acclaim at the summit of their trades. In both cases their success was based on the growing consumption of commercial goods and their particular flair for developing and flaunting ties to royal and noble patrons. Their commercial strategies also resembled each other to a certain extent, as neither Bertin nor Wedgwood sought custom through low prices, both preferring the prestige associated with high prices over the accessibility of low ones.

Wedgwood differed sharply from Bertin, however, in the scale of his production and distribution; unlike Bertin, who focused on a custom-made retail trade, Wedgwood was a merchant manufacturer who used sales agents and smaller merchants to supply a widespread market for his factory-produced goods. One has to wait for the nineteenth century for such large-scale production in the French garment trades.[44]

Another possible comparison is with artists, who were gaining in fame and prestige in the middle of the eighteenth century as autonomous creators, rather than dependent craftsmen. Just as with Bertin, artists allowed their patrons to display taste and wealth, while the artists benefited from the social rank of their clients and the publicity attached to their commissions. This parallel is reinforced by the prominence of a handful of female artists in the late eighteenth century, such as Elisabeth Vigée-Lebrun, who painted a controversial portrait of Marie Antoinette wearing a simple chemise dress made by Bertin (figure 6.5). Another example would be the painter Adélaïde Labille-Guiard, who was herself the daughter of a successful fashion merchant, famous for having employed Louis xv's mistress Madame du Barry as a shopgirl. However, I would follow Antoine Lilti in placing artists in a different category, along with men of letters, because they escaped the taint of the shop and base commerce. What makes Bertin so fascinating is that she combined both roles: observers lauded her artistic skills and talent but also described her as intensely interested in profits and frequently depicted her in her boutique selling goods. This combination of the gifted artist and the profit-seeking merchant constitutes the originality of her self-fashioning.[45]

It is important to emphasize that the queen did not manifest displeasure or anger at Bertin's pretensions. On the contrary, she seems to have acted as an ally in Bertin's endeavor to be publicly recognized as something more than a common merchant. In May 1779 the *Mémoires secrets* noted that Marie Antoinette had given one more proof of the "particular distinction" with which she honored Bertin by ordering that the fashion merchant be given the best seat at a spectacle at the royal palace of Marly.[46] A year later, in the summer of 1780, the queen was reportedly displeased to find that Bertin did not have a good seat at another Marly entertainment and ordered that she be conducted to a prime location.

Outside the court Marie Antoinette obliged the entire royal family to an extraordinary public recognition of Bertin in the streets of Paris. As she rode in a carriage down the rue Saint-Honoré in March 1779, it was reported, Marie Antoinette noticed Bertin standing on a balcony with her workers observing the royal procession: "Ah! There is mademoiselle Bertin, [the queen stated] and

FIGURE 6.5 Marie Antoinette in a chemise dress. Display of this portrait by Elisabeth Vigée-Lebrun at the Salon of 1783 caused scandal because of the informality of the queen's dress. The style was credited to Rose Bertin. *Source*: © bpk, Berlin/Schlossmuseum/Darmstadt/ Art Resource, NY.

at the same time made with her hand a sign of protection, which obliged [Bertin] to respond with a curtsey. The king stood up and applauded her; another curtsey: the whole royal family did the same, and the courtiers aping their master did not fail to bow while passing before her."[47] By personally overseeing Bertin's seating at court festivals and acknowledging her in public, Marie Antoinette included her fashion merchant in traditional forms of aristocratic patronage and sociability. The shock was not merely that she extended such honors to a commoner. She had similarly recognized and welcomed to court Madame Geoffrin, the salonnière whom she had met in Vienna prior to her marriage. However much a departure from the rules for presentation at court, Marie Antoinette's recognition of Geoffrin could be explained by the latter's privileged role as a society hostess and her social relations with court aristocrats. Her relationship to Bertin was not merely vastly unequal in social terms, but was based on commerce.

If Bertin did not correspond to historians' notions of a "credible" merchant, neither did she bear a reputation exclusively shaped by perceptions of female sexual propriety. Indeed, Bertin's private life played surprisingly little role in the stories recounted about her in the memoirs and journals of the day. Instead, her reputation was based on her activities as a merchant, her dealings with clients, and the fashions she created. Her unmarried status might, of course, be read as an implicit acknowledgment of the difficulties of combining an independent career with marriage and family. The only individual noted in an intimate relationship with Bertin outside of her family was a woman named Elisabeth Vechard, an unmarried former shopgirl, who was present when police seals were applied to Bertin's apartment on the rue de Richelieu in Paris after her death. According to the document, Vechard was the "*femme de confiance*" of Bertin and had lived with her since 1778.[48] We might also expect, however, that her unmarried status would make Bertin more vulnerable than other women to accusations of sexual misconduct. Instead, we find relatively little innuendo about Bertin's private life in a period when her royal client endured an onslaught of libels about alleged sexual misadventures. She was so little fazed by the prospect of sexual rumor that she volunteered to create the robes that the notorious cross-dressing Chevalier d'Eon was to don after being ordered to give up male clothing and appear as a woman.

While she was relatively unaffected by sexual slander, Bertin's reputation was still highly ambiguous. Contemporary opinion appears to have agreed on the fashion merchant's remarkable arrogance and pride in dealing with customers. In the outrage, amusement, and pity Bertin provoked, there is some evidence that she did not, in fact, entirely master her self-presentation, just as she did not master the credit relations that both gave her a prestigious clientele and threatened her stability. The cracks in Bertin's façade were exposed in a violent confrontation at Versailles with a former employee. Bertin was furious to discover that, on the strengths of the connections she had forged as Bertin's shop assistant, demoiselle Picot had set up her own business and threatened to steal important clients. In a formal complaint to the police Picot accused Bertin of spitting in her face in the passageway at Versailles as they awaited the royal family's exit from Mass, an accusation Bertin vehemently denied. The affair was reportedly only settled with the queen's intervention on Bertin's behalf.[49]

Bertin's Private Life of Credit

Just as the queen attempted to fashion a new, less formal female sovereignty through appearances, so Bertin sought in her way to forge a new identity for the independent female creative entrepreneur. Both women were testing, from opposite extremes, the edges of the overlap between court and city that had grown over the eighteenth century. Bertin's professional success allowed her to engage in a long series of ancillary financial transactions in which she manipulated financial credit to procure for herself a way of life that approached aristocratic standards. Her ostentatious consumption patterns led her rival Beaulard to note snidely that Bertin conducted herself as a duchess although she did not even belong to the bourgeoisie.

In March 1782 Bertin bought a country house and dependencies in Epinay-sur-Seine, allowing her to divide her time between her Parisian affairs and a rural estate. The price of the house was thirteen thousand livres, three thousand of which she paid in cash as a down payment. In November 1782 she signed a notarial contract for a loan of ten thousand livres in specie from a lawyer at the Parlement of Paris to cover the remaining principal, pledging all of her assets as collateral for the loan. Bertin's country estate was substantial, with a vestibule, kitchen, pantry, dining room, living room, and bathroom on the ground floor, second floor bedrooms for herself and family, and on the third floor rooms for servants and storage. The grounds of the house contained stables, a dove house, a courtyard, terrace, and woodland extending to the Seine River that ran alongside the bottom of the property. Bertin spent a great deal of time there and her two nephews, brother, and a sister eventually took up permanent residence, along with two domestic servants.[50]

She used the home not only for respite from Paris but apparently as a place to entertain noble clients, such as Chevalier de l'Isle, who described Bertin as his "intimate friend" in correspondence.[51] The justice of the peace of the 10th arrondissement of Paris, sieur Godard, wrote a fulsome letter memorializing Bertin in 1816, declaring that "she had several beautiful houses in Paris and the countryside . . . I often saw her dine with Prince Kourakin, Ambassador of Russia and princesses of that nation, who loved her and came to dinner at her place in the country, where I have mine."[52]

In addition to her own accommodations Bertin purchased a series of investment properties. On June 22, 1783, she bought a second house outside of Paris, this time in Pontoise on the grande rue, route de Paris. She agreed to pay the 10,030-livre price of the house in installments. On January 31, 1786, she made the final payment, apparently having avoided the need for a loan for the purchase of the house, which she rented to tenants. In 1788 she purchased an apartment building in Paris, on the rue du Mail, for the impressive sum of 287,700 livres.[53]

Apart from her real estate holdings, Bertin pursued other forms of ostentatious consumption. She rented an apartment in Versailles to facilitate her work for the queen and court. To take her back and forth from Paris to Epinay and to and from Versailles, Bertin kept a carriage and horses with liveried grooms, an essential accoutrement of the aristocrat's lifestyle. Her boutique was large and expensively decorated. In describing a visit to the shop in 1783, the Baronne d'Oberkirch noted that Bertin had her own portrait on the walls, surrounded by the portrait of the queen and the other royal personages that she served. She employed a doorman to greet those who came to her shop, servants to deliver her wares, and had an anteroom with clerks through which clients passed to reach the interior of the boutique. In November 1787 Bertin benefited from the queen's patronage like a court lady when the king agreed to constitute an annuity in Bertin's name paying 1,900 livres annually. In 1789 she purchased a building on the rue de Richelieu from Jean-Baptiste Bochart, the first president of the Parisian Parlement, for 180,000 livres.[54]

Bertin paid 10,000 livres in cash as a down payment, promising an additional 50,000 livres within six months.[55] She financed the remaining 120,000 livres of the principal by establishing a perpetual annuity in favor of the owner of 4,400 livres per year. Her choice of the building appears to have been motivated by a desire to move her shop from the rue Saint-Honoré to the rue de Richelieu. With the opening of the galleries of the Palais Royal, as a result of the Duc d'Orléans's subdivision of the gardens of his estate into arcaded galleries housing apartment buildings and ground-floor luxury boutiques, the shopping center for elegant Parisians had shifted northward toward the rue de Richelieu. Bertin's shop soon opened on the ground floor and second floor, while she lived one flight upstairs and rented the apartments above to tenants. On

April 24, 1789, she borrowed 24,000 livres in cash from Jean-Athias Pasquier, a real estate developer (*entrepreneur de bâtiments*), to furnish her apartment, promising to return the first half of the loan by April 1, 1791.

These purchases predated the outbreak of revolution by only a few months. Bertin did not, in fact, file for bankruptcy in 1787 as the rumors claimed, but as 1789 progressed she must have had growing concerns about the future. By 1792, with France in severe economic crisis and most of her clients long emigrated, Bertin was obliged to sell her property on the rue du Mail for the price of 320,000 livres. In April 1793 she used proceeds from the sale to reimburse some of the multiple debts she had acquired over the years of the revolution. She reimbursed two individuals by constituting for each of them an annuity of 30,000 livres in principal, paying 1,500 livres annually. She also paid 60,000 livres to Louis Denis Moreau, a prominent wholesale merchant from Chantilly, for money borrowed in January 1791, and 20,000 livres to another creditor.[56] In August of that year, she lent 22,000 livres to Jean Charles Marchand to finance his purchase of land formerly belonging to the archdiocese of Paris.[57] Despite this financial activity, when the former owner of her building on the rue de Richelieu had his goods seized by the revolutionary government, it was found that Bertin still owed him 100,000 livres.[58]

Despite Bertin's straitened finances, she began to make new investments, this time speculating on purchases of property sequestered by the revolutionary government. On June 30, 1792, she agreed to purchase for 12,400 livres a property of eighteen apartments in Epinay formerly owned by the Mathurin religious order. On August 14, 1793, after she had left the country, her representative lent 22,000 livres on her behalf to Jean Charles Marchand to be used to acquire additional nationalized property in Epinay. Another notarial contract passed in 1797 refers to two new life-time annuities Bertin constituted, each paying 1,710 livres annually.[59] By 1799, she had rented most of the building on the rue de Richelieu (re-named the rue de la Loi) to Antoine Beauvillier for six thousand francs a year.[60]

Bertin's ambition to elevate herself to a new stratum of elite society was not limited to her own lifetime. Although she did not have children of her own, Bertin formulated generational strategies intended to capitalize on her acclaim and fortune. Bertin was survived by two nephews and the children of her two nieces, all descendants of her brother, Louis Nicholas, the only one of her three siblings who appears to have left heirs. During her own lifetime Bertin brought her two nephews, Nicholas and Claude-Charlemagne, into her business, charging them in their youth with keeping accounts in her boutique's anteroom. Nicholas helped run the business while she left France under the revolution, and she passed it on to him before her death. Claude-Charlemagne's main role seems to have been handling the political maneuvering necessary to ensure that she was not placed on the list of "émigrés," whose property was automatically relinquished to the state.

Bertin's strategies with her two nieces were also business related but in a less direct manner. She married her niece Marie-Catherine-Jacqueline to Monsieur Ibert, a merchant draper with a prosperous business in Paris. The union produced two children, a daughter who married a lawyer and a son who became captain of an infantry regiment and received the *légion d'honneur*. Her second niece, Marie-Louise, was married on February 5, 1790 to Mathurin Chasseriau, scion of a wealthy bourgeois merchant family in Paris. Bertin was apparently extremely proud of this alliance, which she favored with a dowry of 40,000 livres in the form of a 2,000-livre annuity and the pledge to bequeath the bride her royal pension of 1,900 livres. These promises were undone by the vicissitudes of revolution; by 1793 Chasseriau had placed a lien on Bertin's goods for 60,200 livres in unpaid financial obligations. Like his cousin, the son born of this union—the couple's only child—became a military officer and was awarded the légion d'honneur. Thus, whatever her financial distress later in life, Bertin could proudly reflect on her success in lifting the next generation out of the shop and into the established bourgeoisie and military officer classes. She had successfully maneuvered the cultural credit of fashion into financial credit that served as a basis for enduring social credit for her descendants.

Madame Déficit and Her Minister of Fashion

Rose Bertin was not the only individual to be caught up in speculation, expense, and ostentatious display in the 1780s. In these pursuits she emulated, at a much lower level, the activities of the court nobles whom she served. This was a period of spectacular bankruptcies among the nobility and high stakes gambling at court, a favorite pastime of Marie Antoinette among others. Traditionalists at court and the Parisian public, who were well aware of the financial crisis looming over the realm, received this intemperance poorly. Accusations that Bertin no longer recognized her appropriate place thus contained as much reproach for the queen as they did for her fashion merchant. Commentators wondered at the unprecedented intimacy Marie Antoinette accorded Bertin, the many hours spent in consultation with her, and the influence she seemed to hold over the queen. One account circulating even accused her of being the queen's lesbian lover, accusations also directed at the queen's friends Madame de Lamballe and the Duchesse de Polignac.[61]

In recent years historians have devoted considerable attention to the host of such libelous pamphlets directed against Marie Antoinette, starting in the mid-1770s and escalating through the final years of the Old Regime and the onset of the revolution. They have established that pornographic depictions of the queen as sexually voracious and perverted served to support arguments about her undue influence over the king and his government and, by extension, to paint monarchical rule as feminized, corrupt, and decadent. In the figure of Marie Antoinette, therefore, claims about illicit sex and female power were forcefully linked to the denunciation of illegitimate relations of political power.[62]

This analysis is compelling but incomplete. If we widen the scope of investigation to include Rose Bertin and the controversy she aroused, we find that the conceptual circuits in which the queen was caught up also included an explicit critique of fashion, credit, and the transgression of boundaries separating commerce from the court. These circuits were not separate from those attacking the queen's sex life and her political influence; on the contrary, the notion of uncontrolled, illicit, and unproductive circulation was a common thread tying these discourses together. An additional element was, of course, that they were all, through the figure of the queen and her fashion choices, gendered as feminine.

The rhetorical charge surrounding Bertin's relationship with Marie Antoinette thus drew on the fact that it allowed observers to connect several strands of criticism of the monarchical regime. First, it provided a striking example of the lavish and self-indulgent expense for which noble society—and the court in particular—was increasingly criticized. Libels accused the queen of bankrupting the crown through her excessive spending on fashion and of leading many families into disarray and debt as wives and mothers emulated her example. Even those close to Marie Antoinette were sensitive to this charge and, in retrospect, willing to acknowledge its partial accuracy. From the perspective of the postrevolutionary period, Marie Antoinette's own lady-in-waiting, Madame de Campan, shared these sentiments and placed the blame directly on the shoulders of Rose Bertin. Of the court ladies inspired to follow her example, she wrote that "they wanted to have immediately the same outfit as the queen, to wear the flowers, the garlands to which her beauty, which was then in all its radiance, gave an infinite charm. The expense of young ladies was extremely increased; mothers and husbands grumbled about it, some thoughtless women contracted debts; there were unfortunate family scenes, several households chilled or broken; and the general rumor was that the queen would ruin all the ladies of France."[63] Campan thus claimed that the queen's reliance on credit had encouraged a wider dependency on deficit spending among her female subjects. Far from imagining French ladies to hold the upper hand in credit relations, Campan reports rumors that they could be ruined by their obligations to merchants like Bertin. Another commentator wrote of the credit that courtiers ascribed to Bertin and their efforts to have her present solicitations on their behalf to the queen (an echo, of course, of the treatment Marie Antoinette received from courtiers avid for recommendations to the king). Campan ascribes women's consumption to their desire for beauty, but it must also be put into the background this chapter has sketched of the credit dynamics of court society. "Wanting" to have the same outfit from Bertin was partly about social prestige but also about the self-interested need to display allegiance to the queen by visibly following her fashion cues.

The fact that Marie Antoinette was known to have paid her debts to Bertin on at least one occasion with the proceeds of high-stakes gambling did nothing to help her image. In November 1780 the *Correspondance secrète* reported that gambling at Marly had been "murderous," obliging a Monsieur de Calare, who had lost 42,000 louis d'or (or 252,000 livres), to cover his debts with "what was owed to him from gambling by several courtiers. *Madame* was among them for 50,000 écus (150,000 livres), and madame la Comtesse d'Artois for 25,000 (75,000 livres). More fortunate in this instance, the queen had won 7,000 louis d'or (42,000 livres) and summoned Bertin to court the next day to pay her bill."[64] This anecdote confirms one way the newssheets featuring Bertin's name may have served to reassure creditors about her solvency, as well as fueling her celebrity.

Political critics did not view the queen's expenses on gambling and clothing, and her improper ties to a venal commoner and a self-interested coterie of female favorites, simply as the private failings of a flawed consort. Instead, they depicted them as signs of the systematic abuses of absolute authority. The libellist Théveneau de Morande thus derided Bertin as an autocratic "minister of fashion," stating:

> We have one more minister, who will cede nothing to Calonne [the controller general], nor to the Baron of Breteuil [minister of the royal household], if not in administrative capacities, at least for stubbornness in everything that relates to the affairs of her ministry, upon which this great personage in petticoats will never suffer contradiction. This minister is Mademoiselle Bertin, the first fashion merchant of Paris, who has had painted on her sign, in very large letters, that she has the honor to coif and clothe the court, and principally Marie Antoinette; nothing equals the impertinence and the

haughtiness of this demoiselle since she is admitted to the intimacy of the queen, to whom she dictates the laws of fashion, of which she is, she says, the most fervent priestess.[65]

This statement clearly portrays the notion of arbitrary authority attached to Rose Bertin's relations with Marie Antoinette and draws an implicit connection between fashion tyranny and ministerial despotism. Commentators had long mockingly referred to the "empire of fashion," but now this ironic phrase resonated in a more sinister register. The ridiculous notion of a minister of fashion highlighted the innate capriciousness and illegitimacy of ministerial rule as much as it mocked female devotion to fashion. The overtones of religious fanaticism completed the image of wrongful and irrational rule.

In 1785 Marie Antoinette, on the cusp of her thirtieth birthday, began to rethink her previous strategies of display. In February of that year she called Bertin to Versailles, telling her, according to the *Correspondance secrète*, "that in November, she will be thirty years old; that most probably no one would let her [Bertin] know about it; that her intention was to eliminate from her dress those decorations that could only suit the very young; that as a result, she would no longer wear feathers or flowers." Indicating that this change of heart was about more than the process of aging, she declared that she also planned to abandon the series of novel dress styles she had previously adopted and return to more formal court dress. She expected her ladies to follow suit. As the *Correspondance secrète* noted: "We also know that the etiquette for her dresses has changed; that the queen wishes no more *pierrots*, nor chemise dresses, nor riding coats, nor *polonaise* dresses, nor *lévites*, nor *robes à la turque*, nor *circassiennes*; that it is a matter of bringing back more formal dresses: that the princesses have been invited to prohibit all others for ceremonial visits and [been told] that their lady-in-waiting should warn ladies who come in any other dress that they may not be admitted without permission from her highness."[66]

According to the Baronne d'Oberkirch, news of these "great reforms" in the queen's apparel were met not with relief but with consternation: "Here are thirty-year-old women obliged to abdicate, like her, feathers, flowers, and the color pink, the queen having indicated that she will no longer wear it, that it is ridiculous at her age."[67] In seeking to please public opinion the queen had succeeded only in alienating the court. By 1787 the economic crisis had deepened her self-consciousness about the expenses of her wardrobe. The queen was heard making a joke at her own expense, which again made the rounds of the Parisian gossip sheets: "They are repeating this pleasantry of the queen: Mademoiselle Bertin brought her majesty a bonnet in the new style. The queen admired it and asked the price. 'That's much too expensive,' responded her majesty; 'Monsieur d'Eprémesnil [spokesman of the Parisian Parlement] would never allow me to spend so much money on a hat.'"⁶⁸

The queen's alleged financial abuses were not separate from but inextricably linked to her gender and her alleged sexual deviance. The queen's devotion to appearances revealed her to be guilty of the most feminine weaknesses: capriciousness, vanity, self-indulgence, and pride. As she made the wrong choices in female companions, she made the wrong fashion decisions, either parading in overly elaborate and ostentatious outfits or abandoning royal decorum to adopt new styles of shocking informality. Moreover, the queen's vanity was inseparable from the licentiousness and attachment to sensual pleasure of which she was accused. The secrecy of her meetings with Bertin in the privacy of the cabinet thus matched the illicit secrecy of goings-on at the queen's retreat at Trianon, where pamphleteers imagined the most sordid debaucheries took place.⁶⁹ The Diamond Necklace Affair of 1785—in which an impersonator swindled the cardinal de Rohan of an enormous sum to buy a diamond necklace supposedly on behalf of the queen—is another striking example of the way sex, finances, and luxurious consumption intertwined in the discrediting of Marie Antoinette.⁷⁰ The queen could not control herself, she entertained shameful relations with the wrong people, and she squandered the crown in futile expenditures of all kinds. The libidinal economy historians have already identified in portrayals of Marie Antoinette was thus echoed and reinforced by reports of her literal economic relations.

Marie Antoinette's problematic credit presented a conceptual bundle that was extremely useful to critics of the Old Regime. It was an economic problem in that it encouraged nonproductive expenditure for consumption, a political problem in that the weakness of the state was linked to its exhausted credit, a gender problem in that women were squandering money and escaping male control, and a sexual problem in that fashions purchased through credit were used to flaunt a scandalous female sexuality. Ultimately, Marie Antoinette's perceived misuse of credit relations with merchants like Bertin did a great deal to discredit her with the French people, as her capacity to project moral integrity and honesty was fatally compromised by public knowledge of her bad credit. Her extravagant and reckless spending, moreover, became figuratively associated with her supposedly unbridled spending of sexual libido and political influence. In all of this lay not only a condemnation of absolutist rule but a condemnation of new forms of commercial and economic activity, the triumph of fashion over substance, and of the authority women assumed as cultural arbiters of taste and style.

Not "Desacralization" but "Discrediting" of the Monarchy

Rose Bertin's relationship with Marie Antoinette is not of historical interest because it *caused* the French Revolution. The problems confronting the royal government in 1789 were immeasurably taller than the height of the queen's most extravagant hat. The crown's financial impasse stemmed from its enormous military expenditures and an inadequate fiscal structure, which in turn generated high-interest, short-term borrowing and crushing debt service. The late eighteenth-century crisis of monarchy can be said to have originated with the expenses of war under Louis xv and the failure to overcome the structural gridlock in royal finances inherited from Louis xiv, and it can be said to have been exacerbated by the indecisiveness and impotency (literal and figurative) of Louis xvi.

The relationship between queen and merchant is nonetheless significant. It is important in part because it encapsulates in such a striking and provocative manner the intertwining of the numerous circuits discussed in previous chapters. In this sense the two women partook of long-standing traditions for proving credibility and acquiring reputation. Marie Antoinette's advisers were unusually candid and explicit in outlining credit strategies for their distracted pupil, yet their advice could have been applied equally to Maria-Theresa, the Spanish princess who arrived as bride to Louis xiv a century earlier in 1660, or to any female courtier from the reign of Louis xiv onward. The mingling of political credit with financial credit at court, and the use of fashionable appearances and display as one tool to acquire credit, were also standard practices, as we have seen. Innumerable young ladies at court, from the seventeenth through the eighteenth century, must have been scolded by their mothers for the ridiculousness of what they were wearing on their heads, without ever losing their heads as a consequence.

The high stakes attached to Marie Antoinette's fashion addiction were a product of political movements of her time and, to a certain extent, of the exceptional marital circumstances in which she found herself. Her husband's initial impotence and subsequent disinterest in sex endowed her with unprecedented dominance over her husband yet also fundamentally delegitimized her role as royal consort, rendering her vulnerable to lurid slander. It was in part the early failures of her bond with Louis, we may surmise, that led her toward the female coterie, Rose Bertin, and fashion.

And yet the very public intimacy between the two women, a queen and her fashion merchant, was something new and was enabled only by fundamental changes that had taken place over the eighteenth century, which their story helps to illuminate. The growth of consumption and the rise of the marchandes de modes as a distinct trade group created the fashion system that served as such a potent resource for both Marie Antoinette's and Rose Bertin's self-fashioning. It was itself enabled by a spread of commerce fueled by credit, either in the form of shop credit or the annuities, real estate speculation, and other leveraged financing from which Bertin profited.

A second factor was the blossoming of information networks in which news, jokes, and opinions circulated in printed and oral form. One way that women participated in these networks was by the choice of current events to display on their heads. This was trifling frivolity, but it was also a way to disseminate news and, more importantly, to help shape public opinion of which events were the most significant and how they should be interpreted. In her "work" with Rose Bertin, Marie Antoinette laid claim to belonging to this world, to contributing to it, and even to shaping and influencing it. She thus responded to a third factor, which was the modernization of models and practices of rule. Like the ministers attempting to reform the government, whom she despised and whose policies she sometimes opposed, Marie Antoinette tried to bring about a new style of court life, one directly tied to the city, freed from the weight of ceremony and tradition, receptive to outside influences and public opinion. Her failure was not inevitable but bound up in dynamics beyond her control.

The relationship between Marie Antoinette and Rose Bertin did not cause the revolution, but it did serve as a potent crystallizing point for a host of contemporary tensions and conflicts caused by the disjuncture between tradition and change: over growing private and public debt, over women's role in public life, over the court's loss of cultural authority, over its callous disregard for the problems of the tax-paying common people, and over the illicit and despotic relations that seemed to characterize monarchical government. Fashion, credit, and femininity combined in an explosive mixture in the late 1780s as a queen's bad credit and a commoner's overweening credit came to stand for the collapse of credibility of the entire regime.

CHAPTER 7

FAMILY AFFAIRS

CONSUMPTION, CREDIT, AND THE MARRIAGE BOND

*I*n the last decades of the Old Regime, social commentators lamented an apparent decline in marriage rates. Some, like Louis-Sébastien Mercier, castigated single women who chose not to marry.[1] Others located the source of the problem with men, declaring that a growing number of men were scared off marriage. These reluctant bachelors were apparently discouraged by contemporary women's obsession with luxury and fashion, fearing that a wife's uncontrolled spending would drive them into bankruptcy. In his *L'Ami des femmes* (1775), for example, Pierre-Joseph Boudier de Villemert claimed that "men only marry with regret, often very late, and a great number do not marry at all." The reason for this unnatural abstention was clear: "The luxury of women alone makes men fear uniting themselves with them. They fear with reason a splendor that, become a sort of necessity, and always extended beyond the fortune that a wife brings them, threatens to engulf that of the husband."[2]

The preceding chapters have examined intertwined concepts of credit, fashion, and gender and their articulation with daily practices of credit in the fashion industry. In this chapter we turn the problem on its head to investigate women's consumption of fashion on credit. Eighteenth-century concern with women's luxurious ways is familiar from historical studies that have documented the progressive "femininization" of consumption, appearances, and fashion in literary sources of the eighteenth century.[3] Drawing on probate inventories and other archival sources, scholars like Daniel Roche have shown that contemporary representations were at least partially correct: women did in fact take the lead in some forms of consumption, particularly that of clothing and accessories.[4]

Criticism of women's vanity and excess spending ranged from the vitriolic attacks on Marie Antoinette discussed in the previous chapter to the witty satires found in novels, the periodical press, and other sources. What was needed, moralists like Jean-Jacques Rousseau and others argued, was to purify women so that they could lead simple lives devoted to their homes and children while men re-established control of the public sphere. Contemporary fears about bachelors' reluctance to marry thus fits comfortably into scholars' findings of an eighteenth-century project to reform the family, both the private family threatened by women's excessive consumption and the political family in which an impotent king was bankrupted by his extravagant wife.[5]

As familiar as this story now is, it raises pressing questions for the history of credit and its relationship to the law, family, and gender. One of the first points historians emphasized when they began to pay attention to the status of women under the Old Regime was wives' legal subordination within marriage. In his pioneering early twentieth-century study Léon Abensour noted that the Coûtume de Paris endowed husbands with legal control over their families, leaving their wives and children in a position of legal incapacity.[6] In particular, husbands acquired control over the community of property established by Parisian customary law. Although wives could own property, they could not dispose of it without explicit authorization from their husbands. A number of historians have argued that this male domestic authority increased over the early modern period. Most notably, Sarah Hanley has posited a "family-state compact" in which the power of the state and patriarchal families expanded through a process of mutual (albeit fractured and inconsistent) consolidation from the sixteenth century onward.[7]

These marital powers raise a question hitherto unnoticed in the literature but glaring once one considers it: Given the legal controls husbands enjoyed over family property, how was it possible for their wives to drive them into bankruptcy? If wives could not engage debt on their own, why was it not a simple matter for husbands to refuse to authorize excessive spending and be done with it? Why would anyone suggest, even as a polemical statement, that men's inability to enforce the most basic of their marital prerogatives was so extreme that they would avoid marriage altogether? Was the epithet hurled at Marie Antoinette, *Madame Déficit*, not an oxymoron, a legal impossibility?

Studies of women and the family provide limited assistance with this question. In the last twenty-five years historians of women and gender—along with family, economic, and business historians—have discussed in increasingly nuanced ways women's ability to acquire fortune, and to manage, inherit, and transmit it.[8] For all its insights, this reassessment of female financial activities has had two significant limitations. First, scholars have tended, for understandable reasons, to focus either on widows and unmarried women or on wives' actions within the context of marital coverture. By doing so, however, they have on the whole accepted the legal strictures on married women as a practical reality. They have thus left unchallenged basic assumptions about married women's legal incapacity and its restrictive effects on their financial activities.

Second, revisionist studies of female financial roles have largely neglected the question of women's capacity to create and transmit debt. Most studies have concentrated, on the contrary, on the positive aspects of women's economic activity: inheriting wealth, earning money, managing family finances, making investments, running businesses, and transmitting fortune to new generations. Ignoring debt, however, means neglecting what was a central element of most people's economic activities and their daily lives. As Julie Hardwick's important recent study of household economies has shown, debt was ubiquitous among families at all levels of society, and it generated considerable tension and conflicts among spouses and their kin.[9] Debts existed in a myriad of forms, including loans of money, annuities, unpaid rent, back wages to servants and workers, promissory notes, and accounts owed to provisioners of all the needs of daily life purchased on credit (including clothing, food, and fuel). Given the wide array of possibilities, it was extremely rare for people to die without encumbering their estates with debt.[10]

To understand how their wives could drive men, with all the legal powers at their disposition, into insolvency, we must focus attention on married women and their capacity to form autonomous debt. A prime arena in which they could do so, this chapter suggests, was the particular form of debt constituted by shop credit. This was one area where the law created a gray form of financial capacity for married women that has attracted little attention from French historians.[11] Although wives could not sign contracts or engage property on their own, they did retain the tacit capacity to engage their own and their husbands' credit for purchasing food, clothing, and other consumer goods. Legal commentators saw this as a minor loophole intended to facilitate household provisioning. As commodities expanded, fashion cycles accelerated, and even middling and common people aspired to fashionable consumption, this loophole became a gaping breach in the fortress of male privilege.

To make this argument, this chapter examines women's consumption on trade credit from legal, practical, and literary perspectives. We begin by examining the legal restrictions against married women and the loophole offered in the law for trade credit. To clarify the parameters of husbands' authority over their wives—and to balance our account by addressing, if only briefly, the issue of male consumption—we then turn to the archives of Parisian police commissaires who conducted investigations on behalf of wives seeking financial emancipation from their husbands. The next section of the chapter takes up the case of Rose Bertin, and the accounts outstanding she left behind at her death in 1813, as a means to establish the validity of debts married women formed through shop credit. Following Bertin's death, her heirs and their lawyers embarked on a thirty-year effort to recoup the sums owed by former clients. Records from these travails—which consist of copies of her account book and correspondence between Bertin family lawyers and her clients or their descendants—show that elite women engaged themselves for hundreds and thousands of livres of credit for clothing purchases. Not only did Bertin extend them credit but her heirs and her clients' heirs respected the legitimacy of the transactions. Even after the fundamental political and legal transformations of the revolution, both sides treated these as valid debts, encumbering the estate of husband and wife.

These examples suggest that social mores and legal practice gave full credence to the loophole recognized by jurists. This hitherto overlooked right sheds new insight on the nature of the marriage community between husband and wife, revealing that one of the central prerogatives a woman gained through marriage was access to her husband's credit. She may not have controlled cash or been able to conduct formal financial transactions, but she did enjoy the privilege of engaging her husband's name in debts for her own and her family's consumption. A wife's loss of her husband's confidence—and withdrawal of access to his credit—was tantamount to the dissolution of their marital community. In turn, recognizing the existence of female credit helps explain how the consumer revolution itself came into being. Like other sectors of the economy, retail commerce was fueled by credit; its important growth over the eighteenth century drew on women's capacity to receive and bestow credit autonomously, both within and outside marriage. This right not only encouraged the consumer revolution, it profoundly shaped the character of consumption, giving it a notably "feminine" cast and helping to define consumption as a quintessentially female activity.

Women's access to trade credit drew on a long tradition of wives acting as household provisioners, but as the femininity of consumption took on expanded proportions it took on accordingly controversial meanings. The last section of the chapter examines criticism of female consumption on credit. Presumably, in many households women's capacity to use their husbands' credit facilitated household provisioning and occasioned no particular anxiety. For critics who castigated luxury and the decadence it caused, however, women's consumption was a larger cultural and social problem that demanded a solution. Since the law afforded little recourse and contemporary mores took for granted wives' ability to form debts through credit, the answer did not lie in a

FIGURE 7.1 *Watch Out or the Harem in the Boutique*. This early nineteenth-century engraving depicts the fashionable shop as a lascivious "harem" where pickpocketing and robbery combine with the most overt sexual displays. *Source*: Bibliothèque nationale de France.

simple reassertion of marital authority. Instead, we find in moralizing literature of the late eighteenth century the notion that women needed to reform themselves. It was up to elite women to learn their own lessons about self-control, charity, and humility. Wives who could not learn these lessons faced marital disgrace and exile to the provinces. As we will see, however, moralizing texts displayed considerable doubt about women's ability to resist the temptations of the consumer economy.

Shop credit was thus no trivial matter but a crucial point of intersection among social, cultural, and financial credit. Women's access to it affected family honor, both positively through the display of fashion and negatively through the shame of debt. One path toward reestablishing noble credibility lay in noblewomen's self-imposed reform of their use of shop credit. It is tempting to fit this story into the larger narrative, established by scholars such as Joan Landes and Sarah Maza, of an increasing anxiety over female decadence culminating in a revolutionary outburst of misogynist repression. Certainly, criticism of elite women's extravagant consumption mounted in the last decades of the Old Regime, producing a wealth of satirical representations (figure 7.1) and culminating in the attack on Marie Antoinette we have already witnessed. This critique can even be seen to have achieved victory in the austere fashions of the revolution.

Such a conclusion, however, is short-sighted and grants too much credence to political rhetoric, satire, and prescriptive literature. As we will see, criticism of women's consumption on credit dates to the late seventeenth century at least. Luxury consumption quickly returned to the Napoleonic and Restoration courts, and the rest of society followed as far as its means allowed. More importantly, the legality of women's autonomous use of their husbands' credit never came into question. Women continued to use credit to purchase items for their own and household consumption, without male authorization. Thus, a longue durée of practices lay hidden beneath the most apparently stark paradigm shifts. Another important point is that no easy gender distinction existed between consuming women and producing (or paying) men. Credit-wielding merchants, like dissolute consumers, could be found on both sides of the gender divide.

The Legal Parameters of Female Economic Activity

Parisian customary law, followed throughout the jurisdiction of the Parlement of Paris, offered a series of restrictions on women's legal capacity. Two of the most important factors were age and marriage. Minors, both male and female, were under the authority of their major guardian, usually their father. Single women over age twenty-five and widows were legally responsible and could own and control property and sign contracts. Married women fell under the legal control of their husbands.[12]

The logic behind these stipulations was not, according to commentators, that of women's inherent irrationality or incapacity. If that was the case, single women would not have gained autonomy at the age of majority, and widows could not act as tutors to their children. Instead, the restrictions on wives' legal capacity stemmed, as the eminent jurist Pothier explained, from a belief that families, like kingdoms, needed to be ruled by a single leader.[13] Married women's subordination to their husbands had multiple dimensions. In an article on "marital power" the *Encyclopédie* offered the following summary of married women's incapacity: "The ordinary effects of *marital power* in areas of customary law are 1. that the wife cannot pass any obligation, or contract, without the explicit authority of the husband; she cannot even accept without him a settlement, even if she is separated in goods. 2. She cannot testify in court without the consent of her husband, unless she is authorized either by the court if her husband refuses, or if she is separated in goods, and the separation executed. 3. The husband is the master of the community, so that he can sell, alienate, or mortgage all movable and immovable property without the consent of his wife, provided that it is to a competent person and without fraud."[14]

As this definition emphasized, at the center of legal restrictions on married women lay control over their capacity to buy or sell property. Under common law, when women married they entered a "community of goods" with their husbands. At the time of marriage husband and wife customarily signed a marriage contract outlining the property that each spouse owned and what portion of that property entered the marital community. While the couple owned that property jointly, each spouse owned any remaining property outside the community outright. Parisian customary law placed both the communal property and the wife's residual property under the control of her husband. According to article 223 of the customary law of Paris, "the married woman can neither sell, alienate, nor mortgage her inheritance without the authority and explicit consent of her husband. And if she makes any contract without the authority and consent of her said husband, the contract is null as much with regard to her as her said husband, and she cannot be pursued for it, nor her heirs, after the death of her husband."[15] Nevertheless, because the wife retained legal ownership of her property, she would expect to recover whatever she had brought into the marriage when her husband died or to pass it on intact to her heirs if she predeceased him.

Several exceptions existed to these rules. Two main categories of emancipated wives were independent businesswomen (*marchandes publiques*) and women who were "separated in goods" from their husbands. As the Coûtume stated: "A married woman cannot oblige herself without the consent of her husband, if she is not separated or a public merchant, in which case, being a public merchant, she obliges herself and her husband concerning the fact and dependencies of the said public merchandise."[16] As the last clause suggests, a public merchant's autonomy did not extend to personal transactions. However, she did have the capacity to create debt that was binding on both her and her husband and thereby oblige the marital community as a unit.

Wives could also gain financial autonomy by contract or judicial fiat. Although the community of goods was the norm, couples could marry under the Coûtume de Paris without forming a financial community if a "separation of goods" was stipulated in their marriage contract. A woman who married under this stipulation retained her financial autonomy, although with some restrictions, as the *Encyclopédie* definition suggested. This choice was rare among Parisian marriage contracts.[17] If she did not choose separation of goods at the time of marriage, a wife who had married under the community of goods could later pursue a financial separation if she could prove in court that her husband was recklessly squandering her property.

This last possibility was intended to protect the financial interests of a wife and her heirs, but contemporaries feared that it could also serve as a way to hide assets from creditors. Going beyond the stipulations of Parisian customary law, Colbert's Commercial Code of 1673 required marriage contracts establishing a separation of goods to be publicly registered at a hearing of the local commercial court or, in cities lacking such a tribunal, to be announced at a meeting of the city council and publicly posted. Failure to do so, according to the code, would invalidate the separation.[18] The *Journal de Paris* regularly published the names and addresses of couples who registered their financial separation with the merchant court.

Philippe Bornier, a late seventeenth-century commentator on the code, remarked that these stipulations were intended "for the security of creditors, and so that public and judicial authority may prevent the fraud that could be committed by spouses, in departing through secret [contractual] acts from the community of goods [that is] introduced and authorized by customary laws, under the confidence of which creditors might have had dealings with them." He further added that "there is always more danger in lending to a trader whose wife is not in a community [of goods] than to another who is."[19]

Concerns about separated women stemmed from the preferential treatment they received in the event of bankruptcy. Under the normal regime of community property, the wife habitually placed a third or a half of her fortune in the marital community, property that she (or her heirs) could not reclaim until the marriage ended with the death of one of the partners. A woman with financial autonomy, however, could reclaim her property at the moment her husband declared bankruptcy, at which time she became the creditor of first resort up to the total value of the property she brought to marriage. The fact that these rules applied even if the separation took place subsequent to the act of marriage made legal commentators—and the commercial world—extremely suspicious of the potential use of financial separation as a means to shelter property from legitimate creditors.

In addition to the two major categories of separated women and marchandes publiques, Robert-Joseph Pothier's *Traité de la communauté* listed additional groups of women who could be relieved of marital control such as women whose husbands were insane, missing, in prison, or presumed dead. The most important form of exception for the purposes of this chapter, however, was not the separated wife, the businesswoman, or the wife of an incarcerated man but a much more common figure. After discussing a series of unusual and exceptional circumstances placing women outside the control of their husbands, Pothier also mentions the tacit provision that allowed all married women to conduct financial transactions as part of the normal business of provisioning a household. Pothier states: "When a married woman settles the accounts of merchants and artisans, for provisions made for the household, the settling that she does, by the tacit consent of her husband, who customarily charges her with this task, does not need the husband's authorization to be valid; because it is not the wife who is meant to settle these accounts in her name, but the husband who does so through the ministry of his wife."

Pothier's discussion in this passage touched on shop credit, which Parisians used to purchase items for daily consumption, including food, wine, medicine, clothing, and other goods. Once the account reached a certain level, the tradesman or woman would ask the client to sign a formal declaration acknowledging the amount owed on the account, like the fashion merchants we have seen in bankruptcy court. This memorandum (known as an *arrêté*) provided clear proof of debt and could be used in courts of law to pursue payment of outstanding accounts. Since women were legally forbidden from obliging themselves or entering contracts without their husbands' permission, technically they could not sign such documents or enter credit agreements in the first place. Given the demands of daily life, however, husbands could not be expected to preside over all of the mundane transactions necessary to provision a household, and women thus held tacit authority to buy on credit and formally settle accounts.

Pothier described a number of situations that required similar forms of tacit authorization. Wives working in their husbands' business, he explained, could oblige themselves in business-related transactions because they were acting on their husbands' behalf. In the same manner, he added, a master's clerk or shopgirl could oblige him- or herself on his behalf.[20] These provisions were necessary in businesses where the master's wife or employees served customers and dealt with suppliers, while the master directed production in a separate workshop or traveled about the city or further afield to attend to the needs of business. In both cases wives were empowered to engage themselves in service of the husband or the family with the husband's implicit approval.

The exception allowing wives autonomy for credit transactions seems unremarkable as long as one assumption holds true: that these were petty expenses involved in provisioning the household. This may have been true for some families and in an earlier period when finished goods were less plentiful and less tempting. With the growth of market production and the ensuing consumer revolution of the second half of the eighteenth century, however, a new array of commodities became available to female consumers as Parisian shops filled with novel and expensive goods and boutiques became centers for fashionable leisure.

The growth of consumption created new possibilities for married women to exercise their autonomous financial capacity. Pothier's commentary made it clear that wives were not supposed to deal in large sums of money on their own. As he states, even women with a formal financial separation from their husbands were not allowed to borrow "considerable sums" without the husband's explicit authorization.[21] When we examine credit agreements for the purchase of women's clothing, however, we find that these could represent very considerable sums indeed. As we will see, the provision allowing women autonomous credit activity nonetheless remained in force, even when the sums involved were enormous. Acceptance that wives could and would conduct such transactions on their own was so widespread that no one—creditors or debtors—seems to have questioned the validity of such debt. Instead of being a legal problem, female debt generated through trade credit was perceived as a moral problem of temptation and self-control.

Drunken, Debt-Ridden, and Debauched: Bad Husbands

Before examining the consumption of wives on credit, it is worthwhile examining the parameters of husbands' authority over their wives, particularly as it relates to questions of spending and consumption. How much control did husbands exercise over the community of goods created by Parisian customary law between a man and a wife? Could he simply dispose of the couple's property as he wished? If wives who overspent on frivolous fashion were castigated as bad consumers, what kinds of expenditures were considered unethical or irrational for husbands?

The discrepancy between wives' lack of authority in the daily management of their resources and their titular ownership of them could generate substantial conflict within a marriage. In the event that a husband turned out to be a poor manager of household finances, wives were entitled to seek legal action to protect their resources. Parisian police archives reveal that if informal efforts to chastise their husbands did not produce satisfactory results, wives could seek recourse in a formal request to the civil lieutenant at the Châtelet of Paris to dissolve the financial community between themselves and their husbands. Before granting such a separation, the lieutenant would charge a commissaire of police with conducting an investigation into the woman's allegations.

On March 23, 1754, Commissaire Doublon took the initial testimony of a woman seeking to dissolve her financial community with her husband. Her words contain the type of complaints that many women repeated in justifying such requests. Thus, Anne Françoise de la Porte, wife of the master glazier Claude Nicolas Dardet, declared:

> that she would have believed in marrying the said Sieur Dardet to find in him the required and necessary qualities of a husband, but she was utterly mistaken because soon after their marriage was celebrated in the month of April 1747 he revealed himself and made himself known as a man of debauchery, violence, [being both] furious and dangerous, that in fact he never ceases going to taverns where he finds the means to dissipate the dowry she brought him, that while she has always had and has for him, despite this disorder, all the indulgence a wife attached to her husband should have, he nonetheless has had and has only disdain and contempt to the point of treating her as the "lowest of wretches" and hitting her with cruelty; that not content with that, yesterday, Friday the 22nd of the present month, at eight o'clock at night he took her by the arm calling her "bitch, beggar, and whore" and brusquely took her to Sieur Antoine de la Porte her father, concierge of the cemetery of Calamart, where he left her, saying that he could no longer suffer her or keep her and that the said de la Porte her father had but to keep her and feed her as seemed fit to him, that in addition he had the cruelty along the way to take her by the neck and remove her fine garnet necklace as well as her silver snuffbox, that today about half an hour ago she went to find him accompanied by the said Sieur de la Porte her father, that instead of acknowledging his wrong doing he entered into the greatest fury against her and not only refused to receive her but also refused to give her her clothing and linen.[22]

We see here the full range of accusations a woman could muster to present a convincing complaint against her husband: violence, debauchery, drunkenness, financial dissipation, and mental cruelty extended over a seven-year period. She contrasted this scandalous behavior with her own early hopes for the marriage and her unceasing obedience and fealty despite the abuse. The final straw was when she was ejected by her husband from their joint domicile, returned in shame to her father's home, stripped of her finest possessions, and denied access to her personal goods. Despite the complaints of physical violence, what de la Porte sought was a financial separation, intended above all to protect her property. (Wives who believed their lives were in danger from a husband's violence could request a physical separation allowing them to establish a separate household.)

A month later, on April 23, 1754, we find Commissaire Doublon conducting an inquiry on behalf of Anne Couront, a used-clothes seller, the wife of Pierre Derozière, a journeyman ribbon maker. The first witness he interviewed was Jean Fusilier, a twenty-two-year-old journeyman printer, who lived at home with his father, a journeyman blanket maker. He told the commissaire that "he has known the said Derozière for around ten years, knows that he lacks good conduct, that he is much given to drink, that he does not like to work at all, and finally that he contracts debts easily, so that his affairs are in complete disorder." The second witness was Fusilier's forty-five-year-old father, who declared that he had known Derozière for twenty years, "knows that he has undertaken different enterprises in which he succumbed, that he does not behave and does not like to work at all so that his affairs are in total disorder."[23] A third witness, also a journeyman blanket maker, told the same story of excess drink, neglect for work, and failed business undertakings.

Judging by the number of investigations he conducted on behalf of unhappy and desperate wives, it appears that Commissaire Doublon had acquired a reputation as a sympathetic official. The families involved in his cases spanned the social scale. While Derozière was a humble journeyman, other husbands belonged to the Parisian elite. On April 20, 1754, he conducted an investigation on behalf of Marguerite Françoise Roye, the wife of Jean Plainpol de Prébois, a lawyer at the Parlement of Paris. On May 18, 1754, he conducted another inquiry on behalf of Anne Desnoyers, a former widow married to a trader in Saint-Germain-en-Laye.[24] On May 25, 1754, the investigation was for Marie Thérèse Chevalier, the wife of Louis Richer, an attorney at the Châtelet court.

The witnesses' complaints against the accused husbands presented similar themes. With regard to Richer, Jean Baptiste Boucher, a fifty-nine-year-old lawyer at the Parlement, stated "that he has known the said Master Richer for around twenty years, knows that he has dissipated the dowry of the said demoiselle Chevalier his wife without having made any use of it, that he still owes the price of his office of attorney at the Châtelet that he purchased, and that he has contracted considerable debts, such that he is overwhelmed with creditors."[25] Like Pierre Derozière, the journeyman ribbon maker, Jean Plainpol de Prébois was too quick to contract debts that he could not repay. Plainpol's wife differed from the ribbon maker's only in that her husband had the means for a more spectacular failure. According to the witnesses, he had sold the family furniture to raise money and fled the country to escape being jailed for debt, leaving his wife to seek refuge in a convent.[26]

Commissaire Doublon was not the only police official to conduct numerous investigations on behalf of wives seeking financial autonomy. On March 31,

1756, Commissaire Mouricault interviewed witnesses about the conduct of Philippe Nicolas Desloches, bourgeois de Paris, at the request of his wife Jeanne Françoise Téty. She had obtained the right to the inquiry in a judgment handed down by the civil lieutenant of the Châtelet of Paris three weeks earlier, despite the formal opposition of her husband. The commissaire first heard testimony from Elzéar Nicolas Le Bret, a twenty-eight-year-old clerk in the fiscal bureaucracy, who stated that "he has known the said sieur Desloches for three or four years, that he knows him for a dissipated man, given over to gambling, without an estate and without an occupation, that he engages in the pursuit of different lawsuits, [is] the quickest to contract debts, in such a manner that there is reason to fear that the dame his wife will lose part of her dowry." The second witness was twenty-nine-year-old Maurice Roussel, an employee in the tax farms, who stated that "for the six years that he has known him, sieur Desloches has had no estate, he contracts debts and is very much given over to gambling, that he used the pretext of pursuing different lawsuits to contract debts, that it is not surprising given his conduct that the said dame his wife takes all possible precautions to try to avoid the dissipation of her dowry." Finally, a third witness, twenty-eight-year-old Jacques François Meye, a bourgeois de Paris, stated that "for eight or ten years he has seen the said sieur Desloches frequent gambling dens, that he has never seen him with an occupation, that he spends whole days gambling, that he takes two or three months to pay very small debts of six or twelve francs, which denotes a disorder and lack of conduct sufficient to put his wife at risk of losing her dowry if he is not prevented."[27] The testimony of each of the three witnesses stressed the danger that Desloches's conduct posed to his wife's dowry, a theme echoed by witnesses in case after case, especially those involving significant property.

Lest it appear that these wives from the middle of the century were a passing phenomenon, the litany of complaints from a wide spectrum of the social scale may be followed into the 1780s. From January to May 1783, for example, Commissaire Vanglenne conducted separation inquiries on behalf of five women, whose husbands included two noblemen, a bourgeois de Paris, a wine merchant, and a journeyman clock maker.[28] As in the earlier cases, the most important complaint was that the husband squandered the couple's money, thereby placing his wife's dowry in clear jeopardy. These statements suggest the helplessness of wives to prevent their husband from excessive spending and acquiring debts. The husband's authority over the financial community meant that he could pledge his name for anything from credit accounts at the tavern to loans of money, financial credit to operate a business, and gambling debts.

The statements also show that a broad consensus existed among Parisian men of different ages, occupations, and social status across the eighteenth century regarding the appropriate masculine duties of a husband. He was to abstain from excessive indulgence of his pleasures, be they drink, fornication, or gambling. He was also to work hard, refrain from risky enterprises and contracting debts, and thus safeguard the property his wife had entrusted to his care. Failure to fulfill these duties earned the public condemnation of other men. The number of these cases is quite substantial, suggesting separation was an accessible means of recourse against a husband's flagrant failure to fulfill his responsibilities.

Just as important as the number of women who took legal action against their husbands is the absence of any men from the commissaires' archives complaining about their wives' abuse of property. Police records abound with wives legally empowered to seek autonomy from wayward husbands, but my research did not turn up a single case of a man protesting financial misconduct on his wife's part. Certainly wives failed to act as proper helpmeets; they could be disobedient, slatternly, drunken, unfaithful, and spendthrifts. Husbands retained the right to physical violence against disobedient wives (if it did not threaten the women's lives), and they could also, in the most extreme cases, have their wives forcibly confined. These marital prerogatives meant that men were judges and enforcers of the law in case of their wives' dereliction of duty; they did not appeal to local police to enforce their rights, because it was their own prerogative and responsibility to do so. In the case of property, since married women theoretically could not borrow on their own authority, their husbands had no legal justification—and little personal incentive—for appearing before the commissaire to confess their inability to control their wives' use of debt.

They could, of course, make use of civil litigation to protest debts presented by their wives' creditors if they felt that their spouses had acted without appropriate approval. Certainly, the courts could reject any formal document creating debt or any other financial transactions signed by a wife without her husband's written authorization. Notaries were forbidden from passing such contracts, as they were not allowed to draft or witness any document whose stipulations contravened the law.

What, however, of informal debt? Did husbands refuse to pay for purchases on credit because their wives did not have their authorization to make them? Were there limits, either legal or practical, to the loophole permitting wives to purchase on credit on their own authority? If the civil court of the Châtelet did not exercise jurisdiction over women's purchases on credit, what recourse did husbands have against their wives' spending sprees? To return to the quotation that opened this chapter, if men avoided marriage to prevent being bankrupted by a wife's addiction to fashion and luxury, did that mean they were powerless to control their wives' expenses?

Rose Bertin's Clients

One source of insight into the legal status of married women's use of shop credit, and the perceived validity of those debts, is provided by the copies of accounts and correspondence generated by the estate of Rose Bertin. Mademoiselle Bertin herself was doubly protected from legal restrictions on female economic autonomy, for she never married and was also an independent businesswoman (*marchande publique*). For her clients, however, the question of financial autonomy is more ambiguous. The long process through which her heirs sought payment for her accounts provides a case study to test the extent to which the credit she extended to female clients was considered legally binding or not.

To understand the significance of these debts, it is important to recognize that the sums involved could be immense: Bertin's heirs claimed that she was owed a total of 1.5 million livres in outstanding accounts when she died in 1813. To put these sums in perspective, fashion merchants' shopgirls received an annual salary of 150 to 200 livres (which did not include any meals and lodging they might have received as well). The most expensive dresses Bertin sold—for a noblewoman's first presentation at court—cost between 1,000 and 2,000 livres. Individual accounts outstanding ranged from under 100 livres (a relatively small sum but still judged worthy of legal procedures thirty years later) to thousands and tens of thousands of livres.

Whereas tradesmen and women periodically collected accounts throughout their working careers, the revolution brought this process to an abrupt halt for Bertin and her clients. Bertin left France in 1792 on a passport issued by the revolutionary government, returning briefly at the end of that year and departing again near the time of the king's execution. She spent time working for the émigré communities of Frankfurt, Coblenz, Brussels, and London and did not return to France for a number of years. When she did, it was to a vastly reduced business and a largely vanished clientele. At Bertin's death in 1813, she left substantial debts of her own.[29] Bertin was survived by two nephews and the children of her two nieces, all descendants of her brother, Louis Nicholas. In 1815 these heirs began what was to be a decades-long effort to collect her outstanding accounts, a frustrating and expensive task only justified by the number and worth of the accounts.

Whatever else vanished over the course of the revolution and the Napoleonic Empire, property rights did not. It is perhaps surprising to note that despite all the political, economic, and constitutional changes from the Old Regime to the Restoration, the status of private debt endured. Legally formed debts from the 1770s—including trade credit—thus could, in principle, be enforced under the Restoration. A series of complicating factors, however, hampered the efforts of the Bertin heirs. The first was the question of proving the existence of the debts themselves. The surest way for merchants to safeguard debts formed through trade credit was by having a client sign a memorandum recognizing their liability for the total amount due. Lacking such a signed statement, merchants could produce their account books. If maintained in accordance with commercial law, they could be used in court, but they carried much less authority than the memoranda. In many cases all the Bertins had to go on were the account books themselves. They excused this deficit by claiming that Rose Bertin—like many other merchants—trusted her noble clients implicitly and therefore did not bother with the formalities of written statements. Business practices imposed by social deference were thus brandished as a form of honor decades later.

A second obstacle was the age of the debts. According to property laws that remained in force from the Old Regime through the revolution, debts of more than thirty years were invalid if creditors had registered no formal claim to them with authorities. In some cases the Bertin heirs could fall back on the submission of accounts that Rose Bertin had made to revolutionary authorities in 1793 in an attempt to wrest compensation from the sale of noble property, but this was not always the case. The third problem was the disintegration of noble families and fortunes that had taken place under the revolution. Many of Bertin's original clients had died. Some were guillotined under the Terror, some died in exile, and others had returned to France and died of disease and old age. Their fortunes were, in general, much diminished and their families dispersed. Many of the heirs claimed to be unable to satisfy any debts at all, despite their best intentions. Great doubt also existed about the identity and whereabouts of the myriad marquises, duchesses, and countesses in Bertin's account books, who belonged to the entangled branches of the French and European nobility. The series of laws on the confiscation of émigré property under the revolution and for the restitution of such property under the Restoration included provisions intended to help creditors recoup debts attached to noble property, but Restoration governments also passed laws postponing debt collection on restored property.[30]

What is noteworthy in the context of this chapter is the way the heirs of both Bertin and her clients conceived of female debt generated through shop credit. In thirty years of negotiation and litigation neither side ever challenged the authority of her female clients to contract debt with the fashion merchant. The clients' heirs did not raise the issue of female legal incapacity, and Bertin's heirs never responded to any perceived weaknesses in the status of female debt. The tacit provision of the Coûtume de Paris described by Pothier proved remarkably efficacious: despite the fact that the accounts could amount to thousands of livres, no one questioned these married women's capacity to (in effect) borrow money and pledge to repay it without their husband's authorization.

Certainly it was possible for men in other circumstances to make use of the provisions of the Coûtume de Paris to refuse to pay debts incurred by their wives without permission. In a commentary on the status of the marchande publique, Claude de Ferrière included the example of a ruling from April 12, 1604 in which Catherine Chevreu, a marchande publique, refused to refund a sum of one hundred écus that she had borrowed. In her defense she claimed that she had borrowed the money without her husband's authorization. Even though she was a marchande publique, she insisted that the debt was invalid because it was for personal not commercial purposes. The courts rejected her claim, but Ferrière nonetheless concluded that the woman's interpretation of the legal principle was correct. He asserted that all other legal judgments condemning marchandes publiques and their husbands to pay debts had occurred only in cases where the debts stemmed directly from the women's commerce.[31]

And yet, when dealing with married women, the Bertin lawyers consistently insisted that husbands were responsible for the debts their wives had incurred. For example, the Marquis de Chambonas refused to pay his wife's account, explaining that he and his deceased wife had been separated in body and goods for forty-four years and that he was therefore not responsible for her debts. After some investigation the lawyers were able to point out that the separation had taken place after the items were purchased from Rose Bertin. As a result, they declared to the marquis that he "remained a debtor as head of the conjugal society that existed at the time."[32] The question of the marquise's capacity to create a binding debt for her husband was not raised. Both debtor and creditor seemed to agree that only a financial separation would have let the husband off the hook.

When circumstances required, however, they would argue on the contrary that responsibility for the debt resided with the individual female client who created it, not her husband. In one example the lawyers began by contacting the Marquis de Chatenay for payment of an account of 915 livres; when they realized he was dead, they switched course and began pursuing his wife.[33] In another example the Marquise de Champrenits wrote to inform the lawyers that she could not be held accountable for Bertin's bills because she had renounced her father's succession; she was informed that unless she had also renounced her mother's succession she was still responsible for the debt incurred by her mother.[34] As in this example, when pursuing the heirs of a female client, the Bertin lawyers approached both male and female descendants. They showed a tendency to approach by preference the presumed male head of the family, but they also contacted the female clients and their daughters, sisters, or nieces. As women were judged capable of generating debt, they also inherited debts and were responsible for meeting them. Community property really was communal, despite the husband's control.

The Bertin lawyers thus adapted their interpretation and use of the law according to circumstances. They were happy to claim that the debt was a family debt, which belonged to the husband as household head. They were also ready to characterize the debt as an individual debt belonging to the woman in question when there was no husband available to pursue. What remained constant, in these two tactics, was the notion that wives had generated legally valid debt.

It is also important to underline that the law was only one element at work in these cases. In the absence of a formal title the letters appealed to the honor of the family. In an internal correspondence they declared of the Duc de Choiseul, "one can hope that he will pay the debt of his wife."[35] They also appealed to families based on the strict regularity of Bertin's bookkeeping, which—they claimed—left no room for doubt about the validity of the claim. For example, to the son of the Marquise de Carcado, the lawyer declared: "You will appreciate even more this regularity in the books of Mademoiselle Bertin, monsieur, when you see on the copy of the account excerpted faithfully and ordered by date from the said registers, that the bill reached in total the sum of 1,220 livres against which madame la marquise having paid that of 400 livres, the latter sum was exactly carried to the account as a deduction. The rank that you occupy in society, the noble sentiments with which your ancient family has always shown itself to be replete, guarantee me the certainty that you and Mademoiselle de Carcado [his sister], to whom I have the honor of writing by the same messenger, will immediately give orders to the effect of examining my claim and according it the fair solution that it should receive from your loyalty."[36]

A third tactic was their emphasis on the poverty of the Bertin clan, whose survival, they asserted, depended entirely on recovering the accounts. They frequently resorted to all three tactics in the same letter. In 1817 the Bertin lawyers wrote to the Comte de Chabannes to press for 320 livres and 15 sols remaining due from an account of 3,659 livres and 15 sols for merchandise delivered to his first wife from 1782 to 1783 and to his second wife in 1788. As they stated, "Messieurs Bertin in whose name I have the honor to submit this request are in pressing need of money being in a very alarming state of scarcity, with the sole hope that you will hasten to come to their aid by acquitting promptly or in portion this debt so legitimate. . . . Your honorability [*honnêteté*] is for them a sure guarantee of the success of their expectations." Their letter concluded that they had already addressed themselves to the count's present wife for her portion of the account without success.[37] Throughout the correspondence, the Bertin lawyers also reminded their interlocutors of the fashion merchant's respect for her clients' honor. Rather than protecting her accounts, she made it a practice not to harass high-ranking patrons for payment or to charge interest on their accounts. Credit relations between merchant and noble customer had their own etiquette, which Bertin had scrupulously observed. This point aptly demonstrates the intersection of noble credit codes with the credit practices of the mercantile world.

The correspondence between the Bertin lawyers and her clients thus emphasizes the highly personal nature of the credit system. Credit relations took place between merchants and clients who knew each other; the faith of the former in the latter was based on personal knowledge, reputation, and social prestige. It was this personal quality that led Bertin to extend credit up to 1.5 million livres and allowed her in turn to run her own business on credit. Yet the law was also crucial in allowing women—if only by a tacit loophole—to give and receive credit. This case reveals the normality of women's consumption through credit for the hundreds of families who shopped in Rose Bertin's boutique. Despite all the hand-wringing and moralizing discussed below, for elite families before and after the revolution, it was entirely normal and expected that women would generate legally valid debt by making purchases on credit.

Making and Breaking the Family on Credit

While women's use of credit was part of everyday life, it also aroused considerable negative scrutiny. The issue surfaces at several points, for example, in the texts Madame de Maintenon wrote for the orphaned daughters of the nobility who attended her school at Saint-Cyr in the last decade of the seventeenth century. Among the pedantic skits she wrote, one series focused on the proverb "women make and break households." In the second scene Monsieur du Château provides the moral ideal in his description of his modest and pious wife, who "says that she makes it a point of honor not to borrow, to live on what she has, and to give as much as she can to her husband and her children."[38]

The opposing extreme is presented in subsequent scenes. In scene 3 two characters, Madame Duvernois and Madame Clairfait, discuss news of the bankruptcy of Monsieur de Remont. Madame Duvernois tells her friend that rumor attributes the failure to his wife, who entertains a great deal, employs many servants, and keeps a disorderly home. Madame Clairfait protests that the woman's fault consisted only of "a little too much spending on clothing; in truth, you can get a lot for a small sum." Madame Duvernois contradicts her friend's naiveté, emphasizing the dangers of purchasing on credit: "One spends too much on clothing, gambles, does not pay, one buys to please merchants who ruin themselves as well with their greed and sell on credit; one desires a grand lifestyle; poorly paid valets serve poorly; the horses die, one must get others; creditors tire of waiting, there are lawsuits; because one is in the wrong, one loses them and is condemned." This sordid train only ends, as in Monsieur de Remont's case, with the seizure of landed estates. Remont's just anger at his wife's excesses led to the couple's separation, and she became "the contempt of everyone who knows her," including her children.[39] Madame de Maintenon tells the same story from the perspectives of the domestics in scene 4. The character Suzanne implores her friend and fellow servant Justine to find her a place within Justine's household because her ruined mistress can no longer employ her. As Suzanne explains: "My mistress never thought about her affairs; she bought at any expense, she never counted; she gambled on cash and purchased on credit; she slept until noon and stayed up all night."[40]

If we cast forward several decades into the eighteenth century, an anecdote from the memoirs of Madame d'Oberkirch provides one glimpse into the way elite husbands and wives understood matters of consumption. Oberkirch describes a meeting that took place between herself and her future husband when she informed him that she would accept his proposal of marriage. Oberkirch remembered the conversation and the intimate negotiation between the fiancés as centering on issues of dress and consumption. As she recounted: "I was wearing a puce brocade dress, I remember perfectly and a small 'pouf' hat that was then the height of fashion. He complimented me for my dress and quickly added: 'You follow fashion, countess.' 'When I have the time to think about it.' 'Do you strictly follow its whims?' 'Oh, no, do you?' 'I frequently anticipate them.' 'That is what I have heard,' I said smiling, though my heart was beating. 'Does that displease you?' 'Not as long as I am the first to be informed.' 'I hope, countess, that you do me the honor of counting on my courtesy. Are you not the mistress of your own household and could your first servant wear an outfit that did not meet your approval?'"[41]

This tense but witty banter reveals the expectations and anxieties that men and women of high rank brought to marriage negotiations. Among the issues to be discussed included an exchange of confidences about their relationship to fashion and where authority over choices about consumption would lie. In extending his hand in marriage the Baron d'Oberkirch explicitly conferred on his future wife the role of "mistress of her own household" and the capacity to pass judgment on his apparel. Based on the lessons of the Bertin correspondence, it appears clear that one important element of being a household mistress was enjoying access to the husband's credit for purchasing clothing and other goods.

Madame d'Epinay's autobiographical roman à clef *Histoire de Madame de Montbrillant* depicts the possibly bitter denouement of such nuptial promises. Married at nineteen to her cousin the tax farmer Denis-Joseph de la Live d'Epinay, Madame d'Epinay suffered not only from her husband's affairs with dancers and actresses but also from his excessive spending, which destroyed the family finances. In one passage of the novel Madame de Montbrillant records her credit woes in a journal entry dated April 9, 1747: "The cloth merchant sent me this morning a bill for 400 livres that I have owed her for six months and, at the same time, the seamstress brought me one for 200. I did not have three livres in my pocket." Her response to the demand reveals a great deal about the financial relationship between the spouses and its impact on their credit dealings: "My husband, to whom I went straight away to ask for the four months he owes me on my pension of 200 livres, refused to give them to me. I asked him to account at least for the money that he made me lend the Chevalier de Canaple last month; but I could get nothing from him but his regret, he said, to be unable to extricate me from the situation. He spoke himself to the two creditors, and gave them hope for their payment at the beginning of next month."[42]

As husband and head of their financial community, Monsieur de Montbrillant (a stand-in for d'Epinay's own husband) wholly controlled his wife's money. Although she enjoyed a monthly pension, it could be withheld or diverted to a different purpose. Her husband did not disavow her capacity to form debt with merchants, but he did refuse to give her the money to pay them, presumably because his resources were tied up with his own creditors. Monsieur de Montbrillant's response to his wife's predicament was to reassure personally the creditors that the debts would be paid, implicitly exercising his masculine marital authority while simultaneously acknowledging the validity of his wife's debts. This anecdote aptly encapsulates the ambiguous status of credit as a form of debt accessible to married women. In 1748, ten years after her marriage, d'Epinay successfully pursued a separation of goods against her husband to protect what remained of her own fortune.

Although women continued to acquire credit for consumption through and beyond the revolution, this practice attracted new attention in the last decades of the Old Regime. Criticism of women's expenditures in this period belonged to a broader attack on royal and aristocratic consumption. In particular this criticism needs to be viewed within the context of contemporary debates about luxury. The historian John Shovlin describes a shift in these debates around 1750. Prior to that date the critique of luxury had focused on bourgeois imitation of noble consumption, such as Molière's social climbing Monsieur Jourdain and his ilk. Subsequently, according to Shovlin, the term was used to "denounce all uses of pomp to constitute political authority and social rank." Luxury was now a crime of the parasitic aristocracy rather than the overambitious bourgeoisie. Shovlin argues that a "cultural crisis hinging on problems of representation and luxury played a crucial role in destabilizing and delegitimizing the social order of the Old Regime."[43]

In this context the decadence and self-indulgence of aristocratic women became a symbol of the corruption of the regime as a whole. As scholars such as Joan Landes, Sarah Maza, and Lynn Hunt have shown, Jean-Jacques Rousseau and others couched their attack on the Old Regime as an attack on the very women who were Rose Bertin's best clients, including, as we saw in the previous chapter, the queen herself.[44] The strength of this attack lay in its imbrication of the cultural, social, and political: cultural decay was inextricably linked to social disorder and political illegitimacy. It is no surprise, therefore, that hopes for reform lay as much in cultural and social as political change and that the proper education of girls and boys generated so much interest. In his passages on the education of Sophie in *Emile*, for example, Rousseau counsels parents to teach young girls to reject excessive self-ornamentation. Girls should learn that real beauty shines most when it is left unadorned and that a simple and modest toilette is always the most attractive. Rousseau does not wish young girls to neglect their looks—for heterosexual desire is at the heart of his social and political system—but he wishes to discourage the tyranny of artifice and women's addiction to expensive adornments. Just as Emile would learn to control his desires and achieve freedom through self-sufficiency, so Sophie would be taught to subdue her feminine desire for superficial items of fashion.[45] Purging the public sphere of women was not enough; it was also necessary to create a new breed of virtuous women who would prepare boys and girls to fulfill their proper roles in a new society.

Echoing Rousseau, Louis-Sébastien Mercier's *Le Tableau de Paris* attacked women's excessive indulgence in fashionable goods. In a chapter titled "Fashion Merchants" he complained that "the expense of fashion today exceeds that of the table and carriages. The unfortunate husband cannot calculate to what price these changing fantasies will amount; and he needs quick resources, to meet these unexpected whims. He would be pointed out in public, if he did not pay these futilities as precisely as those of the butcher and the baker."[46] In a separate article Mercier explained that such vanity was inculcated in girls by their faulty education:

> From the most tender childhood we impregnate, so to speak, women's souls with vanity and superficiality. Everyone participates; the daddy, the mommy, the maid, and the friends of the household; the dance master comes ahead of the reading master in a young lady's education, and even before he who should teach her to fear God and love her future duties. The fashion merchant and the seamstress are beings whose importance she appreciates, before even having heard of the farmer who feeds her and the weaver who dresses her. Before learning that there are objects she should respect, she knows that she must only be pretty and the whole world will shower praise on her. They speak to her of beauty before teaching her of wisdom.[47]

How did women respond to these critiques? Did attacks on noblewomen's consumption, and their access to credit, register with the women who flocked to Bertin's shop? Did they read these accounts as so much rhetorical bombast without relation to their own lives, or did the criticism hit home? Marie Antoinette, as we saw in the previous chapter, declared a revolution in her relationship to fashion when she turned thirty in 1785. But the record also notes the resentment and hostility that this decision generated among the ladies at her court. Certainly, there is no evidence of a slowdown in orders fashion merchants received until the late 1780s, in a time of generalized financial crisis.

If practices do not seem to have been much impacted by these complaints, they did elicit a set of explicit responses from women writers, who read Rousseau and took up his challenge to reform women through a reconceived education for young girls of the elite. One such individual was Madame d'Epinay, best known today as a salonnière and the patron who lent Rousseau her country estate, l'Ermitage, where he wrote parts of *Emile*, the *Social Contract*, and *Julie ou la Nouvelle Héloïse*. D'Epinay was deeply influenced by Rousseau's writings, until a bitter break in 1757 at the time Rousseau parted company with Diderot and other Enlightenment writers. The text of *L'Histoire de Madame Montbrillant* suggests that the book was inspired by the author's critical reading of *Julie*. In 1773 her *Les conversations d'Emilie* represented an explicit response to the pedagogical concerns of *Emile*.

The book consisted of a set of dialogues between a mother and her young daughter, Emilie, a lively format intended simultaneously to entertain and instruct. Dialogue fifteen introduces the themes of good taste, self-control, and the ethics of consumption. The dialogue begins with Emilie talking to her doll, which she is dressing, while her mother sits nearby embroidering. Emilie scolds her doll: "To be frank with you, Madame, I am outraged to see you in this state of humiliation. You look terrible in that bonnet and despair overtakes me each time I see you so horribly dressed." She promises her doll, that when she is twelve or fifteen, she will have six livres of pocket money to spend and they will together make the acquaintance of Mademoiselle Bertin. And then, she delights: "We will have poufs, bonnets, hats, feathers, pearls, cords, earrings in our ears, watch chains, belts, and we will speak in ecstasy of our taste and our elegance." She concludes her speech by lamenting: "It is very cruel that we are too poor right now to buy anything we need."[48]

Emilie's mother calmly responds to the girl's prattling by saying that she herself is more to be pitied than Madame, because she has none of the fashionable accessories coveted by Emilie. Through a gentle exchange of questions and answers, she leads Emilie to see that the use of extravagant terms such as "horror" and "despair" to talk about bonnets is inappropriate, however "à la mode" such language may be. If Emilie continues to speak in this exaggerated fashion, her mother warns: "you will soon have the reputation of having a false, superficial, and frivolous mind that speaks like a canary sings, without attaching sense or feeling to what you say."[49] She contrasts the inherent bad taste of extravagant language with its current vogue, urging her daughter to develop an inner sense of taste to guide her words and actions.

To drive home the need to distinguish true misery from the pretense of it, Emilie's mother reminds the girl of a walk they had taken the previous summer, in the course of which they encountered a widowed peasant woman at the door of her cottage surrounded by three children. She recalls that the woman was barefoot and appeared very poor, but both agree that she had a "noble air" and that it did not occur to them to offer alms. Rather than decrying her situation, the woman simply stated that her husband had died recently just before harvest time. With those few, simple words, the mother tells her daughter, the peasant woman signified her extreme distress, for without her husband's help it would have been impossible for the woman to bring in the harvest or chop wood, and thus the family faced the prospect of a harsh winter with no income, food, or heat. Touched, the child exclaims that they will have to help the family in need but is reminded by her mother that one needs money to help the poor.

Confronted with the spectacle of deserving poverty, the dutiful daughter repents her previous attachment to finery: "Mama, I would give everything I have to have at my disposition the capital destined for Mademoiselle Bertin." Satisfied that her daughter has learned to value charitable giving over personal adornment, her mother extends the reward of maternal approval: "I understand you. That use seems to me infinitely more noble and satisfying than the project of spending one's capital on fashion." As for the doll, she concludes: "Madame will do without poufs for a little while longer."[50]

D'Epinay's personal biography lends important depth and nuance to the passages cited above. Scholars have identified d'Epinay's investment in representing the idealized conversations between a sheltered young girl and her caring mother as resulting at least in part from the loss of her father at a young age, her mother's neglect and indifference, and her frustration at the mediocre education she received. Her own belief in the pedagogical lessons she delivered is not entirely clear, however. The passages of *L'Histoire de Madame de Montbrillant* that describe motherhood report the title character's resentment at her pregnancies and the lack of satisfaction she experienced in raising children. As for d'Epinay herself, a series of monogamous affairs with Enlightenment writers, rather than childrearing, filled the void left by her husband's infidelity. (Her name does not, however, figure among Bertin's unpaid accounts.)

An even more elaborate curriculum on appropriate female consumption issued from Madame de Genlis, former governess of the children of the Duc d'Orléans, celebrated salonnière, and prolific author. In her pedagogical novel *Adèle et Théodore ou Lettres sur l'éducation* (1782) Genlis offers a fascinating account of the training in appropriate consumption that a mother offers her twelve-year-old daughter.[51] The novel consists of a series of letters describing the educational program implemented by the Baron and Baronne d'Almane when they retire to the countryside of Languedoc to raise their two children. Each day has a rigorously planned schedule of lessons in languages, history, religion, music, invigorating physical activities, and—for Adèle—needlework. Published just one year after d'Epinay's text, Genlis replaced the dialogue form with that of letters with the same intent of combining a lively and enjoyable format with moral instruction.[52]

An important element of the baronne's pedagogic technique consisted of setting a series of practical tests for her daughter in ethics, etiquette, and other crucial elements of the child's education. In each case the girl's inevitable failure elicited a tender lesson from her mother to drive home the intended moral. One of these tests aimed to teach Adèle the dangers of credit and to instill a self-disciplined attitude to consumption. In letter twenty-seven of the second volume, Madame d'Almane describes this test in a letter to Madame de Valmont. She had recently accorded the twelve-year-old Adèle two louis d'or (or forty-eight livres) per month in pocket money, from which the girl was obliged to purchase her own "pins, powder, pomade, shoes, gloves, and writing paper." Intoxicated by this spending money, Adèle wasted the entire sum—equivalent to several months of salary for a working girl—in three days on "superfluities." The next month she again wasted her money, spending her last twelve livres on a wooden box instead of saving to buy a useful writing desk. The girl's enjoyment of her purchase evaporated, however, when a poor woman (secretly sent by her mother) appeared in the kitchen, begging charity for the seven children she had left behind in her freezing garret. Since her mother was asleep and her governess had been forbidden to lend Adèle money, the girl was mortified to find that she could not help the woman. Luckily, her governess was able to assist the poor woman out of her own carefully saved funds.

Further questioning on Adèle's part elicited the fact that the poor woman was a former fashion merchant. She had granted "immense credit" to her clients, who purchased well beyond their income, often without even asking the price of the items they acquired. When her clients failed to pay, the merchant had been forced into bankruptcy, selling off her own belongings to satisfy her creditors honorably. Like Bertin's clients, the husbands of her clients were legally responsible for their wives' debts, but they succeeded in driving down the price and often paid nothing at all. To illustrate her point further, Madame d'Almane tells her daughter the story of Madame de Germeuil, who lives in the provinces, separated from her Parisian husband. The couple's separation, d'Almane explains, resulted from the husband's displeasure over his wife's enormous debts. Adèle wonders how one can be so extravagant. Her mother tells her this is possible: "When you lack justice and reflection, when you accustom yourself to yielding madly to all of your fantasies, when you have the silly and ridiculous pretension to outshine all women by the affectation and elegance of your dress. With such a way of thinking, you have extravagant bills with your fashion merchant, you are cheated, robbed, you ruin yourself, you dishonor yourself, and for a few pieces of cloth, feathers, flowers, gauze, and ribbons, you lose the confidence of your husband, the sweetness of your home, and the esteem of the public."[53]

From this staged encounter, Adèle learns all the right lessons: to abhor extravagant self-indulgence, to moderate her desires, and to resist the temptations of the new array of consumer goods available in the second half of the eighteenth century. She comes to appreciate the virtues of charity and the need to help the poor not only by distributing alms but also by treating debts to tradesmen and women as debts of honor. She learns to value the "confidence" her husband will place in her, confidence a husband apparently needed because law and tradition obliged him to entrust his wife with free rein over his credit. This story is a moral lesson about restraining desire, a cautionary tale about the family breakdowns caused by women's uncontrolled desires, and a social critique of the suffering imposed on female merchants by the abuse of credit among elite clients.

In case this example provided insufficient warning to her readers, Genlis devoted a play, titled *Les Dangers du monde*, to another story of elite dissipation.[54] This play tells the story of the Marquise de Germini, a twenty-one-year-old noblewoman who has been married for a year and a half. In the absence of her husband and the aunt who raised her after her parents' death, the marquise has devoted herself to fashionable society. She has been drawn into a circle of affected women and become the bosom friend of the flighty and self-indulgent Vicomtesse Dorothée. Unable to resist her desire to shine in society—and the blandishments of avaricious merchants—the marquise has run up a long list of debts. At the opening of the play her faithful attendant, Juliette, has chased away a fashion merchant, one of the throng of tradespeople who visit the house each morning. They visit not only to sell their wares but also to press their accounts. Juliette has just received a packet of bills from her mistress's creditors, which includes a bill for five thousand livres to the cabinet maker, another for over eight thousand from a painter, and one for nine thousand nine hundred livres for bracelets, rings, and other adornments. The unexpected arrival of the marquise's aunt after a ten-month absence recalls the young woman to her duties. She acknowledges her departure from the solid morals and useful pastimes her aunt had taught her. And yet the young woman's desire to return to a peaceful and orderly life is undermined by her pleasure in the whirl of Parisian high society and the demands of Vicomtesse Dorothée.

As she ponders her situation, and the mountain of debt she has amassed, the marquise receives a visit from Mademoiselle LeDoux, a celebrated fashion merchant and possible ringer for Rose Bertin. As the merchant and her assistant display their wares, the vicomtesse arrives. She recounts the latest gossip, the downfall of a mutual acquaintance who has gambled away forty-eight thousand livres and risks disownment by her husband and his family. (Later Mademoiselle LeDoux will act on this overheard indiscretion by presenting herself to the woman's parents-in-law to demand payment of her long overdue bill before news of the financial catastrophe reaches other creditors.) Meanwhile, a poor woman from the marquise's estates arrives with her children to beg for charitable aid. Her home has been destroyed by fire and if she does not pay five hundred livres to the bailiffs, her husband will be taken to prison the next day. Given her own debts, the marquise—like the young Adèle—is mortified to admit that she cannot assist the woman. She does not realize that her servant Juliette—like Adèle's governess—has paid the woman in the marquise's name, until her valet comes to demand his overdue wages, having heard from the grateful peasant about the marquise's generosity. The story culminates with a visit from a financier who calculates that the marquise's debts total seventy thousand livres, a sum impossible to meet with her limited funds. Facing disgrace in the eyes of her husband, whose arrival is imminent, the marquise is saved by her aunt, who pays off the entire debt. This sacrifice is the last lesson needed to bring the young wife entirely back to the straight and narrow as she prepares to greet her husband.

It is clear from the text that the abuse of credit lies at the center of the marquise's problems. The faithful Juliette offers a frank summary of her mistress's faults: "You have never examined a statement of accounts or a bill; you know the price of nothing, you have always bought everything on credit: those are the principal causes of the difficulties you are in."[55] Her overreliance on credit is inextricably linked to her dissipated life among other decadent society women, with their obsession with clothing, appearances, and fashion. Only by refusing the life of high society, staying home, tending to her household, and occasionally sojourning on her provincial estates, could an elite lady avoid the temptations of excessive and futile consumption. Interestingly, the marquise's husband never appears during the play, an absence that is plausible given the largely separate social lives noble couples conducted in the period. His absence enables her mountain of debt just as his threatened return sets the drama in motion by obliging the marquise to face up to her debts and devise a solution that will allow her to retain the confidence he has invested in her. However, the crisis—and its ultimate resolution—takes place in a world of female consumers, female friends, and female vendors.

A revealing counterexample of a young woman's use of credit is provided by Félicité de Choiseul-Meuse in her *Récréations morales et amusantes, à l'usage des jeunes demoiselles qui entrent dans le monde*. In one story in the collection the orphaned Mélise visits the shop of her fashion merchant Madame Mallouet. At the doorway she encounters an admirer, the chevalier Muller, who requests permission to accompany her inside the shop. Madame Mallouet greets the pair enthusiastically and encourages Mélise to try on a beautiful coral necklace and earrings. She flatters Mélise on how well the jewelry suits her and urges her to buy the set, declaring "they have not been seen yet and you may be sure that no one in Paris will have anything similar." Mélise passionately desires the pieces but realizes she doesn't have enough money to buy them. The problem is not poverty, for her guardian provides her with "a large allowance for her dress"; however, "she had so little order and so many whims that the quarter was always eaten in advance, and at that moment almost nothing remained for her."[56]

The chevalier steps in at this point to offer to lend Mélise the asking price of the jewelry. He assures her it will be a perfectly legitimate transaction, because he will charge interest, thus indicating a purely financial rather than personal interaction. Mélise demurs, not out of proper outrage at such a proposal but because she is certain her family will want to know how she could afford such expensive items. Demonstrating her familiarity with the pedagogy of female consumption outlined in works by Genlis, d'Epinay, and others, she declares that "they will never believe that I was able to make this purchase without going into debt; I will be scolded, sermonized, and I will defend myself even more poorly because I sense myself that I am a little in the wrong." The fashion merchant resolves this dilemma by declaring that she will give the jewels away as a prize in a lottery, in which the sole ticket will be sold to her client. Mélise accepts this stratagem, while the chevalier hands the merchant her price in silver coin.[57] Unfortunately for Mélise, at the ball where she wears the jewels their rightful owner recognizes them as property that had been stolen some weeks previously. Far from being the only woman in Paris to wear the jewels, as Madame Mallouet promised, Mélise is publicly denounced as a thief. She is forced to return the jewels, refund the chevalier, and leave Paris for several years to escape the ensuing scandal.

As a counterexample of an unmarried woman's relationship to credit and consumption, this story underlines at least two important points. The first is the lack of credit available to minor single women. If Mélise had been married, she would have been able to purchase the jewels she desired without controversy by drawing on her tacit authorization to use her husband's credit. Unlike the fashion merchants in other accounts, who facilitate overindulgence through easy credit, Madame Mallouet does not suggest that Mélise make the purchase on credit. It is only through the chevalier's intervention that she can realize her desires. Second, this story also suggests that, while marriage offered a woman autonomous access to her husband's credit as a central prerogative of her marital status, it was scandalous and dishonorable for an unmarried woman to make use of another man's credit. Precisely because the use of credit belonged to the bonds of marriage, accepting a man's credit implied the existence of intimate relations. This was the same logic that made Marie Antoinette's alleged use of the credit of the Cardinal du Rohan to purchase the necklace at the center of the Diamond Necklace Affair so shocking. The bond of credit so closely overlapped the conjugal tie that it was dishonorable to form credit ties outside of marriage. Even though it was quickly proven that the queen was not involved, the taint of misconduct remained.

What are we to make of Genlis's and other women writers' critique of female consumption on credit? In many ways they echo Rousseau's call for female reform. Like Rousseau, the texts examined here agreed that women's role was to marry, raise their children, and help the poor through charity and good works. The end of Genlis's novel finds Adèle married, pregnant, and setting up a school to teach poor girls a trade.[58] Despite these similarities, there were crucial differences between the two writers' perspectives. While Rousseau condemned female aristocrats from his position outside the court, Genlis was very much a court insider. As governess to the children of the Duc d'Orléans as well as the duke's mistress and mother of two of his children, she was in multiple ways an intimate of the cadet branch of the royal family. Her concern was not to undo the aristocracy but to suggest a path toward its reform. The educational plan outlined in *Adèle et Théodore* thus purported to produce noblemen and women who would lead useful and exemplary lives at the summit of the social hierarchy. Like Rousseau, Genlis emphasized virtue; however, in her vision, this was not a radical, socially transformative trait but a moral and religious position achieved through self-discipline and renunciation.[59] Genlis's critique of female consumption thus did not replicate Rousseau's republican vision. Neither did it correspond to the aristocratic reaction against upstart bourgeois ladies or the horror at dissolving social borders described by Sarah Maza. Instead, Genlis's writings should be seen as an attempt to portray the internal self-critique of a reforming nobility. Madame de Genlis's writing—if not her actual life—thus prefigures the chastised female nobles described by Margaret Darrow, who renounced public life for family in the aftermath of the revolution, finding in the household a new foundation for aristocratic honor.[60]

How widespread was this reaction to women's "excessive" consumption? The immense popularity of Rousseau's *Emile* and Genlis's *Adèle et Théodore* suggests that there was a considerable audience for calls for female reform. *Emile* appeared in sixteen editions in six years, while fourteen editions of *Adèle et Théodore* were issued in four years.[61] The revolution, with the emigration of the nobility and the politically suicidal connotations of conspicuous consumption, appears at first glance to have solved the problem of female credit. Margaret Darrow argued that returning emigrées and their daughters accepted accusations that the decadence and luxury of their prerevolutionary lifestyle played a key role in the downfall of the Old Regime. To regain a place for the nobility in French cultural and political life, they embraced private domesticity as "part of their effort to transform the aristocracy from frivolous, malicious parasites into a natural elite of wise statesmen and administrators and devoted, modest wives and mothers."[62] Madame de Campan's regret over Marie Antoinette's excessive consumption and the example it set to other noblewomen fits perfectly into this scenario.

It would be overly simplistic, however, to conclude that an engulfing cultural tide rose against female consumption and credit in the late Old Regime, culminating in the French Revolution and resulting in a reformed female elite under the Restoration. In practical terms we know that the renunciation of luxurious consumption was short-lived. Whatever their newfound devotion to family and domesticity, wealthy women continued to purchase expensive clothing on credit. A fashion merchant's account book from the First Empire recorded accounts for individual female clients under their married names.[63] Like Rose Bertin, this merchant routinely accorded credit to married women, keeping track of services and merchandise rendered on the left-hand side of the book, while carefully noting sums received on the right-hand page. To judge from this account book, nothing had changed between 1780 and 1812 in terms of married women's access to credit. Designated as the "mistress of the household," the domesticated noblewoman retained responsibility for securing provisions, and maintaining appearances, in an appropriate manner.[64] One needs only to recall the cascade of bills engulfing Emma Bovary to be persuaded of the continuity of this form of female autonomy and the dangers associated with it. This scene of attempted reconciliation between husband and wife could describe the Marquise de Germini as easily as Madame Bovary: "if she had never informed him about the letter [of credit], it was to spare him domestic worries; she sat on his knees, caressed him, cooed at him, made a long list of all the indispensable things taken on credit."[65]

Genlis herself exemplifies the dangers of reading too much into prescriptive literature. During her lifetime observers often remarked on the discrepancy between her written calls for virtue and her considerably less circumspect personal life. This author of appeals for women to submit to the authority of their husbands lived independently of her own spouse for twenty years and had numerous affairs.[66] Madame d'Epinay similarly engaged in a series of long-term, as well as more fleeting, sexual relations with men outside of marriage and seems to have felt deeply ambivalent about motherhood. If it was possible to write one narrative while living another, it is certainly equally likely that readers could enjoy the stories they read without changing their own daily habits.

Moreover, Genlis's writings themselves do not tell a simple story. The errors of the Marquise de Germini, for example, suggest the author's fears of the inadequacy of even the best education. At the age of twenty-one, mistress of her own household, the Marquise de Germini had access to seemingly un-limited credit. Raised with excellent morals, she was still vulnerable to the in-fluence of bad friends and pushy merchants. At the same time that it highlights the dangers of women's access to the market, this cautionary tale raises questions about the ultimate efficacy of education. Pedagogical tales by Genlis and the other authors examined above, furthermore, have a double-edged lesson. While they underline contemporary "anxiety" about consuming women, they also emphasize the centrality of credit to the marriage contract. According to these well-placed observers, women's right to use their husband's credit was at the core of the marital relation. A wife's ability to provision the household and to appear as a proper representative of her husband's estate relied on being able to wield his credit independently. The payoff of patriarchy, of being sub-sumed by the husband's authority, was the ability to represent that authority in dealings with the outside world. Consumption thus gave wives a certain status in the "public" represented by merchants, shops, and credit arrangements. De-priving a wife of this status was equivalent to public disavowal and constituted a devastating loss of face. For husbands, trust in their wives was a question of financial, as well as sexual, probity. Renouncing excessive consumption, in Genlis's stories, did not mean giving up access to a husband's credit but pledg-ing to use it wisely.

As much as Genlis reveals about contemporary fears of female consump-tion, therefore, she also shows how much credit and consumption lay at the heart of marriage and family life. The continued availability of credit to mar-ried women, and the ongoing legal validity accorded to debts formed on credit beyond the revolution, suggests that this was an enduring feature of marriage and marital relations. Beneath the "froth" of revolutionary events, female credit appears as a central element of the longue durée of marriage and family life.

Rose Bertin's faith in her clients' financial resources and in the honor of their word created a mountain of debt that kept lawyers busy over three decades. This striking example was replicated, on a smaller scale but in countless num-bers, in the day-to-day life of Parisian trades. As businesswomen and as con-sumers, women's daily transactions relied heavily on an informal system of trade credit. To understand the way women operated in the interstices of the law and to appreciate their active participation in economic exchange (buying, selling, borrowing, lending, bequeathing, and inheriting), we need to take into account the weight of the credit economy and women's role in it as buyers, as well as producers and sellers.

In their daily transactions with credit married women did not bring their husbands along to authorize their actions. Our long-accepted notion that married women could not contract debt is contradicted by the basic fact at the heart of their daily lives: all families lived with debt, and women often managed it. Debt management was at the center of women's lives, and it formed a central aspect of female financial activity. Women from modest families juggled credit for necessities along with credit for the little extras for comfort or style. Among elite families, women's consumption could take on proportions that far outstripped the limited autonomy envisioned by legal strictures.

Women's access to trade credit has important implications both for the consumer revolution of the eighteenth century and for wives' status within the family. Women's consumption of clothing and other articles of daily life led them to enter credit agreements that bypassed legal restrictions on married women's financial actions. To date, French historians have not drawn connections between women's consumption and their legal status, but it is clear that the growth of consumption in the eighteenth century both relied on and enlarged a sphere of female economic capacity lying alongside or beneath the law. This is a particularly important insight, given the predominant position women played in the consumer revolution of the eighteenth century and, in particular, in purchases of clothing and accessories.

In order to consume such commodities, they made use of trade credit with elite merchants like Rose Bertin, their neighborhood seamstress, or used-clothes sellers. Wives' capacity to engage in trade credit was widely accepted, so much so that no one seemed to notice when it took on proportions that appeared to contradict the provisions of the Coûtume de Paris. A wife's position thus entitled her to engage her husband's credit, even beyond the means of the family. His only recourse was to renounce his wife and send her far from the urban centers of fashionable consumption. As we have seen, this wifely prerogative was so entrenched that it survived the tumult of the French Revolution and the stringent critiques of elite women and their luxurious ways produced by prerevolutionary and revolutionary ideologues. In decades of litigation between the Bertin family and clients, neither vendor nor consumer raised the question of the legal validity of a wife's debts. Based on this evidence, we may conclude that one of the chief perquisites of marriage for women was the guarantee it gave them of their ability to wield their husbands' credit in their own account. Wives may not have had access to money or property on their own, but they enjoyed the capacity to engage their names (and by extension their husbands') for purchases for themselves and their households. Male household authority, so firmly entrenched by law, was a much more fragile and negotiable affair in daily life.

CONCLUSION

CREDIT IS DEAD!
LONG LIVE CREDIT!

One of Louis XVIII's first acts upon his return to France in 1814 was to inquire after the health and whereabouts of Mademoiselle Bertin. To build a legitimate monarchical court, he understood, the royal family and its courtiers needed to dress the part. No one knew better than Bertin how to help him acquire the cultural capital of ostentatious display and leverage it into the political and social credit he so badly needed. Unfortunately for both king and fashion merchant, Bertin had died in diminished circumstances several months earlier in September 1813, almost twenty years after the beheading of her most famous client. Bertin's lawyers spent months, years, and ultimately decades writing letters and knocking on doors in mostly futile attempts to collect the hundreds of thousands of livres her clients still owed, a testimony both to the legal durability of credit despite political, economic, and social upheaval and to the obstacles standing in the way of merchants seeking remuneration for their wares. Bertin and her lesser-known colleagues illuminate and helped shape a particular moment in French history when the "regime of credit" described by the Abbé de Vermond was at its peak.

This book has argued that multiple, intersecting economies of regard operated in Old Regime France. These included political economies of power in court patronage and royal administration, economies of trust and affection within families, economies of prestige and renown within intellectual life, economies of desire in sexual relations, economies of money in the myriad form of stipends, pensions, commerce, and public finance, and economies of information and publicity. Common to all of these economies was the key role of reputation and confidence, the influence they conveyed and the access they opened to resources of many different guises. Like the gift economy described by Marcel Mauss, these economies were simultaneously reciprocal and self-interested, spontaneous and carefully strategized. They also ranged in scale from relatively closed and small-scale networks, in which personal ties and interaction remained paramount, to regional, national, and global circuits of commerce and trade. Alongside the growth of commercial news distribution, eye- and ear-witnessing remained essential methods for transmitting assessments of value, and embodied forms of self-representation, such as fashionable dress, served as crucial tools for acquiring and displaying regard.

The intertwined nature of these economies, as well as their imbrication with social relations and reputation, made it difficult to fix the value of any good (a commodity, a social relation, a favor, to name but a few). This book has posited that constant processes of conversion across economies occurred and that what we perceive today as the discrete realms of politics, economics, culture, and society were intermingled and intertwined. Understanding this point helps the historian see beyond our divided domains of inquiry and appreciate the extent to which strategies for individual and collective advancement worked through many fields simultaneously.

This book has maintained, as well, that, far from being dupes of the processes that shaped their lives, denizens of *le monde* understood all of this very well, so well that they employed a single term to refer to the impact of reputation and the authority it conveyed on multiple, symbiotically interrelated economies. That term was *credit*, which provided a useful shorthand to evoke everything that everyone already knew about how power actually operated. This was not an aspirational principle, like honor or virtue or merit. Philosophers and other writers accordingly paid it little explicit attention compared to those ideals, although their correspondence is replete with frank references to the impact of their own or others' credit standing. Credit was thus the open secret of the Old Regime. Everyone knew that individuals or groups (or literary styles, religious orders, and outfits) that succeeded in gaining recognition from others could realize profits unforeseen by the normative rules; those excluded from the privileges of credit for religious, political, social, or personal reasons denounced the secret with bitterness and contempt. The construction and reconstruction of le monde itself—in other words, the effort to know what "everyone" knew and thus to join the "*on*" of *Le Mercure galant* and other publications—consisted in many ways of struggles to obtain, safeguard, and increase one's own and one's friends' credit while diminishing that of rivals.

It is no accident that both material and nonmaterial connotations combined in the term contemporaries used to encompass the workings of power in human society. The word was so useful precisely because it could convey faith and belief, on the one hand, and loans and debts, on the other. It thus evoked in a nutshell the ambiguous relationship that always existed between reciprocity and obligation. It was a cynical and yet frank summary of their daily experience. It stood in contrast to the language of the gift, which "everyone" (again) knew to be a form of etiquette disguising the underlying reality of credit. To put it more simply, their use of the term *credit* confirms that subjects of the Old Regime were by no means pre-economic; they were fully and deeply economic in the sense of undertaking strategic action to foster the production, development, and management of wealth. By "wealth," however, they meant a variety of different goods; money was prominent among them but still bore the taint of Christian doctrine against usury and suffered from the traditional valorization of land, commensality, gifts, and other nonmonetary goods. In the hands of critics the language of credit could turn both ways: to castigate its holders as lowly traffickers in base materialism or to call for a return to an ostensibly ideal past of disinterested credit based on love and virtue.

These arguments are important, I believe, for several reasons: for summarizing and synthesizing what historians from many different perspectives and approaches have posited about Old Regime France and early modern societies in general, for emphasizing connections among historiographical fields that tend to remain apart, and for insisting on the sophisticated self-awareness and powers of complex calculation possessed by the subjects we study. Beyond offering a new framework through which to make sense of existing interpretations, this book has aimed to expand our understanding of credit systems in a number of ways: first, by examining more closely the roles available to women in dispensing and wielding credit and in particular the capacity ascribed to them of leveraging credit through sex; second, by inquiring into the ways that worldly understandings of *crédit* extended to ordinary men and women of the working classes, both in conceptual and practical terms; third, by positing a close relationship between credit and fashion, which I have characterized as complementary systems for acquiring reputation and for circulating judgments on value; fourth, by providing a case study for the interaction of the elements discussed above—material and nonmaterial forms of credit, fashion, and sex—through an examination of the fashion merchants of Paris. A fifth and final aim—with which I began this conclusion and to which I return in more detail in its closing sections—has been to use the story of credit to provide another perspective on the question of change over time over the long eighteenth century.

To begin with the issue of gender, credit ran through and against normative social and political hierarchies and the (mostly) fixed, quantifiable character of specie. It will be no surprise to gender historians to hear that women enjoyed much more access to the gray markets of credit than to official structures of power and authority. Women played key roles in networks of patronage; their correspondence shows them openly discussing their credit strategies and receiving explicit appeals to mobilize their credit on behalf of others. While noblewomen's capacity to wield credit in the form of patronage does not seem marked by gender, the role attributed to women in libidinal economies and their ostensible capacity to generate sexual credit that could be leveraged into political influence, expensive clothing, and other resources was highly gendered. Indeed, it was the particular opening to other forms of power represented by women's alleged control of circuits of desire—and the unique possibility it allowed for women of the lower classes to form intimate ties to wealthy and powerful men—that led some commentators to call for greater separation and distinction among different forms of credit. In economic terms women enjoyed significant access to credit both as producers and consumers. In particular, married women benefited from the gray area constituted by credit to escape the restrictions of coverture and run up substantial debts with artisans and merchants.

Assessing the meaning of the term for the *"morts sans crédit"* evoked by André Monglond is challenging due to the paucity of sources written by men and women of the working world.[1] We know that reliance on credit for daily purchases of bread and other necessities was ubiquitous, and evidence from my own and other historians' research shows that borrowing and lending money played as crucial a role in humble households as in *hôtels particuliers*. Thus, the issues of social recognition and reputation involved in obtaining and dispersing credit touched nearly all levels of society. Trade credit, a form of borrowing and lending largely ignored by historians, constituted a crucial site for the intersection of social, cultural, and financial capital. With regard to nonmaterial forms of credit, I have argued that worldly writers attributed the possession of political and social credit to leaders among the people and that texts specifically aimed at nonelite readers assumed their audiences would be familiar with the same multiplicity of usages of credit found in elite sources.

This book contends, moreover, that not only were all forms of credit recognizable to plebeian subjects but also that the intersection and interaction of multiple economies described by members of le monde encompassed many sectors of society. The weight of the luxury trades within the French, and especially the Parisian, economy meant that a large proportion of skilled artisans and merchants worked in these industries; their livelihood depended on mastery of the subtleties and intersections of the economies of regard discussed above. More broadly speaking, the politics of reputation, influence, and power shaped access to the resources of institutions at all levels of society from the poor relief of the parishes to the orphanage at the Trinité hospital, from the seamstresses' guild to the Parlement of Paris and Versailles.[2] Thus, whatever the blind spots of historians and their sources, there were few Old Regime subjects who did not recognize and participate in credit systems in some manner, if only as the marginalized whose exclusion helped consolidate the privileges of others.

Credit constituted one set of systems for circulating information about the reputation of members of a group and their capacity to engage in reciprocal exchange; another was fashion. Both systems relied on the eye- and ear-witnessing of the embodied actions of others. They circulated through multimedia information networks that combined traditional modes and sites of transmission such as gossip, letter writing, privileged gathering spots, and objects of material culture with newer commercial forms and arenas of publicity that began to expand in the last decades of the seventeenth century, including published newspapers, manuscript newssheets, advertisements, and luxury boutiques. Through the end of the eighteenth century, personal observation or secondhand transmission from a reliable source remained tremendously important, and printed sources contain fascinating traces of an information culture in which conversation, correspondence, social gatherings, witty stories, rumor, manuscript texts, material goods, gestures, and other oral or embodied modes of communication held more power than the printed word. Studying the circulation of fashion and credit is one way to apprehend the slow transition of information technologies and, in turn, understanding the two as dual information systems helps explain the many affinities between them.

Perhaps more than any other group, the fashion merchants' trade embodied the intersection of multiple economies of regard and the role women acquired in such economies as consumers and as producers of goods, cultural knowledge, reputations, and desire. They show us that independent female retailers and small business owners—in certain trades at least, with predominantly female clienteles—could acquire credit on a par with married couples and with men. They also reveal, however, the gulf separating these modest entrepreneurs from large-scale merchants of cloth, lace, and other expensive materials, who were almost invariably men. Fashion merchants confirm the astoundingly long terms of credit—ranging from several months to several years—that were apparently commonplace in Old Regime retail commerce, particularly in the luxury trades. In the multiple conversions of credit, the final transformation—of shop credit into specie—was the hardest to achieve. Credit was not merely a story of social connections, influence, and reputation but also one of uncertainty, risk, failure, and domination.

The only way fashion merchants could survive such delays was by imposing similar periods on their suppliers and, one presumes, by using their own wares to swap book credit. Successful merchants were not those without debt, but those who scrounged the means to hold off creditors and who were resourceful or fortunate enough to navigate the more or less constant state of cash flow crisis. A key to their survival was the reciprocal bonds imposed by the credit regime. Elite clients needed talented *marchandes de modes* to gain access to the prestige of fashionable dress; in turn, merchants' success depended on the patronage of socially powerful women who could draw in other customers and serve as indirect collateral for the supplies they purchased on credit. Shared risk bound patron to purveyor, even if the risk was extremely unequally distributed.

As the last remark suggests, to cast fashion merchants as the weak link in the chain of credit risks would significantly underestimate their role in economies of regard and, in particular, the historical changes they both revealed and helped bring into being. Fashion merchants built on the success of Parisian and provincial seamstresses, who usurped tailors' guild privileges to build a trade niche serving children and female customers in the second half of the seventeenth century. In 1675 the royal government acknowledged their success with an independent all-female guild, which quickly grew into one of the largest corporations in Paris. Several decades later female fashion merchants similarly emerged from the shadows of the mercers' guild to create a trade specialization in making headwear and accessories for women. In 1776, a century after the seamstresses, fashion merchants obtained a guild of their own, which soon attracted hundreds of female members who employed many more shopgirls, apprentices, and subcontracted laborers. These two acts of female incorporation serve as bookends to the slow rise and the full development of the consumer revolution in France.

For both seamstresses and fashion merchants, the push from the supply of female laborers—who provide a compelling example of the trajectory of Jan de Vries's industrious revolution—fostered significant growth in the production of women's clothing, which simultaneously broadened women's access to new, custom-made apparel and publicized new gendered divisions of labor and consumption. Women's access to credit made it possible for these female entrepreneurs to operate their businesses, and it enabled married women to make choices about purchasing new fashions without authorization from their husbands. The growth of garment trades staffed by women and supplying female customers, in which the majority of purchases were made on account, was a key element of the expansion of credit within the French commercial economy, impacting not only the women themselves but the hundreds of thousands of spinners, weavers, knitters, wholesale merchants, feather collectors, precious stone miners, whale fishermen, and enslaved cotton and indigo producers, among others, who furnished the materials of their trade.

To gain their livelihood, fashion merchants devoted their creative energies to inventing new forms of dress decorations, new items of apparel, and new styles for existing items. Their success in convincing clients to purchase a constant stream of clothing and accessories contributed a great deal to contemporaries' perception that fashion was moving ever more swiftly and encompassing more objects. Their growing numbers thereby made it at once more difficult to follow fashion (because so many more items needed to be of the latest fashion) and easier (because cheaper versions of items were available in public shops that offered professional assistance and guidance). They helped popularize, in both senses of the word, the very notion of fashion and the perceived need to follow it. They were thus key players in the rising commercialization of culture and media. As such, they helped create a new type of cultural capital for artisans and merchants who presented their work as a type of artistic genius rather than manual labor. The eighteenth century was the dawn of the celebrity artisan, who wielded a certain authority over elite clients through ostensibly superior taste and imagination. Fashion merchants, like Duchapt and Rose Bertin, were early virtuosos of the genre.

Reliance on shop credit and the close ties between moral and material credit were obviously not unique to France or even to Europe. Laurence Fontaine has traced the crucial role of credit in economic exchange on a European level and scholars of individual countries, England in particular, have provided details on a national or regional level. These studies have emphasized that moral reputation was an essential prerequisite for financial credit. A merchant's credibility, that is, his or her reputation for probity, solvency, and integrity, were as valuable as collateral. Like their French counterparts, women used their access to credit in England, as Margot Finn has shown, to overcome the strictures of coverture and make their own choices about consumption.[3]

Further research is necessary to understand how these themes played out beyond the French capital, in the provinces, in the rest of Europe, and beyond. Did courtiers at Vienna (or Bavaria or Istanbul) conceive of their favors as a form of "credit" in the same way as those at Versailles? Did they describe fashion and credit as analogous dynamics? How were Parisian networks of credit integrated in wider national and global circuits of financial credit, and how did political and cultural credit interact on a global scale? How did economies of regard help shape France's colonizing projects, and did they lead to distinctive encounters with indigenous peoples' own notions of reciprocal exchange? Beyond the John Law episode, how did credit economies shape French participation in the slave trade and the multiple economic, social, political, and cultural calculations involved in transporting millions of enslaved Africans across the Atlantic and working them to death on plantations? These questions demonstrate that we urgently need wider and more global frameworks of history in which to situate the French "regime of credit" examined in these pages.

Credit Is Dead! Long Live Credit!

A broader spatial perspective is thus necessary to test the saliency of the "credit regime" framework beyond Paris and the royal court. What about the question of time? In his *Psychologie économique* of 1902 the French sociologist Gabriel Tarde offered the following reflection on credit as a form of confidence: "The credit of a man, born of public belief in him is for him a great means of action, and for the public a great safeguard, apparent or real. And economists are correct to speak of credit. But the financial credit of a man, the only one to which they attend is not the only one that demands attention. The confidence that a citizen inspires, as a statesman, a general, a scholar, an artist, is a moral credit, of quite distinct importance than the confidence that some bankers have in his solvency."[4] This passage, which might have been lifted from the pages of Duclos's *Considérations sur les moeurs de ce siècle*, offers striking testimony to the longue durée of concepts of moral credit within French culture. His call for inquiry into the questions of credit and confidence were part of the plea Tarde formulated in this work for a wholly new way of conceiving economics and its relation to the social sciences. Rejecting the labor theory of value of classical economics, Tarde proclaimed that value arose instead from collective and subjective judgments about "the aptitude of objects to be more or less—and by a greater or lesser number of people—believed, desired, or enjoyed."[5] Thus, alongside utility, criteria of beauty and truth were equally important factors in assessments of value. For Tarde, the "goods" at stake in such evaluations consisted not merely of commodities but also different forms of knowledge, aesthetic creations, credit, fame, and power. He thus made a case for an all-encompassing economics in which money was but one, relatively impoverished, measuring system. Such an economics could be fully integrated with the other human sciences, having discarded the notion of the "economy" as an autonomous realm subject to scientific laws. Tarde further insisted on the quantitative nature of processes of evaluation, despite the intangible nature of many of the goods in circulation. Whether it be gold or glory, he claimed, individuals strive to acquire more of any high-value good and anxiously assess how much they possess in comparison to others, whether the amount circulating is rising or falling and whether the value of the good itself has grown or diminished.

Judgments assessed quantitatively must be analyzed in the same manner. Tarde thus dreamt of a "glorimeter" that could measure the multiple, sudden, and fleeting fluctuations in the amount of glory any man possessed. Such a mechanism would measure the number of people who had heard of the individual, how deeply they admired him, and, in turn, the social status and influence of the group of admirers. Just like the highly nuanced mutual assessment of gradations of nobility within the salons of the Old Regime, he tells us, the glorimeter would need to probe the many fine details that shaped the production of reputation in the early twentieth century.[6]

At this point the reader may wonder why Tarde figures in the conclusion rather than the introduction to this book. Given the affinities between the universal economics he proposes and the credit regime studied in the preceding pages, why not begin with Tarde and bring his glorimeter to bear on the marchandes de modes and their worldly clientele? We come to Tarde at the end of this story because, in fact, his own arguments were shaped in direct and explicit opposition to two great inventions of the late eighteenth century: political economy and the liberal state. As Karl Polanyi would argue some decades later, Tarde claimed that the new awareness of the economy as a discrete field was not an empirical discovery of the period, as fledgling political economists claimed, but an invention predicated on belief in an immanent providence capable of producing market equilibrium. He thus dismissed the long and violent debate between proponents of regulation and of free markets as a mirage masking two versions of the same misguided belief. Unlike Polanyi, Tarde insisted that there was no preexisting "society" in which the economy could be embedded; society itself emerged from the same realm of human interests, desires, and beliefs that created economies of value.

What Tarde only hints at, in his reference to the aristocratic salon, is the eighteenth-century credit regime against which political economists formulated their theories. Their self-proclaimed discovery of the economy, this book has suggested, constituted at once a monumental ideological projection and an effacement of the multiple economies of regard in which they struggled to make their voices heard. Ending with Tarde thus allows us a critical vantage point from which to assess the credit regime traced in this book, to understand better the consequences of its disavowal, and to see more clearly the announced destruction of this regime as a construct in its own right rather than an inevitable result of economic and political modernization.

Databases of published sources lend support to the notion that there is something particularly Old Regime about the credit story, suggesting that the period from 1600 to 1850 represented a high point in the cultural saliency of credit, particularly with regard to nonmaterial uses of the word.[7] The social and cultural weight of French court society played a key role in this periodization, as it provided a crucial arena for ostentatious, competitive display and a restricted and centralized milieu in which displaying and witnessing could function as modes for assessing value and transmitting judgments. As court society broadened into le monde of the late seventeenth century, which contained both sword and robe nobles as well as successful writers and non-noble office holders and financiers, these practices became the subject of new kinds of publicity and spread to wider milieus. If worldly salons introduced aspiring men of letters to preexisting modes of aristocratic sociability, as Antoine Lilti has suggested, le monde formed a particularly fertile crucible for the mixing and converting of cultural, social, and economic credit and a meeting point for the court and the commercial world of Paris.

The fact that credit ran so deeply through the operation of power in Old Regime France meant that any efforts at reform, either political or fiscal, inevitably encountered the problem of addressing the role of informal modes of reputation, influence, and their gray-market circulation. Thus, credit reveals to us another logic that structured criticism of the Old Regime; a hitherto undernoticed red thread running from the marginalized and the malcontents of Louis xiv's reign to the projects of the regency (represented by both the John Law experiment and plans for eliminating women's exchange of sex for political influence), to the slander of Louis xv's mistresses and their credit at court, and, finally, to the furor over Marie Antoinette and her exhausted credit. In the context of the explosive monarchical credit crisis of the late 1780s, the story of credit told in this book helps explain why the attack on Marie Antoinette simultaneously targeted her gender, her sexuality, her fashion sense, her accounts with her dressmaker, and her credibility at court and among the people of France. Indeed, one might see the Marie Antoinette moment as an instant of conceptual fusing of all of the intermingled forms of credit onto one female and sexed body, before they were flung apart in the revolutionary maelstrom, henceforth to occupy discrete spheres: political economy, public opinion, women's fashions, personal wealth, republican government, and the intimacy of sex in private bedrooms.

Despite its political discrediting, the language of credit as a form of power and influence continued to appear, if with decreasing frequency, during and well beyond the revolution. The characters of Germaine de Staël's *Delphine*, for example, remark on the credit of the "democratic deputies of the Constituent Assembly." In a letter to her son in February 1808, Empress Josephine lamented: "I see my consideration lower every day while others gain in credit."[8] A spurious memoir attributed to Rose Bertin, published in 1824, justifying Marie Antoinette's actions from a royalist perspective, noted the weakening of the queen's credit as a result of her failure to produce a child in the early years of her marriage and her attempts to use her credit with Louis XVI to prevent him from calling the Estates General in 1789.[9]

To return to dictionaries, it is worth noting that the *Dictionnaire de l'Académie française* published in the early 1930s maintained the nonmaterial sense of the word *credit*. As in previous editions, the academy gave the financial sense of the word first and with numerous details of usage. It followed this definition with the moral connotations of the word inherited from the first edition of the dictionary: "It means in the figurative authority, influence, consideration. *He is in credit, in great credit. Have credit with someone. That put him in credit, acquired credit for him. He used all his credit for it. He has lost much of his credit, all his credit. Make use of, use one's credit. Abuse one's credit. Exhaust one's credit. Make use of the credit of someone. Put one's credit at the service of someone.*"[10] General de Gaulle himself, architect of the French Fifth Republic, devoted many passages of his memoirs to discussing his credit within the Resistance movement and with the French people in the postwar period.

Gabriel Tarde's discussion of credit in 1902 thus fastened on a concept that continued to retain currency within French culture during his lifetime. Yet, as Tarde's plea for a universal economics reveals, the ideological disavowal and historical forgetting of the credit system of the Old Regime was so effective that he could only imagine moral credit as the projected mirror image of its opposite, the tenets of political economy. He makes no reference to eighteenth-century notions of credit, despite their striking affinity with his own.

I have argued that the John Law project was an early effort to strike down the credit regime in order to build a transparent and accountable means of managing government debt. Similarly, political critics like Holbach called for an end to the credit regime as a necessary element of destroying despotism. Enlightened ministers like Turgot struggled to free wealth, trade, commerce, and labor from the obstructive hand of the state, a project finally declared a reality by the revolutionary state. By aiming to set us free from the caprices of credit, from the unstable and unchecked conversion of value across multiple domains of life, political economy and liberal revolution imagined and then reified the economy and the republic as related but distinct entities, both derived from universal laws laid down by nature. To destroy the weight of exclusionary and unequal collectivities—the salons, coteries, and circles so despised by Rousseau—they posited the free and equal individual as the sole locus of rights and privileges. This was the realization of the dream of all those snubbed by worldly salonnières, who lost trials to better-connected opponents, of those who waited years to be paid for the fruit of their labor: to be freed from the whisper of power in one's ear, hissing "you have no credit, you will be crushed."

As a result of their success, connections among political, social, cultural, and economic capital went underground. They did not cease to shape assessments of value and the exercise of power, but no discourse remained within which to discuss and analyze their interaction, except in the frameworks of discredit, shame, and criminality. Modern society thus differs from that of pre-revolutionary France not so much in having abandoned economies of regard but in disavowing and refusing to acknowledge them, a self-imposed ignorance that renders us less canny critics of our own period than the morts avec crédit of the Old Regime. Obviously, many elements of the exercise of power and its relationship to social taxonomies, cultural recognition, and economic capital have fundamentally changed. Today's highly institutionalized multiethnic and multiracial societies, mass consumer markets and politics, and globally integrated economies operate at a scale and with a complexity that far exceeds anything imaginable in the day of Marie Antoinette and Rose Bertin. Safeguards against fraud and corruption, political checks and balances, and processes for ensuring transparency in public affairs are all legacies of the rejection of the credit regime and everything it encompassed by revolutionary and democratizing movements of the late eighteenth, nineteenth, and twentieth centuries.

Nonetheless, reflecting on the Old Regime of credit helps us to perceive the many ways in which the system lives on. If we look closely at our daily lives, we find an ongoing conversion of influence, reputation, and power from cultural to social to political to economic forms, whether it be the role of social connections in gaining places in prestigious schools, the use of corporate money to finance political campaigns, the use of newspapers to smear the reputations of individuals who oppose their owners' views, or attacks on powerful women in the form of criticism of their hairstyles and sexual behavior. Occasionally, an operative in the modern-day credit regime commits an overly egregious act of conversion and his or her subsequent arrest and the ensuing publicity bring forth allegations of corruption and racketeering. Such denunciations apart, we lack the vocabulary or conceptual framework to explain these events as belonging to one end of the spectrum of the normative operating procedures of our society. We have been so well schooled in the existence of discrete spheres of life—politics, economy, society, culture—that we fail to notice, let alone interrogate, the intertwined nature of the forces that shape our lives on a daily basis.

If eliminating the credit regime was a response to centuries of inequality and oppression, some of which is documented in this book, one advantage denizens of the Old Regime held was that they had an honest and sophisticated, if at times cynical and embittered, understanding of the way their society generated value and of how ineffable resources like reputation and glory led to real power. Without such an awareness—without a way of talking to ourselves about the multiple, interwoven dynamics of reputation and influence, how they constantly span behaviors categorized as legitimate or illegitimate and how they act as unspoken systems of inclusion and exclusion—we cannot address how power actually functions in our societies and how to police boundaries between acceptable and unacceptable forms of "credit" manipulation. We do not require a return to the poufs of Marie Antoinette, but we might do well to take seriously the conceptual constructs of her day in order to produce more effective and self-aware analyses of the creation of value and the operation of power in our own. In responding to Gabriel Tarde's call for a reintegration of the "economy" into the full array of human economies, the hidden common sense of the Old Regime provides one starting place for inquiry.

NOTES

Abbreviations Used in the Notes

AN   Archives nationales de France
MC   Minutier central
ET   Etude
AP   Archives de Paris
INHA   Institut national de l'histoire de l'art

Introduction

1 Louis-Sébastien Mercier, *Le Tableau de Paris*, ed. Jean-Claude Bonnet (Paris: Mercure de France, 1994), 1: 1212.

2 Mercier, *Le Tableau de Paris*, 1213. The Caisse d'escompte was a government-backed protobank created by Controller General Turgot in 1776, with the mission of encouraging trade by purchasing commercial paper in exchange for its own bank notes.

3 As always with Mercier, rather than taking him at face value we should read his statement as an ideological projection, perhaps stemming from his hostility to the Physiocrats and their insistence on land as the sole source of economic value. On this element of Mercier, see Steven Laurence Kaplan, *Bread, Politics and Political Economy in the Reign of Louis XV* (The Hague: Martinus Nijhoff, 1976), 1: 591, 603.

4 Trading in shares of the Caisse d'escompte underwent a series of speculative booms and busts in the 1780s as loans forced on the Caisse by the royal government undermined investor confidence. In 1785, Mirabeau denounced the Caisse as an enticement for speculation. On the Caisse d'escompte, see Robert Bigo, *La Caisse d'escompte (1776–1793) et les origines de la Banque de France* (Paris: Presses universitaires de France, 1927).

5 Among the most important texts in French over the past twenty years have been Jean-Claude Perrot, *Une histoire intellectuelle de l'économie politique: XVII–XVIIIe* (Paris: Editions de l'Ecole des hautes études en sciences sociales, 1992); and Jean-Yves Grenier, *L'économie d'Ancien Régime: Un monde de l'échange et de l'incertitude* (Paris: Albin Michel, 1996). In English, see Michael Sonenscher, *Sans-culottes: An Eighteenth-Century Emblem in the French Revolution* (Princeton, NJ: Princeton University Press, 2008) and *Before the Deluge: Public Debt, Inequality, and the Intellectual Origins of the French Revolution* (Princeton, NJ: Princeton University Press, 1990); Paul Cheney, *Revolutionary Commerce: Globalization and the French Monarchy* (Cambridge, MA: Harvard University Press, 2010); John Shovlin, *The Politi-*

cal Economy of Virtue: Luxury, Patriotism, and the Origins of the French Revolution (Ithaca, NY: Cornell University Press, 2006); and Emma Rothschild, *Economic Sentiments: Adam Smith, Condorcet, and the Enlightenment* (Cambridge, MA: Harvard University Press, 2001).

6 Jean Nicot, *Thresor de la langue françoyse* (Paris: David Douceur, 1606), "*crédit.*"

7 See Brigitte Lépinette, "Trois dictionnaires du XVIIe siècle, trois traitements différents de l'etymologie: Richelet (1680), Furetière (1690), Académie (1694)," in *Les Marques d'usage dans les dictionnaires: XVIIe-XVIIIe siècles*, ed. Danielle Bouverot and Michel Glatigny (Villeneuve d'Ascq: Presses Universitaires Septentrion, 1990).

8 Pierre Richelet, *Dictionnaire françois* (Geneva: Chez Jean Herman Widerhold, 1680), "*crédit.*"

9 Antoine Furetière, *Dictionnaire universel* (The Hague: A. and R. Leers, 1690), "*crédit.*"

10 *Dictionnaire de l'Académie française* (Paris: chez la veuve Coignard, 1694), "*credit.*"

11 *Dictionnaire de l'Académie française.*

12 I offer in the following notes a short selection of examples of these pairings but have limited myself to only a few cases. Many more could be cited for each example. For the pair of credit and reputation, see, for example, Michael de Montaigne, *Les essais*, ed. Pierre Villey and V.-L. Saulnier (Paris: Chez Michel Sonnius, 1595), 276, 778; Gabriel Naudé, *Apologie pour tous les grand hommes qui ont esté accusez de magie* (Paris: Eschart, 1669), 16, 456; Jean-Louis Guez de Balzac, *Aristippe ou de la Cour* in *Oeuvres* (Paris: T. Jolly, 1665), 2: 144.

13 See, for example, Saint-Evremond, *Oeuvres Meslées de Mr. de Saint-Evremond* (London: Chez Jacob Tonson, 1705), 1: 447; Alain René Le Sage, *Les avantures de Gil Blas de Santillane* (London: Chez Jean Nourse, 1749), 3: 224. Often the two words are combined in a way to suggest that one ("merit") should be the gauge of the other ("credit"). See, for example, Montesquieu's remark in correspondence: "I am very pleased to hear of his credit in the [Dutch] Stadholder's court; he merits the confidence they have in him" (Charles de Secondat, baron de Montesquieu, *Correspondance de Montesquieu*, ed. F. Gebelin and A. Morize, [Paris: Champion, 1914], 438). Others treat them as separate entities, as we see in the comment by the Abbé Prévost, "one hardly doubts that the credit of his family and his own merit will elevate him one day to the purple [that is, to the nobility]" (Abbé Prévost, *Nouvelles lettres angloises ou Histoire du chevalier Grandisson* [1755; Amsterdam, Paris, 1784], 285).

14 See, for example, Balthasar Baro, *La conclusion et dernière partie d'Astrée* (1627; Geneva: Slatkine, 1966), 91. In a play set at the ancient Persian court, Jean Rotrou's characters complain, with regard to the queen, of the "insolent power that her credit gives her" (Jean Rotrou, *Cosroès: Tragédie*, ed. J. Scherer [1649; Paris: Didier, 1950], 15). Jean-Baptiste de Boyer, marquis d'Argens, depicts the relationship in the opposite sense, referring to "the priests, who publicly avowed the power to hunt demons, and to whom this power gave a great credit" (Argens, *Lettres juives* [The Hague: P. Paupie, 1738], 181). See also Argens, *Lettres juives*, 126, 348, for other references to the power of credit. Other writers referred to credit and power as essentially equal. For example, with reference to the enemies of the Arnauld family and the censure they had procured against the family at the Sorbonne, Jean

Racine comments: "they also thereby gave a great idea of their power and the credit they held at court" (Jean Racine, *Abrégé de l'Histoire de Port-Royal*, in *Oeuvres*, ed. P. Mesnard [Paris: Hachette, 1865], 4: 464).

15 See Jacques Abbadie who discusses the "credit and authority" that Jewish doctors held over their people (Jacques Abbadie, *Traité de la vérité de la religion chrétienne* [Rotterdam: R. Leers, 1684], 157). While Abbadie treats the two as commensurate, the Abbé Dubos places authority above credit. With reference to Clovis, the ancient Frankish king, he writes: "Thus his credit with his subjects had become an absolute authority that he transmitted to his children" (Abbé Dubos, *Histoire critique de l'établissement de la monarchie françoise dans les Gaules* [Paris: Nyon Fils, 1742], 23). Nicolas Lenglet Dufresnoy satirically reversed this order: "And because legitimate wives have so much credit, what authority does a mistress not possess? This has been in all governments the great motive of all great affairs. One gives himself pleasure in according to his mistress what he would feel by duty obliged to refuse to a wife" (Nicolas Lenglet Dufresnoy, *De l'usage des romans, où l'on fait voir leur utilité et leurs différents caractères* [Amsterdam: Veuve de Poilras, 1734], 101).

16 The comte de Caylus suggests that friendship produces greater credit than formal titles. He recounts the tale of an ancient Persian shepherd who had miraculously gained the favor of the king: "Finally, his continual liberality and his eloquence gave him such great credit over the king's mind, that the sovereign made him vizir so as to never be separated from him; however, the confidence and the friendship that the king showed him, gave him even more credit than the charge he was awarded" (Anne Claude Philippe, comte de Caylus, *Nouveaux contes orientaux*, in *Œuvres Badines Complettes* [Paris: Vissem, 1787], 7: 313).

17 See, for example, the thirteenth-century writer Rutebeuf: "Théophile Salatin, my brother, things have come to such a pass that if you knew a means for me to retain my rank, my charge, my credit, I would do anything" (Rutebeuf, *Œuvres complètes*, ed. Michel Zink [Paris: Bordas, 1990], 252). Voltaire treats them as distinct, one as the official title of power and the second as the true holder of power: "a man because he is noble or because he is a priest, is not exempt here from paying certain taxes, all taxes are regulated by a House of Commons, which being [only] second in rank is first in credit" (Voltaire, *Lettres philosophiques*, ed. Gustave Lanson [Paris: Hachette, 1915], 106).

18 See, for example, Blaise Pascal, *Les provinciales, ou Les lettres écrites par Louis de Montalte à un provincial de ses amis et aux RR. PP. Jésuites* (1657; Paris: Garnier, 1965), 220. The Abbé Prévost combined friendship, credit, and glory in the following example: "Even his compatriots take glory in his friendship; they make use of it to establish credit on their voyages and in their affairs, especially in France, where he is no less respected than in Italy" (Abbé Prévost, *Nouvelles lettres angloises*, 356). See also Jean-Jacques Barthélemy, *Voyage du jeune anacharsis* (Paris: De Bure, 1788), 555.

19 See, for example, Arnauld d'Andilly, "all favor and credit passed in a moment to Monsieur de Luynes" (Robert Arnaud d'Andilly, *Mémoires*, in *Collection complète des mémoires relatifs à l'histoire de France* [Paris: Foucault, 1824], 33: 371). Jean de

la Bruyère favored a tripartite composition of favor, credit, and "great wealth." See Jean de La Bruyère, *Les caractères ou les mœurs de ce siècle*, in *Œuvres complètes*, ed. Julien Benda (Paris: Gallimard, 1951), 233.

20 See, for example, Pierre Nicole's *Essais de morale*, vol. 1 (1671; Paris: G. Desprez, 1701), 253: "If we feel that we have not the credit and esteem necessary to have our warnings well received, we should usually believe that God dispenses us from saying what we think about things that appear blame-worthy." Much later, the marquis d'Argenson, who was critical of the demands of the credit system, lamented: "My son works with gentleness and finesse not to be on bad terms with anyone and to advance little by little in credit and esteem with the royal family. Oh what a devil of a country, where it is such a little thing to do one's duty" (René-Louis de Voyer, marquis d'Argenson, *Journal et mémoires 1755-1757* [Paris: Renouard, 1867], 9: 144).

21 See, for example, Madame Lafayette's rendition of this pairing: "The queen, my daughter-in-law, proud of her beauty and of the credit of her uncles, renders no duty to me" (Marie-Madeleine Pioche de la Vergne, Madame de Lafayette, *La princesse de Clèves*, ed. Emile Magne [1678; Paris: Droz, 1946], 105).

22 William Sewell, "The Empire of Fashion and the Rise of Capitalism in Eighteenth-Century France," *Past and Present* 206, no. 1 (February 2010): 119.

23 Avner Offer, "Between the Gift and the Market: The Economy of Regard," *Economic History Review* 50, no. 3 (August 1997): 450–76. For Offer, *regard* is an umbrella term for the rewards from personal interaction that was one goal of exchange (alongside material benefit) in the premarket gift economy and included such forms as "acceptance, respect, reputation, status, power, intimacy, love, friendship, kinship, sociability." Unlike perfect anonymous markets, regard-driven exchange occurs between specific individuals with a personal relationship, and these individuals strive for successful interaction at the cost of exclusion from exchange. Therefore, "real regard is typically not for sale." He argues that the search for regard survives in the market economy in the form of holiday gift exchange and other nonmonetary reciprocity. I believe that Offer's analysis would benefit from explicit consideration of the notion of credit, alongside the gift, as a structuring logic for premarket exchange; however, I retain from his extremely helpful formulation the insistence on a range of nonmaterial benefits accruing from exchange. I also add the implied pun on the French *regarder* (to look), to suggest the importance of appearances and display in the search for benefits from personal interaction in Old Regime society.

24 The pioneering article establishing information as an issue of concern for economics was George Stigler's "The Economies of Information," *Journal of Political Economy* 69, no. 3 (1961): 213–25. This article discussed the costs of "search," which Stigler defined as the effort to acquire information about variance in price for a given commodity and various methods, such as markets, advertising, and specialized brokers, adopted to reduce the time and cost of search. Although the article does not discuss quality extensively, it does note that "'reputation' is a word which denotes the persistence of quality, and reputation commands a price (or exacts a penalty) because it economizes on search" (224).

25 See Delphine Denis, *Le Parnasse gallant: Institution d'une catégorie littéraire au*

xviie siècle (Paris: Honoré Champion, 2001); and Christian Jouhaud and Alain Viala, ed., *Groupe de recherches interdisciplinaires sur l'histoire du littéraire. De la publication: Entre Renaissance et Lumières* (Paris: Fayard, 2002).

26 On the rise of the novel and its relation to the credit economy, see Michael McKeon, *Origins of the English Novel, 1600–1740* (Baltimore: Johns Hopkins University Press, 1987); Mary Poovey, *Genres of the Credit Economy: Mediating Value in Eighteenth- and Nineteenth-Century Britain* (Chicago: University of Chicago Press, 2008); and Ian Baucom, *Specters of the Atlantic: Finance Capital, Slavery, and the Philosophy of History* (Durham, NC: Duke University Press, 2005).

27 Jean-Yves Grenier, *L'économie d'Ancien Régime*, 418. Grenier appears to be drawing on Bourdieu, particularly his comments on economic information in *The Logic of Practice*, trans. Richard Nice (Palo Alto, CA: Stanford University Press, 1992), 64.

28 Robert Darnton, "An Early Information Society: News and the Media in Eighteenth-Century Paris," *American Historical Review* 105, no. 1 (February 2000): 1–35.

29 Pierre Bourdieu, "The Forms of Capital," in *Handbook of Theory and Research for the Sociology of Education*, ed. J. Richardson (New York: Greenwood, 1986), 243.

30 Bourdieu, "The Forms of Capital," 253.

31 Bourdieu, "The Forms of Capital," 242.

32 See Pierre Bourdieu, *The Logic of Practice* and *Outline of a Theory of Practice*, trans. Richard Nice (Cambridge: Cambridge University Press, 1977); Michel de Certeau, *The Practice of Everyday Life*, trans. Steven Randall (Berkeley: University of California Press, 1984).

33 Todd Lowry, "The Archaeology of the Circulation Concept in Economic Theory," *Journal of the History of Ideas* 34, no. 3 (July–September 1974): 429–44.

34 Adam Smith, *An Inquiry into the Nature and Causes of the Wealth of Nations* (London: W. Strahan and T. Cadell, 1776), 1: 346. In *Tableau économique*, published in 1758, François Quesnay explicitly evoked the equilibrium of the circulation of blood in the human body as an analogy to the circulation of money.

35 I am inspired here by Mary Poovey and her disavowal of the model of homologies for understanding eighteenth-century disciplines. It is following her lead that I part company with Michel Foucault's reading in *The Order of Things* of the relationship between the signifying system of language and those of other nascent disciplines, including political economy. See Michel Foucault, *The Order of Things: An Archaeology of the Human Sciences* (New York: Vintage Books, 1994).

36 Barbara Duden, *The Woman beneath the Skin: A Doctor's Patients in Eighteenth-Century Germany*, trans. Thomas Dunlap (Cambridge, MA: Harvard University Press, 1998).

37 On habitus and its relation to practice, see Bourdieu, *The Logic of Practice*, chap. 3.

38 The serial approach to cultural history adopted by adherents of the Annales school in the 1960s and 1970s has been sharply criticized. See, for example, Roger Chartier, *Cultural History: Between Practices and Representations*, trans. Lydia Cochrane (Ithaca, NY: Cornell University Press, 1988). In attempting to read historical actors' intention and values through quantitative analysis, I have drawn on work in Old Regime labor history. See Steven L. Kaplan, *The Bakers of Paris and the Bread Question, 1700–1775* (Durham, NC: Duke University Press, 1996); and Simona Cerutti,

La Ville et les métiers. Naissance d'un langage corporatif (Turin, 17e–18e siècle) (Paris: Editions de l'Ecole des hautes études en sciences sociales, 1990).

39 In tracing this position between the imagined and the real, I am guided by the work of a number of scholars, including Daniel Roche, Roger Chartier, Nicole Pellegrin, and, more recently, Antoine Lilti. As Daniel Roche noted specifically with regard to texts describing clothing and appearances: "Certainly the works never coincide with the gaze direct at the world and at things, in a reality now gone for ever, by the characters put into writing or onto the stage. . . . For the historian of society and culture, it is less a matter of achieving an illustrative metatext on the basis of the original text of the novels, or of assembling from between them the realia, than of understanding the signifying elements of the story and their logic. Thus reality interrogates fiction" (Daniel Roche, *The Culture of Clothing: Dress and Fashion in the Ancien Régime*, trans. Jean Birrell [Cambridge: Cambridge University Press, 1994], 19).

40 Jay Smith, "No More Language Games: Words, Beliefs, and the Political Culture of Early Modern France," *American Historical Review* 102, no. 5 (December 1997): 1434.

41 Smith, "No More Language Games," 1440.

42 Daniel Lord Smail, *The Consumption of Justice: Emotions, Publicity, and Legal Culture* (Ithaca, NY: Cornell University Press, 2003), 146. For a long-term anthropological perspective on debt and credit, see David Graeber, *Debt: The First 5,000 Years* (Brooklyn, NY: Melville House, 2011).

Chapter 1: Credit and Old Regime Economies of Regard

Epigraph: Louis-Sébastien Mercier, *Le Tableau de Paris*, ed. Jean-Claude Bonnet (Paris: Mercure de France, 1994), 1: 631.

1 Pierre Carlet de Chamblain de Marivaux, *La Double inconstance*, in *Oeuvres de Marivaux: théâtre complet*, ed. Edouard Fournier (Paris: Garnier frères, 1878), 286.

2 As Roger Chartier put it in his study of the term *civilité*: "Each use of the word, each definition of the notion, then, sends us back to an enunciative strategy that is also a representation of social relations." A truly rigorous analysis, Chartier reminds us, would require that, for each usage of a term like *crédit* or *civilité*, we reconstruct the entire web of texts in which it was produced and to which it refers, the precise identification of the author in social and cultural terms, and the range of reader responses. For this chapter, even more so than Chartier's article, "the analysis . . . cannot possibly satisfy all these demands" (Roger Chartier, "From Texts to Manners: A Concept and Its Books: *Civilité* between Aristocratic Distinction and Popular Appropriation," in *The Cultural Uses of Print in Early Modern France*, trans. Lydia Cochrane [Princeton, NJ: Princeton University Press, 1987], 73). It is worth noting here that civilité, as analyzed by Chartier, is tellingly different as a concept than crédit; it was a normative concept that inspired long and elaborate treatment in manuals explicitly devoted to turning the rules and expectations ascribed to it into actual behaviors and practices. Crédit by contrast inspired no manuals or treatises; it was a fact of life to be acknowledged and managed, not celebrated or taught as

codes of behavior. Certainly, the letters to and about Marie Antoinette, discussed in chapter 7, show self-conscious and determined efforts to teach a recalcitrant pupil how to acquire and manipulate credit; such advice was kept to the backstage and never formed part of conduct guides for court life or polite society.

3 William Beik, *Absolutism and Society in Seventeenth-Century France: State Power and Provincial Aristocracy in Languedoc* (Cambridge: Cambridge University Press, 1985); Sharon Kettering, *Patrons, Brokers, and Clients in Seventeenth-Century France* (Oxford: Oxford University Press, 1987) and *Patronage in Sixteenth- and Seventeenth-Century France* (Aldershot: Ashgate, 2002); Sara E. Chapman, *Private Ambition and Political Alliances: The Phélypeaux de Pontchartrain Family and Louis XIV's Government, 1650-1715* (Rochester, NY: University of Rochester Press, 2004); Arlette Jouanna, *Le devoir de révolte. La noblesse française et la gestation de l'Etat moderne, 1559-1661* (Paris: Fayard, 1989); Jonathan Dewald, *The European Nobility, 1400-1800* (Cambridge: Cambridge University Press, 1996).

4 Jonathan Dewald, *Aristocratic Experience and the Origins of Modern Culture, 1575-1715* (Berkeley: University of California Press, 1993), 147.

5 Dewald, *Aristocratic Experience and the Origins of Modern Culture*, 157.

6 Jay Smith, "No More Language Games: Words, Beliefs, and the Political Culture of Early Modern France," *American Historical Review* 102, no. 5 (December 1997): 1413-40.

7 Smith, "No More Language Games," 1432.

8 Smith follows Karl Polanyi in making the claim of the gradual emergence of the economy as a conceptually distinct sphere, which led to legislation ending regulation of production and distribution in favor of "free" markets. See Karl Polanyi, *The Great Transformation: The Political and Economic Origins of Our Time* (1944; New York: Beacon, 2001). For my response to Smith's work, see Clare H. Crowston, "Credit and the Metanarrative of Modernity," *French Historical Studies* 34, no. 1 (winter 2011): 7-19.

9 A frequency count per ten thousand words of text eliminates the difficulty of representativity within the database, since some periods are much more heavily represented in ARTFL than others. Concerns for representativity also led me to eliminate the period 1250-99, which had a frequency rate of 0.59 but only because of Rutebeuf's ten uses of the word in one text.

10 A list of French authors ranked purely by the number of times they used the word in the ARTFL dataset is: the Duc de Saint-Simon, Voltaire, Honoré de Balzac, Jean Jaurès, Emile Zola, Louis Blanc, Pierre-Joseph Proudhon, Alexandre Dumas, and Alain. If ranked by use of the term per ten thousand words of text, the results are quite different: Jean-Claude Fernier, Pierre Berthelot, Jean Rotrou, Marie de Gournay, the Marquis d'Argenson, the Abbé de Vertot, Madame de Villedieu, Guy Patin, and Gabriel Naudé (ARTFL database, consulted January 12, 2012).

11 It is worth noting that even for the period 1800-1849, the majority of references in the texts included in the ARTFL were to credit as a form of influence and power, rather than its financial sense. This was true even among authors born during and after the revolution, such as Dumas (who used the word forty-four times in *The Count of Monte Cristo*) and Balzac. As the presence of Balzac, Proudhon, and Zola

on the list suggests, the first half of the nineteenth century was an important moment for critical rethinking of processes for producing value and the intertwined nature of economics, politics, and social life.

12 Saint-Simon's memoirs contain 651 uses of the term.

13 Louis de Rouvroy, duc de Saint-Simon, *Mémoires complets et authentiques du duc de Saint-Simon sur le siècle de Louis XIV et la régence*, ed. Adolphe Chéruel (Paris: L. Hachette, 1856–58), 12: 389.

14 Saint-Simon, *Mémoires*, 13: 43–44. Le Tellier defended himself by saying that of twenty matters brought before the king, his ministers could expect to get their way nineteen times out of twenty. On the twentieth, however, they would certainly be rebuffed by the king. Not only was it impossible to predict which issue would arouse the king's opposition, but it was often the very issue closest to the minister's heart. As he put it: "the king reserves this stroke [to let us feel that he is the master and that he governs]."

15 Saint-Simon, *Mémoires*, 13: 39.

16 Saint-Simon, *Mémoires*, 13: 40.

17 Saint-Simon, *Mémoires*, 13: 41.

18 Madame de Maintenon's affair with the king is believed to have begun in 1675. See Madame de Maintenon, *Correspondance générale de Madame de Maintenon*, ed. Théophile La Vallée (Paris: Charpentier, 1865–66), 2: 13.

19 Madame de Maintenon, *Correspondance générale de Madame de Maintenon*, 2: 80.

20 Madame de Maintenon, *Correspondance générale de Madame de Maintenon*, 3: 110.

21 Madame de Maintenon, *Correspondance générale de Madame de Maintenon*, 3: 139.

22 Both letters cited in Théophile La Vallée, *Madame de Maintenon et la maison royale de Saint-Cyr (1686–1793)* (Paris: H. Plon, 1862), 218.

23 Abbé J. Berthier, ed., *Lettres de Messire P. Godet des Marais, évêque de Chartres, a Madame de Maintenon* (Paris: J. Dumoulin, 1908), 151.

24 See, for example, Sharon Kettering, "The Patronage Power of Early Modern French Noblewomen," *Historical Journal* 32, no. 4 (1989): 817–41; and Sara Chapman, "Patronage as Family Economy: The Role of Women in the Patron-Client Network of the Phélypeaux de Pontchartrain Family, 1670–1715," *French Historical Studies* 24, no. 1 (2001): 11–35. Kettering argues that noblewomen's political and economic power did not dramatically decline in the early modern period, as an earlier generation of women's historians had maintained.

25 References to women's credit abound in historical works and in fictional and non-fictional accounts of foreign empires.

26 Esprit Fléchier, *Oraison Funèbre de Marie-Thérèse d'Autriche*, in *Oraisons Funèbres*, vol. 2 (Paris: A. Dezallier, 1691), 51. Fléchier was a priest and man of letters who gained reputation and court patronage through his sermons and funeral orations. He was elected to the Académie française in 1672 and was named almoner to the dauphine and the bishop of Lavaur (1685), before becoming the bishop of Nîmes in 1687.

27 Fléchier, *Oraison Funèbre de Marie-Thérèse d'Autriche*, 36.

28 Saint-Simon, *Mémoires*, 3: 66.

29 *Dictionnaire universel françois et latin. Reproduction de l'édition de Trevoux* (Paris: Delaulne, 1721).

30 For the late eighteenth-century critique of female power, see Joan Landes, *Women in the Public Sphere in the Age of the French Revolution* (Ithaca, NY: Cornell University Press, 1988).

31 Saint-Simon, *Mémoires*, 13: 34. Her brother was Charles, comte d'Aubigné. In one letter to her brother, Madame de Maintenon clearly stated her refusal to use her influence on his behalf: "I could not make you constable if I wanted to; and even if I could, I would not want to do so. I am incapable of wanting to ask for anything but what is reasonable from him to whom I owe everything" (cited in Jules Soury, ed., *Souvenirs de Mme de Caylus* [Paris: Librairie des bibliophiles, 1883], 74).

32 La Vallée, *Correspondance générale de madame de Maintenon*, 4: 462.

33 Saint-Simon, *Mémoires*, 9: 59.

34 Madame de Lafayette, *Histoire de Madame Henriette d'Angleterre* (Amsterdam: Chez Michel Charles le Cene, 1720), 9.

35 Madame de Lafayette, *Vie de la Princesse d'Angleterre*, ed. Marie-Thérèse Hipp (Geneva: Librairie Droz, 1967), 53.

36 Saint-Simon, *Mémoires*, 4: 93.

37 Guy Patin, *Lettres de Gui Patin, 1630–1672* (Paris: Champion, 1907), 444, December 6, 1644.

38 A century later the memoirs of René-Louis de Voyer, marquis d'Argenson, former minister of foreign affairs under Louis XV, revealed the ongoing mixture of financial and political credit: "The Duc de Saint-Aignan has just received through the credit of Mesdames [the aunts of Louis XV] forty thousand livres in pension from the Estates of Burgundy" (René-Louis d'Argenson, *Journal et Mémoires du marquis d'Argenson, 1755–1757* [Paris: Veuve Jules Renouard, 1897], 9: 37).

39 Roger de Bussy-Rabutin, *Les mémoires de messire Roger de Rabutin, comte de Bussy* (Paris: Chez Rigaud, 1704), 2: 429–30.

40 Bussy-Rabutin, *Les mémoires de messire Roger de Rabutin*, 430.

41 Emile Gérard-Gailly, introduction to *Lettres de Madame de Sévigné* (Paris: Gallimard, 1953), 1:30.

42 The royal government imposed a series of devaluations of the livre between 1690 and 1725 to meet the expenses of the wars of Louis XIV and the lingering financial crises they caused.

43 Patin, *Lettres de Gui Patin*, 330, to M. Spon, September 14, 1643. Spon was a doctor in Lyons.

44 Patin, *Lettres de Gui Patin*, 175, October 6, 1640.

45 Robert Arnauld d'Andilly, *Mémoires*, in *Collection des mémoires relatifs à l'histoire de France*, vol. 33 (Paris: Foucault, 1824), 412.

46 Madame de Sévigné, *Correspondance*, ed. Roger Duchêne, 3 vols. (Paris: Gallimard, 1972–78), 2: 950.

47 Vincent Voiture, *Lettres*, in *Les Œuvres* (Paris: A. Courbe, 1654), 1: 438. Jonathan Dewald's examples also include women in key roles both as litigators and as bearing influence over judicial decisions. See Dewald, *Aristocratic Experience*, 158–59.

48 Charles Sorel, *La Bibliothèque Françoise* (Paris: Compagnie des Libraires du Palais, 1664), 74.

49 Charles de Secondat, baron de Montesquieu, *De l'esprit des lois*, ed. J. Brethe de la Gressaye (Paris: Belles-Lettres, 1958), 57. On the relationship between money and words as signs in this period, see Michel Foucault, *The Order of Things: An Archaeology of the Human Sciences* (New York: Vintage Books, 1994).

50 Sorel, *La Bibliothèque Françoise*, 99. On late seventeenth-century perceptions of the impact of fashion on literary style, see Sylvain Menant, "Les Modernes et le style 'à la mode,'" *Cahiers de l'Association internationale des études françaises* 38 (1996): 146–56.

51 Sorel, *La Bibliothèque Françoise*, 101. On Balzac and contemporary debates about his *Lettres*, see Christian Jouhaud, *Les pouvoirs de la littérature: Histoire d'un paradoxe* (Paris: Gallimard, 2000).

52 Sorel, *La Bibliothèque Françoise*, 127.

53 Gabriel Naudé, *Advis Pour Dresser une Bibliothèque* (Paris: Role le Duc, 1644), 106.

54 Jean-Louis Guez de Balzac, *Dissertations Chrestiennes et Morales*, in *Oeuvres*, vol. 2 (Paris: T. Jolly, 1665), 342.

55 Balzac, *Dissertations Chrestiennes et Morales*, 394.

56 On the role of royal patronage as legitimating literature as an autonomous field, see Jouhaud, *Les pouvoirs de la literature*; and Peter William Shoemaker, *Powerful Connections: The Poetics of Patronage in the Age of Louis XIII* (Cranbury, NJ: Associated University Presses, 2007).

57 Nicolas de Peiresc, *Lettres de Peiresc*, ed. Philippe Tamizey de Larroque (Paris: Imprimerie nationale, 1898), 7: 28.

58 Peiresc, *Lettres de Peiresc*, 35.

59 Voiture, *Lettres*, 1: 109. Mademoiselle Angélique Paulet was a précieuse and a member of the salon at the Hôtel de Rambouillet.

60 Patin, *Lettres de Gui Patin*, 344, November 16, 1643.

61 Molière, *Le Tartuffe ou L'imposteur: Comédie*, in *Œuvres complètes*, ed. Eugène Despois (Paris: Hachette, 1873), 422.

62 Le Père Louis Le Comte, *Nouveaux mémoires sur l'état présent de la Chine* (Paris: J. Anisson, 1696), 70. For a reading of an earlier Jesuit's "ethnographical discourse" on China, see Matthieu Bernhardt, "Construction et enjeux du savoir éthnographique sur la Chine dans l'œuvre de Matteo Ricci S.J.," *Archivum Historicum Societatis Iesu* 79, no. 158 (July–December 2010): 321–44.

63 Le Comte, *Nouveaux mémoires sur l'état présent de la Chine*, 232.

64 Le Comte, *Nouveaux mémoires sur l'état présent de la Chine*, 288. As a point of comparison, Doris Garraway notes the use of the language of commerce and mercantile exchange by French missionaries in the Caribbean to discuss their missionary work. See Doris Garraway, *The Libertine Colony* (Durham: Duke University Press, 2005), 69–70. See also Garraway's comments on natives who donned European dress as a way of making themselves "commendable" to French authorities (71).

65 Le Comte, *Nouveaux mémoires sur l'état présent de la Chine*, 387.

66 Le Comte, *Nouveaux mémoires sur l'état présent de la Chine*, 409.

67 Charles Bonnet, *La Palingénésie Philosophique ou idée sur l'état passé et futur des*

êtres vivants (Geneva: Philibert et Chirol, 1769), 118. On this point, see Arthur Mc-Calla, "From *Palingénésie Philosophique* to *Palingénésie sociale*: From a Scientific Ideology to a Historical Ideology," *Journal of the History of Ideas* 55, no. 3 (July 1994): 421–39.

68 Abbé de Mably, *Parallèle des Romains et des Français* (Paris: Didot, 1740), 73.

69 Abbé Jean-Baptiste Dubos, *Histoire critique de l'établissement de la monarchie française dans les Gaules* (Paris: Nyon Fils, 1742), 563. As in Rome, credit was a means to attract a large cohort of followers. See J. Esprit, *Fausseté des Vertus Humaines* (1678; Amsterdam: P. Mortier, 1710), 129.

70 On Tacitus and his influence on early modern political theory, see Jacob Soll, "Amelot de La Houssaye (1634–1706) Annotates Tacitus," *Journal of the History of Ideas* 61, no. 2 (2000): 167–87. On English readings of Tacitus, see Kevin Sharpe, *Reading Revolutions: The Politics of Reading in Early Modern England* (New Haven, CT: Yale University Press, 2000), 184–86.

71 For example, compare the English and Latin in *Annals*, Book I in *Tacitus Histories Books IV-V, Annals Books I-III* (Cambridge: Loeb Classical Library, 1931) with *Les Oeuvres de Tacite*, trans. Perrot D'Ablancourt (Paris: Chez Thomas Jolly, 1672). For the original: "multaque eo coram adversus ambitum et potentium preces constituta" (p. 372 in the Loeb edition), d'Ablancourt writes: "fit donner plusieurs Arrests équitables contre le crédit des Grands, et leurs brigues" (87). The English is: "many verdicts were recorded in defiance of intrigue and of the solicitations of the great." Another example is: "non obscuris, ut antea, matris artibus, sed palam hortatu" (246), rendered by d'Ablancourt as "non plus comme autrefois par les secrets artifices de sa mère; mais publiquement par le crédit de cette Princesse" (5). The English is: "not as before by the secret diplomacy of his mother, but openly at her injunction."

72 Samuel Richardson, *Pamela: Or Virtue Rewarded* (London: J. Osborn and J. and J. Rivington, 1746), 1: 160.

73 Henry Fielding, *Amelia* (London: Harrison and Co., 1780), 1: 39.

74 Henry Fielding, *Amélie, histoire angloise*, trans. P. F. de Puisieux (Paris: Chez Charpentier, 1762), 1: 122.

75 Richardson, *Pamela*, 263.

76 Fielding, *Amelia*, 2: 124; Fielding, *Amélie*, 1: 158.

77 Albert O. Hirschman, *The Passions and the Interests* (Princeton, NJ: Princeton University Press, 1977), 9. Albert Hirschman's classic study argued for the concept of interest as a "new paradigm" for understanding the history of European thought. Hirschman argued that during the eighteenth century thinkers, such as Montesquieu, Hume, and Adam Smith, rehabilitated "interest" from its negative status in Christian theology as a response to the passions and the unruliness and chaos they had unleashed on European society. For Hirschman, this ideological breakthrough prepared the way for capitalism (and was therefore not a post hoc justification for it). Hirschman's book has been criticized on a number of grounds, including its Eurocentric insistence on the valorization of self-interest as a necessary precondition for the growth of capitalism. From the perspective of this book's story of credit, what is fascinating is his insistence that interest equaled self-interest and

that it was fundamentally motivated by financial interest, or what Hirschman calls the "money-motive." By contrast, I argue that the advantage of the term *credit* for Old Regime French writers was that it provided a single term with which they could conjure up the multiple forms of goods at stake (many of which were impossible to cast in monetary terms) and the processes of collective, social judgment that evaluated and gave access to them. From this perspective, one might argue that Hirschman's account teleologically reads the outcome of capitalism and its conceptual categories back onto a very selective reading of certain texts by certain authors that he constructs ex post facto into an empirically existing canon of liberal political economy. In the English novels cited here, the characters did not refer to interest as "reasonable, deliberate, self-love," to use Hirschman's terms, but instead to forms of social influence and the powers it conveyed.

78 Molière, *Dom Garcie de Navarre*, in *Œuvres complètes*, 246.

79 Madame de Lafayette, *La Princesse de Clèves*, ed. Emile Magne (1678; Paris: Droz, 1946), 11.

80 Pierre Corneille, *Le Menteur*, in *Oeuvres complètes*, ed. Marty-Laveaux (Paris: Hachette, 1863), 193.

81 Esprit Fléchier, *Mémoires sur les Grands-Jours d'Auvergne* (1710; Paris: Hachette, 1862), 30.

82 Jean Chapelain, *La Pucelle* (Paris: A. Courbe, 1656), 263.

83 Molière, *Le Tartuffe*, 457.

84 Molière, *Le Depit amoureux*, in *Œuvres complètes*, 439.

85 Patin, *Lettres de Gui Patin*, 405, to A. Spon, June 13, 1644.

86 Molière, *Le Misanthrope: Comédie*, in *Oeuvres complètes*, 496–97.

87 Quentin M. Hope, "Society in *The Misanthrope*," *French Review* 32, no. 4 (February 1959): 329–36.

88 Madame de Sévigné's models for her correspondence—which circulated in manuscript form during her lifetime—were Vincent Voiture and Guez de Balzac. See Michele Longino Farrell, *Performing Motherhood: The Sévigné Correspondence* (Hanover, NH: University Press of New England, 1991), 27.

89 Roger de Bussy-Rabutin, *Les Lettres de messire Roger de Rabutin, comte de Bussy* (Paris: Chez Florentin Delaulne, 1720), 3: 284, January 4, 1671.

90 Bussy-Rabutin, *Les Lettres de messire Roger de Rabutin*, 3: 343, May 22, 1671.

91 Bussy-Rabutin, *Les Lettres de messire Roger de Rabutin*, 3: 415, September 3, 1671.

92 Bussy-Rabutin, *Les Lettres de messire Roger de Rabutin*, 4: 109, May 7, 1674.

93 Bussy-Rabutin, *Les Lettres de messire Roger de Rabutin*, 4: 128, July 19, 1674.

94 Bussy-Rabutin, *Les Lettres de messire Roger de Rabutin*, 4: 179, May 24, 1675.

95 Bussy-Rabutin, *Les Lettres de messire Roger de Rabutin*, 4: 330, July 12, 1677.

96 Pierre Richelet, *Dictionnaire de la langue françoise ancienne et moderne* (Lyon: J. M. Bruyset, 1728).

97 Madame de Sévigné, *Correspondance*, 2: 971, June 12, 1680.

98 Madame de Sévigné, *Correspondance*, 3: 569, April 4, 1689.

99 Madame de Sévigné, *Correspondance*, 1: 625, November 23, 1673.

100 Madame de Sévigné, *Correspondance*, 2: 207, January 1, 1676.

101 Madame de Sévigné, *Correspondance*, 2: 216, January 8, 1676.

102 Madame de Sévigné had been courted by Fouquet and ran some risk when her letters to him were discovered in his private papers after his arrest.

103 See Madame de Sévigné, *Correspondance*, 1: 465, March 30, 1672.

104 Madame de Sévigné, *Correspondance*, 2: 513, August 3, 1677.

105 Madame de Sévigné, *Correspondance*, 2: 669, spring or summer 1679.

106 Madame de Sévigné, *Correspondance*, 2: 877, March 17, 1680.

107 Madame de Sévigné, *Correspondance*, 3: 4, September 8, 1680.

108 Madame de Sévigné, *Correspondance*, 2: 387, September 2, 1676.

109 Madame de Sévigné, *Correspondance*, 2: 605, April 28, 1678. On Retz, see pp. 50–51.

110 Madame de Sévigné, *Correspondance*, 1: 249, May 6, 1671.

111 Madame de Sévigné, *Correspondance*, 3: 855, April 2, 1690.

112 Madame de Sévigné, *Correspondance*, 1: 488, April 24, 1672.

113 Madame de Sévigné, *Correspondance*, 2: 943, May 25, 1680.

114 Madame de Sévigné, *Correspondance*, 2: 189, December 15, 1675. She was right to be concerned. They ended up with three-hundred-thousand livres of debt that they could only pay by marrying their son to the daughter of a rich financier, considered a misalliance. On this point, see Emile Gérard-Gailly, introduction to *Lettres*, 1: 52–53. This was the occasion of Madame de Grignan's infamous remark: "Once in a while even the best land needs manure."

115 Gérard-Gailly, introduction to *Lettres*, 30–32.

116 Gérard-Gailly, introduction to *Lettres*, 36.

117 See Farrell, *Performing Motherhood*, 137.

118 The quotation is from André Monglond, *Le préromantisme français* (Geneva: Slatkine, 1930), vii. Lucien Febvre lauded the phrase in "Du Goût classique au foisonnement romantique," in *Combats pour l'Histoire* (Paris: Colin, 1953), 273.

119 Cited in Johnson Kent Wright, *A Classical Republican in Eighteenth-Century France: The Political Thought of Mably* (Palo Alto, CA: Stanford University Press, 1997), 158.

120 Jean François Paul de Gondi Cardinal de Retz, *Mémoires*, in *Oeuvres*, ed. A. Feillet, J. Gourdault et R. Chantelauze (Paris: Hachette, 1872), 2: 40.

121 Retz, *Mémoires*, 4: 453.

122 Retz, *Mémoires*, 2: 134.

123 Pierre Carlet de Chamblain de Marivaux, *Les Fausses Confidences*, in *Oeuvres de Marivaux: théâtre complet*, 547.

124 Nicolas-Edmé Restif de la Brétonne, *Histoire de Sara*, in *Monsieur Nicolas* (Paris: I. Lisieux, 1883), 12: 165.

125 Dominique Bouhours, *Les entretiens d'Ariste et d'Eugène* (1671; Paris: Armand Colin, 1962), 102.

126 Louis-Elie Moreau de Saint-Méry, *Description topographique, physique, civile, politique et historique de la partie française de l'isle Saint-Domingue*, 2nd ed. (Paris: Morgan, 1875), 1: 75.

127 Saint-Méry, *Description topographique, physique, civile, politique et historique*, 2: 139.

128 On the *Bibliothèque bleue*, see Thierry Delcourt, *La Bibliothèque bleue et les littératures de colportage* (Paris: Librairie Droz, 2000); Robert Mandrou, *De la culture populaire aux 17e et 18e siècles: La Bibliothèque bleue de Troyes* (Paris: Stock, 1964); and Geneviève Bollème, *La Bibliothèque bleue* (Paris: Gallimard-Julliard, 1980).

129 Anonymous, *Le femme mécontente de son mari* (Troyes: Veuve Garnier, 1738), 45.

130 Anonymous, *Le miroir d'astrologie naturelle* (Troyes: Veuve de Jean Oudot, 1745), 52.

131 Anonymous, *Le miroir d'astrologie naturelle*, 15–16.

132 Anonymous, *L'état de servitude ou la misère des domestiques* (Troyes: Veuve Garnier, 1738), 2.

133 Anonymous, *Fameuse harangue . . . de messeigneurs les savetiers* (Troyes: Veuve Garnier, 1738), 6.

134 Anonymous, *La grande Bible des noëls tans vieux que nouveaux* (Troyes: Garnier le jeune, 1772), 14.

135 Anonymous, *Vie de S. Patrocle* (Troyes: Garnier le jeune, 1772), 31.

136 Thomas-Joseph Moult, *Prophéties perpétuelles* ([Troyes?]: [Garnier?], 1765), 9, 29, 54, 57.

Chapter 2: Critiques and Crises of the Credit System

Epigraphs: Jacques-Pierre Brissot de Warville, *Réplique à la première et dernière lettre de L.-M. Gouy, 10 février 1791* (Paris: Belin, 1791), 7; Marquis de Sade, *Juliette*, trans. Austryn Wainhouse (New York: Grove Press, 1988), 597.

1 Paul-Henri Thiry, baron d'Holbach, *Système social ou principes naturels de la morale et de la politique avec un examen de l'influence du gouvernement sur les moeurs* (London, 1773), 2: 158.

2 See, for example, Roger Chartier, "From Texts to Manners, a Concept and Its Books: *Civilité* between Aristocratic Distinction and Popular Appropriation," in *The Cultural Uses of Print*, trans. Lydia Cochrane (Princeton, NJ: Princeton University Press, 1987), 86, on doubts in the second-half of the seventeenth century about *civilité* as a potentially false mask that disguised base and self-interested characters rather than offering proof of inner virtue. See also the discussion of dissimulation as a theme of early modern culture in Jon Snyder, *Dissimulation and the Culture of Secrecy in Early Modern Europe* (Berkeley: University of California Press, 2009). See also Lionel Rothkrug, *Opposition to Louis XIV: The Political and Social Origins of the French Enlightenment* (Princeton, NJ: Princeton University Press, 1965).

3 Even Madame de Maintenon experienced posthumous apocryphal writings; the letters forged by La Beaumelle, the eighteenth-century editor of her correspondence, also contained much more pointed references to her credit than her authentic letters.

4 Jacques Du Lorens, *Satires* (1646; Paris: D. Jouaust, 1869), 53.

5 Du Lorens, *Satires*, 121.

6 Jean-Louis Guez de Balzac, *Aristippe ou de la Cour*, in *Oeuvres* (Paris: T. Jolly, 1665), 2: 180.

7 Nicolas Faret, *L'Honneste homme, ou, L'art de plaire à la court* (1630; Paris: Presses universitaires françaises, 1925), 39.

8 The terms *merit* and *virtue* appear frequently in Jean de La Bruyère's *Les caractères ou les mœurs de ce siècle*, in *Œuvres complètes*, ed. Julien Benda (1694; Paris: Gal-

limard, 1951), 112 and 120 times respectively (ARTFL database word search, January 23, 2012). La Bruyère does not define *merit* specifically but does include a chapter on "personal merit" that laments the many men of merit whose lack of connections prevent from them obtaining the posts or rank they deserve. He contrasts the inner worth and innate modesty of such men with the showy clothing and behavior of lesser individuals, who nonetheless win greater favor. The passage where he comes closest to an explicit gloss on virtue is in its relationship to nobility: "If nobility be virtue; it is lost by everything that is not virtuous; and if it is not virtue, it is an insignificant thing" (410).

9 La Bruyère, *Les caractères ou les moeurs de ce siècle*, 221. On the genre of the character sketch, see Jacques Bos, "Individuality and Inwardness in the Literary Character Sketches of the Seventeenth Century," *Journal of the Warburg and Courtauld Institutes* 61 (1998): 142–57.

10 La Bruyère, *Les caractères ou les moeurs de ce siècle*, 236–37.

11 La Bruyère, *Les caractères ou les moeurs de ce siècle*, 223–24.

12 La Bruyère, *Les caractères ou les moeurs de ce siècle*, 192.

13 La Bruyère, *Les caractères ou les moeurs de ce siècle*, 193.

14 Thomas Parker, "La Bruyère Gives His Two Cents: Financial Language and Ethical Ideals," *Seventeenth-Century French Studies* 27 (2005): 163.

15 See the comment of François-Xavier Cuche: "La Bruyère seems incapable of conceiving of economic time as a time of growth and multiplication, as a cumulative time, as a time subject to acceleration, at least in the capitalist logic of monetary economics. He thinks of it always in terms of spatial metaphors and this space is that of stability" (cited in Parker, "La Bruyère Gives His Two Cents," 172). See also François-Xavier Cuche, *Une pensée sociale catholique: Fleury, La Bruyère, Fénélon* (Paris: Cerf, 1991), 59.

16 Natalie Zemon Davis, *The Gift in Sixteenth-Century France* (Madison: University of Wisconsin Press, 2000); and Harry Liebersohn, *The Return of the Gift: European History of a Global Idea* (Cambridge: Cambridge University Press, 2009).

17 On this double language, see Jay Smith, "No More Language Games: Words, Beliefs, and the Political Culture of Early Modern France," *American Historical Review* 102, no. 5 (December 1997): 1432.

18 Marcel Mauss, *The Gift: Forms and Functions of Exchange in Archaic Societies* (London: Cohen and West, 1954), 34–35. Mauss continues: "The evolution in economic law has not been from barter to sale, and from cash sale to credit sale. On the one hand, barter has arisen through a system of presents given and reciprocated according to a time limit. This was through a process of simplification, by reductions in periods of time formerly arbitrary. On the other hand, buying and selling arose in the same way, with the latter according to a fixed time limit, or by cash, as well as by lending. For we have no evidence that any of the legal systems that have evolved beyond the phase we are describing (in particular, Babylonian law) remained ignorant of the credit process that is known in every archaic society that still survives today. Of course, one could also envisage a hybrid system in which the regular gift/counter gift cycle co-existed with less regularized forms of exchange."

19 Avner Offer, "Between the Gift and the Market: The Economy of Regard," *Economic History Review* 50, no. 3 (August 1997): 450–76.

20 La Bruyère, *Les caracteres ou les moeurs de ce siècle*, 195.

21 La Bruyère, *Les caracteres ou les moeurs de ce siècle*, 196.

22 See Pierre Bourdieu on the contrast between roulette and capital: "Roulette, which holds out the opportunity of winning a lot of money in a short space of time, and therefore of changing one's social status quasi-instantaneously, and in which the winning of the previous spin of the wheel can be staked and lost at every new spin, gives a fairly accurate image of this imaginary universe of perfect competition or perfect equality of opportunity, a world without inertia, without accumulation, without heredity or acquired properties, in which every moment is perfectly independent of the previous one, every soldier has a marshal's baton in his knapsack, and every prize can be attained, instantaneously, by everyone, so that at each moment anyone can become anything. Capital, which, in its objectified or embodied forms, takes time to accumulate and which, as a potential capacity to produce profits and to reproduce itself in identical or expanded form, contains a tendency to persist in its being, is a force inscribed in the objectivity of things so that everything is not equally possible or impossible. And the structure of the distribution of the different types and subtypes of capital at a given moment in time represents the immanent structure of the social world, i.e., the set of constraints, inscribed in the very reality of that world, which govern its functioning in a durable way, determining the chances of success for practices" (Pierre Bourdieu, "The Forms of Capital," in *Handbook of Theory and Research for the Sociology of Education*, ed. J. Richardson [New York: Greenwood, 1986], 241–42). La Bruyère's reading of gambling as corrosive of traditional social relations is in contrast to Thomas Kavanagh's interpretation of gambling as epitomizing the noble warrior culture of embracing risk and exchanging gratuitous gifts. See Thomas Kavanagh, *Enlightenment and the Shadows of Chance: The Novel and the Culture of Gambling in Eighteenth-Century France* (Baltimore: Johns Hopkins University Press, 1993). On gambling, see also Francis Freundlich, *Le monde du jeu à Paris, 1715–1800* (Paris: Albin Michel, 1995).

23 Blaise Pascal, *Les provinciales, ou Les lettres écrites par Louis de Montalte à un provinciale de ses amis et aux RR. PP. Jésuites* (1657; Paris: Garnier, 1965), 330.

24 Pascal, *Les provinciales*, 280. On Pascal's attack on the hypocrisy of civilité, see Chartier, "From Texts to Manners," 87.

25 Marie Jeanne Guyon, *Récits de captivité* (1709; Grenoble: Editions Jérôme Million, 1992), 119.

26 Voltaire, *Siècle de Louis XIV* (1751; Paris: Charpentier et Cie, 1874), 525.

27 Voltaire, *Siècle de Louis XIV*, 526.

28 Pierre Nicole, *Essais de Morale* (1671; Paris: G. Desprez, 1701), 2: 239.

29 Nicole, *Essais de Morale*, 220.

30 Nicole, *Essais de Morale*, 253.

31 Jacques Abbadie, *Traité de la vérité de la réligion chrétienne* (Rotterdam: R. Leers, 1684), 2: 155.

32 Abbadie, *Traité de la vérité de la réligion chrétienne*, 113.

33 Simon-Nicolas-Henri Linguet, *Histoire impartiale des Jésuites depuis leur établissement jusqu'à leur première expulsion* (Paris: Chez P. G. Simon, 1768), 12.

34 Linguet, *Histoire impartiale des Jésuites*, 399. Referring to a commentary on seventeenth-century prophesying against the Jesuits, he noted that "the time will come when a Jew will have more credit than a Jesuit."

35 Jacques Bénigne Bossuet, *Oraison funèbre d'Henriette d'Angleterre*, in *Œuvres Oratoires* (Paris: Declee de Brouwer et Cie, 1922), 5: 663.

36 *Dictionnaire de l'Académie française* (Paris: Chez la veuve Jean Coignard, 1694), "odieux."

37 Charles de Secondat, baron de Montesquieu, *Lettres persanes*, ed. Elie Carcassonne (1721; Paris: F. Roches, 1929), 76–77.

38 Michael Mosher suggests that Montesquieu points to this middle ground in chapter 22 of book 28, when the text "commends a gender division of power that exactly matches Montesquieu's defense of the separation of power in the political sphere." Derived from chivalric codes of male comportment toward women, Mosher argues, Montesquieu's compromise was to allow women a "sphere of autonomy based on its share in the kind of governance exemplified in 'judgment.'" This compromise assumed and maintained the basic inequality between the sexes, but expressed it in softened terms that affirmed the dignity of the weaker side. See Michael A. Mosher, "The Judgmental Gaze of European Women: Gender, Sexuality, and the Critique of Republican Rule," *Political Theory* (February 1994): 33–36. The term *despotique* was first used in France in pamphlets attacking Cardinal Mazarin during the Fronde. See Roger Boesche, "Fearing Monarchs and Merchants: Montesquieu's Two Theories of Despotism," *Western Political Quarterly* 43, no. 4 (December 1990): 741.

39 Charles-Irénée Castel de Saint-Pierre, *Discours sur la polysynodie, où l'on démontre que la polysynodie, ou pluralité des Conseils, est la forme de ministère la plus avantageuse pour un Roy et pour son royaume* (Amsterdam: Du Villard et Changuion, 1719), 81–82.

40 Mona Ozouf has identified male-female interaction as a key element of French culture in the longue durée. See Mona Ozouf, *Women's Words: Essay on French Singularity*, trans. Jane Marie Todd (Chicago: University of Chicago Press, 1997). This argument generated controversy among historians, particularly due to her own espousal and defense of this pattern as not only "singularly" French but also preferable to what she viewed as the oppositional stance of American feminism. My argument here is not that such relations did exist or were uniquely French but that some authors of the early eighteenth century represented them that way.

41 Castel de Saint-Pierre, *Discours sur la polysynodie*, 85.

42 Cited in Carol Blum, *Strength in Numbers: Population, Reproduction, and Power in Eighteenth-Century France* (Baltimore: Johns Hopkins University Press, 2002), 58.

43 Jacques Joseph Duguet, *Institutions d'un prince, ou traité des qualités, des vertus et des devoirs d'un souverain*, vol. 2 (London: chez Jean Nourse, 1740), 167–75.

44 Jean-Jacques Rousseau, *Politics and the Arts: Letter to M. D'Alembert on the Theatre*, trans. Allan Bloom (Ithaca, NY: Cornell University Press, 1968). Rousseau's attack

on public women is analyzed at length in Joan Landes, *Women in the Public Sphere in the Age of Revolution* (Ithaca, NY: Cornell University Press, 1988). In fact, Rousseau read Saint-Pierre closely and published commentaries on his works.

45 Paul Harsin, *Crédit Public et Banque d'Etat en France du XVIe au XVIIIe siècle* (Paris: E. Droz, 1933).

46 For a detailed account of practices and policies of state finance from the time of Colbert to the death of Louis XIV, see Gary Bruce McCollim, *Louis XIV's Assault on Privilege: Nicolas Desmaretz and the Tax on Wealth* (Rochester, NY: University of Rochester Press, 2012); and "The Formation of Fiscal Policy in the Reign of Louis XIV: The Example of Nicolas Desmaretz, Controller General of Finances (1708–1815)" (PhD diss., Ohio State University, 1979). See also the classic studies of finance in this period, which underline the strong ties between financiers and the court: Daniel Dessert, *Argent, pouvoir et société au Grand Siècle* (Paris: Fayard, 1984); Françoise Bayard, *Le Monde des financiers au XVIIe siècle* (Paris: Flammarion, 1988).

47 On Desmaretz's career as controller general, see McCollim, "The Formation of Fiscal Policy in the Reign of Louis XIV." McCollim suggests that "Desmaretz's hardline on the *comptables, traitants*, and 'les aisez' did not win him any friends, although his struggles to rein them in remained secret so as not to imperil the credit they offered the state" (368–69). Thus, Desmaretz's efforts make him a precursor of the struggle against private, political credit described in this chapter.

48 Philippe de Courcillon de Dangeau, *Mémoires et journal du marquis de Dangeau* (Paris: Mame et Delaunay-Vallée, 1830), xvi, 231–32, November 10, 1715.

49 John Law, *Money and Trade Considered: With a Proposal for Supplying the Nation with Money* (Glasgow: R. and A. Foulis, 1705). See Antoin E. Murphy, *John Law: Economic Theorist and Policy Maker* (Oxford: Oxford University Press, 1997), 115. There is a copious literature on Law; see especially John Law, *John Law: Oeuvres complètes*, ed. Paul Harsin, 3 vols. (Paris: Sirey, 1934); Edgar Faure, *La Banqueroute de Law* (Paris: Gallimard, 1977); and François Velde, "Was John Law's System a Bubble? The Mississippi Bubble Revisited," in *The Origins and Development of Financial Markets and Institutions*, ed. Jeremy Atack and Larry Neal (Cambridge: Cambridge University Press, 2009), 99–120. See also the discussion in Michael Sonenscher, *Before the Deluge: Public Debt, Inequality, and the Intellectual Origins of the French Revolution* (Princeton, NJ: Princeton University Press, 1990); Larry Neal, *The Rise of Financial Capitalism: International Capital Markets in the Age of Reason* (Cambridge: Cambridge University Press, 1990); Thomas Kaiser, "Money, Despotism, and Public Opinion in Early Eighteenth-Century France: John Law and the Debate on Royal Credit," *Journal of Modern History* 63 (March 1991): 1–28; and Charles Kindleberger, *A Financial History of Western Europe*, 2nd ed. (New York: Oxford University Press, 2006).

50 See Thomas E. Kaiser, "Money, Despotism, and Public Opinion," 4.

51 In the aftermath of the bubble, two of Law's former associates published defenses of Law's monetary theory, without naming him explicitly. These were Jean-François Melon's *Essai sur le commerce*, published in 1734, and Dutot's two volume *Réflexions politiques sur les finances et le commerce*, published in 1738. These

defenses of Law spurred the financier Pâris-Duverney, one of the principal providers of state finance and thus a main target of Law's reforms, to publish a scathing attack. On this debate, see Antoin E. Murphy's introduction to Charles Dutot, *Histoire du système de John Law (1716–1720)*, ed. Antoin E. Murphy (Paris: Institut National d'Etudes demographiques, 2000).

52 Cited in Sonenscher, *Before the Deluge*, 160.

53 Sonenscher, *Before the Deluge*, 3.

54 Robert Harms, *The Diligent: A Voyage Through the Worlds of the Slave Trade* (New York: Basic Books, 2002), 48–54. Coercive measures were also employed to recruit French colonists to inhabit Louisiana, including the forced transport of convicts.

55 In a letter to the Comte d'Argenson, Pompadour wrote: "If the post of historiographer falls vacant, I ask it of you for Duclos in case you do not have another engagement." Letter reproduced in Maurice Charles Marc René de Voyer de Paulmy, marquis d'Argenson, ed., *Autour d'un ministre de Louis XV* (Paris: Messein, 1923), 280.

56 A recent critical edition of the text attempted to redress its relative scholarly neglect. See Charles Duclos, *Considérations sur les moeurs de ce siècle*, ed. Carole Dornier (Paris: Honoré Champion, 2005). See also Jacques Brengues, *Charles Duclos (1704–1772), ou l'obsession de la vertu* (Saint-Brieuc: Presses universitaires de Bretagne, 1971) and Jay Smith, *Nobility Reimagined: The Patriotic Nation in Eighteenth-Century France* (Ithaca, NY: Cornell University Press, 2005), 85–90.

57 Charles Duclos, *Considérations sur les mœurs de ce siècle* (Amsterdam: Aux Depens de la Compagnie, 1751), 149–50.

58 Duclos, *Considérations sur les mœurs de ce siècle*, 154–55.

59 Duclos, *Considérations sur les mœurs de ce siècle*, 156–57.

60 Duclos, *Considérations sur les mœurs de ce siècle*, 154.

61 Charles Duclos, *Mémoires secrets sur les règnes de Louis XIV et de Louis XV*, in *Nouvelle collection de mémoires pour servir à l'histoire de France*, vol. 10, ed. Joseph Michaud and Jean Joseph François Poujoulat (Paris: Chez l'éditeur du commentaire analytique du code civil, 1859), 563. This letter is also cited in Kaiser, "Money, Despotism and Public Opinion," 20. On the impact of the Law project on his family, see Charles Duclos, *Considérations sur les moeurs de ce siècle* (1939; Cambridge: Cambridge University Press, 2010), ed. F. C. Green, "Editor's Introduction," i.

62 Duclos, *Considérations sur les moeurs* (1751), 157.

63 Duclos, *Considérations sur les moeurs*, 231.

64 Duclos, *Considérations sur les moeurs*, 140.

65 *Dictionnaire de l'académie française* (1762), "mérite."

66 Duclos, *Considérations sur les moeurs*, 161.

67 Duclos, *Considérations sur les moeurs*, 161–62.

68 Duclos, *Considérations sur les moeurs*, 164.

69 Duclos, *Considérations sur les moeurs*, 165.

70 Duclos, *Considérations sur les moeurs*, 167.

71 Duclos, *Considérations sur les moeurs*, 107.

72 Duclos, *Considérations sur les moeurs*, 120.

73 Duclos, *Considérations sur les moeurs*, 139.

74 Duclos, *Considérations sur les moeurs*, 140.

75 Duclos, *Considérations sur les moeurs*, 141.

76 Duclos, *Mémoires secrets sur le règne de Louis XIV*, 461, 467, 490.

77 Duclos, *Mémoires secrets sur le règne de Louis XIV*, 631.

78 Duclos, *Mémoires secrets sur le règne de Louis XIV*, 654.

79 Even her father's escape from execution was seen as due to the effects of credit. Her father, an employee of the Pâris family of financiers, was sentenced to death by hanging for financial wrongdoing in 1726. According to the memoirs of the Duc de Richelieu: "This Poisson [father of Pompadour] was condemned to be hanged; but because that does not happen when one has a bit of credit and money, and above all the four [Pâris] brothers as protectors, Poisson was able to flee to Hamburg." Louis François Armand Du Plessis, duc de Richelieu, *Mémoires du maréchal duc de Richelieu* (Paris: Chez Buisson, 1793), 8: 165.

80 Pompadour supported Machault and his party at court in opposition to the dévot faction, attached to the royal family, who opposed him and resented his taxation of the clergy. See Evelyne Lever, *Madame de Pompadour: A Life*, trans. Catherine Temerson (New York: Farrar, Straus and Giroux, 2002), 145.

81 On perceptions of Pompadour's influence at court, see Thomas E. Kaiser, "Madame de Pompadour and the Theaters of Power," *French Historical Studies* 19, no. 4 (autumn 1996): 1025–44. See also John Shovlin, *The Political Economy of Virtue: Luxury, Patriotism and the Origins of the French Revolution* (Ithaca, NY: Cornell University Press, 2006), 26–38; and Julian Swann, "Parlement, Politics and the *Parti Janseniste*: The *Grand Conseil Affair, 1755–56*," *French History* 6, no. 4 (December 1992): 435–61.

82 Cited in Argenson, *Autour d'un ministre de Louis XV*, 233.

83 René-Louis de Voyer de Paulmy, marquis d'Argenson, *Journal et mémoires du marquis d'Argenson* (Paris: Chez veuve Jules Renouard, 1867), 9: 173.

84 Argenson, *Journal et mémoires du marquis d'Argenson*, 9: 175.

85 Argenson, *Journal et mémoires du marquis d'Argenson*, 9: 201.

86 Argenson, *Journal et mémoires du marquis d'Argenson*, 3: 230–31.

87 Only a few hundred letters by Pompadour survive, many of them unpublished. For a collection of several dozen letters to her family, see M. A. Poulet-Malassis, ed., *Correspondance de Madame de Pompadour avec son père, M. Poisson et son frère, M. de Vandières* (Paris, 1878). Eighty-five letters from Pompadour to the Comte d'Argenson were published in Argenson, *Autour d'un Ministre de Louis XV*. These letters mostly concern patronage requests for posts overseen by d'Argenson. In them, Pompadour draws on the credit described by the Marquis d'Argenson without using the term explicitly. On Pompadour's correspondence, see Andrea Weisbrod, *Von Macht und Mythos der Pompadour* (Berlin: Ulrike Helmer Verlag, 2000); and Christine Pevitt Algrant, *Madame de Pompadour: Mistress of France* (New York: Grove Press, 2003), 323–24.

88 François Barbé-Marbois, *Lettres de Madame la Marquise de Pompadour, depuis MDCCLIII jusqu'à MDCCLXII inclusivement* (London: T. Cadell, 1772), 1: 64.

89 Barbé-Marbois, *Lettres de Madame la Marquise de Pompadour*, 2: 6.

90 Barbé-Marbois, *Lettres de Madame la Marquise de Pompadour*, 1: 5.

91 Barbé-Marbois, *Lettres de Madame la Marquise de Pompadour*, 2: 54–55.

92 Cited in Robert Darnton, *The Forbidden Best-Sellers of Pre-Revolutionary France* (New York: W. W. Norton, 1996), 221.

93 Darnton, *The Forbidden Best-Sellers of Pre-Revolutionary France*, 221.

94 Jean de La Bruyère, *Dialogues sur le quiétisme*, in *Oeuvres complètes*, ed. Julien Benda (Paris: Gallimard, 1951).

Chapter 3: Incredible Style: Intertwined Circuits of Credit, Fashion, and Sex

1 Charles Pinot Duclos, *Acajou et Zirphile*, in *Le Cabinet des Fées* (Geneva: Barde, Manget et Co., 1786), 35: 77.

2 On fashion, appearances, and court society in the seventeenth century, see Clare Haru Crowston, *Fabricating Women: The Seamstresses of Old Regime France, 1675–1791* (Durham, NC: Duke University Press, 2001), chapter 1; Jennifer Jones, *Sexing la Mode: Gender, Fashion, and Commercial Culture in Old Regime France* (London: Berg, 2004); Daniel Roche, *The Culture of Clothing: Dress and Fashion in the Old Regime*, trans. Jean Birrell (Cambridge: Cambridge University Press, 1994); Philip Mansel, *Dressed to Rule: Royal and Court Costume from Louis xiv to Elizabeth ii* (New Haven, CT: Yale University Press, 2005). On fashion and French identity, see Joan DeJean, *The Essence of Style: How the French Invented High Fashion, Fine Food, Chic Cafés, Style, Sophistication and Glamour* (New York: Free Press, 2005). Michael Kwass has questioned the extent to which fashion became "feminized" over the course of the eighteenth century. See Michael Kwass, "Big Hair: A Wig History of Consumption in Eighteenth-Century France," *American Historical Review* 111, no. 3 (June 2006): 630–59.

3 On criticism of fashion under Louis xiii, see Louise Godard de Donville, *La Signification de la mode sous Louis xiii* (Aix-en-Provence: EdiSud, 1976).

4 Nicolas Faret, *L'Honneste homme, ou, L'art de plaire à la court* (1633; Paris: Presses universitaires françaises, 1925), 39.

5 Faret, *L'Honneste homme*, 91–92.

6 Faret, *L'Honneste homme*, 10.

7 Cited in David Matthew Posner, *The Performance of Nobility in Early Modern Literature* (Cambridge: Cambridge University Press, 1999), 19.

8 Antoine de Courtin, *Nouveau traité de la civilité qui se pratique en France, parmi les honnestes gens* (1671; Paris: Chez Helie Josset, 1672), vii.

9 See Roger Chartier's discussion on Courtin in "From Texts to Manners, a Concept and Its Books: *Civilité* between Aristocratic Distinction and Popular Appropriation," in *The Cultural Uses of Print in Early Modern France*, trans. Lydia Cochrane (Princeton, NJ: Princeton University Press, 1987), 80–82. On the evolution of notions of *civilité* in France from the seventeenth century to the revolution, see Chartier, "From Texts to Manners"; and Orest Ranum, "Courtesy, Absolutism, and the Rise of the French State, 1630–1660," *Journal of Modern History* 52 (1980): 426–51.

10 Courtin, *Nouveau traité de la civilité*, 101.

11 Courtin, *Nouveau traité de la civilité*, 41–42, 23. On disciplining the body and especially the female body and its hair in early modern civility manuals, see James R. Farr, "The Pure and Disciplined Body: Hierarchy, Morality, and Symbolism in France During the Catholic Reformation," *Journal of Interdisciplinary History* 21, no. 3 (winter 1991): 391–414.

12 Courtin, *Nouveau traité de la civilité*, 71.

13 Courtin, *Nouveau traité de la civilité*, 72.

14 Text reproduced in Peter Rickard, ed., *The French Language in the Seventeenth Century* (Woodbridge, UK: D. S. Brewer, 1992), 249.

15 Courtin, *Nouveau traité de la civilité*, 73.

16 Courtin, *Nouveau traité de la civilité*, 74.

17 Jean-Baptiste de La Salle, *Les règles de la bienséance et de la civilité chrétienne*, ed. Philippe Louis Constantin (1703; Paris: Douxfils, 1841), 20. Again, his notion of reason is not that of the philosophers but something akin to "the established rule" as explained by Courtin.

18 See Chartier's discussion on Courtin in "From Texts to Manners," 91.

19 Godard de Donville, *La Signification de la mode sous Louis XIII*, 22.

20 See Norbert Elias, *The Court Society* (Oxford: Blackwell, 1983); Philip Mansel, *Dressed to Rule*, chapter 1; Jones, *Sexing la Mode*; Emmanuel Le Roy Ladurie and Jean-François Fitou, *Saint-Simon and the Court of Louis XIV* (Chicago: Chicago University Press, 2001); and Hélène Himelfarb, "Versailles, source ou miroir des modes Louis-quatorziennes? Sources et Dangeau, 1684–1685," *Cahiers de l'Association internationale des études françaises* 38 (1986): 121–43.

21 *Déclaration contre le luxe des habits, carrosses et ornemens*, November 17, 1660, in François-André Isambert et al., eds. *Recueil général des anciennes lois françaises, depuis l'an 420 jusqu'à la Révolution de 1789* (Paris: Belin-Leprieur, 1821–33), 17: 382–85.

22 Cited in Mansel, *Dressed to Rule*, 1.

23 On his support for the lace industry, see Colbert's letters on the subject in Pierre Clément, ed., *Lettres, instructions et mémoires de Colbert*, vol. 3, *Commerce et industrie* (Paris: Imprimerie imperial, 1861–1882). See also Béatrix de Buffevent, *L'économie dentellière en région parisienne au XVIIe siècle* (Pontoise: Société historique de Pontoise, du Val-d'Oise et du Vexin, 1984); and Paul-Martin Bondois, *Colbert et l'industrie de la dentelle* (Paris: M. Rivière, 1926).

24 On the seamstresses' guild, see Crowston, *Fabricating Women*, chapter 4.

25 One historian described the furor over painted cloth as equaled only by contemporary debates over the liberalization of the grain trade. See Edgar Depitre, *La Toile peinte en France au XVII et au XVIIIe siècles. Industrie, commerce, prohibitions* (Paris: Marcel Rivière et cie., 1912), i.

26 Antoine de Furetière, *Dictionnaire universel* (The Hague: A. and R. Leers, 1690), "*mode*."

27 For one scholar's account of the court's role in creating fashion, see Himelfarb, "Versailles, source ou miroir des modes Louis-quatorziennes?"

28 By the time of Louis XIII in the early seventeenth century, the word *mode* had acquired the significance it holds today, referring to innovations in styles of cloth-

ing or other goods and practices, produced through a constant process of change and renewal. See Godard de Donville, *La Signification de la mode sous Louis XIII*. On *Le Mercure galant*, see Monique Vincent, *Le Mercure galant. Présentation de la première revue féminine d'information et de culture, 1672-1710* (Paris: Champion, 2005); Reed Benhamou, "Fashion in the 'Mercure': From Human Foible to Female Failing," *Eighteenth-Century Studies* 31, no. 1 (fall 1997): 27–43; Susannah Carson, "L'économique de la mode: Costume, Conformity, and Consumerism in *Le Mercure galant*," *Seventeenth-Century French Studies* 27 (2005): 133–46; Jones, *Sexing la Mode*; and Joan DeJean, *The Essence of Style*, 46–59. After Donneau's death in 1710, the new editor, Charles du Fresny, accorded less attention to fashion.

29 *Le Mercure galant* (Paris: Chez Claude Barbin, 1673), 3: 282–83.

30 *Le Mercure galant*, 3: 283–84.

31 *Le Mercure galant*, 284–86.

32 *Le Mercure galant*, 288–92.

33 *Le Mercure galant*, 298.

34 *Le Mercure galant*, 308.

35 *Le Mercure galant*, 322–23.

36 *Le Mercure galant*, 324–25.

37 *Le Mercure galant*, June 1687, 306–7.

38 On cheap versions of luxury goods in the eighteenth century, see Cissie Fairchilds, "The Production and Marketing of Populuxe Goods in Eighteenth-Century Paris," in *Consumption and the World of Goods*, eds. John Brewer and Roy Porter (New York: Routledge, 1993), 228–60. A subsequent edition of the journal provided a similar example with reference to a type of skirt made from linen printed with a lacework design and then combined with taffeta underskirts. Much cheaper than real lace, "these skirts were common from their birth and being found beautiful and inexpensive almost all women have bought them" (*Le Mercure galant* [Paris: Claude Bargin, 1673], 4: 345–46). These examples demonstrate that "populuxe" goods existed well before the mid-eighteenth century, when Fairchilds places their origins.

39 Many of these details were contained in the *Extraordinaire du Mercure galant*, January 1678, 521–47. See also Carson, "L'économique de la mode," 133–46.

40 *Le Mercure galant*, October 1678, 363–64.

41 *Le Mercure galant*, October 1682, 280.

42 *Le Mercure galant*, May 1679, 354.

43 *Le Mercure galant*, July 1677, 257–58.

44 Abraham de Pradel's almanac informed the reader that "cloth of silk, gold, and silver are amply traded by Messieurs Gautier and Regnault, rue des Bourdonnois." See Abraham de Pradel, *Les addresses de la ville de Paris* (Paris, 1691), 25. The business apparently continued well into the eighteenth century. Germain-François Poullain de Saint-Foix in *Oeuvres complètes: Essais historiques sur Paris* (Paris: Chez la veuve Duchesne, 1778) refers to "Gaultier & Dupré," silk merchants at the sign of the Golden Crown (67).

45 *L'Extraordinaire du mercure quartier de janvier 1678*, 508.

46 *Le Mercure galant*, 1672, 1: 275. After Louis XIV's death, the regency relaxed a

number of his rules on court dress and etiquette, including halving the period of required mourning dress. See Kimberly Chrisman-Campbell, "Mourning and *La Mode* at the Court of Louis XVI," *Costume* 39 (2005): 65. See also Lou Taylor, *Mourning Dress: A Costume and Social History* (London: Allen and Unwin, 1983).

47 *L'Extraordinaire du mercure quartier de janvier 1678*, 522.

48 *Le Mercure galant*, October 1682, 275.

49 Françoise Waquet, "La mode au XVIIe siècle: de la folie à l'usage," *Cahiers de l'Association internationale des etudes françaises* 38 (1986): 91–104. See also Godard de Donville, *La Signification de la mode sous Louis XIII*.

50 Disagreements on the moral valence of fashion may be seen as one element of the struggle between the ancients and moderns, the literary quarrel of the late seventeenth century that opposed partisans of classical authors to those who believed contemporary writers had surpassed them. Many of the contributors to *Le Mercure galant* (including Donneau de Visé, Bernard le Bovier de Fontenelle, and Thomas Corneille) championed the modern position, while Jean de La Bruyère and—before his disgrace in the late 1690s—François de Salignac de la Mothe-Fénélon took up the former. On Fénélon as an ancient, see Patrick Riley, "Rousseau, Fénélon, and the Quarrel between the Ancients and the Moderns," in *The Cambridge Companion to Rousseau*, ed. Patrick Riley (Cambridge: Cambridge University Press, 2001), 78–93.

51 La Bruyère, *Les caractères ou les mœurs de ce siècle*, in *Œuvres complètes*, ed. Julien Benda (1694; Paris: Gallimard, 1951), 314. The term *le monde* (also used in English in this period) denoted both geographical and social exclusivity, being located in Paris or at court and in the homes and leisure spaces of the nobility and the wealthy bourgeoisie. See Isabelle Journeaux, "L'entrée dans le monde à travers les romanciers français et anglais du dix-huitième siècle," *Histoire, économie et société* 12, no. 2 (1993): 273–298.

52 Jean de La Bruyère, *Les caractères ou les mœurs de ce siècle*, 354.

53 François de Salignac de la Mothe Fénélon, *Directions pour la conscience d'un roi* (Paris: Chez les frères Estienne, 1775), 22.

54 Fénélon, *Directions pour la conscience d'un roi*, 26.

55 Fénélon, *Directions pour la conscience d'un roi*, 28.

56 Molière, *Le bourgeois gentilhomme*, in *Oeuvres complètes*, ed. Eugène Despois (Paris: Hachette, 1873). On the frequent thematics of gift, money, and debt in Molière, see Richard Sörman, "L'économie de l'incertitude chez Molière," *Seventeenth-Century French Studies* 27 (2005): 91–102; Jean-Marie Apostolidès, "Molière and the Sociology of Exchange," *Critical Inquiry* 3 (1988): 477–92; Sara Kofman and Jean Yves Masson, *Don Juan ou le refus de la dette* (Paris: Galilée, 1991); and Pierre Force, *Molière ou le Prix des choses* (Paris: Nathan, 1994).

57 One scholar attributes the conservative nature of *Le Bourgeois gentilhomme* to the overreaching Molière had done in his previous play, *Les Amants magnifiques*, which diminished royal support for the playwright and his troupe. See Gretchen Elizabeth Smith, *The Performance of Male Nobility in Molière's Comédie-Ballets: Staging the Courtier* (Aldershot: Ashgate Publishing, 2005), 213–14.

58 Dancourt was an actor and playwright of the Comédie française with close con-

nections to the court; during his lifetime his plays—numbering approximately fifty—were performed frequently but to mixed reviews. Dancourt is less known today than Regnard and Le Sage, two other of Molière's successors at the Comédie française, but his plays had received over five thousand performances there by 1969, earning him the rank of sixth most performed playwright at that institution. Dancourt's most successful plays—including *Le Chevalier à la mode* (1687), *Les Bourgeoises à la mode* (1692), and *Les Bourgeoises de qualité* (1700)—presented close counterparts to Monsieur Jourdain: men and women of the bourgeoisie who foolishly aspired to nobility using fashionable appearances as a lever of entry. *La Femme d'intrigues* presented an alternative, much more cynical view of society and perhaps for that reason was less successful with theater audiences. See André Blanc, *F. C. Dancourt (1661-1725): La Comédie française à l'heure du Soleil couchant* (Paris: Editions Place, 1984), 6-9.

59 See the discussion of the "*revendeuse à la toilette*" in Laurence Fontaine, *L'économie morale, pauvreté, crédit et confiance dans l'Europe préindustrielle* (Paris: Gallimard, 2008), 109-15. This figure was both complementary and a foil to the *marchande à la mode*. Aspects of their businesses certainly overlapped, for fashion merchants also sometimes agreed to sell goods for their clients and they also consigned items to intermediaries like the revendeuse à la toilette for sale. They could both be found circulating among the homes of the wealthy, bringing goods, news, gossip, and loans of money. However, fashion merchants made their niche, in contrast to the revendeuse, through their reputation for creating new items, not for recirculating used ones. With their fancy boutiques and, after 1776, guild status, successful fashion merchants strove to distance themselves from the shady reputation of the revendeuse.

60 Florent Carton Dancourt, *La Femme d'intrigues*, in *Oeuvres choisis de Dancourt* (Paris: P. Didot l'ainé et F. Didot, 1810), 172.

61 Dancourt, *La Femme d'intrigues*, 174-75.

62 Blanc, *F. C. Dancourt*, 49.

63 François de Grenaille, *La Mode* (Paris: Chez Nicolas Gasse, 1642).

64 La Bruyère, *Les caractères ou les moeurs de ce siècle*, 391.

65 Louis de Rouvroy, duc de Saint-Simon, *Mémoires complets et authentiques du duc de Saint-Simon sur le siècle de Louis XIV et la régence*, ed. Adolphe Chéruel (Paris: L. Hachette, 1856-58), 1: 182.

66 Saint-Simon, *Mémoires complets et authentiques du duc de Saint-Simon*, 5: 62-63.

67 Saint-Simon, *Mémoires complets et authentiques du duc de Saint-Simon*, 12: 96.

68 Saint-Simon, *Mémoires complets et authentiques du duc de Saint-Simon*, 14: 111-12.

69 Abel Boyer, *Dictionnaire royal, François et Anglois*, vol. 1 (The Hague: Meyndert Uytwerf, 1702).

70 Abel Boyer, *Dictionnaire royal, françois-anglois, et anglois-françois*, vol. 2 (Amsterdam: R. and G. Wetstein and Pierre Humbert, 1727).

71 Jacques Savary des Bruslons, *Dictionnaire universel de commerce* (Geneva: Chez les heritiers Cramer and Freres Philibert, 1742), 2: 50.

72 The fact that such "style" might appear innate and effortless was merely part of the naturalization of cultural capital. Pierre Bourdieu and Jean-Claude Passeron dis-

cuss this phenomenon for the children of the bourgeoisie in modern society. Pierre Bourdieu and Jean-Claude Passeron, *The Inheritors: French Students and Their Relation to Culture*, trans. Richard Nice (Chicago: University of Chicago Press, 1979).

73 This argument also has affinities with Robert Darnton's account of the "information society" of the Old Regime. See Robert Darnton, "An Early Information Society: News and the Media in Eighteenth-Century Paris," *American Historical Review* 105, no. 1 (February 2000): 1–35. On information economies in the seventeenth century, see Richard Scholar, "Towards a Pre-History of the Knowledge Economy: The Case of Pascal," *Seventeenth-Century French Studies* 27 (2005): 71–80.

74 *Le Mercure galant*, July 1677, 257–80.

75 Phillip Hoffman, Jean-Laurent Rosenthal, and Gilles Postel-Vinay, *Priceless Markets: The Political Economy of Credit in Paris, 1660–1870* (Chicago: University of Chicago Press, 2000).

76 Recent studies focusing on the circulation of information, inspired by renewed interest in the history of the book, offer one example of such interest but need to be broadened to include "news" about fashion, insolvency, and other affairs. See, for example, Robert Darnton, *The Devil in the Holy Water or the Art of Slander from Louis XIV to Napoleon* (Philadelphia: University of Pennsylvania Press, 2009); Jacob Soll, *The Information Master: Jean-Baptiste Colbert's Secret State Intelligence System* (Ann Arbor: University of Michigan Press, 2009); Raymond Joad, *News Networks in Seventeenth-Century Britain and Europe* (New York: Routledge, 2008); Filippo de Vivo, *Information and Communication in Venice: Rethinking Early Modern Politics* (New York: Oxford University Press, 2009); and Brendan Dooley and Sabrina Baron, eds., *The Politics of Information in Early Modern Europe* (London: Routledge, 2001).

77 Godard de Donville, *La Signification de la mode sous Louis XIII*, 87.

78 Other factors included the possession of collateral, the stocks held in the warehouse or shop, and family ties.

79 In the grain trade, licensed brokers, or *facteurs*, served as middlemen between wholesale suppliers of flour and retail bakers. As Steven L. Kaplan explains, the credit that brokers extended "was at the core of their relationship with the bakers." They obtained enduring relations with bakers by furnishing extended credit but had to contend with the wholesale merchants who demanded payments. See Steven L. Kaplan, *The Bakers of Paris and the Bread Question, 1700–1775* (Durham, NC: Duke University Press, 1996), 379.

80 On artistic representations of the death of credit, see René Saulnier and Henri van der Zée, "La Mort de credit. Image populaire, ses sources politiques et économiques," *Dawna sztuka: czasopismo poświęcone archeologii i historii sztuki* 2, no. 3 (June 1939): 195–218.

81 *Encyclopédie ou dictionnaire raisonné des sciences, des arts et métiers*, ed. Denis Diderot and Jean Le Rond d'Alembert (Geneva: Pellet, 1778), "cours," 4: 397.

82 On the epistemological model of the clue or trace, see also Carlo Ginzburg, "Clues: Roots of an Evidential Paradigm," in *Clues, Myths, and the Historical Method*,

trans. John Tedeschi and Anne C. Tedeschi (Baltimore: Johns Hopkins University Press, 1989), 96–125.

83 Georg Simmel, "Fashion," *American Journal of Sociology* 62 (1904; May 1957): 541–88.

84 One example to note here is Giovanni Levi's *Inheriting Power: The Story of an Exorcist*, trans. Lydia Cochrane (Chicago: University of Chicago Press, 1988), which illuminates the difficulties encountered by a notary father in transmitting social credit to his priest son.

85 Saint-Simon, *Mémoires*, 2: 223.

86 Saint-Simon, *Mémoires*, 2: 74.

87 Saint-Simon, *Mémoires*, 19: 426–27.

88 In a chapter titled "Les Gens à la mode" Duclos contrasts the old-fashioned, typically French *homme sociable* with the new, fashionable *homme aimable*. The former was frank, helpful, and benevolent, in short "the model citizen," while the latter was "very indifferent about the public good, ardent to please all societies where his taste and fortune throw him and ready to sacrifice any scruple. He loves no one and is beloved by no one at all, pleases everyone, and is often despised and sought out by the same people" (Duclos, *Considérations sur les mœurs de ce siècle*, 122). See also Jean-Francois Marmontel, *Les Contes moraux* (Liège, 1780), 3: 25.

89 Gracian Baltasar, *L'homme de cour* (Châtenay-Malabry: Editions de Kerdraon, 1989), 161.

90 The story of the forced marriage appears in Le Sage's *Le diable boîteux*. Alain René Le Sage, *Le diable boîteux*, in *Romanciers du 18e siècle*, ed. René Etiemble (Paris: Gallimard, 1960), 1: 377. Du Fresny served as editor of *Le Mercure galant* from 1710 to 1713 and again from 1721 to 1724.

91 Charles Du Fresny, *Amusemens sérieux et comiques* (Paris: C. Barbin, 1699), 170–73.

92 Du Fresny, *Amusemens sérieux et comiques*, 226.

93 Du Fresny, *Amusemens sérieux et comiques*, 227–28.

94 La Bruyère, *Les caractères ou les moeurs de ce siècle*, 392.

95 La Bruyère, *Les caractères ou les moeurs de ce siècle*, 265.

96 François de Salignac de la Mothe-Fénélon, *Examen de conscience sur les devoirs de la royauté: Mémoires pour le duc de Bourgogne*, in *Lettre à Louis XIV* (Neuchâtel: Ides et Calendes, 1961), 123.

97 Charles de Fieux de Mouhy, *Les Mille et une faveurs* (London, 1740), 7: 11.

98 On the evolution of elite masculinity in the eighteenth century, see Anne C. Vila, "Elite Masculinities in the Eighteenth-Century," in *French Masculinities: History, Culture and Politics*, ed. Christopher E. Forth and Bertrand Taithe (New York: Palgrave Macmillan, 2007), 15–30.

99 See the recent English translation, Charles Pinot Duclos, *Two French Libertine Novels: "The Story of Madame de Luz" and "The Confessions of the Comte de ***,"* trans. Douglas Parmée (Brooklyn, NY: AMS Press, 2006).

100 On reading the libertine novel, see Pierre Serna, "Antonelle, bonnet rouge, talons rouges, de l'aristocratie des Lumières au penseur de la démocratie representative, ou le double statut en Révolution," *Annales historiques de la Révolution française* 301

(1995): 459. See also the important recent studies on *libertinage*: Michel Delon, *Le Savoir-vivre libertin* (Paris: Hachette Littératures, 2000); and Marc André Bernier, *Libertinage et figure du savoir: Rhétorique et roman libertin dans la France des Lumières (1734–1751)* (Québec: Les Presses de l'Universitée Laval/L'Harmattan, 2001).

101 Claude-Prosper Jolyot de Crébillon, *Les égarements du cœur et de l'esprit*, in *Romanciers du 18ᵉ siècle*, ed. René Etiemble (Paris: Gallimard, 1965), 2: 151–52.

102 Crébillon, *Les égarements du cœur et de l'esprit*, 152.

103 Claude Prosper Jolyot de Crébillon, *La nuit et le moment ou les matins de Cythère, dialogue* (1755; Paris: Les Editions Desjonquères, 1983), 94.

104 For an interesting interpretation of affinities between gambling and libertinage, see Thomas Kavanagh, "The Libertine's Bluff: Cards and Culture in Eighteenth-Century France," *Eighteenth-Century Studies* 33, no. 4 (summer 2000): 505–21.

105 Michel Marescot, *La folie du jour ou la promenade des boulevards* (1754), 1; cited in Journeaux, "L'entrée dans le monde," 274.

106 Marie Françoise Abeille, madame de Keralio, *Les succès d'un fat, nouvelle*, 135–38; cited in Journeaux, "L'entrée dans le monde," 279.

107 Philippe-Auguste de Sainte Foy, chevalier d'Arcq, *Le Roman du jour: pour servir à l'histoire du siècle*, vol. 1 (Amsterdam: Van Harrevelt, 1755), 7–8.

108 Anne-Thérèse de Maguenat de Lambert, *Réflexions nouvelles sur les femmes*, ed. Milagros Palma (1727; Paris: Côté femmes, 1989), 195. Lambert did not intend the work for publication and attempted to prevent the circulation of the edition published without her knowledge.

109 Madame de (Madeleine) Puisieux, *Les caractères seconde partie* (London, 1751). Puisieux was author of two early feminist works, *La Femme n'est pas inférieure à l'homme* (1750) and *Le Triomphe des dames* (1751); she was also Diderot's lover and literary collaborator from 1745 to 1750. She is not the same woman as the Madame de Puysieux of Saint-Simon's acquaintance, described above.

110 Louis de Boissy, *Les Dehors Trompeurs ou l'homme du jour* (Paris: Chez Prault, 1746), 58.

111 *Laïs et Phriné, poème en quatre chants* (Paris: Chez Panckoucke, 1767), 79. The names Läis and Phriné were commonly used in poetry to refer to courtesans, based on classical examples.

112 Antoine Alexandre Henri Poinsinet, *Le cercle, ou la soirée à la mode* (London, 1785), 11. Poinsinet was a librettist for the nouvelle Comédie-Italienne. He was best known for his collaboration with the composer François-André Danican Philidor.

113 The ARTFL database (which contains three thousand published works from the Middle Ages to the late twentieth century) contains thirteen uses of the term *homme à la mode* from 1700 to 1749 and the same number between 1750 and 1799, compared to only two references to *femme à la mode* from 1700 to 1749 and seven from 1750 to 1799 (ARTFL database search performed February 6, 2012). A database containing works in French published in Britain during the eighteenth century shows eighteen works containing the phrase *femme à la mode*, all from after 1750, versus forty-seven texts with *homme à la mode*, almost all post-1750 (search of *Eighteenth-Century Collections Online* performed February 6, 2012). A search of Google Books reveals the following breakdown (search performed February 6, 2012):

DATES OF PUBLICATION	PUBLICATIONS CONTAINING *HOMME À LA MODE*	PUBLICATIONS CONTAINING *FEMME À LA MODE*
1650–1699	34	1
1700–1749	297	17
1750–1799	1,380	351
1800–1849	4,380	2,450
1850–1899	5,540	4,800
1900–1959	1,630	1,260

Each of these databases represents its own issues of representativity and incompleteness. For example, with the exception of ARTFL, they contain multiple editions of many works. Despite their varied drawbacks, the search findings suggest that the cultural currency of the man of fashion was greater than that of the woman of fashion, although the latter seems to have grown in relative importance over the nineteenth century.

114 Stéphanie Félicité, comtesse de Genlis, *Les Petits émigrés ou correspondance de quelques enfans* (London, 1799), 2: 383–84.

115 The ARTFL database has forty-seven uses of the term *femme à la mode* from 1800 to 1849 and twenty-four from 1850 to 1899, compared to forty-two for *homme à la mode* from 1800 to 1849 and fourteen from 1850 to 1899 (ARTFL database search performed February 6, 2012). The top user of *femme à la mode* in the database was Balzac, who used the term twenty-nine times in eighteen different works; he was the second most frequent user of *homme à la mode*, with eight mentions in four different works. The top user of the phrase was Charles Pinot Duclos, at ten references in three publications.

116 Honoré de Balzac, *L'Interdiction* (Paris: Furne, Dubochet et Cie, 1844), 125–26. In his later work *Splendeurs et misères des courtisanes*, we learn that the marquise's lawsuit failed and she was reprimanded by the court. For another contemporary portrait of this type, see Marguerite-Louise Virginie Ancelot, "Une Femme à la mode," in *Les Français peints par eux-mêmes: Encyclopédie morale du dix-neuvième siècle* (Paris: L. Curmer, 1841), 1: 59–65. The book was a collection of character types inspired by La Bruyère. Balzac contributed the essay "Une Femme comme-il-faut" to the same collection.

Chapter 4: Credit in the Fashion Trades of Eighteenth-Century Paris

1 Florent Carton Dancourt, *Les Bourgeoises à la mode* (Paris: T. Guillain, 1693), 18.

2 On credit in eighteenth-century France, see Thomas Luckett, "Credit and Commercial Society in France, 1740–1789" (PhD diss., Princeton University, 1992); Philip T. Hoffman, Gilles Postel-Vinay, and Jean-Laurent Rosenthal, *Priceless Markets: The Political Economy of Credit in Paris, 1660–1870* (Chicago: University of Chicago Press, 2000); "Information and Economic History: How the Credit Market in Old Regime Paris Forces Us to Rethink the Transition to Capitalism," *American Historical Review* 104, no. 1 (1999): 69–94; "Economie et politique: les

marchés du crédit à Paris, 1750–1840," *Annales: Histoire, Sciences Sociales* 49, no. 1 (1994): 64–98; and "Private Credit Markets in Paris, 1690–1840," *Journal of Economic History* 52, no. 2 (1992): 293–306; and Natacha Coquery, *Tenir boutique à Paris au XVIIIe siècle. Luxe et demi-luxe* (Paris: CTHS, 2011). For a European-wide perspective, see Laurence Fontaine, *L'économie morale: Pauvreté, credit et confiance dans l'Europe préindustrielle* (Paris: Gallimard, 2008) and Fontaine et al., eds., *Des personnes aux institutions: Réseaux et culture du crédit du XVIe au XXe siècles* (Louvain-la-Neuve: Académie Bruylant, 1996). On merchants and reputation, see, for example, the work of Craig Muldrew, *The Economy of Obligation: The Culture of Credit and Social Relations in Early Modern England* (New York: St. Martin's, 1998), on early modern English merchants and their cultivation of a reputation for integrity as well as Laurence Fontaine's argument in *L'économie morale* that merchants' *crédit*, was substantively different than that of nobles, the former being concerned with hard work and honesty, while the latter derived from aristocratic rank and ostentatious display.

3 On fashion merchants and their midcentury origins, see Michelle Sapori, *Rose Bertin: Ministre de modes de Marie-Antoinette* (Paris: Editions du Regard, 2003), 28; and Jennifer Jones, *Sexing la Mode: Gender, Fashion, and Commercial Culture in Old Regime France* (New York: Berg, 2004), 91–96.

4 Carolyn Sargentson, *Merchants and Luxury Markets: The Marchands Merciers of Eighteenth-Century Paris* (London: Victoria and Albert Museum, 1996), 11.

5 On the Parisian garment trades, see Daniel Roche, *The Culture of Clothing: Dress and Fashion in the Ancien Régime*, trans. Jean Birrell (Cambridge: Cambridge University Press, 1994); Madeleine Delpierre, *La Mode et ses métiers du XVIIIe siècle a nos jours, 6 mars-31 octobre 1981, Ville de Paris, Musée de la mode et du costume* (Paris: Palais Galliéra, 1981), 247–92; Jones, *Sexing la Mode*, chap. 3; Judith Coffin, *The Politics of Women's Work: The Paris Garment Trades, 1750-1915* (Princeton, NJ: Princeton University Press, 1996), chap. 1; and Clare Haru Crowston, *Fabricating Women: The Seamstresses of Old Regime France, 1675-1791* (Durham, NC: Duke University Press, 2001), chap. 2. William Sewell's "The Empire of Fashion and the Rise of Capitalism in Eighteenth-Century France," *Past and Present* 206, no. 1 (February 2010): 81–120, synthesizes much of the literature on the production of textiles and the rise of fashionable consumption in the eighteenth century to argue for a "design-intensive consumer capitalism" (117) that preceded industrial capitalism.

6 See Crowston, *Fabricating Women*, chap. 4.

7 See Daryl Hafter, *Women at Work in Preindustrial France* (University Park: Pennsylvania State University Press, 2007); Janine Lanza, *From Wives to Widows in Early Modern Paris: Gender, Economy, and Law* (Aldershot: Ashgate, 2007), chap. 1; and Clare Haru Crowston, "Family Affairs, Wives, Credit, Consumption and the Law in Old Regime France," in *Family, Gender, and Law in Early Modern France*, ed. Suzanne Desan and Jeffrey Merrick (University Park: Pennsylvania State University Press, 2009), 62–100.

8 See Clare Haru Crowston, "An Industrious Revolution in Late Seventeenth-Century Paris: New Vocational Training for Adolescent Girls and the Creation of Female Labor Markets," in *Secret Gardens, Satanic Mills: Placing Girls in Modern*

European History, ed. M. J. Maynes, Birgitte Soland, and Christina Benninghaus (Bloomington: Indiana University Press, 2005), 69–82.

9 See Daniel Roche, *A History of Everyday Things: The Birth of Consumption in France*, trans. Brian Pearce (Cambridge: Cambridge University Press, 2000). Cissie Fairchilds also discusses a growth in populuxe fashions in home furnishings such as window curtains, mirrors, bookcases, clocks, and items for drinking tea, coffee, and cocoa in "Marketing the Counter-Reformation, Religious Objects and Consumerism in Early Modern France," in *Visions and Revisions of Eighteenth-Century France*, ed. Christine Adams et al. (University Park: Pennsylvania State University Press, 1997), 31–58. She used probate inventories to establish that households she studied between 1771 and 1789 possessed such goods. On the consumer revolution in England, see Neil McKendrick, John Brewer, and J. H. Plumb, eds., *The Birth of a Consumer Society: The Commercialization of Eighteenth-Century England* (Bloomington: Indiana University Press, 1982); John Brewer and Roy Porter, eds., *Consumption and the World of Goods* (London: Routledge, 1993); Cary Carson, Ronald Hoffman, and Peter J. Albert, eds., *Of Consuming Interests: The Style of Life in the Eighteenth Century* (Charlottesville: University of Virginia Press, 1994); and Beverly Lemire, *Fashion's Favourite: The Cotton Trade and the Consumer in Britain, 1660–1800* (Oxford: Oxford University Press, 1991), 228–49.

10 Cissie Fairchilds, "The Production and Marketing of Populuxe Goods in Eighteenth-Century Paris," in *Consumption and the World of Goods*, ed. John Brewer and Roy Porter (London: Routledge, 1993), 228–60.

11 The expansion of female rural industry, both cottage and large-scale, contributed to a growth in production of fabric and lowered its cost to consumers. See Guillaume Dadin, *Commerce et prospérité: La France au XVIIIe siècle.* (Paris: Presses de l'université de Paris-Sorbonne, 2005), 27–34; and Philippe Minard, *La Fortune du colbertisme: Etat et industrie dans la France des Lumières* (Paris: Fayard, 1998).

12 This development derived from the removal of government bans on imported cotton in 1759, which resulted in a vast expansion of cotton manufacture in subsequent decades. The new emphasis on natural and comfortable forms of living encouraged by Enlightenment writers helped popularize the new fabrics. On the success of the Oberkampf cotton manufacture in the second half of the eighteenth century, which became the leader in new techniques for high-quality printed cotton fabrics, see Serge Chassagne, *Oberkampf, un entrepreneur capitaliste au siècle des Lumières* (Paris: Aubier-Montaigne, 1980). On changing modes of consumption and production, see Michael Kwass, "Big Hair: A Wig History of Consumption in Eighteenth-Century France," *American Historical Review* 111, no. 3 (2006): 631–59; and Carlo Poni, "Fashion as Flexible Production: The Strategies of the Lyons Silk Merchants in the Eighteenth Century," in *World of Possibilities: Flexibility and Mass Production in Western Industrialization*, ed. Charles F. Sabel and Jonathan Zeitlin (Cambridge: Cambridge University Press, 1997), 37–74. Poni describes the crisis in the Lyons silk industry in the 1780s produced by the shift to cotton.

13 Albane Forestier notes that in 1788, there were 3,097 indigo estates and 705 cotton estates on Saint-Domingue in addition to sugar and coffee plantations. See Albane

Forestier, "A 'Considerable Credit' in the Late Eighteenth-Century French West Indian Trade: The Chaurands of Nantes," *French History* 25, no. 1 (2011): 51. See also Jean Tarrade, *Le Commerce colonial de la France à la fin de l'Ancien Régime* (Paris: Presses universitaires de France, 1972), 45, 48.

14 Her career in those decades is documented in bills she submitted to Madame de Bercy, held at the Musée Galliera, see below. It is unknown when she began and ceased working in the trade.

15 Anne-Claude-Philippe, comte de Caylus, *Histoire de Guillaume Cocher*, in *Oeuvres badines complètes* (Paris: Vissem, 1787), 10: 36.

16 *Annonces, affiches et avis divers* (Paris: Bureau d'adresse et de rencontre, 1755), 460.

17 *Annonces, affiches et avis divers*, 644.

18 *Encyclopédie*, vol. 10, 598.

19 See François-Alexandre-Pierre de Garsault, *L'Art du tailleur* (Paris: Imprimerie Delatour, 1769), 54–56; and Abbé Pierre Jaubert, *Dictionnaire raisonné universel des arts et métiers, contenant l'histoire, la description, la police des fabriques et manufactures de France et des pays étrangers* (Paris: P. F. Didot, jeune, 1773), 3: 93. Garsault credits a Mademoiselle Alexandre, "one of the most employed in her talent," with explaining the construction of the mantle and other robes belonging to the trade for which he provides instructions in the book.

20 See Crowston, *Fabricating Women*, chap. 4.

21 AN MC ET XLVI 384, April 8, 1761. These documents indicate that the trade was sufficiently established and recognized by 1751 to have developed institutionalized training arrangements, although training regulated by notarial contract appears to have been rare. Exhaustive indexes of the notarial archives for 1751 and 1761 turned up only these examples.

22 AN Y9390, February 5, 1762. Moiny supplied livestock to feed the household of the bishop of Paris. The document does not specify whether the contract included lodging and other services in addition to training.

23 AN MC ET XLVI 388, April 25, 1762. The daughter's age was not given, but she was declared to be a legal major, that is, at least twenty-five years old.

24 Archives de la Seine D4B6, c. 18, d. 865. Dossier of Marie Denise Prévost in 1758.

25 Archives de Paris D4B6, c. 65 d. 4204. Dossier Marie Anne Defrenay.

26 AN Y 11942, July 1, 1758.

27 AN Y 11942, July 3, 1758.

28 The plumassiers were estimated by Savary to number twenty-four masters in 1750, according to René de Lespinasse, *Les métiers et corporations de la ville de Paris: XIVe-XVIIIe siècles* (Paris: Imprimerie nationale, 1897), 3: 297. On the strife-ridden process of first abolishing and then thoroughly renovating and recasting the guild system, see Steven L. Kaplan, *La fin des corporations* (Paris: Fayard, 2001); and Daryl Hafter, *Women at Work*, chap. 4.

29 AN A.D. XI 25. Arrêt du conseil d'état du roi, July 4, 1777.

30 AN V7 435.

31 Mathurin Rose de Chantoiseau, *Essai sur l'almanach général d'indication d'adresse personnelle et domicile fixe, des six corps, arts et métiers* (Paris: Chez la veuve Duchesne, chez Dessain, chez Lacombe, 1769).

32　*Almanach du commerce et de toutes les adresses de la ville de Paris* (Paris: Duchesne, 1798–1798), 265–66.

33　*Almanach du commerce de Paris, des départements de l'Empire français et des principales villes du monde* (Paris: Chez J. de la Tynna, 1809).

34　See Jean-Jacques Carré, Paul Dubois, and Edmond Malinvaud, *French Economic Growth*, trans. John P. Hatfield (Palo Alto, CA: Stanford University Press, 1975), 12.

35　On this shift from a fashion system whose purpose was to display rank and status to one that focused on individual women's taste and elegance, see Jones, *Sexing la Mode*, 182–83. I differ from Jones only in seeing the "feminization" of fashion that she describes as being much less thorough and far-reaching. Jones's argument is based primarily on her reading of *Le Cabinet des modes*. Its editors strove to present philosophical explanations for fashion, which included drawing on then current ideas, influenced by Rousseau, about women's innate capacity for capriciousness and folly and their essentialist drive for seductive display. A broader reading of reports on fashion in the periodical press presents a less "gendered" image of fashion. To be sure, images of women's garments and accessories predominate but there is no sense that men are exempt from fashion or that worldly men should not be aware of the latest fashions in both male and female attire. Moreover, the journals presumably intended their extensive material on carriages and harnesses for a male audience and presented the many items of "fashionable" furniture and household decoration in a gender-neutral manner. This finding is consonant with Daniel Roche's finding, discussed above, that noblemen continued to consume clothing on a par with noblewomen.

36　Louis-Sébastien Mercier, *Le Tableau de Paris*, ed. Jean-Claude Bonnet, vol. 1 (Paris: Mercure de France, 1994), "Marchandes de Modes," 409.

37　*Journal de Commerce et d'agriculture* (Bruxelles: Chez P. de Bast, 1761), 139–40. On the editor, see "Jacques Accarias de Sérionne, économiste et publiciste français au service des Pays-Bas autrichiens," *Etudes sur le XVIIIe siècle* (Bruxelles, 1974), 159–70. Parts of this article were reprinted in the 1765 edition of Jacques Savary des Bruslons, *Dictionnaire universel de commerce, d'histoire naturelle et des arts et métiers* (Copenhagen: Chez Claude Philibert, 1759–65), 5: 280–281.

38　*Journal de commerce et d'agriculture* (October 1761): 142–43.

39　*Journal de commerce et d'agriculture* (October 1761): 143.

40　*Journal de commerce et d'agriculture* (October 1761): 143–44. Testimony to the European-wide empire of Paris over fashion appears in numerous sources. One example is Carlo Poni's research on the complaints of silk producers in the Netherlands, England, and Italy about the dominance of French silks. See Poni, "Fashion as Flexible Production," 42–45. Poni also discusses the strategies of foreign silk manufacturers to imitate and steal French silk designs.

41　*Journal de commerce et d'agriculture* (October 1761): 144.

42　*Journal de commerce et d'agriculture* (October 1761): 141.

43　Jacques Savary, *Le Parfait négociant ou instruction générale pour ce qui regarde le commerce des marchandises de France et des pays estrangers* (Paris: L. Billaine, 1675), 117.

44　*Journal de commerce et d'agriculture* (October 1761): 142.

45 Under the editorship of Antoine de la Roque, *Le Mercure de France*, as he renamed it, published only six articles on fashion. See Reed Benhamou, "Fashion in the 'Mercure': From Human Foible to Female Failing," *Eighteenth-Century Studies* 31, no. 1 (fall 1997): 27–28.

46 Annemarie Kleinert, *Die Frühen Modejournale in Frankreich. Studien zur Literature der Mode von den Anfangen bis 1848* (Berlin: E. Schmidt, 1980), 60–61.

47 *Correspondance littéraire, philosophique et critique de Grimm et de Diderot*, ed. Jules-Antoine Taschereau, vol. 5 (Paris: Furne, 1829–31), April 1768, 400–401.

48 On the fashion press, see Jones, *Sexing la Mode*, esp. chap. 6, "Selling a la Mode"; and Kleinert, *Die frühen Modejournale in Frankreich*. Both Kleinert and Jones focus almost exclusively on the *Cabinet des modes* and its successors; neither discusses the *Courrier de la mode* or coverage of fashion in the nonspecialized press. On the periodical press in general, see Claude Bellanger et al., *Histoire générale de la presse françcaise*, vol. 1, *Des origines à 1814* (Paris: Presses Universitaires de France, 1969); and Jack R. Censer and Jeremy D. Popkin, eds., *Press and Politics in Pre-Revolutionary France* (Berkeley: University of California Press, 1987).

49 A selection of these prints is reproduced in Stella Blum, ed., *Eighteenth-Century French Fashions in Full Color* (New York: Dover Publications, 1982).

50 *Spectator*, no. 277, January 17, 1711 (Dublin, 1755), 4: 105.

51 *Correspondance littéraire, philosophique et critique de Grimm et de Diderot*, vol. 5, March 1766, 23. On the dolls, see Joan DeJean, *The Essence of Style: How the French Invented High Fashion, Fine Food, Chic Cafés, Style, Sophistication, and Glamour* (New York: Free Press, 2005), 63–67. The Musée de la Poupée in Paris and the Victoria and Albert Museum in London possess collections of eighteenth- and nineteenth-century fashion dolls.

52 Mercier, *Le Tableau de Paris*, vol. 1, "Marchandes de Modes," chap. 173, 21.

53 Caroline Weber, *Queen of Fashion: What Marie Antoinette Wore to the Revolution* (New York: Henry Holt, 2006), 121.

54 *La Feuille nécessaire*, no. 5, Monday, March 12, 1759, 72.

55 *La Feuille nécessaire*, no. 33, Monday, September 24, 1759, 526.

56 See, for example, *Journal des dames*, October 1761, vol. 3 (The Hague, 1761), viii.

57 *Journal des dames*, November 1761, 191. Nina Rattner Gelbart argues that overall the *Journal des dames* displayed less interest in fashion than other contemporary periodicals; its editors—especially the succession of three female editors who ran the journal from October 1761 to April 1775—were determined to steer female readers toward more serious topics. See Nina Rattner Gelbart, *Feminine and Opposition Journalism in Old Regime France: Le Journal des dames* (Berkeley: University of California Press, 1987). Other important studies of the feminine press are Evelyne Sullerot, *Histoire de la presse féminine des origines à 1848* (Paris: Armand Colin, 1966); Suzanne Van Dijk, "Femmes et journaux au XVIIIe siècle," *Australian Journal of French Studies* 18, no. 2 (1982): 164–78.

58 Article reprinted in *L'esprit des journaux, françois et étrangers* (Paris: Chez Valade, 1778), January 1778, 345.

59 *Le Cabinet des modes*, 2e cahier, December 11, 1788, 9.

60 *La Feuille sans titre*, no. 63, Friday, April 4, 1777, 251.

61 *Journal de Paris*, no. 129, Sunday, May 9, 1779, 519.

62 *Journal de Paris*, no. 186, Tuesday, July 4, 1780, 759.

63 *Supplément au Journal de Paris*, no. 13, Tuesday, March 2, 1790, iii.

64 *La Feuille sans titre*, no. 54, Wednesday, March 26, 1777, 1, "Epitre à Beaulard."

65 See *Cabinet des modes*, 21e cahier, June 10, 1788, 162; 32e cahier, September 30, 1788, 251.

66 *La Feuille sans titre*, no. 15, Saturday, February 15, 1777, 9–60.

67 *La Feuille sans titre*, no. 263, Tuesday, October 21, 1777, 325.

68 See, for example, *General Evening Post*, Issue 8553, September 9, 1788 — September 11, 1788 and *World*, Issue 531, Wednesday, September 10, 1788.

69 *Magasin des modes nouvelles françaises et anglaises*, 3e année, 28e cahier, August 20, 1788 and 29e cahier, August 30, 1788.

70 *Magasin des modes nouvelles françaises et anglaises*, 3e année, 30e cahier, September 10, 1788.

71 Savary des Bruslons, *Dictionnaire universel de commerce*, 2: 80.

72 For one example of a partisan of luxury and the role of commerce in French society, see Coyer's *La noblesse commerçante*, published in 1756, which argued that nobles should be encouraged to engage in trade. His treatise brought a vociferous attack from the chevalier d'Arcq in the form of *La noblesse militaire, ou le patriote françois*. D'Arcq argued that Coyer's propositions would disastrously undermine the honor and military vocation of the nobility. A vigorous print debate followed. See Jay Smith, "Social Categories, the Language of Patriotism, and the Origins of the French Revolution: The Debate over *Noblesse Commerçante*," *Journal of Modern History* 72, no. 2 (2000): 339–74; John Shovlin, *The Political Economy of Virtue: Luxury, Patriotism and the Origins of the French Revolution* (Ithaca, NY: Cornell University Press, 2006), 58–65.

73 *La Feuille sans titre*, no. 15, Saturday, February 15, 1777, 59.

74 Mathieu François Pidansat de Mairobert, *Anecdotes sur M. la Comtesse Du Barri* (London, 1775), 14.

75 Crowston, *Fabricating Women*, 106–10. On prostitution in the garment trades, see also Erica-Maria Benabou, *La prostitution et la police des mœurs* (Paris: Perrin, 1987); and Nina Kushner, "Unkept Women: Elite Prostitution in Eighteenth-Century Paris, 1747–1771" (PhD diss., Columbia University, 2005).

76 Savary, *Le Parfait négociant*, 114.

77 Muldrew, *The Economy of Obligation*, 96.

78 Thomas Luckett, "Credit and Commercial Society in France, 1740–1789," 7.

79 For credit practices in specific trades, see Carolyn Sargentson, *Merchants and Luxury Markets: The Marchands merciers of Eighteenth-Century Paris* (London: Victoria and Albert Museum, 1996), 26–33; Steven L. Kaplan, *The Bakers of Paris and the Bread Question, 1700–1755* (Durham, NC: Duke University Press, 1996), 137–51, 377–99; Natacha Coquery, *Tenir boutique à Pais au XVIIIe siècle. Luxe et demi-luxe* (Paris: CTHS, 2011); Laurence Fontaine, *Histoire du colportage en Europe (XVe-XIXe siècle)* (Paris: Albin Michel, 1993); and Crowston, *Fabricating Women*.

80 Kaplan, *The Bakers of Paris and the Bread Question*, 377, 150.

81 Steven L. Kaplan, *Provisioning Paris: Merchants and Millers in the Grain and Flour*

Trade During the Eighteenth Century (Ithaca, NY: Cornell University Press, 1984), 147–53.

82 Coquery, *L'Hôtel aristocratique*, 162.

83 Julie Hardwick, *Family Business: Litigation and the Political Economies of Daily Life in Early Modern France* (Oxford: Oxford University Press, 2009), 136.

84 Muldrew, *The Economy of Obligation*, 148. On regulation and its role in generating confidence, see Philippe Minard, *La Fortune du Colbertisme* (Paris: Fayard, 1998).

85 Philip T. Hoffman, *Growth in a Traditional Society: The French Countryside, 1450–1815* (Princeton, NJ: Princeton University Press, 1996), 78.

86 Craig Muldrew makes this point, arguing that a merchant's wealth was equivalent to his creditworthiness, not the value listed in his inventory (*The Economy of Obligation*, 24).

87 In his study of rural land markets in early modern Italy, Giovanni Levi notes that economic insecurity and limited information made building social networks a safer bet for survival than monetary gain. See Giovanni Levi, *Inheriting Power: The Story of an Exorcist*, trans. Lydia Cochrane (Chicago: University of Chicago Press, 1988), 44.

88 Dancourt, *Les Bourgeoises à la mode*, 20–21.

89 Dancourt, *Les Bourgeoises à la mode*, 22–23.

90 Dancourt, *Les Bourgeoises à la mode*, 30–32.

91 On the allegedly scandalous and dishonorable wealth of Gabriel-François Taschereau de Baudry, see René-Louis de Voyer de Paulmy, marquis d' Argenson, *Journal et mémoires du marquis d'Argenson, 1755–1757*, ed. Edmé Jacques Benoît Rathéry, vol. 2 (Paris: Veuve Jules Renouard, 1859), 381. On his hidden fortune, see Charles-Philippe d'Albert, duc de Luynes, *Mémoires du duc de Luynes sur la cour de Louis XV (1735–1758)*, ed. Louis Dussieux and Eudore Soulié (Paris: Firmin-Didot frères, 1860–65), 14: 144. For details on the de Bercy family, see Charles-Henri de Malon, seigneur de Bercy, "Topographie historique de la seigneurie de Bercy," *Bulletin de la Société de l'histoire de Paris et de l'Ile-de-France* 8 (1882): 18.

92 *Encyclopédie*, 7: 518.

93 Musée Galliera, Fonds de Bercy, nos. 6–10.

94 See Crowston, *Fabricating Women*, 148–50.

95 The correspondence of the firm of the silk merchant Jean-François Barbier, who supplied the king and held one million livres of stock in his warehouses, documents the multifaceted interaction among client, textile merchant, and seamstress or tailor and the reliance on correspondence as a way to obtain fabric samples and submit orders. On Barbier's correspondence, see Mary Boyce Schoeser, "The Barbier Manuscripts," *Textile History* 12 (October 1981): 37–58. On the use of letters to transmit orders for cloth and garments, see Amanda Vickery, *The Gentleman's Daughter: Women's Lives in Georgian England* (New Haven, CT: Yale University Press, 1998); and Miles Lambert, "'Sent from Town': Commissioning Clothing in Britain During the Long Eighteenth Century," *Costume* 43 (2009): 66–84. See also the published sample album of Barbara Johnson in Natalie Rothstein, ed., *A Lady of Fashion: Barbara Johnson's Album of Styles and Fabrics* (New York: W. W. Norton, 1987).

96 I calculated the average time lapse between an order and its payment by designating the date when she ordered one or more garments or accessories as one order and then subtracting that day from the day payment was made. It was impossible to be absolutely precise in these calculations because de Bercy often paid a lump sum in partial satisfaction of the account, which did not correspond to the precise amounts charged on any given set of orders. In those cases I calculated as closely as possible which orders would have been covered by a given payment.

97 Natacha Coquery notes that for the wealthiest noble families over one hundred craftsmen and merchants might serve each family merely to supply the needs of their wardrobe (*L'Hotel aristocratique*, 70).

98 Ernest Labrousse, *Esquisse du movement des prix et des revenus en France au XVIIIe siècle* (Paris: Librairie Dalloz, 1933). On the use of credit to purchase luxury goods, see Jean-Yves Grenier, *L'économie d'Ancien régime: Un monde de l'échange et de l'incertitude* (Paris: Albin Michel, 1996), 319.

99 Marginal notes on the bills submitted by Gaillard and other merchants record the reductions imposed. A rare marginal comment explains: "It was demanded by Madamoiselle Gayard three livres, tens sols for making the stomachers, they were only accorded to her at the rate of 30 sols." This represented a reduction of more than half the bill. Note that the document couches her memorandum as a "demand" rather than a straightforward bill for services rendered. Musée Galliera, Fonds de Bercy, no. 47.

100 Musée Galliera, Fonds de Bercy, no. 58.

101 For this graph, I described as one "order," an order de Bercy placed with one merchant or artisan on a given day; this does not refer, therefore, to the numbers of specific items included in an order, which I grouped together. I also aggregated all of the orders for a given month across the period 1732–72, so that the bars on the graph represent the total orders in a given month across the entire period.

102 "Edit du Roy, servant de règlement pour le commerce des marchands & négocians, tant en gros qu'en détail," in *Conférence des ordonnances de Louis XIV*, ed. Philippe Bornier (Paris: Les associez, 1755), 449.

103 "Edit du Roy, servant de règlement pour le commerce des marchands & négocians," 450.

104 "Edit du Roy, servant de règlement pour le commerce des marchands & négocians," 457.

105 "Edit du Roy, servant de règlement pour le commerce des marchands & négocians," 460.

106 The stipulation that the merchant keep his books "himself" may have been intended to require in-house bookkeeping rather than the literal hand of the master, since it was extremely common for merchants to employ clerks or their own wives or other relatives in a small enterprise to keep the accounts.

107 Savary, *Le Parfait négociant*, 252.

108 Bornier, *Conférence des ordonnances de Louis XIV*, 463.

109 Savary, *Le Parfait négociant*, 248.

110 This discussion puts an interesting spin on studies in accounting history that place bookkeeping practices within a Foucauldian perspective of surveillance and

discipline, particularly as exercised by European states over colonial subjects and workers. In this case Savary believed that accounting should function as a disciplining device for merchants themselves, and he feared that recalcitrant subjects would consciously refuse to submit to their own self-discipline. Studies using Foucault's notion of discipline to discuss accounting include Keith W. Hoskin and Richard H. Macve, "Accounting and the Examination: A Genealogy of Disciplinary Power," *Accounting, Organisations and Society* 11, no. 2 (1986): 105–36; Anthony G. Hopwood, "The Archeology of Accounting Systems," *Accounting, Organisations and Society* 12, no. 3 (1987): 207–34; and Peter Miller and Ted O'Leary, "Accounting and the Construction of the Governable Person," *Accounting, Organisations and Society* 12, no. 3 (1987): 235–65.

111 Bornier, *Conférence des ordonnances de Louis XIV*, 444.

112 Women legally separated from their husbands were forbidden from committing acts that would be grossly contrary to their own interests, as conceived by outside authority. On widows, see Lanza, *From Wives to Widows*.

113 Jacques Savary, *Le Parfait négociant ou instruction générale pour ce qui regarde le commerce des marchandises de France et des pays étrangers*, 2nd ed. (Paris: Chez Claude Robustel, 1715), 2: 241.

114 Seventeenth- and eighteenth-century grain merchants lodged formal complaints regarding bakers' abuse of credit, including the practice of obtaining a legal separation from their wives in order to hide resources from their creditors. See Kaplan, *Provisioning Paris*, 149–50. We return to the question of separation of property in chapter 7.

115 On the rise of the novel and its relation to the credit economy, see Margot C. Finn, *The Character of Credit: Personal Debt in English Culture, 1740–1914* (Cambridge: Cambridge University Press, 2003); Michael McKeon, *Origins of the English Novel, 1600–1740* (Baltimore: Johns Hopkins University Press, 1987); Mary Poovey, *Genres of the Credit Economy: Mediating Value in Eighteenth- and Nineteenth-Century Britain* (Chicago: University of Chicago Press, 2008); and Ian Baucom, *Specters of the Atlantic: Finance Capital, Slavery, and the Philosophy of History* (Durham, NC: Duke University Press, 2005).

116 Garsault, *L'Art du tailleur*, 54.

117 Martine Sonnet, *L'Education des filles au temps des Lumières* (Paris: Cerf, 1987).

118 See Clare Haru Crowston, "L'apprentissage hors des corporations. Les formations professionnelles alternatives à Paris sous l'Ancien Régime," *Annales: Histoire, Sciences Sociales* 60, no. 2 (2005): 409–42.

119 On genteel women's household accounts in England, see Amanda Vickery, *The Gentleman's Daughter: Women's Lives in Georgian England* (New Haven: Yale University Press, 1998); as well as an article drawing out the implications of women's bookkeeping for the field of historical accounting, Lina M. Kirkham and Anne Loft, "The Lady and the Accounts: Missing from Accounting History," *Accounting Historians Journal* 28, no. 1 (June 2001): 67–92.

120 Savary, *Le Parfait négociant* (1675), 249–50.

121 Savary, *Le Parfait négociant* (1675), 119. On the role of information for merchants,

see Gilbert Buti and Wolfgang Kaiser, eds., "Moyens, supports et usages de l'information marchande à l'époque moderne," special issue, *Rives méditerranéennes* 27 (2007).

122 Savary, *Le Parfait négociant*, 117. We unfortunately do not have direct records of the speech of retail merchants; however, we do have the fulsome language of advertising from fashion journals of the late eighteenth century like the *Cabinet des modes* as well as the proud statements attributed to Rose Bertin, discussed in chapter 6. On eighteenth-century Parisian advertising, see Colin Jones, "The Great Chain of Buying: Medical Advertisement, the Bourgeois Public Sphere, and the Origins of the French Revolution," *American Historical Review* 101, no. 1 (February 1996): 13–40.

123 See chapter 5 for evidence on this point.

124 Cited in Kimberly Chrisman Campbell, "The Face of Fashion: Milliners in Eighteenth-Century Visual Culture," *Eighteenth-Century Studies* 25, no. 1 (October 2008): 163.

125 On the nascent phenomenon of celebrity in the eighteenth century, see Antoine Lilti, "The Writing of Paranoia: Jean-Jacques Rousseau and the Paradoxes of Celebrity," *Representations* 103 (summer 2008): 53–83.

126 In two notarial documents of 1751 Duchapt named her deceased husband as Martin Arnaud Loysant, merchant and bourgeois de Paris. See AN MC ET XCIII 513, February 9, 1751, a transfer of the lease on a property on the rue de la Monnaie in Paris and AN MC ET XXXIII 509, June 28, 1751, the lifting of a financial claim on Paul Hippolyte de Beauvillier, duc de Saint-Aignans. See another document featuring Duchapt at AN MC ET VIII 114, March 19, 1761, the release of a financial claim on the duc de Chaulnes, perhaps a client.

127 Memoirs cited in Edmond de Goncourt and Jules de Goncourt, *La duchesse de Chateauroux et ses sœurs* (Paris: G. Charpentier, 1879), 73.

128 Voltaire, *Oeuvres complètes de Voltaire* (Paris: Firmin Didot, 1855), 11: 628. In 1756 he noted that his doctor Tronchin had begun performing inoculations and had achieved "more vogue than Duchapt" (Voltaire, *Oeuvres complètes*, 453).

129 Voltaire, *Oeuvres complètes de Voltaire: Correspondance générale* (Paris: Armand-Aubrée, 1930), 9: 192–93. See Serge Chassagne, *Le coton et ses patrons: France 1760–1840* (Paris: Editions de l'École des hautes études en sciences sociales, 1991), 133n176.

130 Jean-Jacques Rousseau, *Emile, ou, de l'éducation*, in *Oeuvres complètes* (Paris: Gallimard, 1969), 4: 714.

131 Jean-Jacques Rousseau, *Les confessions de Jean-Jacques Rousseau* (Paris: Charpentier, 1869), 335.

132 Anne-Gabriel Meusnier de Querlon, *Sainte Nitouche ou histoire galante de la tournière des Carmelites suivie de l'histoire de La Duchapt, célèbre marchande de modes* (London, 1830).

133 In the ranks of the sex trade the shopgirls of fashion merchants often figure higher than female workers for the seamstresses and linen drapers. The former appear in police reports as the kept mistresses of wealthy men they met in their mistresses'

shops, while the latter are more often found in arrests of streetwalkers or in raids on women who received clients in cheap rented rooms. On this point, see Crowston, *Fabricating Women*, 106–10.

Chapter 5: Fashion Merchants: Managing Credit, Narrating Collapse

1 *Journal de Paris*, no. 125, Saturday, May 5, 1781, 505.
2 AP D4B6, c. 83, d. 5564.
3 These documents are held in the INHA manuscript collection in Paris, France.
4 On *faillites* and the frequency of bankruptcy among Parisian retailers, see Steven L. Kaplan, *Provisioning Paris: Merchants and Millers in the Grain and Flour Trade During the Eighteenth Century* (Ithaca, NY: Cornell University, 1984); Natacha Coquery, "Les Faillites boutiquières sous l'Ancien Régime. Une gestion de l'échec mi-juridique mi-pragmatique (fin XVIIe–XVIIIe siècle)," *Revue française de gestion* 34, nos. 188–189 (2008): 341–58; Jean-Clément Martin, "Le commerçant, la faillite et l'historien," *Annales, économies, sociétés, civilisations* (November–December 1980): 1251–66; and Thomas M. Luckett, "Credit and Commercial Society in France, 1740–1789" (PhD diss., Princeton University, 1992), esp. 69–99. The bias of the faillite sources is also partially balanced by the example of Madame de Bercy, a case that did not rely on documents produced by bankruptcy.
5 The *Dictionnaire universel de commerce* of 1723 states of the daily journal that "each item that one enters in this book should be composed of seven parts, which are the date, the debtor, the creditor, the sum, the quantity and kind [of goods], the action or how payable, and the price." Cited in Stanley E. Howard, "Public Rules for Private Accounting in France, 1673 and 1807," in *Accounting in France: Historical Essays / La Comptabilité en France: Etudes historiques*, ed. Yannick Lemarchand and R. H. Parker (New York: Garland, 1996), 96.
6 Pierre Claude Reynard, "The Language of Failure: Bankruptcy in Eighteenth-Century France," *Journal of European Economic History* 30, no. 2 (2001): 365.
7 In their critical account of economic and accounting historiography, Richard Fleischman and Thomas Tyson note that "many historians of accounting believe that entrepreneurs were inattentive to production costs because profit margins were so substantial." See Richard K. Fleischman and Thomas N. Tyson, "Cost Accounting during the Industrial Revolution: The Present State of Historical Knowledge," *Economic History Review* 46, no. 3 (August 1993): 506. They argue, by contrast, that large industrial concerns did practice cost accounting during the late eighteenth century and in some cases as early as the late seventeenth century. Wedgwood, the pioneering ceramics manufacturer, is one example. My argument here is that small firms, like fashion merchants, were inattentive to production costs in spite of low profit margins, not because of them.
8 Jacques Savary, *Le Parfait négociant ou instruction générale pour ce qui regarde le commerce des marchandises de France et des pays etrangers* (Paris: L. Billaine, 1675), 37–38.
9 AP D4B6, c. 18, d. 865.
10 Musée Galliera, Fonds de Bercy, no. 47.

11 Marie-Claire Grassi, *L'art de la lettre au temps de la Nouvelle Héloïse et du romantisme* (Geneva: Slatkine, 1994), 123–25. See also Dena Goodman, "L'ortografe des dames: Gender and Language in the Old Regime," *French Historical Studies* 25, no. 2 (2002): 191–223.

12 See, for example, Natacha Coquery, *Tenir boutique à Paris au XVIIIe siècle: Luxe et demi-luxe* (Paris: CTHS Histoire, 2011). I thus concur with other historians in finding that there was no significant gender differentiation in bookkeeping and credit management among male and female merchants. See Christine Wiskin, "Businesswomen and Financial Management: Three Eighteenth-Century Case Studies," *Accounting, Business & Financial History* 16, no. 2 (July 2006): 143–61.

13 Laurel Thatcher Ulrich, *A Midwife's Tale: The Life of Martha Ballard, Based on her Diary, 1785–1812* (New York: Vintage, 1990).

14 Reynard, "The Language of Failure," 371.

15 On Rose Bertin, two only partially reliable and unevenly documented early twentieth century biographies exist: Emile Langlade, *La marchande de modes de Marie-Antoinette* (Paris: A. Michel, 1911); and Pierre de Nouvion and Emile Liez, *Un Ministre des modes sous Louis XVI: Mademoiselle Bertin, marchande de modes de la reine, 1747–1813* (Paris: Henri Leclerc, 1911). A more reliable and well-researched recent study is Michelle Sapori, *Rose Bertin: Ministre des modes de Marie-Antoinette* (Paris: Editions du Regard, 2003). See also Caroline Weber, *Queen of Fashion: What Marie Antoinette Wore to the Revolution* (New York: Henry Holt, 2006).

16 AN MC ET LXX 845, March 12, 1813.

17 These documents are held in the manuscript collection of the INHA. It is also unknown if the family discarded dossiers of those who did eventually pay, meaning that we are left with only the clients who were most recalcitrant or impoverished in the aftermath of the revolution.

18 Caroline Amelia Smith De Windt, ed., *Journal and correspondence of Miss Adams, Daughter of John Adams, Second President of the United States; Written in France and England in 1785* (New York: Wiley and Putnam, 1841), 54.

19 Natacha Coquery's study of noble consumption patterns confirms that Bertin belonged to the top rank of Parisian luxury merchants. See Natacha Coquery, *L'Hôtel aristocratique: Le marché du luxe à Paris au XVIIIe siècle* (Paris: Publications de la Sorbonne, 1998), 88. Precise accounts of mercantile fortunes for the purposes of comparison are difficult to obtain. Jean-François Barbier, a merchant mercer specializing in silk cloth, went bankrupt in 1762, with four million livres in assets and debts. He was considered to be such a crucial economic actor that the king himself intervened to save the mercer's business. His son, Jean Nicolas Barbier, referenced in chapter 4, continued his father's trade through the revolution. More commonly, Sargentson found wealthy Parisian merchant mercers in partnerships with a combined capital of more than half a million livres. In a single year, between 1792 and 1793, Bertin claimed to have paid four hundred and seventy-five thousand livres to her creditors based on income from her trade. See Carolyn Sargentson, *Merchants and Luxury Markets: The Marchands merciers of Eighteenth-Century Paris* (London: Victoria and Albert Museum, 1996), 30–32; and Lesley Ellis Miller, "Paris-Lyon-Paris: Dialogue in the Design and Distribution of Patterned Silks in the 18th

Century," in *Luxury Trades and Consumerism in Ancien Régime Paris: Studies in the History of the Skilled Workforce*, ed. Robert Fox and Anthony Turner (Aldershot: Ashgate, 1998), 139–67.

20 This was not the case for the French queen, whose wardrobe was supervised by the *dame des Atours*. This position was filled by the Countess Gramont d'Ossun in the last years of the Old Regime.

21 INHA MS1, Marie-Jeanne-Rose Bertin, ff. 2,066–2,163. Bertin's companion was Elisabeth Vechard, a former shopgirl who lived with Bertin from 1777 until the latter's death in 1813. See chapter 6.

22 INHA MS1, Marie-Jeanne-Rose Bertin, f. 222.

23 AN O1 3792.

24 Comte de Reiset, *Modes et usages au temps de Marie-Antoinette. Livre-journal de Madame Eloffe* (Paris: Firmin-Didot, 1885), 2: 511–12, 521–27.

25 Reiset, *Modes et usages*, 2: 513–19.

26 AN F7 5612, f. 103–6.

27 The list also included sums paid for a "voluntary loan" to the nation, for back payments on a house she owned, and for expenses associated with the brief she submitted to protest her inclusion in the list of illegal émigrés in 1793.

28 See AN O1 3792.

29 "Lettres familières du chevalier de l'Isle pendant l'année 1781," *Mercure de France: Série moderne* 69, December 19, 1781, 287.

30 Sapori, *Rose Bertin*, 44.

31 INHA MS1, Marie-Jeanne-Rose Bertin, f. 374.

32 On Bertin's contacts and travels outside Paris, see Kimberly Chrisman Campbell, "Rose Bertin in London?," *Costume* 32 (1998): 47; and Sapori, *Rose Bertin*, 102–35.

33 Cited in Sapori, *Rose Bertin*, 63.

34 Eight doubtless seems like a very small proportion of the over one hundred account books available. My decision to limit the study to this number resulted from the amount of time required to transcribe the details of each transaction—which included the date, type of transaction, client's name, details on the quantities, colors, materials, styles, and so on of the items sold, price, and so forth.

35 Thomas M. Luckett, "The Sale and Business Strategies of a Parisian Artisan, 1754–1764: The Letters and Accounts of N.-C. Flocquet," *Proceedings of the Western Society for French History* 36 (2008): 94. For Duvaux, see Sargentson, *Merchants and Luxury Markets*, 156.

36 French currency in this period was the livre, with twenty sous equaling one livre and twelve deniers equaling one sol. For the purposes of calculation, I converted all figures to a decimal system. In most cases I have rounded up or down to the nearest livre.

37 I eliminated the 1784 portion of her business for this analysis because it was so brief.

38 This estimate is corroborated by her bankruptcy statement of October 24, 1760, in which Cabaille declared 6,736 livres in unpaid accounts dating from February 1753 to March 28, 1760, which would produce a percentage of paid orders of 59 percent based on the orders in her account book.

39 On credit crises, see Thomas M. Luckett and Pierre Lachaler, "Crises financières dans la France du XVIIIe siècle," *Revue d'histoire moderne et contemporaine* 43, no. 2 (April–June 1997): 266–92. These panics testify to the rapid circulation of information within merchant communities in this period.

40 Jean-Yves Grenier has noted that as periods of growth transitioned to stagnation or recession consumers tended to rely on credit to maintain the same level of purchasing, despite the decline of income, a reliance that merchants encouraged in order to move their stock and obtain revenue, if in delayed form. See Jean-Yves Grenier, *L'économie d'Ancien Régime: Un monde de l'échange et de l'incertitude* (Paris: Albin Michel, 1996), 320. On the French economy in the second half of the eighteenth century, see Louis M. Cullen, "History, Economic Crises, and Revolution: Understanding Eighteenth-Century France," *Economic History Review* 46, no. 4 (1993): 635–57. Cullen rejects Ernest Labrousse's claim for deep crisis extending from the 1770s through 1789.

41 For Bernard, AP D4B6 c. 81 d. 5393 and D5B6 1163 and 1463; for Leveque and Boullenois, AP D4B6 8051; I analyzed the journals AP D5B6 230 and 2511.

42 AP D4B6 c. 83 d. 5564 and D5B6 1295; additional registers exist that I did not analyze. Using her daily journal, I calculated her accounts unpaid to have constituted the significantly higher sum of 51,888 livres, up to April 30, 1781. There are several explanations for this discrepancy. It is possible that she did not note all the payments that she received in her journal or that she made efforts to collect debts in the several months leading to her bankruptcy. It is also likely that she only included in her statement the accounts for which she had issued a formal bill and not the current accounts that had not yet been drawn up and submitted.

43 AP D5B6 1295.

44 AP D5B6 230.

45 AP D5B6 1289.

46 On these and other credit instruments, see Luckett, "Credit and Commercial Society in France, 1740–1789," 9–17.

47 Luckett, "Credit and Commercial Society in France, 1740–1789," 28, 35–38. Luckett calculates the implicit interest rates of commercial paper on the basis of their published exchange rates. This may have been the case in discount markets for financial paper, but it seems that shop credit did not carry interest, suggesting a significant discrepancy between these two forms of credit.

48 Robert-Joseph Pothier, *Traité du contrat de vente* (Paris: Chez Debure, 1762), 1: 247.

49 Savary, *Le Parfait négociant*, 58.

50 Savary, *Le Parfait négociant*, 299.

51 Francisco Gómez de Quevedo y Villegas, *Les visions de Dom Francisco de Quevedo Villegat* (Troyes: Veuve de Jaques, 1711), 129.

52 Stephanie Félicité, comtesse de Genlis, *Adèle et Théodore ou Lettres sur l'éducation* (Paris: Chez M. Lambert and F. J. Baudouin, 1782), 231. See chapter 7 for more on Genlis and consumption.

53 AP D4B6 c. 107 d. 7854.

54 For this analysis, we made use of six merchants' account books, with a total of eight account books included: AP D5B6 230 (Leveque and Boullenois); AP D5B6 306

(Bermont); AP D5B6 581 (Lacroix); AP D5B6 1163 and 1463 (Bernard); D5B6 1289 (Gicquel); and AP D5B6 1295 (Moreau).

55 These statistics were generated by the Illinois Statistics Office of the University of Illinois at Urbana-Champaign. The model used for the analysis was: reduction ~ amount owed + client number + title + length of time after owing money.

56 AP D4B6 c. 109 d. 7751.

57 Coquery, *Tenir boutique à Paris au XVIIIe siècle.*

58 Other fashion merchants similarly owed significantly more than they were owed. Bermont owed 6,906 livres more than he was owed, Cabaille owed 2,424 livres in excess of her accounts, Gicquel owed an excess of 21,849 livres, and Lacroix owed 6,028 livres more than her accounts were worth.

59 On the issue of the *fonds de commerce*, see Alessandro Stanziani, "Shopkeepers and the Legal Price of Goodwill: Parisian fonds de commerce in the Nineteenth–Twentieth Century," paper delivered to the conference "Droit et histoire des enterprises, 18e-20e siècles" (Paris, March 23–24, 2007).

60 AP D5B6 1163 or 1463.

61 Craig Muldrew, *The Economy of Obligation: The Culture of Credit and Social Relations in Early Modern England* (New York: St. Martin's, 1998), 95–47. For one study of credit and social networks in eighteenth-century France, see James Livesey, "Les réseaux de credit en Languedoc au XVIIIe siècle et les origines sociales de la Révolution," *Annales historiques de la Révolution française* 359 (January–March 2010): 29–51.

62 AP D5B6 1163 and 1463.

63 AP D6B6 13, August 12, 1782.

64 AP D5B6 c. 65 d. 4204.

65 Natalie Zemon Davis, *Fiction in the Archives: Pardon Tales and Their Tellers in Sixteenth-Century Archives* (Palo Alto, CA: Stanford University Press, 1987). For highly similar narratives among millers, farmers, grain merchants, and bakers, see Steven L. Kaplan, *Provisioning Paris* and *The Bakers of Paris and the Bread Question, 1700-1775* (Durham: NC: Duke University Press, 1996).

66 AP D4B6 c. 51 d. 3157.

67 AP D4B6 c. 18 d. 865.

68 AP D5B6 c. 104 d. 7409.

69 AP D4B6 c. 44 d. 2551.

70 AP D4B6 c. 28 d. 1510. The notary Mathon drew up a formal settlement on October 10, 1761.

Chapter 6: Madame Déficit and Her Minister of Fashion

1 Suzanne Burkard, ed., *Baronne d'Oberkirch, Memoires de la Baronne d'Oberkirch sur la cour de louis XVI et la société française avant 1789* (Paris: Mercure de France, 1989), 187.

2 Emile Langlade, *La Marchande de modes de Marie-Antoinette, Rose Bertin* (Paris: Albin Michel, 1911), 192–93. This tactic may explain Oberkirch's cryptic observation that at the time of her "bankruptcy" Bertin had demonstrated shocking in-

gratitude to the queen, who accordingly refused to receive the fashion merchant the next time she appeared at Versailles. See Burkard, *Baronne d'Oberkirch*, 187.

3 Florimond Claude, comte de Mercy-Argenteau, was born in Belgium; he served as a junior diplomat in France and then as Austrian ambassador in Turin and St. Petersburg before arriving in 1766 as Austrian representative at the court of France, where he remained until 1792. See Théodore Juste, *Le Comte de Mercy-Argenteau* (Bruxelles: A. Lacroix, Verboeckhoven and Co., 1863). On this correspondence, see Larry Wolff, "Habsburg Letters: The Disciplinary Dynamics of Epistolary Narrative in the Correspondence of Maria Theresa and Marie-Antoinette," in *Marie-Antoinette, Writings on the Body of a Queen*, ed. Dena and Thomas Kaiser (New York: Routledge, 2003), 25–42.

4 Alfred von Arneth and Auguste Geoffroy, eds., *Correspondance secrète entre Marie-Thérèse et le comte de Mercy-Argenteau: Avec les lettres de Marie-Thérèse et de Marie-Antoinette* (Paris: Firmin Didot Freres, 1874), 1: 162, Maria Theresa to Mercy-Argenteau from Vienna, December 1, 1770.

5 *Correspondance secrète entre Marie-Thérèse*, 1: 327, Mercy-Argenteau to Maria Theresa, July 18, 1772; 1: 349; Mercy-Argenteau to Maria Theresa, September 16, 1772.

6 *Correspondance secrète entre Marie-Thérèse*, 1: 369; 2: 5, July 17, 1773.

7 *Correspondance secrète entre Marie-Thérèse*, 1: 301–2, Mercy-Argenteau to Maria Theresa, May 15, 1772.

8 *Correspondance secrète entre Marie-Thérèse*, 1: 304.

9 *Correspondance secrète entre Marie-Thérèse*, 2: 22–23, Mercy-Argenteau to Maria Theresa, August 14, 1773.

10 *Correspondance secrète entre Marie-Thérèse*, 2: 147, Mercy-Argenteau to Maria Theresa, May 17, 1774.

11 *Correspondance secrète entre Marie-Thérèse*, 2: 168, note reproduced in letter from Mercy-Argenteau to Maria Theresa, June 7, 1774.

12 *Correspondance secrète entre Marie-Thérèse*, 2: 169.

13 *Correspondance secrète entre Marie-Thérèse*, 2: 185, Mercy-Argenteau to Maria Theresa, June 28, 1774.

14 *Correspondance secrète entre Marie-Thérèse*, 2: 197, Mercy-Argenteau to Maria Theresa, July 15, 1774.

15 *Correspondance secrète entre Marie-Thérèse*, 2: 99, Mercy-Argenteau to Maria Theresa.

16 *Correspondance secrète entre Marie-Thérèse*, 2: 203, Maria Theresa to Mercy-Argenteau, July 16, 1774.

17 Cited in *Correspondance secrète entre Marie-Thérèse*, 1:1, "Introduction."

18 *Correspondance secrète entre Marie-Thérèse*, lii.

19 *Correspondance secrète entre Marie-Thérèse*, lviii.

20 The first full-length study of Marie Antoinette's relationship to clothing is Caroline Weber's *Queen of Fashion: What Marie Antoinette Wore to the Revolution* (New York: Henry Holt, 2006). Most biographies also focus on this question, including Antonia Fraser, *Marie-Antoinette: The Journey* (New York: Random House, 2002).

21 Cited in Weber, *Queen of Fashion*, 4.

22 Cited in Weber, *Queen of Fashion*, 3.

23 François Métra et al., *Correspondance secrète, politique et littéraire ou mémoires pour servir à l'histoire des cours, des sociétés et de la littérature en France* (London: Chez John Adamson, 1787–1790), 179, January 28, 1775. This is a reprint of *Correspondance littéraire secrète*, possibly printed in Paris with a false London imprint.

24 Robert Darnton, "An Early Information Society: News and the Media in Eighteenth-Century Paris," *American Historical Review* 5, no. 1 (February 2000): 1–35.

25 Métra et al., *Correspondance secrète*, 214, February 25, 1775. See Weber on Marie Antoinette's use of headdresses to comment on public affairs (*Queen of Fashion*, 105–7).

26 Métra et al., *Correspondance secrète*, 226–27, November 4, 1775. The *Journal de Paris* and the other periodicals discussed in chapter 4 did not exist in 1775, so it is impossible to gauge whether this interest in the queen's clothing would have been shared by the periodical press, which generally made little reference to court fashions.

27 Jeanne-Louise-Henriette Campan, *Mémoires de Madame Campan. Première femme de chambre de Marie-Antoinette*, ed. Carlos de Angulo (Paris: Mercure de France, 1988), 88–89.

28 Campan, *Mémoires de Madame Campan. Première femme de chambre de Marie-Antoinette*, 91–92.

29 Campan, *Mémoires de Madame Campan. Première femme de chambre de Marie-Antoinette*, 92.

30 Arneth and Geoffroy, *Correspondance secrète entre Marie-Thérèse*, 2: 293, February 4, 1775.

31 Arneth and Geoffroy, *Correspondance secrète entre Marie-Thérèse*, 2: 302, March 4, 1775.

32 Arneth and Geoffroy, *Correspondance secrète entre Marie-Thérèse*, 2: 307, March 17, 1775.

33 Arneth and Geoffroy, *Correspondance secrète entre Marie-Thérèse*, 2: 307–8, March 17, 1775.

34 *Correspondance secrète inédite sur Louis XVI, Marie-Antoinette, la cour et la ville de 1777 à 1792*, ed. Mathurin de Lescure, 2 vols. (Paris: Henri Plon, 1866).

35 Bibliothèque de l'Arsenal MSS 10 128, March 6, 1773. This document states that Bertin's "beau-frère," a Sieur Doudeuil, made the first declaration of the theft on March 3. This archival reference seems to contradict the Baronne d'Oberkirch's later claim that Bertin worked at the "quai de Gèvres" in her early years in Paris.

36 On female honor, see David Garrioch, *Neighbourhood and Community in Paris, 1740–1790* (Cambridge: Cambridge University Press, 2002), 37–40; Laura Gowing, *Domestic Dangers: Women, Words, and Sex in Early Modern London* (Oxford: Oxford University Press, 1999), 50–52, 128–33; Garthine Walker, "Expanding the Boundaries of Female Honour in Early Modern England," *Transactions of the Royal Historical Society* 6th ser., 6 (1996): 235–45.

37 On the circulation of rumor and gossip in late eighteenth-century Paris and their entry into printed literature, see Darnton, "An Early Information Society"; and Jeremy D. Popkin and Bernadette Fort, eds., *The 'Mémoires secrets' and the Culture of Publicity in Eighteenth-Century France* (Oxford: Oxford University Press, 1998).

38 Antoine Lilti, *Le Monde des salons: Sociabilité et mondanité à Paris au XVIIIe siècle* (Paris: Fayard, 2005).

39 Burkard, *Baronne d'Oberkirch*, 45–46.

40 *Mémoires secrets pour servir à l'histoire de la république des lettres en France depuis 1762 jusqu'à nos jours* (London: Chez John Adamson, 1782), 17: 9.

41 See Nouvion and Liez, *Un Ministre des modes sous Louix XVI*, 29–30. The authors quote the *Correspondance secrète* of April 11, 1778.

42 On marketing and publicity among luxury merchants, see Natacha Coquery, *L'Hôtel aristocratique: Le marché du luxe à Paris au XVIIIe siècle* (Paris: Publications de la Sorbonne, 1998), 93–105.

43 Cited in Kimberly Chrisman Campbell, "The Face of Fashion: Milliners in Eighteenth-Century Visual Culture," *British Journal for Eighteenth-Century Studies* 25, no. 2 (2002): 163.

44 On Wedgwood, see Neil McKendrick, John Brewer, and J. H. Plumb, *Birth of a Consumer Society: The Commercialization of Eighteenth-Century England* (Bloomington: Indiana University Press, 1982), chap. 3, "Josiah Wedgwood and the Commercialization of Potteries."

45 On the role of artists, see Lilti, *Le Monde des salons*, 182. On Labille-Guiard, see Laura Auricchio, *Adélaïde Labille-Guiard: Artist in the Age of Revolution* (Los Angeles: J. Paul Getty Museum, 2009).

46 *Mémoires secrets pour servir à l'histoire de la république des lettres en France*, 14: 72, May 31, 1779.

47 *Mémoires secrets pour servir à l'histoire de la république des lettres en France*, 13: 299, March 5, 1779.

48 AP D2U1, September 22, 1813.

49 See *Mémoires secrets pour servir à l'histoire de la république des lettres en France*, 18: 20, September 8, 1781.

50 Lucien Lazard, "Les lettres de ratification hypothécaires, contribution à la topographie historique de Paris et du Département de la Seine," *Bulletin de la société de l'histoire de Paris* 30 (1903): 39.

51 *Mercure de France: Série moderne* 69, "Lettres familières du chevalier de l'Isle pendant l'année 1781," December 19, 1781, 287. De l'Isle was both a military officer and a man of letters, a conservative opponent of the philosophes, and for a time Parisian literary agent of a German prince.

52 INHA MS1, Marie-Jeanne-Rose Bertin, f. 22.

53 AP, Minutes des lettres de ratifications no. 2369, February 23, 1788.

54 AN MC ET LVII 593, April 24, 1789. At the time of her death, Bertin was living principally at her country home outside Paris and her personal apartments in the building had diminished to a living room and her own bedroom on the third floor and a guest suite on the third floor. This information is noted in Bertin's probate inventory at AN MC ET LXX 845, March 12, 1813. The inventory also testifies to Bertin's straitened circumstances at the time of her death, noting, for example, the presence of a receipt from the municipal pawnbroker for a gold watch, in exchange for which Bertin had received 8,050 francs.

55 According to her probate inventory, Bertin did not pay the 50,000 livres until February 28, 1793. AN MC ET LXX 845, March 12, 1813.

56 AN MC ET IX 840, April 11, 1793. For the original loan from Moreau, see MC ET XVI 886, January 28, 1791.

57 AN MC ET IX 842, August 14, 1793.

58 AN series T 1604, no. 53. Bertin's probate inventory refers to a receipt for payment of the 50,000 livres dated February 28, 1793. See AN MC ET LXX 845, March 12, 1813.

59 AN MC ET XII 780, 29 floréal Year 5.

60 As noted in her probate inventory, AN MC ET LXX 845, March 12, 1813.

61 Campan, *Mémoires de Madame de Campan*, note 126: "The most scandalous rumors circulated on the conduct of Marie-Antoinette, who, in December 1775, wrote to her mother: 'We are in an epidemic of satirical songs. . . . As for me, I have not been spared: they have very freely attributed to me the two tastes: that of women and of lovers.' The Abbé Baudeau, in 1774, speaks of rumors on the relations of the Queen with Mesdames Lamballe, de Pecquiny, etc. Soulavie also echoes these reports: 'The queen was very publicly reproached for having morals that history reproaches to several empresses. . . . They also reproach her with secret liaisons with Mademoiselle Bertin, celebrated fashion merchant of the capital and with demoiselles Guimond, Renaud et Gentil."

62 On pornographic libels of Marie Antoinette, see Jacques Revel, "Marie-Antoinette in Her Fictions: The Staging of Hatred," in *Fictions of the French Revolution*, ed. Bernadette Fort (Evanston: Northwestern University Press, 1991), 111–30; Lynn Hunt, "The Many Bodies of Marie Antoinette: Political Pornography and the Problem of the Feminine in the French Revolution," in *Eroticism in the Body Politic* (Baltimore: Johns Hopkins University Press, 1991), 103–89; *The Family Romance of the French Revolution* (Berkeley: University of California Press, 1992); Sarah Maza, *Private Lives and Public Affairs: The Causes Célèbres of Pre-Revolutionary France* (Berkeley: University of California Press, 1993); and Chantal Thomas, *The Wicked Queen: The Origins of the Myth of Marie-Antoinette*, trans. Julie Rose (New York: Zone Books, 1999).

63 Campan, *Mémoires de Madame Campan*, 73.

64 *Correspondance secrète inédite sur Louis XVI*, 1: 330.

65 This is a quotation from Théveneau de Morande, cited in Langlade, *La Marchande de modes de Marie-Antoinette*, 170–71.

66 Théveneau de Morande, cited in Langlade, *La Marchande de modes de Marie-Antoinette*, 168. For the original, see *Correspondance secrète*, February 27, 1785.

67 Burkard, *Baronne d'Oberkirch*, 396.

68 *Correspondance secrète inédite sur Louis XVI*, 2:171.

69 See Hunt, "The Many Bodies of Marie-Antoinette: Political Pornography and the Problem of the Feminine in the French Revolution"; and Jacques Revel, "Marie-Antoinette in Her Fictions."

70 On the Diamond Necklace Affair, see the classic study of Frantz Funck-Brentano, *L'Affaire du collier* (Paris: Hachette, 1901). More recently, Sarah Maza, "The Dia-

mond Necklace Affair Revisited (1785–1786): The Case of the Missing Queen," *Marie-Antoinette: Writings on the Body of a Queen*, 73–98.

Chapter 7: Family Affairs

1 Louis-Sébastien Mercier, *Le Tableau de Paris*, ed. Jean-Claude Bonnet (Paris: Mercure de France, 1994), 1: 796.

2 Pierre Joseph Boudier de Villemert, *L'ami des femmes, ou la philosophie du beau sexe* (London, 1775), 54–55.

3 See, for example, Clare Haru Crowston, *Fabricating Women: The Seamstresses of Old Regime France, 1675–1791* (Durham, NC: Duke University Press, 2001); Jennifer Jones, *Sexing la Mode: Gender, Fashion, and Commercial Culture in Old Regime France* (New York: Berg, 2004); and Judith Coffin, *The Politics of Women's Work: The Paris Garment Trades, 1750–1915* (Princeton, NJ: Princeton University Press, 1996).

4 Daniel Roche, *The Culture of Clothing: Dress and Fashion in the Ancien Régime*, trans. Jean Birrell (Cambridge: Cambridge University Press, 1994).

5 On critiques of luxury in France, see Philippe Perrot, *Le Luxe. Une richesse entre faste et confort (XVIIIe-XIXe siècle)* (Paris: Seuil, 1995); Sarah Maza, "Luxury, Morality, and Social Change: Why There Was No Middle-Class Consciousness in Prerevolutionary France," *Journal of Modern History* 69, no. 2 (June 1997): 199–229; John Shovlin, "The Cultural Politics of Luxury in Eighteenth-Century France," *French Historical Studies* 23, no. 4 (2000): 577–606 and *The Political Economy of Virtue: Luxury, Patriotism and the Origins of the French Revolution* (Ithaca, NY: Cornell University Press, 2006); and Jeremy Jennings, "The Debate about Luxury in Eighteenth- and Nineteenth-Century French Political Thought," *Journal of the History of Ideas* 68, no. 1 (2007): 79–105.

6 Léon Abensour, *La Femme et le féminisme avant la Révolution* (Paris: Ernest Leroux, 1923). On attacks on Marie Antoinette, see Chantal Thomas, *The Wicked Queen: The Origins of the Myth of Marie-Antoinette*, trans. Julie Rose (New York: Zone Books, 1999); Lynn Hunt, "The Many Bodies of Marie-Antoinette: Political Pornography and the Problem of the Feminine in the French Revolution," in *Eroticism and the Body Politic*, ed. Lynn Hunt (Baltimore: Johns Hopkins University Press, 1991), 103–89; Sarah Maza, "The Diamond Necklace Affair Revisited (1785–86): The Case of the Missing Queen," in *Eroticism and the Body Politic*, ed. Lynn Hunt (Baltimore: Johns Hopkins University Press, 1991), 63–89; and Jacques Revel, "Marie-Antoinette in Her Fictions: The Staging of Hatred," in *Fictions of the French Revolution*, ed. Bernadette Fort (Evanston, IL: Northwestern University Press, 1991), 111–30.

7 Sarah Hanley, "Engendering the State: Family Formation and State Building in Early Modern France," *French Historical Studies* 16, no. 1 (spring 1989): 4–27.

8 Philip T. Hoffman, Gilles Postel-Vinay, and Jean-Laurent Rosenthal discuss the importance of single and widowed women's activity as investors in the Parisian credit markets in "Information and Economic History: How the Credit Market in

Old Regime Paris Forces Us to Rethink the Transition to Capitalism," *American Historical Review* 104, no. 1 (February 1999): 89. Other historians have noted the important roles wives could play in administering family fortune. See, for example, Barbara B. Diefendorf, "Women and Property in Ancien Régime France: Theory and Practice in Dauphiné and Paris," in *Early Modern Conceptions of Property*, ed. John Brewer and Susan Staves (New York: Routledge, 1996), 170–93; Sharon Kettering, "The Patronage Power of Early Modern French Noblewomen," *Historical Journal* 32, no. 4 (1989): 817–41; and Daniel Dessert, *Argent, pouvoir et société au grand siècle* (Paris: Fayard, 1984). On widows, see the work of Janine Lanza, *From Wives to Widows in Early Modern Paris: Gender, Economy, and Law* (Aldershot: Ashgate, 2007).

9 Julie Hardwick, *Family Business: Litigation and the Political Economies of Daily Life in Early Modern France* (Oxford: Oxford University Press, 2009).

10 So important, indeed, was debt as a form of inheritance that legal provisions existed to shelter heirs from creditors. When it was clear that debts outweighed the value of the estate, an heir could simply renounce the succession. Alternately, an heir could accept the succession *sous bénéfice d'inventaire*, meaning that he or she was only responsible for debts up to the limit of the value of the estate. See *Encyclopédie ou dictionnaire raisonné des sciences, des arts et métiers*, ed. Denis Diderot and Jean Le Rond d'Alembert (Geneva: Pellet, 1778), "héritier bénéficiare."

11 For discussions of the use of credit to overcome the restrictions of coverture among English historians, see Margot Finn, "Women, Consumption and Coverture in England, c. 1760–1860," *Historical Journal* 39, no. 3 (1996): 702–22; and Joanne Bailey, "Favoured or Oppressed? Married Women, Property and 'Coverture' in England, 1660–1800," *Continuity and Change* 17, no. 3 (2002): 351–72. Another form of debt that married women formed autonomously, as the moralizing literature discussed in this chapter reveals, was gambling. For women as for men, gambling losses were debts of honor and failure to repay them risked extreme social sanction. To date, the link between married women's theoretical legal incapacity and the frequent reports of huge losses by noblewomen at the gambling table has received no attention from historians.

12 This was the case for women who accepted the *communauté de biens* stipulated by the Coûtume de Paris. They could choose to retain financial independence by stipulating in their marriage contracts that there would be no financial community between the spouses, but this was a much less common occurrence.

13 Robert-Joseph Pothier, *Traité de la communauté* (Paris: Frères Debure, 1774), 8. Pothier explains that there is an essential difference between the incapacity of children and women. Because children's incapacity was based on their lack of reason, it was only temporary, lasting until the age of reason. Because wives' incapacity was based on the need for a single family head, it was permanent.

14 *Encyclopédie*, 13: 558, "puissance maritale."

15 Charles Antoine Bourdot de Richebourg, *Le Nouveau coûtumier général* (Paris: Chez Theodore Le Gras, 1724), 10: 45–46, article 223.

16 Bourdot de Richebourg, *Le Nouveau coûtumier général*, 10: 46, article 234.

17 In a sample of seventy seamstress marriage contracts, for example, only four couples married with a separation of goods. The proportion is strikingly low, given that women with autonomous careers might be expected to insist on financial independence more than other women. In the few cases where seamstresses did choose financial separation, the motivation appeared to have been to protect a bride from the financial burden of a husband's children from a previous marriage. See Crowston, *Fabricating Women*, 354.

18 "Edit du Roy, servant de règlement pour le commerce des marchands & négociants, tant en gros qu'en détail," reproduced in Philippe Bornier, ed., *Conférence des ordonnances de Louis XIV* (1694; Paris: Chez les associés choisis par sa Majesté, 1755), 439.

19 Bornier, *Conférence des ordonnances de Louis XIV*, 651.

20 Pothier, *Traité de la communauté*, 20.

21 Pothier, *Traité de la communauté*, 16. As he states, "sales contracts or exchange of an inheritance, borrowing considerable sums, acceptance or refusal of an inheritance bequeathed to the wife, and generally all acts that do not belong to simple administration, the wife, although separated, cannot validly do them without authorization from her husband or the judge."

22 AN Y 11470, March 23, 1754. I have added punctuation for clarity, although the lack of punctuation in the original aptly reflects the state of mind of the witness.

23 AN Y 11470 April 23, 1754.

24 AN Y 11470, March 20, 1754; May 18, 1754.

25 AN Y 11470, May 25, 1754.

26 AN Y 11470, March 20, 1754.

27 AN Y 14803, March 31, 1756.

28 AN Y 13311, November 20, 1784.

29 Insight into Bertin's business-related debts at the time of her departure from France can be found in AN O1 3792; F7 5612; and F7 4596.

30 For laws on the sale of biens nationaux and restitution of émigrés' property, see Marc-Georges Mallet, *La Politique financière des Jacobins* (Paris: A. Rousseau, 1913), and André Gain, *La Restauration et les biens des émigrés: La législation concernant les biens nationaux de seconde origine et son application dans l'Est de la France (1814–1823)*, 2 vols. (Nancy: Société d'impressions typographiques, 1928).

31 Ferrière, *Corps et compilation*, 3: 363.

32 INHA MS1, Marie-Jeanne-Rose Bertin, ff. 1295–97.

33 INHA MS1, MJB, f. 1318.

34 INHA MS1, MJB, f. 1159.

35 INHA MS1, MJB, f. 1442.

36 INHA MS1, MJB, ff. 1010–11.

37 INHA MS1, MJB, ff. 1243–44.

38 Madame de Maintenon, *Conseils et instructions aux demoiselles pour leur conduit dans le monde*, ed. Théophile La Vallée (Paris: Charpentier, 1857), 2: 15, 3e partie.

39 Maintenon, *Conseils et instructions aux demoiselles*, 16.

40 Maintenon, *Conseils et instructions aux demoiselles*, 18. The writings of François de

la Mothe-Fénélon, a close confidante of Madame de Maintenon until his disgrace in 1697, related to female education, echo these concerns. In addition to his condemnation of luxury in the *Adventures of Telemachus*, he also warned of the dangers of female luxury in his writings on female education. For example, he wrote a long letter advising a couple on their daughter's education, urging—among other pieces of advice—that they should make her understand that luxury confuses social conditions and offered a path of social mobility to the low born. The letter is cited in Révérend Père Mercier, *Madame de Maintenon* (Paris: Lecoffre fils et cie, 1874), 204.

41 Suzanne Burkard, ed., *Baronne d'Oberkirch, Mémoires de la Baronne d'Oberkirch sur la cour de Louis XVI et la société française avant 1789* (Paris: Mercure de France, 1989), 75–76.

42 Louise Florence Pétronille Tardieu d'Esclavelles, marquise d'Epinay, *Histoire de Madame de Montbrillant*, ed. Georges Roth (1770; Paris: Gallimard, 1951), 1: 394. On *Histoire de Madame de Montbrillant*, see Cécile Cavillac, "Audaces et inhibitions d'une romancière au XVIIIe siècle: le cas de madame d'Epinay," *Revue d'Histoire Littéraire de la France* 104, no. 4 (2004): 887–904.

43 Shovlin, "The Cultural Politics of Luxury," 605.

44 Joan Landes, *Women and the Public Sphere in the Age of the French Revolution* (Ithaca, NY: Cornell University Press, 1988); Sarah Maza, *Private Lives and Public Affairs: The Causes Célèbres of Pre-Revolutionary France* (Berkeley: University of California Press, 1993); Lynn Hunt, *The Family Romance of the French Revolution* (Berkeley: University of California Press, 1992), chap. 6.

45 Jean-Jacques Rousseau, *Emile, ou, de l'éducation*, in *Oeuvres completes* (Paris: Gallimard, 1969), 4. On Rousseau, see Jennifer Popiel, *Rousseau's Daughters: Domesticity, Education, and Autonomy in Modern France* (Durham: University of New Hampshire Press, 2008). Rousseau echoed this contempt for fashion and finery in his own life; in 1751 upon recovering from a serious illness, he embarked on a future of avowed "independence and poverty." He began by abandoning all fashionable elements of his wardrobe: "I began my reform with my finery. I gave up my gold trimmings and white stockings, I took a short wig. I laid aside my sword. I sold my watch" (cited in Michael Kwass, "Big Hair: A Wig History of Consumption in Eighteenth-Century France," *American Historical Review* 111, no. 3 [2006]: 631).

46 Mercier, *Le Tableau de Paris*, 1: 409.

47 Mercier, *Le Tableau de Paris*, 47–48.

48 Louise Florence Pétronille Tardieu d'Esclavelles, marquise d'Epinay, *Les conversations d'Emilie* (Paris: Humboldt, 1781), 2: 159.

49 Epinay, *Les conversations d'Emilie*, 170.

50 Epinay, *Les conversations d'Emilie*, 198.

51 Stéphanie Félicité, comtesse de Genlis, *Adèle et Théodore ou Lettres sur l'éducation*, vol. 2 (Paris: Chez M. Lambert and F. J. Baudouin, 1782). Genlis's work drew inevitable comparison with the best-known eighteenth-century pedagogical work, Rousseau's *Emile*. Genlis acknowledged she had been criticized for not praising *Emile* adequately. She praised Rousseau's knowledge of children, his brilliance, and

his sincerity, but she found him morally repugnant and recoiled from his "monstrous and disgusting" *Confessions* (vi).

52 Bonnie Arden Robb, "Madame de Maintenon and the Literary Personality of Madame de Genlis: Creating Fictional, Historical, and Narrative Virtue," *Eighteenth-Century Fiction* 7, no. 4 (July 1995): 356. For a more extended discussion of Genlis, see Bonnie Arden Robb, *Félicité de Genlis: Motherhood in the Margins* (Cranbury, NJ: Associated University Presses, 2008). Genlis wrote a novel about Madame de Maintenon in 1806 in which she presents the founder of Saint-Cyr as a "glorious model of virtue."

53 Genlis, *Adèle et Théodore*, 2: 232–33.

54 Genlis, "Les Dangers du monde," in *Théâtre à l'usage des jeunes personnes*, 4 vols. (Dublin: Luc White, 1781), 1.

55 Genlis, "Les Dangers du monde," 273.

56 Félicité de Choiseul-Meuse, *Récréations morales et amusantes, à l'usage des jeunes demoiselles qui entrent dans le monde* (Paris: F. Eymery, 1817), 70–71.

57 Choiseul-Meuse, *Récréations morales et amusantes*, 73.

58 Lesley H. Walker, "Producing Feminine Virtue: Strategies of Terror in Writings by Madame de Genlis," *Tulsa Studies in Women's Literature* 23 (2004): 224.

59 The Baronne d'Almane criticizes Rousseau's desire to retain girls' natural instinct for cunning—which he thought would help them win over the men on whom their lives depended—and insists that "there is nothing reliable but the constant usage of virtue." If marriage is women's destiny, virtuous and frank conduct is the only way for wives to earn the respect of worthy husbands (Genlis, *Adèle et Théodore*, 1: 41).

60 Margaret Darrow, "French Noblewomen and the New Domesticity," *Feminist Studies* 5 (1979): 41–65.

61 Denise Yim, "*Adèle et Théodore*'s Influence on an English Family's Education," *Australian Journal of French Studies* 38 (2001): 141–57.

62 Darrow, "French Noblewomen and the New Domesticity," 43.

63 Bibliothèque Nationale de France, Manuscript Collections, Nouvelles acquisitions françaises 5931. The merchant's name does not appear in the journal, which covers the period between 1812 and 1816. In addition to serving a long list of noblewomen, this merchant was purveyor to the imperial court; the empress is the first client named in the journal.

64 The phrase *maîtresse de la maison* is from a contemporary source cited by Darrow, "French Noblewomen and the New Domesticity," 58.

65 Gustave Flaubert, *Madame Bovary* (1857; Paris, 1945), 123.

66 Margery Ann Crumpacker, "Three Eighteenth-Century Women Writers: Contravening Authority" (PhD diss., City University of New York, 1998), 255.

Conclusion

1 André Monglond, *Le préromantisme français* (Geneva: Slatkine, 1930), vii.

2 On the Hôpital de la Trinité, the machinations involved in having a child admitted to the orphanage, and the privileges with regard to the guild system provided to its

wards, see Clare Haru Crowston, "L'apprentissage hors des corporations: Les formations professionnelles alternatives à Paris sous l'Ancien Régime," *Annales: Histoire, Sciences Sociales* 60, no. 2 (2005): 409–42.

3 Laurence Fontaine, *L'Economie morale: Pauvreté, crédit et confiance dans l'Europe préindustrielle* (Paris: Gallimard, 2008); Craig Muldrew, *The Economy of Obligation: The Culture of Credit and Social Relations in Early Modern England* (New York: St. Martin's, 1998); Margot Finn, *The Character of Credit: Personal Debt in English Culture* (Cambridge: Cambridge University Press, 2003).

4 Gabriel de Tarde, *Psychologie économique* (Paris: F. Alcan, 1902), 73–74.

5 Tarde, *Psychologie économique*, 60; cited in Bruno Latour and Vincent Antonin Lépinay, *The Science of Passionate Interests: An Introduction to Gabriel Tarde's Economic Anthropology* (Chicago: Prickly Paradigm Press, 2009). Latour and Lépinay make a strong case for the originality and insight of Tarde's plea for a new approach to economics.

6 Tarde, *Psychologie économique*, 71–73.

7 It is worth noting that for the period 1800–1849, the majority of references in the texts included in ARTFL were to credit as a form of influence and power rather than to its financial sense. This was true even among authors born during and after the revolution, such as Dumas (who used the word forty-four times in *The Count of Monte Cristo*) and Balzac. As the presence of Balzac, Proudhon, Zola, and de Staël on the list suggest, the first half of the nineteenth century was an important moment for critical rethinking of processes for producing value and the intertwined nature of economics, politics, and social life.

8 Joséphine de Beauharnais, *L'Impératrice Joséphine, Correspondance, 1782–1814* (1782; Paris: Payot et Rivages, 1996), February 10, 1808, letter to Eugène.

9 Jacques Peuchet, *Mémoires de Mademoiselle Bertin sur la reine Marie-Antoinette* (Paris: Bossange, 1824), 55, 139.

10 *Dictionnaire de l'Académie française*, 8th ed. (Paris: Hachette, 1932–1935).

BIBLIOGRAPHY

Manuscript and Archival Sources

ARCHIVES DE PARIS (AP)

D4B6 — dossiers of merchants who filed *faillite* (with the date of initial filing)

c. 68 d. 445	Allain, Jacques (June 5, 1778)
c. 94 d. 6573	Alleaume, Cécile Sophie (November 23, 1785)
c. 51 d. 3157	Bail, Marie Jeanne (May 4, 1774)
c. 107 d. 7854	Beaulard, Jean-Joseph (August 30, 1789)
c. 64 d. 4179	Bénard, Charles-François (September 15, 1777)
c. 64 d. 4150	Bermond, Jean-Baptiste (June 20, 1777)
c. 84 d. 5393	Bernard, Adélaïde (May 1, 1781)
c. 66 d. 4396	Brocard, Marie Thérèse (January 20, 1778)
c. 22 d. 1101	Cabaille, Barbe Catherine (October 24, 1761)
c. 94 d. 6571	Cautier, Jeanne Françoise Julie (November 22, 1785)
c. 109 d. 7751	Defrance, Louise (March 24, 1789)
c. 105 d. 7463	Duflocq, Jeanne Gabrielle (April 8, 1789)
c. 111 d. 7921	Duluc, Catherine Mélanie (November 30, 1790)
c. 83 d. 5557	Duval, Angélique (November 17, 1781)
c. 75 d. 4954	Evrard, Elisabeth (November 30, 1789)
c. 44 d. 2551	Fremont, Marie Madeleine (December 16, 1771)
c. 109 d. 7722	Gicquel, Marie-Thérèse (May 3, 1790)
c. 68 d. 4444	Girard, Madeleine Charlotte (July 22, 1779)
c. 105 d. 7432	Hébert (March 10, 1789)
c. 70 d. 4638	Henry, Hélène (February 6, 1779)
c. 91 d. 6229	Janson, Marie-Joseph-Antoinette (July 7, 1784)
c. 28 d. 1510	Lacoste, Marie (October 10, 1761)
c. 91 d. 6291	Lacroix, Joséphine Catherine (September 17, 1784)
c. 75 d. 4980	Lametz, Charles (January 13, 1780)
c. 82 d. 5477	Lechard, Elizabeth (July 16, 1781)
c. 104 d. 7347	Ledoux, Marie Charlotte (December 17, 1788)
c. 83 d. 5608	Lemaître, Julienne Angélique (February 7, 1782)
c. 113 d. 8051	Leveque et Boullenois (November 28, 1791)
c. 29 d. 1541	Morand, David (June 2, 1766)
c. 83 d. 5564	Moreau, Jeanne Victoire (August 14, 1781)
c. 24 d. 1251	Moulin, Eléonore Louise (June 17, 1778)
c. 38 d. 2087	Pétard, Marie Elisabeth (July 21, 1770)
c. 92 d. 6329	Petit, Marie Geneviève (December 10, 1784)

c. 81 d. 5399	Poidevin, Marie Anne Elisabeth (January 1, 1780)
c. 84 d. 5649	Possel, Louis (March 1, 1782)
c. 57 d. 3661	Poyet, Marie Etiennette Charlotte (February 1, 1776)
c. 18 d. 865	Prévost, Marie Denise (February 18, 1758)
c. 104 d. 7409	Rondu, Marie Elisabeth (January 28, 1789)
c. 85 d. 5791	Soyer, Alexis (November 25, 1782)

D5B6 —account books deposited during *faillite* proceedings

10; 4327	Anonymous
306	Bermond, Jean-Baptiste
1163; 1463	Bernard, Adélaïde
5307	Cabaille, Barbe Catherine
1289	Gicquel, Marie-Thérèse
581	Lacroix, Joséphine Catherine
2522; 230	Leveque et Boullenois
1295	Moreau, Jeanne Victoire

D6B6 —adjudication of commercial conflicts at the Juridiction consulaire

ARCHIVES NATIONALES DE FRANCE (AN)

Minutier central (MC)—notarial archives

A.D.	printed government documents, including laws and regulations
F7	archives of the post-1789 ministry of police
O 1	documents from the royal household
V7 423	records of royal audits of the Parisian fashion merchants' guild
Y	archives of the police *commissaires* of Paris

INSTITUT NATIONAL DE L'HISTOIRE DE L'ART (INHA)

MS1, Marie Jeanne Bertin—copies of account books and correspondence generated by Marie Jeanne (Rose) Bertin's heirs after the Restoration

MUSÉE GALLIERA

Fonds de Bercy—records from the household of the de Bercy family

BIBLIOTHÈQUE NATIONALE DE FRANCE

Nouvelles acquisitions françaises 5931—an early nineteenth-century fashion merchant's account book

BIBLIOTHÈQUE DE L'ARSENAL

MSS—manuscripts collection, includes reports by Parisian police inspectors

Periodicals

Annonces, affiches et avis divers. Paris: Bureau d'adresse et de rencontre, 1755.
Le Cabinet des modes (later *Magasin des modes nouvelles françaises et anglaises*).
L'esprit des journaux, françois et étrangers. Paris: Chez Valade, 1778.

La Feuille nécessaire

La Feuille sans titre

Journal de commerce et d'agriculture. Brussels: Chez P. de Bast, 1761.

Journal des dames

Le Journal de Paris

Le Mercure galant. Geneva and Paris: Slatkine Reprints, 1982.

Printed Primary Sources

Abbadie, Jacques. Traité de la vérité de la réligion chrétienne. Vol. 2. Rotterdam: R. Leers, 1684.

Almanach du commerce de Paris, des départements de l'Empire français et des principales villes du monde. Paris: Chez J. de la Tynna, 1809.

Almanach du commerce et de toutes les adresses de la ville de Paris. Paris: Duchesne, 1798–1798.

Ancelot, Marguerite-Louise Virginie. "Une Femme à la mode." In Les Français peints par eux-mêmes. Encyclopédie morale du dix-neuvième siècle. Paris: L. Curmer, 1841.

Annonces, affiches et avis divers. Paris: Bureau d'adresse et de rencontre, 1755.

Anonymous. Fameuse harangue . . . de messeigneurs les savetiers. Troyes: Veuve Garnier, 1738.

———. La grande Bible des noëls tans vieux que nouveaux. Troyes: Garnier le jeune, 1772.

———. Laïs et Phriné, poème en quatre chants. London, 1767.

———. Le femme mécontente de son mari. Troyes: Veuve Garnier, 1738.

———. Le miroir d'astrologie naturelle. Troyes: Veuve de Jean Oudot, 1745.

———. L'état de servitude ou la misère des domestiques. Troyes: Veuve Garnier, 1738.

———. Vie de Saint Patrocle. Troyes: Garnier le jeune, 1772.

Arcq, Philippe-Auguste de Sainte-Foix, chevalier d.' Le roman du jour, pour servir à l'histoire du siècle. Vol. 1. Amsterdam: Van Harrevelt, 1755.

Argens, Jean-Baptiste de Boyer, marquis d.' Lettres juives. The Hague: P. Paupie, 1738.

Argenson, Maurice Charles Marc Rene de Voyer de Paulmy, marquis d,' ed. Autour d'un ministre de Louis XV. Paris: Messein, 1923.

Argenson, René-Louis de Voyer de Paulmy, marquis d.' Journal et mémoires du marquis d'Argenson, 1755–1757. 9 vols. Paris: Veuve Jules Renouard, 1859–1867.

Arnauld d'Andilly, Robert. Mémoires. In Collection des mémoires relatifs à l'histoire de France, vol. 33. Paris: Foucault, 1824.

Arneth, Alfred von, and Auguste Geoffroy, eds. Correspondance secrète entre Marie-Thérèse et le comte de Mercy-Argenteau: Avec les lettres de Marie-Thérèse et de Marie-Antoinette. Paris: Firmin Didot Frères, 1874.

Barbé-Marbois, François. Lettres de Madame la Marquise de Pompadour. 4 vols. London: T. Cadell, 1772.

Baltasar, Gracian. L'homme de cour. Châtenay-Malabry: Editions de Kerdraon, 1989.

Balzac, Honoré de. L'Interdiction. Paris: Furne, Dubochet et Cie, 1844.

Barthélemy, Jean-Jacques. Voyage du jeune anacharsis. Paris: De Bure, 1788.

Beauharnais, Joséphine de, empress. L'Impératrice Joséphine, Correspondance, 1782–1814. 1782. Paris: Payot et Rivages, 1996.

Berthier, Abbé J., ed. *Lettres de Messire P. Godet des Marais, évêque de Chartres, à Madame de Maintenon*. Paris: J. Dumoulin, 1908.

Bouhours, Dominique. *Les entretiens d'Ariste et d'Eugène*. 1671. Paris: Armand Colin, 1962.

Boissy, Louis de. *Les Dehors Trompeurs ou l'homme du jour*. Paris: Chez Prault, 1746.

Bonnet, Charles. *La Palingénésie Philosophique ou idée sur l'etat passé et futur des êtres vivants*. Geneva: Philibert et Chirol, 1769.

Bornier, Philippe, ed. *Conférence des ordonnances de Louis XIV*. 1694. Paris: Chez les associés choisis par sa Majesté, 1755.

Bossuet, Jacques Bénigne. *Oraison funèbre d'Henriette d'Angleterre*. In *Œuvres Oratoires*, vol. 5, edited by Joseph Lebarq. Lille: Desclée de Brouwer et Cie, 1922.

Boyer, Abel. *Dictionnaire royal, françois-anglois et anglois-françois*. Amsterdam: R. and G. Wetstein and Pierre Humbert, 1727.

———. *Dictionnaire royal, François et Anglois*. The Hague: Meyndert Uytwerf, 1702.

Buffevent, Béatrix de. *L'économie dentellière en région parisienne au XVIIe siècle*. Pontoise: Société historique de Pontoise, du Val-d'Oise et du Vexin, 1984.

Burkard, Suzanne, ed. *Baronne d'Oberkirch, Memoires de la Baronne d'Oberkirch sur la cour de Louis XVI et la société française avant 1789*. Paris: Mercure de France, 1989.

Bussy-Rabutin, Roger de. *Les Lettres de messire Roger de Rabutin, comte de Bussy*. 4 vols. Paris: Chez Florentin Delaulne, 1720.

———. *Les mémoires de messire Roger de Rabutin, comte de Bussy*. 3 vols. Paris: Chez Rigaud, 1704.

Campan, Jeanne-Louise-Henriette. *Mémoires de Madame Campan. Première femme de chambre de Marie-Antoinette*. Edited by Carlos de Angulo. Paris: Mercure de France, 1988.

Caylus, Anne-Claude-Philippe, Comte de. *Histoire de Guillaume Cocher*. In *Oeuvres badines complètes*, vol. 10. Paris: Vissem, 1787.

———. *Nouveaux contes orientaux*. In *Oeuvres badines completes*, vol. 7. Paris: Vissem, 1787.

Chapelain, Jean. *La Pucelle*. Paris: A. Courbe, 1656.

Choiseul-Meuse, Félicité de. *Récréations morales et amusantes, à l'usage des jeunes demoiselles qui entrent dans le monde*. Paris: F. Eymery, 1817.

Clément, Pierre, ed. *Lettres, instructions et mémoires de Colbert*, vol. 3, *Commerce et industrie*. Paris: Imprimerie imperial, 1861–1882.

Corneille, Pierre. *Le Menteur*. In *Oeuvres complètes*, edited by Marty-Laveaux. Paris: Hachette, 1863.

Correspondance littéraire, philosophique et critique de Grimm et de Diderot. Edited by Jules-Antoine Taschereau. Paris: Furne, 1829–1831.

Correspondance secrète inédite sur Louis XVI, Marie-Antoinette, la cour et la ville de 1777 à 1792. Edited by Mathurin de Lescure. 2 vols. Paris: Henri Plon, 1866.

Courtin, Antoine de. *Nouveau traité de la civilité qui se pratique en France, parmi les honnestes gens*. 1671. Paris: Chez Helie Josset, 1672.

Crébillon, Claude Prosper Jolyot de. *La nuit et le moment ou les matines de Cythère, dialogue*. 1755. Paris: Les Editions Desjonquères, 1983.

———. *Les égarements du cœur et de l'esprit*. In *Romanciers du 18ᵉ siècle*, vol. 2. Edited by René Etiemble. Paris: Gallimard, 1965.

Dancourt, Florent Carton. *La Femme d'intrigues*. In *Oeuvres choisis de Dancourt*. Paris: P. Didot l'ainé et F. Didot, 1810.

———. *Les bourgeoises à la mode*. Paris: T. Guillain, 1693.

Dangeau, Philippe de Courcillon de. *Mémoires et journal du marquis de Dangeau*. Paris: Mame et Delaunay-Vallée, 1830.

De Windt, Caroline Amelia Smith, ed. *Journal and correspondence of Miss Adams, Daughter of John Adams, Second President of the United States; Written in France and England in 1785*. New York: Wiley and Putnam, 1841.

Dictionnaire de l'Académie française. Paris: Chez la veuve Jean Coignard, 1694.

———. 8th ed. Paris: Hachette, 1932–1935.

Dictionnaire universel françois et latin. Reproduction de l'édition de Trevoux. Paris: Delaulne, 1721.

Dubos, Abbé Jean-Baptiste. *Histoire critique de l'établissement de la monarchie françoise dans les Gaules*. Paris: Nyon Fils, 1742.

Duclos, Charles Pinot. *Acajou et Zirphile*. In *Le Cabinet des Fées*, vol. 35. Geneva: Barde, Manget et Co., 1786.

———. *Considérations sur les mœurs de ce siècle*. Amsterdam: Aux Dépens de la Compagnie, 1751.

———. *Considérations sur les moeurs de ce siècle*. Edited by Carole Dornier. Paris: Honoré Champion, 2005.

———. *Considérations sur les moeurs de ce siècle*. Edited by F. C. Green. Cambridge: Cambridge University Press, 2010.

———. *Mémoires secrets sur le règne de Louis xiv, la Régence et le règne de Louis xv*. In *Nouvelle collection de mémoires pour servir à l'histoire de France*, vol. 10, edited by Joseph Michaud and Jean Joseph François Poujoulat. Paris: Chez l'éditeur du commentaire analytique du code civil, 1859.

———. *Two French Libertine Novels: "The Story of Madame de Luz" and "The Confessions of the Comte de ***."* Translated by Douglas Parmée. Brooklyn, NY: AMS Press, 2006.

Duguet, Jacques Joseph. *Institutions d'un prince, ou traité des qualités, des vertus et des devoirs d'un souverain*, vol. 2. London: chez Jean Nourse, 1740.

Du Lorens, Jacques. *Satires*. 1646. Paris: D. Jouaust, 1869.

Dutot, Charles. *Histoire du Système de John Law (1716–1720)*. Edited by Antoin E. Murphy. Paris: Institut National d'Etudes démographiques, 2000.

Encyclopédie ou dictionnaire raisonné des sciences, des arts et métiers. Edited by Denis Diderot and Jean Le Rond d'Alembert. Geneva: Pellet, 1778.

Encyclopédie ou dictionnaire raisonné des sciences, des arts et des métiers, etc. Edited by Denis Diderot and Jean le Rond D'Alembert. University of Chicago: ARTFL Encyclopédie Project (spring 2011 edition), edited by Robert Morrissey. http://encyclopedie.uchicago.edu.

Epinay, Louise Florence Pétronille Tardieu d'Esclavelles, marquise d.' *Histoire de Madame de Montbrillant*. 1770. Edited by Georges Roth. 3 vols. Paris: Gallimard, 1951.

———. *Les conversations d'Emilie*. Paris: Humboldt, 1781.

Esprit, Jacques. *Fausseté des vertus humaines*. 1678. Amsterdam: P. Mortier, 1710.

Faret, Nicolas. *L'Honneste homme, ou, L'art de plaire à la court.* 1633. Paris: Presses universitaires françaises, 1925.

Félicité, Stéphanie, comtesse de Genlis. *Les Petits émigrés ou correspondance de quelques enfans.* London, 1799.

Fénélon, François de Salignac de la Mothe. *Directions pour la conscience d'un roi.* Paris: Chez les frères Estienne, 1775.

———. *Examen de conscience sur les devoirs de la royauté: Mémoires pour le duc de Bourgogne.* In *Lettre à Louis XIV,* edited by Henri Guillemin. Neuchatel: Ides et Calendes, 1961.

Ferrière, Claude de. *Corps et compilation de tous les commentateurs anciens et modernes sur la coûtume de Paris.* Paris: M. Guignard, 1714.

Fielding, Henry. *Amelia.* 4 vols. London: Harrison and Co., 1780.

———. *Amélie, histoire angloise.* Translated by P. F. de Puisieux. Paris: Chez Charpentier, 1762.

Flaubert, Gustave. *Madame Bovary.* 1857. Paris, 1945.

Fléchier, Esprit. *Mémoires sur les Grands-Jours d'Auvergne.* 1710. Paris: Hachette, 1862.

———. *Oraison Funèbre de Marie-Thérèse d'Autriche.* In *Oraisons Funèbres,* vol. 2. Paris: A. Dezallier, 1691.

Fresny, Charles du. *Amusemens sérieux et comiques.* Paris: C. Barbin, 1699.

Furetière, Antoine. *Dictionnaire universel.* The Hague: A. and R. Leers, 1690.

Garsault, François-Alexandre-Pierre de. *L'Art du tailleur.* Paris: Imprimerie Delatour, 1769.

Genlis, Stéphanie Félicité, comtesse de. *Adèle et Théodore ou Lettres sur l'éducation.* 4 vols. Paris: Chez M. Lambert and F. J. Baudouin, 1782.

———. "Les Dangers du monde." In *Théâtre à l'usage des jeunes personnes.* 4 vols. Dublin: Luc White, 1781.

———. *Les Petits émigrés ou correspondance de quelques enfans.* Vol. 2. London, 1799.

Goncourt, Edmond de, and Jules de Goncourt. *La duchesse de Chateauroux et ses sœurs.* Paris: G. Charpentier, 1879.

Grenaille, François de. *La Mode.* Paris: Chez Nicolas Gasse, 1642.

Guez de Balzac, Jean-Louis. *Œuvres.* Paris: T. Jolly, 1665.

Guyon, Marie Jeanne. *Récits de captivité.* 1709. Grenoble: Editions Jérôme Million, 1992.

Holbach, Paul-Henri Thiry, baron d.' *Système social ou principes naturels de la morale et de la politique avec un examen de l'influence du gouvernement sur les moeurs.* 3 vols. London, 1773.

Isambert, François-André, et al., eds. *Recueil général des anciennes lois françaises, depuis l'an 420 jusqu'à la Révolution de 1789,* vol. 17. Paris: Belin-Leprieur, 1821–1833.

Jaubert, Abbé Pierre. *Dictionnaire raisonné universel des arts et métiers, contenant l'histoire, la description, la police des fabriques et manufactures de France et des pays étrangers.* Paris: P. F. Didot, jeune, 1773.

La Bruyère, Jean de. *Dialogues sur le quiétisme.* In *Oeuvres complètes.* Edited by Julien Benda. Paris: Gallimard, 1951.

———. *Les caractères ou les mœurs de ce siècle.* 1694. In *Œuvres complètes.* Edited by Julien Benda. Paris: Gallimard, 1951.

Lafayette, Madame de (Marie-Madeleine Pioche de la Vergne). *Histoire de Madame Henriette d'Angleterre*. Amsterdam: Chez Michel Charles le Cene, 1720.

———. *La Princesse de Clèves*. Edited by Emile Magne. 1678. Paris: Droz, 1946.

———. *Vie de la Princesse d'Angleterre*. 1693. Edited by Marie-Thérèse Hipp. Paris: Minard, 1967.

Lambert, Anne Thérèse de Maguenat de. *Réflexions nouvelles sur les femmes*. 1727. Edited by Milagros Palma. Paris: Côté femmes, 1989.

La Salle, Jean-Baptiste de. *Les règles de la bienséance et de la civilité chrétienne*. 1703. Edited by Philippe Louis Constantin. Paris: Douxfils, 1841.

La Vallée, Théophile. *Madame de Maintenon et la maison royale de Saint-Cyr (1686–1793)*. Paris: H. Plon, 1862.

Law, John. *John Law: Oeuvres complètes*. Edited by Paul Harsin. 3 vols. Paris: Sirey, 1934.

———. *Money and Trade Considered: With a Proposal for Supplying the Nation with Money*. Glasgow: R. and A. Foulis, 1705.

Le Comte, Le Pére Louis. *Nouveaux mémoires sur l'état présent de la Chine*. Paris: J. Anisson, 1696.

Le Sage, Alain René. *Le diable boîteux*. In *Romanciers du 18e siècle*, vol. 1. Edited by René Etiemble. Paris: Gallimard, 1960.

Lespinasse, René de. *Les métiers et corporations de la ville de Paris: XIVe-XVIIIe siècles*. Paris: Imprimerie nationale, 1897.

Linguet, Simon-Nicolas-Henri. *Histoire impartiale des Jésuites depuis leur établissement jusqu'à leur première expulsion*. Paris: Chez P. G. Simon, 1768.

L'Isle, Chevalier de. "Lettres familières du chevalier de l'Isle pendant l'année 1781." *Mercure de France* 69 (1907): 275–89.

Luynes, Charles-Philippe d'Albert, duc de. *Mémoires du duc de Luynes sur la cour de Louis XIV (1735-1758)*. Edited by Louis Dussieux et Eudore Soulié. Paris: Firmin Didot, 1860–1865.

Mably, Abbé de. *Parallèle des Romains et des Français*. Paris: Didot, 1740.

Maintenon, Madame de. *Conseils et instructions aux demoiselles pour leur conduit dans le monde*. Edited by Théophile La Vallée. Paris: Charpentier, 1857.

———. *Correspondance générale de Madame de Maintenon*. Edited by Théophile La Vallée. 5 vols. Paris: Charpentier, 1865–66.

Maintenon, Madame de, and Marie-Anne de la Trémiolle Ursins. *The Secret Correspondence of Madame de Maintenon with the Princess des Ursins*. 3 vols. London: George B. Whittaker, 1827.

Mairobert, Mathieu François Pidansat de. *Anecdotes sur M. la Comtesse Du Barri*. London, 1775.

Marivaux, Pierre Carlet de Chamblain de. *Oeuvres de Marivaux: théâtre complet*. Edited by Edouard Fournier. Paris: Garnier frères, 1878.

Marmontel, Jean-Francois. *Les Contes moraux*. Liège, 1780.

Mémoires secrets pour servir à l'histoire de la république des lettres en France. London: Chez John Adamson, 1783–1789.

Mercier, Louis-Sébastien. *Le Tableau de Paris*. Edited by Jean-Claude Bonnet. 2 vols. Paris: Mercure de France, 1994.

Mercier, Révérend Père. *Madame de Maintenon*. Paris: Lecoffre fils et cie, 1874.

Métra, François, et al. *Correspondance secrète, politique et littéraire ou mémoires pour servir à l'histoire des cours, des sociétés et de la littérature en France.* London: Chez John Adamson, 1787–1790.

Meusnier de Querlon, Anne-Gabriel. *Sainte Nitouche ou histoire galante de la tournière des Carmelites suivie de l'histoire de La Duchapt, célèbre marchande de modes.* London, 1830.

Molière. *Oeuvres complètes.* Edited by Eugène Despois. Paris: Hachette, 1873.

Monglond, André. *Le préromantisme français.* Geneva: Slatkine, 1930.

Montaigne, Michael. *Les essais.* Paris, 1595.

Montesquieu, Charles de Secondat, baron de. *De l'esprit des loix.* Edited by J. Brethe de la Gressaye. Paris: Belles-Lettres, 1958.

———. *Lettres persanes.* 1721. Edited by Elie Carcassonne. Paris: F. Roches, 1929.

Mouffle d'Angerville, Barthélemy-François-Joseph. *Vie privée de Louis XV.* Edited by Albert Meyrac. Paris: Calmann-Lévy, 1921.

Mouhy, Charles de Fieux de. *Les Mille et une faveurs.* London, 1740.

Moult, Thomas-Joseph. *Prophéties perpétuelles.* Troyes[?]: Garnier[?], 1765.

Naudé, Gabriel. *Advis Pour Dresser une Bibliothèque.* Paris: Rolet le Duc, 1644.

———. *Apologie pour tous les grands hommes qui ont esté accusez de magie.* Paris: Eschart, 1669.

Nicole, Pierre. *Essais de morale.* 1671. 2 vols. Paris: G. Desprez, 1701.

Nicot, Jean. *Thresor de la langue française.* Paris: David Douceur, 1606.

Pascal, Blaise. *Les provinciales, ou Les lettres écrites par Louis de Montalte à un provincial de ses amis et aux RR. PP. Jésuites.* 1657. Paris: Garnier, 1965.

Patin, Guy. *Lettres de Gui Patin, 1630–1672.* Paris: Champion, 1907.

Peiresc, Nicolas de. *Lettres de Peiresc.* Edited by Philippe Tamizey de Larroque. Paris: Imprimerie nationale, 1898.

Peuchet, Jacques. *Mémoires de Mademoiselle Bertin sur la reine Marie-Antoinette.* Paris: Bossange, 1824.

Poinsinet, Antoine Alexandre Henri. *Le cercle, ou la soirée à la mode.* London, 1785.

Pothier, Robert-Joseph. *Traité de la communauté.* Paris: Frères Debure, 1774.

———. *Traité du contrat de vente.* Vol. 1. Paris: Chez Debure, 1762.

Poulet-Malassis, M. A., ed. *Correspondance de Madame de Pompadour avec son père, M. Poisson et son frère, M. de Vandières.* Paris, 1878.

Pradel, Abraham de. *Les addresses de la ville de Paris.* Paris, 1691.

Prévost, Abbé. *Nouvelles lettres angloises ou, Histoire du chevalier Grandisson.* Amsterdam, 1784.

"Prospectus" for *Gazette du commerce.* Paris: Prault, 1763.

Puisieux, Madame de (Madeleine). *Les caractères seconde partie.* London, 1751.

Quevedo y Villegas, Francisco Gómez de. *Les visions de Dom Francisco de Quevedo Villegat.* Troyes: Veuve de Jacques, 1711.

Ramsay, Andrew-Michael. *Les Voyages de Cyrus.* Paris: G. F. Quillau, 1727.

Restif de la Brétonne, Nicolas-Edmé. *Histoire de Sara.* In *Monsieur Nicolas.* Vol. 12. Paris: I. Lisieux, 1883.

Retz, Jean François Paul de Gondi de. *Mémoires.* In *Oeuvres.* Edited by A. Feillet, J. Gourdault, and R. Chantelauze. Paris: Hachette, 1872.

Richardson, Samuel. *Pamela: Or Virtue Rewarded*. London: J. Osborn and J. and J. Rivington, 1746.

Richebourg, Charles Antoine Bourdot de. *Le Nouveau coutumier général*. Paris: Chez Theodore Le Gras, 1724.

Richelet, César-Pierre. *Dictionnaire de la langue françoise ancienne et moderne*. Lyon: J. M. Bruyset, 1728.

———. *Dictionnaire françois contenant les mots et les choses*. Geneva: Chez Jean Herman Widerhold, 1680.

Richelieu, Louis François Armand Du Plessis, duc de. *Mémoires du maréchal duc de Richelieu*, vol. 8. Paris: Chez Buisson, 1793.

Rotrou, Jean de. *Cosroès: Tragédie*. 1649. Edited by Jacques Scherer. Paris: Didier, 1950.

Rousseau, Jean-Jacques. *Emile, ou, de l'éducation*. In *Oeuvres complètes*, vol. 4. Paris: Gallimard, 1969.

———. *Les confessions de Jean-Jacques Rousseau*. Paris: Charpentier, 1869.

———. *Politics and the Arts: Letter to M. D'Alembert on the Theatre*. Translated by Allan Bloom. Ithaca, NY: Cornell University Press, 1968.

Roze de Chantoiseau, Mathurin. *Essai sur l'almanach général d'indication d'adresse personnelle et domicile fixe, des six corps, arts et métiers*. Paris: Chez la veuve Duchesne, chez Dessain, chez Lacombe, 1769.

Rutebeuf. *Œuvres complètes*. Edited by Michel Zink. Paris: Bordas, 1990.

Saint-Foix, Germain-François Poullain de. *Oeuvres complètes: Essais historiques sur Paris*. Paris: Chez la veuve Duchesne, 1778.

Sainte Foy, Philippe-Auguste de, chevalier d'Arcq. *Le Roman du jour: pour servir à l'histoire du siècle*. Vol. 1. Amsterdam: Van Harrevelt, 1755.

Saint-Méry, Louis-Elie Moreau de. *Description topographique, physique, civile, politique et historique de la partie française de l'isle Saint-Domingue*. 2nd ed. Paris: Morgan, 1875.

Saint-Pierre, Charles-Irénée Castel de. *Discours sur la polysynodie, où l'on démontre que la polysynodie ou pluralité des Conseils, est la forme de ministère la plus avantageuse pour un Roy et pour son royaume*. Amsterdam: Du Villard et Changuion, 1719.

Saint-Simon, Louis de Rouvroy, duc de. *Mémoires complets et authentiques du duc de Saint-Simon sur le siècle de Louis XIV et la régence*. Edited by Adolphe Chéruel. 20 vols. Paris: L. Hachette, 1856–1858.

Savary, Jacques. *Le Parfait négociant ou instruction générale pour ce qui regarde le commerce des marchandises de France et des pays estrangers*. Paris: L. Billaine, 1675.

———. *Le Parfait négociant ou instruction générale pour ce qui regarde le commerce des marchandises de France et des pays étranger*. 2nd ed. Paris: Chez Claude Robustel, 1715.

Savary des Bruslons, Jacques. *Dictionnaire universel de commerce, d'histoire naturelle et des arts et métiers*. Edited by Philemon-Louis Savary. Geneva: Chez les héritiers Cramer et les frères Philibert, 1742–1744.

———. *Dictionnaire universel de commerce, d'histoire naturelle et des arts et métiers*. 5 vols. Copenhagen: Chez Claude Philibert, 1759–1765.

[Sénac de Meilhan, Gabriel]. *Mémoires de madame du Hausset, femme de chambre de Madame de Pompadour*. Paris: Baudoin frères, 1824.

Sévigné, Madame de (Marie de Rabutin-Chantal). *Correspondance*. Edited by Roger Duchêne. 3 vols. Paris: Gallimard, 1972–1978.

Smith, Adam. *An Inquiry into the Nature and Causes of the Wealth of Nations*. Vol. 1. London: W. Strahan and T. Cade, 1776.

Sorel, Charles. *La Bibliothèque Française*. Paris: Compagnie des Librairies du Palais, 1664.

Tarde, Gabriel de. *Psychologie économique*. Paris: F. Alcan, 1902.

Villemert, Pierre Joseph Boudier de. *L'ami des femmes, ou la philosophie du beau sexe*. London, 1775.

Voiture, Vincent. *Lettres*. In *Les Œuvres*. Paris: A. Courbe, 1654.

Voltaire. *Lettres philosophiques*. Edited by Gustave Lanson. Paris: Hachette, 1915.

———. *Oeuvres complètes de Voltaire. Correspondance générale*. Vol. 11. Paris: Firmin Didot, 1855.

———. *Oeuvres complètes de Voltaire. Correspondance générale*. Vol. 9. Paris: Armand-Aubree, 1930.

———. *Siècle de Louis XIV*. Paris: Charpentier et Cie, 1874.

Secondary Sources

Abensour, Léon. *La Femme et le féminisme avant la Révolution*. Paris: Ernest Leroux, 1923.

Algrant, Christine Pevitt. *Madame de Pompadour: Mistress of France*. New York: Grove Press, 2003.

Apostolidès, Jean-Marie. "Molière and the Sociology of Exchange." *Critical Inquiry* 3 (1988): 477–92.

Auricchio, Laura. *Adélaïde Labille-Guiard: Artist in the Age of Revolution*. Los Angeles: J. Paul Getty Museum, 2009.

Bailey, Joanne. "Favoured or Oppressed? Married Women, Property and 'Coverture' in England, 1660–1800." *Continuity and Change* 17, no. 3 (2002): 351–72.

Baucom, Ian. *Specters of the Atlantic: Finance Capital, Slavery, and the Philosophy of History*. Durham, NC: Duke University Press, 2005.

Bayard, Françoise. *Le Monde des financiers au XVIIe siècle*. Paris: Flammarion, 1988.

Beik, William. *Absolutism and Society in Seventeenth-Century France: State Power and Provincial Aristocracy in Languedoc*. Cambridge: Cambridge University Press, 1985.

———. "The Absolutism of Louis XIV as Social Collaboration." *Past and Present* 188 (2005): 195–224.

Bellanger, Claude, et al. *Histoire générale de la presse française*. Vol. 1, *Des origines à 1814*. Paris: Presses universitaires de France, 1969.

Benabou, Erica-Maria. *La prostitution et la police des mœurs*. Paris: Perrin, 1987.

Benhamou, Reed. "Fashion in the 'Mercure': From Human Foible to Female Failing." *Eighteenth-Century Studies* 31, no. 1 (fall 1997): 27–43.

Berg, Maxine, and Elizabeth Eger, eds. *Luxury in the Eighteenth Century: Debates, Desires and Delectable Goods*. Basingstoke: Palgrave, 2002.

Bernier, Marc André. *Libertinage et figure du savoir: Rhétorique et roman libertin dans la France des Lumières (1734-1751)*. Québec: Les Presses de l'Université Laval, 2001.

Bigo, Robert. *La Caisse d'escompte (1776-1793) et les origines de la Banque de France*. Paris: Presses universitaires de France, 1927.

Blanc, André. *F. C. Dancourt (1661-1725). La Comédie française à l'heure du Soleil couchant*. Paris: Editions Place, 1984.

Blondé, Bruno, et al. *Retailers and Consumer Changes in Early Modern Europe: England, France, Italy and the Low Countries*. Tours: Presses universitaires François Rabelais, 2005.

Blum, Carol. *Strength in Numbers: Population, Reproduction, and Power in Eighteenth-Century France*. Baltimore: Johns Hopkins University Press, 2002.

Blum, Stella, ed. *Eighteenth-Century French Fashions in Full Color*. New York: Dover Publications, 1982.

Boesche, Roger. "Fearing Monarchs and Merchants: Montesquieu's Two Theories of Despotism." *Western Political Quarterly* 43, no. 4 (December 1990): 741–61.

Bollème, Geneviève. *La Bibliothèque bleue*. Paris: Gallimard-Julliard, 1980.

Bondois, Paul-Martin. *Colbert et l'industrie de la dentelle*. Paris: M. Rivière, 1926.

Bos, Jacques. "Individuality and Inwardness in the Literary Character Sketches of the Seventeenth Century." *Journal of the Warburg and Courtauld Institutes* 61 (1998): 142–57.

Bourdieu, Pierre. "The Forms of Capital." In *Handbook of Theory and Research for the Sociology of Education*. Edited by John G. Richardson, 241–58. New York: Greenwood, 1986.

———. *The Logic of Practice*. Translated by Richard Nice. Palo Alto, CA: Stanford University Press, 1990.

———. *Outline of a Theory of Practice*. Translated by Richard Nice. Cambridge: Cambridge University Press, 1977.

Bourdieu, Pierre, and Jean-Claude Passeron. *The Inheritors: French Students and Their Relation to Culture*. Translated by Richard Nice. Chicago: University of Chicago Press, 1979.

Boyce, Mary Schoeser. "The Barbier Manuscripts." *Textile History* 12 (October 1981): 37–58.

Brancourt, Jean-Pierre. "Un Théoricien de la société au XVIIIe siècle: Le chevalier d'Arcq." *Revue historique* 250 (1973): 337–62.

Brewer, John, and Roy Porter, eds. *Consumption and the World of Goods*. London: Routledge, 1993.

Buffevent, Béatrix de. *L'économie dentellière en région parisienne au XVIIe siècle*. Pontoise: Société historique de Pontoise, du Val-d'Oise et du Vexin, 1984.

Burchell, Stuart, Colin Clubb, and Anthony G. Hopwood. "Accounting in its Social Context: Towards a History of Value-Added in the United Kingdom." *Accounting, Organisations and Society* 20, no. 4 (1985): 381–413.

Buti, Gilbert, and Wolfgang Kaiser, eds. "Moyens, supports et usages de l'information marchande à l'époque moderne." Special issue, *Rives méditerranéennes* 27 (2007).

Campbell, Kimberly Chrisman. "The Face of Fashion: Milliners in Eighteenth-Century Visual Culture." *Eighteenth-Century Studies* 25, no. 1 (October 2008): 157–71.

———. "Mourning and *La Mode* at the Court of Louis XVI." *Costume* 39 (2005): 64–78.

————. "Rose Bertin in London?" *Costume* 32 (1998): 45–51.

Carré, Jean-Jacques, Paul Dubois, and Edmond Malinvaud. *French Economic Growth.* Translated by John P. Hatfield. Palo Alto, CA: Stanford University Press, 1975.

Carson, Cary, Ronald Hoffman, and Peter J. Albert, eds. *Of Consuming Interests: The Style of Life in the Eighteenth Century.* Charlottesville: University of Virginia Press, 1994.

Carson, Susannah. "L'économique de la mode: Costume, Conformity, and Consumerism in *Le Mercure galant.*" *Seventeenth-Century French Studies* 27 (2005): 133–46.

Castelluccio, Stéphane, ed. *Le Commerce du luxe à Paris aux XVIIe et XVIIIe siècles: échanges nationaux et internationaux.* Bern: Peter Lang, 2009.

Cavillac, Cécile. "Audaces et inhibitions d'une romancière au XVIIIe siècle: Le cas de madame d'Epinay." *Revue d'Histoire Littéraire de la France* 104, no. 4 (2004): 887–904.

Censer, Jack R., and Jeremy D. Popkin, eds. *Press and Politics in Pre-Revolutionary France.* Berkeley: University of California Press, 1987.

Cerutti, Simona. *La Ville et les métiers. Naissance d'un langage corporatif (Turin, 17e-18e siècle).* Paris: Editions de l'Ecole des hautes études en sciences sociales, 1990.

Chapman, Sara E. "Patronage as Family Economy: The Role of Women in the Patron-Client Network of the Phélypeaux de Pontchartrain Family, 1670–1715." *French Historical Studies* 24, no. 1 (2001): 11–35.

————. *Private Ambition and Political Alliances: The Phélypeaux de Pontchartrain.* Rochester, NY: University of Rochester Press, 2004.

Chartier, Roger. *Cultural History: Between Practices and Representations.* Translated by Lydia Cochrane. Ithaca, NY: Cornell University Press, 1988.

————. "From Texts to Manners, a Concept and Its Books: *Civilité* between Aristocratic Distinction and Popular Appropriation." In *The Cultural Uses of Print in Early Modern France.* 71–109. Translated by Lydia Cochrane. Princeton, NJ: Princeton University Press, 1987.

Chassagne, Serge. *Le coton et ses patrons: France 1760-1840.* Paris: Editions de l'École des hautes études en sciences sociales, 1991.

————. *Oberkampf, un entrepreneur capitaliste au siècle des Lumières.* Paris: Aubier-Montaigne, 1980.

Cheney, Paul. *Revolutionary Commerce: Globalization and the French Monarchy.* Cambridge, MA: Harvard University Press, 2010.

Coffin, Judith. *The Politics of Women's Work: The Paris Garment Trades, 1750-1915.* Princeton, NJ: Princeton University Press, 1996.

Cohen, Matt. *The Networked Wilderness: Communicating in Early New England.* Minneapolis: University of Minnesota Press, 2009.

Coquery, Natacha. "Les Faillites boutiquières sous l'Ancien Régime. Une gestion de l'échec mi-juridique mi-pragmatique (fin XVIIe-XVIIIe siècle)." *Revue française de gestion* 34, nos. 188–189 (2008): 341–58.

————. *L'Hôtel aristocratique: Le marché du luxe à Paris au XVIIIe siècle.* Paris: Publications de la Sorbonne, 1998.

————. *Tenir boutique à Paris au XVIIIe siècle. Luxe et demi-luxe.* Paris: CTHS, 2011.

Coquery, Natacha, ed. *La boutique et la ville. Commerces, commerçants, espaces et clien-*

tèles, *XVIe-XXI siècle: Actes du colloque des 2, 3, et 4 décembre 1999 organisé par l'université François Rabelais de Tours*. Tours: Publications de l'université François Rabelais, 2000.

Crouch, Charles. "The Petite Bourgeoisie of Paris during the Bourbon Restoration, 1814–1830: A Prosopographical Inquiry into the Political and Economic Integration of the Parisian Lower Middle Class." PhD dissertation, University of Illinois at Urbana-Champaign, 1991.

Crowston, Clare Haru. "Credit and the Metanarrative of Modernity." *French Historical Studies* 34, no. 1 (winter 2011): 7–19.

———. *Fabricating Women: The Seamstresses of Old Regime France, 1675–1791*. Durham, NC: Duke University Press, 2001.

———. "Family Affairs, Wives, Credit, Consumption and the Law in Old Regime France." In *Family, Gender, and Law in Early Modern France*, edited by Suzanne Desan and Jeffrey Merrick. 62–100. University Park: Pennsylvania State University Press, 2009.

———. "An Industrious Revolution in Late Seventeenth-Century Paris: New Vocational Training for Adolescent Girls and the Creation of Female Labor Markets." In *Secret Gardens, Satanic Mills: Placing Girls in Modern European History*, edited by M. J. Maynes, Birgitte Soland, and Christina Benninghaus. 69–82. Bloomington: Indiana University Press, 2005.

———. "L'apprentissage hors des corporations: Les formations professionnelles alternatives à Paris sous l'Ancien Régime." *Annales: Histoire, Sciences Sociales* 60, no. 2 (2005): 409–42.

———. "The Queen and Her 'Minister of Fashion': Gender, Credit and Politics in Pre-Revolutionary France." *Gender and History* 14, no. 1 (April 2002): 92–116.

Crumpacker, Margery Ann. "Three Eighteenth-Century Women Writers: Contravening Authority." PhD dissertation, City University of New York, 1998.

Cuche, François-Xavier. *Une pensée sociale catholique: Fleury, La Bruyère, Fénélon*. Paris: Cerf, 1991.

Cullen, Louis M. "History, economic crises, and revolution: understanding eighteenth-century France." *Economic History Review* 46, no. 4 (1993): 635–57.

Darnton, Robert. *The Devil in the Holy Water or the Art of Slander from Louis XIV to Napoleon*. Philadelphia: University of Pennsylvania Press, 2009.

———. "An Early Information Society: News and the Media in Eighteenth-Century Paris." *American Historical Review* 105, no. 1 (February 2000): 1–35.

———. *The Forbidden Best-Sellers of Pre-Revolutionary France*. New York: W. W. Norton, 1996.

Darrow, Margaret. "French Noblewomen and the New Domesticity." *Feminist Studies* 5 (1979): 41–65.

Daudin, Guillaume. *Commerce et prospérité. La France au XVIIIe siècle*. Paris: Presses de l'université de Paris-Sorbonne, 2005.

Davis, Natalie Zemon. *Fiction in the Archives: Pardon Tales and Their Tellers in Sixteenth-Century Archives*. Palo Alto, CA: Stanford University Press, 1987.

———. *The Gift in Sixteenth-Century France*. Madison: University of Wisconsin Press, 2000.

DeJean, Joan. *The Essence of Style: How the French Invented High Fashion, Fine Food, Chic Cafés, Style, Sophistication, and Glamour.* New York: Free Press, 2005.

Delcourt, Thierry. *La Bibliothèque bleue et les littératures de colportage.* Paris: Librairie Droz, 2000.

Delon, Michel. *Le Savoir-vivre libertin.* Paris: Hachette Littératures, 2000.

Delpierre, Madeleine. *La Mode et ses métiers du XVIIIe siècle à nos jours, 6 mars-31 octobre 1981, Ville de Paris, Musée de la mode et du costume.* Paris: Palais Galliera, 1981.

Denis, Delphine. *Le Parnasse gallant: Institution d'une catégorie littéraire au XVIIe siècle.* Paris: Honoré Champion, 2001.

Depitre, Edgar. *La Toile peinte en France au XVII et au XVIIIe siècles. Industrie, commerce, prohibitions.* Paris: Marcel Rivière et cie., 1912.

Deslandres, Yvonne. *Le Costume, image de l'homme.* Paris: Albin Michel, 1976.

Dessert, Daniel. *Argent, pouvoir et société au Grand Siècle.* Paris: Fayard, 1984.

Dewald, Jonathan. *Aristocratic Experience and the Origins of Modern Culture, 1575-1715.* Berkeley: University of California Press, 1993.

———. *The European Nobility, 1400-1800.* Cambridge: Cambridge University Press, 1996.

Diefendorf, Barbara B. "Women and Property in Ancien Régime France: Theory and Practice in Dauphiné and Paris." In *Early Modern Conceptions of Property.* Edited by John Brewer and Susan Staves. 170–93. New York: Routledge, 1996.

Dooley, Brendan, and Sabrina Baron, eds. *The Politics of Information in Early Modern Europe.* London: Routledge, 2001.

Duden, Barbara. *The Woman beneath the Skin: A Doctor's Patients in Eighteenth-Century Germany.* Translated by Thomas Dunlap. Cambridge. MA: Harvard University Press, 1998.

Elias, Norbert. *The Court Society.* Oxford: Blackwell, 1983.

Fairchilds, Cissie. "Marketing the Counter-Reformation: Religious Objects and Consumerism in Early Modern France." In *Visions and Revisions of Eighteenth-Century France.* Edited by Christine Adams et al. 31–58. University Park: Pennsylvania State University Press, 1997.

———. "The Production and Marketing of Populuxe Goods in Eighteenth-Century Paris." In *Consumption and the World of Goods.* Edited by John Brewer and Roy Porter. 228–60. New York: Routledge, 1993.

Farr, James R. "The Pure and Disciplined Body: Hierarchy, Morality, and Symbolism in France During the Catholic Reformation." *Journal of Interdisciplinary History* 21, no. 3 (winter 1991): 391–414.

Farrell, Michele Longino. *Performing Motherhood: The Sévigné Correspondence.* Hanover, NH: University Press of New England, 1991.

Faure, Edgar. *La Banqueroute de Law.* Paris: Gallimard, 1977.

Febvre, Lucien. "Du Goût classique au foisonnement romantique." In *Combats pour l'Histoire.* Paris: Colin, 1953.

Finn, Margot C. *The Character of Credit: Personal Debt in English Culture.* Cambridge: Cambridge University Press, 2003.

———. "Women, Consumption and Coverture in England, c. 1760–1860." *Historical Journal* 39, no. 3 (1996): 702–22.

Fleischman, Richard K., and Thomas N. Tyson. "Cost Accounting during the Industrial Revolution: The Present State of Historical Knowledge." *Economic History Review* 46, no. 3 (August 1993): 503–17.

Fontaine, Laurence. "Antonio and Shylock: Credit and Trust in France, c. 1680–1780." *Economic History Review* 54, no. 1 (2001): 39–57.

———. *L'économie morale: Pauvreté, crédit et confiance dans l'Europe préindustrielle.* Paris: Gallimard, 2008.

———. *Histoire du colportage en Europe (xve–xixe siècle).* Paris: Albin Michel, 1993.

Fontaine, Laurence, et al., eds. *Des personnes aux institutions: Réseaux et culture du crédit du xvie au xxe siècles.* Louvain-la-Neuve: Académie Bruylant, 1996.

Force, Pierre. *Molière ou le Prix des choses.* Paris: Nathan, 1994.

Forestier, Albane. "A 'Considerable Credit' in the Late Eighteenth-Century French West Indian Trade: The Chaurands of Nantes." *French History* 25, no. 1 (2011): 28–47.

Foucault, Michel. *The Order of Things: An Archaeology of the Human Sciences.* New York: Vintage Books, 1994.

Fraser, Antonia. *Marie-Antoinette: The Journey.* New York: Random House, 2002.

Freundlich, Francis. *Le monde du jeu à Paris, 1715–1800.* Paris: Albin Michel, 1995.

Gain, André. *La Restauration et les biens des émigrés: La législation concernant les biens nationaux de seconde origine et son application dans l'Est de la France (1814–1823).* 2 vols. Nancy: Société d'impressions typographiques, 1928.

Garraway, Doris. *The Libertine Colony.* Durham, NC: Duke University Press, 2005.

Gelbart, Nina Rattner. *Feminine and Opposition Journalism in Old Regime France.* Berkeley: University of California Press, 1987.

Ginzburg, Carlo. "Clues: Roots of an Evidential Paradigm." In *Clues, Myths, and the Historical Method.* Translated by John Tedeschi and Anne C. Tedeschi. Baltimore: Johns Hopkins University Press, 1989.

Godard de Donville, Louise. *La Signification de la mode sous Louis xiii.* Aix-en-Provence: EdiSud, 1976.

Goodman, Dena. "L'ortografe des dames: Gender and Language in the Old Regime." *French Historical Studies* 25, no. 2 (2002): 191–223.

Goodman, Dena, and Thomas E. Kaiser, eds. *Marie-Antoinette, Writings on the Body of a Queen.* New York: Routledge, 2003.

Gordon, Alden R. "The Longest Enduring Pompadour Hoax: Sénac de Meilhan and the Journal de Madame du Hausset." In *Art and Culture in the Eighteenth Century: New Dimensions and Multiple Perspectives.* Edited by Elise Goodman. 28–38. Plainsboro, NJ: Associated University Presses, 2001.

Gowing, Laura. *Domestic Dangers: Women, Words, and Sex in Early Modern London.* Oxford: Oxford University Press, 1999.

Graeber, David. *Debt: The First 5,000 Years.* Brooklyn, NY: Melville House, 2011.

Grassi, Marie-Claire. *L'art de la lettre au temps de la Nouvelle Héloïse et du romantisme.* Geneva: Slatkine, 1994.

Grenier, Jean-Yves. *L'économie d'Ancien Régime: Un monde de l'échange et de l'incertitude.* Paris: Albin Michel, 1996.

Hafter, Daryl. *Women at Work in Preindustrial France.* University Park: Pennsylvania State University Press, 2007.

Hanley, Sarah. "Engendering the State: Family Formation and State Building in Early Modern France." *French Historical Studies* 16, no. 1 (spring 1989): 4–27.

Hardwick, Julie. *Family Business: Litigation and the Political Economies of Daily Life in Early Modern France*. Oxford: Oxford University Press, 2009.

Harms, Robert. *The Diligent: A Voyage Through the Worlds of the Slave Trade*. New York: Basic Books, 2002.

Harsin, Paul. *Crédit public et Banque d'Etat en France du XVIe au XVIIIe siècle*. Paris: E. Droz, 1933.

Hautcoeur, Pierre-Cyrille, ed. "Justice commerciale et histoire économique." Special issue, *Histoire et mesure* 23, no. 1 (2008).

Himelfarb, Hélène. "Versailles, source ou miroir des modes Louis-quatorziennes? Sourches et Dangeau, 1684–1685." *Cahiers de l'association internationale des études françaises* 38 (1986): 121–43.

Hirschman, Albert O. *The Passions and the Interests*. Princeton, NJ: Princeton University Press, 1977.

Hoffman, Philip T. *Growth in a Traditional Society: The French Countryside, 1450–1815*. Princeton, NJ: Princeton University Press, 1996.

Hoffman, Philip T., Gilles Postel-Vinay, and Jean-Laurent Rosenthal. "Economie et politique: les marchés du crédit à Paris, 1750–1840." *Annales: Histoire, Sciences Sociales* 49, no. 1 (1994): 64–98.

———. "Information and Economic History: How the Credit Market in Old Regime Paris Forces Us to Rethink the Transition to Capitalism." *American Historical Review* 104, no. 1 (February 1999): 69–94.

———. *Priceless Markets: The Political Economy of Credit in Paris, 1660–1870*. Chicago: University of Chicago Press, 2000.

———. "Private Credit Markets in Paris, 1690–1840." *Journal of Economic History* 52, no. 2 (1992): 293–306.

Hope, Quentin M. "Society in *The Misanthrope*." *French Review* 32, no. 4 (February 1959): 329–36.

Hopwood, Anthony G. "The Archeology of Accounting Systems." *Accounting, Organisations and Society* 12, no. 3 (1987): 207–34.

Hoskin, Keith W., and Richard H. Macve. "Accounting and the Examination: A Genealogy of Disciplinary Power." *Accounting, Organisations and Society* 11, no. 2 (1986): 105–36.

Howard, Stanley E. "Public Rules for Private Accounting in France, 1673 and 1807." In *Accounting in France: Historical Essays / La Comptabilité en France: Etudes historiques*, edited by Yannick Lemarchand and R. H. Parker. 93–110. New York: Garland, 1996.

Hunt, Lynn. *The Family Romance of the French Revolution*. Berkeley: University of California Press, 1992.

———. "The Many Bodies of Marie Antoinette: Political Pornography and the Problem of the Feminine in the French Revolution." In *Eroticism in the Body Politic*. Edited by Lynn Hunt. 103–89. Baltimore: Johns Hopkins University Press, 1991.

———, ed. *The Invention of Pornography: Obscenity and the Origins of Modernity*. New York: Zone Books, 1993.

Joad, Raymond. *News Networks in Seventeenth-Century Britain and Europe.* New York: Routledge, 2008.

Jennings, Jeremy. "The Debate about Luxury in Eighteenth- and Nineteenth-Century French Political Thought," *The Journal of the History of Ideas* 68, no. 1 (2007): 79–105.

Jones, Colin. "The Great Chain of Buying: Medical Advertisement, the Bourgeois Public Sphere, and the Origins of the French Revolution." *American Historical Review* 101, no. 1 (February 1996): 13–40.

Jones, Jennifer. "*Coquettes* and *Grisettes*: Women Buying and Selling in Ancien Régime Paris." In *The Sex of Things: Gender and Consumption in Historical Perspective*, edited by Victoria de Grazia and Ellen Furlough. 25–53. Berkeley: University of California Press, 1996.

———. *Sexing la Mode: Gender, Fashion, and Commercial Culture in Old Regime France.* New York: Berg, 2004.

Jordan, William Chester. *Women and Credit in Pre-Industrial and Developing Societies.* Philadelphia: University of Pennsylvania Press, 1993.

Jouanna, Arlette. *Le devoir de révolte. La noblesse française et la gestation de l'Etat moderne, 1559-1661.* Paris: Fayard, 1989.

Jouhaud, Christian. *Les pouvoirs de la littérature: Histoire d'un paradoxe.* Paris: Gallimard, 2000.

Jouhaud, Christian, and Alain Viala, eds. *Groupe de recherches interdisciplinaires sur l'histoire du littéraire. De la publication: Entre Renaissance et Lumières.* Paris: Fayard, 2002.

Journeaux, Isabelle. "L'entrée dans le monde à travers les romanciers français et anglais du dix-huitième siècle." *Histoire, économie et société* 12, no. 2 (1993): 273–98.

Juste, Théodore. *Le Comte de Mercy-Argenteau.* Bruxelles: A. Lacroix, Verboeckhoven, and Co., 1863.

Kaiser, Thomas E. "Madame de Pompadour and the Theaters of Power." *French Historical Studies* 19, no. 4 (autumn 1996): 1025–44.

———. "Money, Despotism, and Public Opinion in Early Eighteenth-Century France: John Law and the Debate on Royal Credit." *Journal of Modern History* 63 (March 1991): 1–28.

Kaplan, Steven L. *The Bakers of Paris and the Bread Question, 1700-1775.* Durham, NC: Duke University Press, 1996.

———. *Bread, Politics, and Political Economy in the Reign of Louis XV.* The Hague: Martinus Nijhoff, 1976.

———. *La fin des corporations.* Paris: Fayard, 2001.

———. *Provisioning Paris: Merchants and Millers in the Grain and Flour Trade during the Eighteenth Century.* Ithaca, NY: Cornell University, 1984.

Kavanagh, Thomas. *Enlightenment and the Shadows of Chance: The Novel and the Culture of Gambling in Eighteenth-Century France.* Baltimore: Johns Hopkins University Press, 1993.

———. "The Libertine's Bluff: Cards and Culture in Eighteenth-Century France." *Eighteenth-Century Studies* 33, no. 4 (summer 2000): 505–21.

Kessler, Amalia. *A Revolution in Commerce: The Parisian Merchant Court and the Rise of Commercial Society in the Eighteenth Century*. Palo Alto, CA: Stanford University Press, 2007.

Kettering, Sharon. *Patronage in Sixteenth- and Seventeenth-Century France*. Aldershot: Ashgate, 2002.

———. "The Patronage Power of Early Modern French Noblewomen." *Historical Journal* 32, no. 4 (1989): 817–41.

———. *Patrons, Brokers and Clients in Seventeenth-Century France*. Oxford: Oxford University Press, 1987.

Kindleberger, Charles. *A Financial History of Western Europe*. 2nd ed. New York: Oxford University Press, 1993.

Kirkham, Lina M., and Anne Loft. "The Lady and the Accounts: Missing from Accounting History." *Accounting Historians Journal* 28, no. 1 (June 2001): 67–92.

Kleinert, Annemarie. *Die Frühen Modejournale in Frankreich. Studien zur Literatur der Mode von den Anfangen bis 1848*. Berlin: E. Schmidt, 1980.

Kofman, Sara, and Jean Yves Masson. *Don Juan ou le refus de la dette*. Paris: Galilée, 1991.

Kwass, Michael. "Big Hair: A Wig History of Consumption in Eighteenth-Century France." *American Historical Review* 111, no. 3 (2006): 631–59.

Labrousse, Ernest. *Esquisse du movement des prix et des revenus en France au XVIIIe siècle*. Paris: Librairie Dalloz, 1933.

Lambert, Miles. "'Sent from Town': Commissioning Clothing in Britain During the Long Eighteenth Century." *Costume* 43 (2009): 66–84.

Landes, Joan. *Women in the Public Sphere in the Age of the French Revolution*. Ithaca, NY: Cornell University Press, 1988.

Langlade, Emile. *La marchande de modes de Marie-Antoinette, Rose Bertin*. Paris: Albin Michel, 1911.

Lanza, Janine. *From Wives to Widows in Early Modern Paris: Gender, Economy, and Law*. Aldershot: Ashgate, 2007.

Latour, Bruno, and Vincent Antonin Lépinay. *The Science of Passionate Interests: An Introduction to Gabriel Tarde's Economic Anthropology*. Chicago: Prickly Paradigm Press, 2009.

Lazard, Lucien. "Les lettres de ratification hypothécaires, contribution à la topographie historique de Paris et du Département de la Seine." *Bulletin de la société de l'histoire de Paris* 30 (1903): 33–46.

LeMercier, Claire. "The Judge, the Expert and the Arbitrator: The Strange Case of the Paris Court of Commerce (ca. 1800–ca. 1880)." In *Fields of Expertise: A Comparative History of Expert Procedures in Paris and London, 1600 to Present*. Edited by Christelle Rabier. 115–45. Newcastle: Cambridge Scholars Publishing, 2007.

Lemire, Beverly. *Fashion's Favourite: The Cotton Trade and the Consumer in Britain, 1660–1800*. Oxford: Oxford University Press, 1991.

Lemire, Beverly, Ruth Pearson, and Gail Campbell, eds. *Women and Credit: Researching the Past, Refiguring the Future*. New York: Berg, 2002.

Lépinette, Brigitte. "Trois dictionnaires du XVIIe siècle, trois traitements différents de l'etymologie: Richelet (1680), Furetière (1690), Académie (1694)." In *Les Marques d'usage dans les dictionnaires: XVIIe-XVIIIe siècles.* Edited by Danielle Bouverot and Michel Glatigny. Villeneuve d'Ascq: Presses Universitaires du Septentrion, 1990.

Le Roy Ladurie, Emmanuel, and Jean-François Fitou. *Saint-Simon and the Court of Louis XIV.* Chicago: University of Chicago Press, 2001.

Lever, Evelyne. *Madame de Pompadour: A Life.* Translated by Catherine Temerson. New York: Farrar, Straus and Giroux, 2002.

Levi, Giovanni. *Inheriting Power: The Story of an Exorcist.* Translated by Lydia Cochrane. Chicago: University of Chicago Press, 1988.

Liebersohn, Harry. *The Return of the Gift: European History of a Global Idea.* Cambridge: Cambridge University Press, 2009.

Lilti, Antoine. "The Kingdom of *Politesse*: Salons and the Republic of Letters in Eighteenth-Century Paris." *Republics of Letters: A Journal for the Study of Knowledge, Politics and the Arts* 1, no. 1 (May 1, 2009). http://rofl.stanford.edu/node/38.

———. *Le Monde des salons: Sociabilité et mondanité à Paris au XVIIIe siècle.* Paris: Fayard, 2005.

———. "The Writing of Paranoia: Jean-Jacques Rousseau and the Paradoxes of Celebrity." *Representations* 103 (summer 2008): 53–83.

Livesey, James. "Les réseaux de credit en Languedoc au XVIIIe siècle et les origines sociales de la Révolution." *Annales historiques de la Révolution française* 359 (January–March 2010): 29–51.

Lowry, Todd. "The Archaeology of the Circulation Concept in Economic Theory." *Journal of the History of Ideas* 34, no. 3 (July–September 1974): 429–44.

Luckett, Thomas M. "Credit and Commercial Society in France, 1740–1789." PhD dissertation, Princeton University, 1992.

———. "The Sale and Business Strategies of a Parisian Artisan, 1754–1764: The Letters and Accounts of N.-C. Flocquet." *Proceedings of the Western Society for French History* 36 (2008): 93–108.

Luckett, Thomas M., and Pierre Lachaler. "Crises financières dans la France du XVIIIe siècle." *Revue d'histoire moderne et contemporaine* 43, no. 2 (April–June 1997): 266–92.

Mallet, Marc-Georges. *La Politique financière des Jacobins.* Paris: A. Rousseau, 1913.

Malon, Charles-Henri de, seigneur de Bercy. "Topographie historique de la seigneurie de Bercy." *Bulletin de la Société de l'histoire de Paris et de l'Ile-de-France* 8 (1882): 1–106.

Mandrou, Robert. *De la culture populaire aux 17e et 18e siècles: La Bibliothèque bleue de Troyes.* Paris: Stock, 1964.

Mansel, Philip. *Dressed to Rule: Royal and Court Costume from Louis XIV to Elizabeth II.* New Haven, CT: Yale University Press, 2005.

Martin, Jean-Clément. "Le commerçant, la faillite et l'historien." *Annales, économies, societies, civilisations* 35, no. 6 (November–December 1980): 1251–66.

Mauss, Marcel. *The Gift: Forms and Functions of Exchange in Archaic Societies.* London: Cohen and West, 1954.

Maza, Sarah. "The Diamond Necklace Affair Revisited (1785–86): The Case of the Missing Queen." In *Eroticism and the Body Politic.* Edited by Lynn Hunt. 63–89. Baltimore: Johns Hopkins University Press, 1991.

———. "Luxury, Morality, and Social Change: Why There Was No Middle-Class Consciousness in Prerevolutionary France." *Journal of Modern History* 69, no. 2 (June 1997): 199–229.

———. *The Myth of the French Bourgeoisie: An Essay on the Social Imaginary, 1750–1850.* Cambridge, MA: Harvard University Press, 2005.

———. *Private Lives and Public Affairs: The Causes Célèbres of Pre-Revolutionary France.* Berkeley: University of California Press, 1993.

McCalla, Arthur. "From *Palingénésie Philosophique* to *Palingénésie sociale*: From a Scientific Ideology to a Historical Ideology," *Journal of the History of Ideas* 55, no. 3 (July 1994): 421–39.

McCollim, Gary Bruce. "The Formation of Fiscal Policy in the Reign of Louis xiv: The Example of Nicolas Desmaretz, Controller General of Finances (1708–1715)." PhD dissertation, Ohio State University, 1979.

———. *Louis xiv's Assault on Privilege: Nicolas Desmaretz and the Tax on Wealth.* Rochester, NY: University of Rochester Press, 2012.

McKendrick, Neil, John Brewer, and J. H. Plumb, eds. *The Birth of A Consumer Society: The Commercialization of Eighteenth-Century England.* Bloomington: Indiana University Press, 1982.

McKeon, Michael. *Origins of the English Novel, 1600–1740.* Baltimore: Johns Hopkins University Press, 1987.

Menant, Sylvain. "Les Modernes et le style 'à la mode.'" *Cahiers de l'Association internationale des etudes françaises* 38 (1996): 146–56.

Miller, Lesley Ellis. "Paris-Lyon-Paris: Dialogue in the Design and Distribution of Patterned Silks in the 18th Century." In *Luxury Trades and Consumerism in Ancien Régime Paris: Studies in the History of the Skilled Workforce.* Edited by Robert Fox and Anthony Turner. 139–168. Aldershot: Ashgate, 1998.

Miller, Peter, and Ted O'Leary. "Accounting and the Construction of the Governable Person." *Accounting, Organisations and Society* 12, no. 3 (1987): 235–65.

Minard, Philippe. *La Fortune du Colbertisme.* Paris: Fayard, 1998.

Mollenauer, Lynne Wood. *Strange Revelations: Magic, Poison, and Sacrilege in Louis xiv's France.* University Park: Pennsylvania State University Press, 2007.

Mosher, Michael A. "The Judgmental Gaze of European Women: Gender, Sexuality, and the Critique of Republican Rule." *Political Theory* 22, no. 1 (February 1994): 25–44.

Muldrew, Craig. *The Economy of Obligation: The Culture of Credit and Social Relations in Early Modern England.* New York: St. Martin's, 1998.

Murphy, Antoin E. *John Law: Economic Theorist and Policy Maker.* Oxford: Oxford University Press, 1997.

Neal, Larry. *The Rise of Financial Capitalism: International Capital Markets in the Age of Reason.* Cambridge: Cambridge University Press, 1990.

Neuschel, Kristen. *Word of Honor: Interpreting Noble Culture in Sixteenth-Century France.* Ithaca, NY: Cornell University Press, 1989.

Nouvion, Pierre de, and Emile Liez. *Un Ministre des modes sous Louis xvi: Mademoiselle Bertin, marchande de modes de la reine, 1747–1813.* Paris: Henri Leclerc, 1911.

Offer, Avner. "Between the Gift and the Market: The Economy of Regard." *Economic History Review* 50, no. 3 (August 1997): 450–76.

Ozouf, Mona. *Women's Words: Essay on French Singularity*. Translated by Jane Marie Todd. Chicago: University of Chicago Press, 1997.

Pardailhé-Galabrun, Annik. *The Birth of Intimacy: Privacy and Domestic Life in Early Modern Paris*. Translated by Jocelyn Phelps. Philadelphia: University of Pennsylvania Press, 1992.

Parker, Thomas. "La Bruyère Gives His Two Cents: Financial Language and Ethical Ideals." *Seventeenth-Century French Studies* 27 (2005): 163–74.

Perrot, Jean-Claude. *Une histoire intellectuelle de l'économie politique: XVII-XVIIIe*. Paris: Editions de l'Ecole des hautes études en sciences sociales, 1992.

Perrot, Philippe. *Le Luxe. Une richesse entre faste et confort (XVIIIe-XIXe siècle)*. Paris: Seuil, 1995.

Polanyi, Karl. *The Great Transformation: The Political and Economic Origins of Our Time*. 1944. New York: Beacon, 2001.

Poni, Carlo. "Fashion as Flexible Production: The Strategies of the Lyons Silk Merchants in the Eighteenth Century." In *World of Possibilities: Flexibility and Mass Production in Western Industrialization*. Edited by Charles F. Sabel and Jonathan Zeitlin. 37–74. Cambridge: Cambridge University Press, 1997.

Poovey, Mary. *Genres of the Credit Economy: Mediating Value in Eighteenth- and Nineteenth-Century Britain*. Chicago: University of Chicago Press, 2008.

Popiel, Jennifer. *Rousseau's Daughters: Domesticity, Education, and Autonomy in Modern France*. Durham: University of New Hampshire Press, 2008.

Popkin, Jeremy D., and Bernadette Fort, eds. *The 'Mémoires secrets' and the Culture of Publicity in Eighteenth-Century France*. Oxford: Oxford University Press, 1998.

Posner, David Matthew. *The Performance of Nobility in Early Modern Literature*. Cambridge: Cambridge University Press, 1999.

Ranum, Orest. "Courtesy, Absolutism, and the Rise of the French State, 1630–1660." *Journal of Modern History* 52 (1980): 426–51.

Reddy, William. *The Rise of Market Culture*. Cambridge: Cambridge University Press, 1984.

Reiset, Comte de. *Modes et usages au temps de Marie-Antoinette. Livre-journal de Madame Eloffe*. Paris: Firmin-Didot, 1885.

Revel, Jacques. "Marie-Antoinette in Her Fictions: The Staging of Hatred." In *Fictions of the French Revolution*. Edited by Bernadette Fort. 111–30. Evanston, IL: Northwestern University Press, 1991.

———. "Microanalysis and the Construction of the Social." In *Histories: French Constructions of the Past*. Edited by Lynn Hunt and Jacques Revel. 492–502. Translated by Arthur Goldhammer. New York: New Press, 1996.

Reynard, Pierre Claude. "The Language of Failure: Bankruptcy in Eighteenth-Century France." *Journal of European Economic History* 30, no. 2 (2001): 355–90.

Ribeiro, Aileen. *Dress in Eighteenth-Century Europe*. New Haven, CT: Yale University Press, 2000.

Rickard, Peter, ed. *The French Language in the Seventeenth Century*. Woodbridge, UK: D. S. Brewer, 1992.

Riggs, Larry W. "The Formation and Exploitation of Cultural Capital in Molière." *Seventeenth-Century Studies* 27 (2005): 81–89.

Riley, Patrick. "Rousseau, Fénélon, and the Quarrel between the Ancients and the Moderns." In *The Cambridge Companion to Rousseau*. Edited by Patrick Riley. 78–93. Cambridge: Cambridge University Press, 2001.

Robb, Bonnie Arden. *Félicité de Genlis: Motherhood in the Margins*. Cranbury, NJ: Associated University Presses, 2008.

———. "Madame de Maintenon and the Literary Personality of Madame de Genlis: Creating Fictional, Historical, and Narrative Virtue." *Eighteenth-Century Fiction* 7, no. 4 (July 1995): 351–72.

Roche, Daniel. *The Culture of Clothing: Dress and Fashion in the Ancien Régime*. Translated by Jean Birrell. Cambridge: Cambridge University Press, 1994.

———. *A History of Everyday Things: The Birth of Consumption in France*. Translated by Brian Pearce. Cambridge: Cambridge University Press, 2000.

Rothkrug, Lionel. *Opposition to Louis XIV: The Political and Social Origins of the French Enlightenment*. Princeton, NJ: Princeton University Press, 1965.

Rothschild, Emma. *Economic Sentiments: Adam Smith, Condorcet, and the Enlightenment*. Cambridge, MA: Harvard University Press, 2001.

Rothstein, Natalie, ed. *A Lady of Fashion: Barbara Johnson's Album of Styles and Fabrics*. New York: W. W. Norton, 1987.

Sapori, Michelle. *Rose Bertin: Ministre de modes de Marie-Antoinette*. Paris: Editions du Regard, 2003.

Sargentson, Carolyn. *Merchants and Luxury Markets: The Marchands Merciers of Eighteenth-Century Paris*. London: Victoria and Albert Museum, 1996.

Saulnier, René, and Henri van der Zée. "La Mort de credit. Image populaire, ses sources politiques et économiques." *Dawna sztuka: czasopismo poświęcone archeologii i historii sztuki* 2, no. 3 (June 1939): 195–218.

Schoeser, Mary. "Letters to Monsieur Barbier, Parisian Silk Merchant, 1755–97." Master's thesis, Courtauld Institute of Art, 1979.

Scholar, Richard. *The Je-Ne-Sais-Quoi in Early Modern Europe: Encounters with a Certain Something*. Oxford: Oxford University Press, 2005.

———. "Towards a Pre-History of the Knowledge Economy: The Case of Pascal." *Seventeenth-Century French Studies* 27 (2005): 71–80.

Serna, Pierre. "Antonelle, bonnet rouge, talons rouges, de l'aristocratie des Lumières au penseur de la démocratie representative, ou le double statut en Révolution." *Annales historiques de la Révolution française* 301 (1995): 459–66.

Sewell, William. "The Empire of Fashion and the Rise of Capitalism in Eighteenth-Century France." *Past and Present* 206, no. 1 (February 2010): 81–121.

Sharpe, Kevin. *Reading Revolutions: The Politics of Reading in Early Modern England*. New Haven, CT: Yale University Press, 2000.

Shoemaker, Peter William. *Powerful Connections: The Poetics of Patronage in the Age of Louis XIII*. Cranbury, NJ: Associated University Presses, 2007.

Shovlin, John. "The Cultural Politics of Luxury in Eighteenth-Century France." *French Historical Studies* 23, no. 4 (2000): 577–606.

———. *The Political Economy of Virtue: Luxury, Patriotism, and the Origins of the French Revolution*. Ithaca, NY: Cornell University Press, 2006.

———. "Toward a Reinterpretation of Revolutionary Antinobilism: The Political

Economy of Honor in the Old Regime." *Journal of Modern History* 72, no. 1 (March 2000): 35–66.

Simmel, Georg. "Fashion." *American Journal of Sociology* 62 (1904; May 1957): 541–88.

Smail, Daniel Lord. *The Consumption of Justice: Emotions, Publicity, and Legal Culture*. Ithaca, NY: Cornell University Press, 2003.

Smith, Gretchen Elizabeth. *The Performance of Male Nobility in Molière's Comédie-Ballets: Staging the Courtier*. Aldershot: Ashgate Publishing, 2005.

Smith, Jay. *Nobility Reimagined: The Patriotic Nation in Eighteenth-Century France*. Ithaca, NY: Cornell University Press, 2005.

———. "No More Language Games: Words, Beliefs, and the Political Culture of Early Modern France." *American Historical Review* 102, no. 5 (December 1997): 1413–40.

———. "Social Categories, the Language of Patriotism, and the Origins of the French Revolution: The Debate over *Noblesse Commerçante*." *Journal of Modern History* 72, no. 2 (2000): 339–74.

Snyder, Jon. *Dissimulation and the Culture of Secrecy in Early Modern Europe*. Berkeley: University of California Press, 2009.

Soll, Jacob. "Amelot de La Houssaye (1634–1706) Annotates Tacitus." *Journal of the History of Ideas* 61, no. 2 (2000): 167–87.

———. *The Information Master: Jean-Baptiste Colbert's Secret State Intelligence System*. Ann Arbor: University of Michigan Press, 2009.

Sonenscher, Michael. *Before the Deluge: Public Debt, Inequality, and the Intellectual Origins of the French Revolution*. Princeton, NJ: Princeton University Press, 1990.

———. *Sans-culottes: An Eighteenth-Century Emblem in the French Revolution*. Princeton, NJ: Princeton University Press, 2008.

Sonnet, Martine. *L'Education des filles au temps des Lumières*. Paris: Cerf, 1987.

Sörman, Richard. "L'économie de l'incertitude chez Molière." *Seventeenth-Century French Studies* 27 (2005): 91–102.

Stanziani, Alessandro. "Shopkeepers and the Legal Price of Goodwill; Parisian fonds de commerce in the Nineteenth–Twentieth Century." Paper delivered to the conference Droit et histoire des enterprises, 18e-20e siècles, Paris, March 23–24, 2007.

Stigler, George. "The Economies of Information." *Journal of Political Economy* 69, no. 3 (1961): 213–25.

Sullerot, Evelyne. *Histoire de la presse féminine en France des origines à 1848*. Paris: Armand Colin, 1966.

Swann, Julian. "Parlement, Politics and the *Parti Janseniste*: The *Grand Conseil Affair, 1755-56*." *French History* 6, no. 4 (December 1992): 435–61.

Tarrade, Jean. *Le Commerce colonial de la France à la fin de l'Ancien Régime*. Paris: Presses universitaires de France, 1972.

Taylor, Lou. *Mourning Dress: A Costume and Social History*. London: Allen and Unwin, 1983.

Teichgraeber, Richard, and Thomas Haskell, eds. *The Culture of the Market: Historical Essays*. Cambridge: Cambridge University Press, 1994.

Thomas, Chantal. *The Wicked Queen: The Origins of the Myth of Marie-Antoinette*. Translated by Julie Rose. New York: Zone Books, 1999.

Ulrich, Laurel Thatcher. *A Midwife's Tale: The Life of Martha Ballard, Based on her Diary, 1785–1812*. New York: Vintage, 1990.

Van Dijk, Suzanne. "Femmes et journaux au XVIIIe siècle." *Australian Journal of French Studies* 18, no. 2 (1982): 164–78.

Velde, François. "Was John Law's System a Bubble? The Mississippi Bubble Revisited." In *The Origins and Development of Financial Markets and Institutions*. Edited by Jeremy Atack and Larry Neal. 99–120. Cambridge: Cambridge University Press, 2009.

Vickery, Amanda. *The Gentleman's Daughter: Women's Lives in Georgian England*. New Haven, CT: Yale University Press, 1998.

Vila, Anne C. "Elite Masculinities in the Eighteenth-Century." In *French Masculinities: History, Culture and Politics*, edited by Christopher E. Forth and Bertrand Taithe. 15–30. New York: Palgrave Macmillan, 2007.

Vincent, Monique. *Le Mercure galant. Présentation de la première revue féminine d'information et de culture, 1672–1710*. Paris: Champion, 2005.

Vivo, Filippo de. *Information and Communication in Venice: Rethinking Early Modern Politics*. New York: Oxford University Press, 2007.

Vries, Jan de. *The Industrious Revolution: Consumer Behavior and the Household Economy, 1650 to the Present*. Cambridge: Cambridge University Press, 2008.

Walker, Lesley H. "Producing Feminine Virtue: Strategies of Terror in Writings by Madame de Genlis." *Tulsa Studies in Women's Literature* 23 (2004): 213–36.

Waquet, Françoise. "La mode au XVIIe siècle: de la folie à l'usage." *Cahiers de l'Association internationale des etudes françaises* 38 (1986): 91–104.

Weber, Caroline. *Queen of Fashion: What Marie Antoinette Wore to the Revolution*. New York: Henry Holt, 2006.

Weisbrod, Andrea. *Von Macht und Mythos der Pompadour*. Berlin: Ulrike Helmer Verlag, 2000.

Wennerlind, Carl. *Casualties of Credit: The English Financial Revolution, 1620–1720*. Cambridge, MA: Harvard University Press, 2011.

Wiskin, Christine. "Businesswomen and Financial Management: Three Eighteenth-Century Case Studies." *Accounting, Business & Financial History* 16, no. 2 (July 2006): 143–61.

Wolff, Larry. "Habsburg Letters: The Disciplinary Dynamics of Epistolary Narrative in the Correspondence of Maria Theresa and Marie-Antoinette." In *Marie-Antoinette, Writings on the Body of a Queen*. Edited by Dena Goodman and Thomas Kaiser. 25–42. New York: Routledge, 2003.

Wright, Johnson Kent. *A Classical Republican in Eighteenth-Century France: The Political Thought of Mably*. Palo Alto, CA: Stanford University Press, 1997.

Yim, Denise. "*Adèle et Théodore's* Influence on an English Family's Education." *Australian Journal of French Studies* 38 (2001): 141–57.

INDEX

Page numbers followed by f indicate figures.

banking system, 57–59

bankruptcy, 196, 197, 211–19; case studies of, 215–43, 368n4, 370n34, 371n54; cash sales and, 235–38; clientele and, 217–19; court settlements for, 242–43; delayed payments and, 220–24; economic crises and, 221, 371n40; exchanging credit and, 232–33, 235; forms of payment and, 224–25, 244; gender and marital status and, 213–14, 233–35; incarceration for, 237–38; interest and surcharges in, 225–33; legal recourse in, 228–29; narratives of calamities and, 204, 238–43; number of cases of, 212–13; personal expenses and, 204–5, 212, 239; price reductions and partial payments in, 219–20, 226–30; ratio of assets to liabilities in, 229–32, 372n58; records required for, 211–12

banqueroute, 197

Banque royale, 74–78

Barbier, Jean-François, 364n95, 369n19

Barbier, Jean Nicolas, 369n19

Barry, Jeanne Bécu, comtesse du, 92, 165, 252, 270

Baucom, Ian, 12

Baudry, Marie-Angélique-Françoise Taschereau de. *See* Bercy, Marie-Angélique-Françoise de marquise

the *bavaroise*, 173

Beaulard, Jean-Joseph, 159, 213–14, 224, 226–27, 234, 259

beauty: female education in, 305; of Marie Antoinette, 264, 277; of Mme de Pompadour, 89; as opposite of fashion, 110, 192, 304; as source of credit, 7, 60

Bercy, Marie-Angélique-Françoise, marquise de, 20, 141, 169–79; consumption of clothing by, 171–74, 177, 178*f*, 191, 360n14, 365n101; family background of, 169–71, 175, 364n91; household expenses of, 175–76; payment delays of, 174–76, 203, 365n96; price reductions demanded by, 176–77, 365n99; settling of accounts by, 175–79, 368n4

Bercy, Nicolas, marquis de, 171–72

Bermont, Jean Baptiste, 215–25

Bernard, Adelaïde, 216–19, 227, 232, 236–38

Bertin, Claude-Charlemagne, 275–76

Bertin, Louis Nicholas, 275, 297

Bertin, Nicholas, 275–76

Bertin, Rose (Marie-Jeanne), 10, 18, 20, 125, 243–44, 249*f*; appearances in fiction of, 306–7, 309; bankruptcy rumors about, 197, 205, 211, 246–47, 275, 372n2; biographies of, 265, 369n15; boutique of, 206*f*, 214, 265, 274–75; clientele of, 206–9, 244, 265, 272, 297–301, 369n19; communication skills of, 189; credit and debt at death of, 285–86, 297–301, 314–15, 316; employees of, 148, 198, 207, 210–11, 370n21; goods and services provided by, 157, 207; international business of, 210, 214, 265, 297; management of credit by, 196, 198, 205–11, 250, 265, 298, 301, 369n17, 370n27; media coverage of, 159, 250, 267–68, 374n26; memoir attributed to, 326; personal properties and investments of, 273–76, 375n54; physical appearance of, 269; public criticism of, 246–47, 268, 276–80; relationship with Marie Antoinette of, 250–51, 261–64, 267–82; rival of, 159; self-fashioned reputation and celebrity of, 192–94, 196, 250, 265–73, 322; suppliers of, 210–11, 233, 275; visits to elite clients by, 202–3, 247; on "work" of time, effort, and imagination, 202. *See also* Marie Antoinette

Bibliothèque bleue, 50, 52–54, 226

La Bibliothèque françoise (Sorel), 34–35

bills of exchange, 224–25

Boisguilbert, Pierre Le Pesant, sieur de, 73

Boissy, Louis de, 135

Bombelles, marquis de, 215

bookkeeping. *See* management of credit and debt

Bornier, Philippe, 181, 189, 290

Bossuet, Jacques-Bénigne, bishop, 28, 66

Boucher, François, 97*f*, 149*f*, 203

Bouhours, Dominique, 52, 102

Boullenois bankruptcy case. *See* Leveque and Boullenois bankruptcy case

Bourdaloue, Père, 27–28

Bourdieu, Pierre: on economic information, 333n27; on forms of capital, 13–15; on naturalization of cultural capital, 353n72; on political economy of credit, 15–18; on roulette and capital, 344n22

bourgeois de Paris, 213–14

Les Bourgeoises à la mode (Dancourt), 139, 169–71

Le Bourgeois gentilhomme (Molière), 118–20, 139, 169, 304, 352n57

Boutique of Rose Bertin, 206*f*

Boyer, Abel, 123–24, 127

Bussy-Rabutin, Roger de, 20, 22–23, 31–33; correspondence with Mme de Sévigné of, 43–44, 48–49; literary renown of, 44

Cabaille, Barbe Catherine, 215–25, 370n38

Cabinet des modes, 158–59, 161, 186, 361n35, 362n48

Caisse d'escompte, 1–2, 329n2, 329n4

calicoes, 106

Calonne, Charles Alexandre, 247

Campan, Jeanne-Louise-Henriette de, 261, 263, 267–68, 277–78, 313

Cantillon, Richard, 16

capitalism, 8, 12, 339n77, 358n5. *See also* economic capital

the caraco, 158

Caractères ou les moeurs de ce siècle (La Bruyère), 58, 60–64, 78, 117–18, 342n8

Caylus, Anne-Claude-Philippe, comte de, 145, 331n16

celebrity, 367n125; of fashion merchants, 191–93; of the *homme à la mode*, 132

Chambonas, Victor-Louis de la Garde, marquis de, 299

Champrenits, marquise de, 299–300

Chapelain, Jean, 39, 41

charity, 63; as opposite of consumption, 287, 306–9, 312; schools funded by, 104, 187

Chartier, Roger, 104, 334n2, 334n39, 342n2

Chasseriau, Marie-Louise Bertin, 276

Chasseriau, Mathurin, 276

Chateau de Bercy, 171, 172*f*

Cheney, Paul, 16

Chinese credit, 37–38

Choiseul, comtesse de, 90

Choiseul, Etienne François, duc de, 251, 256–57, 300

Choiseul-Meuse, Félicité de, 310–11

chronology of credit, 18–20, 24–25, 333n38

circulation, 1–2, 73. *See also* credit; information exchange

civilité, 57, 101–4, 334n39, 342n2

Clérembault, maréchal de, 129

Club de l'Entresol, 70

Coëffure à l'indépendance ou triomphe de la liberté, 260*f*

Colbert, Jean-Baptiste: Commercial Code of, 167, 180; credit of, 26, 38; fiscal regime of, 71, 74; impact on textile and clothing industries of, 104–6, 143, 145

Comédie française, 352n58. *See also* Molière

commerce. *See* consumer revolution; fashion merchants

Commercial Code of 1673, 105; bankruptcy policies in, 211–13; bookkeeping and accounting requirements in, 180–83, 198, 201, 365n110; on separation of goods in marriage, 290

commercial culture, 167, 175–76, 185, 194

common/ordinary people, 23, 50–55; Duclos's exclusion from discussion of, 85; household credit networks of, 168; plebian credit of, 50–54; spread of *civilité* to, 103–4

economies of regard, 9–10, 21–55, 316–17, 327–28, 332n23; among common people, 50–55; in daily life, 43–50; in foreign societies, 38–41, 339nn69–71, 339n77; gift economy of, 63, 316, 317–18, 343n18; in intellectual life, 34–37; in legal contexts, 33–34; in marriage and family life, 41–42, 45–46; in religious contexts, 37–38, 53–54, 338n64; in the royal court, 21–33, 54

Les égarements du coeur et de l'esprit (Crébillon), 132–34

Eighteenth-Century Collections Online, 17, 356n113

elites. *See* aristocracy and elites; monarchy and court; *le monde*

Eloffe, Mademoiselle, 209–10

Emile (Rousseau), 192–93, 304, 305, 312–13, 380n51

Emma Bovary (character), 313

Encyclopédie: definitions of *cours* in, 127; definitions of credit in, 87, 89, 94; on fashion merchants, 145–46; on fashion neologisms, 162; on legal status of married women, 288–89

Les entretiens d'Ariste de d'Eugène (Bouhours), 52

Eon, Charles de Beaumont, chevalier d,' 272

Epinay, Louise Florence Pétronille, marquise d,' 303, 305–7

L'Esprit des journaux, 154

Estrades, compte d,' 89–90

L'état de servitude ou la misère des domestiques, 53

Examen de conscience sur les devoirs de la royauté (Fénélon), 118

L'Extraordinaire du Mercure galant, 107, 115, 125

faillite, 197. *See also* bankruptcy

Fairchilds, Cissie, 144, 351n38, 359n9

family life. *See* marriage and family life

Faret, Nicholas, 60, 100–104, 116–17, 119

Farrell, Michele Longino, 49

fashion, 8, 96–99, 282; affinities with credit of, 99, 122–28, 136–37, 353n72; creation of economic value with, 124, 151–57, 163, 322, 361n35, 363n72; credibility attained through, 14, 20, 98–104, 113, 118–19, 141, 151, 247–48, 258–64, 277–78, 316, 327, 350n28; definitions of, 107, 122, 124; Donneau's *Le Mercure galant* on, 107–17, 119, 125–27, 129, 151–52, 154; feminization of consumption of, 151, 169, 283–84, 286–87, 361n35; under the First Empire and Restoration, 312–13, 315, 381n63; at the French court, 100–101, 103, 104–5, 107, 109, 111, 113–16, 118, 123; French dominance of, 98, 107, 152–53, 322, 361n40; humans as objects of, 99, 128, 130–31, 135–36, 138; Louis XIV's policies on, 99, 100, 104–6, 113, 258, 350n25, 351n46; Marie Antoinette's relationship to, 258–59; media coverage of, 151–63; in men's dress, 110, 112, 115, 130, 138, 151; relation to social hierarchy of, 10–11, 20, 98–99, 102, 104–5, 108–19, 127–28, 137, 151, 304; sexual credit and, 99, 132–36, 356nn108–9; temporal dynamics of, 115–16, 126, 133, 179, 351n44, 354nn78–97. *See also* criticism of fashion; information exchange; *Le Mercure galant*

fashion dolls, 155–57

fashion merchants, 8–12, 18, 320–22; apprenticeships and training of, 147, 186–87, 360nn21–22; bankruptcy among, 211–12, 215–16, 219–25, 238–43; bookkeeping and accounting practices of, 180–82, 187, 197–205, 219, 365n106, 366n119; celebrity status of, 9–10, 138, 191–93, 322; creation of fashion by, 139–40, 151–53, 157–59, 163; cultural credit conveyed by, 14, 20, 125–26, 139–42, 158, 161–62, 163, 200–201, 322, 354n76; dramatic portrayals of, 139, 142, 154–55, 169–71, 353n59; economic value produced by, 141, 151–53, 163, 322, 361n35, 363n72; education levels of, 187, 203–4; employees of, 148–50, 321; gender composition of, 150, 207; independent guild of, 9, 139, 142–44, 148–50, 184, 321; management of reputation and credibility by, 8, 139–40, 168–69, 180–91, 204–5, 265–67, 364nn86–87; media coverage of, 157–66, 267–68; origins and evolution of, 139, 141, 142–51; private lives of, 204, 212, 213–15, 239; relations with elite clients of, 10–12, 20, 141, 149*f*, 165, 169–79, 194; retail boutiques of, 145–46, 165–66, 187–89; sexual liaisons and, 163–66, 167*f*, 193, 194, 367n133; suppliers of, 184–91, 210–11, 214–15, 225, 233–34, 321–22, 354n79, 364n95. *See also* management of credit and debt

fashion press, 107–16, 153–55, 157–66, 259–61, 267–68, 361n35, 362n48, 362n57

fashion system, 98–99, 145, 258, 361n35

fashion trades, 120–21, 138, 142–44, 211, 243–45, 320–22; advertising and publicity in, 154–57, 259–61, 266–68, 367n122; coordination within, 173–74, 210–11; credit networks in, 233–35; dramatic portrayals of, 113–21; government regulation of, 105, 180–83; Parisian dominance of, 152–53. *See also* management of credit and debt

Les Fausses Confidences (Marivaux), 51

featherworkers, 148, 360n28

La femme d'intrigues (Dancourt), 120–21, 352n58

femmes à la mode, 135–36, 356n113, 357n115

Fénélon, François de Salignac de la Mothe, 118, 131, 352n50, 380n40

Ferrière, Claude de, 299

Feuille nécessaire, 154, 157, 158

Feuille sans titre, 154–55, 159, 161, 267

Fielding, Henry, 40–41

Filliard, Madamoiselle, 155*f*

financial credit, 3, 6, 7, 19–20; Duclos's views on, 86; exchange values of, 33, 63, 337n42; expansion of, 23–25, 29, 335n8; in the fashion industry, 31, 121, 140–41, 142; gender dimensions of, 211; inseparability from other modes of credit, 30–33, 83, 257, 281–82, 317, 327–28; Mme de Sévigné on, 46–49; role in commerce of, 166–69; tools of, 54–55. *See also* money; public credit; shop credit

financiers, 71, 73, 75, 118, 341n114, 346n46; Duclos on, 85–86; Mme de Pompadour's ties to, 88–89, 91, 348n79

First Empire, 313, 381n63

Fléchier, Esprit, 28–29, 41, 336n26

fonds de commerce, 231

Fontenelle, Bernard Bovier de, 107, 352n50

Forbonnais, François Véron Duverger de, 87

foreign credit, 38–41, 339n77, 339nn69–71

Foucault, Michel, 94, 333n35, 365n110

Fouquet, Nicolas de, 31–32, 35, 341n102

France, Louise de, 228

French Revolution, 19–20, 77, 281–82, 325; aristocratic emigration during, 150–51, 275, 297, 298, 312; impact on fashion consumption of, 150–51, 297–98, 304–5, 312–13, 315, 381n63; Marie Antoinette's clothing expenditures during, 208; status of private debt after, 298

friendship, 6, 42; Bussy-Rabutin on, 43–44; Duclos on, 82; La Bruyère on, 60–61; Mme de Sévigné on, 46–47

fripiers' guild, 142

Furetière, Antoine, 4–5, 7, 8, 29, 80, 107, 122

Gaillard, Mademoiselle, 172–77, 178*f*, 203, 365n99

Galerie des modes, 154, 164*f*, 190*f*

Gallica, 17

gambling, 170, 276; debt from, 10, 63–64, 344n22, 378n11; libertinage and, 356n104; Marie Antoinette's losses from, 278–79

garment trades, 142–44. *See also* fashion merchants; fashion trades

Garraway, Doris, 337n64

Garsault, François Alexandre, 146, 185, 360n19

Gautier and Regnault, messieurs, 115, 351n44

Gazette Royale, 107

Gelbart, Nina Rattner, 362n57

gender, 7–8, 318–19, 325; account management skills and, 204, 369n12; availability of financial credit and, 213–14, 233–35, 243–44; bankruptcy and, 213–14, 233–35; in definitions of credit, 5–7, 29, 87–88, 138; expectations of males and, 292–97; in fashion consumption, 128–36, 151, 169, 283–84, 286–88, 292, 301–14, 361n35; of fashion industry debtors, 234–35; in fashion industry work, 9, 98, 112, 138, 211, 244; financial abuses and, 280. *See also* fashion merchants; sexual sources of credit; women

Genlis, Stéphanie Félicité, comtesse de, 135–36, 226, 228, 307–14, 380n51

Geoffrin, Marie Thérèse Rodet, 272

Gicquel, Louis, 214, 234, 238–40

Gicquel, Marie-Thérèse, 202, 214, 216–28, 231–33, 235, 237–40

gift economy, 62–63, 86, 316, 317–18, 343n18

Girard, Madeleine Charlotte, 240–41

Godet des Marais, Paul, 27–28

Goodman, Dena, 204

Google Books, 17, 356n113

Gournay, Marie de, 24, 335n10

grand journal (ledger), 198, 205

Grand Mogol boutique, 206f, 214, 265, 274–75

Grassi, Marie-Claire, 204

Grenaille, François de, 122

Grenier, Jean-Yves, 12–13, 333n27, 371n40

Guez de Balzac, Jean-Louis, 35, 59–60

Guines, Adrien-Louis de Bonnières, duc de, 256–57

Guyon, Jeanne-Marie, 64–65

Hanley, Sarah, 284

Hardwick, Julie, 168, 285

Hardy, Siméon-Prosper, 246

Harvey, William, 16, 73

hats and headwear, 148, 150f, 152, 158, 162–63, 164f, 202, 321, 360n28; cash versus credit payments for, 237f; height of, 261–64; of Marie Antoinette, 259–64; prices of, 236; by Rose Bertin, 207

A Hint to the Ladies to Take Care of Their Heads, 262f

Hirschman, Albert O., 339n77

L'Histoire amoureuse des Gaules, 49

Histoire de Guillaume Cocher (Caylus), 145

Histoire de Madame de Montbrillant (Epinay), 303, 305, 307

Histoire de Sara (La Bretonne), 51–52

Hoffman, Philip, 125, 168, 377n8

Holbach, Paul-Henri Thiry, baron d,' 29, 56–57, 92, 326

hommes à la mode, 356n113, 357n115; Duclos on, 355n88; fashion of, 128–31; seduction and credit of, 99, 132–36, 356nn108–9

honor: commerce and, 200, 301; debt and, 10, 308; Duclos on, 78, 84; of elite clients, 301; familial forms of, 287; female forms of, 301, 311–12, 374n36; juxtaposition of credit and, 6–7, 42, 48

The Human Comedy (Balzac), 136

humoral system, 16

Hunt, Lynn, 304

Ibert, Marie-Catherine-Jacqueline Bertin, 276

imprisonment for debt, 237–38

L'Indicateur, 154

indigo dye, 144, 322, 359n13

industrious revolution, 143, 145, 194, 321

information exchange, 12–13, 333n27; in aristocratic and elite circles, 13, 49–50, 125–26, 266–68, 320, 332n24; credit and fashion as systems of, 8, 99, 125–27, 137, 320; in economics, 12, 168; in the fashion industry, 98–99, 105–16, 125–27, 137, 145, 151, 157–63, 188–89, 194, 203, 259–60, 282; histories of, 12–13, 354n73, 354n76; in markets, 13, 332n24; notaries' roles in, 125; secrecy in, 123; writing, publishing, and communication in, 12–13, 34–37, 151

inseparable domains of credit in daily life, 2–3, 7–8, 47–48, 316–18, 327–28; as common sense, 16–17, 19, 22–23, 125; at court, 25; mingling of the material and nonmaterial in, 54–55, 317–18

Institutions d'un prince (Duguet), 70

intellectual credit, 34–37

L'Interdiction (Balzac), 136, 357n116

interest, 41, 339n77, 371n47; charging in credit sales of, 176, 225–26, 237; creditors' imposition of, 195, 208, 225, 241–42; as English equivalent to *crédit*, 40–41; state payments of, 75. *See also* self-interest

Janinet, Jean-François, 249f

Jansenism, 64–66

Jaubert, Pierre, 146, 360n19

Jeanne d'Arc, 39, 41

Jesuit credit, 66

Jones, Jennifer, 361n35, 362n48

Joseph II, Emperor of Austria, 264

Josephine, Empress of France, 326

Jouanna, Arlette, 23

Journal de commerce et d'agriculture, 152, 153

Journal de Paris, 154–55, 158–59, 160f, 195, 267, 290, 374n26

Journal des dames, 154, 157, 362n57

Journal des savants, 107

Journal étranger de littérature, des spectacles et de politique, 154

judicial decisions. *See* legal parameters

Juridiction consulaire, 196, 198, 212–13, 237–38

Kaplan, Steven L., 167–68, 354n79

Kavanagh, Thomas, 344n22

Kettering, Sharon, 23, 377n8

Kleinert, Annemarie, 362n48

Labille-Guiard, Adélaïde, 270

La Bretonne, Nicolas Restif de, 51–52

La Bruyère, Jean de: on credit, 57, 58, 60–64, 78, 93, 331n19, 342n8; on fashion, 117–18, 122, 130–31, 352nn50–51; inspiration of Balzac by, 357n116

lace, 214–15

La Croix sisters, 216–25, 227, 235–37

Lafayette, Marie-Madeleine Pioche de la Vergne, madame de, 30, 41, 332n21

"Laïs et Phriné" (anonymous), 135, 356n111

Lamballe, Marie Thérèse, princesse de, 257, 276

Lambert, Anne Thérèse de Maguenat de, 134, 356n108

Landes, Joan, 20, 286, 304

Lanza, Janine, 377n8

La Reynie, Nicolas de, 113

La Rochefoucault, princesse de, 215–16

La Salle, Jean-Baptiste de, 104, 118

Latour, Bruno, 382n5

Law, John: assessments of, 76, 81, 346n51; financial project of, 57–59, 73–78, 87, 90, 93, 323, 326, 346n51; impact on Duclos family of, 347n61; on increasing circulation of money, 75–76; on overseas commerce and the slave trade, 77, 347n54

Le Comte, Louis, 37–38

legal credit, 33–34, 337n47

ing and accounting obligations in, 180–82, 187, 197–212, 219, 236, 365n106, 366n119, 368n5; cash sales and, 235–38; Commercial Code requirements in, 105, 180–83, 198, 201, 290, 365n110; delayed payments and, 175–79, 196, 200, 203, 208, 219, 220–24; essential role in commerce of, 166–69; exchanges of credit in, 232–33, 235; *fonds de commerce* and, 231; forms of payment in, 174, 224–25, 244; gender and marital status in, 211, 213–14, 233–35, 243–44, 369n12; incarceration for debt and, 237–38; interest and surcharges in, 208–9, 225–33; legal recourse in, 228–29; narratives of calamities and, 204, 238–43; obligations to workers and suppliers in, 126, 210–11; price reductions and partial payments in, 176–77, 196, 208–9, 219–20, 226–30, 365n99; profit margins in, 199–201, 202, 226, 229, 236, 245, 368n7; records of orders in, 202–3; social contexts of, 201–3, 205–11; success in, 244–45

the mantua dress, 109–10, 112

Manuel des toilettes, 155, 161

Marbois, François Barbé de, 91

La Marchande de modes (Boucher), 149f, 203

marchandes de mode. See fashion merchants

marchanes publiques, 143, 183–84, 197, 238, 289, 299

Maria Theresa, Empress of Austria, 251–56, 263–64

Maria Theresa, Queen of France, 28, 105, 281

Marie Antoinette, Queen of France, 20, 192, 325–26; consumption of fashion by, 208–9, 211, 247, 258–64, 268–69, 279, 305, 370n20; controversial marriage of, 251; credit and power at court of, 247, 250–58, 276–82; Diamond Necklace Affair and, 280, 311–12; fashion debt of, 246, 278; fashion dolls and

mannequin for, 157; female coterie of, 257, 276, 280, 281; financial status of, 209, 246–47; gambling expenses of, 278–79; hats and headwear of, 259–64; Le Petit Trianon of, 261, 280; portraiture of, 125, 248f, 258, 270, 271f; power at court of, 326; public hostility toward, 247, 257–58, 276–80, 284, 288, 313; relationship with Rose Bertin of, 250–51, 261–64, 267–82; rumors on sexuality of, 276–80, 376n61. *See also* Bertin, Rose

"Marie Antoinette, Queen of France" (Vigée-LeBrun), 248f

"Marie Antoinette in a chemise dress" (Vigée-Lebrun), 270, 271f

Marie Leczynska, Queen of France, 255

Marivaux, Pierre Carlet de Chamblain de, 21, 51

market economy, 31, 69, 75, 324, 332n23, 335n8

markets, 2, 14; circulation of information and, 13, 332n24; expansion of, 291; impact of credit on, 167–68; industrious revolution and, 143; mercantilism and, 106; relationship of accounting to, 199; for secondhand goods, 144; women's access to, 314, 318

marriage and family life, 7, 41–42, 45–46, 283–315; availability of credit and, 213–14, 233–35; "community of goods" in, 289–90, 378n12; critics of female consumption and, 286–88, 292, 301–14; emancipated wives in, 289; fashion and consumption as threat to, 283–84; husbands' financial role in, 284, 292–97, 303, 315, 379n21; inheritance of debt in, 285, 299–301, 315, 378n10; legal status of women in, 284–86, 288–92, 299, 315, 377n8, 378n13; physical violence in, 296; separation of goods in, 289–90, 292–96, 299, 379n17; ubiquity of debt in, 285, 319; women's financial autonomy and debt in, 291–92, 297–301, 311–15, 319, 378n11

royalty. *See* monarchy and court

rue Saint-Honoré, 191, 215

Rules for Christian Propriety and Civility (De la Salle), 104

Rutebeuf, 25, 331n17, 335n9

Saint-Aubin, Gabriel Jacques de, 160*f*

Sainte Nitouche ou histoire galante de la tournière des Carmelites suivie de l'histoire de La Duchapt (Meusnier de Querlon), 193

Saint Méry, Louis-Élie Moreau de, 52

Saint-Pierre, Charles-Irénée Castel de, 68–70, 132

Saint-Quentin, Mademoiselle, 158–59, 160*f*

Saint-Simon, Louis de Rouvroy, duc de, 25–31, 51–52, 335n10; on fashion, 123; on the *homme à la mode*, 128–29, 131; influence on Duclos by, 85–88; on the Princesse des Ursins, 56, 87; on the regency, 88; on women's credit, 94

Sargentson, Carolyn, 369n19

satire: in Donneau's reporting on fashion, 107–13, 119, 125–27; of fashion and credibility, 117–21, 192–93; of fashion merchants, 159, 161, 163; of *femmes à la mode*, 135–36; in *A Hint to the Ladies to Take Care of Their Heads*, 262*f*; of *hommes à la mode*, 129–32; of hypocrisy at court, 57, 59–64, 342n8, 343n15

Satires (Du Lorens), 59

Savary des Bruslon, Jacques, 124, 153, 162–63, 166–67; on merchant bookkeeping, 201; on merchant reputation, 200, 365n110; on merchants' appearance, 189; on merchants' sharing of information, 188; on *plumassiers*, 360n28; on the price of credit, 225–26; on shop location and appearance, 187–88; on women's legal independence, 183–84

Scudéry, Madeleine de, 43

seamstresses: Code of Commerce regulation of, 180; guild of, 105, 142–44,

146–48, 215, 258, 321, 367n133; Mme de Bercy's patronage of, 171–77; prostitution among, 367n133; relation to fashion merchants of, 173–74, 185, 194, 207, 210; separation of property among, 379n17

Secret Memoirs of the Reign of Louis XIV . . . and Louis XV (Duclos), 56, 81, 87–88

self-interest: capitalism and, 339n7; criticism of, 42, 57, 65, 68, 93; Duclos on, 78, 81–83, 85–86, 93; the *femme à la mode* and, 136; the *homme à la mode* and, 131; La Bruyère on, 60–62; of Mme de Pompadour, 24; Molière on, 37, 42; in noble worldviews, 24

Seven Years' War, 90–91, 246

Sévigné, Marie de Rabutin-Chantal, madame de, 20, 22–23, 45–46; Bussy-Rabutin's description of, 48–49; on the Cardinal de Retz, 46–47; correspondence of, 33, 43–44, 340n88; financial challenges of, 47–49, 341n114; multiple interactions with credit of, 34, 43–50; relationship with Fouquet of, 32–33, 341n102

Sewell, William, 8, 12–13

sexuality: definitions of credit and, 5; of female fashion workers, 163–66, 167*f*, 193, 194, 367n133; in Louis XVI and Marie Antoinette's relationship, 247, 250, 252; in marital contexts, 41; Mme de Pompadour and, 89–91; rumors of Marie Antoinette and, 276–80, 376n61

sexual sources of credit, 69–70, 119, 266, 318–19, 325, 345n40; for *femmes à la mode*, 135–36; for *hommes à la mode*, 96, 99, 132–36, 356nn108–9; during Louis XV's regency, 67–71, 345n38; Mme Pompadour's use of, 88–92; women's manipulation of, 7–8, 58–60, 67–71, 92, 93–95

shop credit, 5, 9, 140, 141, 166–69, 319, 322; noble consumption on, 5, 10–11, 31, 47–48, 119, 120–21, 168, 169–70;

temporal patterns of, 177–79. *See also* fashion merchants; financial credit; management of credit and debt

shopping, 144, 187, 203, 274

Shovlin, John, 16, 304

silk cloth, 144, 215, 359n12, 361n40

Simmel, Georg, 127–28

slavery, 52; cotton and indigo production and, 144, 322, 359nn12–13; John Law project and, 77, 347n54

Smail, Dan, 18–20

Smith, Adam, 16

Smith, Jay, 18–19, 23–24

social credit, 2–3, 6, 8, 10–15, 20, 25–26; achievement of celebrity and, 9–10, 138, 159, 191–94, 196, 322; individual deployment of, 127–28, 355n84; inseparability from other modes of credit, 31, 317, 327–28. *See also* political credit

social hierarchies: at court, 80–83; impact of credit and fashion on, 10–11, 20, 127–28, 137; performative nature of, 101–2; in power dynamics of credit relationships, 194, 319–20; in power dynamics of merchants and clients, 10–11, 20, 141, 169–79

Sonenscher, Michael, 16, 76–77

Sonnet, Martine, 187

Sorel, Charles, 34–35

specie. *See* money

spelling, 203–4

Splendeurs et misères des courtisanes (Balzac), 357n116

Staël, Germane de, 325–26, 382n7

status. *See* reputation

Stigler, George, 332n24

The Story of Madame de Luz (Duclos), 132

sumptuary law, 105

Système social (Holbach), 56–57

Le Tableau de Paris (Mercier), 1, 151–52, 304–5, 329nn2–3

Tableau économique (Quesnay), 333n34

Tacitus, 40, 339n71

tailors, 142–43, 146–47, 150, 210, 321

Tarde, Gabriel, 323–28, 382n5

Tartuffe (Molière), 37, 41

taste: in fashion merchants' trade, 152–53, 156, 162, 189, 214, 259, 267, 322; of the *homme aimable*, 355n88; individual *vs.* collective forms of, 115, 147, 361n35; for luxury, 119; of Marie Antoinette, 209, 261, 263, 376n61; in Paris, 263; subjection to fashion of, 122, 131; of women, 132, 133, 192, 280, 306

Tatry, Elizabeth, 214, 240–41

terminology of fashion, 162–63

textiles: Louis XIV's policies on, 105–6; price of, 144, 359nn11–13; production sites for, 214–15

the Third Estate. *See* common/ordinary people

Thresor de la langue françoyse (Nicot), 3–4

trade cards, 154, 155*f*, 156*f*

Traité de la Communauté (Pothier), 290–92

Traité du Contrat de Vente (Pothier), 225–26

Treaty of Versailles of 1756, 251

trust, 6, 168, 183, 314, 316. *See also* credit; reputation; risk

Turgot, Anne-Robert-Jacques, 9, 139, 257, 326

Ulrich, Laurel Thatcher, 204

Ursins, Marie Anne de la Trémoille, Princesse des, 31, 56, 87

"The Used Clothes Seller-Fashion Merchant," 154

value, 12; abstraction of, 18–19; as apparent *vs.* real, 33, 163; assessments of, 15, 203, 317, 327; creation of, 35, 328; early nineteenth-century attitudes toward, 382n7; fashion merchants' creation of, 141, 151–53, 157; forms of, 2, 54–55; of French currency, 61, 72, 75–77; impact of fashion cycles on, 230, 241; of infor-

value (*continued*)
mation, 13; production through fashion and credit of, 124, 126, 127; Tarde on, 323–24; volatility of, 126
Vauban, Sébastien Le Prestre, marquis de, 73
Vechard, Elisabeth, 272, 370n21
Verbiest, Père, 37
Vermond, Mathieu-Jacques, Abbé de, 251–56, 316
Vertot, Abbé de, 24, 335n10
Victoire, Princesse of France, 209–10
Vigée-Lebrun, Elisabeth-Louise, 125, 248f, 270, 271f
Villedieu, Marie-Catherine de, 24, 335n10
Villemert, Pierre-Joseph Boudier de, 283
virtue, 93; Duclos on, 58, 78, 82–87, 93–94; the *homme à la mode's* lack of, 129, 131, 133–34; La Bruyère on, 60–61, 64, 342n8; relationship of fashionable appearance to, 100–103, 117; as source of credit, 4, 28–29, 42, 318; of women, 96, 312–13, 381n59
Les visions de Dom Francisco de Quevedo Villegat, 226
Voiture, Vincent, 34, 35, 36
Voltaire, 64, 89, 331n17, 335n10; on the Calas affair in Toulouse, 92; as *historiographe de France*, 78; on Law's financial reforms, 76; on Mademoiselle Duchapt, 192

wages, 106; of fashion merchants' employees, 237, 297; in the industrious revolution, 143–44; as part of debt, 230, 237, 241, 285, 310; of seamstresses, 144, 176, 194
War of the Austrian Succession, 81, 246
War of the Spanish Succession, 67, 71–72
Watch Out or the Harem in the Boutique, 287f
wealth, 4, 15, 64, 65, 318; conceptions of, 168–69; nobility and, 217; relationship

to credit of, 31, 200, 331n19, 364n86; relationship to merit of, 81
weather and fashion, 115
Weber, Caroline, 258–59
Wedgwood, Josiah, 269–70
The Wife Unhappy with Her Husband, 53
women, 7–8, 23, 318–19; access to financial credit of, 233–35, 283–88, 311–12; alleged immodesty of, 118; Commercial Code of 1673 and, 180, 290; consumption of clothing by, 8, 9, 144, 286; Duclos's silence on, 58, 87–88, 96–98; education of, 187; emotional credit of, 42; as *femmes à la mode*, 135–36, 138; the *homme à la mode* and, 99, 132–36, 356nn108–9; humoral systems of, 16; incarceration for debt of, 237–38; intellectual credit of, 36; legal status of, 183–84, 284–86, 288–92, 299, 315, 366n112, 366n114, 377n8, 378n13; manipulation of judicial decisions by, 34, 337n47; marriage and economic autonomy of, 291–92, 296–301, 311–15; moral weakness of, 94–95, 286–88, 292, 301–14, 378n11; power and political credit of, 20, 25, 27–29, 31, 54, 57–59, 66–70, 87–92, 118, 336n18, 336n25; seamstress guild of, 143–44; sexual manipulation of, 7–8, 58–59, 67–71, 94–95. *See also* gender; sexuality; sexual sources of credit; *specific women*
work: credit in world of, 52–55, 243, 318–19; husbands' responsibilities and, 294, 296; illegal forms of, 147–48; performance by fashion merchants and their employees of, 152–53, 185–91, 194, 202, 206–7, 211, 237, 265, 322; of Rose Bertin with Marie Antoinette, 202, 246, 267–69; as source of identity, 204; subcontracting of, 150; of women in the industrious revolution, 143–44

Zola, Emile, 335nn10,11, 382n7